THE STORY OF BRITAIN

The Battersea Shield, 1st century BC, found in the River Thames at Battersea.

THE STORY
OF BRITAIN

From the Romans
to the Present:
A Narrative History

REBECCA FRASER

W. W. Norton & Company
NEW YORK   LONDON

Copyright © 2003 by Rebecca Fraser
First published as a Norton paperback 2006

Originally published in Great Britain under the title *A People's History of Britain*

For information about permission to reproduce selections from this book,
write to Permissions, W. W. Norton & Company, Inc.,
500 Fifth Avenue, New York, NY 10110

Manufacturing by LSC Harrisonburg
Production manager: Amanda Morrison

Library of Congress Cataloging-in-Publication Data

Fraser, Rebecca.
[People's history of Britain]
The story of Britain : from the Romans to the present : a narrative history / Rebecca
Fraser.— 1st American ed.
p. cm.
"Originally published in Great Britain under the title A People's history of Britain"—
T.p. verso.
Includes bibliographical references and index.
ISBN 0-393-06010-1
1. Great Britain—History—Anecdotes. I. Title.
DA32.8.F73 2005
941—dc22
2004026049

ISBN-13: 978-0-393-32902-5 pbk.
ISBN-10: 0-393-32902-X pbk.

W. W. Norton & Company, Inc.
500 Fifth Avenue, New York, N.Y. 10110
www.wwnorton.com

W. W. Norton & Company Ltd.
15 Carlisle Street, London W1D 3BS

7 8 9 0

Contents

Tudor

Stuart

Hanoverian

Saxe-Coburg

Windsor

CONTENTS

Maps by Cartographica

List of Illustrations

The Battersea Shield 1st century BC (© Copyright The British Museum)
Stonehenge
Roman soldiers
Partial sandstone Roman building inscription near Battle, East Sussex (Copyright Dr Gerald Brodribb)
Locker room from Roman bathhouse, Battle, East Sussex (Copyright Dr Gerald Brodribb)
A section of Hadrian's Wall, 2nd century AD (The Bridgeman Art Library)
Angle slaves in the market at Rome
St Augustine converts King Ethelbert of Kent, 597 AD
Christian Irish missionaries setting off for northern Britain
The 7th-century Bewcastle Cross, Cumbria (Copyright Peter Burton)
7th-century Anglo-Saxon helmet, from the ship burial at Sutton Hoo (© Copyright The British Museum)
Iona, an island off the west coast of Scotland
Drawing of the 8th-century Brixworth Church, Northamptonshire
Viking warships
Murder of King Edmund of East Anglia in 870 AD by the Danish Grand Army
9th-century grave marker with seven Viking warriors carved into the surface, from Lindisfarne Priory (© English Heritage Photo Library)
Alfred the Great's Isle of Athelney, Somerset
Page of text from *The Anglo-Saxon Chronicle* in the 11th century (British Library)
Tomb of King Edward the Confessor
The Bayeux Tapestry: King Harold is killed and the English turn in flight; detail from the Bayeux Tapestry (Musée de la Tapisserie, Bayeux, France/Bridgeman Art Library. With special authorization of the City of Bayeux, Giraudon/Bridgeman Art Library)
Bishop Odo of Bayeux
Great Domesday Book, Volume 1, Berkshire (The National Archives)
The Chapel of St John at the Tower of London
A typical Norman keep, Rochester Castle on the Medway
William Rufus
Durham Cathedral

Nineteenth-century engraving of Stonehenge, Salisbury Plain, Wiltshire. Prehistoric monument of standing stones begun by Neolithic people around 3000 BC.

Preface

When I was young there were various histories of Britain which seemed to provide a clear route through our long and immensely complicated past. They were heavily biographical, extremely colourful and full of adventures which made them easy to remember. The most famous of them, *Our Island Story*, was written in 1905 by a New Zealand lady named Henrietta Marshall at the height of empire when Britain was, in the immortal words of *1066 and All That*, 'Top Nation'. Needless to say, the world has moved on and so has the point of view of Clio, the muse of history. What might seem heroic to an earlier generation appears in a different guise today.

But it seemed to me, when I embarked on this book with three young daughters in mind, that some kind of easy framework was still needed to guide the average person through the confusing shoals of disputed facts, to give a broad-brush picture of the past to those not in the van of historical research. The national curriculum today enables many young people to grow up used to handling esoteric historical documents yet without any real chronological sense of the years between, say, the Stuarts and the Victorians. Many children might be forgiven for believing that the Egyptians and the Aztecs once lived on these islands too. The aim of this history is to attempt to return to those old rules of 'who, when, what, how'.

Furthermore, if I may strike a patriotic note, there is a great deal to celebrate about Britain that is owed to the dead Britons of the past. The impact of some gifted individuals was so great that Britain would have been a different place without them. Their actions produced turning points in history. William Wilberforce was the driving force behind the abolition of the slave trade; Florence Nightingale saved the lives of British soldiers condemned to death by the inertia of the army bureaucracy. Despite the cruelty of the Normans or the Tudors, one of the glories of Britain's history is the essentially free-spirited, not to say bloody-minded, nature of her natives. From Boudicca onwards a heady something in the air makes Britons resist their rulers if they go too far. That tradition of defending the rule of law and the rights of ordinary people against despots gave the world Parliamentary democracy.

In my view the history of a people must include the anecdotes which have become embedded in the national psyche, because they reflect the values of that people. I therefore make no apology for re-telling some of the nation's best-loved stories, though the facts on which they rest may be dubious to say the least. The important thing is that they have stood the test of time and continue to be related after hundreds of years. It is surely illustrative of the British people that our favourite anecdotes concern the mighty being willing to stand corrected by the ordinary man or (in Alfred's case) woman in the street.

Ironic, kindly, democratic, humorous, energetic, tolerant and brave, surely these are the best qualities of the British people. If the British over the centuries have thrown up a number of harsh rulers and policies, there seems to have been no shortage of British men and women ready to confront them, from John Hampden to the British missionaries who tried to stop Cecil Rhodes seizing the lands of the Ndebele people and creating Rhodesia. Along with Joe Chamberlain's municipal socialism, the creation of the National Health Service is the greatest testimonial to the best British humanitarian ideals.

Despite considering myself a Scot with Irish roots, and being very conscious of those nations' and Wales' independent histories, most of this narrative has been driven by the story of the English kingdom. Since the Parliament at Westminster remains the chief law-making body for all four countries, and while the United Kingdom remains intact, I believe this is still a valid approach.

Although the errors in this volume are all my own, this book owes more than I can adequately describe to the generous help of the historian Alan Palmer, whose profound and encyclopaedic knowledge of British history has been inspiring. My editor Penelope Hoare has been extremely patient in waiting for this book, as has my inestimable agent Ed Victor. My children Blanche, Atalanta and Honor have put up with historical expeditions during their school holidays, such as tramping across the bitterly cold battlefields of Culloden at Easter, with relative good humour. I want to thank Helen Fraser (no relation), who commissioned this book, Alison Samuel, the publisher of Chatto and Windus, for her encouragement, and my mother Antonia Fraser who has not only read the manuscript at all stages but remained intensely interested in the project. I also want to thank my stepfather Harold Pinter for reading the manuscript in its early stages, as did my late grandfather and grandmother Frank and Elizabeth Longford. I am also very grateful to Patrick Seale for sharing his immense knowledge of the Middle East and to the extraordinarily learned Daniel Johnson for many gifts of books which he thought would be of use. Laura Lindsay of Christie's used her command of British pictures to point me in the right direction with the visual images. I would like to thank the late Dr Gerald Brodribb, who took me round the Roman bathhouse he had unearthed at Beauport Park in East Sussex. Thanks also to Philip Flower for permission to reproduce a part of his grandfather's unique photographic records of the Boer War, to Robert Silver for the inspiration provided by his childhood copy of *The Pictorial History of England*, and to my brother-in-law the artist Coleman Saunders, Lily Richards and Poppy Hampson, in particular, for their picture research. I am also most grateful to Christopher Woodhead for his continued encouragement, to Edward Barker for the views of a teenage history buff, and to Laure de Gramont for a French view of Albion. I am indebted to Dr Munro Price for his help and to Professor Ralph Griffiths for reading the proofs. The book would not be in the shape it is without the brilliant work of Peter James on the manuscript.

Lastly, the greatest thanks of all must go to my husband Edward Fitzgerald who has lived with this book and whose passion for history remains undiminished.

ROMAN

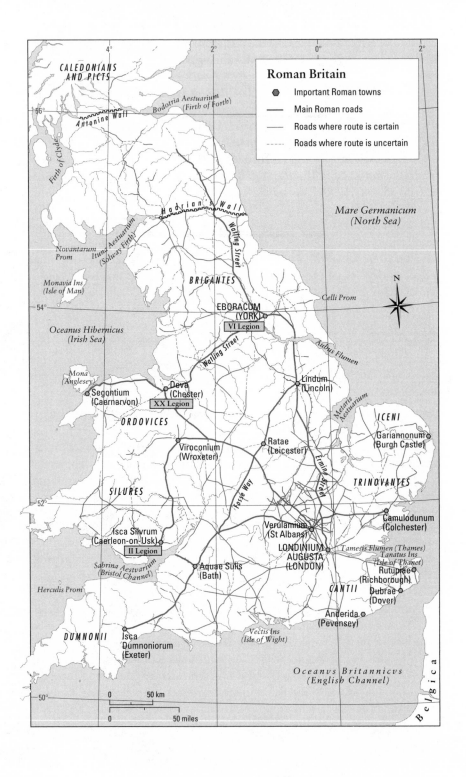

Roman Britain

⬡ Important Roman towns

━━━ Main Roman roads

─── Roads where route is certain

--- Roads where route is uncertain

CALEDONIANS AND PICTS

Antonine Wall

Firth of Clyde

Bodotria Aestuarium (Firth of Forth)

Hadrian's Wall

Mare Germanicum (North Sea)

Watling Street

Novantarum Prom

Ituna Aestuarium (Solway Firth)

BRIGANTES

Monavia Ins (Isle of Man)

Celti Prom

EBORACUM (YORK)
VI Legion

Oceanus Hibernicus (Irish Sea)

Watling Street

Abus Flumen

Mona (Anglesey)

Deva (Chester)
XX Legion

Lindum (Lincoln)

Segontium (Caernarvon)

Metaris Aestuarium

ICENI

ORDOVICES

Viroconium (Wroxeter)

Ratae (Leicester)

Gariannonum (Burgh Castle)

SILURES

Fosse Way

Ermine Street

TRINOVANTES

Camulodunum (Colchester)

Isca Silvrum (Caerleon-on-Usk)
II Legion

Verulamium (St Albans)

LONDINIUM AUGUSTA (LONDON)

Tamesis Flumen (Thames)
Tanatus Ins (Isle of Thanet)

Sabrina Aestvarium (Bristol Channel)

Aquae Sulis (Bath)

Rutupiae (Richborough)

Dubrae (Dover)

CANTII

Herculis Prom

Anderida (Pevensey)

DUMNONII

Isca Dumnoniorum (Exeter)

Vectis Ins (Isle of Wight)

Oceanvs Britannicvs (English Channel)

Belgica

N

0   50 km

0   50 miles

Roman

I have chosen to begin the story of Britain in the year the Romans came, fifty-five years before the birth of Christ, over 2,000 years ago. Before Julius Caesar, the Roman Empire's greatest general, led his first expedition ashore, the country's stormy seas isolated her from the traffic of the European continent. Apart from her own inhabitants, no one knew very much about the place, though there were rumours. How far did it stretch north? Were its forests impenetrable? Was it really an island? Was its mineral wealth extraordinary?

Since at least the fourth century before Christ, that is 250 years before Caesar appeared, the natives had been mining highly prized gold and tin for export at the Island of Ictis (St Michael's Mount) on the extreme south-western tip of Britain, and they had trading links as far afield as the Mediterranean. As a result of this trade, in 300 BC the Greek colony of Massilia, or Marseilles, had sent one of its citizens named Pytheas on a reconnaissance trip to Britain. Pytheas had noted the friendly nature of the inhabitants. It was said that the Britons' relations further east had some secret method of transporting vast blue stones from a more mountainous region. On a great plain north-east of their chief port in Dorset, they or perhaps their gods were said to have erected the enormous circle called Stonehenge which was used for religious ceremonies.

But Pytheas' description is a mere fragment reported in a later work. Since the British tribes could not read or write, they remain as mysterious and fabled as their distant ancestors, the small, dark, long-headed Neolithic or New Stone Age invaders who started to arrive from the Mediterranean in 3000 BC. That British Neolithic man hacked at the soil with deer antlers to grow a little wheat, and that he used flint-headed arrows to kill game for food have had to be deduced from what archaeologists have found in their long barrow graves. It is only when we get to Caesar's *Commentaries on the Gallic War* that we are able to read the first written description of the country known to the Romans for 400 years as Britain.

By the time of Pytheas and Caesar himself the inhabitants of ancient

Britain were mainly what have come to be known as Iron Age Celts. Like the Iberians in Spain and the Gauls in France, they were members of the great military aristocracy which until the rise of the Rome city state in the third century BC were masters of the trade routes between northern and central Europe and the Mediterranean. The Celts were the second wave of invaders to follow Neolithic man to Britain, but they came 2,000 years later, around 1000 BC. Between Neolithic man, whose great monument is the stone-circle temple at Avebury in Wiltshire, and the Celts another wave of invaders had arrived.

These invaders were round-headed Bronze Age people, originally from the Rhineland, who reached Britain in about 1900 BC. They were a stronger, larger race than Neolithic man, though still dark and swarthy, and they swiftly occupied England from the east coast of Yorkshire down to Surrey. This more sophisticated race is sometimes known as the Beaker People because of the drinking vessels found in their graves. They could make tools from bronze; they built Stonehenge; they buried their dead in individual round barrows. But in their turn about 1000 BC their way of life was challenged by a new, more powerful civilization.

From the first millennium BC the Celts of eastern Europe were migrating west. The expansion of the Germanic tribes at their back encouraged them to move into northern and western Europe, particularly into France, Spain and Britain, bringing with them what is known as the Iron Age. Their peoples were sophisticated enough to known the secret of mining iron ore out of the ground – they could extract the iron ore by heating it. Then they worked the more difficult metal by beating layers of it together. This enabled them to achieve a major advance on bronze or flint tools, and with their stronger iron spears they easily defeated the Bronze Age peoples. They could also travel faster in chariots furnished with iron wheels and drawn by horses that they loved so much they had them buried with them in their graves.

Tall and fair skinned with red or blond hair and blue or green eyes, the Celts were not only physically quite dissimilar to Bronze Age man, they also spoke a different language. No one is quite sure why two kinds of Celtic languages developed. Goidel, from which comes the word Gaelic, was spoken in Ireland and Scotland, and Brythonic is the family from which Welsh, Breton and Cornish derive. Unlike the cave-dwelling Neolithic man, the Celts built their own huts with posts sunk in mud and woven branches for the roof. Although at first they lived in hill forts enabling them to command the countryside, they developed ploughs and were soon farming the surrounding land in small square fields, a shape that would continue through Roman times. Some of those who settled in south-west England lived in lakeside villages, island-like enclaves designed for protection. The Celts were ruled by queens as well as kings, and might even be led in battle by women.

By the first century BC Britain (or Britannia, as the Romans called it) had attracted Caesar's hostile attention. He wished to put an end to the use of Britannia as a sanctuary by the leaders of Gaul (a country covering roughly the territory of modern France) rebelling against their Roman overlords. Archaeologists have shown that in the first century AD the inhabitants of Britain's south coast, sailing from their chief port of Hengistbury Head in Dorset, had a great deal of trade with Gaul. Within Caesar's lifetime southern Britain and northern France may have been ruled by a Gallic overlord called Diviacus. Caesar believed that the Britons' powerful religious leaders, the Druids, were also helping to foment trouble. The rebellious Belgae in north-west Gaul, what is now Belgium, had close relations across the Channel in Britain to whom they were in the habit of fleeing in times of trouble. These Belgae, who were now known as Catuvellauni after their leader Cassivellaunus, had settled there from Gaul within living memory. Making Britannia a province of the Roman Empire would finally break the power of the Belgae, whom Caesar was determined to destroy. It would also usefully add to his reputation as a great man by extending the empire even to the edge of the known world. Expanding the empire's territories, rather than administering them, was how glory and power were won in the uniquely militaristic society of Caesar's Rome.

Gathering information about Britain's harbours and landing places was one reason why Caesar sailed across the 'Ocean' (the Channel) on his first expedition in 55 BC. He landed with some difficulty owing to a spring tide which swamped his heavy transport ships. He noted that the houses and inhabitants of Britain seemed very similar to those of Gaul, with the striking difference that rich or poor the British men were shaved of all bodily hair (except for the upper lip, where they grew long moustaches) and painted with a blue dye called woad. Their reddish hair was also worn very long, often with a headband. They knew how to cure hides for export and had a good trade with the continent in iron, cattle and corn, using gold and iron bars in a rudimentary currency system. But as Caesar approached the shores of Kent at what is now Deal the woad-covered Britons looked wild and primitive as they whirled in their chariots on the cliffs above him. Because they wore skins Caesar assumed that they could have no knowledge of cloth-weaving, which to a Roman was one of the marks of civilization. But the ancient Britons' appearance was misleading. They knew how to spin wool, how to weave it into garments and how to dye it with colours from flowers and insects. Indeed they usually wore long woollen tunics, cloaks and robes fastened by intricate articles of jewellery in swirling patterns which their talented smiths made out of gold, silver and enamel. They were half naked when they were first seen by Caesar only because that was their battle costume. Their Celtic relations, the Gauls across the channel, fought completely naked.

Caesar nevertheless continued to believe that, although the people of Cantium (his translation of the name he heard them use for their country – that is, Kent) were in fact fairly civilized and knew how to grow grain, Britons who lived further north did not know how to cultivate crops and lived on what they hunted. It was true that compared to Roman civilization, with its advanced precision engineering which enabled the Romans to build stone bridges, roads and aqueducts, its architectural science which threw up palaces and forts, its military and political science, the Britons seemed childlike, ignorant and superstitious. They were ruled by the white-robed Druids, who regarded mistletoe as sacred and practised human sacrifice, burning their victims in wicker cages. Hares, fowl and geese were also sacred, which meant they could not be eaten – although the Britons liked them as pets. The Britons were said to love poetry, but they were also extremely quarrelsome.

Caesar found Britannia's climate more temperate than that of Gaul, though much wetter, and by his water clock he could confirm that being further north the nights in this strange new country were shorter than on the continent. Moving inland he came upon a great river in the east of the country about eighty miles from the south coast which he called the Thamium, a Latin approximation of the name the ancient Britons gave to what we still know as the Thames. He was impressed by the bravery of the British warriors and by their methods of chariot warfare, describing them in considerable detail. In particular he observed their brilliant control of their horses, which they drove fearlessly down steep slopes at full gallop only to turn them in an instant. They would then run along the pole of the chariot to the yoke and urge the horses onwards.

Despite the apparently lower form of civilization that prevailed in Britain, neither of Caesar's two expeditions reflected much glory on him. His famous wisecrack 'Veni, vidi, vici' (I came, I saw, I conquered), never applied to Britain. His first invasion ended in stalemate because the effect of British tides was unknown to a man brought up in the tideless Mediterranean, and he failed to land enough soldiers to secure the country. He attempted another invasion from Boulogne a year later, in 54 BC with a huge force of twenty-eight warships and 800 transports (built lower for British waters) and this time was more successful. Under the ensuing peace treaty the British tribes were meant to send tribute to Rome once a year, but the invasion ended inconclusively when Caesar had to dash back to Gaul to stamp out a rebellion.

Caesar might say that the Cantii of Kent, the powerful Trinovantes of

Essex and the Iceni of Norfolk had surrendered to him, but unlike when the real conquest of Britain took place under the Emperor Claudius ninety years later he left no garrisons behind. Though he and his legions had crossed the Thames it was only the defection of the Trinovantes of Essex which saved the Romans from being driven out of the country by the sheer weight of the British numbers. For once the squabbling British tribes had united, under Cassivellaunus. In the face of the separate peace reached by the Trinovantes, Cassivellaunus decided it was wiser to make terms with Caesar. But these were hardly onerous. There was no sense that Britain now formed the most westerly outpost of the empire. Caesar himself does not seem to have believed that he had really conquered Britain. He never ordered a Triumph, the traditional way of showing off new acquisitions by parading the natives as slaves around Rome. The only trophy he is said to have displayed was a corselet made of British freshwater pearls (he was very disappointed by the lack of silver in Britain). He may have been pleased to leave a country whose climate the first-century Roman historian Tacitus would call 'objectionable, with its frequent rains and mists', where crops were slow to ripen but quick to grow due to the 'extreme moistness of land and sky'.

Then Caesar's attention was diverted by the Civil Wars back in Italy, and his successors too had more pressing concerns than Britain. For almost a hundred years the Britons under their kings and chiefs were free to carry on the existence of their ancestors, but very subtly and slowly their lives were changing. They were increasingly in contact with Rome at both diplomatic and trade levels. Britain was now selling grain to the Roman Empire and buying olive oil and wine from Roman traders in exchange, as we can tell from their presence in late-first-century BC British graves. Highly wrought artefacts of Roman workmanship – such as the silver cups found at Hockwold in Norfolk – previously believed to have been the property of Roman officers after the invasion are now thought to be gifts to an important pre-conquest British chieftain from the Roman government. Increased contact with Roman-educated Gauls escaping to Britain – for example, Commius, who had helped Caesar with the attempted invasion, but who became king of the Atrebates in the Sussex area – brought more Roman habits into Britain. By the end of the first century BC a number of kings in southern England, including Tincommius, Commius' son, who lived at Silchester in Hampshire, had their own mints. They were striking their own coins inscribed in Latin and calling themselves 'rex' even though they could not themselves read or write.

The most important of these kingdoms were those ruled by the descendants of Cassivellaunus, whose tribe the Catuvellauni had massively extended their territories since Caesar's departure. The lands of the

Catuvellauni stretched in a semi-circle from Cambridge and Northampton down through Hertfordshire to Surrey, south of what became London. By the beginning of the first century AD they were ruled by King Cunobelinus (Shakespeare's Cymbeline), whose coins bear the letters CUNO. The early-second-century Roman historian Suetonius called him King of the Britons. It was because of a row between Cunobelinus and his son Adminius that the far-off and still mysterious country of Britain once more came to the attention of the authorities in Rome. For Prince Adminius, who had been banished by his father, fled to Rome and the court of the Emperor Caligula.

Now that Britain had been put on the map for the Romans by Caesar, conquering it had remained for the Roman government a perpetual but distant ambition: having resisted Caesar the country had acquired a certain glamour. With the arrival of the exiled British prince Adminius, imperial interest was once more aroused. The Emperor Caligula began preparations for a new invasion. He built boats, gathered arms and raised money and troops. Whether he ever really arrived at the cliffs of Dover, and was so put off by their height that he set his disgusted soldiers to gather shells of the seashore as 'spoils of the ocean' in place of 'spoils of war' is not clear. Satirical jokes about the cruel Emperor Caligula were often told, so one cannot be sure whether the report is fact or fiction.

But nine years later, in AD 43, Caligula's preparations were taken up when his cousin, the eccentric but energetic new emperor Claudius, needed a military conquest to secure his shaky throne. It was under Claudius that the subduing of Britain began in earnest, as it was turned into a Roman province held by military garrisons in forts erected systematically across the country. This time the Roman invaders – four legions consisting of 20,000 soldiers plus 20,000 auxiliaries – would occupy the country up to Scotland and stay for four centuries. After his military commander Aulus Plautius had defeated the Britons north of the Medway, Claudius arrived with elephants to make a triumphant progress through Cunobelinus' former capital Camulodunum, or Colchester, in Essex. Conquering Britain brought much-needed political credit to Claudius.

By the end of the first century AD Britain had been completely integrated into the empire as the province Britannia. Roman military tactics and Roman armour had ensured that after only six years of fighting, 40,000 Romans had subdued hundreds of thousands of British Celts, conquering England up to the Rivers Trent, Severn and Dee. However, despite the formidable superiority of the Roman invaders, some hope remained among many ancient Britons of re-establishing their independence and throwing the Romans off their island. The extent of the British tribes' obsession with personal liberty would impress and amaze the sober Romans, who had to crush their many rebellions. But their spirited bravery was not enough. What counted most against them was the tribes' fatal habit of treachery. This meant that their one source of strength – their great numbers – was never used against the Romans. Tacitus believed that 'nothing has helped us more in war with their strongest nations' than the British tribes' 'inability to co-operate'. Their universal tendency was to make separate treaties with Rome and then to turn on one another. Never has there been a better example of Caesar's maxim 'divide and rule' than in first-century Britain. Had the tribes only united as they had under Cassivellaunus, by sheer weight of numbers they might have held the Romans at bay.

Claudius was careful to establish good relations with many British kings and queens. Another method of pacifying Britannia was immigration. Old soldiers started arriving in Britain from Italy to make a new life; as a reward for their thirty years of service to the Roman Empire they were given grants of British land in what were called 'veterans' colonies'. This was the traditional Roman way of turning a country into a Roman province. Nevertheless, for nine long years under another of Cunobelinus' sons, the chieftain Caractacus, a dangerous British patriotic resistance continued in the west on the borders of Wales. These Britons refused to be driven off their land to make way for Roman colonies, and were further enraged by the governor Ostorius Scapula's calls for all the British tribes to disarm.

Caractacus' followers were a tribe called the Silures. Swarthy and curly haired, believed by Caesar to be of Spanish origin, they had a reputation for extreme ferocity. Under Caractacus their fame spread as far as Italy, where it was considered extraordinary that a barbarian chieftain could defy the resources of imperial Rome. Caractacus waged an early kind of guerrilla warfare, moving his men from territory to territory. But having taken cover in Shropshire, the land of the Ordovices tribe, he made the mistake of thinking that, given the vast numbers of Britons flocking to join him, he could defeat the Romans in pitched battle. In words which would win the admiration of Roman contemporaries and confirm their view of the central importance of liberty to the British character, Caractacus told his men that there was no point in living if all they had to look forward to was a miserable existence spent in hiding: they must win their freedom back or they would be enslaved for ever.

Caractacus had chosen the site of his stand well. With looming cliffs behind them, and protected by a river and man-made ramparts, the long-haired, moustachioed, blue-skinned tribes shook their spears at the enemy, whooping and uttering fierce guttural yells. But brave though they were, and though their iron shields and spears were admirably robust, they stood little chance against the Romans' superior battle tactics: their missiles and rocks shattered harmlessly against the Romans' armour and against their famous tortoise formation, in which they placed their shields together like an umbrella. Moving implacably forward the Roman soldiers stormed the ramparts. The battle was over almost before it had begun. The advance party of auxiliaries attacked, throwing javelins, while behind them marched the well-protected infantry in close formation, silently and methodically cutting down all who had escaped the auxiliaries. The surviving British tribesmen had to run for the hills.

Caractacus fled east and threw himself on the mercy of Queen Cartimandua of the Brigantes, the powerful tribe who with the Parisi ruled the part of northern England today called Yorkshire. But Cartimandua had allied herself to the Romans, so Caractacus was shipped off to Rome with his wife and children. There he continued to impress the Romans by his unbreakable spirit. Unlike other captives who marched past the emperor howling for mercy, Caractacus maintained a proud and resolute bearing undiminished by his haggard appearance. Limping after his wife and brothers and his little children, all of them bound in chains, he suddenly stepped out of the procession, approached the emperor's dais and addressed him boldly. Caractacus told Claudius that only fate had given victory to the emperor and not to him, and that the emperor should not be surprised that Caractacus was sorry to lose. The emperor might want to rule the world, but did it follow that everyone else would welcome enslavement? If he had surrendered without a blow neither he nor the fact of his capture would have become famous. 'If you kill me they will be forgotten,' he said, 'but show mercy, and I shall be an eternal reminder of your clemency.' Claudius was so moved by the speech of the barbarian prince that he ordered Caractacus' chains to be struck off, and he and his family freed.

In Britain itself, however, the Romans' humiliating treatment of the conquered tribes continued to arouse resentment. A slave-owning society themselves, the Britons considered that the Romans were treating them like slaves. This was the fault of the first Roman governor of Britain, Ostorius Scapula. The Roman Empire everywhere relied on the co-operation of local chieftains if it was to be successfully administered. What made a difference was the nature of the local ruler, whether he was a sensitive and thoughtful man. Ostorius Scapula did not possess the same diplomatic touch as the emperor Claudius, who had received the friendly British tribes with ceremony and respect.

Ostorius Scapula turned a blind eye to local taxes raised illegally from the inhabitants of Colchester in order to build an enormous statue of the Emperor Claudius – a monument which the religious Britons disliked as a visible sign of the occupying power. He did nothing to prevent ex-servicemen taking Essex land illegally from the Trinovantes for their veterans' colony; indeed he probably profited from it himself. Since the British showed no mercy in their guerrilla attacks on the veterans, the veterans in turn showed no mercy to the Trinovantes, throwing them out of their homes and seizing their land. Normally Roman garrisons were punctilious about making sure veterans' colonies observed the terms of the treaties, but the soldiers in Essex had their eye on British land when their own thirty-year service was up, so they ignored the veterans' misbehaviour. When Ostorius died of exhaustion from battling the Silures, his militaristic successor Suetonius Paulinus did nothing to soothe an already inflamed situation by launching a military attack on the sacred island of Anglesey, the home of the Druids. Paulinus believed that if he could extirpate that nest of rebels the British resistance would die a natural death.

Roman soldiers invaded with Julius Caesar in 55 and 54 BC, but conquered Britain only after 43 AD, under the Emperor Claudius.

By AD 61 relations between the Romans and the British tribes were already in a bad way. It was particularly bad north-east of London around Colchester and in Norfolk where the Trinovantes' neighbours the Iceni tribe had still more to anger them. Their dying king Pratusagus had tried to ensure that his wife Queen Boudicca was protected from the bad treatment being meted out to the Britons by making Rome co-heir to his kingdom with his two daughters. Instead of being satisfied by this the local military commander had flogged the beautiful red-haired queen with rods and raped her two teenage daughters. The Romans then destroyed her houses and removed her household treasures – her silver flagons, engraved mirrors and gold jewellery disappearing into the commander's quarters. Finally he expelled her and the Iceni from their lands, which the Romans at once subjected to an orgy of destruction.

Paulinus, being new to his command, had no sense of the anger burning among the British tribes and failed to see that the real threat to Rome's regime lay not in Wales but in East Anglia. Directly he had turned his back on East Anglia and set off to lay waste Anglesey, across the country the furious Iceni rose. With the queen were the Trinovantes and all the other tribes pushed beyond endurance. While Paulinus and his soldiers were in Wales, building boats to take them across to Anglesey, in Essex Queen Boudicca had gathered an army of 120,000 men, three times the strength of the Roman legions in Britain. These forces surged into the new Roman town of Colchester, which its arrogant settlers had foolishly built without walls. Having destroyed it, including the Temple of Claudius, and routed the Ninth Legion, they streamed on to London (Londinium).

It was the common opinion among the Roman command that had Suetonius Paulinus not rushed back south Britain would have been lost to Rome. As it was, Paulinus sacrificed London to save the province of Britain. The citizens implored him for help but, though Londinium was the trading centre of Roman Britain, Paulinus sent no troops. He regarded London as indefensible because it was really a collection of merchants' settlements, being unwalled and not garrisoned. Having massacred its citizens, the vengeful Britons put London to the torch. So great was the heat that Roman buildings were reduced to a layer of red clay which to this day lies thirteen feet deep below the city's pavements. A part of it can be seen where it has been exposed by archaeologists beside the Barbican, near the Museum of London.

Meanwhile the British horde swept on. They are estimated to have killed 70,000 Roman settlers, but they looted indiscriminately and never thought of destroying important military targets like forts and garrisons. Queen Boudicca, standing in her chariot spear in hand, a heavy yellow torc round her neck, and her red-gold hair in two long plaits held in place by a headband, made a series of magnificent speeches as she drove around the tribes drawn up on the battlefield. But, despite their enormous numbers, when they met Paulinus in the Midlands the Britons once again came to grief in pitched battle against the Romans. The assembled chiefs could not agree on a battle plan and around 80,000 of their men were killed by

10,000 Roman soldiers. Refusing to allow her beloved girls to fall into the hands of the Romans again, Boudicca forced them to drink poison from a golden cup and then drank it herself. When Paulinus found her, the great queen was dead, but she looked as peaceful as if she were asleep, clasping her daughters in her arms.

Two thousand extra Roman troops had to be rushed over from Germany to ensure that the victory in southern Britain was permanent. Because there had been no one left to look after the crops, famine weakened the resistance of the British tribes, but nothing seemed to crush their spirit or curb their sharp tongues. When the emperor sent an ex-slave named Polyclitus with still more troops to advise Paulinus on the better management of the province, the Romans were astonished by the way the Britons even in their darkest hour clung to the idea of freedom and dared to jeer at the spectacle of such a great general as Paulinus having to obey a slave. But Wales and northern Britain remained unconquered. By the late 60s, raids by the Parisi tribe of Humberside, the Brigantes of Yorkshire (who had turned hostile) and the Silures and Ordovices of Wales made it necessary for further Roman onslaughts to subdue the recalcitrant British tribes.

From AD 68 onwards, successful campaigns by a series of Roman governors brought the rest of the island, up to southern Scotland, at least temporarily under imperial control. Roman forts to garrison the con-quered areas were established at York, Caerleon and Chester in the early '70s and new northern roads carved their way across the landscape from York to Corbridge to Newstead and as far as the River Tay. The most famous of these first-century governors was Agricola, who in seven great campaigns between 74 and 84 completed the conquest of north-west Britain and established a sturdy system of roads and forts to defend her. By AD 78 he had defeated the Ordovices in Shropshire, conquered Anglesey and stationed the Twentieth Legion at Chester in a new fortress; the next year he constructed a road from Chester to Carlisle (which he fortified) and placed garrisons between the Solway Firth and Tyne. He next took his legions as far as the Moray Firth in Invernesshire, and at the Battle of Mons Graupius defeated the massed tribes of the Caledonians, as the Romans called the northern Picts. He went on to build a series of forts in southern Scotland between the Firth of Clyde on the west coast and the Firth of Forth on the east, and this line formed the Roman frontier. Agricola also established a naval base at Dover for a new British fleet, sent an expedition to northern Scotland that rounded the north coast and visited the Orkneys, and may even have contemplated invading Hibernia – the Roman name for Ireland.

Agricola was in Britain for only ten years, before being recalled in AD 84 by the jealous and cruel emperor Domitian who feared that the great governor might be about to make a bid for the imperial throne. Agricola did much to reconcile the Britons to their fate as a Roman province. He kept a weather eye open for rebellion but did not humiliate the tribes. The southern garrison towns of Roman Britain became centres of enlightenment and improvement for the British. The warlike Celts were transformed into Roman citizens who took pride in wearing the toga, as Agricola's son-in-law Tacitus reported with some surprise. Agricola destroyed enmity from within. He deliberately took the sons of British chiefs and educated them in the Roman curriculum, the Trivium (grammar, rhetoric and dialectic or logical argument) and the Quadrivium (arithmetic, geometry, astronomy and music), the classical liberal arts. This upbringing, and the adoption of the Roman language, created a new generation of Britons tied to Rome by invisible but unbreakable bonds.

Agricola made a point of using members of this elite in the Roman civil service as administrators, for he admired what he considered to be the Britons' naturally fearless character. Once trained he believed they made better civil-servant material than the more servile Gauls. He thus created what amounted to a fifth column in Britain among the wealthier classes. The new southern Romano-Britons' loyalty was to Rome only. They delighted in the new Roman way of life. Agricola had a governor's palace and basilica built in London and during his period as governor the grand Roman palace known as Fishbourne was built.

The Roman concept of the market place or forum encouraged trade to flourish in the new towns Agricola built. A spate of building produced Exeter, Lincoln, Cirencester and St Albans, with their public baths, amphitheatres and forums after the Roman fashion. Noble stone and marble façades enclosed splendid courts of justice where the written Roman law was consulted and measured out. It was an entirely different experience from being tried in a forest glade by Druids. Roman law relied on knowledge of what had been done in the past, a much quicker and fairer way to reach decisions.

Wealth began to flow into Britain as the Romans oversaw the export of lead and tin, which the country had in abundance – particularly in the south-west. Classical observers like Tacitus were dismayed by the ease with which the ancient Britons took to a grander lifestyle, for they had admired their primitive vigour which compared so favourably to the decadence of imperial Rome. As the new Roman Britons of the south gloried in the modern conveniences such as public baths, it was lucky for them that Agricola remained alert for trouble, for the British tribes of the north and west were a constant threat.

Agricola had had a profound effect on Britain. In the south-east the

2nd to 3rd century AD Roman partial building inscription near Battle, East Sussex, site of what was probably a major Roman ironworks.

country became very similar to the rest of the Roman Empire, with Latin as the official written and spoken language. Much of the population learned to read and write, as education was highly valued by the Romans. The landscape too was transformed, as dark, thickly wooded oak forests near which lurked the Celts' small damp wood-and-wicker huts gave way to great clearings and plains. Here magnificent towns were built, busy with the commerce made easy by the laying of swift, straight roads, for the Roman system of government was essentially municipal. In the towns or just outside them were the elegant stone villas in which lived the wealthy Britons who were allowed to hold public office and be magistrates or senators. Their homes, which had running water brought to them by pipe and aqueduct, were heated by hypocausts and their walls were decorated

Locker room from Roman bathhouse, Battle, East Sussex.

with coloured frescoes, of the kind that can be seen at Pompeii. These leading Britons organized the raising of taxes to be sent back to the imperial coffers in Rome, and slaves and freedmen worked for them in the fields outside the cities, growing crops and tending sheep to produce the delicate Roman wool.

It was the Romans' policy to allow the countries they conquered to worship their own deities, although they would not tolerate the ancient Britons' practice of human sacrifice. The Celts' religion was pantheistic – that is, they saw gods or spirits everywhere, in streams and trees and so on. Over time their shrines came to merge with those to Roman deities. At Bath, where the Roman baths survive as grandly as they did 2,000 years ago, the shrine to Minerva was erected on the site of an ancient Celtic shrine. Something similar happened with aspects of the Britons' civic organization. Outside the Roman towns the councils of the old Celtic tribes like the Silures and Atrebates were adapted so that they could continue almost like local councils of the imperial administration.

Many of the English names of the months date from the Roman occupation. January derives from Janus, the two-faced deity who looks backwards and forwards to the past and coming year, and who was actually adopted by the Romans from the Egyptians. March comes from Mars the God of War, July from Julius Caesar and August from his nephew Augustus, another great emperor for whom the Latin poet Virgil wrote the *Aeneid*. Although the later Anglo-Saxon invasions meant that the names of Anglo-Saxon gods were applied to several days of the week, much that is of Roman origin remains. Many British customs and sayings derive from the Roman occupation: several wedding customs, including the wedding cake, the ring, bridesmaids and pages and the bride's veil are Roman. So are a number of our funeral customs, including putting flowers on the grave. The cypress and yew trees we plant in graveyards were the trees of mourning in Rome. The Romans said the Latin for 'bless you' when somebody sneezed – even the emperors used it. They also believed that your ears burned if somebody was talking about you; and the shriek of the screech owl in Rome was always considered a sound of ill omen.

Despite the complete Romanization of southern Britain it was never possible to regard the whole province as a secure Roman possession because of the constant rebellions in the north and Scotland. The province would always require a garrison of 50,000 soldiers to hold it – three legions plus auxiliaries were permanently stationed there. So skilled at warfare were the British tribes that at times 10 per cent of the empire's entire army was employed in Britain.

All British Roman towns (the major ones being Colchester, Lincoln, Gloucester, York and St Albans) were built with walls to keep out the barbarian tribes, especially in Wales. Though nominally conquered, the British continued to attack the Roman centres. This was quite unlike Gaul, where walled towns were the exception rather than the rule. Indeed, in contrast to Britain, Gaul was so completely Romanized that the old Celtic tongues died out except in Brittany, and were replaced by Latin – which accounts for the greater number of Latin words in the French vocabulary. In Britain the Celtic tongue lived on in Wales and Cornwall, and in the countryside outside the Roman towns and cities.

Despite Agricola's brilliance he never really conquered Scotland, and nor did the Roman rulers who came after him. By AD 87 Rome had conceded that Agricola's plan to hold southern Scotland up to the Tay was impracticable, so the fortress Agricola had built on that river for the Twentieth Legion was abandoned and the Roman legions pulled back to Agricola's Forth–Clyde frontier. But even that was gradually regarded as too ambitious and the slow withdrawal of the Roman legions from Scotland continued. It was the especially dangerous attack of the combined forces of the Brigantes and Picts on the Ninth Legion at York in AD 118 that decided the realistic Emperor Hadrian not only that the frontier of Roman Britain had to be placed much further south, but that it had to be of the most formidable kind. Hadrian's solution was an immense defensive wall, eight foot broad and twelve foot high, dotted at every Roman mile with a fort containing Roman soldiers: it would run through Cumbria and southern Northumberland between the Solway Firth and the Tyne.

In the following centuries three Roman emperors tramped up to Scotland to attempt to extend Roman rule further north in the troublesome province of Britain, in an attempt to bring credit to themselves and to enhance their political power. But though the emperor Antoninus Pius would build a turf and clay wall in AD 140 between Agricola's forts (the Antonine Wall), the real boundary of Roman Britain remained the extraordinary feat of engineering begun on Hadrian's orders when he visited Britain in 122.

Unlike other emperors, Hadrian was not grandiose; he thought Rome would do better by limiting her power rather than expanding it. For over thirty years the great wall he had designed was slowly built – eighty miles long, bristling with military lookout towers and, at greater intervals, large forts with their own shops, military hospitals and temples, much of which can still be walked along today. Until Christianity became compulsory in the early fourth century throughout the empire, the soldiers on the wall and in their forts at York (Eboracum), Caerleon (Isca Silurum) and Chester (Deva) had their own religion: they worshipped an eastern deity from Persia named Mithras in the bowels of the earth whose rites were secret. Hadrian also built a fort at London.

If Hadrian's Wall is the largest and most visible of the surviving symbols of the Roman occupation of Britain, the second must be the famous Roman roads. They were built 2,000 years ago to link garrison with garrison, enabling help to be brought swiftly to the legions at York,

Hadrian's Wall begun in AD 122.

Caerleon and Chester. Watling Street ran from Dover (Dubrae) to London and then via St Albans to Wroxeter (Viroconium) on the Welsh border. Although a branch was pushed south to Caerleon just north of Newport, and another branch carried on east to Carnarvon, the principal road continued north to Chester and then crossed over to York. Ermine Street was the road stretching down the eastern side of Britain from York to Lincoln (Lindum) and then to Colchester and on to London. The Fosse Way ran from Lincoln to Exeter (or Isca Dumniorum – the Dumnia were the local Celtic tribe), crossing Watling Street on its way.

Thanks to the Romans, Britain grew rich as her citizens benefited from an economy based on bronze and gold coinage. A rubbish pit uncovered beneath the City of London's pavement suggests a wealthy and sophisticated populace who walked in elaborate sandals and enjoyed a delicately coloured pottery. Merchants now reckoned their sums on wax tablets with bone and wooden styluses, and bobbins for weaving show that Britons now rejoiced in the art of producing fine patterned linen. Britain also embarked on greater cultivation, aided by the crooked plough, and the Romans drained the marshes of East Anglia. Britain became one of the best sources of corn in the empire, with her own special warehouses in Rome. By the fourth century the emperor Julian had built warehouses in the rest of his empire to receive British wheat. British tin and iron ore, which the Iron Age Celts had done well by, became extremely profitable for the Roman Empire. In fact there is good reason to believe that the third largest imperial ironworks was in the eastern part of the Weald at Battle near Hastings. To this day the shape of its vast slagheap of iron waste from the iron industry which served the Roman fleet in Britain can be seen buried under the grass and trees which have grown over it during the past twenty centuries. A magnificently preserved Roman bath for naval officers has been discovered beside it in the grounds of the Beauport Park estate, its changing room amazingly still furnished with rare examples of 'lockers', of which only four others have survived from the old Roman Empire.

For 200 years Britain was ruled strongly from Rome. But, as the third century AD wore on, the leadership in Rome became complacent and allowed territories to slip out of their control. Local commanders of distant provinces given too much independence began to think of carving their own kingdoms out of the empire. Britain's distance from Rome made her attractive to such adventurers. Thus in 287 a Roman admiral named Carausius, who had been sent to clear Saxon pirates out of the English Channel, seized power in Britain. With the support of the Roman garrisons there he proclaimed himself emperor. Carausius had embarked on the conquest of northern Gaul when he was assassinated in 293. His murderer was his chief subordinate, Allectus. Allectus ruled Britain until 296 when he in his turn was killed by Constantius I, the warrior father of the Roman emperor Constantine the Great, who rushed from Rome to liberate a besieged London from Allectus and his Frankish mercenaries.

Constantius I's title was the Caesar of the West. This position had been invented as part of the Emperor Diocletian's reforms to bring stability back to the empire and so see off rebellious military leaders as well as the invading German tribes from the east. Recognizing that extensive changes were needed if the empire was to continue, Diocletian brought in a system of two emperors, the 'Augusti', and two 'Caesars', or junior emperors, who automatically became emperors on the death of the Augusti. These four rulers divided the eastern and western empires between them. Countries within the empire were now called dioceses, ruled by vicars. Britain herself became a diocese, consisting of four provinces, though it was only part of a much larger unit known as the Praetorian Prefecture of the Gauls.

Constantius after duly succeeding as Augustus marched from York to Tayside on a campaign against the Picts and Caledonians. But he died at York, and there famously his son, the half-English Constantine, was proclaimed emperor by the legions in 306. Constantine was one of the most important Roman emperors, whose espousal of Christianity in 313 changed the nature of the Roman Empire and of the European world. Constantine believed that the Christian God, who had appeared to him in a vision and told his soldiers to wear crosses on their shields, had given him victory at the famous battle of Milvian Bridge which had reunited the empire. Constantine shifted the empire's capital to the 'Christian Rome', the new city he built at Constantinople, and made Christianity the state religion, believing it would be a unifying force in the empire. The wealth the pagan temples had accumulated for centuries became the property of the Christian Church, which itself became an important pillar of the Roman Empire's organization. In addition, Constantine gave local bishops judicial powers above the local magistrate.

Though Constantine continued also to worship the sun, he had been brought up a Christian by his English mother Helena. At the beginning of the fourth century members of the small but charismatic Christian sect who had renounced earthly power and riches in favour of heavenly ones were being horribly persecuted by Diocletian, for he believed that the troubles of the empire were due to neglect of the ancient gods like Jupiter and Minerva. Britain had become a safe haven for fleeing Christians, because its ruler Constantius was married to a Christian and had some sympathy for their beliefs. Although Constantius demolished the British churches, or basilicas as they were called, he did not execute their devotees. Even so, Britain had three early Christian martyrs, St Julian, St Aaron and St Alban. Especially well known was the wealthy Romano-British youth St Alban from Verulamium in Hertfordshire, who was executed in 305 for sheltering a Christian priest and refusing to sacrifice to the ancient gods. Verulamium took the name St Albans in his honour.

By the time that Constantine was taking a personal interest in deciding doctrine there were already enough Christians in Britain to send three bishops to the Council of the Church in 314 at Arles. The Britons had their home-grown version of heresy in Pelagianism: the British thinker Pelagius had boldly disputed with the great African Church Father St Augustine of Hippo, and had insisted that the doctrine of original sin was mistaken. The Scots and Irish Churches sprang from the work of two Romano-British Christian saints: St Patrick, who famously converted Ireland to Christianity and who had created the papal see of Armagh by 450, and St Ninian, the north-countryman who began the conversion of the Caledonians and Picts in the early fifth century.

Yet, although the Romano-British Church produced some very great missionaries, Roman Christianity had shallow roots in England. Celtic deities continued to be worshipped alongside Christ. To some extent Christianity probably depended on the personal beliefs of individual lords of the great villas characteristic of Britain in the fourth century. There are surviving examples of the chi-rho Christian sign in mosaics, wall paintings and silver cutlery of such wealthy villa-owners in this period, notably in Dorset. The heathen Saxons, even now priming themselves on the other side of the North Sea to invade Britain, would succeed in almost completely erasing Christianity from England. Only in Cornwall and Wales, where pockets of Christian Romano-Celts hid themselves away from the invaders, did Christianity survive. By the seventh century, after 150 years of Saxon settlements, England herself would have to be converted anew to Christianity by Roman, Scottish and Irish missionaries.

For by the first decade of the fifth century, most of Britain's protectors against the Pictish and Saxon threat, the Roman legions, had either been withdrawn or were in the process of being withdrawn to defend Rome against the German tribes. In 402 the Visigoths under Alaric had entered Italy. Despite the structural reforms of Diocletian and Constantine the Roman Empire was no longer in command of its frontiers. It had been gravely weakened by civil war between Constantine's sons, but the chief danger facing it in the fourth century was a demographic phenomenon: the barbarian migrations or folk wanderings of the land-hungry German tribes. These aggressive military people from east of the River Danube in central Europe – the Visigoths, the Ostrogoths, the Vandals, the Alans, the Suevi, the Alemanni – had begun putting unbearable pressure on the outer Roman territories a hundred years before. In the mid-third century they had breached the Roman Empire's frontiers of the Rhine and the Danube and had been thrown back only by Diocletian's reforms.

After 375 when they were defeated in Russia by the terrifying Huns, a savage tribe from central Asia also on the move west, the alarmed German tribes would no longer brook the imperial government's refusal to let them in. In 376 the Visigoths and Ostrogoths, who lived on the eastern side of the Danube, begged the Emperor Valens to give them sanctuary by allowing them to cross the Danube and be federated within the Roman Empire. In return for land and sanctuary against the Huns, they said they would serve in the imperial armies. Though their subsequent slaughter of Valens two years later at Adrianople was a grim portent, the imperial government recognized that the pressure of the German tribes was such that it was best to have some of them on its side. Treaties were made and land was granted, some of it in north Gaul.

In 402 Rome decided to pull more soldiers out of Britain and bring them home. They were needed in Italy to defend the imperial city against the barbarian Visigoths under Alaric who were now encamped in the north of the country. If many more Roman soldiers were withdrawn the Britons would be completely at the mercy of their own enemies who were attacking with renewed vigour: the Picts from beyond the now scantily defended Wall in the north, the Scots from Hibernia, attacking Galloway, Wales and Cornwall, and the Saxons from across the North Sea, a northern branch of the German tribes putting such pressure on the Roman Empire.

Since the third century the more daring members of the population of what we now call north Germany and Denmark had been forming raiding parties to cross the North Sea and the Channel to Britain in ever larger numbers. By then the Roman army in Britain increasingly contained Gauls and Germans, Spaniards and Moors, and it seems that the little groups of Saxon ex-soldiers settling in Britain attracted by the good farmland and clement weather reported back to their relatives that here was a country ripe for the plucking.

By now Britain felt very remote from the imperial government, a remoteness which was emphasized by her being part of the Gallic Prefecture. Britain thus became a magnet for imperial pretenders, not least Magnus Maximus, one of the Emperor Theodosius' generals, who after a victory over the Picts was proclaimed emperor by his legions and successfully became ruler of the Praetorian Prefecture of Britain, Gaul and Spain until 387. Pretenders were welcomed by the vulnerable British if they seemed likely to protect them from their own barbarian enemies better than their Roman overlords.

It was under the British imperial pretender Constantine III that Britain severed her links with Rome for good. Constantine III had been elevated to the emperorship by the army in Britain on account of widespread dissatisfaction with the way the province was being treated by Rome. Since 402 Rome had not even paid the salaries of the imperial troops or civil servants remaining in Britain. But by 406, the year the barbarians crossed the Rhine, Rome had no time to think about Britain: she was concentrating on defending her homeland. As with many of her more distant provinces, the imperial government may no longer have been able to afford the wages, or perhaps the chaos arising from the war against the barbarians prevented the money being shipped to Britain. Whatever the reason, this failure greatly angered the local magnates and the wealthier classes of Britain on whose shoulders the fiscal burden now fell. Constantine III, who had invaded Gaul and Spain, was at first allowed to retain his north-western empire by the Emperor of the West, Honorius. But his yen for external conquest meant that his soldiers were not stationed in Britain to ward off the newly vigorous attacks by the Irish, Saxons and Picts. Infuriated by Constantine remaining in Spain when he was needed at home, it seems that in 409 British leaders expelled the last remnants of his purportedly imperial administration.

But the feeling was mutual. In 410 the sack of Rome by Alaric and the

Goths obliged Rome for the moment at least to wash her hands of the distant province. Honorius sent a formal letter to the British cities telling them that they could no longer depend on the Romans for their defence against the Picts. Henceforth they must rely on themselves. Citizens should now carry weapons, which hitherto had been forbidden. Local British rulers sprang into existence to fill the power vacuum left by the collapse of the imperial administration.

At first this was a relief. The British magnates had loathed the regulations requiring conscription into the Roman army, brought in recently to make up for the lack of slaves as the empire ceased to expand by conquest. Conscription drew on their own source of labour and robbed their fields of men just when they were needed for the harvest. They were delighted that they no longer had to pay the heavy Roman taxes that the enormous bureaucracy of the top-heavy imperial government needed if it was to maintain itself. Contemporary historians write of how the British people threw off all Roman customs and Roman law. To begin with they were happy to rely on Saxon mercenaries for all defensive purposes where previously they had used the Roman legions. They would soon learn, as the Romans had, that it was better not to place yourself in the power of the barbarians unless you had time to train them to adopt your habits and customs.

The Roman style of life continued among quite a few of the British magnates and well-to-do townspeople for a couple of decades after the withdrawal of the legions. In 429 St Germanus, on a visit to Britain with other bishops to dispute the Pelagian controversy, encountered a wealthy society which still had all the hallmarks of Roman civilization: its members were richly dressed and highly educated and could speak Latin. St Patrick, who died in 461, came from one of these landowning families.

But, despite the British people's Roman habits, the dissolution of the empire was changing their way of life even before they were assaulted by the Anglo-Saxons, reliance upon whose arms was storing up a terrible fate for them. As the empire was replaced worldwide by individual German territories, its sophisticated global economy and long-distance trade based on a 400-year-old Roman peace slowly came to an end. By the 420s coinage was starting to die out in Britain. Within a generation in many places Roman cemeteries like the one at Poundbury in Dorset had become deserted. Roman laws requiring burial outside the town walls for health reasons were no longer obeyed because there were no longer Roman officials to enforce them. Furthermore the trade and employment in the cities that the Roman legions and civil government had brought to Britain had gone. Without large numbers of soldiers needing goods and services, towns declined. Without a central taxation system, many of the allurements of Roman civilization, like roads, baths and government, simply fell away. The famous pottery factories, which gave so much employment because the Romans used pots the way we use plastic bags, as containers and transporters for every kind of commodity, vanished – and so did the art of making glass.

Within thirty years the combined effect of the attacks by the Saxons and the decay of towns meant that the inhabitants of Britain were soon living in a far more primitive fashion than their grandparents had. But the decline of sophistication caused by the deterioration of the global economy was a fact throughout the Roman world. In Britain and other former Roman provinces trade became local and was reduced to barter. By 481 there would no longer be a Roman emperor in the west. Rome had been sacked for a second time and Rome herself would be controlled by the eastern tribe, the Ostrogoths. The Roman Empire which had ruled the whole of the Mediterranean and had ranged from Britain in the west to Romania (hence the name of that country and her Latin language) in the east had shrunk to Constantinople and some surrounding lands. On the continent in the empire's place various tribes ruled: the Ostrogoths (east Goths) in Italy, the Franks and Burgundians in north and middle Gaul, the Visigoths (west Goths) in southern Gaul and Spain, the Vandals in north Africa.

It was in about 447 that the former Roman province of Britannia, already adrift from Rome, began to experience her own concerted attack by the Teutonic tribes of the Jutes, Angles and Saxons. Although this was an era for which contemporary written sources do not exist (that is why it has been called the Dark Ages), there is evidence to suggest that the beginning of this great invasion was sparked off by an ambitious British tyrant. After the Roman fashion he imported Germanic tribesmen in the 430s to act as mercenaries against his fellow British kings and to protect his territory against the Picts, who had become increasingly troublesome ever since the legions deserted their positions along the Wall. As a reward for the Saxon mercenaries' services this British king – whom England's first historian, the great eighth-century Anglo-Saxon monk the Venerable Bede, said was called Vortigern – seems to have encouraged them to settle on land of his in Kent and near London. But a combination of rising sea levels along the north German coast, reports of the fertile lowlands and mild weather in England compared to their cold climate and the obvious inability of the Britons to defend themselves meant Vortigern and his fellow Britons got more than they bargained for. The chief deities of the Jutes, Angles and Saxons were Woden the God of War and Thor the God of Thunder – in other words, they were fierce warrior peoples for whom glory was to be won by fighting, not by building towns.

Beginning round mid-century, waves of Germanic tribesmen moved over the next fifty years to Britain in such numbers that they pushed the Romano-British out of their native lands into the west. Instead of being content with their own small kingdom, these Saxons under their dynamic leaders – whom legend names Hengist and Horsa – turned on their British host when he refused to increase their holdings and murdered him. They started seizing more areas of England for themselves, beginning with Thanet and Kent, then moving west to the Isle of Wight and east Hampshire. Coastal south-east Britain would become known as Sussex, the land of the South Saxons. By 527 a new wave of Saxons had gone east of London and called the land they settled the country of the East Saxons – Essex. Meanwhile the Angles, whose own country lay so nearly opposite across the North Sea, seized what would become known as the country of the East Angles, or East Anglia.

The British Romano-Celts took shelter in the south-west in the old territories of the Ordovices and Silures which the Angles and Saxons called Wales, meaning land of the foreigner. Some went north to the three British kingdoms established above Hadrian's Wall around 400 – Strathclyde, Gododdin and Galloway. As early as 460, after ten years of bitter fighting, the Anglo-Saxon force had slaughtered many of the Romano-British, sacked the main cities and taken over much of the south and east of the country. By 495 the first part of the English settlement was completed and the Anglo-Saxon kingdoms reached as far north as York and as far west as Southampton.

History tends to be the story of the successful, but for two centuries the Anglo-Saxon conquerors were incapable of recording their actions. The fair-haired, pale-eyed Angles, Saxons and Jutes were illiterate north German tribespeople from the neck of the harsh windswept Cimbrian peninsula, the modern-day Denmark, Schleswig and Holstein. Unlike the Germanic peoples taking over the territories of the former Roman Empire in France and Italy, most of these bloodthirsty invaders of Britain had never felt its civilizing influence: though a number of Saxons from the German Bremerhaven coast were to be found in the Roman armies, more of them were pirates and enemies of the empire. These peoples' remote northerly geographical position (Jutland is on the same parallel of latitude as Aberdeen in northern Scotland) ensured that most of them had escaped contact with the Roman Empire, which had educated their fellow Teutonic tribes from further south.

Moreover, the Teutonic tribes such as the Burgundians, Visigoths, Vandals and Franks, had been deeply affected by Roman civilization when they had settled within the empire. As their power grew and that of the empire weakened, the civil administration of the Roman government on the continent tended to remain in place and was taken over wholesale by the new rulers. In Britain, on the other hand, the expulsion of the Roman government left no proper central political or economic structures for the Saxons to adopt. The wild Germanic tribes arriving in Britain were quite unaffected by the already withering Roman civilization they encountered. In addition, the transition to Anglo-Saxon rule was brutal, bloody and sudden. Most of England would be depopulated or her inhabitants slaughtered or subdued, so no classical influences modified the Anglo-Saxons' savage ways. In Britain there was no time for a considered handover. The small individual kingdoms of Saxons established their own unadulterated institutions.

We do not know how the Romano-British reacted to the German peoples setting up homes at such bewildering speed on their fertile lands in the south and east while many were even forced to live in caves in Wales or Cornwall. The few contemporary references are mainly glancing asides by foreign historians, like the sixth-century Byzantine writer Procopius. For the most part, therefore, English history of this very early period has to be deciphered from the physical evidence of settlements unearthed by archaeology and from references to ancient practices preserved in the Anglo-Saxon laws which began being written down in the seventh century. It can be augmented by hearsay and folk tales handed down over the centuries, and sought out by the Venerable Bede. It was only with the reconversion to Christianity of the Anglo-Saxons at the end of the sixth century that learning returned to England, though it had meanwhile continued in Wales and Cornwall. Anglo-Saxon monks and priests then began writing down accounts of life in their new country which would be collected in the late ninth century as their official record, *The Anglo-Saxon Chronicle*. The nearest Briton we have as an eyewitness of the horrors his country endured at the hands of the pagan Anglo-Saxons is the mid-sixth-century Romano-British monk Gildas, who recounted the story in his book *Of the Destruction of the British*. But even he is writing a hundred years after the first Anglo-Saxon invasion.

By about 460, the deRomanization of Britain had become very noticeable to contemporaries abroad. Much of the country had been entirely taken over by the Saxon tribes, and all feared the worst for its former inhabitants. Some of the British community still considered themselves Roman enough in the late 440s to send a plea for help to the ruler of what remained of the Roman Empire, the great general Aetius, who was trying to keep Attila the Hun and his horde out of Gaul. They headed their letter to him, 'The Groans of the British'. 'The Barbarians drive us to the sea,' they wailed; 'the sea throws us back on the Barbarians: thus two modes of death await us; we are either slain or drowned.' But Aetius had too much to handle nearer home to think of Britain. It was not until 451 at the Battle of the Catalaunian Plains that he was able to halt Attila decisively and drive the Huns out of France. One Roman who did return to help was St Germanus, who led the Britons in battle and told them to shout 'Alleluia!' as they fought the enemy. But it was not enough.

Under the onslaught of the Germanic tribes the only hope for the Romano-British was to abandon their villas and their cities. As the Saxons set fire to their houses and murdered those who fled, some Roman Britons buried their family silver beneath their cellars, thinking that one day when the invaders had been expelled they would be able to come back for it. Some of that silver may now be seen in the British Museum, having been found centuries later, for its original owners never returned. The solid Roman British citizens, able to dispute legal points with the best lawyers in Rome, were forced to take refuge behind the palisades of the ancient hill forts which their far-off primitive ancestors had built in the Iron Age 400 years before. Now they had to refortify them with timber as so few of them knew how to work stone, thanks to the rapid decline in the art of Roman stonemasonry.

Everywhere fanatical barbarians with their manes of long hair – a mark of their warrior caste – fell on the British and put them to the sword. Invoking the names of Thor and Woden, whose ravens fed on human blood, they went on the rampage. Priests, women and children were all horribly murdered, often before the very altars where they had sought sanctuary. So many were killed that there were not enough people left to bury them. Those making for the Welsh hills were butchered in heaps, and even those who surrendered had no guarantee of mercy. Thus in the first years of the Saxon invasion the old population of England was very nearly destroyed.

Many fled to the British colony of Armorica in Gaul, which had been established at the time of the pretender Magnus Maximus in the late fourth century. They found some comfort in a country by the sea which so nearly resembled the one they had left behind. So many Romano-British made their home in Armorican Gaul, and so powerful were they, that to this day their descendants speak a version of the ancient British tongue – and that piece of France, Brittany, is still named after them. Britannia, the name of the Roman province, disappeared from people's lips and was replaced by the word England, as in Angle-land, until the anglicized name Britain was revived in 1707 to describe the union between England, Scotland and Wales.

Writing a century after the first invasions, Gildas would note that all the Roman cities remained abandoned: 'our cities are still not occupied as they were; even today they are dismal and deserted ruins'. Having become a literate people, highly educated by the Roman curriculum and trained to be clerks and administrators in the Romano-British towns, accustomed to underground central-heating systems, with glass in their windows and pavements at their feet, the Britons had lost the hardy spirit which Roman commentators had so admired. After 400 years of Roman occupation, the wild Celts whose ancestors had been those fierce, half-naked charioteers had been replaced by courteous Latin-speaking Roman settlers. As Romano-Celts worshipping the gentle God of the Christians who abhorred violence, they were helpless against the Angles and Saxons.

Fortunately two outstanding leaders appeared on the scene to transform the British into an army of resistance between the first onslaught of the Anglo-Saxons and the end of the century. The first was a high-born Roman, perhaps an ex-general, called Ambrosius Aurelianus, whom Gildas calls 'a modest man who of all the Roman nation was then alone in the confusion of this troubled period left alive'. The second, a Romano-Celtic leader who arose in the west in the late fifth century after the Saxons had been in Britain for a generation, and who may have been Aurelianus' son, managed to hold the Saxon foe at bay for thirty years. He pushed the West Saxons back out of Dorset into the middle of Wiltshire in a series of clashes culminating in the critical Battle of Mons Badonicus (which may now be marked by the town of Liddington) in about 500 or 516. This leader, whose beginning and end are wreathed in fantastic mystery, and whose tomb has never been found, is believed to have kept the west a separate British kingdom until a new wave of Saxons in about 550 finally completed the takeover of England. He may have been the original of the great Celtic leader now known as King Arthur, about whom by the ninth century very many stories were circulating, and he may have lived in the large Iron Age fort at South Cadbury in Somerset, which was heavily refortified during the fifth and sixth centuries (remains of its kingly hall have been found).

What can be said for sure is that the myths and legends which have inspired the writers and poets ever since cluster the most thickly in those parts of Britain which became the refuge of the fleeing southern British – that is, in Cornwall and Wales. The tales are curiously uniform in suggesting that King Arthur is not dead but merely sleeping, perhaps in a cave in Wales, perhaps in the fairy isles of Avalon, and would one day awaken to help Britain in her darkest hour. Apart from their obvious Christian symbolism, they imply that the Romano-British Celts were a desperate but not yet despairing people who believed that they would one day return to their homes. But it was not to be.

Thanks to the victories of the Romano-Celt 'Arthur' there was peace for about fifty years from Mons Badonicus until the mid-sixth century – we know that because Gildas was writing in a time of peace. But only ten years later, in about 550, a new invasion of the Saxons began, so that by the end of the sixth century Saxon kingdoms were permanently established throughout most of England up to the Scottish Lowlands. Two tribes of Angles colonized eastern England from the Humber northwards. The southern kingdom called Deira approximated to Yorkshire; north of it stretched the kingdom of Bernicia, which ran from the Tees to the Firth of Forth. By the early seventh century Bernicia and Deira had been combined in the kingdom of Northumbria. Below spread the kingdom of the middle English or Mercians, which ran from the northern border of Wales in the west to the kingdom of the Angles in the east. At its foot began the kingdom of Wessex or the West Saxons, which, thanks to the valour of its chieftain Ceawlin, by the early seventh century reached as far as the lower Severn. Only Wales and the west country held out against the Saxons, Cornwall resisting until the mid-ninth century. Meanwhile in the north the Irish tribes had taken advantage of the Roman absence to establish a kingdom of Scots to the west of the Picts above the northern Roman provinces. Thanks to the impact St Patrick had made upon Ireland, in 563 a monk from one of the monasteries he had founded there, St Columba, would finish the work of St Ninian, converting the Scots and Picts to Christianity from his island of Iona off the west Highland coast.

In Wales, Cornwall and Ireland the Christian Celtic Church preserved some of the classical habits. Thanks to the Church and the education perpetuated by the new monasteries, writing in Latin continued and manuscripts were copied for wider circulation. But, burning with hatred for their oppressors, the Romano-British kept themselves to themselves and refused to have anything to do with converting their Anglo-Saxon neighbours to Christianity. Its civilizing influence would have to come from abroad. Fortunately for the future of England the Angles and Saxons were not to remain in a state of savagery for long.

In the last years of the sixth century, it is said (this is reported as a national tradition by Bede in the eighth century), the powerful new pope Gregory the Great was reminded of the lost Roman Christian province of Britannia when he saw some handsome slave children, blond and blue-eyed, in the market at Rome. On asking who they were and being told they were Angli or Angles, the pope is said to have remarked thoughtfully, 'Non Angli sed angeli' (Not Angles but angels). What is certainly true is that in 597 Pope Gregory, who was breathing new life into the papacy, despatched a slightly reluctant mission to convert King Ethelbert of Kent to Christianity. The pope suspected his legate Bishop Augustine might obtain a hearing because the king was married to a Christian Frank, the former Princess Bertha. Thus began the reconversion of England to Christianity and the country's return to a higher form of civilization. It would bring England back into the fold of a Europe where for the next thousand years a common religious culture called Christendom took the place of the Roman Empire, unifying the whole.

6th-century Angle slaves in the market at Rome. To the future Pope Gregory the Great, they looked like angels and reminded him of the need to reconvert Britannia.

ANGLO-SAXON

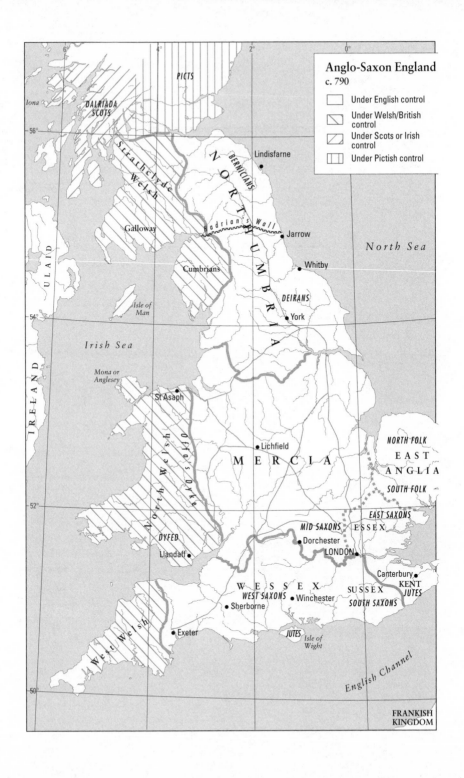

Anglo-Saxon England
c. 790

Under English control

Under Welsh/British control

Under Scots or Irish control

Under Pictish control

PICTS

Iona

DALRIADA SCOTS

Strathclyde Welsh

Galloway

Cumbrians

ULAID

Isle of Man

IRELAND

Irish Sea

Mona or Anglesey

St Asaph

North Welsh

Offa's Dyke

DYFED

Llandaff

West Welsh

Exeter

NORTHUMBRIA

BERNICIANS

Lindisfarne

Hadrian's Wall

Jarrow

Whitby

DEIRANS

York

North Sea

MERCIA

Lichfield

NORTH FOLK

EAST ANGLIA

SOUTH FOLK

EAST SAXONS

ESSEX

MID SAXONS

Dorchester

LONDON

Canterbury

KENT

JUTES

WESSEX

WEST SAXONS

Winchester

Sherborne

SUSSEX

SOUTH SAXONS

JUTES

Isle of Wight

English Channel

FRANKISH KINGDOM

Ethelbert of Kent to the Viking Invasions
(597–865)

When the papal mission arrived on the Island of Thanet in 597, its leader St Augustine was extremely nervous about meeting the Saxons. If King Ethelbert of Kent resembled any of the other German barbarians such as King Clovis of Gaul, his wife's grandfather, he would be a fierce, soldierly type. King Clovis had said that if he had been present at Christ's crucifixion he would have avenged it, which was rather missing the point. Despite Augustine's fears Pope Gregory was insistent in a series of letters that the mission be accomplished. At the end of the sixth century Ethelbert was the most important king, the bretwalda, of the Anglo-Saxon kingdoms into which England was divided. If Ethelbert's country was converted to Christianity he might influence the other kingdoms to copy him.

The Roman mission of St Augustine to King Ethelbert of Kent, in AD 597, begins conversion of the southern English to Christianity.

King Ethelbert lived up to expectations. Though the small group of forty travel-weary monks were unarmed and wearing homespun brown habits bearing before them a silver cross of the suffering Christ, he treated them as if they were wizards or magicians. He insisted on meeting them in the open air where their magic would be less potent to prevent them casting spells, and he would not allow them to leave the island. However, one of the conditions of King Ethelbert allying himself to the powerful royal house of the Franks had been that his wife Queen Bertha was to be allowed to practise her religion. So, living among the worshippers of Woden and Thor, she did not forget her faith. An old Roman church to St Martin was still standing on the eastern side of the king's capital of Canterbury, and there she and her spiritual adviser Bishop Luidhard were allowed to pray.

After a while, having observed that the monks, who had brought him a richly decorated Bible and jewels from the pope, were quiet and well behaved, King Ethelbert allowed them off the island to worship in the queen's church. Soon Ethelbert would be so impressed by their preaching of a future eternal life at a time when even a king could do little against illness, by their reading and writing and by their care of the poor, that he himself was baptized. By the end of the year, 10,000 of his people had been baptized as well.

Under the influence of the Roman missionaries, who received regular advice in letters from Pope Gregory, for the first time in the England of the Anglo-Saxons a code of laws was written down in 616. But this time it was in English, not Latin. Unlike the Romano-British the Anglo-Saxons could understand only their own language. These first English laws of Ethelbert's, which were much influenced by the Franks, protected the new clergy and the land the king donated to them for church-building. By the end of the seventh century the churches would be free of taxation. Augustine built the monastery of St Augustine (which became the burial place of the early Anglo-Saxon kings of Kent), as well as founding the church that became Canterbury Cathedral. In the monastery the letters from Pope Gregory would be preserved, as well as other precious written materials. The Roman missionaries built further monasteries, which developed into centres of learning for the people of Kent. A fashion developed for wealthy noblemen to have their sons taught to read and write in monasteries for whose foundation they gave money and land. In 602 the pope created the archbishopric of Canterbury for St Augustine.

Pope Gregory had intended there to be twin archbishoprics in England, at Canterbury and York, because he still thought of England as the Roman province – one of whose centres would be the important Roman city of Eboracum, or York. But York was now part of the kingdom of Deira, which was entirely separate from Kent even though Ethelbert's lands stretched as far as Deira. York and its environs would therefore have to be converted separately, as would all the other kingdoms of Anglo-Saxon England. Another bishopric was created in 604 at nearby Rochester, whose 'chester' or 'ceaster' suffix denotes in the Anglo-Saxon way an old Roman city; a further bishopric, for the East Saxons, was created the same year at the old settlement of Londinium, known to the Saxons as Lundenwig.

Though he knew that Ethelbert was the most important king in the country, Pope Gregory was unaware of the extent of the changes that had taken place in England since the departure of the Romans. As we have seen, England had long ago lost all vestiges of her Roman national administration. The country was now divided up into the separate lands of small tribal peoples who themselves were in the process of being subsumed by the more warlike kings. Thus the heads of the small tribes became underkings or what the Anglo-Saxons called ealdormen (the word for military leader) of the larger kingdoms. By the end of the seventh century there were seven kingdoms altogether, known as the heptarchy; they were Sussex, Kent, Essex, East Anglia, Wessex, Mercia and Northumbria. Historians have to make educated guesses about these tribal peoples because they were not literate. But surviving references to ancient practices in later documents, literary fragments and law codes have brought them to the conclusion that the early Anglo-Saxons still shared many characteristics with their Germanic ancestors of the first century AD, characteristics which had been observed by Roman commentators.

The most important feature of the social organization of the Germanic peoples was the family, or to use an Old English word the kin. Loyalty to one's kin was a key concept. The kin had an obligation to kill the murderer of one of their own. Even by the first century, however, this had been commuted to a money payment, the so-called wer-gild or price of a man (literally man-gold), which had the effect of making society more peaceful. If payment was not made, the custom was that the victim's kin must either kill the perpetrator or be paid not to do so. In addition a man's kin were expected to swear an oath to support him in court if he was accused of a crime. By the tenth century the kin was responsible for a criminal family member's future behaviour. Over the centuries kings and their nobles, who began to take charge of the village courts, would accept the evidence of the community to balance the evidence of the kin when it came to establishing the facts about a crime. By the ninth century kings like Alfred the Great would be changing the law to make sure that duty to one's lord took precedence over duty to one's kin. But, with these shifts of emphasis, loyalty and the sacredness of oath-taking continued to form the bedrock of Anglo-Saxon society.

Most of the Angle and Saxon invaders settled in England in tribal groups of free peasants under separate leaders, not under one national king; over those separate peoples overlord kings and bigger kingdoms would arise. This can be seen by the many place names in England that end in 'ing', which means 'people of' – thus Hastings signifies 'the people of Haesta' and Woking 'the people of Wocca'. A famous tenth-century document drawn up for taxation purposes, the so-called Tribal Hideage, identifies many of these peoples and the amount of land they held in 'hides', the Old English unit of landholding and assessment for taxation. Depending on which kingdom you inhabited, a hide consisted of between 40 and 120 acres.

King Ethelbert's law code reveals that the people of Kent were used to discussing local affairs in popular open-air assemblies under the direction of the more learned or wealthy. Since the late sixth century there seems to have been a tribal court for every hundred hides, about 4,000 acres or more. They were probably the origin of the 'hundred' courts to which there are documentary references by the tenth century. By then the courts of the hundred were held on a monthly basis to sort out breaches of the customary and Church law and to adjust taxes, reflecting the fact that all the English kingdoms were now divided into administrative units called hundreds. For many centuries the judges were chosen by the local people rather than by the king. In contrast to the Roman way of life, early on among these primitive Anglo-Saxon peoples there were genuinely democratic customs, even though they themselves had slaves.

A small class of nobles formed the wealthiest level of Kentish society, but the most numerous element in that kingdom at the end of the sixth century was the free peasant or ceorl (churl), whose rights were protected by law and whose immediate overlord was not a noble but the king himself. In Kent the ceorl was worth a hundred golden shillings to his family: that was the price of killing him, the wer-gild. The disruption caused by the ninth-century Viking invasions ruined many of these people, so that they had to labour for the local lord to pay the swingeing tax bill of Danegeld, or to pay for the protection of the lord's soldiers when war threatened his home and crops. At the same time many Anglo-Saxons managed to cling to the financial autonomy of their distant ancestors, valuing the independence of mind it allowed.

The late-seventh-century laws of King Ine of Wessex give us further information about the western cousins of these men. They were required to serve in the fyrd, the Anglo-Saxon militia which was called out against national enemies at times of crisis; and there was a special law imposing heavy penalties on anyone who penetrated the hedge around another's property when the fyrd was out. With their fellow villagers they had to support the king by paying a feorm – that is, an ancient royal food rent, originally a certain amount of ale, oxen, honey and loaves which was later commuted into a money rent or tax. With a contribution assessed by hideage, it seems that from the earliest times the Anglo-Saxons were expected to help build local bridges and walls and the king's fortresses if called upon. By 700 the kings of the separate kingdoms of England each had their own council of wise men called the Witan. Members of the Witan, who tended to be the great landowners of the kingdom, witnessed the king's acts of state, whether it was giving land to a noble, or declaring that a monastery need not pay rent. They could elect a king from a royal line if they chose, but their chief role was to advise him.

Just as they had settled England in tribes, the Anglo-Saxon peasants tended to live in small villages. Their fields were quite different from the rectangular ones of the Celtic Iron Age, being laid out in long curving strips. In some kingdoms some land was farmed in common, in strips scattered over open fields. In others, such as Kent, land was organized in a more self-contained way. All over England woods on the outskirts of villages tended to be held as common land where everyone could put their pigs, sheep and cows out to pasture.

These blond, big-boned Angles and Saxons had heavier, stronger ploughs than the ancient Britons, whose lighter ploughs had led them to prefer high ground and lighter soil. So the Anglo-Saxons were unafraid of the richer, heavier, alluvial valley soil of the midlands. Increasing numbers of them therefore began to spread along the Ouse towards the Tyne and Tees, enlarging the kingdoms of Mercia, Deira and Bernicia. By the early seventh century the latter two would be united by the powerful King Ethelfrith into the kingdom of Northumbria (the people north of the Humber).

The Anglo-Saxon peoples regarded the ruins of the vast Roman buildings they came upon with wonder. They were primitive builders themselves who could handle only wood and brick. The skills required to build the towering marble temples, the immense stone Roman baths, the aqueducts that littered England were so far beyond them that they could not believe they had been constructed by humans. 'The work of giants' is how their literature repeatedly describes Roman architecture. It used to be thought that the Anglo-Saxons avoided Roman cities because they believed superstitiously that they contained ghosts. But the latest research suggests that, while at first the Saxons and Angles may have preferred to carry away superior Roman bricks to build their own settlements, by the end of the seventh century the old Roman cities were beginning to attract a new population of Anglo-Saxon city-dwellers. These cities, such as York and London, never contained more than a few thousand people, as most Anglo-Saxons preferred to live in the country as farmers. However, the farmers would build a king's hall, a royal manor or tun, which survives in the place names Wilton, Walton and Kingston. These edifices were impressive (if crude) wooden buildings which functioned as administrative centres and which had to be large enough to receive the local hundred when they brought their goods to support the king.

But the king's hall, whether it was the home of a king's ealdorman or the king himself, was also a warm cheerful place where mead was passed round in a horn from person to person at a vast log table, with a fire burning in the enormous hearth and clean green rushes on the floor to sweeten the air. Although most Anglo-Saxons had settled down to farm they still retained a folk memory of their ancestors, the north German warriors, which found expression in the vigorous songs which bards sang for them in the great hall, recounting the exploits of Beowulf for example.

Loyalty, revenge and death were some of the favourite themes of Anglo-Saxon literature, but perhaps most popular of all were poems about the loyalty between the king and his men, the devoted noblemen known as thanes. Like the bond between kin, the bond between a king and his bodyguard was sacred. It was a disgrace for a man to allow his lord to fall in battle without avenging him by his own death. The early history of England is full of heroic examples of thanes who refused to change sides even if their lord was dead, like those of the eighth-century King Cynewulf of Wessex who avenged his slaying by laying down their own lives.

As the seventh century dawned in England, outside Kent most of the country remained wedded to the heathen gods and pagan way of life. It would take men of tremendous conviction to woo them from the powerful deities after whom they had named many features of the landscape – Thundridge in Hertfordshire meant Thunor's or Thor's ridge, and so on. The Church would become one of the pillars on which the English kingdoms were built, the essence of the civilization of the middle ages. But the raw material the Church was battling with was rough, pagan and insensitive. The monks seeking to convert the Saxons to Christianity often had to adapt their prayers and stories to attract an audience which admired strength and found it hard to admire the Christian reverence for suffering.

Nevertheless, thanks to the force and energy of Augustine's Roman missionaries, and of other missionaries from Ireland and Scotland, within less than a century the Church had converted the whole of the savage country of England to Christianity. It would go on to transform the Anglo-Saxon people and their culture in an astonishing way. From bloodthirsty warriors, the Anglo-Saxons became a people whose sons learned to read and write Latin and thus had access to the knowledge of the ancients. For 150 years in England, from the 660s to the 820s, there was an extraordinary revival of learning in the new monasteries which swept

Christian Irish missionaries setting off across the Irish Sea.

rapidly over the country. It would reach its peak in seventh-century Northumbria, as seen in the illuminated Lindisfarne Gospels, and a scholarly and artistic renaissance would spread from England to the kingdom of the Franks. Links were created between the continent and England not seen since the early fifth century. After 300 years of constructing simple wooden dwellings, the Anglo-Saxons started to put up great numbers of elaborate churches and monasteries as it became socially prestigious to erect buildings to the glory of God. Thanks to French and Italian artists whom the late-seventh-century Archbishop of Canterbury Theodore of Tarsus brought to England, the Anglo-Saxons would be exposed to far more sophisticated workmanship than the wattle and daub of their native Denmark and northern Germany.

English buildings would become splendid again under the influence of the Christian Church with its links to a higher continental civilization. Streets began to be paved, and the floors of kings' halls were made out of tiny pieces of decorative stone. Cloth of gold was the material once more seen on their interior walls, as it had been in the days of the Caesars. Glass-making would return to England after three centuries, thanks to the English Church's strong links with Gaul, for the Gauls had kept that Roman art going. At the end of the seventh century, the warrior and nobleman Benedict Biscop would be the first person to import Gaulish glass-makers to the monastery he had founded at Jarrow on the Tyne. Glass, soon to be stained glass, appeared in church windows for the first time in Anglo-Saxon England.

But early English Christianity was a very fragile plant, dependent on the patronage of a strong ruler. After King Ethelbert of Kent died in 616, his son and successor Eadbald was so hostile to Christianity that Kent trembled on the edge of paganism again. Members of the Roman mission became so dispirited that many decided to quit Kent for France. According to tradition it was only because the Prince of Apostles, St Peter, appeared in a vision to one of their number, Bishop Laurentius, that they returned. In a rage St Peter set about the bishop, beating him ferociously, reminding him all the while of the parable of the Good Shepherd and insisting that he should not abandon his sheep to the infidel wolves. The next day Eadbald was so alarmed by the weals St Laurentius showed him that he reformed and the other bishops returned.

We would have little knowledge of the story of how the astonishing changes took place in the lives of the wild Anglo-Saxons were it not for the detective work of the eighth-century monk from the monastery at Jarrow who is always known as the Venerable Bede. This great writer, the father of English history and one of the most influential writers of the first millennium in Europe, was born about 670. His tomb may still be seen at Durham Cathedral. Bede made it his business to search out the facts as opposed to the myths and legends about the origins of the English people. He was hard working, scientifically rigorous and wide ranging in his investigations. Though he consulted eyewitnesses where he could, every piece of information he presented as a fact had to be backed up by documentary evidence, for which he scoured ancient documents in England as well as sending to the papal registers at Rome for information. He also perfected the system invented by Dionysius Exiguus of chronological dating, taking the birth of Christ as the beginning of modern time. Bede's books became so famous throughout eighth-century Europe that owing to his influence the letters AD (Anno Domini, 'in the year of Our Lord') were adopted for presenting dates everywhere.

The story of the transformation of England is set down in Bede's book *The Ecclesiastical History of the English People*. From it derives the greater part of our knowledge of the fifth-century invasion and the sixth-, seventh- and eighth-century kingdoms of England. The next most important conversion of the peoples of England after Kent was that of the kingdom of the Northumbrians. Although the new Bretwalda of England on the death of Ethelbert was Raedwald, the King of East Anglia, it was owing to an exiled prince of the northern kingdom of Deira (modern Yorkshire) at Raedwald's court, Edwin (the future founder of Northumbria), that the most influential movement of English Christianity began.

Though most early Anglo-Saxon kings are covered in obscurity, Raedwald is one about whom rather a lot is known. In the summer of

The Bewcastle Cross, Cumbria (7th or 8th century). One of the best examples of Anglo-Saxon preaching crosses that were sometimes used instead of churches.

1939, just before the Second World War broke out, what is generally acknowledged to be his tomb was found on what was formerly the Suffolk coast at Sutton Hoo. The magnificent remains, which are thought to date from circa 621–30 and are now on display in the British Museum, further amplify our picture of seventh-century Anglo-Saxon rulers like Raedwald himself and his client Edwin of Northumbria. At the top of a hundred-foot headland, not unlike the funeral pyre of Beowulf, 'high and broad and visible to those journeying the ocean', was found a burial chamber made out of a ninety-foot longship, the kind of vessel in which Raedwald's Angle ancestors had famously appeared.

What is especially interesting about Raedwald's tomb is that it shows that there had been a revival of international trade in Europe, which for two centuries after the fall of the western Roman Empire had decayed to local barter. Raedwald's helmet and armour were made in Sweden, while his drinking bowls were the product of Middle Eastern craftsmen. The many different kinds of foreign coin show what complicated and far-reaching trade Raedwald was involved in, taking in Constantinople and Alexandria.

Sutton Hoo also reveals that, despite Raedwald's veneer of Christianity, his deepest beliefs were as pagan as those of Tutankhamun. For he was buried with quite as much grave furniture as any of the ancient Egyptians, with an enormous cauldron and an immense mead horn beautifully mounted in silver for drinking in the halls of Valhalla. Gold belt buckles weighing more than a pound each, with intricate designs of stylized hunting animals like falcons, indicate that there were brilliant smiths at work in seventh-century England who had developed the art of cloisonné to a peak it would be hard to reach today. But what is outstanding about this man is his appearance as a warrior. His wonderful iron helmet covered with a layer of bronze sculpted with fighting figures, with menacing slits for the eyes and flaps to protect the ears, could only strike fear in those who encountered him.

Edwin of Northumbria was a warrior of this kind too. In the seventh century, when most of the Anglo-Saxon kingdoms were in a constant state of war, battling for territory, it could only be with the support of such a man that Christianity could become permanently established. With Raedwald's help Edwin had defeated his enemy Ethelfrith, who had united the kingdom of Deira round York with Bernicia as far as the Scottish borders and thus became king of the whole of Northumbria. But it was his marriage to Ethelbert of Kent's Christian daughter Ethelburga that was the other crucial feature of Edwin's reign. For she brought with her to the Northumbrian court a Roman Christian monk of intense and determined personality named Paulinus. A potent combination of intellectual argument and magnificent papal gifts such as a silver looking-glass and a gilt ivory comb of exquisite Italian worksmanship, as well as a shirt of extraordinarily fine wool, successfully appealed to the king's taste and to his sense of his kingly rank.

King Edwin's conversion was a very serious matter which was evidently not embarked on without discussion among – and in effect with the permission of – his nobles and his leading heathen priest. It prompted one of the most famous passages in the literature of the Anglo-Saxons, written by Bede, which gives us a rare portrait of the seventh-century Anglo-Saxon ruler's life. After the high priest Coifi of Northumbria had frankly admitted that even he had not gained from sacrificing to idols, one of the king's chief men spoke out as follows:

Early-7th-century Anglo-Saxon iron helmet from the ship burial at Sutton Hoo, Suffolk, believed to be that of King Raedwald of East Anglia.

> This is how the present life of man on earth, King, appears to me in comparison with that time which is unknown to us. You are sitting feasting with your ealdormen and thegns in winter-time; the fire is burning on the hearth in the middle of the hall and all inside is warm, while outside the wintry storms of rain and snow are raging; and a sparrow flies swiftly through the hall. It enters in at one door and quickly flies out through the other. For the few moments it is inside, the storm and wintry tempest cannot touch it, but after the briefest moment of calm, it flits from your sight, out of the wintry storm and into it again. So this life of man appears but for a moment; what follows or indeed what went before, we know not at all. If this new doctrine brings us more certain information it seems right that we should accept it.

Utterly convinced, the high priest borrowed a horse from the king and rode off to destroy the shrine of the idols to whom the Northumbrians were still sacrificing herds of cattle.

Once Edwin had converted to Christianity, his people followed. It was as a community that on Easter Sunday 12 April 627 the nobility and a large number of ordinary people, as well as King Edwin, received baptism at York in a little wooden church built by Paulinus where York Minster now stands. Paulinus then travelled up and down the country performing mass in all the Northumbrian rivers. In fact there was such a fervour to be christened among the Northumbrians that for thirty-six days Paulinus had to work day and night in order to complete his task of baptizing people who had travelled for days from the furthest-flung villages and hamlets throughout the land. By the 630s Northumbria had become a byword for peace among its violent neighbours.

But Edwin, who became bretwalda on the death of Raedwald, had earned the hatred of the old Britons, that is the Welsh under their king Cadwallon of Gwynedd, because Northumbria was increasing its territory at their expense. Despite being a Christian, Cadwallon had chosen to combine his army with that of Penda, the warlike heathen King of Mercia.

The bitter enmity between the Roman missionaries and the Celtic Church meant that no Welsh bishops counselled Cadwallon to refrain from attacking his fellow Christian King Edwin. St Augustine had assumed that the Welsh bishops would be directed by him once his mission had arrived in England, for he had orders to set up two archbishoprics and twenty-four bishoprics. But the Welsh saw him as a foreign usurper who should bow to their more ancient faith. The conference Augustine called in order to reason with them ended with harsh words on both sides. Augustine denounced the Welsh bishops as heretics, warning of dire consequences if the Church was not united. These seemed to be fulfilled when Edwin was killed at the Battle of Hatfield in 633, and the west British swarmed all over Northumbria, burning villages and churches and almost wiping out Christianity despite their common faith. Cadwallon's soldiers spared neither women nor children, so Bishop Paulinus had to gather up Queen Ethelburga and her household, together with a large gold cross and a wonderful chalice studded with jewels, and escort her south to her brother's more peaceful kingdom of Kent. From being Bishop of York Paulinus ended his days as Bishop of Rochester, dying (for once we have a precise death date) on 10 October 644.

The devastation came to an end only when the son of Ethelfrith of Northumbria, Oswald, returned to his old country, drove out Penda and Cadwallon and forced the Welsh Britons as far as their kingdom in Cumbria to acknowledge him as their overlord. Oswald's reign was brief, since he was murdered by Penda in 642. But it was memorable for his association with another great early churchman, St Aidan, who transformed the Northumbrian Church by exposing it to Irish Christianity and its twin traditions of classical scholarship and passionate Celtic evangelism.

St Aidan was a monk at the famous monastery of Iona off the west coast of Scotland where King Oswald himself had been educated and which had been founded in 563 by the Irish monk St Columba to convert the Scots. The monastery had maintained the best traditions of classical education, which had survived in Ireland because it had been left undisturbed by the German migrations. Irish Christianity was a markedly scholarly movement because its monasteries had been the preservers of a significant part of the European classical heritage that had perished in Italy and France under the onslaught of the German tribes. Classical manuscripts, many of them the legacy of Greek civilization to the Romans, once the common reading matter of Roman citizens, continued to be copied in Ireland by industrious monks.

When Oswald returned to Northumbria he brought with him the Irish-educated monks from Iona to re-establish Christianity in his shattered kingdom. St Aidan was made the bishop of the Northumbrians. In typically ascetic Irish and Scots fashion he chose to build his episcopal seat, cathedral and monastery off the Northumbrian coast on the small tidal island of Lindisfarne, or Holy Island, just south of Berwick-on-Tweed.

Iona, an island off the west coast of Scotland where in 563 the Irish St Columba founded the monastery whose monks brought Christianity to the Picts and the Northumbrians.

Despite St Aidan's importance as head of the Northumbrian Church, the buildings on Lindisfarne had thatched roofs of reeds, after the Irish fashion.

Under St Aidan's influence, King Oswald's court became known throughout the rest of the Anglo-Saxon kingdoms for its higher way of life. The nature of the Anglo-Saxon rulers and ealdormen began to change, guided by their priests into better behaviour. Many of the nobility began to copy St Aidan's example of fasting on Wednesdays and Fridays. Instead of an ethic based on the rule of the strong, which was the code of the Anglo-Saxons, Oswald became notable for his care of the poor. Bede tells many stories of the great novelty of the king's selfless generosity, such as giving away his Easter lunch, a silver dish full of dainties, to the poor in the streets.

When Oswald was succeeded by his formidable brother Oswy, who regained the bretwaldaship for Northumbria, the Christian way of life established under St Aidan and Oswald was exported with even greater momentum. Oswy made a point of encouraging missionaries from Northumbria to visit other kingdoms. Thanks to the activities of the Northumbrian monk St Ceadda or Chad, the population of Penda's famously heathen Mercia also began to turn Christian, including Penda's own son Peada. By 700 the whole of England had been converted to Christianity. The missionaries' origins varied: in East Anglia it was the inspired preaching of a Burgundian which did it, while in Wessex it was a Roman from Kent. But in the main the impulse was coming from Northumbria, from Lindisfarne and from Iona. The Yorkshire monk Wilfrid of Ripon converted the South Saxons, while Cedd, who was Chad's brother, reconverted the East Saxons.

By 698 the new monastery on Lindisfarne had produced an extraordinary monument to the new Northumbrian Christian civilization in the form of the Lindisfarne Gospels. This was a version of the Four Gospels of the New Testament but was decorated with beautiful illuminated letters and patterns, patterns which mingle Celtic designs and the sort of Anglo-Saxon shapes found on the buckles of the East Anglian Raedwald.

The Lindisfarne Gospels were made by monks living in communities which were becoming very much the rule in England by the end of the seventh century. Irish Christianity was notable for its monks' austere way of life. The earliest Irish and Scottish monasteries tended to be sited in remote places like islands or on hills, and the monks' cells would be beehive shaped, pleasant in summer and freezing cold in winter. But with the spread of Christianity, as a result of intermarriage between English rulers and of the energy of the Northumbrian and Irish missionaries, monasteries of a more sophisticated kind were built. They grew into large, powerful institutions, with many different rooms such as the scriptorium, where manuscripts were copied, and herb gardens outside. They provided schooling and were increasingly important communities in themselves. They started to have their own farms of sheep and dairy, particularly as the wealthy bequeathed land to monasteries in return for the monks' saying Masses for their souls. Seventh-century women participated too. Soon there were many communities of what were called 'double monasteries', foundations where men and women lived side by side but in separate buildings. The Old English word for monastery is minster and towns with 'minster' at the end suggest that they were once religious communities – for example, Westminster, Minster Lovell and Upminster.

It was owing to the energy of King Oswy that the English Church achieved a much needed national unity, for there was constant quarrelling between the different Christian sects of the Roman, Celtic and Scots and Irish Churches. The dominant issue in their quarrel was the date of Easter, but the real problem was that the Church in England lacked a harmonious national organization. Although he was only a simple warrior, or perhaps precisely because he was a warrior, Oswy decided in 664 that how to calculate when Easter fell and a host of other matters should be determined once and for all.

Oswy called a national Church Council at the monastery built by the Northumbrian princess Abbess Hilda at Whitby on the windswept east coast of Yorkshire. Hilda was a great administrator whose abbey became a training school for Church statesmen. Her monastery produced at least five outstanding ecclesiastics including Wilfrid of York and became a place where kings and princes sought advice on government. Here too in the 680s lived Caedmon, a humble lay brother who would compose some of the earliest extant Anglo-Saxon religious poetry.

Bede described the shyness of this poor lay brother attached to the abbey who, because he was uneducated, performed all the tasks of a servant. In the refectory or dining room at meal times (for monks and lay brothers ate together to emphasize the brotherhood of man) the educated monks would amuse themselves inventing elegant verse. Caedmon was always too embarrassed to speak when he saw the harp coming round the long table towards him. He would quickly find an excuse to leave. One night in the stable where he slept in order to take care of the monastery's horses he had fallen into a melancholy sleep, all too aware of his ignorance. Suddenly someone appeared to him in his dreams and said, 'Caedmon sing some song to me.' Caedmon replied that he could not sing and that was why he had left the hall. But the other insisted that he should sing. 'What shall I sing?' asked Caedmon. 'Sing the beginning of created things,' said the other. And Caedmon, in the muck of the stable, found that the most beautiful verses were coming out of his mouth as he sang the praises of God the Father who had made and preserved the human race. The story goes that when Abbess Hilda heard the exquisite poetry he was speaking she ordered that Caedmon should no longer be a lay brother but should be given a proper monk's habit.

It was at this abbey that the churchmen of the many separate kingdoms in England bowed to the power of the bretwalda Oswy and assembled in what was the first British conference, the Synod of Whitby, attended by all the great figures of seventh-century British Christendom in a bid to stop the bickering between the Irish and Roman Churches. The Irish Church had become a law unto itself during the Dark Ages when it lost contact with Rome. By 664 it was in effect a separate and rival organization which frequently disagreed with the papacy, whether on the date of Easter or on the tonsure – Irish monks were tonsured (shaved) at the front from ear to ear while Roman monks were tonsured on top. In daily life as the Church began to occupy an increasingly central position within the Northumbrian state this was beginning to create a number of practical problems.

With St Aidan's death and the accession of the fiery Bishop Colman to Lindisfarne and the bishopric of York, the issue led to a ludicrous antagonism between the two branches of the same faith. Some people had been converted by Irish Scots and some by Roman missionaries, so that their disputes were beginning to take up energies better used elsewhere. At the Synod of Whitby Wilfrid of Ripon was in favour of the Roman way of reckoning. 'Why', he asked with some resonance, should a small number in 'the remotest of two remote islands, the Picts and Britons, be different from the universal Church in Asia, Africa, Egypt, Greece, Italy and France?'

It was left to King Oswy to decide. He came down in favour of the Church founded by St Peter, in preference to what had in effect become a detached Church founded by St Columba. But at this pronouncement Bishop Colman, who was a strict adherent of St Columba, flew into such a rage that he resigned his bishopric at Lindisfarne, stormed back to Iona and eventually returned to Ireland. Oswy's Synod had done the English Church a great service. Christianity in England was now run by the Roman Church, which had the virtue of being an efficient, permanently staffed, wealthy international organization as opposed to the Irish Church's reliance on the enthusiasm of individuals. A few years later the country benefited from the pope's choice of a brilliant priest from what is present-day Turkey named Theodore of Tarsus as Archbishop of Canterbury.

Despite the importance we attach today to the ancient archbishopric, hitherto the Archbishop of Canterbury had had little actual power outside Kent. But over the next twenty years Archbishop Theodore's organizational skills transformed the English Church into a rationalized whole. In 672 its first canons gave Theodore and his successors at Canterbury authority over all the English Church, with power to create dioceses and make new bishops, a landmark in English religious history. All the bishops (the planned total of twenty-four had now been reached) of the different kingdoms, Mercia, Northumbria and so on, were to be under the authority of the Archbishop of Canterbury. Training schools were set up to ensure that each bishop had so many monks and priests to help with his work as well as schools for gifted children, whatever their means. As a result of Theodore's Greek-speaking background Greek and Latin were taught again to the inhabitants of England as well as the ancient curriculum of the Seven Liberal Arts: the Trivium and the Quadrivium.

The English Church gained a sense of national unity from the Church Councils which Theodore called on a regular basis. As religious enthusiasm swept the country with the aid of the well-to-do, a large number of monasteries were built all over England, particularly in Northumberland. The monks began to produce alliterative religious poetry like the Germanic verse of their forefathers. Talented poets in their midst were most likely responsible for the fusion of Christian values and the Saxon warrior past, which by the eighth century had produced two of the greatest Anglo-Saxon poems, *The Dream of the Rood* and *Beowulf*. If they were not written by monks they were certainly copied down in manuscript by monks in their scriptoriums and transmitted as the Anglo-Saxon version of Christian culture to future generations. They also memorialized the lives of those around them. They painted pictures not of the fabulous monsters of their Nordic ancestors' dour imaginations but of the real people they saw around them: English ceorls working in their fields or hunting hares with ermines, nobles on their horses flying hawks from their wrists. As the wealthier classes' children were educated in monasteries, their pleasures became more cultivated. They wrote gnomic verses, simple poetry. Once they had been taught to read and write by the Latin-speaking monks, the cleverer might enjoy Anglo-Saxon riddles derived from Latin literature, as well as that literature itself, including Virgil's *Aeneid* (which Bede had certainly read) and Pliny's *Natural History*.

Christianity had become a power throughout the Anglo-Saxon kingdoms, as important as the kings and their lords. Other than the monastic communities themselves, the key element in each diocese was not the parish priest, of which there were few, but the bishop, who then had an itinerant preaching role. At first there were very few parish churches because they took time and money to build. In areas where there were none, Archbishop Theodore of Tarsus allowed people to worship in the fields, which is why standing crosses were often erected instead of altars.

Elaborately decorated with new foreign motifs like the Byzantine-style vineleaves of Theodore's craftsmen, they may still be seen at Bewcastle in Cumbria and at Durham.

Some Saxon churches, like the important example at Brixworth in Northamptonshire and the *Lorna Doone* church St Mary the Virgin at Oare in Somerset, survive to this day. But the majority were either destroyed by the Danes or rebuilt by the Normans. As the centuries went on, parish churches tended to be erected as private buildings by wealthy individuals. From this came the large number of lay patrons in England who derived their right to appoint a priest from having built the church on their own land. By the late tenth century, the tithe, a tenth of the farmer's crops, was legally owed to the Church to support the parish priest. A hundred years later the English lord saw it as part of his duty to give the Church a third of his manor lands' income.

On the death of Oswy in 670 Northumbria began to lose her position as the dominant kingdom in England to Mercia. Oswy's son Egfrith had

8th-century Brixworth Church, Northamptonshire, one of the chief meeting places for the Mercian kings and their people.

not inherited his father's practical nature and wasted his kingdom's resources on fruitless attempts to expand north into the country of the elusive Picts. The eighth century in England is generally known as the period of the Mercian Supremacy under two powerful kings – Ethelbald (716–57) and Offa (757–96).

The period was also to be celebrated for the flowering of the Northumbrian Church in what has been called the heroic age of Anglo-Saxon Christianity as the traditions established by the zealously pious Northumbrian kings and monks at Lindisfarne came to fruition. Its Irish roots gave it a strong pietistic strain as well as the profound sense of mission of its great founders like

St Aidan. By the late seventh century the English Church was sending missionaries back to Germany to convert the lands of their heathen forebears. The mission to Saxony was begun by the Bishop of York Wilfred of Ripon, when he was wrecked off the coast of Frisia. It was continued by his pupil St Willibrord and by Willibrord's contemporary St Boniface.

Strong links were also established between the Northumbrian Church and the new regime in France, where the great tradition of English scholarship of the eighth century helped create a revival of western learning – what is called the eighth-century Carolingian Renaissance. Among the fruits of these contacts was the Palace School founded by the greatest of the Carolingian kings, Charlemagne, where young Frankish nobles and promising boys from poor families could be educated. The blond, magnificent Charlemagne, who could neither read nor write himself, set great store by education. The heathen German Saxons who were given a choice of 'Baptism or death' by his conquering soldiers would have been surprised to know that Charlemagne slept with a slate beneath his pillow, hoping to learn by osmosis the magic letters he found so difficult.

In England the power of Mercia meant that for the first time King Ethelbald began to style himself King of All South England, while Offa his successor simply called himself King of the English. This he was certainly in a position to do: except in Northumbria and Wessex, where the ancient house of the West Saxons continued in very reduced circumstances, King Offa directly ruled most of the rest of the country. A superb soldier who introduced a magnificent struck coinage with fine silver pennies in imitation of Roman currency, he also adopted Roman methods to keep the Welsh British out of England, constructing his famous Dyke from sea to sea which can still be seen today. Offa was a notable protector of the Church, which he encouraged as a source of stability and education, supporting it with grants of land and building many abbeys.

During the long reigns of the two strong Mercian kings which between them covered almost the whole century, England prospered as never before. From being the barbarians of Europe, the English had become renowned for their orderly way of life and exemplary scholarship. Charlemagne corresponded with Offa and called him 'brother', an epithet he accorded to very few people, and Offa made the first extant European trading treaty on behalf of the English with Charlemagne. It provides for reciprocal rights of free passage for merchants visiting France or England to be enforced by local officials.

In 787 with great pageantry and ceremonial King Offa's daughter Eadburgha was married to Beohtric, the King of the West Saxons. The marriage brought even more of the West Saxons' territory within Offa's orbit: he had already annexed all the West Saxons' land north of the

Thames. Such was Offa's prestige that he could persuade the pope to split the see of Canterbury in two in order to give Mercia its own archbishopric at Lichfield in Staffordshire. However, despite King Offa's unique position abroad and at home it was during his reign that an external force of far greater magnitude first began to threaten England.

Shortly after his daughter's magnificent nuptials in Wessex, three enormous ships appeared off the Dorset coast, each of them almost eighty feet long and seventeen feet wide – the size of a large house or hall. The ships, which had sailed from Denmark, put in to the harbour at Portland, full of strange, grim men from the north. Instead of responding civilly when one of King Beohtric's officials asked them to accompany him so that they could be registered in the nearest town of Dorchester, as was the practice in those peaceful times, the foreigners turned on the customs official and killed him. 'These', says *The Anglo-Saxon Chronicle* ominously, 'were the first ships of the Danishmen which sought the land of the English nation.' There were many more to come.

Those three ships are the first mention in English history of a fearsome Scandinavian people called the Vikings. For the next 200 years they would destroy much of the newly erected structure of medieval Christendom by their lightning raids. The Vikings' name came from the old Norse word *vik* meaning creek or fjord and they themselves were land-hungry young men from the creeks of Norway, Sweden and Denmark. Brilliant sailors at a time when the nations of north-west Europe had forgotten the art of seamanship in favour of agriculture, the Vikings were also enthusiastic

Viking warships which from 787 onwards raided the coast of England.

traders and adventurers who roamed the seas, bartering hides from their own countries with whatever took their fancy in foreign ports. But they also had the bloodlust that Christianity had damped down in the Angles and Saxons. The Vikings sacrificed to their cruel old gods of Thor and Odin with death and destruction, believing that only by bloodshed would they reach the afterlife.

For some time in the early years of the ninth century rumours had been sweeping the Scandinavians that Charlemagne's conquest of the Frisians, the north German policemen of the Baltic, meant that there were no longer any Frisian warships protecting western seas. Very rich pickings were to be had there. At the same time there had been a rapid increase in the numbers of Scandinavian people, something of a population explosion. The Vikings were landless young men who took to raiding to feed themselves as there were not enough fields to support them beside their narrow Norwegian fjords. Self-sufficient and independent, used to ruling themselves in their isolated hamlets and lonely forests, they were irked by the strengthened powers of the monarchy under powerful kings in Denmark and Norway, like Harold Fairhair, the first King of Norway. Pastures new were what they needed, and these they sought with a vengeance. The coasts of eastern England and the north coast of the Frankish Empire, as Charlemagne's sprawling lands were known, were now at the mercy of any Viking expedition strong enough to overcome resistance at the point where they landed. And again and again they would come, from the icy capes of the Baltic to Britain's fertile and warmer shores.

Fifty years earlier in 732, western Christendom had just succeeded under Charlemagne's grandfather Charles Martel in defeating the Muslim warriors who had conquered Spain, beating them in the Pyrenees and throwing them out of France. But now Christian European civilization was in danger again as the Viking ships harried the north European coasts.

The 300-year era when the Vikings overran Europe displays many similarities to the earlier 'Dark Ages'. Once again, particularly during the ninth century, much of the learning which had been cultivated so pains-takingly to replace the devastation of the German migrations vanished. The light given to Europe by Christianity flickered and very nearly went out. Today it would be as if all our public libraries and publishing houses and schools were burned to the ground systematically, with never enough time to rebuild them.

Unfortunately for England many of her most important monasteries which were centres of learning like Lindisfarne were especially vulnerable to the Norsemen, owing to their founders' wish for solitude. Situated on unprotected promontories jutting out to sea, or on islands far away from the king's soldiers, they were sitting ducks. The Vikings had no sense of their sacredness but thought only of the chapels' famous gold chalices and jewelled ornaments.

The Norsemen's shallow-draught boats were designed to travel swiftly up rivers and estuaries. Their longboats with their vast striped single sails, their snapping dragon-head prows, their shields hung out over the side and huge chainmailed warriors became the sight on the horizon most dreaded by coastal dwellers. The Vikings were stealthy fighters and often moved by night. They would put down their oars, take up their broadswords, disembark and kill the helpless monks even if they were at prayer, before seizing all the gold and silver which the monasteries had collected over two centuries. They would then be off, leaving buildings in flames behind them and despair among the survivors.

Ninth-century Vikings in England and Ireland were responsible for the loss of very nearly all of the priceless monastery libraries, built up by monks painstakingly copying manuscripts by hand. Before printing was invented that was the only way to make a copy of a book. Thousands and thousands of illuminated manuscripts whose great initialled letters occupied a whole piece of vellum and took a year for a monk to paint, became ashes beneath the fallen masonry. Only a tiny number of early manuscripts survived the onslaught of the Vikings, such as the Lindisfarne Gospels and the eighth- or ninth-century *Book of Kells*, which was probably made on Iona but carried over to Ireland. Both are now on display in the British Library. Lindisfarne itself, the great centre of English religious life for two centuries, was destroyed in a Viking raid in 793 and the helpless monks slaughtered. It was followed a year later by Jarrow, birthplace of Bede, and the next year by Iona.

It is hard for us to imagine today how frightening the Viking threat seemed. But the thought of their ships lurking offshore began to prey on the confidence of the peoples of England and France. To the terrified inhabitants of England the burning of Lindisfarne was a sign that God was angry with them, for Lindisfarne was an especially holy place. Why had He let it be destroyed? The Viking plague and their barbaric ways – 'Where we go the ravens follow and drink our victims' blood!' they sang as they disembarked in their horned helmets – made them bogeymen to the Christian nations. It was no wonder that the Mass each Sunday began to include the heartfelt prayer: 'From the fury of the Vikings, save us O Lord!'

There were three kinds of Vikings and they moved in three separate directions. While the Swedish Vikings swept east in their thousands under their chief Rurik to found the Kievan Rus or first Russian state, the Norwegian Vikings sailed west and founded Greenland. Two centuries later, about the year 1000, they would discover North America, putting in at what is now New England, which they called Vinland. They sailed down the west coast of Scotland and across to Ireland, where they founded Viking cities like Dublin and Cork and laid waste almost all the wealthy monasteries in the north of the country. They descended on the Orkneys, Caithness, Ross, Galloway, Dumfries, the Isle of Man, Cumberland, Westmorland, Cheshire, Lancashire and the coast of South Wales. Whirling their double-headed axes, against which there was no response, they carried many of the inhabitants into slavery.

The third kind of Viking, known as the 'inner line', concentrated their unwelcome attentions on the southern coast of England and the north coast of continental Europe. These Vikings were Danes from Denmark, whose ancestors had moved into the districts left empty by the Angles when they went to England in the fifth century. At first the Danish Vikings came only in small bands, for during the first thirty years of the ninth century a strong Danish monarchy and the remnants of Charlemagne's diplomacy protected southern England and France from the worst of danger. But the collapse of the Danish monarchy with the death of King Horik removed the last constraint, and the mid-ninth century saw the high tide of Danish Viking expansion, spearheaded by Ragnar Lodbrok (Ragnar Hairy Breeches) and his myriad warrior sons.

As the Vikings became more successful, their fleet on the high seas grew dramatically. At the height of their power in the 860s it numbered 350 ships. With one hundred fighting men on board each craft and the experience of thirty years of warfare, the Danish Vikings were a lethal striking force and increasingly daring and aggressive. From merely being coastal raiders, who in a sense could be lived with, the Vikings of the mid-ninth century started to spend the winter in the countries they raided, showing their utter contempt for the local community.

Vikings began to anchor large fleets in the loughs and estuaries of Ireland and build forts on her eastern shore. Their intention was not just to raid, but to drive out the native population and settle. It was on Holy Saturday 845, the day before Easter, that the full extent of Viking ambitions were understood. On that Easter eve even the most notorious Viking of the ninth century, the fearsome chief Ragnar Lodbrok, sailed up the Seine and sacked Paris. The citizenry fled and the churches were abandoned. Ragnar Lodbrok had successfully struck at the heart of the kingdom which had dominated Europe so recently under Charlemagne. Before the appalled eyes of the Frankish king Charles the Bald, Ragnar Lodbrok hung 111 citizens from trees and let another hundred go only when he was paid 7,000 pounds of silver. Then, his red beard glinting in the pale spring sun, he made a sarcastic bow to the terrified king and took himself off to the open seas once more. But there was no doubt among the watching crowds where power lay. It was certainly not with the king.

From now on Danish Viking armies took up more or less permanent quarters on the Rhine, the Scheldt, the Somme, the Seine, the Loire and the Garonne. In 859 Vikings were fighting in Morocco and carrying off prisoners to their Irish bases. The sons of Ragnar Lodbrok sailed to Luna in Italy and captured it under the illusion that they had come to Rome itself. The Vikings now had all but encircled Europe with their raids, for in the year 865 the Swedish Vikings who founded Russia laid siege to Constantinople.

It was against this background in 849 that the man was born at Wantage in Berkshire who was to save England from the Vikings. He is known to history as Alfred the Great, and he was a prince of the royal house of Wessex.

Alfred the Great to the Battle of Hastings
(865–1066)

Wessex was the kingdom of the West Saxons. According to folk memory its founders were chieftain Cerdic and his son Cynric in 495 when they landed at what is now Southampton but which they called Hamwic. (The suffix 'wic' comes from the Latin word *vicus* meaning a place, hence Ipswich and Norwich.) The eighth-century supremacy of the Mercian kings had put an end to Wessex occupying the valley of the lower Severn, but this kingdom – which began in the lush and rolling pastures of Hampshire – still ended at Bristol to the north, and incorporated all of Dorset and Somerset. The West Saxons were not only good military strategists. They were a reflective and organized people. One of their most important kings was Ine, who at the end of the seventh century had issued a code or accumulation of the West Saxon laws.

By the third decade of the ninth century the Mercian supremacy in England had yielded to that of Wessex as, benefiting from vigorous rulers, the kingdom continued to grow rapidly. In 825 Alfred's grandfather Egbert decisively defeated the Mercians at the Battle of Ellandune and thereafter the old Mercian tributaries of Kent, Essex, Surrey and Sussex became permanently part of the kingdom of Wessex and had no further separate existence. Egbert, who ruled for thirty-seven years, also finally put an end to the West Welsh or Cornish as an independent power by occupying Devon up to the Tamar; henceforth the Cornish paid Wessex an annual tribute. Only East Anglia, Mercia, Wales and Northumberland remained separate from the kingdom of Wessex but acknowledged Egbert as their overlord. And when Egbert obtained Kent he became the protector of English Christianity because it was the seat of the Primate of all England.

The expansion of the Wessex kingdom was played out against the background of the increasingly daring raids of the Danish Vikings. As we have seen, they were beginning to pose a real threat to the peace and security of the whole of England from the 830s onwards; over the next thirty years there are records of at least twelve attacks, and there were probably many more. But as the records were mainly chronicles kept by monks they tend to be incomplete because so many were destroyed during the raids. In the 840s Vikings devastated East Anglia and Kent, attacked Wrekin in Mercia and in 844 killed the king of Northumbria. But at least they went away again, taking their booty with them.

Ten years later the situation was worse. The Vikings were moving in greater numbers, operating in concert with one another, as opposed to the single-ship raids of earlier years. To contemporaries they had taken on the appearance of a 'pagan army'. In 851 King Ethelwulf, father of Alfred the Great, defeated a fleet of Vikings several hundred ships strong attacking Canterbury and London which had driven King Beorhtwulf of Mercia into exile. Another Wessex prince, Ethelbert, one of Alfred's brothers, who ruled Kent for his father, defeated a Danish army off the coast at Sandwich. Despite these successes, in 855 a large Viking fleet took up permanent winter quarters on the Isle of Sheppey, menacingly close at the end of the Medway to the mouth of the River Thames. The Vikings began building forts there. Many Londoners feared that, just as the Vikings had sailed straight up the Seine to Paris, it was only a matter of time before the Vikings sailed up the Thames and took London. As a result of his family's victories over the Danes, the Wessex that King Ethelwulf handed on to his sons was the most important kingdom in England. But the whole country continued to live in the shadow of another Viking invasion. Ten years later what had been feared for so long came to pass. In 865 a 'Great Army' of Danish Vikings landed in East Anglia with the obvious intention of conquering and settling the whole of Anglo-Saxon England and making it a Danish Viking kingdom.

Although there had been isolated raids on England the Viking attack on Jarrow in 794 had not been an altogether triumphant experience as it had resulted in the death by torture of the expedition's leader. This may have made the Vikings more wary of England. Certainly for much of the ninth century they tended to concentrate their larger numbers on France and Ireland. In about 855 Ragnar Lodbrok, who had forced the French king Charles the Bald to hand over 7,000 pounds of silver, at last fell into the hands of Aelle, the King of Northumbria. Ragnar Lodbrok had been raiding Northumbria with impunity, and seeking ever greater speed (according to legend) had built two boats so large that they proved unmanageable. Cursing his folly, the greatest Viking of them all was wrecked off the coast.

Ragnar Lodbrok was captured, tortured and thrown into a dungeon where he died a lingering and painful death among poisonous snakes, humiliated by the mocking faces of the Northumbrian court who came to gloat over the giant red-headed Viking. But even as he wasted away on his filthy palliasse and the Northumbrians congratulated themselves on their capture of the man who had terrified half Europe, Ragnar Lodbrok would not expire quietly. From his prison deep below the castle walls the old sea king could be heard roaring terrible songs of death and glory and prophesying the reign of terror that would begin when his sons came for his murderers. 'Many fall into the jaws of the wolf,' he sang, 'the hawk plucks the flesh from the wild beasts.' But while he would soon be enjoying feasts in the halls of Valhalla, 'where we shall drink ale continually from the large hollowed skulls', his sons would soon be drinking from the Northumbrians' skulls. Meanwhile, as the snakes rustled beneath him, he called on his sons to avenge him: 'Fifty battles I have fought and won. Never I thought that snakes would be my death. The little pigs would grunt if they knew of the old boar's need.'

And the little pigs did more than grunt as they grew up. Ten years later those little pigs, Ivar the Boneless, Halfdan and Ubba arrived at the head of the Danish Great Army and exacted a terrible price for the death of their father. Landing on the coast of East Anglia in 865 they laid waste the countryside until they had obtained provisions and horses from the terrified farmers. Then they galloped north up the Roman Ermine Street, which still ran so conveniently along the east coast of England, to York, the capital of Northumbria. By 867 the whole of Northumbria, its government already weakened by civil war, was in the hands of the Danish Great Army. They had their revenge, killing both King Aelle and his rival and eight of their military leaders or ealdormen. A puppet king named Egbert was put in to rule the former kingdom of their father's executioner.

But Ivar the Boneless and Halfdan were not content just with Northumbria. Now the Great Army, which was many thousands strong, wheeled about, crossed the Humber and went south to take possession of Nottingham, the capital of once powerful Mercia. Although an army came up to help from Wessex, because the Mercian king Burghred was married to Alfred's sister Ethelswith, the Danes cunningly refused to come out from their defensive earthworks. In the end the Mercians had to agree to pay them to go away. After wintering again in York and causing misery to its citizens, the Great Army moved back south to East Anglia. On the way the Vikings destroyed the beautiful and ancient monastery at Medeshamstede (Peterborough), killing the abbot and monks and burning the celebrated library. In East Anglia the brave young King Edmund led an army against them. But he was taken prisoner and then horribly murdered at Hoxne, twenty-five miles east of Bury St Edmunds: he was tied to a tree where he was used for archery practice before being beheaded. The abbey of the town of Bury St Edmunds was erected in the murdered king's honour over his burial place. East Anglia too was now another kingdom of the Vikings.

In five years three of the Anglo-Saxon kingdoms, all the land north of

Murder of King Edmund of East Anglia by the Danish army in 870.

London – that is Mercia, East Anglia and Northumbria – had fallen to the Danes like ripe apples off a tree. Only Wessex remained Anglo-Saxon. The others were now in effect a huge Danish kingdom run according to Danish law. Thanks to poor and haphazard military organization and no fleet to protect their coasts they had been easy meat for any enemy with a standing army and an urge to conquer. Although the fyrd required men to spend forty days a year fighting, it was unpopular and its call often ignored. Of those who did respond most of its members preferred not to fight beyond their kingdom's boundaries. Rather like jury service today the forty days might come at the worst possible moment, perhaps when the peasant farmer was desperate to bring his harvest in before it rained.

If the isolated raids earlier in the century had been terrible, the permanent presence of the marauding Danish Great Army gave daily life the oppressive feel of a never-ending nightmare. The Trewhiddle Hoard, an important collection of early church silver (now in the British Museum), was hidden in a tree by a priest who never came back for it. It is a mute memento of the continuous slaughter that took place and the destruction of a culture which had developed over two-and-a-half centuries. There is a chronicle written by an eyewitness, a monk of Croyland in the Fens, which gives a typical account of the arrival of a Viking war-party as it was experienced throughout England and describes how the soil shook beneath the pounding hooves of the heathen Danes' armoured horses as they travelled from Lincolnshire to Norfolk. The abbot of Croyland and his monks were at their morning prayers when a terror-stricken fugitive ran in to tell them that the Vikings were on their way. Some of the monks took to their boats and rowed away from the monastery praying that in the mists and marshes of the Fens they would not be found. But the rest were slaughtered where they stood.

9th-century gravestone from Northumbria, showing Viking invaders with axes raised. From Lindisfarne Priory.

By the autumn of 870 the Danes decided to conquer the last of the kingdoms of Anglo-Saxon England which remained independent, namely Wessex. But they had finally met their match. Although the present king of Wessex, Ethelred, was not gifted with determination and was more concerned with his spiritual life than with preserving the safety of the kingdom, his younger brother and co-commander Alfred, who was soon to succeed him, was the heir to all the best qualities of West Saxon kingship. Alfred was the fourth and youngest son of King Ethelwulf, who had passed on to him a strong sense of his duty to resist the destruction of Christendom by the Vikings. Ethelwulf had also inspired Alfred with memories of the most constructive sort of Christian kingship handed on to him by his own father Egbert, who had spent his early life at the court of Charlemagne. Alfred was taken to Rome by his father at least twice on pilgrimages to invoke God's goodwill towards Wessex and protect her from the Viking plague. Reflecting fears among the West Saxons that Christian civilization might die out in England because of the repeated attacks of the Danes, Ethelwulf had designated one-tenth of his kingdom's revenues to be given to the Church to ensure that learning continued.

The sense of learning's almost irreversible decline, now that so many monks and priests had been killed, was a subject which would obsess Alfred himself. Once king he would embark on an extraordinary programme to re-educate the English. In later years he would remember that during his childhood 'there was not one priest south of the Thames who could understand the Latin of the Mass-book and very few in the rest of England'. As a result Alfred himself did not learn to read until the age of twelve, and then only by his own efforts because there were no monks left to teach even a king's son.

Alfred's dictum, 'I know nothing worse of a man than that he should not know', reminds us that as a result of four decades of Viking raids knowledge could no longer be taken for granted. Latin was the language of learning but as there was no one to teach him Latin – Alfred only learned it when he was forty – much was lost to him, as it was to many other English people. The Welsh monk Asser, who became bishop of Sherborne, wrote a famous contemporary life of Alfred in which he relates that the king told him 'with many lamentations and sighs' that it was one of the greatest impediments in his life that when he was young and had the capacity for study he could not find teachers.

Thus when the Danish army decided to turn their unwelcome attentions on Wessex by capturing the royal city of Reading at Christmas 870 they encountered resistance to the death, for to Alfred this was a battle to save English civilization. But it was touch and go. Just when the actual king of Wessex, Ethelred, ought to have been marshalling the attack on the Danes on the Ridgeway in Berkshire, he insisted on listening to the end of the Mass. While Alfred was lining up his part of the army in the famous Anglo-Saxon battle formation called the shieldwall, Ethelred refused to come out of his tent, declaring that as long as he lived he would never leave a service before the priest had finished. Meanwhile the terrifying Danish army were hurling their javelins at the Wessex men below their ridge and keeping up a deafening noise by banging their shields. Ethelred continued to listen to the incantations of the priest as the twenty-one-year-old Alfred took the offensive and charged up the escarpment. His men fought so fiercely around a stunted thorn tree that quite soon, despite their mail shirts, many leading Vikings lay dead on the ridge. The rest soon fled.

Although this was far from being a conclusive engagement (it would be many years before the tide finally turned for the English under Alfred), it was the first time that the Danes had been beaten in open battle. When Ethelred died in his twenties and Alfred became king in 871 he bought time to recover from the Danes by signing a peace treaty. The Danes themselves were glad of a temporary lull. They were exhausted by the ferocity of Alfred's attacks whenever they ventured out of the fortress they had built at Reading. Fortunately the Great Army was then distracted by a revolt in their northern possessions and, having put it down and hammered the kingdom of Strathclyde in south-west Scotland, half of its soldiers under their leader Halfdan decided to tangle no more with Wessex. They would remain in the north and make it a proper Danish kingdom instead of ruling through a native puppet. Under Halfdan as king the Danish Vikings took over much of the old kingdom of Northumbria, corresponding approximately to Yorkshire today (as is shown by the concentration of Danish place names in that county: the suffixes '-wick', '-ness', '-thorpe', '-thwaite' and '-by' are all indications of Scandinavian settlements). Danish soldiers became farmers. They made their capital at Yorvik and organized the land for taxation purposes in the Danish way by *wapentakes* instead of by hundreds as in the Anglo-Saxon kingdoms.

By 874 the Danish army had further consolidated its hold on the rest of occupied England. Most of Mercia other than the small area to the west of Watling Street was parcelled out between Danish nobles. Thus the whole of England from the Thames to the Humber was ruled by Danes in a federation of settlements called the Five Boroughs: Lincoln, Stamford, Nottingham, Derby and Leicester.

But the other half of the Danish army which had not settled in the north still had their eye on the rich southern lands of Wessex, that is Berkshire, Hampshire, Dorset and Devon, which were slowly recovering from the Great Army's depredations. After four years of inactivity the rest of that army decided to return to the fray under its king, Guthrum. Accordingly it moved south to Grantabridge (which we call Cambridge) and began to harass Wessex again. It now occurred to Alfred that the only way to stop the Vikings calling for help and reinforcement from their cousins' fleet in the Channel off France was to defeat the Vikings at sea before they reached land. He therefore sent for the Vikings' old enemies, the Frisians, and invited them to show the English how to build their style of ships, which had previously been a match for the Vikings. The ships which resulted were faster and longer than those of the Vikings. Alfred can justly be said to be the father of the Royal Navy.

While Alfred laid siege to Exeter, where the enemy was currently holing up, sailors on the new ships were appointed to watch the coast and prevent Guthrum's Great Army from obtaining supplies by sea. Undaunted by rumours about Alfred's navy, the Danes sent messages for help to their Viking relations in France, who under their leader Rollo were in the middle of forcing the Franks to grant them what in 911 would become the kingdom of Normandy (or the kingdom of the Norsemen). The new navy's first encounter was with a massive force of 120 French Viking ships crossing the Channel with some 10,000 men. Fortunately poor weather played into Alfred's hands. For once the indomitable Vikings were tired out by battling with storms. They were defeated by Alfred's navy and their fleet destroyed off Sandwich on the coast of Dorset. Guthrum and his army were allowed to ride out of Exeter and travel to Gloucester in Danish Mercia after they had sworn solemn oaths that they would leave Wessex alone.

But the Danes were not men of their word. They soon broke the Treaty of Exeter. Guthrum had drawn up a plan with Ubba, Ragnar Lodbrok's youngest son who was now king of Dyfed and was laying waste South

Wales, whereby they would both attack Wessex. At Christmas 878, believing that the Danes would abide by their oaths, Alfred had told all his thanes to return to their estates. Meanwhile he was alone with his young family in the royal palace at Chippenham, dangerously close to Gloucester. Just after Twelfth Night a messenger brought him the news that an enormous Danish army was 'covering the earth like locusts' and on its way to Chippenham.

By midnight the Danish army had occupied Chippenham, and the king and his family had only just escaped them by fleeing to the unnavigable marshes of east Somerset. The submission of most of the West Saxon nobles followed. They were exhausted by the unending war. Many left their lands to flee abroad, ruined by the obligation to feed the occupying army. Alfred the Great, however, would not submit. While the Danes once more divided up Wessex between them he stayed in hiding with a few nobles on the Isle of Athelney in Somerset. This was dry ground at the confluence of the Tone and the Parrett, surrounded by marshes and impassable rivers where no one could enter except by boat. In the Ashmolean Museum in Oxford may be seen a wonderful little artefact of the most exquisite Anglo-Saxon workmanship. Made of enamel, gold and precious stones and decorated with Christian symbols it bears the legend 'Alfred me fecit', which means 'Alfred had me made' in Latin. Alfred must have dropped the jewel there when he was camping on the island, for 1,100 years later it was dug up on Athelney by a local farmer.

On the island Alfred and his men lived roughly with few of the necessities of life except what they could forage openly or stealthily by

Athelney in Somerset where Alfred took refuge from the Vikings.

raids. The king himself lived in a hut belonging to one of his cowherds. To this period belong many famous legends about him. One day the wife of the cowherd was preparing cakes (scones probably) for the oven and Alfred, who was still only in his twenties, was sitting at the hearth trimming his arrows and dreaming of the day when his country would be free. The goodwife asked the disguised king, whom, in his homespun clothes, she took to be another shepherd cluttering up her house, to keep an eye on the cakes while she went for some water from the spring near by. But Alfred was so lost in thought planning the next attack that the cakes burned quite black without his noticing – to the fury of the cowherd's wife, who shouted crossly at him as if he were a kitchen boy. The horrified cowherd had not told his wife who their guest was, but he now revealed his identity and she was covered with confusion. But King Alfred only laughed and told her she had been right to scold and that he should have been minding the cakes. Years later when he was restored to his kingdom he sent for the couple and rewarded them for helping him in his hour of need. Alfred continued to resist the Danish by guerrilla raids and built an impregnable fort on the island where his family could be safe. It is said that he even went into the Danish camp disguised as a harper. He wandered from tent to tent playing and singing but also secretly noting the number of men and the position they occupied.

Thanks to Alfred's perseverance news spread among the West Saxons that all was not lost and that the king was secretly gathering an army of Wessex men on the twenty-four acres of the island. Support for Alfred grew so rapidly that by the seventh week after Easter 878 a huge number of West Saxon men from Somerset, Wiltshire and Hampshire came out of hiding to meet him at Egbert's Stone, now Brixton Deverill in Wiltshire.

Alfred met the enemy at Edington near the Danish camp at Chippenham. After a siege of fourteen days he won the decisive engagement of the war. It was said that the Danish standard, a raven with outstretched wings which had been woven by the daughters of Ragnar Lodbrok in a single day, drooped and did not fly before the battle. It was an omen of the defeat to come by the White Horse of Wessex, the emblem which adorned Alfred's banner. So complete was the rout of the Danes that Alfred was finally able to dictate the sort of terms which pleased him, including forcing the Danes to accept Christianity. The Danes made a treaty, wrote the chronicler, 'such as they had never given to anyone before'. By the Treaty of Wedmore in Somerset the pagan army had to vacate Wessex and surrender southern and western Mercia to Alfred. Guthrum, the pagan king, would have to be baptized, with Alfred standing as godfather. Guthrum, who was given the baptismal name of Athelstan, thus became

Alfred's adopted son, and there was now a relationship between them which would be taboo to break.

Although Alfred had won a major victory, his kingdom was still surrounded by hostile Danish territory. And that autumn yet another Viking force under a leader named Haesten appeared at the mouth of the Thames aided by Guthrum, despite his treaty with Alfred, and proceeded west up the river to make its winter headquarters at Fulham. Though it disappeared briefly to Ghent after two years of terrorizing Fulham, the Viking fleet then sailed back and forth between England and France laying waste to Kent and besieging the city of Rochester in 884. Only the bravery of Alfred's army succeeded in frightening it off for good.

Alfred had learned a valuable lesson from the siege of Rochester. His towns needed to be better defended and should be able to function as fortresses. The fyrd also had to be reformed into a more reliable army with a longer period of service. Alfred's solution was to divide it into two, with one half on active service, the other on home leave. He also created a network of defences in southern England which had never been attempted before, centred on fortified walled towns called burhs (from which derives the word borough). These were built in a girdle round Wessex so that no member of the kingdom would be more than twenty miles from a refuge against the Danes. There were about thirty of them and they ranged from Southwark in the east through Oxford, Cricklade and Malmesbury to Pilton in north Devon and all along the south coast from Halwell in Devon to Hastings in east Sussex.

In tandem with the invention of burhs went Alfred's reform of local government in Wessex. Made autocratic by the desperate nature of his situation he increased royal power by overriding the ancient boundaries of the hundreds, and divided the country into official shires. Each shire's government was centred on a burh containing a shire court, the shire and burh being run by one of Alfred's royal ealdormen, whose powers could override those of the local lord. These men were responsible for implementing royal commands to raise taxes or call out the fyrd and would be expected to find men to garrison the burh in time of war as well as to undertake general public works for the shire such as repairing bridges or the walls of the burh itself. As the house of Wessex took over more of England the shire system spread throughout the country, so that by the beginning of the eleventh century the whole of England south of the Tees was divided into shires.

The local bishop was as important a figure in the shire as the royal ealdormen, who in time saw their powers transferred to the shire reeve, or sheriff. The bishop would help preside over the shire court and would often have partial responsibility for the money supply because, as fortified places created by a charter from central government, the burhs usually contained a mint.

Despite the strengthening of the monarchy under Alfred, like every Anglo-Saxon king since the most ancient times he continued to rule and pass laws with the approval of the institution known as the *witena gemot*, the king's council. As the Wessex kings took over more and more of the country the witan acquired the character of a national assembly.

By 866 Alfred had become a symbol of hope for the English. He had reconquered their most important city, London, from the Danes – burning many of the Danish settlements there to teach the treacherous Guthrum a lesson. London could once again be the entrepôt of English national and international trade. This was the first time that other Englishmen realized that the Danish occupation was not necessarily a permanent state of affairs, but might one day be reversed. Alfred gave permission for the Danes to remain in a ghetto, the Aldwick (that is, Aldwych, commemorated by the church of St Clement Danes), but he rebuilt London to emphasize its importance as a centre of English life. He founded much of the area of today's modern city, creating new streets between Cheapside and the Thames and building a palace for himself at Old Minster. Instead of leaving it as the undefended open settlement it had become under the Mercians, running along the side of the Thames in the area now covered by the Strand and Fleet Street, he moved the city back within the Roman walls. He also founded Southwark to protect the river at its shallowest point, as that was the main route into London.

The English Mercians asked Alfred to be their overlord in return for his protection. But the king thought it best to be tactful about ruling their territory, which had such a proud history. He therefore made a Mercian nobleman, Ethelred, the ruler of the Mercians with rights over London, and married him to his daughter Ethelflaed. Many of the Welsh princes thought it wise to follow suit, so he became their overlord too. He was described by a contemporary as 'king over the whole kin of the English except that part which was under the power of the Danes'. Many authorities see this moment, when Alfred is acknowledged as a leader of the English against the Danes, as an important stage in the advance of the English peoples towards political unity, a unity which had been forged by national danger. Alfred was the first person to call the English 'Angelcynn', which means the 'English folk'. However it would not be until the end of the tenth century in the reign of Alfred's great-grandson Edgar that the concept of 'Englaland' as a political unit would be adopted.

A second treaty, known as Alfred's and Guthrum's Peace, between Wessex and the cowed Danes provided a new boundary between Alfred's kingdom and the Danish territory, or Danelaw. West Saxon Mercia was to consist of the land north of the Thames to the River Lea on the frontier of Guthrum's kingdom of East Anglia, up to Bedford where it followed the old Roman road of Watling Street before ending at Chester on the Welsh borders. The boundary of Wessex with Danish East Anglia was redrawn at the latter's expense. Though the area Alfred controlled was large, the Danelaw was larger still, but such was the respect the Vikings had for the king of Wessex that the treaty also secured the rights of English subjects living within Guthrum's Danelaw so that there was no discrimination against them in law.

As the first king to defeat the Vikings Alfred's fame spread all over the continent. He was so highly esteemed by the pope as a Christian hero who had driven off the heathen that the Anglo-Saxon school in Rome was not taxed and the pope sent him what was supposedly a piece of the True Cross on which Christ had been crucified – the greatest honour he could bestow. Now that Alfred had secured the kingdom against further external and internal threats the rest of his reign could be dedicated to rebuilding a kingdom whose institutions had been almost destroyed by the Danish wars. Half the royal taxes were donated to the Church each year to rebuild monasteries at home and abroad and so begin the revival of learning, while, since so few of the English people knew any Latin, the king personally oversaw the translation into Anglo-Saxon of books he considered important. Alfred himself translated Bede's *Ecclesiastical History*, saying it was 'one of the books most necessary for all men to know', as well as Orosius' history of the world. His translation of Pope Gregory the Great's suggestions for pastoral care in the running of a parish was distributed to every bishop with instructions to make copies of it. Alfred also added notes to his translations where he thought it might help the reader, for he believed that everybody should have access to knowledge whosoever they were. His translation of Orosius contains descriptions of the ninth century's idea of the geography of northern and central Europe, obtained from adventurous Scandinavian visitors to his court, such as a Norwegian named Ohthere who had lived inside the Arctic Circle, as well as from his own sailors whom he urged to explore the unknown. In order that his people should enjoy what he had sorely missed Alfred paid for scholars to come from abroad – Frisians, Franks and the Welsh – to help him raise educational standards. Asser remembered him remarking sadly that 'Formerly people came hither to this land in search of wisdom and teaching and we must now obtain them from without.'

One of his first acts as king was to build a monastery on the Isle of Athelney, where he had been sheltered. It was the first part of his plan to revive the monastic life, which in Asser's words had 'utterly decayed from that nation'. Though some monasteries were still standing, no one directed their rule of life in a regular way. Most English people had lost all their old reverence for the Church. Alfred would have to mount a national recruiting campaign to find men and women to become monks and nuns. Even then the condition of the English clergy was at first so poor that the abbot for the new monastery on Athelney had to be brought in from Frisia in northern Germany. Alfred's younger daughter Ethelgiva became a nun, and he founded a convent for her near the eastern gate of Shaftesbury.

As part of his programme of repairing the Viking destruction of English life, Alfred commissioned a history of England called *The Anglo-Saxon Chronicle* to help his people acquire some knowledge of themselves and their history. And to make sure that every English person did read it, for he wished all English boys to know their letters, he commanded that it should be written in the language everyone could understand, that is Anglo-Saxon. Copies of the history were distributed to every important church in the country. Containing a brief description of the important events of each year since the mid-fifth century and influenced by Bede in its use of records, the *Chronicle* was continued in various monasteries after Alfred's death up until the twelfth century. Along with Bede's history it is one of the most remarkable of the early histories which any European people possesses.

Pages from an 11th-century continuation of the *Anglo-Saxon Chronicle*. The first history of the English people in their own language, it was begun in the reign of Alfred the Great.

Alfred believed that kings should have good tools to work with. He wrote, 'These are the materials of a king's work and his tools to govern with; that he have his land fully peopled; that he should have prayer men and army men and workmen.' The prayermen had been taken care of. Now Alfred turned his attention to some of the workmen, particularly the judges. The normal machinery of English life had been badly disrupted by the war with the Danes. The Anglo-Saxon law dispensed every month in the local hundred courts was based on ancient custom. But as a result of the wars many people were no longer clear what the ancient customs consisted of. To make up for these gaps Alfred updated the West Saxon laws for the nation, including whatever he thought helpful in the codes of Ethelbert of Kent, Ine of Wessex and Offa of Mercia. The introductory preface announced that he had showed them to his witan, whose members had agreed that the laws should be observed.

Scholars believe that Alfred was personally responsible for a new emphasis on laws to protect the weak. And he himself said that one of his functions was to be the defender of the poor (who received a quarter of his income), because they had no defenders. He imposed further limitations on the destructive custom of the blood feud and emphasized the duty of a man to his lord. Up to Alfred's day there were no prisons but such was his desire to reintroduce a peaceful and civil society where a man's word really was his bond that anyone who broke his oath was to be given forty days' imprisonment.

Alfred's laws had a strongly religious flavour. They opened with the Ten Commandments and included many biblical references to persuade the English to hold them in greater respect. His judges, the local lords, were told that they would either have to improve their legal knowledge or resign. Asser reports that, though most of the judges were 'illiterate from their cradles', in fear and admiration of their great king they frantically set about studying. Since so many of them could not read, most of them adopted King Alfred's suggestion of having the laws read out to them by a son or slave 'by day and night', whenever they had the leisure. Alfred often looked into their judgements. If he disagreed with them he summoned the judge in question and asked why he had come to such a conclusion. 'Was it ignorance, malevolence or money?' he asked frankly on one famous occasion.

Mindful of his grandfather's descriptions of Charlemagne's famous Palace School, Alfred established his own school at the royal court. This was to educate the cleverest boys in the kingdom, regardless of their origins, as future clerks for his civil service so that he would be able to draw on the largest pool of talent in the country. Holy and devout, Alfred invented the first English clock, a horn lantern with candles so that he could divide his day satisfactorily into three eight-hour parts, one for praying, one for governing and one for sleeping. Upon his death in 899, aged only fifty, he was buried in the New Minster he had built in his capital of Winchester.

King Alfred was one of the most important English kings, whose defence of English civilization has rightly earned him the soubriquet the Great. He was succeeded by a worthy soldier son Edward the Elder, who continued the fightback against the Danes that his father had begun. Despite all Alfred's achievements, Edward the Elder still inherited a kingdom which confronted land occupied by the bloodthirsty Danish armies all the way to Whitby in north Yorkshire. Moreover, when the Danes settled they settled in armies rather than kingdoms, so that the threat of another invasion was always present. Further danger threatened because the Norse kingdom of Dublin in Ireland was forever casting covetous eyes at the Danish kingdom of York, which was becoming an important Scandinavian trading post.

As a military strategist, Edward knew that for the sake of England's security he would have to launch a series of pre-emptive strikes against the Danish kingdoms which surrounded him. He should try to capture as many as he could or at least neutralize them and show that there was no point in building a war chest against him. With the help of his sister Ethelflaed, who was known as the Lady of the Mercians because she ruled them after her husband's death, and by constant fighting Edward pursued Alfred's ambition of making England a single state. They strengthened the frontier with the Welsh and Danes by making use of Alfred's device of the burh or fortified town, and they had reconquered the rest of the midland part of the Danelaw, starting with the five Danish boroughs of Derby, Stamford, Nottingham, Leicester and Lincoln, by the time Ethelflaed died, worn out by the constant campaigning. Edward appointed no successor to his sister but took over the government of both Danish and English Mercia, roughly speaking what we call the midlands today, further unifying the country. The midlands were followed by the reconquest of East Anglia and then of a great deal of Northumbria after a lengthy northern campaign. In the process a fresh line of fortresses was built eastwards from Chester along the line of the River Mersey.

By 923 the rest of the princes of Britain accepted they could no longer resist a great West Saxon king who was never happier than when leading the attack in his buckskin trousers and gripping his small shield. Edward and his descendants became overlords to the Scots and Welsh and began to enjoy greater status abroad as a result. Edward the Elder's son, the golden-haired Athelstan, was fêted with expensive gifts by the greatest European rulers of the age, who made a point of intermarrying with the house of

Wessex. The German Henry the Fowler, king of the East Franks, married his son Otto, the future emperor, to Athelstan's sister Edith, while another sister married the king of France. Alfred had long favoured Athelstan because of his beauty, graceful manners and love of poetry. He had given his grandson a special Saxon sword to remind him to be proud of his ancestry, and a scarlet cloak, and Edward had deliberately educated him in his aunt's household in Mercia to bind that kingdom closer to the West Saxon monarchy. Athelstan's campaigns drove out the line of Danish princes ruling York. Although in 937 some Welsh princes, the Scots king Constantine and Vikings from Dublin revolted against Athelstan, they were conclusively defeated at the Battle of Brunanburgh and did not rebel again.

Under the rule of the Wessex kings England over the next fifty years became a unified country. The expansion of the royal house of the West Saxons into a national monarchy was helped by the Danes' destruction of the old dynasties of Mercia and East Anglia, and by the fact that for almost a hundred years there were no fresh Danish invasions. For the great period of Viking invasion was now over – not only in England but on the continent. In 911 Rollo and his Norsemen had been granted a kingdom in the basin of the lower Seine which soon became known as the Duchy of Normandy, on condition that they defend the Frankish kingdom against attack. They were baptized and became subjects of Charles the Simple; Rollo himself married Charles' daughter. Throughout Europe there seemed to be peace at last from the Vikings' marauding ways, though the French cleric Abbé Suger would presciently remark that 'The Normans, in whose fierce Dansker blood is no peace, keep peace against their will.' One hundred years later England would feel the force of that statement.

Like so many of the Wessex kings Athelstan died young, aged only forty, in 940. He was followed by his brother Edmund, who successfully quelled Danish rebellions in Mercia and Deira and brought Scotland under King Malcolm into a closer alliance with England in return for forcing the Welsh to give the Scots Cumberland. Somewhat to the surprise of the English, after half a century the Danish now settled down to being constructive neighbours: once tamed the Vikings would enrich the blood of Europe and England. They had always been merchants as well as pirates, as scales found buried with battleaxes in their tombs show. With the war over, town life in what was becoming known as Yorkshire began to revive. Rural life was invigorated too. These fearless people, who would put to sea in any weather, did not exterminate the local populations as their Anglo-Saxon predecessors had done, but used their English neighbours' knowledge of the land to become excellent farmers. Viking ancestry may account for the famous hardness and cussedness of the people of Yorkshire, that nation within England. The English as a whole would learn a great deal from Viking military success: they borrowed the Vikings' disciplined wedge formation to fight on land, as well as their metal mesh shirts, which would become the chainmail body armour of the English knight.

In 946, after only six years on the throne, King Edmund was murdered while gallantly saving a guest from a roving band of outlaws who had managed to get into the royal banqueting hall. Although he left two small sons they were too young to ascend the throne, which now passed to Edward the Elder's youngest son Edred. Although Edred was in poor health his chief minister was one of the great figures of the tenth century – the monk St Dunstan, Abbot of Glastonbury. St Dunstan had a powerfully ascetic nature, sleeping in a cave by the side of the church of Glastonbury, where the ceiling was so low that he could not stand upright. Like Alfred he was determined to encourage a monastic revival in England to rebuild the civilization destroyed by the Danes. But as well as remodelling the English monasteries on the lines of the Benedictine reforms at Fleury on the Loire, Dunstan guided Edred in expanding the boundaries of his kingdom, and by 954 Edred had decisively reconquered Northumbria from the Danes. He was soon calling himself the Caesar of the British. More than ever the English and Danes had been blended into one people, a process speeded up by the conversion to Christianity of most of the inhabitants of the Danelaw. Dunstan had the farsightedness to allow the Danes in the northern Danelaw a certain amount of independence, enabling them to run their county in their old manner through earls, as they called their rulers. On the death of Edred in 955 his nephew Edwy became king, but he quarrelled with Dunstan and drove him into exile. Dunstan had in any case made many enemies for himself at court by his attempts to expel the married secular canons who, owing to the dearth of English monks, had taken over what were previously monasteries. Their relations at court benefited from livings that passed from father to son and they influenced the king against Dunstan.

Without Dunstan to guide him Edwy's rule was both weak and harsh. Mercia and Northumbria rebelled against him and insisted that his younger brother Edgar become king of their countries. Dunstan returned in triumph to crown the new king with the sacred oil known as chrysm, for the first time in England's history, to show that Edgar was the Lord's Anointed. That ritual is still part of the coronation ceremony today. Although Edwy remained king of Wessex, upon his death Edgar became king of the whole of England. He ruled from 959 until 975 and is most famous for being rowed on the River Dee at Chester by six under-kings who all acknowledged him as overlord: the king of Scotland, the king of

Cumberland, the Danish king of the Isle of Man and three Welsh kings. Advised by St Dunstan, who had been made Archbishop of Canterbury, Edgar avoided the destructive border wars with the Scots by making the king of Cumberland vassal to the Scots king, and by giving Scotland Lothian, which until then had been part of the kingdom of Northumbria. As Archbishop of Canterbury St Dunstan was now in a position to address the low standards of behaviour in English monasteries and ensure that there was once again a thoroughgoing obedience to the rule of 'poverty, chastity and obedience' first laid down by St Benedict in the sixth century. Many of the secular canons were replaced by monks.

Edgar's reign was the high point of the West Saxon monarchy, before the years of its decline under his son Ethelred, famously nicknamed the Unready, who reigned from 978 to 1016. Ethelred inherited the throne after his elder half-brother, King Edward the Martyr, the successor to Edgar, was stabbed to death on the orders of Ethelred's mother Elfrida.

To the chroniclers it seemed that the crown taken in blood brought nothing but misfortune to the king who wore it and to the country he governed. Contemporary observers were savage about Ethelred: one said that he had occupied the throne for thirty-seven years rather than ruling it, and that his career had been cruel at the beginning, wretched in the middle and disgraceful at the end. Archbishop Dunstan was forced by Elfrida to crown her son king to lend the coronation an air of legitimacy. But the murderous queen mother had reckoned without Dunstan's powerful conscience and strong sense of justice. As the ceremony began St Dunstan could not refrain from giving public vent to his feelings of outrage. As he lowered the crown over the head of Ethelred he prophesied, 'Thus saith the Lord God, the sins of thy abandoned mother, and of the accomplices of her base design, shall not be washed out but by much blood of the wretched inhabitants of England; and such evils shall come upon the English nation as it hath never suffered from since the time it came to England.'

Dunstan did not live to see his prophecy fulfilled. But in the fourth year of Ethelred's reign it seemed to come to pass when after almost a century of absence a new Danish army arrived in England. These Vikings landed at Southampton in 982, as piratical and cruel as their ancestors of a hundred years before, probably inspired to invade by rumours that England was ruled by boy-kings and priests. In the next decade the whole of the south coast and East Anglia were continually attacked.

Ethelred had none of his great-great-grandfather Alfred's iron will. In 991 after a Danish victory at the Battle of Maldon in Essex he notoriously made the first payment of Danegeld in England's history – that is, he paid the Danes to go away. The first payment was £10,000, an enormous sum, and was taken from everyone, regardless of their ability to pay. But

£10,000 was not enough. Encouraged by the ease with which they had obtained it, the Danes soon returned for more. They demanded £16,000, then £24,000, then £32,000 – the equivalent in today's terms of millions of pounds. Having to find the money for the Danegeld tax led to a dramatic increase in the number of free peasants forced to become serfs: many had to abandon their own subsistence farming and become farm labourers tied to the manor's fields in order to pay back the tax money lent them by the local landowner.

The word Danegeld has become infamous ever since in English culture as shorthand for a cowardly and ultimately shortsighted course of action. Ethelred tried to buy freedom when he should have fought for it, never thinking that the Danes would ask for more when the money ran out. During his reign, the English lost the old fighting spirit that had defeated the Danes before. Morale plunged. Out of the thirty-two English counties, the Danes had soon overrun sixteen.

The whole country groaned under the assaults from the sea and the oppressive taxation. Ethelred now became known as Ethelred the Redeless or Unready. The meaning of this soubriquet has changed in the centuries since it was coined, for the English were making a rude pun out of his name. In Anglo-Saxon *Ethel* meant noble or good and *rede* meant counsel or advice. The name Ethelred thus meant good counsel. But because his actions always seemed the result of poor counsel Ethelred became known as Ethelred the Redeless, or Ethelred No Counsel.

To compound the feeling of hopelessness in England, Ethelred now married a Viking himself in order to curry favour with the Danes. He took for wife Emma of Normandy, whose father the duke was an ally of the aggressive Danish kings behind the new Viking raids. But Ethelred was incapable of a consistent course of action. In 1002 he turned on his Danish subjects living in the old Danelaw, giving secret orders that on 13 November, the feast day of St Brice, all the Danes in England should be butchered. Neighbours were told by the shire reeve to kill neighbours, hosts to massacre their Danish guests. It was a despicable act, violating all laws of hospitality, as well as intensifying racial divisions.

Gunhildis, the king of Denmark's sister, was then living in England as the wife of an English nobleman. Unlike her brother King Sweyn Forkbeard, Gunhildis was a Christian and had pledged to improve relations between the Danes and the English. Though she threw herself on her knees before Ethelred crying for mercy and reminding him of all she had done for her adopted country, he commanded that she and her son be beheaded just the same.

But Ethelred had made the most disastrous miscalculation of his reign in refusing to spare the king of Denmark's sister and nephew. Outraged by these murders and those of his fellow Danes, Sweyn Forkbeard avenged them by invading England in 1013. After ten years of softening England up by means of coastal raids while he made preparations for a full-scale invasion, Sweyn arrived in person at the head of an immense army. Showing as little mercy to the English as Ethelred had showed to the Danes, he killed all the English he encountered as he marched through East Anglia to Northumbria. Having received the submission of most of the country, he then besieged London – which was sheltering King Ethelred. The citizens of London, who then as now were known for their independence of mind, were preparing themselves to fight to the last man to save Ethelred.

But there was no need. The minute he saw Sweyn's tents going up round the city walls, Ethelred, who was as indolent as he was cowardly, announced that he could not endure the boredom of a long siege. He fled in the night to Normandy, where he had sent his wife Emma and their two children to be protected by her brother. Sweyn would have become ruler of England had he not died suddenly, leaving Denmark and England to his son Cnut, a superb military strategist. But the English still harboured fond thoughts of their ancient West Saxon monarchy. At their invitation a reluctant Ethelred returned to England to lead the resistance against Cnut. When Ethelred died soon after, in 1016, the struggle was carried on by his son Edmund, offspring of an earlier marriage to an Englishwoman, and thanks to his tremendous physique known as Edmund Ironside. After six battles the two kings realized that they were so evenly matched that it was better to come to a power-sharing agreement. By the Treaty of Olney, a small island in the Severn river, Cnut became king of Northumbria and Mercia while Edmund Ironside remained King of Wessex. On Edmund's death in November 1016 the ealdormen of Wessex chose Cnut to be their king as well and England was once again ruled by a single monarch.

To give greater legitimacy to his reign Cnut now married Ethelred's widow Emma of Normandy, the mother of the future king Edward the Confessor. Although Cnut did not kill any of the old Anglo-Saxon heirs to the throne he did the next best thing. He despatched Edmund Ironside's two sons to the king of Sweden with orders that they be executed. In the event they were preserved on account of their innocent appearance before being sent south-east to the court of the king of Hungary; their descendants married into both the Hungarian and Scottish royal families. Meanwhile the only other two serious claimants to the English throne, Emma's sons Alfred and Edward, were protected in Normandy by their uncle Duke Richard. They were growing up more Norman than English.

England prospered under Cnut. By 1027 he had successfully invaded Scotland, forcing the king of the Scots, Malcolm II, to do homage to him as his vassal or under-king. Quite soon Cnut felt sure enough of his position in England to despatch home the remnants of the Danish army with which his father had seized England. Unlike the old West Saxon kings, however, he was perpetually watched over by a giant palace guard, his 3,000 Danish 'housecarles', and he still had a large standing navy. But though Cnut gave a good deal of English land to fellow Danes, there was no dispossession of the native aristocracy as there would be later under the Normans. He relied on English advisers to help him rule.

Cnut was in many ways very similar to the old German kings. He loved the military life, and evenings were passed relating campaigns in his great hall. But as a simple soldier what mattered to him was the truth, and he despised the flattery that many English courtiers used to curry favour with him – as the best-known story about him illustrates.

The king with several Englishmen was walking by the sea. 'Your Majesty,' said the boldest and most sycophantic Englishman, 'we were thinking that Your Majesty is so powerful that everything in our country obeys you. Why, even the waves would obey you if you commanded them.' At last Cnut had had enough of their absurdities. Turning on them he told them to bring a chair down to the waves and set it a little way from where the tide was coming in. 'Now,' he said, seating himself on the throne and watching the waves wet his feet, 'I bid the waves retreat, but they pay no attention to me. I am not a fool, and I hope that next time you embark on silly compliments that you expect me to swallow, you will remember this and hold your tongues.'

The diminutive Cnut gave England an important new legal code. It reinforced the position of the Church and restated many of the ancient English customs as well as innovatively requiring every freeman to be part of the hundred and the tithing (a ten-man grouping within the hundred). By making its subjects responsible for preventing criminal activities by their fellows the kingdom became more orderly. Cnut was anxious to differentiate himself from other Vikings and to join the commonwealth of Christian nations. Attracted by the splendour and ancient nature of the Church, he went on pilgrimage to Rome to attend the coronation of Conrad II as Holy Roman Emperor, and could not resist exploiting the occasion to get customs relief for English pilgrims. The Danes who had accompanied him to England were made to adopt Christianity and he sent English bishops to Norway and Denmark to convert their populations. Cnut's insistence that Sunday be kept as a day of rest and his enforcement of Church tithes soon won him the support of the Church bureaucracy, as did his sense of his royal duty as a moral preceptor.

The Danegeld Cnut exacted from his English subjects was enormous. Nevertheless some important Saxon families came to prominence during his reign. Cnut was often called away from England to rule his immense Nordic empire overseas, which consisted of Denmark, Sweden and Norway, as well as the Hebrides, and his English advisers had to rule in his absence. One particular Saxon family, the Godwins, who were thanes from Sussex, began a rise to power which would eventually lead to the throne. They profited from Cnut's decision to divide England for administrative purposes into four earldoms, covering areas which followed the old Anglo-Saxon kingdoms – East Anglia, Mercia, Northumbria and Wessex. Unfortunately these earldoms had the effect of undoing much of the political unity of England created by Alfred and his descendants. Regional loyalties revived around them and became a source of weakness when a national will to resist was needed against the Normans. At first the earldom of Wessex was ruled by Cnut himself, but by 1020 the energetic and crafty Godwin had flourished sufficiently to become earl of Wessex. And as a result of his friendship with Cnut he was married to a Danish lady connected to the court.

Cnut died in 1035 aged only forty, like many a campaigner worn out by a life in the saddle, and his empire died with him. It had been held together partly by fear of his formidable personality. But its break-up was also a sign of changing times. For the previous 200 years the dominant force in Europe had been Scandinavian, whether it was the landless Vikings themselves or their kings. But for the next century European history would be shaped by those descendants of the Vikings, the Normans, who had settled in northern France after receiving a grant of land from the French king and theoretically becoming his vassals. Thirty-one years after Cnut's death, the military genius of the Normans would conquer England, and their Duke William would become known as William the Conqueror.

The Normans were first alerted to the possibility of England as a new fiefdom when they heard news of the struggle for the royal succession in that kingdom. Their informants were the Norman servants of Cnut's widow Emma. Was the rightful heir to the English throne Cnut's eldest son, the Dane Harold Harefoot, who did briefly succeed his father, or was the better claim that of Alfred and Edward, the sons of the last Saxon king of England, Ethelred? There were also in Hungary the sons of the heroic Edmund Ironside, potential heirs to the royal West Saxon throne. Matters were further complicated by Cnut's favourite son Harthacnut, by Emma of Normandy, whom Earl Godwin had fixed on as a suitable pawn to further his own ambitions, though he claimed to be representing the interests of a fatherless son.

Godwin now took Queen Emma and the considerable royal treasures into what he called 'safe custody' and began to promote Harthacnut's cause. Thanks to the backing of the Danes and the city of London Harold

Harefoot had taken the crown and he expelled Emma and Harthacnut to Bruges. Only a few years later, when Harold Harefoot died in 1040, Ethelred's elder son Alfred ventured out of hiding in Normandy to claim the throne in London before Harthacnut could return. But the masterful Earl Godwin was having none of that. On his secret orders Alfred was arrested, blinded, incarcerated and subsequently murdered in the monastery at Ely, and Harthacnut was crowned king.

Godwin, whom the chroniclers describe as a man 'of ready wit', managed to overcome the feeble Harthacnut's protests at the death of his half-brother by paying him some of the treasure he had accumulated over years of plotting. But on the death of Harthacnut in 1042, which ended the short line of Danish kings, Godwin moved rapidly to become the mentor of Ethelred's younger son Edward. Known to history as Edward the Confessor, he was also living in Normandy and was now the outstanding candidate for the throne.

But Edward, whose nickname arose out of his religious disposition, as he was said to go to confession at least once a day, was not the natural material of which rulers are made. It is said that, lost in uncertainty, he threw himself on his knees before the burly Godwin and asked what he should do. Godwin promised that if Edward would place himself entirely in his hands, grant great offices of state to Godwin's sons and marry Godwin's daughter, he would shortly see himself acclaimed king.

And so it proved. Controlled by Godwin, on Easter Sunday 1043 Edward the Confessor was crowned with tremendous pomp at his ancestor Alfred's capital of Winchester, specially chosen to remind the country of his royal West Saxon blood. Edward married Edgitha or Edith, Godwin's beautiful and cultured daughter, but he remained more like a monk than a husband, and indeed more like a monk than a king. Above all, the new monarch was a Norman first and foremost. Far from being proud that he was an Anglo-Saxon king, Edward's passion was for everything Norman. Norman monks had brought him up when his mother decamped to live with Cnut; the Norman language and Norman customs were what he was used to and what he preferred. As soon as he came to the throne, he surrounded himself with Norman advisers, which helped protect him against the overpowering Godwin, of whom he was always afraid given the rumours about his role in the terrible death of his brother Alfred. As a celebration of Norman culture Edward soon began to build a great church in the Norman style on the north bank of the Thames which would become Westminster Abbey.

The English royal income was prodigious by now for under the strain of the Danish wars and then of Danegeld the raising of taxes had become immensely efficient. Ethelred the Unready had created the rudiments of a civil service of clerks to raise money from the shires. These royal officials communicated with the shire reeves so frequently that a special form of letter from the king to the shire court called a writ had developed before anywhere else in Europe. It was identified by the king's seal attached to it and had the force of law. By the eleventh century it was the shire reeve or sheriff who oversaw the shire court and was the king's official representative (even if that meant conflict with the local earl), in charge of ensuring that the king received the taxation owed to him.

The colossal sums which these improved fiscal methods raised should have been spent on maintaining England's shore defences; instead they were used by Edward to buy relics, or the bones of saints, in silver caskets shaped like miniature churches. He did not keep up the small permanent navy that had become an important guarantee of England's security. The Confessor's days were passed at Mass in the company of the Normans he had imported. They were avaricious, disciplined men who watched the king like hawks and were always looking for ways to get rid of the over-powerful Godwin and his sons.

Quite soon two bitterly opposed parties grew up at Edward's court, the Normans versus the English magnates headed by Godwin. The Normans, with their almost oriental courtesy, disliked the free and frank ways of the English, who did not stand on ceremony. They also objected to the arrogance of the Godwin family, who seemed to place themselves on a level with the king. The Godwins frequently ridiculed Edward's holy simplicity – and even did so in his hearing, as shocked observers noted. Godwin's hold over the king enabled his sons to take huge areas of England into their fiefdoms. Thanks to Godwin's pressure on the king, Sweyn, Godwin's bad-penny son now had an earldom embracing shires from Mercia and Wessex, while his eldest child Harold had been made earl of Essex.

For their part the Godwins, especially Godwin himself and his most able son Harold, resented the arrival of more foreigners at court and detested their growing influence over the king. Normans took over many of the great offices of state, though few of them could speak English, and the Norman monk Robert of Jumièges was made Archbishop of Canterbury. Norman clerks were employed in the royal secretariat, so it came to be believed that only those who spoke Norman French had their petitions heard. In one part of the palace Queen Edith's father and brothers and their supporters spoke English and wore the Anglo-Saxon long mantle. In another part the Normans laughed openly at the Saxon earls' beards and moustaches. The Saxons were permanently in a fever to wipe the supercilious smiles off the Normans' clean-shaven faces. Shaving was an affectation, said the angry Saxons, which made them all look like priests anyway.

It was a situation which could ignite at any minute, and it soon did – with the Godwins to fan the flames – when Edward's brother-in-law Count Eustace of Boulogne paid England a visit in 1051. Like all Franks Count Eustace regarded Saxons as born slaves, despite their common Teutonic ancestry. On his way to London he spent the night at Dover. There, instead of paying for an inn, the count told his men to dress in full armour and demand accommodation from the townspeople at the point of a sword. The burghers refused point blank, and were promptly attacked by Count Eustace's knights. Though they were mainly shopkeepers, they managed to kill nineteen of his professional soldiers.

The incident developed into a full-scale diplomatic row. An angry Edward turned on Earl Godwin within whose domain Dover lay and asked him to visit the port with summary justice – that is, to execute the men involved without holding an inquiry. But instead Godwin the over-mighty subject raised an army from the south coast against Edward, for his lands stretched from Cornwall to Kent, and started for London. It was only when two of the other great earls, Leofric of Mercia (whose wife Godiva became famous for her charitable work) and Siward of Northumbria began moving south with superior forces to support the king that Godwin saw that he should back off. He was forced to attend a meeting of the witan at London, and was exiled with his sons Harold and Tostig and his wife, while Sweyn was condemned as an outlaw. Meanwhile Edward turned on his wife Edith, Godwin's daughter. He renounced her, stripped her of her jewels and had her locked up in a monastery.

At last out of Godwin's shadow, Edward was now free to make his own decisions about the future of the English throne. He almost certainly came down in favour of his cousin William, the bastard son of the Duke of Normandy, in preference to his half-nephew Edward, the son of Edmund Ironside, whom he had never seen. The same year, 1051, most unusually William left his country to pay Edward what was probably a state visit to settle the succession in his favour. The Norman chroniclers of the period all agree on this, and William the Conqueror's many later assertions that he planned to rule England according to the customs of the old English kings, 'as in the days of King Edward' himself, suggest that he saw himself as the legitimate heir. Nevertheless Duke William had no popular support in England, and those who met him in 1051 found him forbidding; he was described as a 'stark man'. Despite the king's own Norman leanings, the Normans were very unpopular in the shires, where they were increasingly being appointed as sheriffs. Since most of them could not speak English, they appeared to have little interest in procuring justice in the shire courts.

Taking advantage of this a year later, Godwin was back on a high tide of anti-Norman feeling. This time he had an enormous navy at his back and numerous enthusiastic seamen recruited from coastal towns. Having obtained the support of the City of London, he surrounded the king's ships at Southwark and dictated terms to the weary king, whose only enthusiasm now was for the building of Westminster Abbey. To the mortification of the king, whose spirit never recovered, an open-air meeting of the witan voted to restore Godwin to his previous position. Many Normans were expelled from England and the queen came back from her convent to resume her rightful place at court. The Norman Archbishop of Canterbury Robert of Jumièges left the country and much of the archepiscopal land was redistributed to the Godwins. The Anglo-Saxon Bishop Stigand, a supporter of the Godwins, was appointed to Canterbury in his stead, without papal permission. The Godwins were now in complete control of the country. With the unusual appointment of Tostig Godwin as earl of Northumbria on the death of the famous Siward, the family's rule stretched over the length and breadth of England.

The ambitious founder of this upstart house passed away soon after his return from exile, during a banquet. Legend has it that his death occurred just after King Edward had asked him, 'Just tell me something, did you really put out the eyes of my brother Alfred and kill him?' Godwin replied, 'May God strike me dead if I did,' whereupon he choked on a piece of meat.

Despite the death of the master plotter, Edward the Confessor's childlessness meant that the succession continued to be a live issue for the Godwins and those who received their patronage. They were determined that the throne should not be settled on Duke William. At their insistence, now that the Norman party had fallen from power, King Edward at last sent for his half-nephew Edward to name him heir to the throne. Mysteriously this rival to William the Conqueror died shortly after arriving in England. Although Edward left a son, Edgar the Atheling, children were almost never crowned under the Anglo-Saxon monarchy and thus once again Duke William seemed the most likely heir.

Despite the king's own leanings toward Normandy, Duke William's claim was not clear cut. There was in fact no obvious natural successor to Edward the Confessor. Meanwhile the evident weakness at the heart of the English monarchy which Godwin's rebellious behaviour had betrayed had aroused considerable interest in England from abroad. In Norway the ambitious young King Harold Hardrada now revived a claim to the throne as Cnut's heir. Meanwhile the friendship between Tostig Godwin, the new earl of Northumbria, with Malcolm III of Scotland did not bode well for the future. It might lead to a Scottish-backed invasion of England.

The last years of the Anglo-Saxon monarchy saw a struggle against Gruffydd ap Llywelyn, the increasingly powerful king of Gwynedd and

Powys. Gruffydd had united most of Wales under him. He had been encouraged by the disgruntled Aelfgar of Mercia, many of whose hereditary possessions had been given to Gyrth, the youngest Godwin, to invade England in alliance with a fleet from Norway. At this moment of national danger Harold Godwin began to attract attention for his daring Welsh campaign, which crushed Gruffydd and annexed his provinces to the English state in 1063.

Three years later, on the death of Edward the Confessor, to the witan Harold as head of the Godwins seemed the best possible English candidate for the throne. Apart from what remained of Mercia the Godwin family in effect ruled most of England. Though Harold was not of royal blood he was the natural choice to defend England from the threat of foreign invaders with claims to the crown, and as an Englishman he was far more welcome to the witan. By then the Godwins' chief rival Aelfgar, the head of the still powerful house of Mercia, was dead, so Harold Godwin's election went through unopposed. During the tenth century so

Tomb of King Edward the Confessor in Westminster Abbey which he founded.

many heirs to the throne had been minors at the time of the king's death that the old English monarchy had become far more elective. There was precedence for this in the Holy Roman emperorship, but it followed a natural tendency in a country where from its most ancient beginnings Anglo-Saxon kings had tended to have their decisions approved by a council of lords. By the time of the Conquest the witan was well used to being consulted on major national issues. The assent of its members – thanes, bishops and sheriffs from every part of the country – to new laws, new taxes, military measures and foreign alliances was sufficiently important to be recorded as part of the ruling process.

Edward died on 5 January 1066 and was buried in the crypt of his new church, Westminster Abbey. The external situation was considered so dangerous that the very next day Harold was crowned king. Though quite contrary to precedent, since the Godwins were without a drop of royal blood in them, it indicated the family's immense influence. But Harold's was to be a very short reign. By Christmas of the same year William the Conqueror was being crowned in the same abbey.

For William of Normandy was convinced that he was the rightful heir to Edward the Confessor. Not only had the former king told him so, but according to the Norman version of events, which is all that survives, as Edward weakened over Christmas 1065 Harold sent a message to William on behalf of the English government declaring that the duke should be ready to receive the crown of England as soon as Edward breathed his last. When William, who was hunting in the forest of Rouvray outside Rouen, received word from England that Harold Godwin had been illicitly crowned in his stead, his rage knew no bounds.

The situation was further complicated by an unfortunate accident which had befallen Harold some years before. In exchange for being ransomed by William, Harold, who was prisoner of the local count after a shipwreck on the French coast, had been forced to swear to be William's liege man, that is his servant. He had sworn an unbreakable oath of loyalty to William on a reliquary containing the remains of some of Normandy's most holy saints and martyrs. In the period in question, when national law was rudimentary and legal charters were in their infancy, the orderliness of society was guaranteed by the sacred nature of the oath; oathbreaking was punishable by forty days' imprisonment. William thus believed that he had been doubly insulted by Harold, who ought in any case to yield the throne to his liege lord.

Throughout 1066 William sent threats to the new king of England to remind him of his broken vow and to warn him that before the year had expired he would come and claim his inheritance. But Harold refused to take any notice, claiming that in return for vowing to be the duke of Normandy's man he had been betrothed to William's daughter, and that his oath was now void because she had since died. Unfortunately Harold seems to have had a reputation for being a slippery character like his father. One chronicler noted that he had a tendency not to respect the sacredness of his word. He was said to be 'careless' about abstaining from a breach of trust 'if he might by any device whatever, elude the reasonings of men on this matter'.

Although Harold had gained the throne he never captured the imagination of the nation, and neither did the rest of the Godwins. His brother Tostig was unpopular enough to have been expelled from Northumbria after a popular uprising, and had to be replaced by Morcar, brother of Edwin of Mercia, who had succeeded his father Aelfgar. Mercia and Northumbria were thus controlled by two members of a rival and hostile family. The lack of countrywide support for Harold would be a fatal element in the next nine months, as would be the air of illegitimacy that continued to cling to the new king and his family. The Godwins' impetuous replacement of the Norman Archbishop of Canterbury by the Anglo-Saxon Stigand without approval from Rome would enable William of Normandy to present his invasion as having a higher moral purpose: the duke announced that he planned to remove the illegal archbishop and replace him with the approved papal candidate. Archbishop Stigand had in any case caused offence by his independent behaviour, not least refusing to send the Church collection money called Peter's Pence to Rome. The pope was happy to provide a papal banner for the expedition, beautifully decorated with pearls and jewels, to spur the duke's men on.

William had also taken care to obtain the support of the other most important international figure in western Christendom, the Emperor Henry IV. Ever since 800 when the title Emperor of the West was created for Charlemagne by the papacy as a rival to the power of the Byzantines, the emperor had been the earthly magnate designated protector of the Church. With both emperor and pope onside, Duke William's soldiers were united by a sense of the rightness of their task. Such a feeling was not present in an increasingly fragmented England. William's soldiers also had a leader of great military renown who had seen off all comers from the kingdoms bordering Normandy, including France. This enabled him to be confident that the duchy would not be attacked in his absence, if he kept it short – particularly given that his greatest enemy, neighbouring Anjou, was wracked by civil war.

William of Normandy had perfected a new method of warfare which would make the conquest of England surprisingly easy to achieve. His Normans fought on horseback and at short intervals threw up primitive castles made out of earthworks to hold the surrounding countryside. His great reputation meant that the expedition, for which he began building boats in the summer of 1066, attracted landless Norman knights of Viking origin in large numbers. Under the sacred papal banner at the ancient town of Lillebonne, with its old Roman amphitheatre, William assembled his force of 5,000 of the most daring men in western Europe. From Brittany, Flanders, Sicily, central France and Normandy itself they flocked to a man who promised them English land and English wives in exchange for their help in conquering England – for he had no gold to offer them. They loved to fight and saw a real prospect of gain for themselves across the Channel in England.

But so did many others. In May 1066 Harold's brother Tostig – at the head of a menacing Norwegian fleet sent by Harold Hardrada of Norway – appeared off the Isle of Wight. From there he moved northwards up the east coast burning ports until he was seen off by Earl Edwin and Earl Morcar and fled north to sanctuary in Scotland.

To make matters worse, by midsummer Harold's spies had confirmed that there would soon be an attack from Normandy. Harold frantically started rebuilding the neglected English navy, and kept the kingdom's militia on standby, for across the sea the duke of Normandy was building more ships than had ever been seen together, perhaps a thousand in all. Though they were not much bigger than fishing smacks they would be more than adequate for their task. We can see them in the Bayeux Tapestry, which was commissioned by William's half-brother the bishop of Bayeux to commemorate the occasion, and which shows them being dragged to the sea by ropes and loaded with horses and armour. In order to bind his men more tightly to him, the duke increased their pay and promised more. By August 1066 the dusty fields of Picardy were full of soldiers waiting for a propitious wind to carry them across the Channel from the port of St Valéry. For a month they lay in their tents as the great harvest moon waxed and waned and the black night sky filled with smoke from their campfires. But still no signal came.

Towards the end of September the soldiers began to mutter nervously that the lack of wind was a sign that God opposed the expedition. At this the brutal Duke William caused the body of St Valéry to be exhumed and paraded round the town while the soldiers watched. At last, a few days later, on 27 September, William got the wind he had asked for. As the soldiers knelt in thankful prayer William was already at anchor midway across the Channel waiting in his crimson-sailed ship for the other vessels to join him. Soon the invasion force was blown lightly across to England, where they landed at Pevensey (the Anglo-Saxon name for the former Roman port of Anderida). The remains of a Roman fort stood there, and William in the Norman fashion immediately made of it a rough defensive castle of ditch and earthwork to protect his troops. In fact the superstitious Norman knights might already have been disheartened, for William had tripped when he landed and sprawled his full length. But as they inveighed against the ill omen the duke leaped up with earth clutched in his fists, and exclaimed that he had only wanted to grasp his new kingdom more closely.

But what of King Harold? Why was he not there to repel the warriors clattering unopposed down the wooden gangplanks? Why was there no one to stop the whole host moving off east down the coast to Hastings, where William's scouts had told him that the land was hillier and would be easier to hold? Indeed why had there been no ships in the Channel to stop the Norman fleet? By the most unfortunate of coincidences, the same wind conditions which had prevented the Normans from sailing had allowed

Tostig and his ally the king of Norway, Harold Hardrada, to invade the north of England. On 25 September, two days before William and his troops arrived at Pevensey, Harold had defeated Tostig and Harold Hardrada at the Battle of Stamford Bridge near York. It would take Harold at least ten days to reach the south coast and meet Duke William. But his men were exhausted from a battle in which so many of them had been wounded.

Worse still, after 8 September the English fleet had had to be disbanded because its sailors and the militia had been guarding the Channel ports since early summer and it was feared that they might mutiny if they continued to be left to their own devices. The militia was allowed to be called out for only forty days, and that period had elapsed. So the Channel had been left quite empty, with the English navy withdrawn up the Thames to London.

With characteristic energy but rather too great impetuosity, the minute he heard the Normans had landed Harold began to march south from York. But he lacked the full complement of troops he needed. The men of the earls of Northumbria and Mercia did not accompany him as they were still recovering from Stamford Bridge and so could not provide the great reinforcements which might have held off the Normans. Nor can the enmity between the Godwins and Edwin and Morcar have helped. The army which faced William consisted mainly of Harold's own bodyguard, the 3,000 housecarles invented by Cnut, men supplied by his brothers Gyrth and Leofwine, and Londoners, thanes and churls living near enough to Sussex to join the host immediately.

Harold seems to have decided not to wait for the full English militia to be assembled before he moved on Hastings. It would have taken too long to go through the motions of summoning it out again from more distant shires, many of which were several days' journey away. Perhaps in the confusion of those September days there was little time to think clearly, with danger facing him from north and south, and Harold was himself exhausted.

The Battle of Hastings was to be a very uneven contest, of highly trained Norman knights against a tired and disorganized English force. Too many of them were peasants in woollen shifts called straight from the fields. They were untrained in warfare but forced by the institution of the fyrd to do service perhaps with just a pitchfork, with a spear if they were lucky. They stood little chance against warriors on horses which were trained to rear and attack. The defeat of the English at the Battle of Hastings hinged on the quality of William's knights. They could follow military orders in a disciplined manner owing to the Norman practice of educating males in warfare from childhood onwards in the castles of the great lords. It was a way of life which was soon to become commonplace in England.

The Bayeux Tapestry made to celebrate the Norman Conquest in 1066. King Harold is killed at the Battle of Hastings and the English turn in flight.

Hearing from his headquarters, a temporary wooden castle at Hastings, that Harold was fast approaching down what is today the A21, William seized the day. Moving his troops forward the Duke of Normandy made the English king halt at the highest point in the area, then called Senlac, while he positioned his own men on a ridge opposite. Harold had to draw up his forces round the royal standard in an uncomfortably narrow space with little room for manoeuvre. As soon as the sun rose on 14 October 1066, after the Normans had received Holy Communion from a silver chalice, William sent his knights down the hill towards the English while Harold and his men struggled to get into formation after the Saxon fashion, the king's housecarles positioned in the centre, and all of them on foot – already a disadvantage against the mounted Normans. The Saxons were armed with their great battleaxes which they whirled round their heads. Closely packed next to one another and creating a wall with their long kite-shaped shields, they formed such an impenetrable mass that even horses could not get near them – so long as they did not break ranks. Harold particularly warned his men to resist the temptation to pursue the enemy, for then they would be lost.

In the very middle of the shield wall stood King Harold and his two brothers with the royal standard of England between them, so that no one would dare flee the battle when the king was in the middle of it. Flanking the shield wall on both sides were two wings of the lightly armed local farmers from Sussex and Kent. Among them were monks from Winchester:

after the battle, as they lay dead on the field, their brown habits were discovered concealed within their armour.

At first the advantage seemed with the Saxons, because the steepness of the ground made frontal attack by the invaders very difficult. The Normans fought in the style they had brought back from the east – that is to say, making use of the Arab stirrup. This invention freed a rider's arms to fight while the lower part of his body was secured to the horse. Again and again the Norman cavalry charged up the slopes of the hill where Harold was positioned, but each time it failed to break through the Saxon shield wall.

For six hours the battle was undecided, though victory seemed imminent for the more technically advanced Normans. William now threw his main energy into attacking the more lightly armed Saxon troops on the wings. His archers sent repeated flights of arrows over their heads. This inflicted heavy losses among the ranks of the English peasantry, who were not protected by the chainmail of the housecarles; nevertheless they stood their ground. Then the cunning duke gave his knights a signal. The whole cavalry wheeled round and appeared to flee. This was too much for the Saxons in the shield wall. With shouts and whoops they broke formation and began to pursue the enemy down the hill, heedless of Harold's shouted orders to stay where they were.

As soon as the Saxons began to follow them, with a great roar the Norman knights turned back and rode them down. Soon the valley between the two hills was filled with the screams of dying men and horses. Bravest of all the Saxons that day was Harold Godwin. It was only when William realized that his troops would never get near the top of the hill, where Harold and his housecarles still kept the shield wall packed in tight formation, that he again ordered his archers to fire their arrows straight into the air over their heads. One of those arrows entered Harold's brain through the eye and killed him.

The duke of Normandy was no less brave. His was the voice in the thickest of the fray urging his men on. He was always the first to rush forward and attack. Eyewitnesses said he was 'everywhere raging, everywhere furious', and, as with Harold, several horses were killed under him that day. He fought until night fell and crowned him with complete victory. As he made his way in the misty twilight across the battlefield he came to where the fighting had evidently been fiercest on the Saxon side, as could be seen by the bodies strewn over the frozen ground. There among them, covered by the now ragged and torn royal standard, lay Harold.

William was so moved by the terrible bloodshed that he decreed that henceforth Senlac would be known as Battle, or Bataille, one of the many Norman words which were to transform the language of England. On the spot where Harold lay William caused the high altar of the new Battle Abbey to be raised as a memorial to the king, which can still be seen today.

Although the Battle of Hastings was a watershed in English history, at the time it was not clear whether the country would rally again either under Edwin and Morcar in the north or under the new party for Edward the Confessor's great-nephew Edgar the Atheling developing in London. For a month the Conqueror, as he would be known to later generations, bided his time, securing the country round Dover and Canterbury. Then he moved west out of Kent to London, encouraged by the submission of Winchester led by Edith, Harold's sister and widow of Edward the Confessor.

Though the Conqueror burned Southwark – a constant feature of its history – he could not break through the guard into the walled city at the crossing which is now London Bridge. He therefore decided that the best way of taking London, then as now the key to England, was to ride west. He would lay waste the countryside round it on which the Londoners depended for their food. Great stretches of Surrey, Berkshire and north Hampshire, the fertile country that the people of Reada and Wocca had settled 600 years before, were set alight by descendants of England's old enemies, the Vikings. When the duke crossed the Thames at Wallingford, apparently intending to return to London again and renew the attack, at the urging of Archbishop Stigand those leading the resistance decided to give in.

Edwin and Morcar had never meanwhile moved their troops south to rally the country. There was no real focus for a national resistance, and William the Conqueror benefited from that. Wealthy London magnates who had earlier declared the youthful Edgar the Atheling king, now accompanied Edwin and Morcar to meet William at Berkhamsted in Hertfordshire in the shadow of the Chiltern Hills just west of what today is Hemel Hempstead. There they offered him the crown. Having sworn an oath to be the Conqueror's men and hostages for peace, they watched as before their eyes William burned every grain of wheat between Berkhamsted and London, a distance of almost thirty miles, to make sure that there was no backsliding when he arrived in London.

On a bitterly cold Christmas Day in 1066 William the Conqueror became King William of England in Westminster Abbey. Although he had taken the crown by military conquest, initially he was very anxious to be considered the legitimate heir and to have the consent of his new subjects. At the moment of coronation he therefore ordered the Englishman Ealdred, archbishop of York and the Norman bishop Geoffrey of Coutances, who were jointly crowning him, to ask the people in the abbey if they accepted him as their king. Although it was unlikely that the English would say no when the abbey was ringed with William's knights, the shouts of acclamation in English and Norman French alarmed those very knights. In a panic they started setting fire to the buildings surrounding the abbey. As the congregation rushed out, the Conqueror and the priests were left alone at the altar. Despite the confusion without, there was deep silence within. William was anointed king according to the Saxon tradition instituted by St Dunstan, and took the oath of the Anglo-Saxon kings to rule his people justly.

Although the Conqueror's intention was to live in peace with his new subjects he could not disguise the fact that England was a country held by military garrison. Within three months William had built the White Tower out of earth and timber to overawe the inhabitants of London, which today is part of the complex known as the Tower of London. It was just one of the series of castles thrown up all over England to prevent rebellions.

For several hundred years the elective kingship of Anglo-Saxon England and the existence of the witan had given England consultative traditions. But the new Norman king did not consult. He dictated. There was to be no more asking for the approval of the witan. The role of the new curia regis, the court of the king, was to implement, not to advise. In March 1067, six months after the Battle of Hastings, the two remaining great magnates of Anglo-Saxon England, Edwin and Morcar, as well as Edgar the Atheling and Archbishop Stigand, were forced to accompany the new master of England over the Channel to Normandy, where they were paraded in triumph.

In charge of England in the Conqueror's absence were the new Norman earl of Kent, formerly Bishop Odo of Bayeux, William's half-brother, and William FitzOsbern, William's seneschal or steward who became earl of Hereford. And soon, as the native English landowners began to rebel against harsh treatment by the Normans, William would return to extirpate the old English ruling class and replace them with a Norman military aristocracy. Most Anglo-Saxon buildings in brick and wood, especially the churches, were replaced by Norman stone. The Saxons became an underclass whose language, as we shall see, was the despised argot of the stable. French became the language of the new aristocracy.

Bishop Odo of Bayeux, half brother of William the Conqueror. He commissioned the Bayeux Tapestry.

The Normans inherited a country with the strongest government in eleventh-century Europe, whose distinctive efficiency continued to be outstanding despite the weakness of the last Old English kings themselves. The English administrative system would form an excellent base for the new Norman government. William was keen to be seen as the legitimate successor of Edward the Confessor and everything was done in the name of that king to wipe out the year of the usurper. But, whatever the justification, the inescapable fact remained that foreigners now ruled the land.

NORMAN AND
ANGEVIN

William I

(1066–1087)

Though peace had succeeded the Conquest, it was not to last. Outbreaks of resistance continued to flare up particularly as the new rulers turned a deaf ear to complaints from the Anglo-Saxons that Norman men-at-arms were abusing their positions, stealing from the English and carrying off their wives or turning humbler thanes out of their family homes. More dangerous were the attempts of regional leaders such as Edwin, Morcar and Edgar the Atheling and their supporters to regain control of the country by seeking assistance abroad. At Rouen William heard rumours that the king of Denmark and even his own cousin the count of Boulogne had been approached by the English to help them get rid of the Normans. In the west of England three sons of Harold who had been hiding in Ireland started laying waste the country. In the north a widespread resistance movement began, led by the northern earls. But once again, as at the Battle of Hastings, the failure of all these parties to make common cause would mean they could never succeed.

It was enough of a threat at the time, however, to oblige William to leave his wife Matilda of Flanders to govern Normandy with his eldest son Robert, while he returned to London. Impressing contemporaries by his refusal to wait for campaigning weather in the milder spring, at the beginning of January 1067 he sent one army north while he personally marched the second west. His progress through the country to Exeter was marked by the throwing up at regular strategic points of characteristic Norman castles. These were towers or keeps erected on top of a man-made mound, or in Norman French *motte*, and surrounded by a moat, their purpose to control the countryside. The use of slits for windows and the forbidding absence of decorative features proclaim their strictly military purpose.

Having successfully besieged Exeter and built the castle of Rougemont outside it, William hurried north to confront the greatest threat to his rule. Early in 1069 the Saxons massacred William's governor in Durham, Robert de Comines, and all but two of his 500 men as they slept. The English population of York soon followed suit, rising against its foreign garrison and destroying it and burning York Minster. When Harold's sons landed again at Plymouth while the fleet of the King of Denmark sailed unopposed up the Humber river alongside ships loyal to Edgar the Atheling, William's control of his new domain seemed suddenly in doubt. But, acting with his usual decisiveness, he bought off the Danes and persuaded them, with the English leaders, to retreat up to the Tyne. Then he himself proceeded to York where the local Saxon leader Waltheof, Earl of Huntingdon had been directing operations and in fact doing much of the fighting himself.

This massive slayer of Normans so impressed William that he took him into his service and married him to his niece Judith. But he loosed a dreadful vengeance on the Northumbrians for their defiance. At Christmas, the season of goodwill, the Conqueror sat in grim and solitary state in the empty city of York planning wholesale destruction for a hundred miles around. Every day Norman soldiers were sent out to kill every living thing in the area: men, women, children and all their livestock. Houses and all fruits, conserves and grain were to be burned, ploughs broken and the country from the Humber to the Tees, from the Wear to the Tyne, to be made a desert. Fourteen years later, in the Domesday Book – the celebrated record of landholding in England compiled for tax purposes – all of that country had only the terrible Latin word *vasta* (meaning ruined or destroyed) to describe it. For fifty years nothing grew there. This episode became known as the Harrying of the North. It was intended to ensure that its inhabitants never rose again against the Norman occupying power.

Nevertheless, thanks to an indomitable Lincolnshire thane named Hereward the Wake, one little place in England held out against William and all his military devices until 1071. That was the tiny Isle of Ely in Cambridgeshire, which was then surrounded on every side by impassable marshes and wild fens. It became a symbol of English national resistance. That its leader's name Hereward the Wake passed into semi-mythical folklore on the level of Robin Hood and King Arthur indicates the strength of emotion surrounding him. Unlike those characters, however, Hereward was a real person whose existence is solidly documented. He had returned from abroad to find his mother turned out of the family home by Norman upstarts who were now themselves living in it. Enraged by her treatment Hereward began harassing the Normans. After the Harrying of the North had driven the two northern earls Edwin and Morcar out of their country they joined him with their followers and Ely became the centre of English resistance.

In the end William could trust only himself to defeat the wily Saxon. He blockaded the Wash for weeks and every little inlet that led into the Fens, trying to starve the English out. But though by then Hereward and the rest of the resistance were living on roots they never gave up. They were so successful in ambushing William's men when they tried to build a causeway to the island that it began to be rumoured that Hereward had magic powers. In fact the Normans might never have captured Hereward at all had not the monks on the Isle of Ely betrayed him. Unlike Hereward they missed their luxurious diet of fine white bread and venison and good French wines. They sent a message to William revealing the existence of a secret passage which ran between the island and the Normans' camp. In the middle of the night William and his men poured on to the island, capturing Hereward as he lay hidden in the reeds.

This marked the real end of the English national resistance. Hereward was treated leniently as William was impressed by his courage, and he is believed to have died on one of the king's campaigns in France to secure the borders of Normandy. But since England continued to be periodically shaken by regional rebellions, minor though they were, William retreated from his policy of using the Anglo-Saxons to govern England for him. The Conquest was still a very recent event and had yet to take permanent root among the people. Owing to the interest neighbouring countries like Denmark and Flanders continued to take in rebel conspirators' plans, in 1074 when the earls of Hereford and Norfolk and the treacherous Earl Waltheof tried to seize power, William's attitude to his newly acquired country changed.

Previously, in exchange for paying a redemptive tax or geld many Saxon thanes had been permitted by the Normans to retain their old lands. The shires and shire courts had continued to be largely administered by English officials. Although there had been some land redistribution to reward William's followers it was on a relatively small scale. But from 1075 onwards the 4,000 thanes who had been the important landowners in England under Harold began to be dispossessed of their ancient estates. Their fields, pastures, meadows and forests would be consolidated into far larger blocs and transferred to the ownership of 200 Norman barons and their own small armies of soldiers. William now believed that only Normans could be trusted to control the rebellious country of England for him, through the military landholding system called feudalism.

Under the Saxon kings land had been owned freely, despite the ancient defensive obligation of the fyrd and the duty to maintain roads and bridges. The Duke of Normandy introduced to England the Norman legal custom in which all landholding carried a military obligation. It was described as being 'held of the king'. Land was granted by William to his followers on the specific condition that its owner served the lord above him in war. It bound the whole of England into one military unit and could have been achieved only in a revolution such as had just taken place in

England. For each unit of land or 'fief' that the new Norman landowner held in England, he was obliged to put an armed soldier or knight at William's disposal to fight for him for so many days a year, and he had to take an oath to be faithful to the lord he held it of, called the oath of fidelity or fealty. The man who took it did homage to the man above him, who was called his liege lord.

The Norman feudal system had accounted for the ease with which William the Conqueror had raised his invading army in 1066. He had called on the knights' service owed to him by the great Norman lords who held land from him, which meant they had to be ready for war, complete with arms and horses, at all times. The king was at the top of the system and below him were the most powerful nobles called the tenants-in-chief, each bound to supply him with up to 1,500 knights. Many of those 1,500 knights would be supplied from among the tenants below who owed the lord above them knight service.

By 1085 not only had all the land been redistributed, but the official or government class responsible for royal business in the shires was now composed of all Norman Frenchmen rather than English. Shires had also been renamed counties, after the Conqueror's local representative, the vicomte, who to begin with took over the functions of the sheriff. But, though county remains another word for shire, the office of vicomte soon melted away, and the title sheriff returned. Over the previous ten years the population of England had become used to the sight of large numbers of Norman French officials guarded by soldiers arriving from London to gather information to facilitate the transfer of land in their area. The Normans called up what became known as juries (from the Latin *juro*, I swear) – that is, panels of inquiry which sat in the open air on the village green to determine what the boundaries, the ancient rights and the labour obligations were for each estate, whether belonging to a lord or a churchman.

The Normans' claim to England was based on conquest. At the same time they were natural lawyers and immensely businesslike. They were obsessed with legitimacy and believed in doing everything by the book. Even though a Norman lord might be taking over a Saxon property, they intended services and dues to carry on as before or 'as in the days of King Edward', in that phrase so resonant of legitimacy for the Normans. William was particularly keen to sort out the large estate owners' rights when it came to the law of the land. The legal powers of the King of England were far greater than those of other western European monarchs. Although the Anglo-Saxon lord was entitled to hold his own courts to judge disputes over land in his domain, to punish thieves and to assess stolen goods, the English national custom had been established for centuries that those rights were granted by the king. The king and his officials were considered to be responsible for keeping the peace. Moreover, the King of England was entitled to raise taxes in every part of the country. When his instructions or writs came to the shire court, now called the county court, the English tradition was that they were to be obeyed. There was no need for soldiers to enforce his writs.

At Christmas 1085, with the land transfer complete, the king held the last of his tri-annual councils with all the most important new landholders or tenants-in-chief. William was recorded as having 'held very deep speech with his council about this land – how it was peopled, and with what sort of men'. He was now in a position to send further posses of government officials among the newly Normanized English to set up an enlarged version of the shire court in every county. They were to assess everyone for tax, from cottagers to lords, and once again to obtain evidence on oath about every item of the countryside from a gathering of the propertied locals, evidence relating both to twenty years before, in 1066, and to the current year, 1086. The court consisted of local lords, members of all the hundred courts within the shire and six of the wealthier peasants, as well as the sheriff. The Norman commissioners were to have no interests in the particular shire and the facts were to be checked by another group of commissioners.

The survey with its descriptions of the land twenty years before in 1066, and at the present day reveals how completely during that period the native

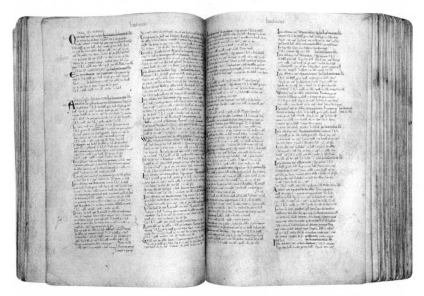

The Domesday Book, the detailed Norman investigation of their English subjects' landholding begun in 1085. This is from the volume called the Great Domesday Book, Volume 1 describing Berkshire.

aristocracy had been displaced by Norman warriors. It also demonstrates the Normans' powers of organization and their interest in statistics, which were without precedent in medieval times. Indeed not until the nineteenth century would such attention to detail be displayed again. The survey rapidly became known to the irreverent English as the Domesday Book. Affronted by the level of detail required by the Norman commissioners, down to how many geese and pigs a cottager owned, one Anglo-Saxon wit remarked that it was as close a record as the Recording Angel would make at the crack of doom on the Day of Judgement, or Doomsday.

Although some counties are missing from the Domesday Book, it gives us an amazingly detailed picture of England, listing all the woodland, pasture, millponds and fishponds, towns and villages and even the names of the inhabitants, English and Norman alike – many of which remain the same today. Reflecting the redistribution of land among a smaller number of Norman warriors England is treated as a country which from now on was to be organized in terms of manors. Each manor is the basis for an assessment of subordinate hides. The Norman commissioners divided the majority of the population into the following main categories: villein, cottars or cottagers, and slaves. The largest group were the villein or villeins. Although by the thirteenth century villeins had become synonymous with serfs, who being the property of their landlord had no independent legal existence, in 1086 they were free men. They ranged from tenant farmers, who held their land in return for services to their landlords, to small landholders, who owned the title to their land outright. Rents, labour services and plough teams were all assessed to see whether William could get any more money out of his new country.

Thanks to Domesday survey, which is held in the National Archives in London, England has the most complete picture of a country in Europe at that time. Completed in a little over a year it is a monument not only to Norman efficiency but to the tremendous tradition of English local government which had flourished since Alfred's time. The already extremely well-organized and mature institutions of Anglo-Saxon local government with its hundred and shire courts could not have been better suited to William's autocratic purposes. But the sort of changes William was rushing through, albeit in an orderly fashion, created such a volume of parchment that by the end of his reign the king's writing office, inherited from Edward the Confessor, could no longer be attached to the royal household. It had to become an independent department called the royal Chancery, staffed by clerks trained to draft the king's directives and send writs to the shires.

In August 1086 William considered that the process of settling England in the Norman way had been completed. He called an assembly at Salisbury of all the chief landowners in the country and the smaller barons who held land from the tenants-in-chief. Although not every single landowner could attend, a significant number were there, and each swore a personal oath of allegiance to William, on his knees before his king, who held the man's hands between his own. This was the remarkable innovation of William the Conqueror and demonstrated the exceptional nature of English feudalism, that all were made aware that they owed their loyalty to the king above their immediate liege lord.

The extraordinary scene on Salisbury Plain of all the landowners in England kneeling before the by now extremely corpulent figure of the Norman king represented a triumphant climax to the Norman Conquest. The rebellions had all petered out and the Danes had finally abandoned their claim to the throne, their last attempt at an invasion being the year before. William had pushed back the frontier with Wales, built a castle at Cardiff and made the Welsh princes and the Scottish king do homage to him or risk further warfare and damage to their countries. All of this was an indication of the strength of the Norman hold on England, and it should also remind us that William had brought peace to England. Most of the English might be in a disadvantaged position, but the fact was that for almost a century England had been at the mercy of powerful foreign invaders. By the 1070s she was the protected centrepiece of a great trans-continental empire as widespread as Cnut's had been. Unlike Cnut's, however, William's empire tore England away from her Scandinavian and Germanic roots. With great consequences for her future she was thrust back into the heart of Latin civilization and the traditions of scholarship which stretched from Roman times.

Nevertheless, for all the positive long-term effects of the Conquest, whatever their circumstances, most Englishmen and women suffered under the Normans. One of the most dramatic effects of Norman rule was the gradual enserfment of the free English tenant farmers, who in 1066 consisted of almost half the population. They who for centuries had played an important part in local government in the hundred and shire court were by 1200 denied access to the king's courts because they were no longer allowed to call themselves freemen. The term villein had come to mean a serf who was tied to his lord's domain by the services he performed for him, whose disputes could be judged only in the manorial court. Thus although under the Normans the Saxon practice of slavery died out, because Norman ecclesiastics found it offensive, for 40 per cent of Englishmen and women their freedom was greatly curtailed. Under the Normans the manor court slowly replaced the ancient hundred court, and the lord of the manor alone now decided what previously had been decided by a group of small farmers and landowners together.

Most English saints' days were suppressed by the new Norman priests, while English went into temporary abeyance as a written language. Whereas poetry and histories like *The Anglo-Saxon Chronicle* had been written in Old English, books in Norman England were now written in French, as that was the language of the court. *The Anglo-Saxon Chronicle* itself, which had been written in monasteries since Alfred's time, falls silent by the mid-twelfth century. For the next hundred years English went underground, becoming the language of the uneducated.

Even their native forests were taken away from the English, owing to William's passion for hunting. Until the Conquest, firewood and wild game from the vast forests still covering the country had been a traditionally free source of fuel and food. But William introduced laws forbidding the use of bows and arrows within them, and the presence of hunting dogs. Anyone who cut firewood from the forest or poached deer might be blinded, mutilated or executed. 'He loved the tall stags as if he were their father,' declared *The Anglo-Saxon Chronicle*.

To make matters worse the Conqueror destroyed churches and towns in Hampshire over a distance of thirty miles in order to create what we still call the New Forest, though it is now 900 years old. Deer roamed while people starved. William's new forest laws incurred much hatred among the English, but his love of hunting made him unwilling to proceed in his usual cautious fashion. He turned the forests all over England into royal reserves that only he and his friends could hunt in.

William the Conqueror's tendency was to scatter the manors of his chief men all over the country to prevent regional loyalties becoming a threat. However, for the dangerous border lands with Wales and Scotland this arrangement was modified. For many centuries they would be in a state of perpetual warfare. On the marcher lands, so called because they marched with the Welsh frontier, lords like Roger de Montmorency were allowed to own huge estates concentrated in one area. There the local landowner was responsible for what was in effect a private army keeping the Welsh at bay. These territories were known as the palatine earldoms, and their rulers were far more like the independent barons of Normandy. But once again William's subtle mind saw a way of cutting down on the power of the palatine earls: where possible he made churchmen palatine rulers. The most famous of these was the Prince Bishop of Durham. By Norman law priests were forbidden to marry and have children, so they could not become a dynastic threat to the eminence of the king's own family.

The last great change the Norman Conquest brought to England was the reform of the English Church. One of the justifications for the Norman invasion had been the Godwins' abuses. Having obtained the papal blessing for the Conquest William had to fall in with the wishes of the papacy, which under the direction of Pope Gregory VII (formerly known as Hildebrand, archdeacon of Rome) had embarked on a hard-hitting programme of reforms. In any case they corresponded to the Duke of Normandy's own austere disposition. William was a deeply religious man and disapproved of corruption. But he waited until the country was quiet before removing the illegitimate Stigand, who had used his influence among the English to secure a peaceful acceptance of the Conquest.

From Normandy William imported his friend the great churchman Lanfranc, Abbot of Caen, to become Archbishop of Canterbury. Lanfranc made a great many changes to the Church organization. In recognition of population shifts, the residences of English bishops were transferred to what had become the leading towns of dioceses – with the Bishop of Lichfield, for example, moving to Chester – and Lanfranc replaced the slack English clergy with the better-trained Normans, thereby depriving the English of parish priests who spoke their own language. Lanfranc was an Italian lawyer who had attended the law school of Pavia and who very late in life had been seized by the religious impulse. He had made the monastery at Bec in Normandy one of the great centres of religious learning of the eleventh century. Possessed of a subtle mind to match his master's, he reformed the practices of the English Church along Hildebrandine lines. One of Gregory's VII's profound beliefs was that the priest should be better behaved than other men – in view of his high calling he should adhere to a more exacting law than ordinary people. Corrupt practices such as simony – that is, selling pardons for sins – were no longer permitted. He insisted on a return to the ideal of celibacy in the clergy. The priest's wife and children, who had been a common sight in every village, were seen no more.

The marking out of the clergy as a separate caste meant that the Norman Conquest put an end to the seamless robe of government between king and churchmen that had prevailed in Anglo-Saxon England – although priests and clerks continued to serve until the sixteenth century as what were in effect civil servants. Bishops no longer presided over the shire courts as they had under Anglo-Saxon kings. The Church obtained her own courts from William, with jurisdiction to try men in holy orders, disputes over marriage, and any spiritual matters.

Two systems of law thus developed side by side in England. Canon law, practised in the ecclesiastical or Church courts, contrasted strongly with what became known in the thirteenth century as the common law, which was by and large ancient English custom. Canon law derived from the principles of Roman law, which had continued to be studied at centres of learning such as Pavia on the continent where Lanfranc himself had been trained. And it was canon law in which the Church clerks, who until the sixteenth century would provide the trained minds essential for the nascent

English civil service, were educated.

In contrast English common law had always had a common-sense aspect to it, since it had always been adjudicated by tenant farmers. It was never particularly precise in legal terms. That imprecision was increased by the fact that the justice meted out by the early Norman kings from what became called the King's Bench was at first fairly informal. It was decided after a discussion with whatever baron happened to be attending court at the time. Members of the royal council or Curia Regis might send clerks into the counties and there take evidence from the sheriff about a dispute which would be deliberated on locally or perhaps brought back to London for a meeting of the Council.

The higher level of education enjoyed by the Church's trained clerks was useful to the Normans in an infinite number of ways. But one feature of the far-reaching Hildebrandine reforms was less pleasing to William. Pope Gregory's belief in the superiority of the clergy to the ordinary man led him to make repeated attempts to liberate the Church from the power of the secular or earthly ruler, by ending their right to confer on bishops and abbots the ring and staff which were their badges of office. He had already clashed with the emperor Henry IV over this principle in the struggle known as the Investiture Contest which rocked Germany and Italy for nearly fifty years.

In William Pope Gregory believed he had a captive ruler. Gregory claimed that not only should the Duke of Normandy abandon the episcopal investiture ceremonies but he should do homage to the pope: the duke's appeal to the Church Curia to support his invasion of England was an implicit acknowledgement of the jurisdiction of the papal court. In a typically ingenious and complicated piece of exposition the best legal minds in Rome further sought to argue that since England had previously paid a tax to Rome known as Peter's Pence this proved that England had previously been the vassal of Rome.

But William the Conqueror was far too shrewd to be caught by Pope Gregory. Just as with the Norman barons he had every intention of limiting the Church's power. In a brief note to Rome he let it be known that he would pay Peter's Pence, which he acknowledged had been in arrears for some time, but that the ancient custom of the English kings prevented him doing homage as the pope's vassal. From then on William did very much as he pleased. He gave orders that no pope should be recognized in England until the king himself had done so. Church councils were not to pass laws without the king's express permission; likewise papal bulls and missives from the pope to the people were to be distributed only when the king had decided that he approved of the content.

The pope generally tolerated William's behaviour because he advanced the cause of the Church much more than he damaged it, not least in the way he used the clergy as clerks to handle the increasing amounts of government business. He therefore allowed William to invest English bishops with their badges of office even though the German emperor was not permitted to do so. For her part the Church, as one of the most important underlying forces which kept society together, promoted Norman government among the English people.

Owing to the Conqueror's alliance with the Church the Normans were tremendous builders of churches and abbeys. Many of England's most famous cathedrals were begun or built just after the Conquest. During the 1070s, Canterbury Cathedral was rebuilt, and Lincoln Cathedral and Old Sarum Cathedral, which lies in ruins above the town of Salisbury, begun. Huge stone churches which looked more like fortresses, in the style called Romanesque that the Normans introduced, sprang up all over England. Romanesque churches, which had little or no decoration other than chevron cross-hatching, were characterized by immensely thick pillars, rounded arches and a very long nave. Visible a long way off, they dominated the landscape almost as much as the Norman castles. The next decade saw the grey stone Norman cathedrals rise at Ely, Worcester and Gloucester. Tewkesbury Abbey was also built, and the cathedrals at St Albans and Rochester were restored.

At the same time the Normans pushed on with their equally distinctive programme of castle-building. In the process they knocked down most Saxon country houses, which is why so few remain. In their place they erected strong forbidding castles in the Norman fashion, some in stone. Towns and commerce likewise flourished under the influence of the energetic Normans, who like their Viking ancestors were keen traders. Jewish merchants returned to England after an absence of 600 years, having left with the Romans.

The Chapel of St John built around 1080 in the White Tower at the Tower of London.

Despite the sufferings of the Saxon

people, the Normans had found plenty about England which they admired enough to want to adapt, particularly the Anglo-Saxon political institutions. Within a generation mixed marriages between Normans and Saxons, especially Saxon heiresses, were common. One of the most famous Conquest artefacts, the Bayeux Tapestry, is of entirely English workmanship, even though it was commissioned by William's half-brother, the Norman Bishop Odo. It shows the high level of artistry in tapestry-making in England and was probably sewn in Canterbury. Two hundred and fifty feet long by twenty feet wide, full of verve and drama, it is also a subtle depiction of the story of the Conquest.

A typical Norman keep, Rochester Castle built 1087 on the Medway.

As such it is one of England's most important pieces of historical evidence.

In 1087, the year after the Domesday Book was completed, the mighty duke returned to Normandy for what turned out to be his last campaign. He died attempting to conquer a disputed area of land, the county of Maine, which abuts Normandy. Twenty years before at the time of Hastings the King of France had been weak. But by 1087 a new king, Philip I, was on the throne. This mischief-maker was delighted to help William's eldest son Robert, the heir to Normandy, stir up trouble against a father who gave him no responsibility, who kept the reins of power firmly in his own hands, and who, to punish him, had deliberately arranged for the kingdom of England to be inherited by his son William Rufus. Now there was open warfare between the conqueror and the French king.

William had always been intending to attack the city of Mantes which had previously belonged to Normandy. But legend has it that the King of France made a cruel joke about William's grossness which got to his ears. The size of his stomach by now was indeed making it hard for him to keep in his saddle and he no longer got about as he had in his younger days. At Rouen, confined to his palace, the duke heard Philip of France's mocking bon mot: 'The King of England keeps his bed like a woman after she has had a baby.' William sent a deceptively mild message in return. 'Tell Philip that when I go to Mass after the confinement, I'll make him an offering of 100,000 candles.' A month later he had surrounded Mantes. Then he set fire to it – a hundred thousand candles indeed.

WILLIAM RUFUS.

This gesture proved William's undoing. His horse stumbled on an ember and threw him so badly that he suffered fatal internal injuries. Watching over his deathbed was William's favourite son Henry, later to become Henry I. His calculating and legalistic tendencies were always appreciated by a father who had similar qualities. But meanwhile the Duke of Normandy's stout son William Rufus, named for his red hair and red face, the heir to the English throne, had immediately hightailed it to England to make sure no Anglo-Saxon seized the crown before he did.

William II

(1087–1100)

The reign of William Rufus was a very different affair from his father's. Superficially he resembled him in so far as he was a fearless and victorious warrior and strong king. He was adroit enough to make himself popular among the English by freeing important English leaders like Morcar. He added to his French possessions, and was even more of a threat to the Welsh and Scottish kingdoms than the Conqueror had been. He defeated and killed Malcolm Canmore, King of the Scots, who was constantly invading England, and in 1092 he reconquered Cumberland, formerly an independent principality founded by the Strathclyde Welsh. Carlisle became an English city, and obtained its own bishop in the next reign. At William Rufus' cosmopolitan court the abacus was used for the first time

Durham Cathedral, begun 1093, finished 1280.

to calculate what was owed the king. During his reign the construction of Durham Cathedral began, the first western European building to use ribbed vaulting for the roof.

But it soon became clear that the new king was a poor version of his great father. He was a greedy man who had none of the sense of fairness which had informed his father, harsh though he was. Although he built Westminster Hall in 1097 as the place where he and his advisers could mete out justice, William Rufus' judgements were generally rather self-interested. Lacking his father's self-discipline and continence, the new king was always in need of money to finance his extravagant lifestyle. Aided and abetted by an equally unscrupulous minor Norman clerk named Ranulf, who soon became his justiciar (or chief minister), a term used for the first time in English history, William Rufus was soon causing the country to groan under his demands. Ranulf was nicknamed Flambard, because, reported the monk Ordericus Vitalis, 'like a devouring flame he tormented the people, and turned the daily chants of the Church into lamentation'. He encouraged the king to swell his coffers by interpreting the Domesday Book information more stringently, especially in relation to the monasteries, to which they felt the old regime's inspectors had been too lenient.

Thanks to Flambard's low but ingenious mind the two introduced new ways of making the country yield more gold for the king than ever before. Feudal dues that William I had demanded only where the estate could bear them were used to enrich the king at the expense of his barons. As with death duties today, feudal law stipulated that on the death of an important landowner or tenant-in-chief a 'relief' or tax was payable to the king before the heir could inherit his father's estate. These were now demanded without mercy. Under William Rufus the property of minors supposedly in the king's safekeeping until they came of age were run to rack and ruin or their woods cut down and sold for the king's profit. Heiresses were married against their will to cronies of the king.

In 1088, a year after he succeeded to the throne, William II's strenuous demands provoked an unsuccessful rising by his tenants-in-chief in the name of his weaker brother Robert, who was now ruling Normandy. Led by the king's half-uncle Odo of Bayeux, these barons made the revolt an excuse to terrorize the country. Alarmed at their strength William cleverly defeated them by promising the humbler people of England that the forest laws would be less harshly enforced and some of the more stringent taxes lifted, with the result that those who had no wish to be at the mercy of marauding armed horsemen supported the king. Subsequently many of the most important tenants-in-chief lost their lands and were banished overseas. In 1095, however, a new rebellion broke out, led by Robert de

Mowbray, the Earl of Northumberland and directed against the king's tyranny. This too was unsuccessful. Even so, William failed to make de Mowbray surrender his castle of Bamburgh, so he ruthlessly built alongside it a new castle which became known as Malvoisin or Evil Neighbour. When eventually de Mowbray was forced to leave the castle, the soldiers of Malvoisin pounced and captured him. This was the last challenge to the king during his reign.

Because of William Rufus' strong-armed approach to his tenants-in-chief, many of the Norman adventurers who still had that Viking zest to conquer decided to try their luck beyond the king's reach by invading Wales and seizing land from the Welsh princes. Like the palatine earls they became a law unto themselves. These marcher lordships became the equivalent of little independent countries, run from the local castle – an economical way of using the energies of Norman knights, whose educational training was for warfare. They also had the advantage of keeping down the Welsh. From this period date the lordships of Montgomery, Brecon and Pembroke.

Not only did William Rufus antagonize the great barons. He also shocked and disgusted the English by his treatment of the Church, which he delighted in mocking from the decadent environs of his court. On Archbishop Lanfranc's death the king refused for four years to appoint a new incumbent at Canterbury. This remissness, instigated by Ranulf Flambard, enabled him to benefit from the right of regale, by which all the rents of the wealthy archdiocese came into the king's hands for as long as the see remained vacant. It was only because William became extremely ill unexpectedly and came to believe that he was on the point of death that he was frightened into good behaviour and agreed to appoint the best possible candidate for the archbishopric.

This was Abbot Anselm, from Lanfranc's old Abbey of Bec in Normandy. The saintly Anselm did not want to come to England, because he was sure there would be a personality clash. He was, he said, 'a weak old sheep, who should not be yoked to a fierce young bull like the King of England'. But William would not be denied, and he was soon ruing his decision. The new arch-bishop was appalled by the state of the English Church under the Conqueror's son and by the immoral quality of the court, where the questions of greatest interest seemed to be whether the king crimped his hair and

whether one should copy the new ram's-horn shoes he had designed, whose toes curled up so extravagantly that they were almost impossible to walk in. Meanwhile, though Canterbury was now occupied, a great many other sees remained empty so that their rents could go to the king. Although Archbishop Anselm was a mild-mannered man, as head of the Church of England he could not countenance this continued abuse of Church lands. But the king thwarted his attempts to call a council of bishops to censure his behaviour, and said that the abbeys were his in any case – to which Archbishop Anselm replied that they were his only to protect, for they belonged to God.

Unlike the case with Lanfranc and William the Conqueror, neither side was capable of seeing the other's point of view. The mounting irritation between king and archbishop reached new heights on the election of Pope Urban II. Owing to the continuing battle for power between the papacy and the secular ruler in the investiture contest, the German emperor had named his own rival pope, Clement. Archbishop Anselm was determined to receive the *pallium*, the badge of office, from Urban, but the red-faced Rufus flew into a rage and forbade him to leave the country because he had recognized neither Urban nor Clement as pope. In 1095 the king called a council of all the tenants-in-chief and all the bishops at Rockingham Castle, to determine whose authority over the archbishop was greater, the pope's or the king's. No solution was reached. Opinion was evenly balanced, with the barons wishing to limit the authority of William Rufus and the bishops anxious to curry favour with him. Most importantly every encounter with William II convinced Anselm that he should not yield to him.

Relations continued to deteriorate until 1097 when Archbishop Anselm refused point blank to send the money and the soldiers that feudal dues required of him for one of William Rufus' campaigns against the Welsh. When William threatened to take the archbishop to court, Anselm responded that only the pope had sufficient authority to settle their dispute. Then the archbishop fled to Rome, fearing that the king was so incensed that he might have killed him. He remained there for the rest of William's reign, leaving the Church in England once more without a head and enabling William to seize all the archbishopric's property again.

Ambitious and energetic, for some time William Rufus had been casting covetous eyes at his elder brother Robert's hereditary duchy of Normandy. Robert's financial incompetence soon played into his hands. The sale by the duke of some of Normandy's most important possessions – the Cotentin Peninsula and the Avranche – to William Rufus' younger brother Henry gave the English king the perfect excuse to invade Normandy. Objecting to Henry's hold over their common ancestral lands, he was paid off with a large portion of eastern Normandy. And Duke Robert soon surrendered the rest of Normandy into his younger brother's hands, temporarily at least, by mortgaging it to him in order to finance a crusade against the Muslims in the Holy Land.

Like many of his contemporaries throughout western Europe, including Edgar the Atheling, Duke Robert was obsessed by the idea of liberating Jerusalem from its new Seljuk Turk overlords. Where previously Christian pilgrims had been allowed to visit the Holy Places, the Garden of Gethsemane, Mount Calvary and the tomb of Christ, the Turks were making access almost impossible. Moreover, Christian pilgrims were being killed and sold into slavery all over the east. In 1095, preaching in the market place of Clermont to an enormous gathering of nobles, burghers and farmers, Pope Urban II launched what became known as the First Crusade, urgently demanding soldiers for Christ to liberate the Holy Land from the Infidel, or Unfaithful.

All knights were to have a red cross sewn on to their surcoat over their chainmail, representing the cross Christ had died on, to show that they were Crusaders. In return for fighting a holy war they would be absolved of some of the sins that would prevent them entering heaven. In an era dominated by the Church there could be no greater appeal for the Norman military caste whose existence was dedicated to warfare. The First Crusade was a great success. By 1099 it had expelled the Turks and set up a Latin Kingdom of Jerusalem under Godfrey de Bouillon. Meanwhile in his brother's stead, his creditor William was returning Normandy to order. He had recaptured Le Mans, attacked France and to the French king's alarm seemed about to take over the sprawling lands of Aquitaine. The Duke of Aquitaine wished like Robert to raise money for the Crusade and had decided to follow suit and mortgage his lands to William. This would have brought within the King of England's control all territory down to the Spanish border.

But at the height of his power William Rufus died out hunting on 2 August 1100, the victim of an anonymous arrow in the New Forest. Although legend accords Walter Tyrrel the role of bowman, if he fired the arrow it seems far more likely that he was acting at the behest of the king's younger brother Henry, who was one of the party. The suspicious circumstances and lack of ceremony which surrounded William Rufus' end suggest that his killing may have been the result of a conspiracy. For this powerful king was left to die alone while all his courtiers and his brother Henry abandoned him. He was found at the spot still marked Rufus Stone today by a humble charcoal-burner, the lowest occupation in Norman England. The charcoal-burner, whose name was Purkess, lugged the king's body to nearby Winchester on a crude wooden cart. But even in Winchester there was no public mourning and William Rufus' body was buried without a service inside the cathedral.

The dead king's brother Henry was already at Winchester by the time the cart arrived. He had galloped as fast as he could to the royal Treasury, which ever since the Wessex kings had been kept in that city, for traditionally whoever held the Treasury could be crowned. He persuaded local nobles to proclaim him king as was customary in the Anglo-Saxon monarchy. Henry was only just in time, for his brother Robert's man arrived immediately afterwards, intent on claiming the throne on behalf of the duke. By 5 August Henry had been crowned.

Henry I

(1100–1135)

Court historians later noted that as a child Henry I had enjoyed seeing his brothers squabble among themselves because then he knew he would get the better of them. The new king's every action was cautious, premeditated and calculated to serve his own ends. Though he was no scholar the nickname Beauclerk, which was applied to him from the fourteenth century, suggests a reputation for natural cleverness. Henry was less impetuous than William Rufus. Although he was just as grasping, he saw that he should proceed more shrewdly than his brother if he wished to rule peacefully.

Henry had inherited his father's deep respect for acting within the letter of the law. His first action was to restore the Norman kings to popularity in England by publishing a Charter of Liberties in which he promised to end William Rufus' oppressive practices and return to the days of Edward the Confessor. As an earnest of this he threw Ranulf Flambard into his father's White Tower and married Princess Edith of Scotland, sister of King Edgar and great-granddaughter of Edmund Ironside. This united the ancient West Saxon blood with that of the new Normans and was another instance of Henry's far-sighted calculation. The closeness thus achieved between the two courts also had the unlooked-for effect of peacefully opening up Scotland to Norman adventurers. Edith changed her name to Matilda, to make herself sound more Norman, while her second brother David (who succeeded Edgar) married the daughter of Earl Waltheof and did homage to Henry as his overlord.

Within the year these measures designed to win popularity among Henry's subjects had paid off. For encouraged by the ingratiating Ranulf Flambard, who somewhat surprisingly had succeeded in escaping from the Tower, Duke Robert made a bid for the throne, landing at Portsmouth with an army raised from many of the Norman barons who held land in both countries. As a hero of the First Crusade and elder brother to Henry, Robert could have been a most dangerous rival.

But Henry's Charter had done its work. The Church, which had been left alone by the new king, encouraged the English to rally to Henry, a sign of its favour being the return of the Archbishop of Canterbury from exile in Rome. Archbishop Anselm put himself at the head of the English people, declaring that they were not afraid of the Normans and would fight them if their English Henry would lead them. When Robert saw that he had no hope of defeating the massed ranks of the English he made a truce with his powerful brother and signed a legal document in which he abandoned his claim to the throne. Then, in return for a pension, he gave his lands in the Cotentin to England and meekly retired to Normandy, leaving the Anglo-Norman barons who had supported him to face Henry's wrath.

Because he was a thoughtless sort of fellow Duke Robert had not understood the terrible risk his followers had taken. To set them all an example not to meddle with him again, Henry destroyed the massive holdings of a great baron named Robert de Bellême, whose lands covered much of Sussex, a great deal of Normandy and the semi-independent palatine earldom of Shrewsbury adjoining Wales. De Bellême's private army, given royal permission to keep the Welsh behind their borders, was too much of a threat to the king, and Henry now mounted a concerted attack on him. He seized all his castles, including the one which still stands at Arundel in West Sussex, laid siege to his newly built fortress towering over the Severn at Bridgnorth, abolished the palatine earldom of Shrewsbury and finally drove de Bellême himself out of the country and back to Normandy.

Like most Norman barons, however, de Bellême was too powerful and restless a character to remain quiet for long. Once in Normandy he began making war on Duke Robert and taking parts of the duchy for himself. This gave Henry the perfect excuse for interfering in Normandy, which under his brother was dissolving into anarchy. In 1106 at Tinchebrai Henry decisively defeated Duke Robert in battle, condemned him to thirty years' captivity in Cardiff Castle and formally annexed the duchy to England. Henceforth for almost a hundred years, until 1204 when Henry I's great-grandson John lost the duchy to the French king, England and Normandy were ruled by the same government.

These upsets prejudiced Henry against the feudal barons, whose heroics his cold and rational character in any case despised. His firm actions had convinced them not to revolt again. For the rest of his reign he would make a point of surrounding himself with men of more modest birth, knights and clerks chosen for their learnedness who were reliant on his patronage to advance them, rather than on the threat of a thousand men-at-arms. Henry's reign saw the rise of educated men like Roger of Salisbury and the emergence of a far more businesslike government. Roger, who became Bishop of Salisbury, was Henry's justiciar. But he was a very different character from Flambard, being possessed of a superbly constructive organizing mind. Thanks to him the early twelfth century saw the appearance of the first national law courts, as well as the government department called the Exchequer, the precursor of the Treasury.

The Curia Regis, or king's court, had arisen out of the deliberations of the king with his most intimate friends, the leading barons, in council, and these embraced the hearing of legal disputes. William Rufus had built Westminster Hall to allow the king's judgement to be given in full view of the people. But in the reign of Henry I the rapid expansion of legal training, particularly on the continent, and of canon law in the separate Church courts began to influence the development of the criminal law. A new professional class of lawyers grew up, better equipped to deal with legal problems along the lines of universal principles. Trained judges in London started taking the place of the king in determining the legal issues of tenants-in-chief or deciding disputes appealed from the shire or county court. The tradition was begun, which is still carried on today, 800 years later, of justices going on circuit round the country to dispense the king's justice locally. The king's justice tended to be more impartial or disinterested, and by the time of his death the improvements he had introduced to the justice system ensured that Henry would be known as the Lion of Justice.

The new government department known as the Exchequer collected tax. It was called the Exchequer for a very simple reason. Unlike the Arab world, the western Europeans had yet to discover the number zero. This made even simple arithmetic a difficult exercise. The way to get round it was to use either an abacus or, as Henry did, a chequered cloth. On this cloth, which looked not unlike a chessboard, counters representing units of money were moved about: this was how twelfth-century national accounting was performed. In the new stone hall of Westminster, business continued even when the court was travelling. Twice a year, under the chairmanship of the king or his justiciar, officials called the barons of the Exchequer sat at a table with counters and the chequered cloth, going through with all the sheriffs the taxes, rents, fines and debts due to the crown. Every penny had to be accounted for.

In every way Henry's reign marks a greater precision in the practice of government. Thanks to Bishop Roger of Salisbury's methodical nature, for the first time in English history since the Roman occupation we can actually read the government accounts. By 1130 they were written down on a very long piece of parchment or fine hide which was then rolled up for easy storage. As this resembled a pipe, the accounts are known as the Pipe Rolls. For the first time too, we have a clearer idea about life at the royal court in the early twelfth century, because we possess a record of the duties of the royal household written after Henry's death. This record is particularly important given that, on his death, England fell into chaos and records were not kept for a while.

Unlike today, when the monarch and her chief minister live at fixed addresses, Henry was always travelling round the country in the fashion of his new circuit judges, staying at the royal residences such as his abbeys or his hunting boxes. Like all the Norman kings he was addicted to the chase, and built a walled park at Woodstock in Oxfordshire to hunt exotic breeds. But the king would also expect to be put up by his tenants-in-chief, sometimes for weeks at a time. To feed and house the court, which might consist of hundreds of soldiers and courtiers, could be ruinous. Especially in William Rufus' time the arrival of the court would be dreaded because its members were so badly behaved. We are told by the chroniclers that local landowners would hide themselves in the woods until the court had passed by after getting no answer to their request for beds for the night.

On the other hand it was a great honour to have the king to stay because it meant that a young man of the house might become a page in the royal household and from there rise to great heights as a minister. For, despite the increasing specialization and professionalism, the king's household continued to be the centre of government. The king's chancellor was head of all the clerks studying to be priests, who as we have seen performed the role of the civil service, doing much of the scribal work needed by the king's business. The chamberlain was the other prize position at Henry's court. Although his name indicates that he presided over the king's bedchamber the chamberlain also supervised the king's Treasury. This arose from the fact that in ancient times the Treasury had been kept in a chest in the king's bedroom. Other king's servants were the steward, who looked after the king's hall, and the constable, who looked after the outdoor servants – including, as his name suggests, the horses in the king's stable.

Out of these domestic positions would eventually grow the great offices of state we know today, though over the centuries their roles have subtly altered. The chancellor of the Exchequer now presides over the Treasury. At the royal Opening of Parliament the bearers of these offices, some of which like the lord chamberlain have become hereditary or have devolved on to one particular family, can be seen today walking in the procession behind the monarch. Great lords would actually pay the king to take their sons into his household because of the career opportunities it offered. A page in Henry I's household who showed willingness and ability in putting out the king's clothes or even his food might find his route to high office smoothed by being chosen to help the king's chaplain. He would then usually become a chaplain himself, opening his way to being part of the king's secretariat.

Henry's court was conducted with regularity and precision, even down to noting what food was owed the courtiers. However high or low, every person at court, whether chancellor or royal laundress, was allocated a certain amount of money, food, wine and candles to live on. For example, the chancellor received the following stipend: five shillings a day, a simnel cake (a rich fruit cake decorated with marzipan), two salted simnels, a form of flour for bread, a measure of clear and ordinary wine (because water, except from springs, was too dirty to drink). Because he spent his life poring over letters the chancellor was allowed the large number of forty candle ends and a thick wax candle to light his room. In contrast the king's watchmen who guarded Henry's palaces received double the chancellor's rations for their more physical work but few candles because they would not be concerned with reading or auditing accounts. They were allowed a supplement of two loaves in the morning, an extra dish in the evening and a gallon of beer to while away the long hours as they watched for the king's enemies.

Henry's close alliance with the Church, which was enhanced by having Bishop Roger as his first minister, meant that the continued struggle for supremacy between Church and secular ruler was resolved amicably for a while, though on less advantageous terms than William I had achieved. During Archbishop Anselm's exile in Rome the contemporary papal spirit of independence had converted him to the idea of the supremacy of the clergy over the prince. Though the archbishop had led the domestic support for Henry against Duke Robert, in 1103 he publicly backed the new pope Pascal II when he renewed the investiture crisis and added that anyone in holy orders was forbidden to do homage to a lay ruler. Although Anselm had already done homage to Henry he refused to perform the act again, withdrawing to Rome for a second time. Once again England was left without a head of the Church, this time for four years. Naturally Henry could not agree to a directive that seemed to strike at his royal power. It would have prevented a large number of the English population swearing an oath of allegiance to him, for holy orders of course covered ordinary clerks as well as bishops and priests.

A satisfactory compromise was reached between Anselm and Henry. Royal authority over the Church in England was preserved at the cost of the king losing the right to perform investitures. All ordinary clerks were once more allowed to perform homage to the king, while bishops would do homage to the king for what were known as their temporal possessions, that is their Church lands, and swore as the king's vassal to produce the soldiers which this entailed. This compromise pleased all parties, and indeed the European investiture contest would end along similar lines. But there was always the possibility that under less suave representatives of Church and state the question of whose authority was the greater might boil up again. Thirty years later, under Henry I's grandson Henry II, it did just that.

Though he was not loved by the English, Henry reconciled them to Norman kings. But on his death the peace he had enforced throughout the island was shaken by civil war. A simple stroke of fate had upset all his careful plans. The tragic, premature death of his only son William saw the throne devolve to his daughter, the Empress Matilda, who had married the Emperor Henry V. Yet the Norman barons and the Anglo-Saxons themselves had never been ruled by a woman – Boudicca had been a Celt and had been queen only of a south-eastern tribe – and all sides were hostile to such an idea.

William's death was entirely avoidable. After the formal annexation of Normandy to the English crown in 1106 the royal household shuttled between the two countries. Unfortunately on the way back to London after a four-year sojourn in Normandy in the autumn of 1120 the heir to the throne, William, was drowned in the Channel just off Barfleur with many members of Henry's court. When the terrible news was brought to the king he gave a cry of agony and fell senseless to the floor. It is said that after this tragedy he never smiled again. He took another wife soon after, Adeliza of Louvain, in hopes of producing more male heirs, but none came. By 1126 he was therefore obliged to make his daughter, the widowed Empress Matilda, his heir. In a formal ceremony his tenants-in-chief did homage to the empress, as they had done to her brother William, and swore to be her liege men. In 1135 Henry I died in Normandy from too many lamphreys, an indigestible form of eel which his doctor had warned him against. But the English crown did not pass to Matilda. Instead Henry's nephew, his sister Adela's son Stephen of Blois, was proclaimed king. Although Stephen had personally sworn the oath of loyalty to his cousin Matilda, he rushed from his home in Blois to England to claim the throne before the empress could arrive there from Anjou.

Stephen of Blois
(1135–1154)

The new king had been sure that the half-Norman barons would be too proud to allow themselves to be ruled by a woman, whatever they may have said to her father. Moreover the Empress Matilda's unpopularity had been compounded after the barons had paid her homage by her second marriage to the Count of Anjou. Although Henry I's aim in arranging this marriage had been to make peace between Normandy and her neighbour Anjou, Anjou's fierce and scheming counts were the hereditary enemies of the Norman barons. Stephen reckoned correctly that the combination of Matilda's sex and her marriage to an Angevin would be more than the great Anglo-Norman magnates could stomach.

As he had hoped, all the most important tenants-in-chief as well as the increasingly powerful London merchants backed his claim, as did the supremely important figure of Bishop Roger of Salisbury. By winning over Henry's justiciar and the organizing genius of his reign, Stephen had secured the loyalty of Henry's network of government officials, the clerks and all the new judges. Stephen's brother, Bishop Henry of Winchester, who had enjoyed his uncle Henry's patronage, helped garner the support of the Church, which made his brother's usurpation seem more legitimate. When Stephen and his soldiers arrived at Winchester after he had been acclaimed king in London, Bishop Henry played a crucial role in ensuring that the new king secured the Treasury.

Stephen had obtained mastery over a country that had recovered from the misery of war and was now enjoying unprecedented growth thanks to the trade links with the wealthy Norman Empire. During Henry I's lifetime the king's peace had been enforced on the country and the barons brought to heel. Peace encouraged prosperity and cultural advances: towns, the religious life and the arts had a chance to flourish. Merchant guilds and craft guilds, for cobblers and weavers, were established for the first time to set standards in trade. Guild members would have sold their goods at what became the greatest cloth fair in medieval England, Bartholomew Fair, started up in 1133. Ten years before that the London hospital we know as St Bart's, or St Bartholomew's, was founded. The Empress Matilda would probably have worn the new materials brought back by English Crusaders or by the merchants accompanying them from the east, such as cotton muslin. Wealthy ladies like herself would have enjoyed the increasingly elaborate patterning embroidered on cloth that merchants imported from Palestine. In Yorkshire the newly founded Cistercian order commissioned the delicate pointed arches of Rievaulx Abbey which not only reveal the influence of eastern architecture but also show that Romanesque church fortresses were no longer quite so necessary. The English were exposed through Norman links to Paris, where the monk Abelard was altering the study of philosophy with his promotion of logic, and what is often known as the twelfth-century renaissance of learning was beginning. Scholars came to England to give lectures, and continental manuscript traditions bore fruit in English monasteries like those at St Albans, Canterbury and Winchester, which began to achieve new heights in the art of illuminated books.

But under Stephen this prosperity began to falter. King David of Scotland repeatedly invaded Northumberland on behalf of his niece Matilda, bringing the years of peaceful coexistence between England and Scotland to an end. The Scottish king was finally driven out of England after his defeat at the Battle of the Standard on Cowton Moor in 1138, at the hands of the elderly Archbishop Thurstan of York, who on his own initiative had raised the northern fyrd. As an independent-minded Yorkshireman Archbishop Thurston had little time for Norman innovations. Not only did his army fight on foot in the old fashion which had been discredited by the Battle of Hastings, he went into battle displaying the banners of Stephen and three of Yorkshire's most famous saints on a farmer's cart to inspire his fellow countrymen. His faith in old-fashioned methods was rewarded, and his troops defeated the Scots cavalry by breaking their charge.

Although Matilda's uncle had been held at bay, later that year civil war broke out between the empress and Stephen after the king made the mistake of sacking Roger of Salisbury. The quarrel between Stephen and Bishop Roger seems to have been born out of the sensitive king's personal insecurities. He saw Roger of Salisbury's family monopoly of ministerial positions – Roger's two nephews held the bishoprics of Ely and Lincoln, while his son was the royal chancellor – as a threat to his own power. When they refused to give up some of their castles, Stephen, by confiscating their great possessions, irrevocably broke with the family whose powerful network of patronage effectively ran the government. Less than a month after Roger had been driven from office in 1138, the Empress Matilda's half-brother Robert of Gloucester landed in England to stir up rebellion against Stephen. Gloucester was a cultivated man who was the patron of

Geoffrey of Monmouth, an historian and popularizer of the Arthurian myths.

A year later, in September 1139, Matilda herself arrived in the west near Bristol. For the next ten years the English people suffered as the two parties battled it out, winning a little territory here, a little territory there, but neither side prevailing. Despite Stephen's attempt to win popularity by abandoning the new forests created by Henry I, he had never seized the public imagination.

The only people who profited from the anarchy that ensued were the barons. As the royal government's control of England diminished, their power expanded until their position was very different from what it had been under the first three Norman kings. None of them was interested in Stephen or Matilda winning and none of them threw his weight behind either candidate. This prolonged the war (it was to last ten years), and Stephen had to resort to importing Flemish mercenaries, which did nothing for his popularity. Over the next fifteen years hundreds of castles and fortified buildings were erected illegally. In those days, because castles were potential instruments of war, a licence for them had to be obtained from the king. They replaced the Norman manor houses as the predominant form of domestic architecture, indicating that English life at that time was lived in a state of siege. Their dungeons often concealed scenes of unspeakable suffering. Peasants were carried off there and tortured when they would not pay the extortionate new dues that the barons began to demand now that the sheriff was not there to prevent them. So many agricultural workers were imprisoned that crops began to fail all over the country: no one knew whom the barons would seize next or whose house would be set on fire to make the owner relinquish his hoard of silver. The chronicles of the time are full of lamentation. 'They took all who had any property and put them in prison,' reported *The Anglo-Saxon Chronicle*, 'and some that were once rich men went about begging their bread. They robbed churches and churchmen, and though the bishops and clergy were ever cursing them, they cared nothing for their curses. The land was all undone with their deeds and men said that Christ and His Saints slept.'

In return for their support some enterprising barons demanded a vast part of the crown lands from Stephen, which his predecessors had been at such pains to acquire. Geoffrey of Mandeville showed particular greed and joined first Stephen and then Matilda, gaining more territory each time he changed sides. Stalemate marked the struggle: Matilda's supporters held on to the west near Bristol and Gloucester because they were the territory of her half-brother Robert of Gloucester, while Stephen's partisans controlled London and the south-east. At last, in 1141, the stalemate was broken when Robert of Gloucester and his son-in-law the Earl of Chester captured Stephen, who was laying siege to Lincoln. When Bishop Henry of Winchester, Stephen's own brother, declared that this was a sign from God that Stephen's claim to the throne was illegitimate some of the most important magnates elected Matilda queen. All would have been settled had it not been for her haughty personality and the independence of Londoners.

Londoners, who were already pro-Stephen and were less than impressed by the empress's lack of warmth, unexpectedly refused to agree to the barons' wishes. They rose up and drove Matilda out of their city in the most humiliating way, in the middle of the night. What had appeared clear cut was once again all confusion. Bishop Henry received further supernatural guidance to suggest that the Almighty was perhaps coming round to Stephen's claim. He changed sides and led a new rebellion to try to free the imprisoned king. Matilda remained uncrowned, and Robert of Gloucester, her brilliant commander-in-chief, was captured during a battle at Winchester, leaving her to command her own forces.

The empress not only lacked the common touch; without her brother she had no sense of tactics. She was soon on the run. Narrowly evading Stephen's forces at Devizes in Wiltshire – disguised, it is said, as a corpse in grave clothes – she ended up besieged in Oxford Castle. In December 1142, when it became clear that her men were going to have to surrender because food had run out, she managed to escape again. In the early hours of the morning, dressed in long white robes so that she would not show up against the snow that lay thickly on the ground, she climbed out of a window and slid down a rope suspended from one of the castle towers. By a secret postern gate she and three knights left the castle compound and slipped through the enemy lines without any of the soldiers realizing that the shadowy form melting into street corners was their prey. On account of the freezing weather there was a very thick crust of ice on the River Thames and the empress was able to walk all the way along it to the safety of Wallingford.

The two sides now agreed to exchange their two most important prisoners of war, Robert of Gloucester and Stephen, and the war continued up and down the country. But Matilda's cause was now a rather half-hearted one, particularly since Londoners had prevented her from being crowned. With the death of Robert of Gloucester in 1148 much of her support faded away, and she swept back to Normandy, never to return. Stephen remained nominally King of England, though he controlled very little of the country that the Norman kings had subjugated. The Welsh were invading the lands of the marcher lords, and the north of England was the fiefdom of King David of Scotland. So the anarchy continued even though the war was over.

In 1153, however, the arrival of the empress's son Henry of Anjou to demand his mother's throne signalled a new era for England. He captured Malmesbury, and his cause was given an additional fillip by the support of the Earl of Leicester, which meant that Henry held the whole of the midlands. Although Stephen had not been defeated unequivocally, he was by now tired of so much warfare. On the recommendation of his advisers he agreed by the Treaty of Wallingford in that year that he would rule until he died, but that Henry was to succeed him. Stephen's son Eustace was paid off with considerable lands.

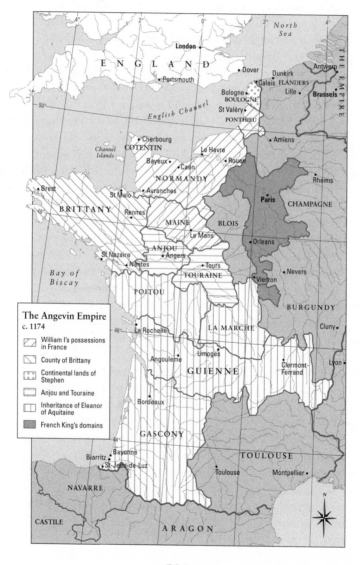

The Angevin Empire
c. 1174

- William I's possessions in France
- County of Brittany
- Continental lands of Stephen
- Anjou and Touraine
- Inheritance of Eleanor of Aquitaine
- French King's domains

Henry II
(1154–1189)

Although he was only twenty-one years old at the beginning of his reign in 1154, Henry II would be one of England's greatest kings. He was a worthy representative of the twelfth-century renaissance, a period of startling innovation and growing self-confidence, when there was a sudden explosion of written sources, of histories, biographies and political treatises. Much of the framework of English national law that Henry II set up has lasted down to the present day.

In 1154 the country was still reeling from the disorder of Stephen's reign. But Henry's vigorous supervision saw to it that by the end of the decade England was once again being run along the well-oiled lines of his grandfather Henry I. Supporters of both his mother and Stephen, such as Roger of Salisbury's nephew Nigel, Bishop of Ely, were willing to sink their differences in order for the bitterness of civil war to end. The Curia Regis began to function again; itinerant justices dared to venture out of their homes. Above all, Henry's aim was to limit the power of the barons so that the sort of destructive anarchy which the country had experienced would never be visited on England again.

In fact Henry II was not a man any baron would wish to trifle with. Not only was he in the fierce, energetic mould of the Norman kings and possessed of a powerful personality, thanks to his marriage to Eleanor of Aquitaine he also ruled the whole of western France from the Loire to the Pyrenees on the borders of Spain, as well as Normandy and Anjou, inherited from his mother and his father respectively. (Eleanor had brought him Aquitaine, Poitou and Auvergne.) The new king of England was thus the greatest monarch in western Europe. No baron was going to argue when he ordered that the 1,115 illegal or 'adulterine' castles be pulled down, given that Henry could call on an unlimited number of soldiers from his vast continental possessions to do the job for him. Although England was not the largest part of his possessions it was the most important because it gave him a crown. This meant he outranked all his tenants-in-chief on the French continent. It also made him the feudal equal of the King of France. Though technically Louis VII was Henry's overlord for

Normandy and Anjou, the French king ruled an area that was not even one-eighth the size of what the English king held in France.

Henry's most pressing task was to restore order to England and reduce the power of the barons to what it had been in the past. He brought the royal power back to the level his grandfather had known by leading military expeditions against the Celtic borderlands of the country, Wales and Scotland. Although Gwynedd remained independent, most of the Welsh princes once again did homage to the English king as overlord, and the English marcher lords resumed their old territories. The ancient separation between Welsh and English Christianity was done away with when the Welsh bishops agreed that the Archbishop of Canterbury should head their Church too. Henry's first cousin Malcolm IV of Scotland, meanwhile, had to return Northumbria to England and was made to do homage to him as his overlord. Henry strongly impressed the official class of England by his firm measures. All foreign soldiers, like the Flemish mercenaries Stephen had used who were still at large in rapacious bands, were packed off to their countries of origin, and all the crown lands Stephen had granted away were restored to royal control. The king insisted on spending time travelling from county court to county court 'judging the judges', as one chronicler put it; this would result in a complete shake-up of the legal system.

The first twenty years of Henry II's reign saw the considerable expansion of the Angevin Empire – that is, the empire of Anjou – with the acquisition of Brittany and of the overlordship of Toulouse; he also obtained the submission of the Irish kings. Despite his Norman ancestry Henry's character owed just as much to his father Geoffrey, who had made the counts of Anjou a rising power in what is now France. By 1144 Geoffrey of Anjou had brought enough of the Duchy of Normandy under his sway to have become its duke by conquest. But because his son Henry had a legal claim to it through his mother, all government business tended to be done in the name of his son. Thanks to his father's interest in education Henry II was one of the best-educated princes of the day, exposed to the finest European learning. Fond of verse and reading, he was also interested in philosophy and, though not a lawyer himself, he absorbed the advances in the law being made at the new universities on the continent and applied them to England. His father being the Count of Anjou, Henry II was the first Angevin king of England, but after his son John lost Anjou Henry's descendants became known as the Plantagenets.

Henry II combined in his person the best and worst sides of his genetic heritage. He had the cunning Angevin mind with its flair for diplomacy, as well as the Angevins' violent temper, and this was allied to the forcefulness of the dukes of Normandy. In addition to the education his father had provided he had also responded well to the training in statecraft he received from his uncles King David of Scotland and Robert of Gloucester. In sum Henry II was one of the most formidable men ever to sit on the English throne, a marvellous warrior and a great statesman. Physically he took after the Angevins, being slightly thick set with famously muscled calves because he was in the saddle so much, and he had a square, lion-like, ruddy-complexioned face. When he was irritated, which was much of the time, the chroniclers noted, his eyes seemed to flash lightning.

Henry's vast inheritance from his father, the Angevin Empire, brought its own problems. Much of his energies and those of his sons would be inextricably bound up with a battle with the King of France for mastery of French territory. To begin with the King of France controlled only a very small area round Paris, but the struggle would end with the loss of the northern empire to France at the beginning of the thirteenth century when the Angevins found a worthy opponent in the French king Philip Augustus.

But the empire also brought great advantages to England, as it led to the establishment of close relations between England's southern ports, London, Bristol and Southampton, and the equally busy Angevin entrepôts of Bordeaux, Rouen and La Rochelle. English merchants were able to import at advantageous rates the French wine and salt which were the preservatives and therefore the great commodities of the middle ages. Water was too dangerous to drink until the purification techniques developed in the nineteenth century, so wine or beer was the drink of choice, small beer being drunk by all classes throughout the day from breakfast onwards. Although vines were grown in southern England during the middle ages, England's ownership until the mid-fifteenth century of Aquitaine and her great region of Bordeaux gave rise to a tradition of the English drinking Bordeaux that was perpetuated until the Napoleonic Wars (when Britain's ally Portugal temporarily replaced France as the main source of British alcoholic beverages).

Ruling such a great empire needed a man of tremendous energy prepared to travel long distances, for what gave the disparate parts of the Angevin Empire their strength and unity was the figure of the king. Fortunately, Henry was suited to the task; he was consumed by curiosity and was famous for his lack of pomp and his indifference to his surroundings. The whole court might find themselves wandering lost in an unknown forest while the king galloped ahead. 'Frequently in the dark,' remembered Peter of Blois, 'we would consider our prayers answered if we found by chance some mean filthy hut. Often there were fierce quarrels over these hovels, and courtiers fought with drawn swords for a lodging that it would have disgraced pigs to fight for.'

Henry's addiction to hunting, shared with so many Normans, meant that much of the king's business was done in the country, although with the establishment of permanent law courts at Westminster London was becoming the seat of government. The king was perpetually busy, and his astonished courtiers observed that he never sat down except to eat, and even then he bolted his food. He found it so hard not to be doing things that he used to draw pictures all through the Mass which as a devout Christian he heard every day. Priests deputed to say the royal Mass were chosen for the speed with which they could get through the service, for everyone dreaded Henry's rage.

One of the king's first appointments in England was his elevation to the chancellorship of a talented and charismatic secretary in the household of the Archbishop of Canterbury named Thomas à Becket, the son of a Norman merchant in London. Becket's natural brilliance and sharp debating skills, which had marked him out when he was only a page, had been honed not only by legal studies in Theobald's household but by being sent to study Roman and canon law at the University of Bologna in Italy. Since then he had been entrusted by the archbishop with many important missions abroad, having shown himself to be a clever and energetic diplomat.

But Becket became more than just Henry's chancellor. As a foreigner the young king needed information about England, and this was supplied by the articulate Thomas. They became boon companions, spending most of their time together. Contemporaries noted how extraordinarily close they were. For a decade the two men – Thomas was some ten years older – ruled almost like brothers, with Thomas taking a starring role in defending the ancient rights and lands of the crown and as chancellor supervising every royal instruction or writ. Henry relied on Thomas for everything, to an almost excessive extent, as they ate every meal together and romped and wrestled more like boys than king and minister. On one occasion Henry rode his horse into Thomas's hall and jumped over the table to sit and dine with him. One writer said, 'Never in Christian times were two men more of a mind. In Church they sat together, together they rode out.' Unlike the king, who was always rather plainly dressed, perhaps because he was rarely to be seen off a horse, the ambitious Thomas à Becket was known for his love of display and heavily embroidered cloaks. Although Henry liked to puncture pretension in anyone else, it amused him in Thomas.

The chancellor was as full of ingenious ideas as the king. He probably encouraged Henry to rely on the increasingly widespread custom of scutage, or shield money (from *scutum*, the Latin for shield), the payment of two marks in lieu of knight's service by those of his tenants-in-chief and their vassals who could not spare the time to fight. Henry was forever having to wage wars to maintain his territories in France, where they were threatened by the meddling activities of the French king Louis VII, who was uncontrollably jealous of his too powerful vassal. It was much easier to depend on the skills of professional soldiers paid for with the shield money. Moreover, to a ruler anxious to reassert royal authority, scutage had the additional advantage of diminishing the military power of the barons. Becket himself enjoyed fighting just as much as the king, and in 1159 he was on his charger at Henry's side as his master attempted to subjugate the county of Toulouse. Becket's subtle mind may also have dreamed up a marriage treaty between the daughter of the King of France and Henry's eldest son as a means of obtaining for England the coveted Vexin region, midway between Rouen and Paris. Certainly it was he who conducted the negotiations. Since the bride and groom were six months and four years old at the time, Louis VII assumed that the event would not take place for at least ten years, although the baby princess went to live at the court of Henry II. But to Louis' rage a couple of years later in 1160 the children were married to one another, now aged six and two, and the Vexin thus once more became part of Henry's empire.

Thomas grew enormously wealthy as Henry granted him the revenues of many religious foundations. When he was sent as ambassador to negotiate the transfer of the Vexin, his equipage was so magnificent that all the French ran out to see it. One thousand knights accompanied him, and 250 pages sang verses to his glory and waved banners. Priests rode two by two alongside the relics from his own chapel which accompanied him; behind them monkeys rode on the saddles of the horses bearing gold for the French king.

In 1162 Archbishop Theobald died. The infatuated king decided that the magnificent Thomas, whose views were so close to his own, should controversially (since he was not an ordained priest) be appointed head of the English Church, namely Archbishop of Canterbury. At the same time he would remain head of the king's Chancery. Like all rulers of the time Henry had been dissatisfied by what seemed the increasingly aggressive demands of the Church. Thomas à Becket might have been the Church establishment's candidate for the chancellorship, but during his eight years in office he had completely identified with the king when it came to collecting taxes imposed on the Church for royal wars. The appointment seemed to be a master stroke which would bring the Church more tightly under royal control.

The years of anarchy and the weakness of the crown had enhanced not only the power of the barons but also the position of the Church. When the king's writs to the shire court had more or less dried up, Church courts had taken their place. By the time of Henry II Church lawyers had been drawing into their courts all aspects of ordinary life, and had begun to argue that cases involving debt belonged to them. Church lawyers appealed to Rome in ever increasing numbers about property, as opposed to the spiritual issues their courts were intended for. In addition these lawyers were using their expertise to boost the revenues of the Church so that its income was now greater than the king's.

The success of the Church in expanding its power had been aided by the activities of a group of Englishmen at Rome, including John of Salisbury, the political philosopher and Becket's future biographer, and Nicholas Breakspear, who became Pope Adrian IV in 1154. The twelfth century was internationally the great century for the development of law and these men were among those leading the advance of canon law. Like Thomas à Becket, John of Salisbury had become a member of Archbishop Theobald's household, and under his influence a more thorough legal training began to be offered to clerks throughout the country.

But for Henry II the most controversial issue relating to the Church was its expansion into the criminal law. Its argument that it reserved to itself the right to try anyone in holy orders was allowing murderers and thieves off scot free. Royal judges who called for clerks in holy orders to appear before them were being insulted, and the miscreants were refusing to accept their authority. At this period the term holy orders meant not just priests but any person trained by the Church. Any man who could write Latin could say he was a clerk, and thus come under the category of clergy. So could anyone who simply had the top his head shaved in a tonsure. Because Church courts could not hand down a death sentence, a great number of 'criminous clerks', as Henry would call them, were escaping proper punishment. They usually avoided prison too, as the Church did not like to pay for it, arguing that its penalty of degrading a man from holy orders was punishment enough. As part of Henry's drive to restore harmony and regularity to his new kingdom these anomalies had to be addressed. By appointing Thomas à Becket archbishop he believed he would draw the too independent and powerful Church into subjection.

However, Thomas was extremely reluctant to accept the post, partly because he foresaw a clash of interests. Despite his great worldliness he knew himself well enough to see that he always pursued his tasks wholeheartedly. He is said to have told the king, 'If I become Archbishop of Canterbury, it will be God I serve before you.' Thomas was in any case unpopular within the Church hierarchy itself for his hard line on making ecclesiastical lands pay scutage; many churchmen in addition were appalled that a mere deacon, who therefore could not say Mass, should become head of the Church. Those who knew Becket greeted his appointment with scepticism, unable to believe that this proud and arrogant chancellor could become a saintly archbishop and forswear a life of revelry and extravagance. But, much to the world's surprise, that is just what he did.

As soon as he became archbishop, having been ordained priest, his behaviour underwent a transformation. He spent his nights in prayer and mortification of the flesh. Beneath his gorgeous vestments he wore a prickly shirt made of goat's hair which swarmed with vermin so that he would always be suffering as Christ had done. For contemporaries and for many later observers, this metamorphosis was evidence that God and his august position had worked a great change in him. Modern historians, however, have been less inclined to take a view so strongly coloured by religious faith. It has been pointed out that once he became archbishop Thomas behaved in an extraordinarily antagonistic fashion to his patron. Despite his notably spiritual life he used his position to interfere in the king's business as obstructively as he had been helpful before. It was as if he was testing his power against the man who had appointed him, though only months before they had been the closest friends.

Although the potential for a quarrel had been building up for some time, it burst out in 1163 when the king informed his bishops in council at Westminster of his intention to end the legal loophole known as 'benefit of clergy'. He intended to make it the law that 'criminous clerks' convicted in the Church courts would be degraded from holy orders and punished by his judges, for it was now obvious that an informal understanding that convicted clerks be retried in the royal courts was not working. When Becket himself refused to give permission for the retrial of a canon, Henry struck. Claiming his right according to the ancient customs of England, in January 1164 he drew up the Constitutions of Clarendon as a restatement of the position of the English Church's organization.

However, the Constitutions of Clarendon went a great deal further than the immediate issue at hand, and a great deal further than ancient custom. They dealt not only with criminous clerks but with Henry's attempt to restrict the Church's power and define relations between Church and state: priests were forbidden to leave the country without royal permission; nor could excommunication be used against the king's barons without his permission; all disputes over land were to be decided in the king's courts even if they concerned the Church; disputed debts were also to be confined to the king's courts; appeals to Rome were to be made only if Henry allowed them.

Although most of the bishops, led by Gilbert Foliot, the Bishop of London, were at first angered by the Constitutions, they came round to them – persuaded by the king's threats of violence against them. The exile from Rome of Pope Alexander III prevented him from doing anything that might annoy the King of England. Henry II was one of Alexander's chief supporters against his rival Pope Paschal, the candidate of the emperor Frederick Barbarossa. Barbarossa, named for his red beard, had driven

Alexander out of Italy, and Alexander would do anything to prevent the King of England going over to the emperor's side in the long struggle for power that was the investiture crisis.

Becket refused to sign the Constitutions, on the ground that they infringed the liberties of the Church. This was hugely embarrassing because if the Constitutions were to become law they required the seal of the Archbishop of Canterbury.

The king's anger knew no bounds, though he was also hurt by Thomas's strange behaviour and wound up by his jealous rivals in the Church. He confiscated the archbishop's property and removed his eldest son Henry from his guardianship. He then set about ruining him. When the king's Great Council met at Northampton in October 1164, Henry demanded that all the money which had passed through Becket's hands when he was his chancellor should be accounted for. Thomas replied that he had spent it all in the king's service. He enraged the king still further by carrying a large crucifix to indicate that the only protection he claimed was God's. Like everything about the archbishop, to his enemies this seemed absurdly dramatic behaviour. But to his supporters like John of Salisbury it was courageous and showed the astonishing miracle that God was performing in Becket's heart.

The king's bullying only increased Thomas's stubbornness. Despite pleas from the bishops that he sign the Constitutions, Thomas insisted on arguing with Henry face to face, and there was an angry exchange of words. Henry exclaimed that he was appalled by Thomas's ingratitude. He had raised him to the pinnacle of honour in the land, yet Thomas did nothing but oppose him. Had he forgotten all the proofs of his affection? Thomas responded that he was not unmindful of the things which God, bestower of all things, had seen fit to bestow on him through the king. He did not wish to act against his wishes, so long as it was agreeable to the will of God. Henry was indeed his liege lord, but God was lord of both of them and to ignore God's will in order to obey the king would benefit neither him nor the king. For as St Peter said, 'We ought to obey God rather than man.' When the king retorted that he wanted no sermons from the son of one of his villeins, Thomas said, 'It is true that I am not of royal lineage, but neither was St Peter.'

As the archbishop still refused to sign, Henry's justiciar pronounced him a traitor. At last appreciating that with the King of England as his enemy his life was in danger, Thomas escaped from Northampton in the middle of the night and fled abroad to appeal to Pope Alexander III. He remained out of the country for six years.

For Henry the situation became intolerable. It embarrassed him at home and internationally for England to be without a head of the Church for so long. By 1170, however, the archbishop had returned, following intervention by the pope. It was believed by both sides that a reconciliation had been effected. At a meeting in France the king promised to allow the archbishop back into the country.

Thomas returned in December, taking up residence once more in the Archbishop's Palace at Canterbury. His occupancy lasted less than a month. Although at their meeting Henry II had never mentioned signing the Constitutions of Clarendon the king had assumed that this would take place and begin the process of reform. But the archbishop was as obstinate as ever. He refused to lift the sentence of excommunication he had imposed on the Archbishop of York who on Whitsunday in Thomas's absence had crowned Henry II's eldest son, the young Henry. This was a medieval custom intended to ensure the loyalty of the barons in the future, but performing the ceremony was the special right of the Archbishop of Canterbury. In fact that December Becket re-excommunicated all those who had been involved, seven of the most important men in England including the justiciar and Gilbert Foliot, the Bishop of London, with nine other bishops.

For a brief period there was a lull. December passed awkwardly, with king and archbishop not on speaking terms. The king's temper was not improved by the pope suddenly taking Thomas's side. A papal bull or message arrived if not excommunicating at least suspending all the English bishops who had taken part in the young king's coronation, leaving the English Church in a state of chaos.

On Christmas Day news reached Henry II, who was spending the festive season in icy Normandy, that Thomas had struck again. He had now excommunicated Ralph de Broc, who had been steward of the diocese of Canterbury's lands during his absence. Maddened by this constant thorn in his flesh, raising his hands to heaven the always impulsive Henry said furiously, 'Can none of the cowards eating my bread free me of this turbulent priest?'

No sooner were the rash words out of the king's mouth than four knights who had always disliked Becket, Hugh de Morville, Reginald Fitz Urse, Richard le Breton and William de Tracy, left the hall and made for England. Having touched down at the home of Ralph de Broc, they went on to the Archbishop's Palace at Canterbury.

On 29 December, on a dark winter's afternoon with the pale sun scarcely penetrating the freezing skies, the archbishop was reading quietly in the library when there was a great commotion at the gate. Pursued vainly by palace servants – priests and serving boys – the knights burst into the archbishop's room and demanded he withdraw the excommunications. The archbishop ignored them. Saying that he was only obeying the pope, he then set off for the nearby cathedral, followed by his cross-bearer Edward Grim, who lived to tell the tale.

The knights paused to put on their armour – though why they needed this was unclear since their only opponents would have been the unarmed monks singing Vespers. Ahead of them now in the gloom of the cathedral they could see Thomas's white garments glimmering as he prepared to listen to Mass before the high altar. 'Where is the archbishop? Where is the traitor?' they shouted. 'Here am I,' said Becket, turning to meet his murderers, 'not traitor but archbishop and priest of God.' Then he meekly bowed his head as if for the first blow. One of the knights remembered his Christian upbringing sufficiently to want to kill the Archbishop of Canterbury outside consecrated ground, ground where for over 500 years the English nation had worshipped. He tried to drag the archbishop out. But Thomas refused to go. He clung so hard to a pillar in the north transept just below the north aisle left of the choir that the knights decided that they would have to kill him where he stood. The first blow missed him and hit the cross-bearer, but then all the knights piled in. The Archbishop of Canterbury was butchered before the High Altar.

This deed of blood perpetrated by four Christian knights apparently on the orders of the Christian King of England became the scandal of western

The martyrdom of St Thomas à Becket in Canterbury Cathedral in 1170 by four knights of Henry II. From an English Psalter circa 1200 AD.

Pilgrim going to Canterbury to the shrine of Thomas à Becket.

Europe. Although Henry II probably had no idea that his exasperated outburst would be seen as an order to murder (we know from contemporary records that the king was planning to have him tried for treason), the world preferred to believe otherwise. The murder of the head of the English Church at the behest of the King of England had enormous reverberations. The cult of St Thomas the Christian martyr – for the pope promptly canonized him – spread as far as Iceland.

Thomas dead was far more powerful than Thomas alive. All his former misdeeds were forgotten, and he was venerated as the Church's champion against injustice. The shrine erected to the former archbishop became one of the most popular in Europe – thus in *The Canterbury Tales* the Pilgrims are seeking the 'blissful holy martyr'. It was also the most richly adorned, having a great reputation for miraculous cures effected by his lacerated body. If the archbishop had been wrong to resist the punishment of the clerks, there was some justification for him opposing such a naked assertion of royal power against the Church. But though Thomas à Becket passed into English folklore as a hero, the view taken of him today is less enthusiastic. His martyrdom put back the reform of an abuse for 300 years.

For all the animosity of the previous few years Henry II was a genuinely devout man and he was appalled by the murder. He burst into loud cries when he heard the news, put on sackcloth, rubbed his face with ashes and, as was noticed by the Bishop of Lisieux, behaved more like a friend than the sovereign of the dead man – which of course he had once been. Shutting himself up in his room for three days, he would not eat and fell into stupors so that for a while the country feared it might lost its king as well as its archbishop. Even though Thomas's own erratic behaviour had to some extent brought his fate upon him, his hideous murder cast a stain over the rest of Henry's reign from which he never quite recovered. The golden reputation and some of the zest for life faded. Despite his great legislative achievements from 1173 onwards his life was marred by rebellions throughout his far-flung possessions, stirred up by his sons whose enmity was used by the King of France to expand his territory at England's expense.

Henry II was the first English king to extend Norman power to the next-door island of Ireland. Although Irish monks had preserved much of the classical corpus in their monasteries and Irish Christianity had been substantially responsible for the conversion of the Anglo-Saxon kingdom, the great days of early Irish civilization were over. Many monasteries had been destroyed in the ninth-century Viking raids that created the settlements of Dublin, Cork and Limerick. The arts and letters were no longer flourishing in a country ruled by a large number of kings who were in effect tribal chieftains. Bloody vengeance and constant war were now the custom of the country.

It was Dermot, King of Leinster who provided the open door to allow the Normans into Ireland. In 1166 he was expelled from Ireland by an alliance of his rivals, their pretext being that he had carried off Devorgil, the beautiful wife of the chieftain of Breffny in neighbouring Connaught. Dermot fled to Henry II's court, which was then at Bristol, to ask for troops to win his kingdom back. Although the king turned down his request for aid, he gave Dermot a letter authorizing him to recruit any of his English subjects. In return King Dermot pledged his homage to Henry as his overlord. It soon became clear to Dermot that the place to recruit Norman adventurers or mercenaries was among the marcher lords of South Wales, who were on active service pushing back the frontiers of the fierce Welsh kings' kingdoms. In the Norman system of strict primogeniture landless younger sons who would do anything for money and land were just the breed needed to reconquer Dermot's kingdom.

Richard de Clare, the palatine Earl of Pembroke, volunteered to be leader of the Norman expedition to Ireland. His reputation as a warrior was so great that most people knew him by the nickname of Strongbow. In return for his help King Dermot promised the hand in marriage of his lovely daughter Eva and the throne of Leinster when he died. A painting can be seen at the House of Commons today which shows the wedding ceremony of Eva and Strongbow, marking the moment when Ireland began to be ruled from England, as it was for the next 800 years. It was up to Strongbow to recruit his own men, and he gathered together a very efficient band of Norman knights as the advance guard of the expedition. The most important of them were the family known as Fitzgerald and their half-brothers the Fitzstephens. They were all the sons of a Welsh princess named Nesta (daughter of Rhys ap Tudor) by Gerald of Windsor, a Norman knight with royal connections. Accompanying these warriors to Ireland was their youngest brother, a scholar known to history as Giraldus Cambrensis (Gerald of Wales – Cambrensis means Welsh in Latin). He described the expedition to Ireland in tremendous detail.

Despite the Normans' small numbers – and even though Strongbow himself had remained in England – their superb discipline and battle tactics stood them in good stead against the Irish tribes and Danish kingdoms.

Celtic individualism and traditions of tribal warfare made it just as difficult for twelfth-century Celts to band together and forget their historic enmities as it had been for first-century AD Celts in Britannia against the Romans. Though the Irish matched the Normans for bravery, they were quarrelsome and disorganized and found it so difficult to accept leadership, to forget their endless grudges and stop warring against one another to combine against a far more dangerous foe, that the important towns of Wexford and Dublin quickly fell to the Norman adventurers. In 1170, after two years of fighting led by William, Raymond and Maurice Fitzgerald, Strongbow at last crossed the Irish Sea, took the town of Waterford and married Eva. When Dermot died the following year, Strongbow became King of Leinster. For all their exploits the Norman lords' hold on Ireland was fairly tenuous. The Norse relations of the citizens of the Norse town of Dublin soon began to attack them, crossing from the Isle of Man. Though the Normans drove them off, they were then attacked by King Dermot's Irish enemies.

Fortunately for Strongbow, in 1171 Henry became alarmed at the threat an independent Norman kingdom in Ireland might pose to his own empire. The continuing furore over Becket's death may have been an additional spur prompting him to assert his rule over the neighbouring island and its warring inhabitants of Irish, Danish and Norman lords. The number of soldiers available to the master of the Angevin Empire was of course far larger than Strongbow's forces. In consequence, little attempt was made to stand up to the first English king to regard himself as ruler of Ireland, and Henry soon set up an English administration in Dublin. The Irish chiefs in fact welcomed the king as protection against the Norman adventurers, while the Norman rulers' submission was soon secured, and the Irish bishops at the Synod of Cashel likewise acknowledged Henry as their liege lord. Henry garrisoned the towns of Waterford and Wexford with his soldiers, brought Anglo-Norman merchants, Anglo-Norman law and Anglo-Norman monks to the country, and built a palace in Dublin. Here he passed the winter. He would have done more had he not been forced in 1173 to deal with a rebellion which had broken out throughout the empire in his absence, instigated by his wife and sons.

As a result the impact of the Norman invasion of Ireland, unlike that of England, was not very far reaching. It was really limited to the conglomeration of what became in effect self-contained little Norman kingdoms around Waterford, Wexford and Dublin. The territory where the crown's writ ran came to be known much later as the Pale (from the Latin *palum*, a stake, used to mark a boundary; this Irish usage gave rise to the expression 'beyond the pale'). This territory was never a very well-defined area. In the fourteenth century it included Louth, Meath, Trim, Kilkenny and Kildare. By the beginning of the sixteenth century the chieftains and their clans had made enormous inroads into the Pale, while the old Norman families like the Fitzgeralds (whose leader was the Earl of Kildare) became so powerful and independent that the Tudors would feel the need to invade Ireland afresh in order to prevent the country becoming a base for a Yorkist revival (see below).

The revolt which forced Henry II's return before he had accomplished his Irish mission was part of a pattern which would dog him for the rest of his life. It was the consequence of having a large empire, too many enemies in Scotland and France and too many sons. In 1173 and 1174 the rebellion against Henry stretched from the Tweed in the Borders to the Pyrenees, as all his enemies took advantage of his unpopularity after Becket's murder and banded together.

By 1173 Henry's elder sons were grown up. His passionate marriage to Eleanor of Aquitaine, the former wife of King Louis VII of France, was faltering despite eight children in fifteen years. Queen Eleanor was a forceful, sophisticated woman of literary tastes whose patronage encouraged the flourishing romantic secular literature which was a striking new feature of the twelfth century and who had considerable political influence owing to her personal power over Aquitaine. She was now estranged from her husband, who had openly taken a mistress in Rosamund Clifford, the daughter of a Welsh marcher lord.

Where his grandfather had imported wild animals, Henry had built within the grounds of his favourite palace at Woodstock in Oxfordshire a private lodge of intricate eastern design. Known as Rosamund's Bower, it had a water garden and could be approached only through a maze. Round the maze the king is believed to have planted the most ancient rose in the world, striped in dark pink and white, which had been brought back by the Crusaders from Damascus. He christened it the Rosamundi, as it is still known today, the rose of the world, as a tribute to his mistress. Fair Rosamund, as she came to be called, died young, and legend has it that Queen Eleanor persuaded one of the king's men to betray the secret of the maze to her. One evening, it is said, when Fair Rosamund heard the sound of bugles and hoofs and went flying to the door, expecting the king's arrival after hunting, she met only Queen Eleanor, who stabbed her to the heart.

What is certainly true is that Queen Eleanor took her sons' part against the king. Like their father they were energetic, active and commanding personalities in the Angevin and Norman tradition. In 1169, four years before, Henry II had divided up his empire between them. His eldest son, known as the young King Henry, received England, Normandy and Anjou. Eleanor's own Duchy of Aquitaine went to her favourite son, the brilliant, generous but violent warrior known to history as Richard the Lionheart (or

Coeur de Lion). Brittany, which Henry II had conquered from its duke, went to the third son Geoffrey. Nevertheless – rather like King Lear – despite this apportionment Henry II had no intention of relinquishing the actual government or income of these lands into their supposed owners' hands.

By March 1173, encouraged by the king of France Louis VII, whose greatest ambition was to break up the Angevin Empire, a conspiracy had been hatched among these sons. They could call on the soldiers of disgruntled barons, particularly in Aquitaine, such as the Count of Poitou whose legal rights (including holding courts and minting money) had been steadily eroded by Henry II's reforms. That month all over the Angevin Empire attacks were mounted against the king's forces. When the rebellion began Queen Eleanor had been stopped, disguised as a man, while fleeing to the French court to join her three sons. She was thrown into prison at Falaise in France with her companion, one of the rebel barons, Hugh of Chester. There she remained until Henry II died. Louis VII tried to invade Normandy, while the young King Henry set sail with a French fleet to attempt, with an equal lack of success, an invasion of England. Barons throughout Aquitaine attacked Henry's garrisons, and once again Scotsmen under William the Lion went marauding through Northumbria. All the rebels were made more confident by the continuing reverberations from the murder of Becket. It is astonishing to record that the king, despite the enormity of the rebellion, defeated them all.

He achieved this with the aid of soldiers who remained loyal to him throughout the Angevin Empire. As has been seen, Henry II was naturally devout. In 1172, the year before the revolt broke out, he had finally reached an agreement with the pope known as the Compromise of Avranches. In order to be cleansed of his sins, he had accepted that appeals to Rome would not be stopped in his lifetime and he revoked the Constitutions of Clarendon, which Archbishop Thomas had refused to sign. As a result, until the Reformation in the sixteenth century any man who could read Latin could claim 'benefit of clergy' to save him from being tried in the king's courts for any crime, however heinous. To some extent this restored the king to respectability, since England had the threat of papal interdict lifted. The clergy – many of whom had disapproved of Thomas à Becket – were reconciled to Henry, and this ensured that the whole civil service of clerks and government officials remained loyal to him. Almost none of the ordinary people of England joined the barons' revolt, as they had little to gain and much to lose from a new anarchy.

After a year of fighting, despite holding off his enemies from abroad in 1174 and quelling the revolt in Aquitaine, Henry II's affairs were still unsettled and England continued to be in a state of uproar. On 12 July 1174, impelled by a genuine desire to atone for the sin of murder, which he believed was preventing God from granting him victory, the great king went on a pilgrimage to Canterbury, to do penance at Thomas's shrine and beg forgiveness. It was a gesture that seized the (very inflammable) popular imagination. The king was barefoot like the poorest pilgrim and naked but for a shirt. When he got near the shrine, to symbolize his utter mortification Henry approached his friend's grave on his knees. As he shuffled forward the monarch who was the Caesar of his day, as Giraldus Cambrensis called him, was scourged by monks wielding rods. He then spent the whole night lying before his former friend's shrine in constant prayer. When amid what were now cheering crowds he reached London the next day, he discovered to his delight that while he had been on his knees at Canterbury the wily king of the Scots, William the Lion, had been captured during a raid on Alnwick in Northumberland.

Henry would always be lenient to his sons, but towards Scotland he was more hard-hearted. Ever since the days of Edward the Elder, kings of the Scots had been forced to acknowledge the king of the English as their overlord, though most of them secretly seized every opportunity to stir up trouble. But by the draconian Treaty of Falaise, which forced William the Lion to do homage to him, Henry II made sure that the overlordship meant what it said, planting garrisons in the main castles of Scotland – at Edinburgh, Stirling, Berwick, Roxburgh and Jedburgh. After this success Henry's morale improved. With his old decisiveness he marched off to Framlingham Castle in Suffolk, which is still standing, to besiege Hugh Bigod, one of the most important leaders of the English barons' rebellion. With Bigod's capture, the threat of disorder at home also died down.

The next decade saw a period of internal consolidation within England, in contrast to the expansion which had marked the first part of Henry's reign. The Assize of Arms of 1181 (an assize was a legislative ordinance), which revamped the laws for calling out the fyrd, was a reflection of Henry's trust in the ordinary Englishman who had not risen against him during his sons' revolt. Every freeman was ordered to keep arms in his home to defend his country or to suppress revolts against the king. This reform was also an attempt to shift military power away from the barons because, as with scutage, the Assize made Henry less dependent on their calling out their feudal levy. As a sign of the king's new respect for his English subjects, from 1181 he stopped using foreign mercenaries in England, and employed them only abroad.

It was the next century which saw the development of professional English lawyers, trained at the infant universities of Oxford and Cambridge or at schools of higher learning based in cathedrals such as Exeter and York. Nevertheless, following a series of legal reforms implemented by Henry, England saw a rapid development in legal definition which by the thirteenth century would be termed the common law. In the penultimate year of Henry's reign, in 1188, an anonymous writer calling himself Glanvill published a groundbreaking written summary of the laws and customs of the English, *De legibus et consuetudinibus regni Angliae*.

This itemized what were now the standard practices throughout the king's courts in England. Glanvill's importance was that he showed that there was a law 'common' to the whole of England available to freemen which could be appealed to over the separate manorial, baronial and ecclesiastical courts. Although it was Henry I who had first instituted the practice of travelling royal judges, under Henry II the system was formalized, and in 1176 England was divided into the same six circuits we have today. The king's judges were now under a duty to visit every shire in the country, and hold an eyre (from the corrupt Latin for *iter*, a journey) or hearing in the shire, or county court so that every part of England could have the benefit of the king's justice. Judges travelled on circuit on a six-monthly basis, co-ordinated by the legal bureau at the royal court at Westminster, which by then had become differentiated into two systems. The Court of Common Pleas dealt with land disputes and disputes between private individuals – that is, civil matters common to the whole kingdom. The Court of the King's Bench tried criminal cases – which, as the name suggests, were sometimes heard in front of the king. The eyre was replaced in the thirteenth century by what was called the assize court or the assizes (from the Norman French *asseyer*, to sit). These continued for 700 years until 1971, when their name was changed to crown court.

Most of Henry's laws made the country much safer for travel. The sheriff, whose office and functions the Normans had taken over pretty well wholesale from the Anglo-Saxons, while remaining the king's financial agent in the county court, had his powers of law enforcement enhanced. To arrest a thief the sheriff could now enter anyone's land, even if it was within the jurisdiction of the lord of the manor – a privilege hitherto limited to the lord or abbot. Sheriffs now resembled an early police force who were expected to co-operate with one another even outside their shire. Henry II also put a prison in every shire and attached a sergeant to every sheriff with the right to arrest suspects and bring them before a court and to break up fights in the village. Every citizen had a duty to raise the hue and cry if he saw a crime being committed and was required to chase after the criminal.

The reign of Henry II also saw the development of the jury trial we know today. From 1179, by the Assize of Northampton, a trial before twelve property owners could take the place of the Norman method of resolving land disputes known as the ordeal by battle. By the late twelfth century the growing numbers of trained lawyers – some of whom were being taught in the town of Oxford since being banned by Henry II from the University of Paris after 1167 when Louis VII sheltered Becket – introduced a new rationalism into the intellectual climate. The ordeal, which assumed that the miraculous intervention of God gave victory to the rightful owner, had begun to look absurd. After all, a man might simply be a stronger fighter. The new system of trial by jury made allowances for the old, for the weak and for women, and it was offered only by the king's courts. By the beginning of the next century opinion in the Church itself rebelled against the old practice. In 1215 by a directive from the Lateran Council in Rome all priests were forbidden to have anything to do with trial by ordeal, and the custom died out soon after.

But Henry did not completely do away with all the ordeals which the Normans had introduced – indeed he produced some of his own. The ordeal by water for criminal trials was brought in in 1166. This required the accused to have his legs and arms tied before he was lowered into a vat of water blessed by the local priest. If the accused sank he was innocent, if he floated he was guilty. Another proof was the ordeal by hot iron; here, the accused was made to carry a piece of heated iron and if it made no mark then he was guilty. In general, however, for most freemen the trend was towards a more rational form of justice under the royal courts.

Henry II also gave England the new office of coroner, which still does much the same work today. Elected in the county or old shire court, the coroner was responsible for carrying out inquests on the bodies of those whose death was suspicious – if it was sudden or accidental or if there was reason to believe it had been murder. By law the coroner's inquest had to be constituted very soon after the death, while the evidence was still fresh in the mind of witnesses.

At the time of the Conquest England had long had a fairly law-abiding population accustomed to the ancient tradition of the hundred and shire courts. Ever since the days of Cnut it had been compulsory under Anglo-Saxon law for each man to belong to a tithing for the purpose of maintaining good order. The process was refined when William the Conqueror imposed the heavy murdrum fine where a Norman was murdered and the hundred could not produce the murderer. Since the hundred might cover a very large area this became impractical, and by the end of the twelfth century a sort of self-policing known as the frankpledge was being practised in the smaller area of the tithing – that is, a community of ten men who were responsible for one another's good conduct. The duty of the tithing was to bring any criminal they suspected before the hundred court. Under Henry II it also became one of the sheriff's functions to make sure that every man in the shire belonged to a tithing.

Although he was incapable of devolving responsibility to his sons, Henry was a generous-spirited man full of family feeling. He had been furious with his elder sons for rebelling against him, but nonetheless decided to believe their protestations of regret and restored them to their lands. His wife, however, remained under lock and key. After he had defeated the revolt there was no question but that Henry II was the greatest monarch of the age. His daughters, moreover, were married to the most powerful kings in Christendom. The system of informal royal alliances that this inaugurated between England on the one hand and Castile (the most important country in Spain), Germany and Flanders on the other set the pattern of foreign alliances for several hundred years.

Similarly the enmity with France continued to be a main theme of English policy. In 1180 the succession of Philip II, known as Philip Augustus, to the French throne brought a far more cunning enemy of the Angevin Empire into play. The last years of Henry II were very sad ones. One of the reasons for the first rebellion against him had been the favouritism he showed towards his youngest son John, to whom he had begun making over castles which belonged to the young King Henry. Ten years younger than his nearest brother Richard, John was a short (five feet five) black-haired youth who was known as Jean Sans Terre or John Lackland because he had no obvious lands to inherit, unlike his elder brothers. He has had a very bad press down the centuries, given his odious moral character and his liking for physical cruelty, but modern historians are impressed by his administrative competence and his interest in justice.

Contemporary historians, however, detested him. At the time the historian Geraldus Cambrensis did not mince his words about the mistake John's doting father Henry II had made in deciding that his new possession, Ireland, might make up for John's lack of lands. In 1185 he sent him as lord of Ireland to govern the country, though he was aged only eighteen, having tried and failed to persuade Richard to yield Aquitaine to John – the death of the young King Henry meant that Richard was now heir to Normandy and England. But he was forced to withdraw John from Ireland within the year on account of his grotesque behaviour. Paying no attention to older advisers and keeping company only with foolish young men of his own age, John failed to behave to the Irish kings with the courtesy they deserved. He pulled their long beards, which were the fashion in Ireland (an oddity to clean-shaven Normans) and granted their lands to his favourites. Despite all this, the infatuated king continued to push the cause of John, at the expense of Richard the Lionheart.

Eleven years after the first revolt of Henry's sons in 1183, another rebellion threatened in Richard's own Duchy of Aquitaine. The proud and restless barons there had felt Richard's firm hand for too long. They were easily encouraged by the young King Henry and his next brother Geoffrey of Brittany to rebel against their overlord. It was a revolt which again threatened to dissolve the Angevin Empire when Toulouse and Burgundy sent aid. So dangerous was the situation that Henry II gave orders that all the barons who had taken part in the first revolt should be locked up. With the sudden death of the young King Henry from dysentery, the rebellion died away almost as quickly as it had sprung up. But the new heir to the throne, Richard, had an even more stormy relationship with his father.

The golden-haired, blue-eyed Richard was cast in a heroic mould. Attractive, generous, fiery and impulsive, he did not have his father's brains, but he had his temper and his military flair. Though Richard was now the heir presumptive to England, Normandy and Anjou, Henry's secret plan was to make these lands John's. After failing to obtain Aquitaine for John, for four years Henry refused to name Richard his heir. He would not have him crowned as he had his elder brother, nor would he make the necessary arrangements to hurry up his marriage to Princess Alice of France, the sister of the young King Henry's widow.

Henry's refusal to treat Richard properly would lead to the beginning of the end of the Angevin Empire. It not only gave the new King of France, Philip Augustus, an excuse to begin hostilities against his over-powerful subject, the King of England. It drove a bitter Richard permanently into Philip's camp. As will be recalled, the return to Henry II of the Norman Vexin was dependent on the marriage between Philip's sister and the young king. This dowry was now transferred to Alice, the next sister, but Henry's foot-dragging meant that she was still not married to Richard. When neither the Vexin nor his sister returned to France, Philip Augustus had a perfect excuse for war. Though it ended in a truce, Richard was soon responding again to the French king's overtures.

Relations became thornier than ever between father and son on account of Henry's behaviour over the Third Crusade, in 1189. Richard the Lionheart, as he soon became known, passionately wished to go on this Crusade to rescue the Latin Kingdom of Jerusalem, which had fallen to the brilliant new Muslim warlord the Kurd Saladin, Sultan of Egypt and Syria. But in such an uncertain situation he would have been foolish to depart unless and until his father named him as heir; this Henry II continued to refuse to do. Richard therefore not only publicly did homage to the French king for his lands in France but simultaneously joined with the French king to invade Henry's Angevin holdings.

By mischance his father was in France, but did not have enough loyal English troops with him to fight on so many fronts. He ran out of gold to pay his mercenaries, who therefore deserted him. Henry's tenants-in-chief in Maine and Anjou all went over to the victorious young kings, and he was driven out of Le Mans too. But some atavistic sentiment made him reluctant to leave his native land of Anjou for Normandy, where he would have found greater loyalty. Perhaps he was too tired to make a last stand, for he was also ill with a debilitating fever. From an old Angevin stronghold, the castle of Chinon, perched on rocky heights above the River Vienne, he was forced to come to a humiliating treaty with Philip and Richard which granted their every demand. He was so unwell when he arrived at the meeting at Colombières, shaking and trembling, that Philip offered him his cloak and suggested he sit on the grass, but the old king angrily refused.

Afterwards, back in his bed at the castle of Chinon, the king scanned the names of the rebels whom Philip and Richard demanded should now do homage to Richard as their liege lord instead of to himself. When at the top of it he saw the name of his beloved son John he turned his face to the wall and was heard by his courtiers to cry, 'O John! John!' Then he said dully, 'Let things go as they will. I no longer care for anything in this world.' He died three days later. In his last agony he was heard by those about him to mutter, 'Shame, shame on a defeated king.'

In his palace at Winchester, Henry had commissioned a painting which to him summed up the last years of his life with his sons grown up: three young eagles were attacking their parent bird, while a fourth was standing on his neck ready to peck out its eyes. It proved all too prescient.

When he was dead he was borne through the rolling Angevin hills to the Abbey of Fontevrault, where you can still see his tomb. Beside him lies Queen Eleanor. Enemies by the end of their lives, they were united in death. But although (as one historian has said) Henry was a lion savaged by jackals, so great were his achievements that many of the methods of justice and government that he designed endured for eight centuries. His superb bureaucracy ensured that England continued to flourish for some time after his death, despite the worst efforts of his two careless sons.

Richard I
(1189–1199)

Once he had assumed the throne Richard's behaviour underwent a marked change. One chronicler reported that when he approached his father's body at the start of the funeral procession the corpse started to spew blood from its nostrils as a sign that the murderer of the dead man was near by. But Richard was a man transformed. He fell into paroxysms of grief, punished all those who had rebelled with him except his mother, whom he released from prison in Winchester, and rewarded his father's most loyal supporters, including William Marshall who had once challenged him to single combat on behalf of the old king. His close relationship with Philip Augustus would shortly become one of bitter enmity.

As far as Richard the Lionheart was concerned, the single most important event of his day was the fall of the Christian Latin Kingdom of Jerusalem to Saladin, the new Muslim warlord ruler of Syria. A Kurd from Mesopotamia (today Iraq), Saladin the Great was overlord of much of the Middle East and was in the process of expelling all the Latin or western European settlements from Palestine.

Palestine, as the cradle of the world's three most important monotheistic faiths, was and is a land of great religious significance. By strange coincidence the tiny city of Jerusalem was the site of many of their separate revelations. It was the scene of Christ's death, just as Palestine was the scene of his life, and contained the Holy Sepulchre, site of his tomb in the rock. On the very same spot as the Holy Sepulchre were the ruins of the destroyed Temple of Solomon, sacred to the Jews. It was also believed that it was there that Abraham had been narrowly saved from sacrificing Isaac by seeing a ram in the thicket. And the same piece of ground was believed by Muslims to have been the very spot from which Mohammed was taken to Heaven. In honour of Mohammed, the Dome or Mosque of the Rock had been built by Muslims – who were the country's most recent conquerors.

The triumphant First Crusade of 1095–9, which had been launched to liberate the Holy Land, had established the Latin Kingdom of Jerusalem as well as the counties of Edessa, Tripoli and Antioch under an Angevin relation of Henry II named Count Baldwin. Since Henry was the head of the Angevin family, on the fall of Jerusalem the Patriarch Heraclius arrived in England on a special mission to implore him and his many armies to liberate the city. But Henry remained unconvinced. For all his religious devotion, mounting a Crusade was a lengthy, dangerous and extremely expensive business. In his view the Angevin Empire was not in sufficiently good shape to be left without a ruler. Since 1166 there had already been a tax for the Crusades of a penny in the pound for every freeman; in response to the patriarch, Henry now imposed the severe Saladin tax or tithe, one-tenth of all freemen's personal goods to raise money for the Crusade.

This action failed to satisfy contemporary opinion, which would have liked the king to lead a Crusade but did not wish to pay the Saladin tithe. In the end the majority of the Crusaders would go off as private citizens. It was what one historian has called an 'armed pilgrimage', in return for which Pope Urban II promised spiritual indulgences to smooth the way to heaven. The Crusades were the closet thing to a mass movement in the intensely religious middle ages. At a time when Bible stories were the only universal literary stimulus, liberating the places where Christ had passed his life – Bethlehem, Nazareth, Canaan, Galilee, Mount Calvary – had an almost unbearable emotional resonance.

Richard Coeur de Lion was no more immune from the lure of the great Crusade adventure than the next man, especially as his chief calling was to be a soldier of great strategic brilliance. He had honed his military skills in reducing the powers of the wild southern barons of Aquitaine, and he believed that he could be particularly useful at avenging the honour of the Christian west after the Second Crusade, to liberate Edessa and led by the French and German armies, had ended in disaster. Perhaps, too, like many a Crusader he had a yen to see the world.

The new king more than made up for his father's reluctance to expose his lands to the dangers of his absence on the Third Crusade. In the ten years of his reign Richard I visited England only twice – first to be crowned, and second to raise money. He had none of his father's interest in good government or in eradicating corruption. The office of sheriff was openly put up for sale in every county; by paying Richard 10,000 marks the Scottish king William the Lion was allowed to annul the Treaty of Falaise. The new justiciar of England, William Longchamp, the Bishop of Ely, was a long-term official of the Angevin civil service, but in the new climate it was

Richard the Lionheart

rumoured that he had purchased his office. Richard himself joked that he would have sold London itself if he could have found a buyer. Nevertheless the great administrative structures set up by Henry II proved their worth: England was governed very successfully without a king during all those years of the Lionheart's absence.

Despite this southern Frenchman's cavalier treatment of precious institutions and his evident lack of interest in the country, there has never been a King of England who arouses quite such enthusiasm as Richard. Somehow the gaiety and generosity of his character, his devil-may-care spirit and his endless adventures continue to blind many to the less attractive sides of his nature. At the beginning of his reign his easy gesture of granting a general amnesty to all those in prison, particularly those who had been prosecuted for the forest laws, has endeared him in popular myth ever since, linking him indissolubly with that mythical prince of forest thieves Robin Hood and hinting at the insubordinate native British desire to sympathize with the rebel. But it was under this great warrior that there began the worst persecution of the Jewish community in English history, after a mob had attacked Jewish leaders attending Richard's coronation.

After their expulsion from Israel by the Romans towards the end of the first century, the Jewish people dispersed round the world, an event known as the Diaspora. In twelfth-century England, whose population was about two and a half million, the Jews were a tiny minority of perhaps 5,000 individuals who tended to be mobile traders, merchants and moneylenders. Their skill in finance meant that they were one of the medieval equivalents of banks for European governments, and they were protected by the post-Conquest Norman and Angevin monarchs who relied on them for loans and taxed them at will. They lived in a separate quarter in towns, and spoke Hebrew among themselves. They were noted for their different foods, taboos and religious rituals, which were far more strictly observed 900 years ago than they are today.

Jesus Christ, the founder of the Christian Church, was the most famous Jewish man in history, while the Apostles and Disciples whose writings Christian scholars argued about were converted Jews. But during the Crusades, when the papacy was preaching an armed campaign against unbelievers of all kinds, parish priests were encouraged to attack Jews from the pulpit. The Christian Church began to dwell on the old belief that the Jewish population of Jerusalem more than a thousand years before had elected to crucify Christ. The parish priest also told his congregation that the practice of loaning money for interest was the sin of usury – even though this was secretly engaged in by Christian moneylenders, and is of course standard banking procedure today.

Until the Crusades the average English person had very little to do with the Jews, apart from those in the merchant fraternity, though there was a Jewish presence in most important southern English towns as well as York. But the need for money to finance a Crusade changed relations between the two communities. For the first time landowning knights who wished to go on crusade needed large amounts of cash. The quickest way of finding it was to raise mortgages on their land, and the best people for cash tended to be Jewish moneylenders, who could tap their overseas contacts to offer extra liquidity. Inspired by religious enthusiasm the Christian knights borrowed immense sums which they often were scarcely in a position to repay.

Although anti-Jewish feeling had been growing for the past century, since the start of the Crusades, concrete manifestations of it began at Richard the Lionheart's coronation. Anti-Jewish prejudice was increased by the handling of the interest on the Crusaders' debts. Knights would return from the Crusades to be told that the interest rate had changed in their absence. If it unexpectedly rose to say 50 per cent on a loan or higher, which it not infrequently did, a small landowner who could not service his debt would find that half his land passed to his creditors. Cash poor, used to a feudal rural life and a barter economy, the Crusaders had no understanding of interest and compound interest. They were aware only of the apparently unfair use of it to make money.

And it was on the Jewish rather than the Christian moneylenders that the Christian English knights vented their ire. As a minority the Jews became a scapegoat for the improvidence of small landowners, who had forgotten that if they borrowed money they would have to pay it back. Inevitably, when the day of reckoning came, Crusaders resented having to sell land to pay off their debts.

At Richard I's coronation banquet the arrival uninvited of the most important members of the Jewish community with splendid gifts seems to have been the spark for the shameful conflagration that swept England. The mass of London's citizenry – many of whom were smaller merchants in debt to Jewish moneylenders – as well as the smaller barons turned on the Jews. They drove them out of the banqueting hall, severely injuring many of them in the process. The king and his soldiers made an attempt to halt them, but the mob swarmed towards the Jewish quarter, hanging its inhabitants and burning their houses. Afterwards not enough was done by the king to seek out and punish the rioters.

This probably encouraged people up and down the country to turn on Jews in the towns, inventing lies about their customs. During the autumn and winter there were massacres at Norwich, Stamford, Lincoln, Bury St Edmund's and elsewhere. It was at York, however, that the worst outrage took place, when 500 Jewish men, women and children who took refuge in the city's castle against a band of armed men were attacked with the aid of the warden's retainers. Many committed suicide, and those who did not were slaughtered where they stood. Their murderers were motivated not only by ethnic hatred, but more sinisterly by a desire to wipe out the great debts they owed the Jews. Many of them were the men-at-arms of important local families. They had been instructed to go straight to the Minster, where the Jews had deposited the bonds which Crusading families had given them for debt, and burn them all. They did so in a large bonfire in the Minster. At a stroke huge debts were wiped off many of the Crusaders' estates.

Although the perpetrators of the massacre at York were sternly punished by William Longchamp, the justiciar, the Jewish communities never recovered their former confidence, or indeed their wealth. They remained in England for another hundred years, continuing to be protected as moneylenders by the crown until, in another fit of Christian religious enthusiasm, Richard's great-nephew Edward I expelled them in 1290.

Though England had been left with excellent regents in William Longchamp and the king's mother Queen Eleanor, the long absence of

Lincoln Cathedral, founded 1092, rebuilt in the Gothic style from 1192 onwards by Bishop Hugh of Lincoln.

Richard in Palestine meant that the good order of the country was soon threatened. The opposition was headed by his brother John and the great barons themselves. They resented the power of the justiciar Longchamp. Like many of those who served the Angevins, Longchamp was a man of natural ability who had not sprung from the baronial classes. In the treacherous and scheming John the barons found a perfect foil for their plans. A struggle against the royal administration involving parts of the country in civil war began shortly after Richard the Lionheart left the country. Despite John's nickname of Lackland, the king's brother now ruled much of south-west England. He had been left in charge of it by Richard, who had a low opinion of John's military abilities and no interest in his compensating cunning.

Richard was careless in most things and, though his legacy to England was a series of useful alliances encircling the Angevin Empire, he generally believed force to be the superior of diplomacy. As the French and English armies travelled east to the Holy Land he chose to ignore a new hostility in his old comrade, the French king Philip Augustus, who resented his new position as head of the Angevin Empire. Far from conciliating him, the English king had not only failed to marry Princess Alice but insulted the French by substituting an alliance with the kingdom of Navarre in northern Spain to protect the empire's southern tip. At Messina in Sicily, where the French and Angevin imperial troops were gathering on the last leg of their journey to Palestine Richard publicly repudiated Princess Alice and married the beautiful Princess Berengaria of Navarre, yet continued to hold on to the Vexin.

In the Holy Land, Richard's outstanding qualities as a military tactician aroused the envy of his fellow monarchs. For over two years they had been besieging without success the Latin citadel of Acre, formidable on its promontory. On the plain below its towering yellow battlements stretched the armies of Christendom and row after row of tents. On the heights above them were Saladin's armies, whose presence was causing the Crusaders' supply of food to dwindle: the besiegers were besieged.

In contrast to the European heavy armour which gave many Crusaders sunstroke in the intensely hot weather, the Syrians', or Saracens', headpieces were not hot metal but turbans in bright colours which protected them from the sun. The Christian west's military advantage over the Muslim east lay in the crossbow – but it availed them very little on the Third Crusade: Saladin was on home territory, and his men were used to desert conditions. They had supply lines to the interior, better horses (the swift Arab breed then unknown to Europe) and a lighter sword, the curved scimitar, which could find its target more quickly than the unwieldy three-foot-long weapon used by the Crusaders. In contrast to Saladin's armies, most of the Crusaders were in very poor health. An epidemic had raged through their poorly situated camp with its bad drainage, killing many, including such important figures as the Archbishop of Canterbury and Ranulf Glanvill.

Nevertheless with Richard present manoeuvres took on a new momentum. Superior management of siege engines beat down the Saracens' resistance. Unlike the other European kings, Richard the Lionheart led from the front, exhibiting the personal valour that made his men worship him. He fought hand to hand and used his crossbow with perfect accuracy, picking Saracens off against the skyline. Under the Lionheart Acre was captured from Saladin.

But the first significant victory against the Muslims for fifty years only added to the tensions already troubling relations between the different national camps of the vast, sickly and bored European armies. The French and English kings quarrelled over their opposing candidates for the crown of Jerusalem. Morale was poor among the German soldiers, whose emperor had been drowned on the journey to Palestine. The Austrians had played little part in relieving Acre but were anxious to share in the glory of liberating it. They were especially annoyed, after they had hung Austrian flags over the citadel's battlements, to find that English soldiers tore them down and threatened to throw the Austrians over the battlements if they put up any more. When their leader Duke Leopold complained to Richard, he did nothing to discipline his men: once again he was not concerned with diplomatic relations. Though the English king had fallen victim to the camp's terrible shivering fever which had decimated the Christian army, he insisted on pushing on to Jerusalem. By August 1191 the short and dark Philip Augustus had had enough of standing in the charismatic Richard's glorious shadow and decided that Coeur de Lion's obsession with the Crusade made it the perfect moment to stir up trouble in England's continental dominions. Pleading illness, he left abruptly for France.

Weak from camp fever, though in high spirits now that it was on the move again, the bedraggled army started tailing its painful way south along the coast before turning up to the rocky heights where stood Jerusalem. As they marched the Crusaders chanted their battle cry: 'Help, help, help for the Holy Sepulchre!' By the camp fires each night, one man would start the call and then it would spread throughout the tents, rousing the soldiers to forget their suffering and fulfil their mission to free the Holy Places.

At the Battle of Arsuf, exploiting his still formidable infantry and brilliant crossbowmen, Richard the Lionheart snatched victory from Saladin, who had never previously been defeated in the open field. This event sent waves of hope across Europe and raised Richard's stock even higher among the men. But in the end, though the Lionheart twice led his troops within twelve miles of the Holy City, he was stymied by the failure of his supply lines and the exhaustion of his men. Saladin's army remained largely unbroken.

Forced to retreat, because he had decided it would be madness to besiege Jerusalem, Richard achieved a treaty in 1192 whose terms Saladin would have granted to no one else – a mark of the great eastern warrior's respect for his generalship. Christians were once again allowed to visit the Holy Sepulchre and to do business all over the city, and Joppa and its district became Christian. But when the courteous Saladin invited Richard to visit the Holy City himself, the king refused. He would not enter the city which God had not permitted him to deliver.

Although Richard had fought Saladin to a standstill over Jerusalem, the Third Crusade like its predecessor was a consummate failure. It did not achieve its immediate objective, which was to bring the Holy Places under Christian control; and in the course of it the previously allied French and English kings became the deadliest of enemies. On the other hand the social intercourse with the Arab world which the Crusades encouraged transformed western Christendom. In a great many respects the Arab culture was far in advance of the Christian. The transfer of superior technology from the west to the east which was to be such a feature of the nineteenth and twentieth centuries was then in the opposite direction. Western Europe benefited enormously from contact with scientific Arab medicine, which very slowly undermined the superstitious practices of the west. Arab science and mathematics introduced the zero and the decimal point, while the Arab use of spices showed the west how to preserve food. In European architecture the ogee or narrow twisting arch so characteristic of the thirteenth century was a direct transmission from Arab architecture.

With the end of the Third Crusade, Richard began to make his way back as fast as possible to England and to an empire threatened by the plots of his younger brother. Word had reached him that it was no longer safe to travel through France because of the French king's hostility. He therefore had to take the long route north through Germany. At home John was making common cause with Philip Augustus. Just as Philip had drawn Richard into his schemes when he was the heir to the throne, the French king now offered John the spurned hand of his sister Princess Alice. In return his overlord proposed that John should have the English continental possessions, though this was hardly a straightforward proposition. In Richard's absence the French king had been exhorting the barons of Normandy to become his liege men and throw off English rule.

England meanwhile was racked by sieges and rebellions led by John and the barons, who had found support in the country owing to the ever higher rate of taxation demanded to finance the Crusade. By 1191 the opposition was sufficiently powerful to bring about the justiciar Longchamp's downfall. Fortunately, just at this moment one of Richard's most trusted advisers, Hubert Walter, Bishop of Salisbury, arrived back from the Crusades to be appointed the new justiciar, as Richard had directed, before one of John's men could take his place. Nevertheless, events seemed to be moving in John's favour. For at the beginning of 1193, King Richard fell into the clutches of his envious fellow Crusader, the Duke of Austria, who then sold him on to the emperor Henry VI.

The story of Richard's captivity, his charm, his bravery, his carelessness – attempting to cross Austria in disguise, he forgot to remove his beautiful royal gloves – sparked a thousand legends. Most famous is the story of Blondel, his minstrel. For three months it seemed that the Lionheart had vanished into thin air. Warned by Philip Augustus, John had begun circulating the rumour that the great Crusader was dead. Blondel set out to search the whole of Europe for the friend whose death he refused to accept. In Aquitaine they had spent long hours together writing verses in celebration of the virtues of the Christian knight. According to legend, as Blondel walked through the mountains overlooking the Danube Plain he was by chance singing one of the troubadour ballads he and the king had composed together. To his astonishment, floating over the trees from where the forbidding castle of Durnstein loomed above him he heard a great bass voice singing the next verse.

Whether or not it was Blondel who brought the news of the king's whereabouts back to England, the emperor Henry VI demanded the immense sum of 100,000 marks for his release – a formidable imposition on a country already reeling from taxes levied to pay for the Crusade. Nevertheless, under the leadership of the masterful Queen Eleanor, most of it would be found a year later, in 1194. Chalices and crucifixes in every church were melted down for their silver, while every freeman paid the colossal amount of one-quarter of his earnings to the government. The Cistercian monasteries pioneering the farming of sheep in Yorkshire were forced to yield up their entire takings from that year's sheep sales.

There was no question of the ransom not being paid. Henry VI was threatening that, if it was not met, he would hand Richard over to the King of France, which would mean the end of the Angevin Empire. Much of that was anyway tottering under Philip Augustus' incursions. His attempts to detach Normandy from England had been unsuccessful while Richard was free: as a Crusader, the Lionheart commanded a good deal of loyalty. But the minute Richard was captured the situation became more nebulous. Philip Augustus succeeded in overrunning the Vexin, which guarded the southern entrance to Normandy, and even got as far as its capital Rouen before being thrown back.

There was thus in 1193 a distinct window of opportunity for the two plotters. John was convinced that the moment to usurp the throne had come – Richard was still in captivity and, despite the harsh measures taken to raise the ransom, the English government had not yet completed the task. John now showed his hand. He crossed the Channel to meet Philip in Paris and did homage for England's French possessions, and possibly for England too. Then he put into effect their joint plan. John mounted his own rebellion in England against his brother's government, while the French king began stockpiling boats to invade across the Channel.

England was saved by the emperor's fear of France's ambitions. An alliance was arranged: in order to secure his freedom, Richard had to do homage for England to the emperor and hold it as the emperor's fief. In practice this amounted to very little. Richard was released from this obligation on the emperor's death and the ransom was never paid in its entirety. The important fact was that the empire and England were now allied against France, and it was in France that Richard spent the last five years of his life, attempting to regain the advantage from Philip Augustus.

With the news that Richard was returning, the French invasion of England and John's rebellion collapsed. John received a brief note from the well-informed Philip that said succinctly, 'Look to yourself, the Devil is loose'; shortly afterwards John left for Normandy. The takeover had never been a foregone conclusion. Queen Eleanor had shown courage and decision in rallying the English people to her eldest son and putting the country's defences into a state of alert. English ships vigilantly patrolled the Channel. But no sooner had Richard returned to England than he left it, though not before raising more taxes and undergoing a second coronation ceremony to remind the people who was king. He never saw the country again.

In charge of the government the king left his efficient justiciar, Hubert Walter, whom he had also made Archbishop of Canterbury. The nephew of Ranulf Glanvill, Walter had been part of Henry II's administration at the end of the great king's life. Trained in the law, he was the perfect administrative instrument to devise higher taxes for the rising numbers of professional soldiers required for the French campaigns, for building defensive castles, and for paying the princes of the Low Countries and north Germany to remain allied to England against France. But a spirit of revolt was growing among the English, whose wealth in many cases had been seriously depleted by the king's ransom. For the next four years England was groaning with the cost of the war to win back Angevin territory from France.

In 1198, the year before the Lionheart died, the barons were again provoked into revolt by a demand that they provide more soldiers for

Richard under their feudal obligations. In question among the tenants-in-chief was how much service they were required to give the king by the feudal levy which had developed from the old fyrd. Defending their native land from attack was one thing, but endless foreign service seemed another. Moreover, they were being asked to provide more than forty days per year. They were joined by many more disinterested characters like the saintly churchman and administrator Bishop Hugh of Lincoln. Hugh of Lincoln protested at the strain these demands were imposing on the tenants of his own episcopal lands and refused to insist upon them. It was therefore a triumph for him when Hubert Walter was dismissed as justiciar and replaced by Geoffrey Fitz Peter, the Earl of Essex.

But Richard was not really interested in the anger of the English. His campaign to push the French armies of Philip Augustus back into their own country was working, and he had regained most of his territories east of the Seine, as well as the Norman Vexin. To protect Normandy from further invasion by Philip Augustus, he built a great castle high on a cliff overlooking the Seine near the town of Les Andelys, whose noble ruins you can still see today. The frontier castle is another testament to the king's outstanding engineering skills, and was built extremely swiftly, in just under a year. The king gazed at the finished building with immense pride and said, 'Is this not a saucy babe that at twelve months can keep the King of France at bay?' The French for saucy was *gaillard*, and it was known ever after as Château Gaillard.

For all Richard the Lionheart's military genius, his violent temperament and natural inclination towards war sometimes led him into launching attacks on vassal barons in disputes that were not worth the cost of the campaign. In the course of one such escapade in April 1199 Richard I met his death. A vassal of his at Chalus, deep in the Limousin in the centre of the Aquitainian territory, had found an enormous silver treasure trove buried in the earth. When he refused to surrender it to Richard as his overlord, the king went to war against him. While he watched the siege on horseback, a bolt from a crossbow, that weapon he himself had made so famous, flew out from one of the castle's slit windows and buried itself in his chest. Attempts to remove it by an incompetent surgeon were unsuccessful, and the wound became infected because of the king's own impatient efforts to wrench it out. As the Lionheart lay dying, his men captured the castle, which had been defended by only seven knights and eight serving men. Generous as ever, Richard insisted on pardoning his assailant, though once he had died his men were not so magnanimous.

On his deathbed Richard the Lionheart called all his most important tenants-in-chief to him and made them swear allegiance to John, since he and Berengaria were childless. Richard's nephew Arthur was his natural heir, as the son of John's elder brother Geoffrey of Brittany. But the Norman and Angevin kings had kept up the tradition of the old English monarchy of choosing a more suitable heir as long as he had royal blood. With the support of his mother Queen Eleanor, by the end of May 1199 John had at last achieved his heart's desire and been crowned King of England.

John
(1199–1216)

Until the late nineteenth century, John's reputation was one of the lowest. His decadent personal habits and taste for cruelty, which was egregious even in a brutal age (he had an appetite for ordeals and executions), cast a long shadow. In addition, his quarrel with the papacy turned all monk chroniclers against him. As the curator of the once formidable Angevin Empire he was soon to be humiliated by the loss of Normandy and all his northern French possessions. England was left only with the Channel Islands as the last remnant of the Norman duchy, and Queen Eleanor's country of Aquitaine.

In some ways John was in fact a better ruler of England than his brother. But personal habits aside, he lacked Richard's glamour as a holy warrior in an age when war was dominant – indeed he had had a purely ecclesiastical education in the typical way of a younger son. Partly as a result of his unwarlike nature, he ended up spending the greater part of his life in England, the longest period of any Norman king since William the Conqueror. Like Henry II he became intimately concerned with every detail of English life, and having the Angevin passion for royal administration he was forever journeying through his new realm. He also shared his father's fascination with justice, and was noted for exercising his right to hear the cases of the King's Bench. Though myth paints him as the venomous foe of the outlaws of Sherwood Forest, in fact King John took care to make the forest laws of his forefathers less harsh. Aged thirty-three when he came to the throne, he had matured from the silly youth of fifteen years before who had pulled the Irish elders' beards.

Even so, John was a tyrannical, greedy and lawless ruler. Like William Rufus he was unscrupulous when it came to other people's property, and made permanent enemies of the Church and the barons by his constant scheming to appropriate their wealth. By the end of his reign so deep was the distrust he inspired that men said he kidnapped the heirs to great fortunes and murdered them.

Although John's accession to the English throne had been painless, it was a different matter in France. In 1199 war broke out between the two countries when the French king Philip Augustus decided to recognize as head of the Angevin Empire the thirteen-year-old Arthur of Brittany, John's nephew. This did not get Philip very far, and the following year he had to accept John's homage in relation to his French possessions. But the war he desired in order to dismember his greatest rival on French territory soon broke out again. John, who had just repudiated his childless wife Isabella of Gloucester, hit on the idea of marrying Isabella of Angoulême, which brought her territory into his empire and provided access to Aquitaine. Unfortunately Isabella of Angoulême had been engaged to an unruly and well-connected Poitevin baron named Hugh de Lusignan who was affronted by the King of England's seizure of what he believed to be his property. He soon found many other turbulent Poitevin barons who resented the erosion of their powers by John's autocratic ways.

Headed by de Lusignan they appealed to Philip Augustus as John's overlord to right the wrongs being done to them by the King of England. This gave Philip his final chance to break up the Angevin Empire and he took it. John refused to answer the charges brought against him in the French king's court, and in 1202 the court declared that he had forfeited all his lands in French territory. To ensure that the message was clear, Philip Augustus then recognized the fifteen-year-old Arthur of Brittany as the ruler of Brittany, Anjou, Maine, Touraine and Aquitaine. With French armies Arthur invaded those territories himself, while Philip went into Normandy, his real objective, as capturing the duchy would give him control of the north coast – the natural hinterland for his capital of Paris.

At this point there occurred the event which blackened John's name through history. Following his nephew to Poitou, where Arthur was besieging his grandmother Eleanor of Aquitaine with the help of the Poitevin barons, John defeated him in battle – to everyone's surprise, for Richard's low opinion of John's military capabilities was universal. He then imprisoned his nephew in his castle at Falaise, before moving him to Rouen, the capital of Normandy. By 1203 Arthur was dead, almost certainly murdered. Contemporaries believed that it was John himself who had performed the deed, by night and in disguise, probably in one of his famous Angevin rages.

Whatever the truth about Arthur's death, it was of no benefit to his uncle John. Philip's forces swiftly overran Anjou, Touraine and Maine, while Brittany came over to France out of anger about Arthur's murder. By 1204 Normandy too belonged to the French crown. Theoretically, of all the English possessions the duchy was the most difficult for France to seize. It had a long connection to England, and the pro-English feeling was greatly strengthened by the trading links between the two countries. What was more, many of its barons were Anglo-Normans who held property on both sides of the Channel. It had magnificent defences against France, the greatest of which was Richard's Château Gaillard. But the barons were very disaffected, and Philip Augustus was a better strategist than John, who tended to procrastinate and stayed in England when he should have been fighting in Normandy. Although Château Gaillard held out for six months until early March, John had really abandoned Normandy long before that. When his mother Eleanor died the following month, the last feelings of Norman loyalty towards the English crown evaporated. By Midsummer Day 1204 all the great possessions in northern France that King John had inherited from William the Conqueror and Geoffrey of Anjou were lost.

The loss of Normandy was an event of central importance for England. Although it was viewed as a disaster at the time, it forced the great Anglo-Norman barons to choose whether their loyalties were to England or to Normandy, for they could no longer hold land in both. The Norman Conquest was superseded by the renewed development of the English as a nation and a unified state under an exclusively English king. No longer linked by the Angevin Empire, the Duchy of Aquitaine, which was all that remained of the English crown's French possessions, became in effect an independent English colony.

A permanent English navy to guard the Channel became a matter of pressing importance, as it had not been since 1066. Until 1204 much of the coast facing southern England belonged to friendly Normandy, so most of the ordinary business of guarding the coast in peacetime could be handled by the towns known as the Cinque Ports – Hastings, Romney, Hythe, Dover and Sandwich (Winchelsea and Rye became *six et sept* later). By a longstanding arrangement, in exchange for freedom from taxes and the right to tax within their own walls, they were legally required to provide fifty-seven ships for use by themselves and the king. But after the loss of Normandy these measures were supplemented partly by impressment and partly by the turning over to the royal government of any merchant ships captured in the Channel.

If the king now had a reputation for being unlucky, after his quarrel with the papacy he was believed to be cursed. In 1205 Hubert Walter, who had remained Archbishop of Canterbury, died. Although technically it was the right of the monks of the Cathedral Chapter of Canterbury Cathedral to elect the head of the Church in England, it had been generally accepted since William the Conqueror that the king would play a large part in the choice. Unfortunately the monks behaved foolishly. They secretly elected their undistinguished sub-prior Reginald without the king's permission and sent him to Rome to receive the *pallium* from Pope Innocent III. But, though Reginald had been warned not to boast about his new position until the pope had confirmed it, the sub-prior, being both indiscreet and vain, insisted on travelling very slowly in tremendous pomp towards Rome as befitted his new dignity, attended by priests and outriders. As a result, the king soon found out what was going on and despatched his own royal candidate to Rome instead, the Bishop of Norwich, who was equally unworthy of this great office.

Neither of these choices satisfied the great pope of the middle ages, Innocent III. He insisted that the monks' chapter elect Cardinal Stephen Langton, a distinguished English theologian living in Rome, and he then invested him as Archbishop of Canterbury. But John did not take this lying down, and refused to allow the new archbishop into the country. There was some justification for this: in all the battles between the papacy and the English kings no pope had ever dared to appoint the head of the English Church against England's wishes. Nevertheless, John's stand derived less from principle than from his desire to have his own creature running the Church who would help milk the tantalizingly wealthy Church lands. A stalemate ensued, since the pope for his part would not recognize the Bishop of Norwich. It was broken by Innocent III putting the whole country under an interdict. All religious services were forbidden.

This was only the beginning of the pope's campaign to use all the weapons at his disposal to bring the King of England to heel. Although the interdict meant very little to the irreligious John, it was a catastrophe for ordinary people. Churches were closed. Weddings could not be celebrated. The dead were buried in unconsecrated ground to the great distress of the population. Only the first and last rites of baptism and extreme unction (the sacrament of the dying), out of fear for the soul, were permitted. Church bells, which in days without clocks marked the passing hours, were eerily silent as if in reproach.

But the impatient king, unmoved by what to everyone else seemed a curse, used the interdict as an opportunity to seize the property of the wealthy abbeys and bishoprics. When in 1209 the pope went further and excommunicated the king himself, John appropriated the lands of England's archbishoprics. With the income from these estates the king raised large armies of mercenaries and settled any quarrels he had with the Scots, Welsh and Irish to his satisfaction. He made Llywelyn Prince of Gwynedd submit to him; then, crossing to Ireland, he divided the east into counties on English lines and reduced their barons to order.

John had not understood quite what a formidable enemy he had made. In 1212, incensed by the King of England's behaviour, Pope Innocent decided to use the final and most potent weapon in his repertoire. For some time the Curia at Rome had claimed that, if a ruler of a Christian country failed to obey the pope, the rest of the princes of Christendom might depose him. Innocent now issued the threat of deposition against John and entrusted the mission to his greatest ally, King Philip Augustus. It was a task the French king was more than happy to take on.

At the news that Philip was preparing an invasion, King John performed a remarkable about-turn. He could not run the risk of an invasion which might lose him the throne: he was unpopular among ordinary people because of the interdict and the English barons were discontented after the loss of their Norman lands. Though the king sent messages to the pope that he would accept his nominee Stephen Langton as archbishop, with Philip Augustus' forces at his back, Innocent could make the King of England accept sterner terms. Not only was Stephen Langton to be Archbishop of Canterbury, but all the priests John had expelled because they had obeyed the interdict and refused to say Mass should be allowed to return to England. Most important of all, John was to yield up the crown of England into the hands of the papal legate, Pandulf. In return for swearing to be the pope's vassal he would receive the crown back but would rule England as a fief of the papacy. England was to pay a thousand marks a year to Rome for this privilege.

John agreed to all this. At least it meant that England was free from the threat of invasion. John had not given up all thought of wresting back his old patrimony of Anjou as well as Poitou. With his nephew the new Holy Roman Emperor Otto, who had himself been deposed by the pope, he continued with a confederacy of northern European princes to attack the French king. But the attempt foundered on John's military irresolution or, as it seemed at the time, his cowardliness. He retreated south from a battle for Anjou with Philip's son Louis that he might have won, while the confederacy's armies with an English contingent were heavily defeated by Philip himself, at the Battle of Bouvines in 1214.

The Battle of Bouvines was final confirmation that the Angevin Empire was lost forever to England: henceforth the French monarchy would become one of the four great powers of western Europe. It also marked a turning point in John's domestic fortunes. Humiliated once again, he now had to return home and face the demands of the baronage and the Church. In his absence abroad they had united under the inspiring leadership of the new Archbishop of Canterbury, Stephen Langton. At his suggestion, they insisted that John issue a new charter of the laws of England like that of Henry I to restore confidence in the increasingly tyrannical crown. When the king refused, the barons mustered for war – with Langton's active support.

Two thousand of them, and the soldiers and knights holding land from them, gathered at Stamford in Lincolnshire and began moving south. The vast array of armed men and horses was composed of all the groups in

England which previously had had nothing in common – the northern and southern barons, the marcher lords, the civil service or official nobility created by Henry II and the tenants-in-chief. Once London had been captured by the rebels, John realized that he would have to give in to their demands in order to fight another day. On 15 June 1215 on the long, low plain of Runnymede near Windsor, on an island in the middle of the Thames, King John reluctantly fixed his seal to the remarkable document known to history as Magna Carta, or the Great Charter.

In many ways Magna Carta is a document of its time. It was a restatement of the existing rights and laws which the English had enjoyed since charters issued under Henry I and II, but it also reflected the grievances of the barons and the erosion of their rights under the Angevin kings. Magna Carta contained their demands for a greater share of power. At the same time, it contained many clauses which have a timeless appeal. Addressed 'to all freemen of the realm and their heirs for ever', it may be seen as a document addressed to all classes. As such, it is generally considered to represent the beginning of English liberties.

Superb administrators though the Norman and Angevin kings were, and though they had made England part of a progressive European civilization, they had ruled as despots. Magna Carta changed all that. It legally limited the power of the king, forbidding him to ignore the law and authorizing a council of twenty-five barons to enforce it by all possible means, including imprisonment, if he did try to overrule it.

The leaders of the rebellion arranged that a copy of Magna Carta should be read by the sheriff to a public meeting in each county in England. Every

The island and meadow of Runnymede on the south bank of the Thames between Staines and Windsor, where King John accepted Magna Carta in 1215.

163

important church and town in the kingdom was to have a copy, so that everybody could know what their rights were and what they should take for granted. Over the next eight centuries the rights proclaimed by Magna Carta powerfully informed not only England's national consciousness but many cultures influenced by Britain and British emigrants, including those of the United States, India and Australia. Magna Carta has been one of England's greatest contributions to political thought, an early expression of the democratic ideal that the rule of law ensures rights for everyone by virtue of their humanity and regardless of their wealth or poverty.

Among its many clauses, the charter guaranteed the rights and liberties of the English Church, not only to prevent future quarrels over the appointment of the head of the Church but also to allow chapters in cathedrals to elect their bishops. The rules of inheritance were emphasized, to stop John from ignoring them as was his wont; the procedure for collecting scutage was laid down; the urgent early-thirteenth-century problem of the indebtedness of the knightly class to Christian and Jewish moneylenders was ameliorated; and certain weights and measures were standardized.

The barons made no attempt to limit the jurisdiction of the king's courts, though they had curtailed some of their own. The Great Charter also enunciated some fundamental principles of justice which have echoed down the centuries, like Clause 40, 'to no one will we sell, deny or defer, right or justice'. But it also expressed the reverence for the rule of law which was the spirit of the age. Clause 39 guaranteed for the first time in English history that no freeman could be imprisoned, deprived of his property, outlawed or molested without a trial according to the law of the land in which he must be judged by his peers. Most importantly for future generations, the king was prevented from raising new taxes on the people without the permission of the council of barons.

But, though John sealed Magna Carta, slippery as ever he had no intention of holding to it. The war between king and barons began again when he fled to the Isle of Wight. From there he appealed for help to his liege lord the pope, having further ingratiated himself with him by hastily taking the Crusader oath. He begged him to free him from Magna Carta, which he said insulted the crown and therefore the Holy See. Nothing loath, Innocent III declared the Great Charter illegal, and suspended the Archbishop of Canterbury Stephen Langton for refusing to excommunicate the English bishops and barons who had produced it.

With an army of foreign mercenaries John escaped from the Isle of Wight, made his way through England and marched into Scotland to attack King Alexander I, who had supported the rebels. Behind him he left a large number of foreign troops to harry the barons' estates; this they did so successfully that the barons decided to ask Philip Augustus for help and to offer his son the crown of England. Speciously asserting that John's murder of his nephew Arthur of Brittany required that he be deprived of the English crown, Philip's son Louis invaded England – claiming the throne in the name of his wife Blanche of Castile, Henry II's granddaughter and John's niece. In November 1215 some 7,000 Frenchmen sailed up the Thames to support the barons and citizens of London.

The real possibility that England would undergo a new French conquest was averted by the death of the already unwell king. Having led an expedition north to capture the important city of Lincoln, in October 1216 John passed away at Newark in Nottinghamshire after a gastric upset caused by a supper of peaches and new cider. Though his heir Henry III was only nine years old, he had the advantage of youth and innocence to make him a rallying point for national enthusiasm and he was endorsed by the papal legate, Guala. To nobles like William Marshall, Earl of Pembroke and Hubert de Burgh, he was the acceptable face of Plantagenet legitimacy. With the support of the Church, they would rule in his name for eleven years.

Henceforth until the end of the fourteenth century when a new dynasty seized the throne, the kings of England were known by a different name. They could not be called Angevins, since they no longer held the land in France which entitled them to. Instead, because the family badge of the Angevin counts was the yellow broom called in French *plante genêt* (genista to us today) they became known as the Plantagenet kings.

John was and remains England's most unpopular king. Despite his competence he had the reputation for being both cruel and unlucky. Not only did he lose Normandy, so earning again the title Jean Sans Terre which his father had affectionately given him, or John Lackland as later generations called him when English became the spoken language instead of French. He is also said to have lost the crown jewels of England when, in October 1216 shortly before he died, his baggage train was sucked down in a whirlpool formed by the incoming tide as it crossed the channel of the Welland. At a point still known as King's Corner between Cross Keys Wash and Lynn, as the king supposedly watched from the northern shore, half his army disappeared beneath the waters of the Wash and the crown of England was never seen again. This episode would enable many schoolchildren to joke that John had lost the crown of England in the Wash.

PLANTAGENET

Henry III

(1216–1272)

Henry III succeeded to the throne as a small boy. Despite his immensely long reign there always remained something weak and childlike about his personality. He had a reputation for 'simplicity'. This was not a compliment in the context of a king required to rule over strong and turbulent barons already used to a limited monarchy and to getting their own way. The abiding passions of Henry's life were his religious faith, which often caused him to neglect regal duties, and his devotion to his greedy French and Italian relations. Their demands for office, which his father John had always happily complied with, meant that a constant theme in England during his fifty-six-year reign was a hatred of foreigners. Henry was thus a poor head of state. On the other hand his strong aesthetic sense did much to advance the arts in England. The country's churches

Henry III, who rebuilt Westminster Abbey, supervising his masons.

benefited from being adorned by the skilled continental craftsmen he so admired, but his greatest monument is Westminster Abbey, the rebuilding of which in the English Gothic style over twenty years was a passionate personal project. Ultimately, however, one of the most significant developments of his reign was that in 1265 the first prototype of the House of Commons was convened.

William Marshall, the elderly Earl of Pembroke, who had been a wise counsellor to Henry's grandfather Henry II, became regent, and his pragmatic actions did much to restore the royal fortunes. He remained alive long enough to ensure that Louis and his French armies were expelled from England and that his youthful charge was backed by the papacy. Then, to end the civil war and secure the barons' allegiance, he cleverly reissued Magna Carta on behalf of the boy king. But, although the French threat to the throne had evaporated, the next ten years were turbulent ones resembling the anarchy under Stephen. When William Marshall died, his place as chief adviser to the young king was taken by Hubert de Burgh. De Burgh's time was soon occupied ridding England of John's foreign favourites, noblemen who had been granted enormous amounts of English land as a reward for helping John but were now riding roughshod over English customs, imprisoning judges and ignoring the law. De Burgh besieged many of the foreigners' illegal castles and chased most of them out of the country.

But in 1227 the situation changed for the worse when the pope declared that Henry III's minority was at an end and that he was of an age to rule. Henry turned away from de Burgh and restored to power, as justiciar, one of John's most grasping ministers, Peter des Roches, who had been both chancellor and Bishop of Winchester. Henry continued blithely to hand out land and offices in unprecedented quantities: Peter des Roches' nephew, for example, became sheriff for no fewer than ten counties: York, Berkshire, Gloucester, Somerset, Northumberland, Devon, Lancashire, Essex, Hampshire and Norfolk. In 1233 the English lost their patience. William Marshall's son Richard tried to force the king to dismiss Peter des Roches. Civil war followed. Though Richard Marshall was treacherously slain when the bishops threatened to excommunicate the king if he did not remove des Roches, Henry eventually gave way. In 1234 he dismissed des Roches and his Poitevin supporters and restored Hubert de Burgh to his estates.

But the king did not learn from these encounters. Though he was far more English in his tastes than any of his line and named his children after English saints, he soon brought a whole new set of foreigners to power when in 1236 he married Eleanor of Provence and adopted her Savoyard relations as his own. Under their influence he attempted to rule without any kind of council of English barons. The country was also plagued by interference from the papacy. Previously, under more resolute kings, the increased assertion of papal power had been resisted. To Henry III, surrounded as he was by French and Italian advisers, there seemed little wrong in allowing the pope to supersede ancient electoral rights and remove incumbents from their positions.

As a result a great number of French and Italian priests became absentee bishops and abbots, taking very little interest in their parishioners. The queen's uncle, the Savoyard Boniface, became a loathed Archbishop of Canterbury on the death of the saintly Edmund Rich in 1240 but hardly bothered to visit England. The unpopularity of these foreigners was not helped by a massive hike in taxation ordered by Pope Gregory IX to pay for his war against the emperor Frederick II, which Henry's religious nature impelled him to obey. The only important figure in the English Church who had the courage to protest was Robert Grosseteste, the Bishop of Lincoln. But a single voice had no impact.

BENEDICTINE NUN.

Despite or perhaps because of the influence of so many foreigners, a new sense of Englishness had been growing in the country. The several reissues of Magna Carta in every shire town helped convey to English people some idea of their rights. The new orders of mendicant or begging friars were another unifying development, acting in effect like newspapers carrying news of the latest events from town to town and enabling those living in isolated villages and hamlets to feel part of the whole. The mendicant friars were travelling brothers, usually Dominicans and Franciscans, who breathed a new ardour for truth into the Church by the sermons they preached at market crosses in the open air. Unconnected to vested interests, they had more critical minds than the regular clergy.

The sense of nationhood was further encouraged by the burst of intellectual energy at the universities of Oxford and Cambridge. There intelligent youths from every region were able to exchange ideas and learn from outstanding lecturers such as Robert Grosseteste, Bishop of Lincoln (who arrived in Oxford around 1230 and set up the Franciscans there) and his fellow Franciscan Roger Bacon. The towns too were now flourishing. A highly profitable trade in raw wool flowed between England and Flanders, from where it was dispersed to continental weaving towns to become cloth. And there had been a resurgence of writing in English: the song 'Sumer is icumen in' dates from this period, written in the language known as Middle English.

Yet in the hands of careless foreigners the efficient government of England was decaying. The Welsh princes once again began to expand south under Llywelyn ap Iorwerth and his grandson Llywelyn ap Gruffydd. Hitherto English kings had been able to rely on income from crown lands, but Richard I and Henry's father John had sold so much that there was little left. The crown was so bankrupt that a number of the king's servants were even convicted of highway robbery because he had not paid their salaries. Bad feeling against the king was becoming universal.

The discontent was fanned by a last attempt to get back the Angevin Empire. Henry III was an exceptionally devoted son. On John's death his mother Isabella of Angoulême had married the son of John's Poitevin enemy Hugh de Lusignan. By 1242 under the French king Louis IX the kingdom of France was continuing to expand dramatically at the expense of the traditional rights of the Poitevin barons. In response to the pleas of his mother and stepfather, Henry took an English army to invade Poitou. He was defeated so conclusively at the Battle of Taillebourg that by the next generation Poitou was directly ruled by the King of France. In 1259 by the Treaty of Paris the king accepted what had been fact since 1214, that only the Gascon region of Aquitaine remained to England. With this defeat yet another wave of foreigners, more of Henry III's numerous half-brothers and sisters, arrived in England. They too had to be accommodated like the Savoyards, with offices and bishoprics.

When Henry III took it upon himself, as a good son of the Church, to pay for the papal wars against the emperor, the country bent under new taxes. Although Frederick II was dead, the papacy was still determined to break up his empire. In return for English money, Henry's second son Edmund had been promised the kingdom of Sicily, while Henry's brother Richard of Cornwall was elected King of the Romans with papal support in 1257. The price tag for these grandiose plans was an enormous £135,000, which Henry had no hope of paying without raising fresh taxes. And by virtue of Magna Carta he could not raise those taxes without obtaining the permission of the Great Council of twenty-five barons. In 1258 he was duly forced to call a meeting of the Council.

The king's perpetually impoverished state meant he called the Great Council together on a regular basis to borrow from it. As these meetings became more frequent it began to be so much the custom for barons to have their say in the affairs of the realm that the Council began to be referred to as a Parliament (from the French *parler*, to talk). By the 1250s the barons were quite clear on their objectives. The closed court circle prevented them obtaining any influence. If the king wished to raise more taxes he must reconfirm the Charters and restore the offices of justiciar, chancellor and treasurer which Henry had done without since 1244.

Thus it was that early in 1258, when the king asked for that £135,000 to meet the cost of the pope's Crusade, the barons and knights rebelled. At the Great Council or Parliament at Westminster they declared that no more cash would be forthcoming from them until the government of England was reformed.

The leader of the revolt was a baron named Simon de Montfort, a Frenchman who had inherited the earldom of Leicester through his mother. De Montfort had begun his life in England as one of the unpopular foreign favourites, and had at first risen high because he was married to Henry III's sister. A fierce and passionate character, in 1248 de Montfort had been entrusted with restoring order to the last remnant of the Angevin Empire in mainland France, the southernmost county of Gascony, where he was made seneschal or governor. He was the son of the Simon de Montfort who had terrorized the Albigensian heretics in that region of France a generation earlier, and he used the same strong-armed techniques to subdue the independently minded towns and tempestuous nobles. But success was achieved at a price. The weak-minded king grew alarmed at the Gascon complaints about the severity of de Montfort's methods and began to take their side. The bitter and disillusioned Simon de Montfort rapidly became a rallying point for opposition to the king.

Simon de Monfort, leader of the barons in the civil war against Henry III.

In June 1258 a second Parliament met at Oxford, with the barons ready for war should Henry III not accede to their demands. Although the king and his cronies dubbed it the Mad Parliament, the Parliament's demands were coolly rational. There was to be a new agreement to supplement the conditions laid down in the Great Charter. Known as the Provisions of Oxford this stipulated that an inner circle or Council of Fifteen was to be chosen by Henry and the barons to administer the country with the king.

The Provisions of Oxford represented a further advance in limiting the royal powers. Their revolt was justified to de Montfort and others by the longstanding Judaeo-Christian doctrine of the righteousness of resisting tyrants, and the concept of the commonweal or good of the community. The Fifteen forced the king to expel all the foreigners (including the king's Poitevin half-brothers) from their official positions, appoint Englishmen as ministers and put an end to his expensive foreign adventures.

The rule of the Fifteen nominally lasted from 1259 to 1263. Jealousies among the barons saw it degenerate into a battle for leadership between de Montfort and Richard of Gloucester and resulted in what are known as the Barons' Wars. Soon the Lord Edward, Henry III's decisive eldest son, the future King Edward I, was intriguing to create a royalist faction within the Fifteen, where his chief accomplice was the Earl of Gloucester. With their backing Henry revoked the Provisions of Oxford, had the pope annul his obligations and went to war. But both sides were so evenly matched that the French king Louis IX was appealed to for judgement. The Mise of Amiens of 1264 was the result, which denounced the Provisions of Oxford as illegal.

But Simon de Montfort and his supporters would not abide by the Mise of Amiens and were determined to continue the war. At Lewes in Sussex on 14 May 1264 the decisive battle of the campaign was fought. Earl Simon, who was a brilliant general, captured both the king and his heir, and by a treaty called the Mise of Lewes the king's power was handed over to a committee of nine. In reality England was ruled by the great earl. However, the royalist opposition had not completely given up. With the Welsh marcher lords gathering for the king, and the queen raising a force on the French coast among her relations, Simon de Montfort saw that he had to act swiftly to get the whole of the country behind him. He therefore summoned in 1265 what is – misleadingly – known as the first English Parliament.

Unlike the earlier Parliaments, that of 1265 was not just a council of barons, but something which approximated more closely to the modern Houses of Parliament. A precursor of the Commons was convoked to discuss the government of the country with the barons and bishops (the Lords). Not only was every shire to elect two knights to give their views at the meeting, but a number of cities and boroughs in England were invited to send two representatives, who by the end of the century had become known as burgesses. The English were used to giving their views on a regular basis to the king, whether via sheriffs who reported on the results of a grand jury inquest or via merchants when the king wished to borrow money. But these were informal gatherings. The Parliament of 1265 was the first time in English history that all the estates of the realm met in the same place. But they did not merely give their assent to taxes. During their meeting all present contributed their views on matters of public policy. This would rapidly become a valued tradition.

A year later Simon de Montfort's rule came to an end. In the course of a de Montfort-led expedition to put down a royalist insurrection among the Welsh marcher lords on behalf of the captive Lord Edward, the king's son managed to escape. Many barons now joined their soldiers to those of the

Welsh marchers and swung to the side of Henry III. De Montfort was forced to recross the Severn and, on a blisteringly hot day in August 1265, face Edward and the marcher lords at the Battle of Evesham. Edward, who was soon to be famous as 'the Hammer of the Scots', outgeneralled de Montfort by surrounding him on all sides. As he surveyed the scene and saw that death was near, Simon said half admiringly, 'By the arm of St James they come on cunningly; God have mercy on our souls, for our bodies are the Lord Edward's!'

That was certainly true for Simon de Montfort, as his body was disembowelled and his head stuck on a pike before the Tower of London. Nevertheless his ideas lived on. The Lord Edward would himself adopt many notions of government that he had learned from Earl Simon. Though Henry III remained king until 1272, real power was now in the hands of his accomplished son.

By 1267 Edward had unified the country by pardoning most of the rebels by an agreement called the Dictum of Kenilworth. Large fines restored them to their confiscated estates. Under the Treaty of Shrewsbury, the new power in Wales, Llywelyn ap Gruffydd, who had allied himself to Simon de Montfort, was apparently bound to the new regime, entitled to call himself prince of all the country of Wales and head or overlord of the Welsh magnates. England, which had had rebels in every shire, was now so peaceful that the Lord Edward was able to depart for the Fourth Crusade for four years. On word of his father's death in 1272 he made a very leisurely return. Appointing regents, Edward I did not reappear in England until 1274, evidently having no fear of further revolts.

Edward I

(1272–1307)

Edward I was thirty-three years old when he succeeded to the throne. He is known as Edward I because he was the first Plantagenet king with that name though there had been two Anglo-Saxon predecessors, Edward the Elder and Edward the Confessor. He was nicknamed Longshanks for his great height, a feature which helped save him from being wounded in battle because his long arms gave him an advantage with a lance and opponents could never get near enough. He was a brilliant soldier, the man who finally broke the power of the Welsh rulers – which no one, not even the Romans, the world's finest soldiers, had succeeded in doing before. Holding the country down by a ring of famous castles which still stand today, he brought Wales permanently under English rule. In place of Llywelyn ap Gruffydd he made his eldest son the Prince of Wales. On his large but austere tomb of Purbeck marble in Westminster Abbey, itself a reflection of his stern personality, an unknown fourteenth-century hand scrawled the words 'malleus Scotorum', the Hammer of the Scots. But though Edward I hammered Scotland he never completely conquered her, and died within sight of that independent land.

The new king was named Edward because Henry III so greatly admired Edward the Confessor. Yet no one could have been less like that mild saint. Edward I more closely resembled his forbidding and decisive ancestor William the Conqueror. His experiences during his father's reign and in the course of what was in effect an apprenticeship in politics under Simon de Montfort had convinced him that the great earl's broad-based Parliament was the best way of uniting the country. The immediate challenge of Edward's reign came from Llywelyn ap Gruffydd, whom it took two Welsh campaigns to destroy. But the king's energies were chiefly bent on a series of legal reforms designed to put the royal government on a firm footing after the anarchy of the previous seventy-five years, and above all to limit the power of the magnates.

Edward I was inspired by a chivalric ideal of good kingship which had come to dominate the mindset of the age through the courtly romances of the previous century. He took a keen interest in King Arthur, whose supposed bones were reburied in a special ceremony performed before him and his queen at Glastonbury Abbey and he was famous for his Round Table banquets. The legendary devotion that existed between him and his wife Eleanor of Castile in an age when many marriages were dynastic affairs reveals a man of strong feelings. She accompanied him on most of his military campaigns, even attending him on his Crusade to the Holy Land in 1270. The legend that she saved the life of Edward there when he was wounded probably indicates that she had brought with her from her native Castile some of the superior medical knowledge of its Arab doctors. When Queen Eleanor died at Harby in Nottinghamshire in 1290, most unusually her distraught widower followed her cortège all the way to Westminster Abbey. He erected the celebrated series of Eleanor Crosses – twelve in all – to mark the places where her body rested as it was carried south. Some of them are still standing, though the best known, which gave Charing Cross its name, is a copy.

But Edward I was not just a romantic warrior, he was also immensely practical. He drew up new laws to encourage foreign merchants and reformed the coinage. He had a political motive here too, because he understood that if he promoted the mercantile interest or trade it would balance the power of the barons. Visiting his French territories on the way back from the Crusades, he was struck by the lawlessness of Guienne in Gascony. He therefore made it a policy to found new towns named *bastides* to encourage the growth of a law-abiding middle-class population of merchants and lawyers. No less practically, one of his first actions was to make sure the crown profited from England's growing wool trade, which had hugely expanded thanks to the Cistercian monks' pioneering work clearing forests to breed sheep. In 1275 he instituted a royal tax on every sack of wool, sheepskin and leather exported to northern Europe.

Under Edward I, more than ever the area round the Tower of London became the seat of government. He moved the mint there from Westminster and built the medieval palace we know today next to the White Tower. The plainness of his quarters, with the little chapel off his bedroom, at a time when the English decorative arts were at their richest suggests the hard purposefulness and lack of frivolity in his character which contrast so dramatically with his father's sensuous and artistic nature.

In 1274, the year of his coronation on his return from the Holy Land, Edward relaunched throughout the country that old Norman admini-strative tool, the inquest. Owing to the careless nature of his father's administration many of the baronial courts had taken over the jurisdiction and rights of the royal courts to the detriment of the king's power. Undertaking an investigation known as *Quo warranto* (Latin for 'by what right') royal commissioners travelled throughout the country inquiring into what rights each baron claimed for himself and whether they were justified. This could mainly be achieved through the production of a charter or piece of parchment sealed with the king's Great Seal, though in some places of course the right to hold a court stretched back to Anglo-Saxon times and was treated as being based on immemorial custom.

The First Statute of Westminster of 1275 summarized the results of this inquiry, while the Statute of Gloucester in 1278 curtailed many former baronial jurisdictions and replaced them with royal courts. The Third Statute of Westminster, generally known as *Quia emptores*, further weakened the power of the feudal party by allowing the sale of land without feudal obligation to the seller. Instead the buyer became the vassal of the seller's own lord – frequently the crown. The responsibility of the hundreds in England to prevent crime within their boundaries was reinforced by the Second Statute of Westminster, which also set down new arrangements for managing the fyrd – from now on to be known as the militia.

Edward I also attempted to check the authority of the Church. He put an end to the annual payment to the pope established by John as Rome's vassal, and laid down that the Church courts should never encroach on the jurisdiction of the common law. By the Statute of Mortmain of 1279 (from the Latin for dead hand, *mortua manu*) men and women were prevented from leaving their property to the Church without the crown's leave. All these measures made Edward I richer than his father had been and enabled him to do without the wealth of the Jewish community. Edward's passionately Christian religious convictions stimulated an anti-Semitic streak in him. Objecting to the high rates of interest the Jewish community charged for loans and accusing them of using foreign coins instead of the sterling he insisted upon, in 1290 he expelled the Jews from England. They did not return for three and a half centuries, when Oliver Cromwell asked them back.

In another display of force, complaints about the judiciary persuaded the king to have every one of the royal judges tried in 1289. All but four were dismissed from office. From 1292 advocacy was put on a more professional basis with the introduction of a rule that only lawyers trained by judges could appear in the royal courts. And the Inns of Court, which all barristers must belong to, date from this era as centres of legal education.

But the wars against Wales and Scotland were the dominating feature of Edward's reign. His campaign against the Welsh under Prince Llywelyn ap Gruffydd began as early as 1277. Prince Llywelyn had used the Treaty of Shrewsbury as an opportunity to enhance his powers. His aim was to overrun the lands of the English marcher lords and double the size of his dominion. When Edward heard that Llywelyn, who was engaged to Simon de Montfort's daughter Eleanor, was claiming to be the spiritual heir of the great rebel, he marched an army into north Wales. By the Treaty of Conway Llywelyn lost the overlordship of Wales and was reduced to being a petty prince once more. Most of his territory was put under English law with no regard for Welsh custom.

Oppressing the Welsh population, with English soldiers placed in every district, soon provoked another rebellion, led by Llywelyn and his brother Dafydd. Once again Edward led an army into north Wales and blockaded Prince Llywelyn in Snowdonia. But Llywelyn managed to flee through the English lines and escape to the upper Wye. There Prince Llywelyn made his last stand with the support of many of the ordinary people of the marches. But on 11 December he was killed at the Battle of Orewin Bridge.

This time Edward was less merciful in his dealings. Llywelyn's head was cut from his body, mounted on a pike and crowned with willow in cruel mockery of the way the Welsh used to crown their kings. In the tradition of the age it was left rotting outside the Tower of London as a warning. Though Prince Dafydd held out for a year longer, hidden in the woods and secret valleys around his home, by 1283 he too had been executed at Shrewsbury.

North Wales was organized along the lines of English local government. The Marcher lands remained semi-independent feudal fiefdoms until the sixteenth century, but most of Wales, particularly the north and coastal regions, was reorganized on the English model. It was divided into six

Harlech Castle, part of the ring of castles begun by Edward I in 1283 to hold down Wales after the conquest.

counties (Anglesey, Carmarthen, Caernarvon, Merioneth and Cardigan, the sixth being invented by Edward I and named Flintshire), each with its own sheriffs. The country was fenced off by a series of impregnable white castles, among them Caernarvon, Conway and Harlech. Edward's surviving eldest son, the future Edward II, was born at Caernarvon Castle in 1284. Legend has it that Edward shouted to the crowds assembled below, 'I will give you a prince who speaks no English,' and produced the newborn babe at the window. From 1301 the title Prince of Wales has always been given to the eldest son of the English monarch.

The conquest of Scotland, though achieved more rapidly than that of Wales, would in fact be a short-lived affair. By the end of the thirteenth century Scotland was a large, unified area ruled by one king and running from the Highlands in the north, which were populated by Celtic tribes who had intermarried with Norman settlers, down to the River Tweed in the south. In the south west the kingdom reached down from Galloway to the old Welsh kingdom of what is today known as Cumbria or the Lake District. So extensive a territory might prove a haven for enemies of England. On any reading, statecraft suggested that it might be better under English control.

The English and Scots had lived in peace for more than a hundred years since the Treaty of Falaise in 1174. But in 1286 the situation became far more volatile: King Alexander III, the last in the line of old Scottish kings, whom tragedy had deprived of his two male heirs within two years of one another, died unexpectedly. This left his seven-year-old granddaughter Margaret, the Maid of Norway, the only heir to the throne. But when she too died four years later, there was then no obvious heir. No fewer than thirteen claimants to the Scottish throne registered their claim. The most important were John Balliol and Robert Bruce, who were both descended in the female line. Their claims were sufficiently contentious for there to be a very real possibility of civil war. The Scottish magnates, many of whom held land in England, decided that Edward I was best placed to name the new king. But Edward would do so only at a price. Ever since Richard the Lionheart had commuted the Treaty of Falaise for money, so that the Scottish king only did homage to the English for his lands in England, the notion of the English king as overlord of the Scots had fallen away. Edward I agreed to judge the contest on condition that all the Scottish nobility and the claimants themselves first performed an act of homage to him as overlord of Scotland.

The chief claimants and the magnates were so anxious to secure Edward's support that they agreed. Assisted by 104 judges, Edward tried the suit for the succession to the Scottish throne. After much deliberation the crown was finally granted in 1292 to John Balliol, who was proclaimed king at Berwick-on-Tweed, then a Scottish town. Almost immediately, however, this apparent solution was thrown into doubt when war broke out once again between France and England over the English possessions on the Continent. Edward I led an English army to Gascony to defend it against the French king Philip IV, while Philip used his agents to stir up rebellion against his English enemy in Wales and Scotland. Although the Welsh rebellion was quickly put down, the Scots threat was far more powerful. From 1293 dates the series of diplomatic treaties and close links between Scotland and France against their mutual enemy England which is known as the Auld Alliance.

A certain amount of antagonism towards Edward I had already been aroused among the Scots barons. Legal appeals by ordinary Scotsmen from the local feudal courts to the royal courts of England were becoming common, partly because of the reputation for fairer, more professional justice in England. But the Scots were also angry at being asked to form part of the English feudal levy against the French army in Gascony. John Balliol was despised as a poor leader of men who was too much in the English king's pocket. He was now more or less supplanted as ruler of Scotland by a committee of twelve nobles similar to the Council of Fifteen which had ruled England for Henry III.

Threatened on all his borders, Edward I followed Earl Simon's example before him. By summoning in 1295 what is known as the Model Parliament he involved the whole English nation in the looming crisis and ratcheted the political organization of the country up another level. The Great Charter had limited the powers of the king by law. But Edward went a step further and stressed that in England the king's government was by the assent of the governed. The writ requesting the attendance of two elected representatives from each shire, and from cities and boroughs to join with the barons and bishops includes the celebrated phrase: 'What touches all should be approved of all.' The document went on, 'It is also very clear that common dangers should be met by measures agreed upon in common.'

Edward had been used to calling upon Parliament since the beginning of his reign. But this was the first time he accepted that, in return for voting new taxes for the war, he should allow the nation to enter into the councils of state. With the large sums of money voted him by the Model Parliament in 1296 he embarked on bringing Scotland to heel. Faced with Edward's huge invading army John Balliol gave up the crown of Scotland, Edward pronounced himself king, and the country was divided among his lieutenants on English county lines. To mark the change of rule, the great Stone of Scone or Stone of Destiny, where Scottish kings since the sixth century had been enthroned, was carted south to lie beneath the English king's throne in Westminster Abbey. There it remained until 1999, when in honour of the new Scottish Assembly, it came home after 700 years.

Edward I's throne in Westminster Abbey, built to hold the Scots' Stone of Scone.

The king now marched south, having apparently disposed of both of the King of France's allies, to prepare for war in Gascony. But in England he found that his war plans were resisted by both the clergy and the baronage. They had evidently taken Edward's injunction that what touches all must be approved by all strongly to heart. The Archbishop of Canterbury, Robert Winchelsea, declared that in accordance with Pope Boniface VIII's most recent bull the English clergy would pay no more taxes to the lay ruler. The Constable of England, Humphrey Bohun, Earl of Hereford, and Roger Bigod, Earl of Norfolk and Marshal of England, and most of the rest of the great magnates meeting in Parliament at Salisbury in 1297 refused to go to Gascony as ordered. Edward stormed off there by himself. Denied money by the estates of the realm he financed the French expedition by the illegal tax known as the Maltolt: this entailed his soldiers confiscating all the merchants' wool and releasing it in return for gold.

But the English magnates were the king's equal in decisive behaviour. As soon as Edward was in Gascony, encouraged by the Archbishop of Canterbury, Bohun and Bigod took his son Edward of Caernarvon prisoner and refused to release him until the king had reissued Magna Carta. They also insisted on the addition of new provisions: that the Maltolt be abolished and that henceforth it be deemed illegal to raise taxes without the permission of Parliament (in place of the twenty-five barons of Magna Carta). This process is known as the *Confirmatio Cartarum*. Edward I was in no position to refuse, and authorized the Confirmation without further ado.

His troubles were far from over. A great popular rebellion in Scotland brought Longshanks hurrying back from the continent. Under a Scottish knight named Sir William Wallace (known as Braveheart) a series of risings had broken out all over the country, and at the decisive battle of Stirling

Bridge in September 1297 Wallace dramatically defeated the king's representative in Scotland, Earl Warenne. By the end of the year Scotland had expelled the English, and Wallace was burning all their border towns.

Wallace's supporters tended to be ordinary people, rather than Scots nobles who frequently held estates in England as well as Scotland and therefore had every reason for not antagonizing the English king. Indeed, most of his ragged army were so impoverished that they could not afford a horse. But Wallace himself was a tactician of genius, and the Battle of Falkirk the following year was a very close-run thing. Only Edward I's employment of archers trained in the esoteric art of the longbow, whose superiority he had first observed during the Welsh wars, defeated Wallace's use of squares and pikes designed to impale the superb English cavalry.

Problems with the baronage soon required the king's presence in the south. It was not until 1303 that he could return to the north and make sure of his Scottish kingdom. By now he was a sick man. Though he was in his late sixties, an elderly man by the standards of those days, he refused to be borne in the litter that his advisers felt would be appropriate for the long journey north. Instead he rode at the head of the army to besiege Stirling Castle, the key to the country's defences. So close was the king to the castle walls during the siege that a crossbow bolt lodged itself in his saddle. But, though his men begged him to retire, the stiff-backed old warrior refused, and sat on his charger day after day watching as the Scots threw Greek fire and boiling oil at their attackers.

When Stirling at last fell, the conquest of Scotland seemed a foregone conclusion. Wallace was captured, taken south and hanged, drawn and quartered, and his head joined Prince Llywelyn's above the gate at the Tower of London. English rule was reimposed. Scotland was divided into four areas to be governed overall by Edward I's nephew John of Brittany, while Edward left for the south. But no sooner had he departed than a new revolt broke out, led by another of Scotland's greatest heroes, Robert the Bruce.

Bruce, grandson of John Balliol's rival, had initially been one of the Scots nobles who supported English rule in Scotland, until the brutality with which English soldiers treated the Scots aroused his ire (great ladies like the Countess of Buchan had been humiliated by being kept in cages suspended from castle walls). In 1306, during an assignation between Bruce and John Comyn in a lonely church in Dumfries to hatch a plot against English rule, the hot-tempered Bruce murdered Comyn. Comyn also had a claim to the Scottish throne and Bruce seems to have been unable to prevent himself seizing the moment to put paid to his rival. Although Bruce was rendered an outlaw by this act, which was made more heinous by being committed on holy ground, the ordinary people began to rally to him, with many joining him at his hideout in the hills. From there an irresistible momentum seized the Scots. Fighting broke out everywhere, the English were expelled from the country, and at the end of that year Robert the Bruce was crowned King of Scotland at Scone.

Although Edward I was by now almost seventy years of age and his health was poor, his will was as strong as ever. For the third time he set out from the south to enforce his rule on the recalcitrant Scots. But on 7 July 1307 he died at Burgh on Sands within sight of his goal. The fierce old king had demanded that his bones be boiled down so they could be carried before the English army when they crossed the border on their way north. His son, Edward II, was made of rather different stuff. Despite his promise to his father to continue his campaign, he abandoned it and retreated south to the company of a handsome Gascon knight called Piers Gaveston.

Seal of King Robert the Bruce, who defended Scottish independence against Edward I.

Edward II

(1307–1327)

Edward I had managed the baronage or feudal party fairly well. But the son who inherited the throne had none of his father's strategic skills nor the English Justinian's serious-mindedness. As might have been expected with such a father, Edward II had been well educated in warfare and kingship, but his character remained incurably frivolous. Although his reign lasted twenty years, he reigned rather than ruled, and early on lost the battle for power.

Edward II was twenty-three years old when he came to the throne. He was nearly as tall and handsome a man as Longshanks, but he had inherited nothing of his strength of character and was very easily influenced. He admired Piers Gaveston for his ready wit and sharp tongue, though the Gascon's insolence was precisely what made him loathed by the English baronage. Upon his father's death Edward II's first action after abandoning the Scottish campaign was to recall Gaveston, whom his father had banished for his decadence, back to court. He married him to his niece and reinstated him with full honours and estates and the royal earldom of Cornwall. But Gaveston's relentless search for pleasure with his boon companion the king soon had the royal government grinding to a halt, and by 1308 the barons in Parliament were calling for his expulsion from the kingdom.

Edward II hurriedly ensured Gaveston's removal from the country by appointing him to the governorship of Ireland, and offered many concessions to Parliament if the Gascon knight were allowed back to England. But, though Gaveston was permitted to return, by 1310 the barons in Parliament were insisting on a new programme of reforms to be set out by a steering committee of the baronage and bishops called the Lords Ordainers. A year later this new committee pronounced that Gaveston was to be exiled permanently, that all ministers were to be appointed on their advice and that the king was not to make war or leave the country without their permission. Though Edward ordered Gaveston back into the country, the barons besieged the favourite in Scarborough Castle and soon after murdered him. Edward II made a few feeble attempts to avenge himself on the baronage, but he was more dependent on them than ever to push back the Scots who, under Robert the Bruce, were threatening to occupy northern England.

According to the story, the audacious Bruce was encouraged to persevere in his campaign under almost impossible conditions when he was hiding out in an old croft in Galloway watching a spider spin its web. By 1314 he and his followers had conquered most of Scotland and crucially won over the majority of the Scottish baronage to his side. All the castles with which Edward had garrisoned the country were in his men's hands except for Stirling, a stronghold of enormous strategic value because it was the gateway to the Highlands. Even the languorous Edward II saw that he would have to lead an army north to rescue his garrison. In the meantime Robert the Bruce, though considerably outnumbered, had prepared the ground to draw the English army into a trap. He would defeat them before they could relieve the siege.

The Scottish army was drawn up in a strong position on rising ground behind the little stream or burn of the Bannock, a tributary of the River Forth. Separating the two armies was a very marshy piece of land full of bogs and pools which Bruce had made more treacherous by secretly digging pits and lining them with stakes. All went according to Bruce's plan: the English cavalry charged and came to grief on the sharpened stakes. Meanwhile the Scots cavalry destroyed the formidable English and Welsh bowmen, Edward having failed to protect them with infantry.

The English army was already in a state of panic-stricken confusion when over the horizon appeared what seemed to be fresh Scottish reinforcements, though they were only camp followers dressed up. The English nerve broke completely. The king himself set a poor example to his men when his armoured figure, the distinctive gold crown encircling his steel helmet, was seen hurrying away from the battlefield. At this his armies also turned and ran. It was a total rout. Next day the exhausted English garrison of Stirling Castle opened its gates to Robert the Bruce. He was king of an independent Scotland in fact as well as name.

The humiliation of the Battle of Bannockburn put more power than ever into the hands of the Lords Ordainer, who were now controlled by Edward's first cousin Thomas of Lancaster, son of Edward I's brother Edmund. Under Lancaster's influence the Lords Ordainer proved just as inadequate as the king at governing efficiently. The rule of law on which Edward I had prided himself began to fall away, as private wars between the king's and Lancaster's retainers took the place of peace. The whole of the English administration began to collapse, and the north of England was increasingly subject to lightning border raids by the Scots. To add to the atmosphere of catastrophe and chaos, 1315 and 1316 were years of famine, with incessant rain throughout those summers preventing the corn from ripening. Even the royal household experienced difficulties in obtaining bread. Thousands of people died and the misery was intensified when cattle disease broke out all over the country. The beasts were slaughtered in their thousands to prevent it spreading further.

A moderate party now arose among the barons headed by the Earl of Pembroke, who sought to control the king by a new council and curtail Thomas of Lancaster's activities. But Edward II began to favour over the rest two barons of Pembroke's party, brothers named Despenser, showering them with titles and lands. In 1321 a full Parliament met, led by Thomas of Lancaster, to launch an attack on the Despensers and banish the new favourites. Showing unexpected spirit, the king went to war against Lancaster's chief supporters and the Despensers' chief enemies, two marcher lords named Roger Mortimer and the Earl of Hereford (son of the magnate who had resisted Edward I). He crossed the Severn, crushed Mortimer and recalled the Despensers in triumph, while Thomas of Lancaster fled north. But at Boroughbridge the king's men caught up with Lancaster, dragged him out of the church where he was claiming sanctuary and struck off his head before his castle at Pontefract.

Edward and his new favourites now seemed secure. All the leaders of what could have been a serious rebellion were either in the Tower, like Mortimer, or dead. For the next four years the Despensers ruled England in the weak king's name. Courting popular favour for their support, at a Parliament held at York in 1322 they annulled the ordinances imposed on the king by the Lords Ordainer on the ground that they had been passed by a Parliament of barons only. They declared the 'commonality of the realm' – that is, shire knights and burgesses – had to be involved in such decisions if they were to become law. This was another important step in the development of the powers of the Commons.

Nevertheless the Despensers had many of the faults which had made Piers Gaveston loathed. They were arrogant and greedy and just as keen to accumulate any lands and titles in their master's gift. In order to end the chaos caused in the Borders by the Scots raids, Edward II made an attempt at invading Scotland, only for it to end in humiliation. The Scots chased him out of the country having refused to do battle, and very nearly took him prisoner at Byland Abbey. In 1323 a truce was effected between the two countries, a *de facto* admission that England recognized Robert the Bruce as king. Meanwhile under the Despensers' lackadaisical rule the infrastructure of the government appeared to be rotting before the nation's eyes. Taxes were not paid, the courts did not pursue justice and officials were detested.

The situation needed only a leader to turn this simmering resentment into rebellion. In 1324 such a leader emerged in the shape of the marcher lord

Roger Mortimer, Lancaster's old henchman, when he escaped from the Tower of London to join many exiled Lancastrians in Paris. By coincidence Edward II's estranged wife Isabella was there with her son, the future Edward III, visiting her brother, the French king Charles IV, so that Edward might do homage for Gascony and Ponthieu. She and Mortimer were united by their hatred of the Despensers: the queen because of their power over her husband, Mortimer because they had confiscated his estates.

A natural alliance was soon supplemented by passion. Ignoring the king's pleas to return, Queen Isabella began to live openly with Mortimer and plot the invasion of England to rid the country of the Despensers. But the flagrant behaviour of the wife of the King of England with a rebel aroused great unease at the French court, and beyond. Charles IV was only too delighted to obey the pope and expel his sister, who was becoming known as the 'She-wolf of France'. Taking her thirteen-year-old son Edward with her, Isabella went to Hainault and betrothed him to the Count of Hainault's daughter Philippa. Given such an alliance to the important country of England, the count was only too glad to provide soldiers for Isabella's and Mortimer's invasion of England on behalf of Prince Edward.

Proclaiming that she and Mortimer had come to liberate the nation from the tyranny of the Despensers, in 1326 Queen Isabella landed at Orwell in Essex and advanced to London. She was rapidly joined by all the most important magnates of the kingdom, including Thomas of Lancaster's brother Henry. Meanwhile Londoners not only opened their gates to Isabella and Mortimer but murdered one of Edward II's envoys, the Bishop of Exeter. Against such a united opposition, the king's party was powerless. Edward II and the Despensers now made for the west hoping to reach the safety of the Despenser estates in Glamorgan, but all were captured. The two Despensers were summarily executed, the younger brother's mutilated body being hung from gallows fifty feet high. Edward was brought back in chains to London and his reign declared to be at an end. Prince Edward, a gauche but soldierly youth apparently under his fascinating mother's spell, was declared Edward III.

Edward II was meanwhile transported under heavy guard from one castle in the west to another. Before long the new government decided that alive he offered too much of a rallying point to their enemies, and in 1327 he was put to death at Berkeley Castle in Gloucestershire by means of a red-hot poker which was stuck up him. It is said that his screams as he died were so loud that they could be heard for miles around. In order to pre-empt claims that he had been murdered, Mortimer – who was in effect the ruler of England – ordered Edward II's naked corpse to be exhibited. And indeed there was no visible mark on it. After this, the body was buried quietly in the Abbey Church of Gloucester.

Edward III

(1327–1377)

Edward III would rule England for fifty years, but he is most remembered as the great warrior who with his son the Black Prince led the English to victory after victory in the Hundred Years War. The Battle of Agincourt won by Edward III's great-grandson Henry V was an apparent vindication of this protracted attempt to claim the French throne. It enabled Henry to marry the French king's daughter Katharine, and his infant son Henry VI was briefly both King of England and King of France. Moreover, Edward III's victories secured Aquitaine for England and thus almost a quarter of the territory of today's France, as well as gaining the important French Channel port of Calais. The immense popularity the war brought him meant that the crown's authority was never in doubt for much of his reign, and the barons' energies were taken up by the French campaign. At the king's extended Gothic castle at Windsor countless great feasts and tournaments took place which appealed to the spirit of the age, modelled on the hundred-year-old cult of King Arthur, the Dark Age chieftain who had been transformed by the courtly romances into a perfect gentle knight and the summit of the chivalric ideal.

The booty from the Hundred Years War paid for an ambitious and popular royal building programme which reinforced the sense of Englishness reviving across the country. Edward III's age marks the beginning of the peculiarly English style of late-Gothic architecture named Perpendicular. In contrast to the flowing lines of the contemporary Gothic style prevailing on the continent, English building whether at Gloucester Cathedral, St George's Chapel Windsor or Winchester Cathedral, is constructed on sterner, more geometric lines. From 1362 onwards English officially replaced Latin as the language of the English law courts. One of England's greatest writers, Geoffrey Chaucer, was born

William of Wykeham, the founder of New College, Oxford, in 1379 and Winchester School, in 1382.

around 1344. A member of a well-to-do family of wine merchants, Chaucer had a cosmopolitan upbringing and spoke at least four languages. His fascination with French poetry and with the writings of Dante and Boccaccio was intensified by a career as a diplomat in the royal service. So influential were his own works, such as *The Book of the Duchess* (which marks the death of John of Gaunt's wife Blanche of Lancaster) and ultimately *The Canterbury Tales*, that by the end of the fourteenth century English had permanently replaced Latin and French as the language of England's litera-ture. William Langland's *Piers Plowman* and the anonymous *Sir Gawain and the Green Knight* also testify to the new creative spirit abroad.

Despite the era's military glory and the king's personal popularity, Edward III's reign was also a time of considerable social misery. In 1348 the bubonic plague known as the Black Death arrived to wreak havoc on the population of England as it did in the rest of Europe. Carried by the black rat on Genoese ships, this curse of God (or so it seemed to contemporary observers) had originated in Asia, where the Republic of Genoa's vast trading operation had its most extensive dealings. In England it killed an astonishing one-fifth of the population with-in the year, ultimately being responsible for

Geoffrey Chaucer, author of *The Canterbury Tales* and a diplomat in the service of Edward III.

the deaths of one-third of the population. In France and Italy half the population died. The pessimism that this brought to the succeeding European generation was similar to that experienced after the First World War. The death of labourers able to produce food ensured that the English population declined for almost a century. It would not be until the mid-fifteenth century that numbers began to increase again.

The shortage of labour undermined the system of serfdom or villeinage introduced by the Normans which forbade families to move from their local lords' domain. So many landowners were desperate for men to work their fields that a 'no questions asked' policy towards runaway serfs was widely operated, and by the end of the fourteenth century the institution was in tatters. But attempts on the part of agricultural workers to better themselves by demanding a living wage were met by swingeing government legislation. The Statute of Labourers of 1351 kept wages down to the level prevailing before the inflation prompted by the Black Death. Many landowners took the decision to turn their fields over to sheep runs because grazing required little labour. Former serfs were grateful if they could find any work at all. This discontent was mirrored in risings or *jacqueries* all over western Europe, and is reflected in *Piers Plowman*.

For numerous landowners sheep-farming was a swift route to profit. The thirteenth and fourteenth centuries were the high point of English wool export, and by Edward III's reign woollen textile manufacture was replacing raw wool as England's chief export or staple. East Anglia did not have the hills and rushing streams that would see the thirteenth-century invention of water-powered mills make areas like the Yorkshire and Lancashire Pennines, and the west country, centres of woollen manufacture for hundreds of years. But the region's soft water (integral to the textile production process) and the fine wool from its native sheep resulted in a much admired material known as worsted after the Norfolk village of that name – a direct result of Edward encouraging Flemish weavers in 1331 to initiate the English into the secrets of fine cloth. The immense personal riches of individual clothiers who controlled the wool staple, the customs entrepôts of the export wool trade, enabled them to take over the Jewish community's position as moneylenders to the king.

The first three years of Edward's kingship were dominated by the regency of his mother Isabella and Roger Mortimer. But their hold on power was not to last. Mortimer's greed, his open attempt to make himself the overlord of Wales where the Mortimer estates were based and the irregularity of the couple's union soon made them extremely unpopular. Their failure to prevent the French king Charles IV seizing most of Gascony added to a feeling of disorder and betrayal. Though Bordeaux and Bayonne remained, the important and historic English wine trade – at a time when wine was the equivalent of clean water for drinking – was dramatically curtailed.

In 1330 Edward seized power. He had just fathered his first child, the warrior known as the Black Prince, and was far more confident and able to stand up for himself. While Isabella and Mortimer slept at Nottingham Castle, the young king – accompanied by a band of armed soldiers – stole in through an underground passage and dragged Mortimer from his bed, closing his ears to his mother's cries for mercy. Mortimer was hung at Tyburn Tree, the gallows for common criminals which until the late eighteenth century stood at the junction of Edgware Road and Marble Arch. Queen Isabella was exiled to the manor of Castle Rising, where she lived on for another thirty years.

Almost immediately the young king was hurled into war. On the death of Robert the Bruce his son David had become King of Scotland, but by 1332 King David lost his throne to John Balliol's son Edward. The following year Edward III recaptured Berwick-on-Tweed from the Scots at the Battle of Halidon Hill and made the border town permanently part of England. But on the outbreak of the Hundred Years War, once the bulk of Edward III's soldiers were across the Channel, David returned and was recognized once more as king of the Scots.

In many ways the Hundred Years War was simply a continuation of earlier wars between France and England over the remains of the Angevin Empire on French soil, such as the conflict recently lost by Isabella and Mortimer. Pride and the wine trade made it impossible for Edward III to put up with the continuous attacks on the French kings on Gascony. Likewise the French kings could not abandon their longstanding policy of uniting all the territories on the French continent under the French crown. The diplomatic situation was made more volatile by the threat of the French king's support for the Bruce cause. But a freshly complicating factor was the struggle for mastery over France's north-east neighbour, Flanders – England's biggest trading partner.

The immensely lucrative clothing trade of Flanders was run by powerful, independently minded merchants. They had little use for their impoverished count, whose feudal rights over them seemed irrelevant relics of an almost forgotten age. Their interests were with England, whose wool had made them rich. But the Count of Flanders, who remained nominally their overlord, was the vassal of the French king. For some time there had been disagreements between the Flemish burghers or clothing-town leaders and the count over their liberties and powers. When the count opted to settle them by force with the aid of French troops, the Flemish burghers' leader James van Artevelde declared independence and in 1338 made a separate alliance with Edward III. The vigorous English king would give the Flemish clothing towns and their trade the protection they needed.

The Battle of Sluys, which is said to be the first naval battle in English history, is generally accepted as the beginning of the Hundred Years War. In 1340 a large French fleet of over 200 men-of-war (including warships from the Norman and Genoese navies) crowded the sea at the port of Sluys to block all English ships reaching Flanders for the war effort. Against the advice of his Great Council the king sailed up in person to attack it. He had gathered a smaller fleet in the Orwell Estuary made up in a more haphazard fashion, from every ship he could find at anchor in the southern ports of England. The chance of ridding the country of the French naval menace was too good to miss.

The battle secured the freedom of the Channel for the next thirty years. It was the first occasion when the French got a taste of the longbow, the weapon which (though developed by the Welsh) would make the English armies invincible in pitched battle for the best part of a century. No contemporary weapon had the same capacity for rapid fire, and in the hands of a master it defeated the more technologically advanced crossbow.

The longbow was so difficult to use that archers had to be brought up practising the art from boyhood to develop the muscles in the arm required for the enormously heavy weapon. At six feet long and three feet broad when drawn back to the ear, the longbow was taller that most Welsh and Englishmen. Lacking the craft traditions which could transform a piece of elm into a perfectly balanced bow, and which had made archery a national sport in England, the French army was never able to master the longbow. Once this became clear, in order to secure a continuous supply of longbowmen Edward III forbade all sports other than archery on the village green.

At Sluys the hail of English arrows drove so many Frenchmen to jump overboard or dive for cover that all 200 ships were captured. So embarrassing was this episode for France's naval prestige that her commanders did not dare tell Philip VI. It was left to his jester to inform him. 'The English are cowards,' he told his royal master as he waited for news of the battle; 'they did not have the courage to jump into the sea like the French and the Normans.'

With the Channel secured, Edward III could afford to make a truce with the French, though he returned to England to raise more money for a new land campaign against them. The war meanwhile had shifted into a game with higher stakes. Through his mother Isabella, Edward III had a strong claim to the French throne since Isabella's brother King Charles IV had died without male heirs. The French crown therefore passed to the head of the more distant Valois branch of the family, who ascended the throne as Philip VI. But it was arguable that Edward, as the former king's nephew, had a nearer claim.

In 1340 Edward III had revived his claim to be King of France. This was partly to please the Flemings, who did not like being seen to rebel against their feudal overlord. If Edward III was their overlord, their rebellion was given legitimacy. But pride also convinced Edward that the war could not be dropped as long as his claim existed. For the next century the English and French were in a state of constant warfare. Indeed, it would not be until the nineteenth century that the English crown abandoned its claim to the throne of France. Until that date in the King of England's coat of arms the fleur-de-lis or lilies of France are to be seen side by side with the lions rampant of England.

In 1346 Philip VI's forces launched such a fierce attack on Edward's garrison in Gascony that the English seemed in danger of being expelled from the continent for ever. As a diversionary tactic Edward invaded northern France on the Cotentin Peninsula of Normandy. At first he was successful. Philip abandoned the Gascon campaign to counter the English army, which was sweeping through Normandy under the command of the English king. With him was his son, the sixteen-year-old Prince of Wales, whose black armour earned him the nickname the Black Prince. Laying waste to the country, they moved up the Seine until they were in sight of the French king's capital of Paris. But Philip VI now rallied. Edward was forced to turn north-east towards the coast and the friendly Flemish frontier, with the French armies in hot pursuit. Beating off the French cavalry which guarded the ford that emerged at Blanche Taque at low tide, Edward crossed the Somme. Then he decided he could flee no longer. He must stand and fight. He took his stand at the little village of Crécy in his hereditary county of Ponthieu.

The Battle of Crécy made Edward III's reputation on the European continent. His men were outnumbered by over two to one, yet by clever positioning and the use of the longbow alongside the infantry the French army was destroyed. Crécy established the superiority of English tactics to the French cavalry charge. Thanks to this great victory, Edward was able to secure the strategically crucial port of Calais to the east. This became a pivotal English stronghold as both entrepôt and garrison. It was not until 1558 that the town which gave England command of the Channel was returned to its rightful owners.

Choosing where to give battle gave Edward III an extra edge at Crécy. He elected to do so on ground that sloped up to a windmill, from where he himself watched the battle. The Welsh and English archers were drawn up in a pattern like a chevron so that those behind could fire over and at the same time cover their colleagues below. The cavalry on whom the French were relying for victory would have to charge uphill – no easy task for warhorses with knights in armour on their backs. Try as they might, charge as they might, in the way that had made them famous, the French cavalry were mown down in mid-gallop by the English archers. Fifteen times they started out again, fifteen times they were forced back by the longbowmen under the command of the Black Prince.

The next morning among the many thousands slain were found to be the King of France's brother, the Duke of Alençon, and the old blind King of Bohemia. The latter had insisted on joining the battle and had told his knights to lead him to the front line of the battle, 'that I too may have a stroke at the English'. Edward III and the Black Prince found the sightless king's body and the helmet surmounted with the Bohemian crest of three ostrich feathers which had rolled a little way away. The Black Prince was so moved by the blind king's gallantry that he took the three ostrich feathers for his own crest, as well as the king's motto '*Ich Dien*' (German for 'I serve'). Both crest and motto have been the Prince of Wales's ever since. Crécy, as Edward III said, was the day that the Black Prince won his spurs.

Though war was cruel and ruthless its perpetrators considered it to be leavened by what is known as the spirit of chivalry. Deriving from the French word for 'mounted knight' and influenced by the Arab east, chivalry was a formal code that insisted on the protection of the weak and the victor's honourable treatment of his defeated enemy. Some of our more humane instincts, such as the strict rules governing the treatment of prisoners of war laid down in the Geneva Convention, derive from this code.

To the barons and knights of the fourteenth century one of the most admired examples of the chivalric code in operation was exemplified by the conduct of all the chief participants in the siege of Calais. Five of the town's leading burghers had offered their lives to Edward III if he would spare the rest of the citizens. Edward coldly sent a message that he would receive them only if they were naked but for their shirts and were holding the rope halters from which they would be hanged. His wife Queen Philippa was impressed by the nobility of the burghers, however, and begged him to spare them. Edward complied: the courtesy of deference to the weaker sex which was also part of the knightly code secured their lives.

On his return to England in 1348, Edward III celebrated Crécy by creating the Order of the Garter, made up of twenty-four knights and the king himself. Legend has it that its motto derives from the tie or garter used to hold up ladies' stockings. One night at a ball held at Windsor, Edward is supposed to have wrapped round his arm a garter which had fallen from the leg of his dancing companion. When he saw the shocked faces of his guests the expansive king is said to have quipped, 'Honi soit qui mal y pense' ('Shame to him who evil thinks'). Whatever its origins the Garter remains one of Britain's highest honours, and continues to be in the personal gift of the sovereign. Every year in June a service to commemorate the order takes place at Windsor in the Chapel of St George, where it was founded.

During these years many an impoverished English knight took unofficial advantage of the English claim to the French throne by joining what were called the Free Companies. These were armed companies of Englishmen who roamed the continent ostensibly fighting for the English king but in fact making their fortune from plunder. Since the ideals of chivalry were at their height, to be a knight and relentlessly involved in warfare had the elements of a vocation; this was only encouraged by the king's personal cult of the tournament.

The activities of these adventurers guaranteed that hostility between the two countries would flare up into war again. In September 1356 the Black Prince had led a small army of around 1,800 men from Bordeaux up the Garonne into central France, penetrating as far as the Loire Valley, and was returning to Gascony laden with his new war chest when the new King of France, Philip VI's daring son John, cut him off with 8,000 troops at Poitiers. Though he was heavily outnumbered, the day was the Black Prince's. The French fell into the same trap of setting their cavalry against the English longbow, and once more came to grief. In the heat of battle the impetuous and brave warrior King John was captured and was later taken to England in triumph to join the king of the Scots in captivity (David II had been taken at the Battle of Neville's Cross in 1346). It was a considerable humiliation for the French when their king, riding a cream charger, was led through the bunting-decorated streets of London. Because chivalry demanded that the French king be better horsed than the Black Prince, John's conqueror trotted beside him on a small pony.

With the French king in his hands Edward III had the leverage in 1360 to negotiate the extremely advantageous Treaty of Brétigny. The whole of Aquitaine (including Poitou and the Limousin) was to be returned. Edward was also confirmed in possession of Ponthieu and Calais, as well as being granted a ransom in gold so enormous that it was never paid in full. In return he abandoned his claim to the French throne.

But this was the peak of English triumph. Hatred of the English, who for twenty years had ruined French agriculture with their wars, began to unite the whole of France behind the new king Charles V, and the ancient regional loyalties from which the English had benefited were further eroded when the desperate French were devastated by a new wave of the bubonic plague in 1362, and by the famine which followed in its wake. In 1369 Aquitaine revolted against the Black Prince.

Edward the Black Prince's most recent adventure in Spain, to restore Pedro the Cruel to the throne of Castile, had been inconclusive and very expensive. When he attempted to pay for the expedition by new taxes on Aquitaine the magnates outside Gascony, who had become used to thinking of themselves as Frenchmen, seized their chance. They had not wished to be vassals of the fierce and warlike prince, as agreed by the Treaty of Brétigny. They called to Charles V for help. On the grounds that the treaty had not been completely implemented and that he was still the Aquitainians' overlord, Charles summoned the Black Prince to answer the charges before the Parliament of Paris. When Prince Edward responded that he would debate with Parliament with a helmet on his head and 60,000 men the war began again.

This time, however, it was an even more pointless and destructive affair. The Black Prince had contracted a wasting disease on the Spanish campaign and was too ill to sit on a horse. Instead he was jolted in a litter from city to city, burning and plundering in the name of his father who had revived his claim to the French throne. In 1370 the sack of Limoges, capital of the Limousin which had revolted against him, blackened his reputation for ever. When he ordered every man, woman and child to be massacred by his soldiers in front of him, it gave the lie to the notion of war as a chivalrous pursuit.

For the rest of Edward III's reign the French showed that they had learned their lesson. Under Charles V and his superb Breton commander Bertrand de Guesclin, they refused to meet the English in pitched battle and instead allowed them to wear out their strength in fruitless local campaigns – which just added to the bad feeling against the English. The Black Prince returned to England to die and was replaced by his younger brother, Edward III's fourth surviving son John of Gaunt (for Ghent, where he was born), Duke of Lancaster.

But the trail of ruin John of Gaunt left as he marched in 1373 from Calais on the north-east coast down to Bordeaux in the south-west achieved nothing. It also killed half his soldiers, who succumbed to hunger and exposure. When the French seized control of the Channel with the help of the Castilian navy and prevented reinforcements reaching the English troops, the war petered out. By the time of Edward III's death in 1377 the achievements of the great battles of the earlier part of his reign had been completely undone. For all the excitement of war, other than Calais the English possessions were less now than they had been under Isabella and Mortimer, consisting only of the few coastal towns of Bayonne, Bordeaux, Brest and Cherbourg.

From the early 1370s on, Edward III declined into premature senility. The country was ruled meanwhile by the squabbling factions in the King's Council – the supporters of John of Gaunt versus those of his elder brother, the dying Black Prince. Just as the main participants in the triumph of England were dead or decaying, the country itself was in crisis. Ever since the Black Death had killed a third of the population in the year 1348–9, chaos had prevailed at all levels of life. A series of droughts and poor harvests had reduced food supplies in England and Europe to dangerously low levels in any case, and even before the plague much of the European population had been suffering from malnutrition. So they were less able to resist the deadly disease, which began with black boils erupting from under the skin in the groin and armpits. In almost all cases it ended with death a few hours later.

But 1348–9 was not the end of the plague in England. In 1362 it returned, as it did in France and elsewhere, and again in 1369. The figures speak for themselves. Before the Black Death the English population is generally estimated to have been about five and half million. By the end of the fourteenth century there were two million fewer. The optimism which had accompanied the material prosperity of the years before 1348 was replaced by an anger and discontent that could not be assuaged by religion and would soon give rise to the Peasants' Revolt. The flow of international trade which had been so profitable for everyone had already been faltering under the impact of the war. Now it fell to a trickle.

The natural order of centuries was overthrown when serfs and land-owners were carried off so fast and in such numbers that there was no one left to remember the feudal arrangements, which had often been maintained by oral tradition. Attitudes to authority were changed too, as the English became less naturally deferential. When the response to the plague of wealthy bishops and barons was to shut themselves up in their castles or leave for the continent, they lost the instinctive respect of the locals. Even the parish priests no longer commanded much automatic obedience, though their behaviour during the Black Death had been exemplary. They had persistently nursed their highly contagious flocks after their families abandoned them, with the result that the death rate among priests was higher than among ordinary folk.

Such is the perversity of human nature that in an age before scientific medicine this was taken as a sign that priests were no holier than other men. Not only had they not been spared from what was commonly considered to be God's vengeance on a wicked race but they were being singled out by him. By the late fourteenth century their self-sacrifice had produced a great shortage of priests to serve in parishes. Very few were left to preach against the dark pessimism and obsession with death seen in the paintings and poetry of the time.

Moreover, for some time in this country there had been a growing anti-clerical sentiment. Ever since 1309 when a French pope removed the Papal Court or Curia to Avignon in southern France, all the popes elected had been French, so that for the next sixty years until 1378 the papacy had come to be seen by the English government as an appendage of their enemy the French king. At Edward III's behest the Statute of Provisors and the Statute of Praemunire asserted English independence from the pope over Church appointments and banned appeals to foreign courts. In 1366 Parliament itself demanded the revocation of King John's agreement to be the pope's vassal and put an end to the annual tax sent to Avignon instead of Rome.

In this feverish religious vacuum and unsettled atmosphere the stress on personal responsibility of a new group of preachers named the Lollards offered an attractive new direction for the disillusioned. The Lollards were followers of a radical Oxford theologian named John Wyclif, whose teachings anticipated many elements of the Reformation. Wyclif believed that the ultimate source of religious authority was not the priesthood but the Bible. With his regular denunciations of the clergy, he also provided a convenient weapon for John of Gaunt in the continued struggle for control of the King's Council.

Thanks to his first marriage to the hugely wealthy northern heiress Blanche of Lancaster, John of Gaunt was now the greatest magnate in the country. He was anyway a swaggering figure with a private life of such epic dimensions that it aroused the antagonism of the English bishops, who formed part of the Black Prince's faction. Gaunt was therefore leader of the anti-clerical party. Using as intellectual justification Wyclif's theory that priests should not be involved in politics, Gaunt got Alice Perrers, Edward III's mistress, to dismiss most of the bishops who, following the long-standing English custom, filled the government offices. William of Wykeham, Bishop of Winchester, and the rest of the clerical party were now at daggers drawn with John of Gaunt's party.

In fact the real corruption at court, the bribes in return for favours, monopolies and offices, was the work of John of Gaunt and his accomplices – Alice Perrers, a London merchant named Richard Lyons, and Lord Latimer. Although he could control most of the government appointments, Gaunt could not control what was now known as the Commons, the elected members from the boroughs and shires, who from the 1330s were congregating apart from the Lords. And the Commons was hard to handle because it was there that the Black Prince's supporters were especially strong. At last in 1376 the bishops and Commons together in what became known as the Good Parliament publicly attacked the court party of John of Gaunt. The Commons then elected what they called a Speaker (the first instance of this title being used), and the man they chose, Sir Peter de la Mare, launched the first case of impeachment in English history, against Gaunt's leading accomplices. De la Mare himself acted as prosecuting counsel for the Commons, while the House of Lords took the part of judges – this remained the standard method of conducting a political trial until the eighteenth century. The Lords found Latimer and Lyons guilty of bribery and corruption, and Alice Perrers, who was also held to be guilty, was ordered to be removed from the king's palace as an evil influence. Just before sentence was pronounced, the Commons' greatest protector the Black Prince died. John of Gaunt was thus able to use his now completely unopposed influence in the country to call a new parliament, and abolished the acts passed by the Good Parliament.

Edward III finally expired on Midsummer's Day 1377. For a long time his own glorious summer had been a fading memory. As he was breathing his last, ungrateful courtiers ran from the palace to attend to the new powerbrokers in the land. Even Alice Perrers, who had been such a feature of the great Edwardian tournaments where she had appeared as the Lady of the Sun, deserted him – though not neglecting to pull the rings off his fingers first. The man who had been the greatest prince of the Europe of his day and England's most popular king for two centuries would have died alone had not a priest happened to be passing. He gave the old king the last rites before his soul departed.

Richard II

(1377–1399)

Richard II (or Richard of Bordeaux as he was known, after the town where he was born) was ten years old when, as the eldest son of the Black Prince, he succeeded to the throne. A contemporary painting shows a slender boy-king with pale yellow hair, but these appealing images should not blind us to the fact that once Richard grew up it became clear that he had inherited the violent and imperious nature of his father. Unlike his grandfather Edward III, he had no sense of the importance of carrying the nation with him, of ruling with the help of Parliament. Nevertheless at the first great crisis of his reign, the Peasants' Revolt, though he was only fourteen years old he showed courage and presence of mind.

Little had changed with the accession of a new king. The country was still ruled, through the council, by Richard's uncle John of Gaunt, the Duke of Lancaster, and the government remained deeply unpopular. The truce with France came to an end and was not renewed, and English trade, English shipping and English coastal towns began to suffer from French raids. There was even a possibility that the French might invade, though this threat disappeared in 1380 when Charles V was succeeded by another boy-king Charles VI. Then in 1381 a very widespread popular rising broke out as a protest against the new poll tax. This is known as the Peasants' Revolt. The government had demanded that every male, rich or poor, over the age of fifteen should pay the same tax per head (or per poll). At this grotesquely unfair request the underlying frustrations of small farmers and labourers who still fell within the category of villein came

King Richard II, who succeeded his grandfather Edward III because his father the Black Prince predeceased him in 1376.

to a head. For forty years the gradual breakdown of respect for authority had spread a sense of the outworn nature of traditional institutions. The socially conservative Church was further undermined by the confusion created by the papal schism of 1378, as there were now two popes in Christendom – one at Rome and one at Avignon.

Furthermore Wyclif had now broken with John of Gaunt. Instead he and his followers the Lollards or 'babblers' had turned to taking their message to the people in the countryside, and their russet-coloured robes were becoming a familiar sight in villages all over England. At the same time, one of these Lollards made the first translation of the Bible into English, for Wyclif believed that everyone should be allowed to read the Holy Scriptures and make up their opinion about their meaning.

His philosophic conclusion that 'dominion' was to be found in all good people regardless of whether they were priests had revolutionary implications. Although there were few Lollards among the peasants themselves, Wyclif's emphasis on each man's worth seeped into the current climate.

In 1381 all these discontents came together in a march on London led by a master craftsman named Wat Tyler (or Wat the roofer). Tyler was at the head of a large number of marchers setting off from Kent, a county which

The theologian John Wyclif whose followers became known as the Lollards.

since the Jutes had a reputation for more democratic traditions. Though there was no villeinage in Kent they demanded an end to villeinage for all Englishmen and refused to pay the poll tax. At the same time revolts broke out all over the country. In Essex a travelling priest named John Ball had been preaching on the theme of his well-known rhyme:

> When Adam delved, and Eve span
> Who was then the gentleman?

In the south the uprisings had a particularly anti-clerical tinge, as most of the participants were serfs from the properties of great abbeys and monasteries. The majority were armed with the agricultural tools they had been using in the fields when word started to spread about the march to

London – billhooks for pulling fruit off trees, shears and axes. The uprisings seem to have been quite spontaneous without any political organization behind them. They were nevertheless extremely dangerous. The rebels swarmed across London on either side of the river, setting fire to Southwark and convincing the city guards stationed at the Tower that they were no match for such numbers. They then murdered the Archbishop of Canterbury and the chancellor, and burned John of Gaunt's Thames-side Savoy Palace to the ground.

In the midst of the mayhem the boy-king Richard was the only member of the government to keep his head. While his ministers dithered, with great courage Richard agreed to meet the rebels and listen to their grievances. At Mile End he promised charters of liberty to abolish serfdom if the crowds would disperse. Then, accompanied by the lord mayor of London William Walworth and only sixty horsemen, he rode out to Smithfield to deal with Wat Tyler and the 2,000 Kentish men he had brought with him. With Richard was his popular mother Joan, the Fair Maid of Kent, whose association with their own county he may have felt would make the rebels readier to listen to him.

After some time talking face to face about the people's complaints Wat Tyler laid a hand on the king's bridle. He had a dagger in his other hand, though he seems to have had no intention of using it. But at a time when much of the city was on fire and two members of the government lay dead, Walworth the lord mayor may be forgiven for thinking that Tyler was about to murder the king. At any rate he reacted by plunging his sword into the rebel leader. At this the Kentish folk surged forward and seemed about to seize Richard, while those with bows trained their arrows on him. But Richard's own courage saved the day. Spurring his horse he galloped up to Tyler's followers crying 'Come with me and I will be your captain. Wat Tyler was a traitor.'

Uncertain how to proceed, since Tyler's oratory had been instrumental in getting them to London, the protesters followed Richard's slender figure into what were then the fields of Islington. But they were surrounded by a thousand soldiers hurriedly gathered by Walworth, and many sank to their knees to beg the king's pardon. By nightfall every single one of London's unwelcome visitors had left the city walls and was heading home convinced by the king's apparently sympathetic manner that serfdom would be abolished.

Eventually a general pardon would be issued to all those who took part in the Peasants' Revolt as part of the celebrations to mark Richard II's marriage in 1382 to the pious Anne of Bohemia, sister of King Wenceslaus. But in the short term the rebels were punished and their wishes ignored. John Ball was executed at St Albans, home of that first British martyr, while the charters abolishing serfdom were never issued because they had been obtained under duress. Although it took another hundred years for villeinage to die out entirely, in practice many lords gave the villeins their freedom and commuted their service to a money payment. The continued shortage of labour meant it was either that or having a very uncooperative workforce.

But Richard II never regained the esteem he won in 1381. John of Gaunt's absence from the council pursuing the throne of Castile by right of his wife Constance should have meant a fresh start for the country. But Gaunt and his cronies were soon replaced by equally venial men who were Richard's favourites, the most important being Robert de Vere, Earl of Oxford, whom Richard made Duke of Ireland, and the chancellor Michael de la Pole, a merchant who became Earl of Suffolk.

Richard and the new court party were just as careless of the law and parliament as John of Gaunt had been. Like his father the Black Prince the king had a taste for luxury and a splendid court. To finance it, sudden and illegal taxes were demanded without reference to Parliament. Under Edward III's youngest son Thomas of Woodstock, Duke of Gloucester, a parliamentary party began to rally against the court. In 1386 the trouble came to a head when Parliament asked Richard to dismiss Chancellor de la Pole for corruption. The king replied that he would not dismiss the meanest scullion in his kitchen just to please Parliament. In response Parliament impeached the chancellor and appointed eleven lords ordainers to rule the country, as had been done in Edward II's time.

Richard II was made of sterner stuff than his great-grandfather. Having persuaded the courts to proclaim the Lords Ordainer illegal because they interfered with the royal prerogative, he declared war on the parliamentary party. But in February 1388 at the Battle of Radcot Bridge in Oxfordshire his army was scattered and he himself was forced back to London. At the Parliament known as the Merciless Parliament, five lords including Richard's uncle the Duke of Gloucester and his first cousin, John of Gaunt's son Henry of Lancaster, accused the royal favourites of treason. These lords appellant as they were known, because they launched the Appeal of Treason, then executed many of the king's favourites.

The lords appellant now ruled the country through the council. But the fluidity and the personal nature of relationships at court meant that within the year Richard was asserting himself again, and once he had gained the support of the respectable old clerical party he was ruling on his own. Stability was cemented by the return from Spain of his uncle John of Gaunt, whose influence smoothed the way for less antagonistic politics, and before long two of the five lords appellant – Gaunt's son Henry of Lancaster and Thomas Mowbray, Earl of Nottingham – came round to the court party. Abroad too there was peace for almost thirty years, after Richard's marriage in 1396 to the daughter of the French king Charles VI – following the death of his wife Anne of Bohemia – led to a truce between the two countries.

But the king's sorrow at the death of his wife Anne touched off the most violent and uncontrollable elements in his rather unstable character. He razed to the ground the palace where he had lived with Anne, and when the Earl of Arundel – one of the lords appellant – arrived late for the queen's funeral, the outraged king publicly struck him in the face.

But Richard II was a subtler character than he appeared. For almost ten years after the Merciless Parliament he bided his time, secretly calculating how to have his revenge on the lords appellant. The year after Anne of Bohemia's death, he suddenly arrested three of them – his uncle Gloucester, Arundel and the Earl of Warwick. Surrounded by 4,000 soldiers of the king's personal bodyguard, the Cheshire Archers, Parliament had no choice but to bow to his wishes and condemned the three for treason. In a display of summary justice, Arundel was tried, convicted and beheaded on the same day, while Gloucester was murdered in Calais prison. Warwick escaped death only by the payment of massive fines.

By 1399 the English had had enough of their tyrannical king, and a mass movement to depose him was led by Henry of Lancaster, or Bolingbroke as he is sometimes known. The two cousins met in north Wales at Flint,

Richard II abdicating to Henry Bolingbroke (the future Henry IV) in the Tower of London, 1399.

and when Richard saw that he had no supporters he surrendered. At a meeting of Parliament, Henry of Lancaster stood before an empty throne and claimed the crown. He was careful not to claim it by right of Parliament, because what Parliament gave Parliament might take away. Likewise he did not claim it by right of conquest, for that too might be challenged by another conquest. But his claim was understood to be founded on a mixture of the two. Thus the Lancastrian revolution, which put the descendants of John of Gaunt on the throne, was achieved almost bloodlessly.

The new king, who was crowned Henry IV, had probably not planned to kill his predecessor. But when at Christmas that year a conspiracy to restore Richard to the throne was uncovered, it became clear that there was no room for two kings in one country. Richard, who was being held prisoner in Henry's Lancastrian stronghold Pontefract Castle, was accordingly murdered, and it was disingenuously announced that he had perished from self-inflicted starvation.

LANCASTRIAN
AND YORKIST

Henry IV

(1399–1413)

Despite the profound instability the Lancastrian revolution caused, in the first twenty years of the new dynasty Parliament reached a peak of influence to which it would not return for another 200 years. The rightful heir was the Earl of March, grandson of the childless Richard II's senior uncle Lionel of Clarence, who was Edward III's third son. The usurper Henry IV therefore had particular need of the Lords' and Commons' support – so the meeting of Parliament became an annual event. Ever since Magna Carta the tradition had grown up that the power of the king was limited by the need to confer with the King's Council. Now consultation became more important than ever.

A key part of that Parliament was the House of Commons. For more than 150 years lawyers, well-to-do townsmen, merchants and small landowners had been responsible through the Commons for raising the king's taxes in the shires. Although the aristocracy with their vast estates and private armies continued to be the crown's advisers, the Commons' control of taxation left the kings of England no option but to listen to the middle classes' petitions. Uniquely in Europe, by the early fifteenth century it was firmly established that the Commons as well as the nobility or the king were the initiators of new laws. By the beginning of Henry V's reign in 1413 it had become the accepted custom that when the House of Commons sent a bill for the royal signature the king might throw it out but he could not change its form to suit himself. English freedoms versus continental royal absolutism became a matter of pride for educated Englishmen.

Since the Commons consisted of both the country gentry and the commercial classes, there was never in England the sense of separate castes that prevailed abroad. Instead common interests bound together the small landowner or country gentry and the merchant. The English class system always surprised foreign observers by its flexibility, with people moving swiftly up and down the scale through marriage and successful careers. In particular, the merchant's daughter had become an instrument for increasing the family fortune, as the merchant class benefited from expanding trade, improved education and better health and as the population and the economy at last recovered from the effects of the Black Death. The men who ran the wool trade took over the building of richly decorated parish churches from the lords of the manor – these may be seen in the 'wool churches' of East Anglia, of which the finest examples are at Long Melford, Sudbury and Lavenham.

The wealthier merchants were also putting up large townhouses, often of brick – a material not used since the Romans. The architecture became domestic rather than defensive – the castle was dying out as a rich man's home. The broad windows in such castles as were built in this period, for example at Herstmonceux in Sussex, indicate that the crenellations above them were added purely for decoration.

As these fortunes were being made from England's growing share of international trade, which was increasingly regulated by treaty, towns and cities became much more sophisticated and complex organisms. Incorporated by royal consent or charter into legal entities, they had their own governments, with powers to make their own laws and hold their own elections, which the king had to respect. Wealth created a more defined class system in towns, which became more oligarchical – controlled exclusively by well-to-do tradesmen, especially clothiers, who elected one another. Trade became standardized too. The craft organizations – the guilds – had powers to perform spot checks on merchants' and craftsmen's premises to make sure that standards were being complied with.

But the guilds' powers were not just regulatory. Along with the town corporations, they were patrons of a new standard of English urban civilization. They provided charitable functions for the poor, and city grammar schools for their own children. They arranged the processions and music which were so constant an accompaniment to fifteenth-century life. Everybody, whatever their circumstances, knew the Bible stories thanks to the celebrated guild plays, of which the best known are those at York, performed on large wagons moving around the city. In the City of London the immense wealth of the Fishmongers', the Goldsmiths' and above all the Mercers' or clothiers' guilds were made dramatically visible in the magnificent halls that still stand today; the guilds continue to manage fortunes in real estate accrued over the centuries, enabling them to carry out generous charitable work. Like their magnate equivalents, the heads of guilds were allowed to wear their own uniforms or livery. No less than the individual merchants, the guilds were responsible for a further transformation in church architecture in the erection of chantry chapels, tacked on to the main body of churches to house the many guild altars. This led to an increase in the numbers of church personnel, as altar priests were specially engaged just to chant masses all day long to ease the afterlife of the souls of departed members.

As more and more sons of clothiers, merchants and shopkeepers such as butchers and bakers benefited from education, scriveners or copiers were kept busy writing out books for their burgeoning audience – until close English trade links with the Burgundian Netherlands brought a printer named William Caxton to England with a printing press with movable type. When he imported one of the presses in 1474, invented by the German Johan Gutenberg, middle-class literacy took off as never before, and the homes of small tradesmen soon contained as many books as those of the upper classes.

Despite all these progressive tendencies, another strong current in fifteenth-century England was the return of feudalism, or the rule of barons, thanks to the weakness of the crown. The Lancastrian kings' reliance on Parliament increased the powers of the Lords, bringing bloody inter-generational factionalism and the sort of anarchy not seen since Stephen. Traditionally the two places where feudalism remained almost unadulter-ated were the border lands guarding England from Wales and Scotland, where independent armies and a palatinate system had prevailed since the early Norman kings. It was from the border lords that the first challenge to the new regime came.

As the name suggests the power base of the Lancastrian dynasty was in the north-west, where Henry IV owned huge swathes of Lancashire and Yorkshire. Indeed Henry of Lancaster had secured the throne with the aid of his fellow northern magnates, above all the soldiers of the Percys of Northumberland. It was the Percys' loyalty during the uneasy early days of the new regime that had kept the Scots out of England – but Henry IV had not rewarded them as they considered their due. Full of pride in their family – as the old saying went there was only one king in Northumberland and that was not the king of England – they were soon nursing a grievance. In particular, they had not become the key advisers in the King's Council they had been led to believe they would. Thus, when a Welsh rebellion broke out within a year of Henry's accession, a desire for revenge and kinship links persuaded the Percys to join it.

In 1400 a new Welsh war for independence was touched off by a quarrel over land resolved in the English law courts in favour of the English marcher baron Lord Grey of Ruthin and against the Welsh landowner Owen Glendower. Glendower's calibre as a general and the disaffection the Welsh felt for their overlords were a potent combination, and Glendower became so confident that he summoned a Welsh Parliament, acknowledged the French pope at Avignon instead of Rome and made a legal treaty allying himself as Prince of Wales to the French king Charles VI, father-in law of the deposed Richard II. When a French troopship arrived at Carmarthen Bay and the Earl of Northumberland's son Harry Percy, who had been sent to Wales to put down the rebellion, started intriguing with the conspirators the Welsh revolt became an attempt to overthrow the new dynasty. By 1403 its leaders were aiming not only for an independent Wales but to reinstate the rightful heir to the throne of England, the Earl of March. Chief among the disaffected nobles was the marcher lord Sir Edmund Mortimer. Himself descended from Edward III through his grandfather Lionel of Clarence, he linked the Percys and Glendower to the Earl of March: he was respectively Harry Percy's brother-in-law, Owen Glendower's son-in-law, and uncle to the Earl of March.

In July 1403 at the Battle of Shrewsbury on the Welsh borders Henry IV intercepted the Percy armies led by Hotspur (as the Scots had admiringly named Harry Percy) on their way to join up with the Welsh under Glendower. Hotspur was killed by his former pupil, Henry IV's son Henry of Monmouth, the future Henry V. The immediate threat of a general rising was temporarily beaten off, though Glendower escaped. But in 1405 a new rebellion broke out, this time led by Hotspur's father the Earl of Northumberland. Since the Archbishop of York, Richard Scrope, the second most important churchman in England after the Archbishop of Canterbury, was one of the northern leaders it had to be crushed with the utmost severity. To considerable disquiet Scrope was executed, even though as a churchman he was not subject to secular law.

By the deaths of Richard II and Archbishop Scrope, Henry IV had shown he was quite capable of ruthless acts to safeguard his dynasty, but it was at great mental cost. Henry of Lancaster was not the natural material of which usurpers are made, being of a melancholy and religious disposition, and he never attempted to root out the Clarence Plantagenet line by killing March. He was said to have been struck with leprosy in 1407 at the moment that Archbishop Scrope was executed. By all accounts the rapid decline which ended with his death at the age of forty-six began with a nervous breakdown that year.

As the king became steadily more incoherent and unaware of his surroundings, power devolved to his close family circle. His son, the future Henry V, with the help of his half-uncles, the ambitious Beaufort sons of John of Gaunt, began to take control of the King's Council, undermining the influence of Henry IV's chief adviser, the Archbishop of Canterbury, Thomas Arundel. In 1413 the king's health finally gave out and he died in the Jerusalem Chamber of the Palace of Westminster – thus fulfilling an old prophecy that he would die in the Holy Land.

Henry V

(1413–1422)

Though Henry V inherited his father's strong religious convictions, in the new king's case they served to reinforce his sense of himself as a born ruler. Unlike his father, he had no blood on his hands. A deep inner conviction of the rightness of any cause he adopted, such as his grandfather's claim to the French throne, gave boldness to a decisive and obsessively disciplined character. His wiry physique had been honed in the saddle since the age of thirteen in the Welsh campaigns. Though his reputation when he became king was that of an outstanding warrior who had got the better of Hotspur, in the best-known portrait of him he more resembles a priest with his cropped hair and solemn, austere look. Although numerous legends suggest a wild youth as Prince Hal, including an incident in which he is said to have struck his father's chief justice Sir William Gasgoigne, many of them seem to have been invented after his death.

What can be said for sure is that Henry V had the ability to move his audiences to follow him anywhere. Oratorical gifts and outstanding military abilities, which enabled him to recapture the ancient English territory of Normandy and make his son the next King of France, inspired feelings of profound devotion among the English. Like his father, Henry had only a short reign, but those nine years were exceptionally glorious, and his victories in France attracted the enthusiastic support of the House of Commons, which raised taxes for each new war without argument. The unique popularity of the hero-king gave the Lancastrian dynasty an emotional sanction and legitimacy it had previously lacked.

The new Lancastrian king had succeeded to the throne without a hitch, but his first task was to restore peace at home. To this end he mollified his potential opponents, granting a free pardon to Owen Glendower and his supporters, releasing the Earl of March from prison and putting up a magnificent tomb to Richard II at Westminster Abbey. Although Henry V had replaced his enemy Archbishop Arundel as chancellor with one of his Beaufort relations, the king shared Arundel's conservative views.

Under Henry V the Lollard heresy was pursued far more strenuously than before. Even his old friend and fellow campaigner the Welsh marcher knight

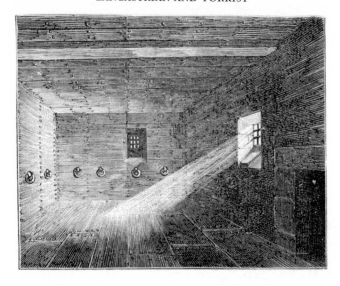

The Lollard Prison, Lambeth Palace.

Sir John Oldcastle, a keen follower of Wyclif who may have been the model for Shakespeare's Falstaff, was tried and arrested for heresy in the second year of his reign. After attempting to lead a rising known as the Oldcastle Plot, intending to take the king prisoner at his palace at Eltham in south London, Oldcastle escaped to his hereditary lands in the Welsh marches. With his subsequent recapture and execution at the Tower of London, the Lollard threat to orthodoxy was extirpated, and the doctrines of the Catholic Church were not to be challenged again for over a hundred years. Henceforth Lollardy became an underground movement with a considerable following in the West Midlands and among some better-educated artisans. Though something of its independent spirit dripped quietly into the English bloodstream, it no longer had a following within the establishment.

With peace at home, Henry V turned his energies abroad, convinced of the need for a just war on behalf of his royal patrimony. In 1360 by the Treaty of Brétigny Edward III had agreed to give up his claim to the French throne in return for Aquitaine. Yet the treaty had never been fulfilled – Aquitaine had never been returned, while its rump Gascony was being reduced, so the English claim to the French throne remained in place. Henry was determined to have the whole of Aquitaine at the very least, and if possible Normandy as well, and now was a good moment to act.

The intermittent madness of Charles VI, which had been afflicting him for over thirty years, had badly weakened the French administration. It was made more ineffective still by the internecine rivalry within the royal family, in particular between the king's brother, the Duke of Orleans, and the king's cousin, the Duke of Burgundy, known as John the Fearless or Jean Sans Peur. In 1407 Orleans was murdered at Burgundy's behest, and a civil war erupted. On one side were the Armagnacs, the Orleanist party headed by the Count of Armagnac, whose home was in southern France near Aquitaine; on the other side were the Burgundians, whose power base lay in the north east of Paris.

Embassies came and went between England and the two French parties, but in terms of territory returned to the English little progress was made. By 1414 Henry V's patience was wearing thin, and he soon concluded that the only way to break the deadlock was to send an English invasion force to France. There was considerable support for war. The City of London with its Gascon trade raised large loans for Henry, and Parliament granted extra taxes to help recover his rightful possessions from Normandy down to Aquitaine – both Houses had been convinced by an address he gave them that his claim to the French throne should be enforced. A new fleet was assembled at Southampton, and the truce which had begun with Richard II's marriage came to an end – the Hundred Years War resumed. By the summer of 1415 the ships and the guns, the heralds and the trumpeters, the drummers and the minstrels, were ready, and in early August the king and his troops sailed for Harfleur in Normandy, the gateway to northern France. This force of 9,000 men was intended only to open the campaign – it was not a full-scale invasion. But things did not go according to plan, and it was not until late September that the port yielded. Food was always hard to come by in enemy territory, and the effort of besieging and an epidemic of dysentery had greatly weakened the men.

As a result the campaign had to be abandoned in favour of making for the greater safety of the English port of Calais. But to reach it the English had to march through hostile territory. Following the course that his grandfather Edward III had taken before Crécy, Henry V and his exhausted army made their way north. After crossing the Ternoise river at Blangy they found their way to Calais blocked by a great French army, at least 40,000 strong. It was drawn up at a little village named Agincourt. In those late October days the odds were against the English. But the French commanders made one significant mistake which would give the English the advantage: they had chosen to fight on a very narrow plateau surrounded by hedges which did not allow them enough room to manoeuvre their formidable forces.

Despite Henry V's personal austerity, he took the greatest care of his soldiers. He introduced surgeons into the army, his archers had horses to ride and, in imitation of Caesar, pontoons or portable bridges were always carried so that English soldiers stayed dry and comfortable crossing rivers.

Unlike other armies English besiegers were housed in weatherproof wooden huts built by the siege train of engineers, carpenters and joiners. Henry always personally oversaw the victualling, to ensure that his men were well fed. Wherever the English army marched, on the nearest sea a flotilla of boats groaning with provisions followed. For the king knew, as Napoleon is said to have remarked centuries later, that an army marches on its stomach. He also took steps to prevent his vital longbowmen running out of arrows. Geese were specially reared on common land throughout England in order to provide the feathered tips for the million arrows the royal armies ordered each year. And it was forbidden by royal decree to use ashwood for the wooden clogs that most country dwellers put on against the mud. This was because ash provided the best wood for the arrows' shafts.

The night before Agincourt Henry did what he had always done ever since he was a young commander: he slipped from group to group under the dripping trees, quietly rallying the men. Then he made an electrifying last speech which was talked about by old campaigners for years to come. If the genius of Shakespeare transformed his words, much of its content was derived from contemporary accounts. In particular, the democratic themes that the playwright puts in Henry V's mouth had a basis in reality. It was a fact that the English archer was more valuable in battle than his social superior the knight, as his skill at archery was responsible for the storms of arrows which protected the knight and which fell so thickly that they reminded observers of snow showers. In the French army strict notions of caste prevailed, just as they did in France itself: the higher social class of the knight segregated him from the peasant archers. But the English knights dismounted before battle and sent their horses to the back. Then they and archers fought side by side on foot. Even if Henry did not precisely say that 'he today that sheds his blood with me, shall be my brother; be he ne'er so vile this day shall gentle his condition', it was clearly implied.

Not only was the small force of English outnumbered by nearly five to one, they also looked outlandish and wild compared to the exquisitely caparisoned French knights. Practicality determined the English costume. The longbowmen had all taken off one shoe and ripped one stocking so that they could have greater purchase in the oozing mud and grip with their naked toes. They had also torn off one sleeve of their sword arm for greater freedom of movement. We may imagine that half naked, they looked an unkempt and inefficient enemy to take on the French. The French knights' armour, on the oher hand, shone brightly from ceaseless polishing. The English and Welsh must have seemed almost as savage as in the days of Boudicca.

But, despite the contrast in the appearance of the two armies, the French knights were not fooled. The English longbowmen continued to be such a source of dread that during battles French knights would swoop by the archers waving their swords to try to cut off the archers' two drawing fingers. In return the English longbowmen would hold up two fingers, a gesture of defiance which continues to be used today.

When battle commenced, Henry ordered the archers at the front to move forward towards the French so that their arrows would not fall short. The French turned to one another in delighted disbelief at the English stupidity before advancing to ride down the longbowmen. But unknown to them sharpened stakes had been planted in the ground in front of them, and there was a huge pile-up of warhorses, their unseated knights thrashing uselessly beneath them as their heavy armour caused them to sink into the mud. At once the English archers ran forward and in their usual cold-blooded fashion set about slitting their enemy's throats.

Many of France's greatest nobles were killed that day in the broken cornfields. One of the reasons for the enormous numbers of French casualties – perhaps 6,000 versus fewer than 300 English dead – was that Henry ordered that all the French prisoners of war should have their throats cut, because the rumour had gone round that there was a danger of attack from the rear. That was where the royal baggage train held the royal crown of England, the Chancery seals without which no official document was complete and the sword of state. Even though permanent government

The Battle of Agincourt, 1415, won by Henry V, one of the great victories of the Hundred Years War which led to the conquest of Normandy.

departments had grown up at Westminster, like his predecessors Henry V went to war accompanied by all the visible signs of his office and majesty. His prompt if unchivalrous action in killing the prisoners caused much grumbling in the English ranks – not on humanitarian grounds, but because dead knights would not elicit the lucrative ransoms that made so many English fortunes in the Hundred Years War.

The way was now open for Calais and London. The hero king was chaired by the crowds when he landed on English soil and was accompanied by exulting citizens all the way to London, where Henry Beaufort, Bishop of Winchester, celebrated Mass. Agincourt was a sign that God was on the side of the English, and the king paid for a Mass to be said in perpetuity on St Crispin's Day, the day of the battle. The mood of national ecstasy continued with Parliament surrendering to Henry V – and to him only – their right to discuss taxation with him and granting him the customs for life.

It was the climax of the love affair between the Lancastrian king and Parliament. Henry became the greatest prince in Europe, so influential that his support of the Emperor Sigismund brought to an end the papal schism which had been plaguing Christendom for over a hundred years: the two popes had become three and were now reduced to one, Martin V. Meanwhile to demonstrate its commitment to orthodoxy, the General Church Council burned at the stake the heretical Jan Hus, a follower of Wyclif's in Bohemia. For the next few years, buoyed by taxes and by loans, the king concentrated on returning Normandy to the English crown. By 1419, after a series of gruelling sieges, he had achieved his objective, and Normandy was once more under English rule. The English were back in force on the lower Seine, as threatening to the French as their Viking ancestors had been 500 years before.

At last the warring Burgundians and Orleanists realized the danger they were facing. They made overtures of peace to one another, but even at this moment of peril the feud between them took precedence. At a meeting on the bridge at Montereau on the Yonne between the dauphin (the name given to the eldest son of the French king), who was head of the Armagnacs or Orleanists, and Jean Sans Peur, Duke of Burgundy, the duke was assassinated. The feud blazed into life again. But Burgundian anger at the Orleanists was to England's lasting advantage, for Jean Sans Peur's son, the new duke, Philip the Good, allied himself comprehensively with the English. In order to prevent the Orleanist dauphin ruling France, by the 1420 Treaty of Troyes with the Duke of Burgundy Henry V was to marry the French king Charles VI's daughter Catherine and become regent during his mad father-in-law's lifetime. Last and best, under the treaty Henry and his heirs were to be the next kings of France, though France was to remain a distinct kingdom, maintaining her separate French laws and a French council.

The dual monarchy promised by the Treaty of Troyes proved hard to enforce. North of the Loire and round the Paris area, the French might hate the Orleanists and welcome the English king presiding over a session of the Estates General and English garrisons manning the Louvre and the Bastille; south of the Loire, however, was a different story. There the dauphin was viewed as France's rightful ruler and future king. When in 1421 Henry V's brother, the Duke of Clarence, was killed attempting to enlarge England's French realm further south, Henry left his infant son and wife Catherine in England and returned to France himself.

Detail of the king on his charger, from Henry V's tomb in Westminster Abbey.

A year later the hero-king was dead. The dysentery which was a hazard of those long campaigns had killed him, and he left as heir that unlucky thing for England, an infant. Worse still, despite his superb sire, little Henry VI had inherited many more genes from his French side. The madness of his grandfather Charles VI was very much to the fore.

What would have happened if Henry V had lived to be an old man is one of the great hypotheticals of history. Those dissatisfied with the few rather solemn paintings of the king and who wish to see some remnant of his spirit should visit his chantry tomb in Westminster Abbey. There, high up, is a most unsacred image of the king on his warhorse charging full tilt at Agincourt.

Henry VI
(1422–1461)

By strange coincidence the French king Charles VI died in 1422 within months of Henry V, leaving the infant Henry VI king of both England and France. In practice both countries were ruled by his royal uncles. Henry V's able soldier brother John, Duke of Bedford became regent. But he returned to France to try to enforce the Treaty of Troyes and left the task of governing England to his ambitious younger brother Duke Humphrey of Gloucester in tandem with the King's Council.

Bedford was as far-sighted as his brother Henry V and he saw that the only way to rule France was through the goodwill of the Duke of Burgundy, Philip the Good. His support was vital as the Burgundians controlled most of the northern part of the country, especially around Paris. Bedford shored up his nephew's kingdom by establishing an Anglo-Burgundian alliance and signing a treaty with the Duke of Brittany. This left him free to extend the Anglo-French kingdom south of the Loire into the Orleanist–Armagnac territory of central and southern France, where the dauphin was acknowledged as king.

Bedford's campaigns were constantly interrupted by the need to return home to sort out the King's Council, in which the jealousies and intrigues between Duke Humphrey and the baby king's equally ambitious great-uncle Henry Beaufort, Bishop of Winchester, often brought government business to a standstill. By 1429 Duke Humphrey was demanding that Beaufort be expelled from the Council as an agent of the pope following his election as cardinal. Bedford therefore deemed it more sensible to crown the seven-year-old Henry VI king than allow Duke Humphrey to remain as protector. From then on Cardinal Beaufort's influence in the royal Council became paramount.

Bedford had already begun a more serious attempt at rooting out the dauphin by laying siege to the town of Orleans, which controlled one of the few bridges on the fast-flowing Loire river and was considered the key to the south. Had he succeeded in taking Orleans, the Anglo-Burgundian forces could have swarmed into central France. However, at this point the fortunes of France were transformed by Jeanne d'Arc or, as the English call her, Joan of Arc, a young peasant girl from Domremi between Champagne and Lorraine in the north-east.

Although Domremi was separated by many miles from Orleanist France in the south, Joan of Arc made her way across enemy country to reach the dauphin at his castle at Chinon, desperate to tell him of her vision that he was to be crowned King of France at Rheims in the heart of English-occupied France. Having pushed her way into his presence she proceeded to put steel into this self-indulgent man. No greater contrast could be imagined than that between the gorgeously dressed and cynical veteran of the French court and the naive Joan in her wooden sabots and home-made woollen garments. But her conviction that France's greatest saints had appeared to her while she was watching her father's sheep and thinking of the suffering of her divided country was so overwhelming that the dauphin too was swept away by her astonishing prophecy.

In an age of symbolism and allegory Joan of Arc, clad in the suit of white armour the dauphin had had made for her and with her hair shorn, seemed the embodiment of a holy angel descended to earth to fight for France. She changed the army's mood from pessimism to inspired patriotism. On a horse from the royal stables, Joan of Arc was allowed to lead a brigade of French soldiers to relieve the defeatist garrison at Orleans. To the Orleanists' astonishment, she managed to fight her way through the English besiegers and clambered within the battlemented walls of the city. Soon after she drove off the English by capturing one of their siege forts.

The siege of Orleans was lifted, and the townsfolk claimed Joan as their own, with the result that ever since she has been known as the Maid of Orleans. Shortly after, she won a pitched battle against the English at Patay, and a new determination was restored to the Orleanist army. It enabled the Maid to lead the dauphin north through Anglo-Burgundian France and have him crowned at Rheims as his ancestors had been since time immemorial. Although the dauphin had to escape south again as soon as the ceremony was over, something had happened to him in the echoing cathedral. When he received the sacred oils of kingship as the Archbishop of Rheims traced the sign of the cross on his forehead, the new king Charles VII was transformed into the Lord's anointed for whom no sacrifice was too great.

Urged on by Joan, who had stayed in the north with the Orleanist troops, even the French inhabitants of the Anglo-Burgundian regions began openly to resist their foreign overlords. For though the Maid had accomplished her first purpose and the dauphin was now the figurehead for an increasingly united France, she had yet to achieve her second objective: that was to drive the English out of France.

It was then that the Maid's luck turned. Her great merit had been the strength of her faith, but she was no trained general. She became over-confident and marched on Paris. When she utterly failed to take it, the mutterings against her grew louder among the dauphin's advisers, who were already jealous of her influence. In May 1430, against military advice, she rashly tried to relieve the town of Compiègne, a former Burgundian possession on the dukedom's western border which had rebelled against its overlord and which Duke Philip of Burgundy had surrounded. Having been wounded, she was on her way back to camp when she was captured by Duke Philip's men-at-arms. Her white armour had made her all too visible.

Joan was thrown into prison, while the English and Burgundians considered ways of eradicating her with the least fuss. In her absence her enemies prevailed over the weak dauphin. In the end it was a French ecclesiastical court at Rouen under the Bishop of Beauvais that did the dirty work. The heroine of France was condemned to be burned to death for witchcraft. The dauphin did nothing to save her. Refusing to alter anything she had said about her visions the Maid of Orleans, weak and pale from captivity, was led out from her underground dungeon and tied to a stake in the market square at Rouen in Normandy. Logs were piled around her and set alight. St Joan, as she was to become, quietly muttered prayers to herself and never cried out during her final agony. Her ashes were thrown into the Seine.

However, the spirit of patriotism that Joan had released lived on after her. Twenty years later the English presence in France had been reduced to the port of Calais. Though Bedford brought Henry VI to France to be crowned in the year of her death, anti-English feeling prevented the ceremony being performed at Rheims. Instead he had to make do with Paris. But the coronation had little effect – in fact, it only encouraged the growth of French patriotism, and even the Burgundian-ruled northern towns turned against the English.

The process was made swifter by the death of Bedford's wife, who was the Duke of Burgundy's sister. Anglo-Burgundian relations had been strengthened by their personal ties, but they never really recovered after Bedford married Burgundy's vassal Jacquetta of Luxembourg without his former brother-in-law's permission. Was England planning to control Luxembourg too? From now on Burgundy allied himself to Charles VII, and threw his influence behind him to establish the French king at Paris.

Though fighting continued sporadically in France, marked by longer and longer truces, Bedford's death in 1435 allowed a peace party to flourish in England, led by Cardinal Beaufort, and the Truce of Tours in 1444 was cemented by Henry VI's marriage to the strong-willed Margaret of Anjou, a cousin of the French royal family. However, Beaufort's wise policy did not jibe with the national mood, which was vehemently anti-French. When he died in 1447 his follower the Duke of Suffolk became a lightning rod for public opinion. As ever Duke Humphrey – though he had been exiled from court, disgraced by his wife's alleged attempts to use witchcraft to bring about Henry VI's death – continued to exercise his populist touch speaking out against the French marriage. His death under suspicious circumstances after he had been arrested by Suffolk created a public outcry.

But that was nothing to what was felt to be the national humiliation of the loss of Normandy and Gascony three years later. By now Suffolk was Henry VI's chief minister. One of his principal councillors was Cardinal Beaufort's nephew, Edmund Beaufort, Duke of Somerset, who held the position of governor of Normandy. Somerset disgraced Suffolk's administration by failing to make sure of Normandy's defences and by 1450 the duchy had passed back into French hands for good. Even in Gascony the patriotism Joan of Arc had first inspired finally prevailed. When French soldiers invaded, none of the Gascons took up arms against them. Even those towns with strong trade links to England, Bordeaux and Bayonne, went over to the French.

However, the Gascons were used to a greater degree of independence than their new masters were willing to allow, so in 1451 the elderly but distinguished commander John Talbot, Earl of Shrewsbury, whose war service stretched back to the Welsh wars of Henry IV, was despatched to aid the Gascons round Bordeaux. Unfortunately, in the half-century since Owen Glendower's revolt there had been a few military developments which had passed the gallant Talbot by, and one of them was artillery. French artillery accordingly won the Battle of Castillon in the Dordogne in 1453, the engagement which at last ended the Hundred Years War. The once unbeatable longbow was finally outclassed. Perhaps because of his age, Talbot made a textbook error, leading a cavalry charge uphill against a fortified camp defended by 300 cannon. One in ten of his troops was killed before they reached the palisades, including Talbot himself. From that day the only English possession left in France was the staple town and port of Calais.

But the initial loss of Normandy and Gascony, even before Castillon had been fought, was enough in 1450 to get Suffolk impeached. There were suspicions that he intended to engineer the succession to the throne for his son, that he was in collusion with the French and that Somerset too was a traitor. So furious was the public mood that Henry VI was forced to banish Suffolk to prevent him being imprisoned. Even so, the duke was murdered on his way to exile in Calais. His headless body was washed up days later on the English coast.

Worse was to come. Only weeks later, Henry VI, who was said to be utterly at the mercy of his fierce French wife Margaret of Anjou, was forced to flee from the capital to escape an invasion by the men of Kent, led by an obscure Irishman named Jack Cade. Rebellion was their response to the government's attempts to punish them, for they were commonly believed to have been behind the murder of Suffolk. They camped out on Blackheath and when they had defeated the king's soldiers sent to round them up they went into London and exacted summary justice on royal favourites. It was only when wilder elements began to loot the fine shops that Londoners turned against Cade. Soon afterwards he was murdered, and the king returned from Kenilworth where he had been hiding.

Who was behind Jack Cade? Unlike the Peasants' Revolt, Cade's uprising included deeply dissatisfied burgesses and gentry, the so-called political nation, protesting against high taxes, incompetent government and the French débâcle. Cade claimed to be a Mortimer, that Welsh marcher family which was so closely connected to the Clarence Plantagenet line. There are some suggestions that the revolt had been orchestrated as a challenge to the Lancastrian line by the royal duke Richard of York. Through his mother Anne Mortimer (who was Lionel, Duke of Clarence's heiress), Richard of York represented the senior branch of Edward III's family. Thus according to strict arguments of heredity, if inheriting through the female line was no obstacle, York was the rightful heir to the throne. In fact not long after Cade's death Richard, Duke of York did appear in London from his estates in Ireland, where he had been banished for the previous three years by Suffolk. He now became the focus of opposition to the Lancastrian regime.

There had been considerable enmity between Henry VI and his putative heir for some time, and relations had not been improved by York's attempt through Parliament to have himself named as the then childless king's successor. Nevertheless, at least initially, York does not seem to have intended to seize the throne. But in 1453 the birth of a son to Margaret and Henry altered his position vis-à-vis the crown. Now that he was no longer the automatic heir his feelings hardened towards Henry. Moreover, events began to play into his hands. The kindly Henry VI lost his reason. One chronicler reported that when the new Prince of Wales was put into his arms he kept looking down at the ground and seemed incapable of seeing the child.

Although the king's madness was concealed and the King's Council continued to rule for him, there was a distinct mood of disenchantment in the country. In 1454, Somerset was dismissed from government and the popular York was elected protector of England. Months later, however, the king's sanity returned and he once more appointed Somerset to lead the Council, from which York was now excluded. York's response was to raise an army against the king. At the first Battle of St Albans in Hertfordshire in 1455 he killed Somerset and captured Henry VI. The king was not capable of withstanding this new assault on his dignity and he lost his mind. Once again the Duke of York was named protector.

The first Battle of St Albans is generally taken to mark the beginning of the thirty years of sporadic civil war between the two branches of the Plantagenet kings known as the Wars of the Roses (in Sir Walter Scott's phrase). A red rose was one of the badges used on their livery by the House of Lancaster, while a white rose was worn by the House of York.

Tomb of Edward III in Westminster Abbey displaying some of the thirteen children whose claims to the throne erupted in the Wars of the Roses.

The Duke of York had married into one of the most ambitious of the English magnate families, the Nevilles, the tentacles of whose Yorkshire clan twined round the power structure of northern England. The Nevilles became completely identified with the cause of York, owing to their long-running rivalry with their fellow northerners, the Percys, the traditional allies of the House of Lancaster. Especially important figures among the Nevilles were the Duke of York's brother-in-law Richard Neville, Earl of

Salisbury and above all his son who by marrying into the Beauchamp family became Earl of Warwick, known to history as Warwick the Kingmaker. The Beauchamp lands made him the wealthiest noble of the time.

Warwick and Salisbury had played key roles at the Battle of St Albans. Warwick was rewarded by being made captain of Calais, a position he kept despite the return of Henry VI to his senses in 1456, which meant the end of York's protectorship. York remained a member of the King's Council, which soon descended into feuding, and all over England the governmental structure began to collapse, and with it the rule of law. Fighting for booty in France had created an appetite among the nobility that did not die with the loss of Normandy and Gascony.

It became the habit for great lords to support retinues of soldiers dressed in their badges, a custom known as livery and maintenance. It would have been a common if unwelcome sight to see such bands of forty men or more – who pledged themselves like so many others to ride with their lord and 'take his part against all other persons within the realm of England', as one oath had it – galloping across the landscape in pursuit of vengeance. In many areas the local law courts stopped functioning, since these private armies simply overturned judgements in the local court that they disagreed with. As the local administration fell apart, the nobility indulged in raids against one another and in small wars. In a period of anarchy the strong man wins, at least temporarily. As captain of Calais, Warwick became a popular hero for using his personal wealth to attack the French.

In 1459 war between the Yorkists and Lancastrians broke out again. This time it was begun by the energetic queen deciding to make a preemptive strike against the Yorkists, whom she had been steadily trying to drive out of the King's Council. Out of the blue she and her troops attacked the Earl of Salisbury but were defeated at the Battle of Blore Heath in Staffordshire. The action now moved to the Welsh marches and the heart of Mortimer country where Warwick was gathered with the Duke of York and his father the Earl of Salisbury preparatory to a fresh attack. Henry VI now showed unexpected decisiveness and, marching at the head of his troops, forced the unprepared conspirators to escape abroad – York to his estates in Ireland and the Nevilles to Calais. Queen Margaret then had Parliament declare all the Yorkist leaders attainted. That meant that they were sentenced to death and all of their property forfeited to the crown.

This aggressive action only upped the stakes for the Yorkists – now it was all or nothing. The following year, 1460, when Warwick and Salisbury returned at the head of an army containing the Duke of York's eldest son, the future Edward IV, their aim was to make his father king instead of protector. At the Battle of Northampton, Warwick the Kingmaker captured Henry VI, who was wandering incoherently about the battlefield and their victory seemed complete. The queen was forced to escape north to Scotland.

York lost no time in crossing over from Ireland to demand the crown before Parliament, but the Lords refused him. Instead he again had to be contented with the title of protector, though he was now styled heir to the throne and made Prince of Wales. Whatever his titles, York was the real ruler of the country; Henry VI lived quietly in the Tower of London. But at the end of the year the protector was forced to hurry north to put down a revolt by Lancastrian Yorkshire magnates. At the Battle of Wakefield in

Eton College, founded by Henry VI in 1440 to give free education to 70 poor scholars.

December 1460 the Yorkists were severely defeated, and some of the most important Yorkist nobles lost their lives – including the duke himself. Warwick's father Salisbury was publicly executed at the Lancastrian stronghold of Pontefract and York's second son, the Earl of Rutland, was killed. York's head was cut off after death, crowned with a paper coronet and stuck on the city of York's walls as a dreadful warning.

Meanwhile Queen Margaret was making her way down from Scotland accompanied by Scottish soldiers to join up with the northern Lancastrian army which was now heading for London. The Scots had driven a hard bargain – in return for their aid Berwick was to be given back to Scotland. At St Albans in Hertfordshire on the road to London, the queen encountered Warwick who had marched north to stop her from reaching the capital. There she won a great victory and recaptured her husband.

KING'S-COLLEGE CHAPEL, CAMBRIDGE.

As a foreigner Queen Margaret had not understood the national feeling about Berwick and the historic enmity between the Scots and the English. As the Scots travelled down through England they behaved like an invading army, which in many ways they were. Their looting and burning of English property in the end proved the French queen's undoing, as the south began to turn against her. Londoners prevented the food carts bearing provisions for the queen's army from reaching her, and Margaret herself hesitated to march straight into London for fear of the reception she would get.

The nineteen-year-old Edward, the former Earl of March – he had inherited his maternal uncle Edmund Mortimer's title and, since his father's death, Duke of York – seized the moment. Summoning an immense gathering of his retainers from the Mortimer estates in Wales and the Welsh marches, he advanced eastwards. Having defeated a Lancastrian army at the Battle of Mortimer's Cross in Herefordshire in February 1461 he met up with Warwick and his army and reached London before Queen Margaret. At Westminster Hall a month later he was acclaimed king. He became Edward IV.

Edward IV
(1461–1483)

Although Edward IV had been acclaimed king, the Lancastrians had not abandoned hope and they continued to fight. Edward was an astute general and saw that their huge army had to be routed immediately or it would remain a threat. At Towton near Tadcaster in Yorkshire he caught up with the Lancastrian forces. In what was becoming a north–south divide the Battle of Towton was fought on Palm Sunday, March 1461, in a blinding snowstorm, the private armies of northern border lords such as the Cliffords and the Percys clashing with retainers from Edward IV's Mortimer estates in Wales and Warwick's soldiers from the midlands. The Lancastrians were comprehensively defeated. Six of their most important magnates were killed, leaving the cause almost leaderless, while some 37,000 of their followers were killed. Their blood stained the snowdrifts red. Many of their bodies fell into a ravine running alongside the battlefield and were never recovered.

It was not in Queen Margaret's nature to give up, however. She retreated to Scotland with the bewildered Henry VI and from there encouraged rebellions in northern England. In 1464 Edward, at last provoked into engaging with what remained of the Lancastrian forces, put an end to the insurrections at the Battle of Hexham. In its aftermath Henry VI, who had been part of the raiding party, became a fugitive and was captured wandering in the Pennines. He was then brought to the Tower of London. The Scots had by now abandoned him, and they made a peace treaty with Edward IV, who began to put the country in order and restore the government. But by the end of the decade a new threat to the Yorkist regime had arisen. This time it came in the somewhat surprising shape of the Earl of Warwick. The Yorkists' former chief adviser had been crucial to their achieving the throne and his influence throughout his own immense estates scattered all round England was a significant factor in ensuring the smooth transition to the Yorkist regime. Warwick had swiftly moved his relations into positions of influence at court, one of his brothers being made Archbishop of York and the other assuming the old earldom of the attainted Percys. His own reward was to be recognized as an international statesman. It had become his conviction that an alliance with France as opposed to the traditional links with Burgundy would now be more useful to England.

Warwick's vanity was flattered by the cunning new King of France Louis XI, Charles VII's son. Louis was determined to limit the power of the dangerous rival perched on his eastern borders, so an alliance with England made perfect sense. He suggested that Edward should marry Bona of Savoy, his wife's sister. But by now Edward IV was older and anxious to be less dependent on the over-controlling Warwick and the Nevilles. He had his own political ideas. The rupture between him and his advisers began when Warwick's French marriage plan forced the king to reveal that he was in fact already married to the exquisite Elizabeth Woodville, the daughter of Lord Rivers and widow of Sir John Grey, a Lancastrian supporter. She had triumphed where other court beauties had failed. The fair and handsome Edward IV was a young giant who stood six feet three in his stockinged feet, a man of great personal charm and a well-known pursuer of the ladies.

Queen Elizabeth, despite her delicate appearance, was no ingenue but an experienced woman of the world, older than the king and the mother of two children by her first husband. The revelation of the secret marriage became the signal for the wholesale filling of positions at court with her grasping relatives, and Warwick and his brother the Archbishop of York were soon excluded from the king's counsels. Moreover Edward deliberately pursued a foreign policy which was the opposite of Warwick's. He renewed the Anglo-Burgundian alliance by marrying his sister Margaret of York to Charles the Rash, Duke of Burgundy.

For so proud a magnate as Warwick to be publicly humiliated in this way was intolerable. He therefore determined to use the private armies of his vast territories to revolt against the king. His scheming mind soon fixed on a new vehicle for his vigorous ambition in the king's younger brother, the impressionable and greedy George, Duke of Clarence. Like everyone Clarence disliked the Woodvilles, and was soon lured into marrying Warwick's elder daughter Isabella, who stood to inherit the Kingmaker's great estates. Thwarted by Edward IV, the Kingmaker now proposed to make Clarence king and his own daughter queen.

In 1469 a series of rebellions began on the Warwick and Neville properties in the midlands. At the Battle of Edgecote Edward IV himself was temporarily taken prisoner by Warwick, though bad feeling among the Lords forced the Kingmaker to release him. A year later Warwick orchestrated another rising, but this time it was absolutely routed by Edward. Clarence and Warwick were forced to flee abroad to the court of the French king Louis XI.

There the restless Warwick's plans took a different form under the influence of the equally crafty Louis XI, who was determined to hit at Burgundy by reinstating the Lancastrian dynasty. Since France was also home to the exiled Queen Margaret and her son Edward, Prince of Wales, Louis managed to effect an amazing reconciliation between the bitterest of enemies – the Lancastrian queen and the former Yorkist Warwick. Once again, Warwick's vanity drew him into a new plot to lead an invasion of England to restore Henry VI to the throne. In return his second daughter Anne Neville was to marry Queen Margaret's son, the Prince of Wales. Anne now became the focus of Warwick's hopes of seeing his flesh and blood on the throne.

In the autumn of 1470, with troops paid for by the French, Warwick and Clarence landed in England. While Edward IV was in the north, they released a puzzled Henry VI from the Tower of London and proclaimed him king. Then with the French army they drove Edward IV into exile at his brother-in-law's court in Burgundy. The speed with which Warwick's expedition had reached London meant Edward had no time to rally his defences.

Henry VI's restoration lasted for six months between October 1470 and May 1471, but it was really the restoration to power of Warwick the Kingmaker and his Neville relations. Henry VI's whirligig of fortune, which might have upset the equilibrium of a more stolid personality, was far too much for him and he became almost imbecilic. One chronicler unkindly reported that he was 'as mute as a crowned calf'. But the Kingmaker's day was drawing to a close. In March 1471 Edward of York landed at Ravenspur on the Humber river, just like that earlier pretender Henry IV, and steadily fought his way to London.

The civil wars had been going on intermittently for over fifteen years. By and large its battles scarcely affected the ordinary citizen, despite their killing perhaps a third of the nobility. Although Edward did not achieve the nationwide enthusiasm which had been crucial for Henry IV's revolution, support for the Yorkist cause had always tended to be concentrated in the south and east, in Kent and Sussex, and on the Welsh marches. Edward IV had extremely warm relations with the merchants of London owing to his keen interest in money. When the city opened its gates to him, Henry VI went back to the Tower and Edward was acclaimed king once more. By his side was Clarence, who had finally realized that his best hope lay with his brother now that Warwick was promoting the cause of Lancaster.

On Easter Sunday, 14 April 1471, the decisive Battle of Barnet was fought in what is now north London. Edward defeated Warwick and the Lancastrian army in no uncertain terms and Warwick himself died on the battlefield. As at the Battle of Towton, freak weather conditions prevailed, with such low-lying mist that it was almost impossible for the soldiers to see.

Although Edward IV's main enemy had been disposed of, there remained the threat of the Prince of Wales and Margaret of Anjou, who had just landed in the west. Had Queen Margaret arrived a little earlier she might have done better for her son, but since the Yorkists had triumphed so conclusively at the Battle of Barnet the country rallied behind Edward. On 4 May Edward IV caught up with the queen and her son, and fought them at the Battle of Tewkesbury. A final, brutal slaughter marked the end of the hopes of the Lancastrians and the triumph of the white rose. Queen Margaret was imprisoned, but the Prince of Wales was murdered in cold blood – as were all the Lancastrian nobles, even though they had surrendered. As for Henry VI, Edward IV at last came to the conclusion that the threat he posed to his dynasty made him too dangerous to live. On the day that Edward returned to London from Tewkesbury it was officially proclaimed that Henry had died in the Tower 'of pure displeasure and melancholy'.

For the rest of his reign, Edward IV ruled as a strong monarch. Law and order returned. He summoned Parliament as little as possible to avoid enhancing the power of the nobility, but so many of their scions had died in the wars that there was no real opposition. The king was very popular with the commercial classes for refusing to tolerate the nobles' habit of private war, even though to escape Parliamentary demands he returned to a form of the Maltolt now known as a benevolence, a forced loan paid mainly by the merchants. His close links with their community were cemented by his longstanding relationship with Jane Shore, the wife of a London merchant.

Now that London was no longer the scene of warfare it benefited from the growing volume of international trade and from cheap and mobile labour, for villeinage had at last withered away. It also helped that the seas round England were safer since Edward IV had stamped out piracy. Instead of fighting suicidal wars among themselves the European kingdoms had begun to turn their energies outwards, exploring the unknown. By 1460 the Portuguese king and grandson of John of Gaunt, Henry the Navigator, had discovered the north-west coast of Africa. In 1481 Bristol merchants sailing west into the Atlantic hit on what they called the isles of Brasil, which may have been Newfoundland. And only a decade later Christopher Columbus became the first European to set foot on the unknown continent later called America.

Edward IV supported the printer Caxton, enabling him to set up his press in the shadow of Westminster Abbey in 1476. This revolutionary development meant that what people read was no longer controlled by the

Church. There now circulated in England the uncensored literature of the ancient Greeks and Romans, which had been frowned on since the days of the Church Fathers as well as romances and histories. It was the beginning of what is known as the Renaissance or rebirth of western culture. Spread by scholars like the Dutchman Desiderius Erasmus and John Colet, the Dean of St Paul's and founder of its School for Boys, the humanist movement took hold in England. The study of man unmediated by religion marked the end of the middle ages and saw the beginning of the modern world.

In the turbulent north, to suppress the Lancastrians and keep out the Scots Edward relied on his brother Richard of Gloucester, who as well as being a talented commander – as he had shown at the Battle of Tewkesbury – was also a very good administrator. The Yorkist king soon felt secure enough to invade France in order to punish Louis XI for his part in Warwick's uprising, but the Anglo-Burgundian alliance was damaged almost at once when the king's brother-in-law Charles the Rash failed to send enough troops to ensure success. Burgundy's existence as an independent country was in any case near its end. In 1477 Charles the Rash was killed at the Battle of Nancy against the Swiss. It was the signal for Louis to invade Burgundy and make it part of France, as it has been ever since.

In 1483 Edward IV suddenly died of a stroke. He was only forty, still golden haired but with a tendency to plumpness. His death was generally put down to a life of self-indulgence which had started to verge on debauchery. In his last years he had moved against his troublesome brother Clarence by means of a bill of attainder. Clarence had learned little from his adventures. He had already aroused the enmity of his brother Richard of Gloucester, who had recently married Clarence's sister-in-law Anne Neville after the murder of her husband, the Prince of Wales. Despite Gloucester's expectations Clarence had attempted to make sure that the immense Warwick possessions were inherited by himself alone. Eventually, in 1478, it was given out that Clarence had drowned in a vat of Malmsey wine. He was most likely murdered.

On the death of Edward IV the crown passed to his thirteen-year-old son, who became Edward V. He and his brother, the eleven-year-old Duke of York, are known to history as the ill-fated Princes in the Tower.

Edward V
(1483)

Since Edward V was not of age, on his father's death the same factional struggle for power that had marred Henry VI's reign erupted between the Woodvilles and the older nobility. To Edward's ministers, the real threat to the government of England was not Richard of Gloucester, whom posterity knows as the murderer of the princes, but the Woodville family. It seemed clear that the Woodvilles were about to mount a *coup d'état*: Queen Elizabeth had removed the king's treasure into her safekeeping, her brother Sir Edward Woodville had commandeered the Fleet, and her son the Marquis of Dorset started rallying his troops on his estates. Ministers lost no time in urging Richard of Gloucester, Edward IV's representative in the north who had been named the young king's guardian by his dying brother, to come south and to take up his position as protector or regent, to which the royal Council had nominated him, as quickly as possible.

The triumph of the Woodvilles at Edward IV's court had driven many former courtiers out of the King's Council and back to their estates. Chief among their enemies was the Duke of Buckingham, brother-in-law of the queen. When it became clear that Elizabeth had decided that the new king should be crowned as soon as possible to prevent Gloucester assuming power as protector, Buckingham acted on Gloucester's behalf to prevent the coronation. The Woodville riding party escorting the new king rapidly into London from the west was ambushed by Gloucester and Buckingham. These two men then proceeded with Edward V into London, which they reached on 4 May 1483.

With 24 June being mentioned as a date for Edward's coronation there was a real possibility that Richard of Gloucester's Protectorate might end before it had begun. In considering what happened next it is hard to achieve a completely objective view of Gloucester, his character having been so blackened by Tudor propagandists, including Shakespeare. Even his appearance counted against him. What seems to have been simply one shoulder a little higher than the other has been exaggerated into a hump back – 'crookback Dick' – and equated with moral deformity. Richard of Gloucester was secretive by nature, one of life's loners. But though he was

King Edward the V.
The Original is in Lambeth Library.

The Seal & Autograp of Rich.ᵈ Duke of Gloucester ——
Protecter to K. Edward the 5.ᵗʰ

From the Original Instrument in the Possession of
John Thane.

Edward V, who did not live for his coronation, was the elder of the
Princes in the Tower.

not personable and charming like his elder brother he was admired for his statesmanlike qualities, and in contrast to his brother Clarence he was always devoted to his brother Edward IV's interests. His austere religious nature was viewed as a welcome contrast to the frivolity of the queen and indeed of Edward IV himself. In the north, which he had governed for the previous twelve years, he had acquired a reputation for exceptional competence, his dutifulness, his rebuilding of the local administration after the anarchy of war and his rooting out of corruption attracting a great deal of personal loyalty.

Until June 1483 in fact Richard of Gloucester seems to have led an exemplary life. Nevertheless it cannot be disputed that he was the moving spirit in the sinister events of that summer. The facts speak for themselves. By 6 July Gloucester had assumed the throne as Richard III in Edward V's stead and been crowned in Westminster Abbey. The disinheriting of his nephew had been carefully prepared. An influential preacher Dr Ralph Shaw had given a public sermon at St Paul's on the theme that 'bastard slips shall not take root'. Shaw's argument was that, owing to Edward IV's pre-contract with another lady before he married Elizabeth Woodville, the marriage was invalid. Edward V and his brother the Duke of York were therefore illegitimate. Two days later Buckingham repeated this theory in a speech to the Mayor of London and important citizens in the Guildhall. Coming from the elder line, Clarence's son would have taken precedence over Gloucester, but his father's treachery disqualified him. The real heir to the throne therefore was Richard of Gloucester.

Edward V's uncle,
Richard III.

In the meantime any potential opposition had been ruthlessly disposed of by Gloucester. Most importantly, two leading Woodvilles had been executed without trial. Next some 20,000 of Gloucester's soldiers descended from the north and began encircling London. Their presence and threats of violence persuaded Queen Elizabeth to release the Duke of York from protective sanctuary in Westminster Abbey so that he could be prepared for his brother's coronation. However, once the eleven-year-old duke had joined his brother in the Tower of London the ceremony was mysteriously postponed until November. Richard was then invited by the Lords in Parliament to accept the crown – they could hardly do otherwise, with his troops surrounding London – and he took over the coronation planned for his nephew. The two little boys vanished into the Tower and after the autumn of 1483 appear never to have been seen again.

Much ink has been expended over whether Richard III had his nephews murdered there. The rumour was first given chapter and verse in the next reign. In the time of Henry VII, Sir James Tyrell – who had been a follower of Richard III and was a well-known conspirator – supposedly confessed to their murder when he was arrested on another charge. He claimed to have been commissioned by Richard III to drug the princes' jailers in the White Tower and smother the children at night in their beds while they slept. While Sir James waited outside the Tower in the moonlight the murderers crept into their room and then disposed of their bodies by thrusting them under the stairs into the foundations. Certainly in 1674, almost 200 years later, workmen digging beneath the staircase of the White Tower discovered a wooden chest containing the bones of two children, one aged about twelve or thirteen, the other about ten. Pieces of rag and velvet were still sticking to their bones.

It was, however, impossible to sex the bones or really date them and now they are no longer in very good condition. In any case, where the Tower complex stands has been a population centre for at least 2,000 years – it was a fort even in Roman times. A laundry list itemizing children's clothing and dated September 1485, by which time Richard had been replaced by his Tudor successor Henry VII, is sometimes quoted as evidence that the boys came to their deaths at his hands. Alive the boys were just as much a threat to the Tudor dynasty as they were to Richard III. However, the weight of the evidence points to Richard as their murderer.

Richard III
(1483–1485)

In the autumn of 1483 a series of revolts against the new king Richard III by pockets of gentry all over the country seems to have had as one of its objects the rescue of the rest of Edward IV's children from Westminster Abbey, to prevent them coming to harm. Evidently many believed something had happened to the two princes. Most of the rebels had previously been pillars of the Yorkist establishment and many were ex-sheriffs. Something very heinous must have taken place that summer to turn them against a Yorkist king. Yet Richard made no attempt to disprove the rumours by producing the boys alive. Although the two princes may have been alive until October 1483, round about then they seem to have fallen out of sight. Tradesmen calling at the Tower stopped seeing them practising at archery in the Tower Garden. Their figures were apparently no longer glimpsed even 'behind the bars and windows'. By then there were definite and damaging rumours that the boys were dead. Richard was evidently seen by many as accursed, the author of royal infanticide. Even by the different standards of the fifteenth century, this was a crime that made men shudder.

One of the most serious rebellions was headed by Richard's former associate the Duke of Buckingham. His is one of the names mentioned in connection with the deaths of the princes because he was the Constable of the Tower, but some time in the summer of 1483 there was a falling out between him and Richard III – perhaps because of the murders, perhaps because of his own distant claim to the throne. He now claimed it for Henry Tudor, the son of the heiress Lady Margaret Beaufort. After the deaths of Henry VI and the Prince of Wales this part-Welsh nobleman was the last and distant hope of the Lancastrian line. His mother the redoubtable Lady Margaret had attended Richard III's coronation, but Henry Tudor himself had been smuggled abroad to Brittany in 1471 as his life was believed to be in danger.

Primed by Buckingham, Henry Tudor duly set out with a small fleet from Brittany to claim the throne but had to turn back when it became clear that the uprising had no hope of succeeding. Buckingham, however, was captured, and executed in the market square at Salisbury. But the disaffection aroused against the king was becoming so widespread that the Yorkists and Lancastrians started to plot together. It was agreed between Queen Elizabeth Woodville and Lady Margaret Beaufort that Princess Elizabeth of York should be married to Lady Margaret's son Henry Tudor.

Henry Tudor's father Edmund, Earl of Richmond, had been a member of one of the Welsh families closely linked to Owen Glendower's revolt. They had emerged from obscurity when Henry Tudor's grandfather Owen Tudor had pursued and married the French queen Catherine after the death of her husband Henry V. Since his father had died before Henry Tudor was born and his mother had then remarried, he had been brought up in Wales at Pembroke Castle by his uncle Jasper Tudor. Much of his early life, he would later remark, had been passed in seclusion or exile.

Exchanging Brittany for France after discovering that the Bretons had planned to betray him for a large ransom, Henry Tudor was soon joined by an increasing number of heads of southern English families who had taken part in rebellion. The confiscation of their property and Richard's plantation of his friends on their old lands meant they had nothing to lose and everything to gain from a new king. The death of Richard III's adored only son in April 1484 and of his wife Anne Neville less than a year later gave a doomed air to the regime. An ancient prophecy circulated that in the Year of Three Kings great disaster would come upon the kingdom.

In fact it was the death of Anne Neville that spurred the Lancastrian king-in-waiting and the Yorkist exiles into action. At the end of spring 1485, a rumour reached them that Anne Neville's death had been no accident. Richard III had poisoned his wife in order to underpin his tottering regime by marrying his niece Elizabeth of York. As the daughter of Edward IV she would lend him the legitimacy he lacked.

But, as we have seen, Elizabeth of York was also the central figure in the plan to put Henry Tudor on the throne. Henry's claim through his mother Lady Margaret Beaufort had serious weaknesses. Although the Beaufort line had been legitimized, the family had originally been barred from the royal succession. The male line had died out when the Duke of Somerset was killed at the Battle of Tewkesbury, and there was the usual prejudice against descent through the female line – the basis of Henry Tudor's claim. Marriage to Elizabeth of York would strengthen that claim. The threat that Richard might marry her instead roused the refugees into speeding up their plans.

The haemorrhage out of the country of the very gentry on whose unofficial network English kings traditionally relied ensured that in a civil war Richard III would be almost completely dependent on the great magnates and their men-at-arms. By 1485, if he was to keep the throne he would need the loyal support of the three most important magnates in England, whose armies could turn the tide either way. They were Henry Percy, Earl of Northumberland, the Duke of Norfolk and the Cheshire magnate Lord Stanley. In the event Norfolk fought on Richard's side. The other two deserted him. The Percys were in any case usually Lancastrian supporters, and Northumberland had been angered by Richard's decision to use the Earl of Lincoln and the Council of the North to keep order in the traditional Percy heartlands.

It was one of Richard III's greatest problems that the third element, Lord Stanley, was an unknown quantity. Stanley was Constable of England but this appointment had only been made to bind him more closely to the Ricardian government. For Stanley was also the third husband of Lady Margaret Beaufort. Richard must have believed that Stanley was aware of his wife's constant plotting, but he was too frightened of a rebellion in the north-west to imprison him.

Where Lord Stanley's allegiance lay proved to be the pivot on which Richard's defences turned. When at the beginning of August Henry Tudor landed at Milford Haven in the far west of Wales his path into England lay north-east, close to the Stanley estates in Cheshire. There Lord Stanley controlled perhaps 4,000 men who could have prevented Henry Tudor and his 2,000 troops leaving Wales – but they allowed them through.

By 22 August Henry Tudor's army was in Leicestershire, the heart of England, at Market Bosworth where the last battle of the Wars of the Roses was fought. He had successfully capitalized on his Welsh roots and Welsh loyalties, and his cause was seen as a Welsh resurgence. As he travelled east towards his destiny at the Battle of Bosworth Field he was hailed by the Welsh bards as a true Prince of Wales whose coming had been foretold by ancient prophecies. His supporters had swelled considerably in the march through Wales and across the midlands. In contrast the allies Richard was counting on were not there. As news spread of the invasion, only Norfolk came up to scratch. Northumberland remained in the north. Richard III had taken the precaution of holding Stanley's son Lord Strange hostage so that he would not help the rebels.

As a result, although he was plainly responsible for letting Henry Tudor through Cheshire, Lord Stanley continued to give assurances of support to Richard. But there was more than a hint of defeat in the wind for Richard. The night before battle – when the usurper king, apparently haunted by strange phantoms, was unable to sleep – many of his supporters secretly decamped to Henry Tudor's side. Meanwhile Stanley had positioned himself on a hill midway between the two armies, so that it was not clear whether his army belonged to the royal forces or to the rebels. The cunning Stanley, caught on the horns of a difficult dilemma, would play a waiting game.

Without Northumberland's troops morale was not good in the king's camp, and it was lower on the morning of battle after the defections had been discovered. When the despairing Richard personally led a cavalry charge against Henry Tudor, bringing his standard with the red dragon of Wales crashing to the ground, the Stanleys at last threw their weight behind the pretender. The day was Henry Tudor's.

Shakespeare has Richard III coming off his charger and shouting in vain, 'A horse! A horse! My kingdom for a horse.' This was based on fact: the muddiness of the ground was responsible for his not being able to keep his seat. But whatever else Richard was, he was no coward – it took a great many Welsh soldiers piling on top of him to kill him. After the battle his body was stripped naked and flung across a horse to remind all that he was no longer the Lord's Anointed. Richard had been wearing a thin gold crown around his helmet. When it was found under a hawthorn bush, where it had rolled, the quick-witted Lord Stanley there and then placed it on the head of Henry Tudor and hailed him as King Henry.

Richard III's naked body was tossed into an unmarked grave at Leicester while the new king Henry VII marched to London. There he later married his distant relation Elizabeth of York. Indicating the depths of suspicion with which the former king was regarded, one chronicler wrote, 'In the year 1485 on 22nd August the tusks of the Boar were blunted and the red rose, the avenger of the white, shines upon us.' It was through the red rose of Lancaster, through his Beaufort blood, that Henry Tudor claimed the throne. The union of England through the two families was symbolized by the Tudor rose – the white rose of York superimposed on the larger red rose of Lancaster. It is still to be seen at the Tower of London on the uniform Henry VII designed for his new bodyguard, known today as the Beefeaters.

Henry VII gave his name to a whole new dynasty – the Tudors. For the first time since the sixth century and King Arthur, England was proclaimed to have a king from her most ancient race. Arthurian echoes were to the fore, since Caxton had just published Sir Thomas Malory's *Morte d'Arthur*. Henry VII even called his eldest son Arthur after the ancient British king. At the coronation such evocations were exploited by the new king and his supporters. In particular, prophecies were once again cited to establish the new king's legitimacy. To underline the unity of the realm the queen was carried off to give birth at Winchester, the ancient seat of the West Saxon kings. Meanwhile, to remind everyone of his Yorkshire title as Earl of Richmond, at the river near Sheen Henry built Richmond Palace.

It was not all romance. Henry VII had no intention of ruling as a constitutional Lancastrian monarch limited by Parliament. He was a monarch, and he had himself crowned before Parliament met. Thereafter, like Edward IV, he summoned Parliament as seldom as possible. By the next century under his descendants the Tudor House of Commons had become an instrument of royal power, the so-called Tudor despotism, which saw the growth of the nation state.

Early days of printing. Caxton in the Almonry, Westminster.

TUDOR

Henry VII
(1485–1509)

The formidable, charismatic and politically gifted Tudor dynasty which ruled England uninterruptedly for a little over a century coincided with massive shifts in the way Europeans viewed the world and themselves. The discovery in 1492 of the unsuspected American continent between Europe and Asia during the reign of the first Tudor, Henry VII, is sometimes said to be the beginning of the modern era, because it coincided with the overthrowing of so many other orthodoxies of the middle ages. With immense ingenuity, medieval philosophers had specialized in reconciling all knowledge within a religious context. For example, before the discoveries of the fifteenth century, European Christians believed Jerusalem to be the geographical centre of the world. After the Portuguese had rounded the coast of Africa and the Spanish had found the Americas it became impossible to hold to this belief.

What is more, by the end of the fifteenth century scholars lacked the will to perform their dizzying feats of argument. Disenchantment with the papacy, which had started with the three popes, was accelerated by a seismic change in the learning process prompted by the study of Greek, a subject little taught to Latin Christians since the Dark Ages. With the fall of Constantinople to the Turks in 1453, hundreds of Byzantine scholars went into exile and thus reintroduced western Europe to the lost world of the ancient Greek classical philosophers. The classical revival in the arts, the Renaissance, had been under way since the fourteenth century, but when the study of Greek philosophy took root at the universities, it liberated scholars from the constraints Christianity had imposed on logical thought and set off a chain reaction. The translation of ancient Greek texts revolutionized the way people studied. Greek scholarship known as the New Learning revealed an early Church in the New Testament which bore no relation to the corrupt and power-hungry papacy. The effect of all these events together was electrifying. In a generation the stranglehold which the Church of Rome had maintained on Christians was thrown off. During the lifetime of the second Tudor, Henry VIII, the awakening of thousands of individual consciences resulted in the Reformation and the break from Rome of various Protestant Churches, including the Church of England.

By the end of the sixteenth century, during the long reign of the fifth Tudor, Elizabeth I, the bitterness of the conflict between what had emerged as Protestant and Catholic powers had become a world war. A growing internal conviction about the rightness of Protestantism polarized Europe and England herself into hardened ideological positions. Spain, newly united in 1469 and expelling the last of the Moors from Granada after 700 years, became Catholicism's champion. For all the serpentine diplomacy and peace-loving nature of the great Queen Elizabeth, by 1588 and the defeat of the Spanish Armada England stood revealed as a firmly Protestant power and Catholic Spain's most important opponent. Last but not least, the discovery of America began the move away from the axis of the Mediterranean that had dominated the world for 2,000 years, revolutionizing trade routes to the advantage of those powers with an Atlantic coastline – that is, Portugal, Spain, France and England. It was these countries that in the next century would begin the path to empire.

But in 1485 at the end of the Wars of the Roses none of these tumultuous changes could have been predicted nor the thrall that the Tudors would

Tombs of Henry VII and his wife Elizabeth of York sculpted by Torrigiano in the Lady Chapel Henry VII built, Westminster Abbey.

have over their adopted kingdom. The Tudors were upstarts, and Henry VII's most pressing task was to establish his dynasty on a firm foundation. He succeeded admirably over the next twenty-odd years, with the result that his son Henry VIII succeeded to the throne without a murmur of protest. But as a usurper Henry VII inevitably spent the first part of his reign dealing with potential threats to the crown. In fact the new king had married the only real Yorkist claimant, the tall, exquisite and golden-haired Elizabeth of York. The only other possible claimant, the disgraced Clarence's son Warwick, was in the Tower. This did not stop people making mischief. Henry VII's particular *bêtes noires* were his wife's aunt Margaret of Burgundy, sister of Edward IV, at whose court all pretenders found a welcome, and the Irish, headed by the Fitzgerald family, the earls of Kildare. The Irish were traditionally Yorkist supporters because the Yorkist Mortimers had estates in Ireland.

The first serious attempt against Henry was made in 1487 by a discontented consortium masterminded by Margaret of Burgundy and led by one of Richard III's chief supporters, Francis Lovel. A young boy named Lambert Simnel landed in Ireland claiming to be the Earl of Warwick freshly escaped from the Tower. Despite being crowned king rather presumptuously in Ireland, his paltry invading force (a few of Lovel's men and some German mercenaries) was easily defeated by Henry at the Battle of Stoke, and Simnel himself was captured. The real Earl of Warwick was taken out of the Tower and paraded to show that he was alive. Henry was so unworried by Lambert Simnel that he simply put him to work in the royal kitchens turning the spit.

Perkin Warbeck, the next pretender sent to England by Margaret of Burgundy, proved to be a good deal more of a threat. He gave out that he was the younger of the princes in the Tower, Richard, Duke of York, and that he had the backing of a party of disaffected English nobles. Not only was Warbeck's claim recognized by the French king, as well as by Margaret of Burgundy, but he was warmly welcomed into Scotland by James IV. James IV even married him to his cousin Lady Catherine Gordon and invaded England on his behalf.

In turn the large taxes raised in England for a war against the Scots became the excuse for a rising in Cornwall in 1497. Cornishmen believed they were too far from Scotland to have to pay for northern England's defence. A Cornish army camped out on Blackheath in London, and Warbeck – who by this time had been expelled from Scotland by James IV out of fear of an English invasion – seized this golden opportunity to land in the west and march on London, only to be roundly defeated at Taunton. After taking refuge in the Cistercian Priory of Beaulieu (now Lord Montagu's museum of car-racing fame) he was captured, brought to

London and beheaded in 1499 along with the unfortunate Warwick, who seems to have been innocent of anything very much except that he was the outstanding heir to the throne.

This encounter has been called the final episode of the Wars of the Roses. By the end of the century careful diplomatic negotiation and judicious use of warfare had enabled Henry VII to establish the Tudor dynasty securely on the throne. Alliances with France's enemies, Ferdinand of Spain and Maximilian of Austria, an invasion of France and a threat to prevent the export of English wool to the Netherlands ensured that Warbeck could not find a safe haven across the Channel. The 1496 Magnus Intercursus Treaty bound the Netherlands and England together, restoring trade links and forbidding both countries to harbour the other's enemies. A further treaty in 1506, occasioned by Maximilian's son the Archduke Philip being shipwrecked on the English coast, amplified this with advantageous terms for English merchants.

Marriage was another string to Henry's bow. Fear of France, whose absorption of Brittany threatened the southern English coast, persuaded Henry to hitch England to the rising power of Spain by marrying his elder son to Ferdinand's daughter Catherine of Aragon. In 1501, after much toing and froing of ambassadors and bargaining about dowries, Catherine was married to Arthur, Prince of Wales. Only a year later, however, Arthur died – to the great distress of his parents. Marrying a brother's widow was forbidden by Church law, but Henry so desired a Spanish alliance that he asked for a special ruling by Pope Julius II so that his next son, the future Henry VIII, could marry Catherine. With incalculable consequences the ruling was granted, and the wedding took place of the new Prince of Wales, the blond and lissom Henry, to the stiff, devout Spanish infanta.

Catherine of Aragon's father, the cunning and astute Ferdinand of Aragon, had not only unified the Spanish peninsula by his own marriage to Isabella of Castile and by expelling the last of the Moors in 1492, but had achieved mastery at the western end of the Mediterranean by controlling the kingdom of the Two Sicilies, the boot of Italy from Naples southwards. Marriage into the Spanish royal family made the new Tudor dynasty appear respectable abroad, and for forty years adherence to Spain would be the first principle of English foreign policy. By marrying his daughter Margaret Tudor to the Scottish king James IV, Henry VII hoped to rupture the Auld Alliance between France and Scotland after 200 years. It would be the great-grandson of that alliance who would inherit the throne when Elizabeth, the last of the Tudors, died childless.

But it was France, after so many centuries as a disunited collection of feudal principalities, that was the great power of the age. In 1488 the last piece of the French jigsaw had fallen into place when the young king

Charles VIII married the heiress of the Duchy of Brittany, and the duchy thus became incorporated into France. Secure at home, in 1494 Charles outraged the Italians by capturing Naples. For half a century French policy existed in a time warp, dictated by a notion of the European economy as it had existed before the discovery of the Americas, when real wealth and power lay in controlling the Italian peninsula and thus the trade routes of the Mediterranean basin leading to the Levant. So France exhausted herself in battles as she attempted to claim the kingdom of Naples and the Duchy of Milan through Angevin and Visconti forebears and allowed herself to become caught up in the ceaseless internecine struggles of the great Italian princes and the papacy. It was a policy which would end in a century-long battle with Spain.

Well set up abroad, at home Henry VII restored the authority of the crown, which had decayed in all parts of his new realm during the disorder of the later fifteenth century. Wales was anyway welcoming to a Welsh prince, and he revived the Council of Wales which was overseen by the Prince of Wales's Council. In Ireland Henry attempted to bind the Irish more tightly to England by sending Sir Edward Poynings over to replace the Earl of Kildare as governor. In 1494 Poynings' Law prevented the by now semi-independent Irish Parliament passing laws without the approval of the King's Council in England and made all laws passed by the English Parliament applicable to Ireland. But Poynings' Law tended to be more honoured in the breach than in the observance, and the Irish chieftains and the Norman Irish continued to lead their lives of semi-autonomy. Poynings is said to have remarked wearily that 'All Ireland could not rule the Earl of Kildare,' at which Henry VII retorted, 'Then let the Earl of Kildare rule all Ireland.' Poynings was withdrawn and matters continued much as they always had done.

At home, despite his Lancastrian roots, Henry followed the Yorkist method of seeing very little of Parliament and raised money by forced loans or benevolences which were in theory illegal. But the English had had enough of weak factional rule and liked the way he clamped down on the power of the barons. One of Henry V's first acts had been to outlaw the practice of livery and maintenance of private armies, which had caused such mayhem during the previous century. The practice nevertheless continued. The story goes that Henry VII went to stay with the Earl of Oxford and, as he was leaving, asked in an admiring way how many servants he kept about him. 'Two hundred at least,' said Oxford proudly. Thereupon the king asked him for 10,000 pounds in fines.

The imposition of massive fines was how Henry enforced the law – to the great benefit of the royal coffers. The royal Council, which had always been partly a law court, adopted a more executive role overseeing the common law as the Court of the Star Chamber. (It took its name from the stars on the ceiling of the room in the Palace of Westminster where it convened.) But though the Star Chamber would become notorious under the later Tudors as a way of executing summary justice, in Henry VII's time it intervened if it had evidence that a lord had brought undue influence to bear on a local court. This was another part of Henry's policy of weakening the powers of the nobility, for the practice of intimidating juries was not ended immediately by Henry's laws against livery and maintenance. Another way of strengthening the crown was to increase the powers of knights of the shires as justices of the peace; this was necessary because by the end of the fifteenth century sheriffs tended to be the preserve of great families and their clients.

Henry VII died in his early fifties in 1509, having succeeded in making the crown very wealthy. But this came at the price of tremendous unpopularity, thanks to the activities of two of his favourite advisers, Richard Empson and Edmund Dudley, who applied their ingenuity to dreaming up new taxes. No less ingenious in this respect was Henry's Archbishop of Canterbury, Cardinal Morton, who was also his chancellor and was sourly remembered for the tax device known as Morton's Fork, which caught the unwary whichever way they turned. Morton's view was that if a man was extravagant, he was not paying enough taxes to the king and had room for more. On the other hand, a man who was not flashing his money around was probably hiding it away in a miserly fashion and should be compelled to share it with the king.

Henry had taken a keen interest in the voyages of discovery to the New World that were beginning so tentatively at this time. Portugal, the great maritime innovator of the fifteenth century, had strong links to Bristol, and it was Bristol merchants in partnership with the king who paid for the Venetian John Cabot to sail west and so discover the coast of Labrador in what is now Canada. But just why had such astonishing discoveries been taking place at this time? One reason lay in the steady advance westward through the Balkans during the fifteenth century of the Turkish or Ottoman people. Hitherto the spice trade had been Europe's most lucrative pursuit, because in the days before refrigeration spices were used to preserve food, and they had to be imported from the hot countries of the east (predominantly India) via the Mediterranean. On this trade the Italian republics of Genoa and Venice, so conveniently situated between east and west, had grown rich. But once the Turks began to interrupt the traffic of the Mediterranean it became urgently important to find a sea route to India which would avoid the traditional overland route from the shores of the eastern Mediterranean.

Portugal, the nation leaning into the western Atlantic and furthest from the Mediterranean, was convinced that she could seize this profitable trade from the Mediterranean nations if a new route could be found to the Indies (as India was called). Their enthusiasm was contagious, and their Spanish neighbours became just as eager. Christopher Columbus, a Genoese sailor, decided that the best route to India lay to the west. Sponsored by Ferdinand and Isabella, he set sail in 1492 and eventually discovered the islands in the Caribbean which continue to be known as the West Indies – though they are of course nowhere near India. He had discovered the New World. Following a papal declaration that all of that unknown country a hundred leagues west of the Azores belonged to Spain and Portugal, Spain under Cortes conquered the Aztecs and created New Spain in Mexico, while Portugal took Brazil.

Meanwhile the other great effect of the Turkish move west, the dispersal of Greek scholars to western capitals and universities, fleeing from the catastrophe of the fall of Constantinople, was slowly having dramatic effects among the educated, as we have seen – most of all in their understanding of religion. Spread by the contemporary technological revolution of printing, a great change occurred in the way people thought – for the religious impulse had not died under the widespread anti-clericalism. The combination of this devotional religious movement and the outrage provoked by the scholarly discoveries of the New Learning led at last to an upheaval in Germany provoked by a monk and professor of theology named Martin Luther. Luther was already disgusted by the irreligious nature of the Church, but in 1517 his anger boiled over when he met a Dominican friar raising money to build the new Church of St Peter's in Rome by selling papal indulgences – which provided absolution from one's sins – from a red velvet cushion.

On 31 October that year Luther nailed his ninety-five theses or criticisms of papal teaching to the door of the Catholic church at Wittenberg, and so sparked off the religious revolution known as the Reformation. Though many had been feeling the same way, it was the first time that the pope's power had been challenged publicly, and Luther's action shook Christendom to its foundations. There were peasant riots, Luther was excommunicated and an official debate took place at a meeting called the Diet of Worms (a diet was an imperial council; Worms was a Rhineland town) between Luther and the Holy Roman Emperor Charles V, who was also the King of Spain and the pope's champion. There Luther refused to retract his views. His belief that man's salvation lay in his own faith and not in the Sacraments of the Church conferred by priests remained unshakeable. By 1530 eight of the north German princes had adopted the Lutheran faith, or Protestantism as it became known after their Protestation against the emperor. And in 1534 Henry VIII of England,

Henry VII's son, became the first king to break officially with Rome, the Lutheran princes having meanwhile tried to reconcile their Church with papal authority.

Henry VIII

(1509–1547)

When the Reformation began in 1517, the English king who created the national Church and broke from Rome, the twenty-seven-year-old Henry VIII, was still a very devout Roman Catholic. As Henry VII's able second son, the fresh-faced Henry may have been educated for a career in the Church, and his reaction to the Lutheran movement on the eve of the Diet of Worms in 1521 had been to write his own learned attack on Luther's position, defending the seven Sacraments. For this the pope gave him the title 'Defensor Fidei' or 'Defender of the Faith'. (By a curious historical anomaly the British monarch bears the title to this day – hence the letters 'DF' on the pound coin – even though as Supreme Governor of the Anglican Church he or she cannot be the defender of the Roman Catholic faith.) Two years after his accession to the throne Henry VIII eagerly joined Pope Julius II's Holy League and later invaded France as part of the papal crusade to drive the French out of Italy. For his sterling work he was soon high in the affections of Rome. He was sent a golden rose as a sign of papal favour, and in 1515 his chief adviser, the lord chancellor and Archbishop of York Thomas Wolsey, was made a cardinal. Moreover Henry was married to the pious Catherine of Aragon, daughter of the very Catholic monarchs Ferdinand and Isabella.

In theory, therefore, there was no less likely candidate to lead the English Reformation and break away from Rome than Henry VIII. That, nevertheless, is what he did. It was the need for a male heir and his passion for a court lady named Anne Boleyn that propelled him into a religious and political revolution.

Henry VIII's father was a cultured man and like all the Tudors he had taken an unusual amount of care with his son's education. The new king could speak several languages, and was an accomplished musician and even composer. One of England's favourite folk songs, the haunting 'Greensleeves', was said to have been written by him. A true son of the Renaissance, who certainly composed two five-part Masses and was a good lutenist, Henry VIII encouraged his court to become a centre of the New Learning. A more scientific approach to health was marked by his establishment of the Royal College of Surgeons and Physicians, and the rebuilding of St Bartholomew's Hospital, while the Regius professorships he founded at Oxford and Cambridge still remind us of his patronage. Henry VIII was fond of exercising his wits against scholars such as his friend Erasmus, one of the most important of all the humanists (that is, students of the New Learning), and his court was as splendid as any in Europe.

The gravely realistic portraits of the outstanding north German painter Hans Holbein seized the king's fancy, and Holbein was persuaded to move to London as the court artist for twenty years. A large gallery of the chief figures of the reign, now housed mainly in the National Portrait Gallery, testifies to Henry VIII as a Renaissance patron of the arts. He brought the celebrated Italian sculptor Torrigiano to London to build the tomb of his mother and father in Westminster Abbey, and by the end of his reign the monarch lived not only at Richmond Palace at Sheen but also in several new palaces, including Hampton Court, Whitehall, St James's and Nonsuch, an exquisite timber palace in Surrey.

As well as the foreign artists the king encouraged to come to England, Italian poetry began to filter into the country, brought back by the young noblemen's sons for whom a voyage to the sights of classical Rome was the

Henry VIII.

end of their education as a gentleman. The Duke of Norfolk's poet son, the Earl of Surrey, and Sir Thomas Wyatt introduced the sonnet form and blank verse – both of which were Italian inventions – to England and they slowly spread outwards in ever increasing circles until they met their greatest expression in the poetry of the Elizabethan genius William Shakespeare. As part of the new interest in classical writing, Latin plays became the fashion at the universities, and in 1545 Henry VIII appointed the first official responsible for playhouses – the Master of the Revels. Henry VII had been the most frugal and careful king England had ever known and had succeeded in restoring the crown finances after a hundred years of war. Perhaps as a reaction to his severe father, Henry VIII was one of the most extravagant. He spent a fortune on glittering costumes embroidered with gold thread and on superb jewellery, as well as on the musicians and feasting that he liked to indulge himself with at all times.

The king was also very athletic, dancing, playing tennis and hunting with equal vigour. He presented a complete contrast to his father, taking after his mother's Yorkist style of golden beauty or perhaps after his grandfather Edward IV. Standing well over six feet in his stockinged feet – as his enormous suit of armour in the Tower of London reminds us – he had great affability and charm as a young man, though like his grandfather he ran to fat as he grew older. Even on his accession, however, the new king displayed an innate ruthlessness. One of his first acts was to execute his father's servants Dudley and Empson on the unspecific charge of treason – his true motive was to make himself popular. In all things Henry VIII was as cunning and masterful as his portraits suggest, the very model of the Renaissance prince described by the sixteenth-century Italian writer Machiavelli.

Henry VIII had a natural feel for politics which would be inherited by his daughter Elizabeth. Both understood the need to be loved by their subjects; both saw that to rule successfully an English monarch must appear to listen to the people by consulting Parliament. They recognized, too, that to be popular they had to make themselves known to their subjects. And known the new king was, whether he was addressing the House of Commons with vigour, wit and élan or going about the countryside to reinforce allegiance to what he was conscious was still a young dynasty. Despite that youthfulness, however, Henry VII's determined efforts had ensured that his son had inherited a secure throne. There were no pretenders with a better claim than his. As an energetic fellow he soon excited the national imagination, as he was easily lured by the glamour of foreign affairs and war abroad. Though he attacked France in the name of the Holy League, his real motive was the old English dream of regaining Normandy and Gascony.

Henry VIII's anxiety to play a role on the world stage prompted him to turn his attention to England's defences. All over the south coast round towers and walls sprang up, for example at St Mawes in Cornwall, to show that the English lion was well protected. Moreover Henry was the first king since Alfred to build up the Royal Navy. In the first two years of his reign two enormous ships were constructed to terrify the French – the *Great Harry* and the *Mary Rose*. In 1545, however, tragedy struck: the *Mary Rose* sank with the loss of all 500 hands on board when, in action against the French and with her portholes open, she attempted too swift a turn. In 1982 she was raised fom the sea-bed, where she had lain for almost 450 years, and her sixteenth-century timbers can be visited at Portsmouth today. Henry also established the royal dockyard at Woolwich and Deptford and set up the Navy Board system to administer it.

At first Henry relied on his father's ministers to run the government. But the vigorous prince soon found that in the chaplain to the Archbishop of Canterbury, a young man named Thomas Wolsey, he had the sort of minister who was as ambitious as he was himself. Wolsey was energetic, charming and fascinated by international diplomacy. His plans for the aggrandizement of England, hitherto not a European power which counted compared to France or Spain, appealed to the king. By the use of shrewd diplomacy and by changing sides, England should guard her own interests by never having permanent alliances, permanently maintaining instead a balance of power between the powerful European states. Though the king enjoyed winning over the House of Commons with speeches, he was easily bored by detail, whereas Wolsey relished going down to Parliament and extracting loans for Henry's wars.

An opportunity for Henry VIII and Wolsey to stretch their wings arose early in the reign. In 1511 the confusing game of international musical chairs, with nations grouping and regrouping to obtain possession of vulnerable Italian states, came to an end when the pope Julius II created a Holy League to drive the French out of Italy. As part of the assault on the French, Henry was to distract them in 1513 by attacking

Cardinal Thomas Wolsey who fell from power because he failed to arrange Henry VIII's divorce from Catherine of Aragon.

France in both the north near Calais and the south. The defeat of the French in an engagement known as the Battle of the Spurs (because more spurs were used than swords as the French ran away), where Wolsey himself fought as a knight, resulted in peace with France. This was strengthened by the marriage of Henry's sister Mary to the aged Louis XII of France.

In that same year the Scots, whose alliance with the French required them to attack the north of England, were dramatically defeated at the Battle of Flodden. James IV and the flower of the Scottish nobility were slain just inside the English border. Thus by 1514 the partnership of Henry and Wolsey and their policy of not being bound by an alliance with Spain seemed to be succeeding. The king was secure in his borders, with Scotland ruled by his sister Margaret Tudor on behalf of her son James V, and France by his sister's husband.

Wolsey's theory of the balance of power would dominate England's approach to European politics for the following four centuries. It made even greater sense over the next few years when a series of deaths left the nephew of Queen Catherine, King Charles V of Spain, ruling most of Europe and the New World. The Holy Roman Emperor – as he soon became, despite the reluctance of the Electors to grant him the title, given his already considerable power and wealth – was the dynastic phenomenon of the sixteenth century. Empire indeed was the right term for the lands Charles V inherited. The Netherlands came to him through his grandmother Mary of Burgundy and the Habsburg lands in Austria through his grandfather the Emperor Maximilian, while his mother Joanna, sister of Catherine of Aragon, brought him not only Spain, but the Aragonese kingdom of the Two Sicilies. In addition to his land empire, as the heir to Spain Charles V was cash rich beyond the dreams of avarice. The discovery of silver mines in the New Spain of Mexico and Peru meant that by the middle of the century his income was far greater than that of the rest of the European states put together.

As Charles was master of the Netherlands, to whom some 90 per cent of England's chief export wool was shipped, it was more or less obligatory for Henry to be on good and peaceful terms with him. Nevertheless there was potential for leverage thanks to the intense rivalry that developed between Charles and the new king of France, Francis I. Francis was the same kind of magnificent Renaissance prince as his fellow monarch across the Channel, and he had designs not only to re-establish France's Italian territories but to be elected Holy Roman Emperor in Charles V's stead. Though the emperorship no longer bore any relation to the title of the Caesars – the incumbent was customarily chosen by seven German Electors, or heads of principalities, who now more or less always bestowed the title on the House of Habsburg – it was still of some significance.

As Francis and Charles clashed again and again in the years 1520–9 over Italian territory, Wolsey remained convinced of the necessity of a relationship with France. The balance of power would be achieved by weighing in on France's side against Charles V – from being France's sworn enemy England would from time to time be her friend. The most notable of these diplomatic rapprochements was a meeting between Henry VIII and Francis I in 1520 known as the Field of the Cloth of Gold. Masterminded by Wolsey, the encounter took place in a field between the English territory of Calais and the French king's domain, in ornate tents specially made for the occasion and furnished with gorgeous rugs. The scene was so splendid and grand – there were fountains running with wine – that the whole field

The Field of the Cloth of Gold in France, scene of the meeting of Henry VIII and Francis I in 1520. Artist unknown.

seemed made of cloth of gold. A famous painting commemorating the extravaganza can be seen at Hampton Court, the palace Wolsey had begun building a few miles beyond Richmond.

The two young kings, in the prime of life, behaved more like brothers than fellow sovereigns, stealing into one another's tents in the early mornings and even wrestling together. Nevertheless, despite these shenanigans, in the end the weight of the Netherlands wool trade and the fact that the emperor was Queen Catherine's nephew meant that nothing much changed. England remained the enemy of France and the ally of the Emperor.

As long as all went well for the king, Wolsey was an untouchable favourite and enjoyed a most regal way of life. He was made Archbishop of York and Bishop of Lincoln, and received the income of two other bishoprics too. Carried away by his own importance, Wolsey built himself not just Hampton Court Palace but another at York Place which became the Palace of Whitehall. When he became a cardinal in 1515, Wolsey was able to override the Church's hierarchy and to have his own way in

everything, despite not being Archbishop of Canterbury and thus head of the Church. In the same year Henry also made him lord chancellor. Wolsey was therefore the most powerful official in England, since he presided over both Church and state. He was feared and disliked for his busybody ways and for his ruthlessness in dealing with Parliament. When Parliament finally refused point-blank to grant any more money to the king, Wolsey refused to recall it for seven years, depending instead on 'gifts' from wealthy citizens.

Wolsey's extravagant way of life and the airs he gave himself increased his unpopularity – even his cook was reported to wear damask satin with a gold chain round his neck. As for the cardinal himself, he could only wear red robes of the finest silk trimmed with fur. All his plates were made of gold, and every day his 500 servants sat down to dinner at three great tables in one of his vast new houses. The cardinal's appearances in public were spectacles of flamboyance, as even the most informal moments apparently necessitated an elaborate procession. The tallest and most handsome priest would walk in front of the cardinal, bearing in his outstretched arms a pillar of silver on top of which was a rather small cross. Next came the cardinal's hat, carried on a purple cushion held by a bare-headed nobleman and accompanied by ushers who shouted as they came, 'Make way for my Lord's Grace!' Then at last appeared the cardinal, his face wearing a modest half-smile, his eyes cast down, perhaps admiring feet shod in golden shoes decorated with pearls. But, for all the grandeur of this apparition, always visible in the background would be an inelegant mule. For, said Wolsey, since he was but a humble priest, it was fitting that he should travel by mule rather than by horse.

But Wolsey was not only a show-off. He was also a serious intellectual, a supporter of the New Learning who was the protector of the Cambridge scholar William Tyndale – the first Englishman since the Lollards to translate much of the Bible into English. Tyndale had smuggled 3,000 copies of his translation into England with the help of Martin Luther. Despite his arrogance, and like all men of intelligence at that time, Wolsey believed that the Church was in need of drastic reform. Many of the monasteries, particularly the lesser ones, were contributing little to the spiritual life of the nation. If they were closed down, the money from selling their lands could be used to found schools which would do much more to spread learning. So in 1523 Wolsey sent in commissioners to investigate some of these smaller monasteries, and the dismal way of life they found there, with little or no religious impulse, led to the break-up or dissolution of several of them. With the proceeds Wolsey founded a splendid new college at Oxford which he called Cardinal College, later known as Christ Church.

The end came for Wolsey quite suddenly. In 1526 the king's eye was caught by a bewitching, black-eyed nineteen-year-old girl named Nan Bullen or Anne Boleyn, whose mother was the sister of the Duke of Norfolk. Henry had begun to despair of his union with Catherine. A papal dispensation had been required to allow him to marry his brother's wife. Now the absence of any surviving children save Lady Mary, after many miscarriages and stillbirths, convinced him that the marriage was cursed. Henry was obsessed with obtaining a son for a dynasty that was still less than half a century old. Anne Boleyn and her uncle were equally obsessed with the king marrying her and not merely making her his mistress, as her elder sister Mary had been. The answer was to get the pope, Clement VII, to declare the original marriage invalid – which was how all divorces were resolved in the middle ages. Unfortunately, though, the international situation and Wolsey's diplomatic machinations meant that Henry was hardly in a position to influence the pope.

At the beginning of 1527, angered by the pope's support for France, Queen Catherine's nephew Charles V had captured and sacked Rome, and Clement VII became his prisoner. Two years earlier, during the interminable struggle with France in Italy, Charles had also managed to capture Francis I at the Battle of Pavia. This striking event had convinced Wolsey once more to assert his theory of the balance of power, and Henry had agreed to make peace with Francis and become his ally instead of the emperor's. But in the context of what was becoming a real crisis at the English court, with the king determined to have his way, this diplomatic revolution could not have come at a more inconvenient time.

When the imprisoned pope failed to dissolve immediately Henry VIII's marriage to Catherine but instead instituted a Decretal Commission to inquire into the situation, Henry's anger knew no bounds. For a scapegoat he turned on the great instigator of the pro-French alliance, Wolsey, who had also been in charge of the diplomatic negotiations with the Vatican. Evidently, despite his cardinal's title, Wolsey had no sway at Rome. When the Papal Commission moved back to Rome for further hearings after gathering evidence in London, including the impassioned testimony of Catherine of Aragon that her marriage to Henry's elder brother Arthur had never been consummated, it was the end of Wolsey.

Thwarted and showing the furious temper which was to become such an overwhelming characteristic of his later years, Henry VIII turned on his former favourite. He was encouraged by Anne Boleyn and her uncle the Duke of Norfolk, who both believed that Wolsey disapproved of the Boleyn marriage. The affection, even love, which the king had borne for his chancellor vanished in the twinkling of an eye. All the cardinal's property, Hampton Court and York Place and Cardinal College, was seized by the king, who soon occupied Hampton Court himself. Wolsey sought refuge in his archdiocese at York, and had he not died at Leicester in 1530 on his way south to the Tower to be tried for treason, he would have been executed. As the lieutenant of the Tower waited by his bed the cardinal told him of his fears for England now that he sensed death was near. Who would curb the king's strong will? he said. There was no one now in the Council who would dare to. Wolsey's last words were 'Had I served God as carefully as my king, he would not have given me over in my grey hairs.'

MARTIN LUTHER.

But events in England were moving swiftly onward, propelled by the king's passion for Anne Boleyn – who, her enemies whispered, had a sixth finger on one hand, the sure sign of a witch – and by the excitement abroad aroused by the Reformation. It was becoming increasingly obvious that the pope, still held captive by the Emperor Charles V, was going to find every reason why he should not grant a divorce against the emperor's aunt Catherine of Aragon. The answer therefore, as far as Henry was concerned, was to show that the pope was wrong. Henry began his campaign by canvassing learned opinion among scholars at the universities.

This radical solution would have been unthinkable before the sixteenth century. But just as the papacy was profoundly unpopular in Germany, it was also profoundly unpopular in England. The Church at Rome had always been an intrusive institution, taking a great deal of money out of the country. But just when the English were beginning to flex their muscles again and take pleasure in their national life and culture, its power seemed especially irksome, particularly when the clergy were a byword for laziness and corruption. For many centuries awe and respect for the hallowed institution that St Peter had established had kept England within the Church of Rome. But now in the changed atmosphere of the New Learning among the educated – whether at the universities, the inns of court or Parliament – a harsh daylight had been let in which had destroyed what was left of the papacy's magic. The climax had come with the pope's imprisonment by the emperor. More than ever before the papacy simply seemed a foreign, secular institution whose peculiar law courts were places where murderers in holy orders could still take refuge from English justice.

But scholars rarely give single-line answers, and in response to Henry's revolutionary consultation they gave a most inconclusive and useless reply. The king therefore decided to put pressure on the clergy themselves. In all his doings Henry had no intention of creating a Church doctrinally different from the Church of Rome; his Church of England was to be Catholicism without the pope. First Henry alarmed the clergy sitting in their national gatherings known as Convocation of Canterbury and York, by telling them that they had broken the ancient Statute of Praemunire by recognizing Wolsey as papal legate. For this he was levying on them a colossal fine of some £100,000. Next, in order to assuage his anger, the clergy had to acknowledge that he was the supreme head of the Church of England. At this point the king still hoped that Pope Clement or his successor Paul III would see reason and grant the divorce, but they did not do so.

By a series of acts over the seven years from 1529 to 1536, passed by what is known as the Reformation Parliament, Henry VIII separated the Church in England from the pope in Rome and created his own Church, the Church of England. By 1534, with the Act of Supremacy, Henry had completed the separation of England from the Roman Catholic Church, and all the incomes hitherto due to Rome were now paid to the crown. The

Statute of Praemunire, which had existed from the fourteenth century but which had been honoured more in the breach than in the observance, was reinforced so that no appeals were allowed from England to Rome. It was made treason to deny Henry's headship.

These acts were pushed through Parliament not against its will, but with its active participation. The members of the Reformation Parliament were keen to assert themselves as independent Englishmen, and felt that by casting off the pope they were carving out their uniquely English destiny. Though Henry's reign might slowly degenerate into tyranny and terror, the gift he had of handling his Parliaments, his hail-fellow-well-met manner and his larger-than-life magnificence meant that in some way he continued to represent an ideal Englishman. This ensured his continuing popularity, a vital matter for him. For what historians call Tudor despotism or absolute rule, unlike the despotism of continental powers, was effected without a standing army. Just as English kings theoretically needed popular acclamation to ascend the throne, control over England was to be had by the support of the local gentry whom Henry charmed in Parliament and made his allies. They enforced his rule in their counties in their capacities as justices of the peace.

Under Henry VIII that sense of Englishness which had been growing since the Hundred Years War and had been given voice in the Reformation Parliament would be reinforced by weekly attendance at Church service. By the end of Henry's reign the Creed, the Lord's Prayer and the Ten Commandments were all spoken in English. Moreover from 1540 an English Bible was placed in every parish church, with effects almost as incalculable for the national literature as Caxton's return to England with a continental printing press. It was in fact Tyndale's version revised by Miles Coverdale, with a preface by Archbishop Cranmer. Henry VIII had completed what is known as the nation state.

With the demise of Wolsey, for the rest of his reign Henry relied on advice in religious matters from a sensitive and eager-to-please Cambridge scholar named Thomas Cranmer. Cranmer, whom Henry made chaplain to Anne Boleyn's family, became head of the new Church of England in 1533 as Archbishop of Canterbury. He announced that the king's first marriage to Catherine of Aragon had

Thomas Cranmer, Archbishop of Canterbury during Henry VIII's English Reformation.

been invalid. The king was therefore free to marry Anne Boleyn – who was about to have a baby, the future Queen Elizabeth I.

Thomas Cromwell, a fuller's son from Putney who had helped develop the theory of Royal Supremacy, was now the king's right-hand man in governing the country. It soon occurred to him that the immense wealth of the monasteries accumulated over the previous 600 years – they owned perhaps one-third of the land in England – might be used to ensure the loyalty of the people who counted in the Tudor state. If he closed them down and redistributed their land among the upper and middle classes – the magnates, gentry, lawyers and merchants – he would under-pin the new Church and destroy the last bastions of loyalty to the pope.

The majority of the monasteries had long ago lost their power and influence. There were fewer than 10,000 monks and nuns to contend with, and they were un-worldly, gentle people. In a spirit of triumphant nationalism inspired by Wolsey's earlier suppression of certain monasteries, Cromwell dissolved all the smaller ones and embarked on an investi-gation which would result in the disso-lution of the rest. And with the dissolving

Thomas Cromwell who piloted the break with Rome through Parliament.

of the monasteries and the carving up of their lands among some 40,000 people the Protestant Reformation was secured on property. Many great English families, such as the Cavendishes and Russells, merchants, lawyers and shire knights, acquired their fortunes in the lands once owned by the monasteries. They made stately homes out of the ancient abbeys – for example, the Russells, later the dukes of Bedford, received Woburn Abbey. As far as these people were concerned, there would be no going back to Rome if it meant the end of their country estates.

The English Reformation had been accomplished upon the sturdiest and most durable of foundations: land. Nevertheless, despite the fear the king inspired as an increasingly bloody tyrant, the royal revolution had not been achieved quite as smoothly as Henry wished, particularly in his immediate circle at court and in government. He might be a religious conservative who disagreed as much as ever with Luther and who burned heretics for promulgating advanced Protestant ideas, but his chancellor Thomas More and the aged John Fisher, Bishop of Rochester, could not accept the king as substitute for the pope. Their historical sense and Catholicism refused

Sir Thomas More, made Lord Chancellor on Wolsey's fall, was executed for resisting Henry VIII's supremacy over the Church.

to let them. So when the 1534 Act of Royal Supremacy required the clergy and government officials to swear an oath of loyalty to Henry as supreme head of the Church of England, More and Fisher refused. They would take the Oath of Succession – that is, they would swear loyalty to Anne Boleyn's children – but to the king's embarrassment and fury they also declined to accept Anne Boleyn as Henry's lawful wife. Both men were promptly sent to the Tower.

The spectacle of More – so recently the equivalent of prime minister and one of the leading figures of English life, a scholar, a notably eloquent lawyer and a member of Parliament internationally renowned for his learning and for his book *Utopia* – being dragged in his shirt through the streets from the Tower to his trial for treason at Westminster increased the atmosphere of terror that began to surround the king. Until very recently More had been a close friend of his. Henry had often been seen walking in More's lovely garden in Chelsea (the Chelsea Physic Garden today) with his arm affectionately round his chancellor's shoulders. It had even been the king's habit to turn up unexpectedly at More's house after dinner to chat and pass the time in a merry way. He had seemed so good tempered on these occasions that More's son-in-law Thomas Roper had remarked that the king's growing reputation for ruthlessness seemed ill-founded. More had responded wryly, 'Howbeit,

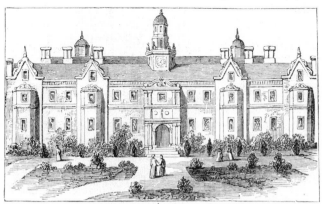

SIR THOMAS MORE'S HOUSE, CHELSEA.

son Roper, I may tell thee I have no cause to be proud thereof, for if my head could win him a castle in France it should not fail to go.' There is an echo of this in Henry's response to the news that the pope had made Fisher a cardinal. When he heard this the king remarked, 'The Pope shall soon have his head in Rome so that he can put the cardinal's hat on it himself.'

Henry was dreading the effect of More's famous eloquence at his trial, fearing that he would rally the country against his reforms. Unlike Fisher who was too old and tired to mount a defence, which ensured a rapid guilty verdict and his immediate execution, More showed that his luminous intellect had been unimpaired by prison. Although he was bowed and his hair had turned grey over the summer of his incarceration, mental torture had robbed him of none of his natural authority. His defence was clear and to the point. He had not offended against the law nor tried to oppose the king's wishes. All he had done was to remain silent, and silence had not yet been declared treason. But nothing could avert his fate. As soon as the sentence of death was pronounced More declared that the Oath of Supremacy was indeed unlawful. 'How can you argue with the whole of England?' one man called from the crowd, amazed at More's courage. 'Ah, but I have the whole history of Christendom behind me,' said More smiling.

On 6 July 1535 a messenger came to More's cell to tell him that he would be taken out and executed. More was utterly composed, pausing only to pen a quick farewell letter to his wife and daughter, begging them to 'pray for me, as I will for thee, that we may merrily meet in heaven'. Then he strolled over to Tower Green just outside his lodgings as calmly as if he were about to have his breakfast, and when the executioner told him that as a special personal favour of the king he would only have his head cut off, not be disembowelled too, as was the usual practice for traitors, More quipped, 'God preserve my friends from all such favours.' But the king had also issued another order. Sir Thomas More was to be allowed no last speeches to the crowd. Even at that last moment, Henry feared More's power. So More simply said that he died a faithful subject to the king and a true Catholic before God. Then the executioner silenced his silver tongue for ever.

In 1536, a year after the execution of More and Fisher, there was a series of risings in the north called the Pilgrimage of Grace. The northern counties of Yorkshire, Lancashire and Lincolnshire still had a monastic tradition which inspired respect among their inhabitants and were far removed from the New Learning and the new ideas which had entered England via the south-eastern seaports. Under the leadership of a Yorkshire country gentleman named Robert Aske, a great gathering at Doncaster demanded that Cromwell be dismissed and the country return to the old faith. But Henry handled the crisis with his usual aplomb. The

Duke of Norfolk, who was generally acknowledged to be the leader of the more Catholic faction at court, was sent up to promise that the king would listen to the rebels' requests if they would disperse peacefully, which they did. The momentum was lost. When the next year rioting began again, it provided the excuse to execute Aske and the rest of the leaders. A Council of the North staffed by Tudor officials removed most of the last vestiges of the old Catholic families' influence, though it did not destroy their attachment to the ancient faith.

Ruins of Tintern Abbey, which fell into disuse after the Dissolution of the Monasteries.

With the Dissolution of the Monasteries the Henrician Reformation shifted into a more radical phase. It became common practice to loot shrines for their jewels on the grounds that they encouraged superstition and idol worship and distracted from true religion. St Thomas à Becket's shrine at Canterbury, one of the most famous places of medieval pilgrimage, was stripped of all its gold and silver. Two groaning wagonloads carried this booty to the eagerly awaiting king. Under the crude and greedy hands of Cromwell's men village churches were frequently ransacked for their plate and chalices. In 1545 Henry dissolved the chantries, those characteristic buildings of medieval England often founded by guilds as well as the colleges of secular clergy. This removed many a source of education, hence the proliferation of schools still flourishing today which were founded in the reign of Henry's son, Edward VI.

A Carthusian monk, whose communities were destroyed by Henry VIII.

Yet despite Cranmer's readiness to appoint advanced Protestants to vacant sees, including Hugh Latimer, the king himself continued to behave like a Catholic. He remained fearful that the pope might give the command for Catholic countries to invade England and bring her back to the true faith, while his superb political antennae forced him to take note of the meaning of the Pilgrimage of Grace. He knew that the bulk of the nation was instinctively Catholic and silently resentful. So, even though he had patronized the translation of the Bible into English, he still asked Charles V to pursue Tyndale its translator as a heretic. Three years after the Pilgrimage of Grace, by publishing the Act of the Six Articles which punished with death anyone who did not believe that Christ was present in the Communion wafer, Henry showed England and the pope that in all essentials he was a most orthodox Catholic.

For by this time the religious debate raging in Europe had moved on. Thinkers such as the Frenchman Jean Calvin and the Swiss Ulrich Zwingli had taken Luther's dismissal of most sacraments many steps further. In Henry VIII's reign the greatest controversy was the issue of the Mass itself. Zwingli held that examination of the texts suggested that Communion was not a sacrament but simply a commemoration of the Last Supper: Christ's body and blood were not present in the host and wine. Although to the end of his days Cranmer could not decide what he believed, Henry was quite emphatic that he believed in the Real Presence at the Mass. At Smithfield the king burned any Protestant heretics straying into England who purveyed the new ideas percolating through Europe. Nevertheless the battle for the soul of the Protestant Reformation continued for the rest of his reign and beyond. And in the king's lifetime the Catholic and Protestant factions within the Church of England each gained a little advantage according to the king's marital state.

The gilded youth who had won the nation's hearts was rapidly degenerating from the attractive Renaissance monarch into both a tyrant and a serial wife-killer. No one in England, whatever their position in the establishment, was safe. In 1538 on the grounds of conspiracy Henry executed two close royal cousins, the Marquis of Exeter and the Countess of Salisbury, mother of the Catholic Cardinal Pole who was in exile at Rome. The seventy-year-old countess's end had been especially frightful.

Once on the scaffold the vigorous old lady ran round and round the block declaring, 'My head never yet committed treason, you must take it as you can.' The axeman had to hold her down over the block himself to chop her head off.

But the axe also fell on Anne Boleyn just three years after her coronation. Instead of the hoped-for male heir the queen had only produced a puny red-headed little girl who was born alive. Henry, by now very bloated from over-indulgence in food and drink, convinced himself that this was a sign that this marriage too was cursed. Despite the many ornamental testaments to his passion for Anne, the entwined initials HA he had had carved all over Hampton Court and St James's Palace, the king began to look for another wife. The lively Anne, who was hated by many for her insolence and her Protestantism, suddenly found herself arrested and accused of adultery.

Anne was removed without ceremony from the royal palace at Greenwich to the Tower. She went by barge and began screaming as soon as she saw the Barbican Gate and realized where she was heading, an eerie and horrible sound, which could be heard on the south bank of the river. The Constable of the Tower tried to comfort her by saying that she would be lodged not in a dungeon but in the apartments she had stayed in before her coronation. But she gave a loud mocking laugh, and an even more mocking one when he told her sincerely that she could be certain that every inhabitant of King Henry's realm could be assured justice. Anne Boleyn then seems to have lost control of herself. The screaming, alternating with hysterical laughter, went on for the next few weeks until she was condemned to death for treason. As a last favour from her husband a special sword was sent from Calais to cut off her head because she had expressed a fear to her jailers that a blunt axe would hurt her little neck.

The very day after Anne Boleyn stepped on to the scaffold and wound her long black hair up into a white linen coif so that the executioner might see her neck more clearly, Henry married his new favourite, the quiet Jane Seymour. At last the king was lawfully married and in 1537 Jane produced the longed-for boy, a new Prince of Wales who was christened Edward. But his mother died only twelve days after his birth. Once more there was a vacancy at the king's side. Out of genuine sadness and respect for his dead wife no one filled it for two years.

Jane Seymour's family were convinced Protestant supporters of the New Learning, particularly her two brothers, who were close to Cranmer and Cromwell. In the late 1530s the Protestant influence round the king appeared to be at its height when he acquiesced in Cromwell's suggestion of Anne of Cleves as a new bride. Her brother was the Protestant Duke of Cleves, on the Lower Rhine, and it looked as if England would soon be publicly allied to the north German princes of the Schmalkalden League who had strenuously embraced Protestantism against the emperor.

The king was in any case beginning to tire of Cromwell and was increasingly inclined towards the religious conservatives, Stephen Gardiner, Bishop of Winchester and Edmund Bonner, Bishop of London. The many real reforms that had been achieved by Cromwell such as introducing parish registers of births, deaths and marriages, did not make up for the government's unpopularity. When Anne of Cleves arrived in London, the marriage having been arranged on the basis of a flattering portrait by Hans Holbein because the king was too busy to meet her, Cromwell's career began to take a downward path. For Anne of Cleves looked nothing like her portrait, which may be seen at the Louvre in Paris. To Henry she seemed big, raw-boned and ungainly; moreover she could speak only a very few words of English. 'A Flanders mare, I like her not,' Henry is said to have hissed angrily at Cromwell when he first met her. Meanwhile despite the grandeur of the wedding, no alliance was forthcoming from the League of Protestant princes. Although the king could not withdraw from the marriage Cranmer swiftly produced suitable reasons as to why it was invalid, and Queen Anne of Cleves retired on a pension, presumably glad to have escaped with her head.

The king soon yielded to the Catholic faction's petitions, led by the ambitious and unscrupulous Duke of Norfolk, to dismiss Cromwell. Having presided over the trial of one niece Anne Boleyn, he was dangling another, Catherine Howard, before the king as a future bride. When in the summer of 1540 it was discovered that a Protestant preacher named Dr Barnes was Cromwell's confidential agent to the German Protestant princes, it seemed good evidence that Cromwell was the agent of Protestant heretics in England. Within weeks Cromwell too had been executed, deserted by all his friends save Archbishop Cranmer, who begged the king to show clemency to a man who had been such a faithful servant. It was to no avail.

The atmosphere in England by the 1540s was one of muted terror. Cardinal Pole would rightly ask, 'Is England Turkey that she is governed by the sword?' Protestant and Catholic martyrs were dragged on the same hurdles to Smithfield for burning, for if it was treason to recognize the Papal Supremacy it was also treason to deny Catholic doctrine! The court was full of the manoeuvring of the two implacably opposed religious parties, who frequently informed against one another.

The Catholic faction were delighted when in the very month of Cromwell's execution the king at last took as his fifth wife the lovely little Catherine Howard. All were hopeful the marriage would last – but it was not to be. In Catherine Howard's case, for once there was good reason for the king's suspicious mind, now as inflamed as his massive leg with its running ulcer, to doubt her. The new queen, aged only eighteen, could not help finding the young blades at court more attractive than her fifty-year-old husband, as the king observed. Less than two years after Catherine had married him, the king vanished after dinner at Hampton Court and departed for his new palace at Whitehall. He never saw the queen again. A few days later, one icy mid-November morning, men came for Catherine and arrested her at Hampton Court. There, in the so-called 'haunted gallery' which links the chapel with the State Apartments, a woman dressed in white is said to haunt the long corridor, crying and moaning as she walks – the ghost of Catherine Howard.

After a period of house arrest at Syon House in Chiswick, the queen – like her cousin Anne Boleyn – was executed for treason on the grounds of adultery. During her captivity her jewels were ripped from all her splendid clothing and sent back to the outraged king. All her friends had been interrogated and she herself had secretly confessed to Archbishop Cranmer, thinking it might help her if she made a clean breast of things and pleaded youth and foolishness.

Henry VIII's sixth and last wife, whom he married a year later in 1543, was Catherine Parr. She was much older than his other wives and a pragmatist with a good sensible head firmly screwed on to her shoulders. She managed to keep it there by outliving the king. She was also a very good nurse, which was by far her most important quality to a king crippled by thrombosis. By the late 1540s Henry VIII had long lost the athletic prowess of his youth; the hunting and music-making were a thing of the past. Though he still managed to lead his troops to the siege of Boulogne in 1544, mostly he had to be wheeled round his palaces in a mechanical contraption, so enormously swollen had his legs become. Too unfit even to sign his own name, a rubber stamp had to be invented to do the job.

The new queen was kind and dutiful to her stepchildren, Mary, Elizabeth and Edward. The two girls, having both been declared illegitimate by Henry, had been brought up in penniless obscurity far from court. To an unenthusiastic Henry, Catherine insisted that the nervous and religious Lady Mary and the clever Lady Elizabeth, whose mother's head had been cut off when she was under three, should come to live with her and the king. Catherine Parr made sure that after years of neglect they were treated as befitted their rank as their father's daughters.

As the king's ill-health signalled that the end of his life was approaching, members of the court began jockeying among themselves for power. Most significant were the two brothers of Jane Seymour, Edward and Thomas. As uncles of the sickly nine-year-old-heir Edward they hoped to rule the country, with the elder uncle Edward Seymour becoming lord protector.

Meanwhile, however, rumours had reached the king's suspicious ears that the Duke of Norfolk, who had now been uncle to two queens, and his son the Earl of Surrey were openly stating that their royal blood showed that on the king's death Norfolk would be the best regent. Surrey indeed had taken to wearing the arms of Edward the Confessor. For this *lèse-majesté* Surrey was executed on 19 January 1547 and Norfolk would have been executed on the 28th had Henry VIII not died the day before. The king passed away holding the gentle Cranmer's hand. It was one of the few of Henry's relationships that had endured.

The succession to the English throne of a minor had always tended to be a recipe for disaster. On the other hand the kingdom Edward VI's father bequeathed to him was more unified under royal government and more closely linked to Westminster than ever before. As partly Welsh with lands and a following in Wales, it had been a relatively easy matter for Henry by the 1536 Statute of Wales finally to do away with the ancient marcher jurisdictions, and the whole country was finally organized into shires along the English model. In Ireland a Fitzgerald rising proved the perfect excuse for Henry to send in an army to reduce the country to some semblance of order. He extended the Reformation to Ireland on the same principles as he had done in England, giving Irish lords the extensive lands of the monasteries in return for their loyalty. Since Lord of Ireland had been a papal title, Henry now called himself King of Ireland.

However, Henry's heirs also had a great many problems on hand. The government's way of raising money during lean times had been to clip the coinage or mix copper into the gold and silver. Edward Seymour, or the Duke of Somerset as he immediately became, who had duly become the lord protector, faced a country in revolt against a very debased coinage, for in order to counteract the devalued coinage shopkeepers put up their prices. The dissolution of the monasteries might have enhanced the fortunes and secured the loyalty of thousands of well-to-do English families, but it had also created pressing social problems. The new owners of monastic lands had none of the kindliness of the old monks, nor their sense of community. The hospitals and almshouses for the poor vanished, and rents became much higher.

Above all, the enclosure system took even more ferocious root. Land which previously had been allowed for the use of the community was hedged round for the new owners' private use. At the same time the high price of wool meant unemployment for thousands as arable farming was abandoned in favour of sheep farming. Skilled men found themselves without homes, as that most profitable of animals, the sheep, required only one shepherd for a large flock. As early as 1516, with the publication of *Utopia*, Sir Thomas More had warned of sheep eating men. Now it was a situation raging out of control and creating landless yeomen who wandered from parish to parish desperate for work.

In contrast to the dead king, Somerset was a convinced radical Protestant – as was the severe young king himself. Henry VIII's Reformation had been carried out in a very gingerly fashion by a monarch conscious of the tightrope he was walking between Catholic powers abroad and natural conservatism at home. The new rulers had none of the old king's instincts.

Edward VI

(1547–1553)

Despite his dislike of extreme Protestants, Henry VIII had so respected their learning that he had left the upbringing of his precious son and heir in the hands of distinguished Protestant divines such as Roger Ascham. The result was a solemn little boy who had inherited a good deal of his father's willpower and who was dedicated to taking the new religion many steps past where his father had intended it to end. One of Edward VI's favourite preachers was the former Bishop of Worcester, Hugh Latimer, the friend of Protestant martyrs under Henry VIII, whom Henry had deprived of his see for holding views that were too radical. Under the influence of Protector Somerset and the boy-king, the court became a quieter, more solemn place than it had been under the late king. Instead of the gaudy colours and slashed velvet doublets of Henry VIII's reign, most Protestant men and women dressed in the dark colours which would soon be identified with the Puritans.

Court life was dominated by the struggle between the protector himself and members of the royal Council to control the ferociously intellectual but sickly young king. But it was also a struggle between the protector and his brother Thomas Seymour. The sheer force of Thomas Seymour's magnetic personality had thrust him to the heart of the royal establishment. Six months into the new reign Seymour swept the late king's widow Catherine Parr off her feet and married her, living much of the time at Sudeley Castle in Gloucestershire. Seymour, who was by now an admiral, thus instantly had control over a possible heiress to the throne, the Lady Elizabeth, who had continued to live with her stepmother after her father's death.

Thomas Seymour was a rumbustious adventurer whose swashbuckling manner and over-familiar treatment of the young Elizabeth led to rumours that he even had plans to marry her himself and thereby seize the throne. His reputation was not good. He was said to have made money by clipping the coinage and even to have benefited from piracy by abusing his position as an admiral. Wild stories proliferated about him. Servants claimed to have seen him romping in Elizabeth's bed in the early morning when both were wearing only nightshirts. He was said to have cut one of her dresses off her on the grounds that black did not suit her, and to have been seen kissing her. When Catherine Parr died in childbirth in 1548, there were even rumours that he had deliberately poisoned her in order to marry Elizabeth.

In fact Seymour had bigger fish to fry: he hoped to persuade his nephew the king to make him protector instead of his elder brother. Whatever his intentions, he began to muster men for a rebellion. When Somerset got wind of it Seymour was executed. On hearing of his execution the thirteen-year-old Elizabeth remarked coolly to her governess Kate Ashley, 'This day died a man with much wit and very little judgement.'

But Somerset's position was not shored up by the execution of his brother. Trouble was brewing, stirred up by the wholesale changes of the previous ten years. Not only was the enclosure system beginning to bite, but under Edward the Church of England moved dramatically away from its old rituals, which Henry VIII had been keen to preserve for the sake of continuity. It took on a severely logical new shape which satisfied purist intellectuals, but took no account of popular sentiment.

Cromwell had begun the process of stripping shrines and churches, mainly to benefit the Treasury. But the Edwardian government took the spoliation of churches to extremes – its aim not so much pecuniary as to rid the Church of the superstition which polluted Roman Catholicism. Thus it was that government agents rushed into churches and whitewashed the stained-glass windows depicting saints and miracles – many old English churches still bear traces of this whitewash. They also dragged out elaborate altars, rood screens and statues and attacked them with hammers. This process, known as iconoclasm, was made lawful by an act against books and images. Longstanding ceremonies and holidays which were an enjoyable part of the village year, such as Candlemas on 2 February, being smeared with ashes on Ash Wednesday, and carrying palms in memory of Christ's entry into Jerusalem on Palm Sunday, were abolished by law as papal inventions. And once again priests were allowed to marry.

In 1549 the enforced use of the first new prayer book (commissioned by Henry VIII and in preparation for several years under Cranmer) triggered uprisings all over the south-west and in the eastern counties of England. Though the two protests were quite distinct – the south-west calling for the restoration of the Mass in Latin and the area round Norwich under Jack Ket for the pulling down of the enclosures – they both signalled the great unpopularity of the government. Managing them proved to be the downfall of Protector Somerset. He was a kindly man and had too much sympathy with Ket's grievances to suppress his rebellion with the severity the rest of the King's Council felt it merited.

While Somerset hesitated, his rivals in the Council struck. John Dudley, son of Henry VII's executed minister, disposed of the eastern counties rebellion with great despatch, hanging Jack Ket from the parapet of Norwich Castle while his followers dangled from what they had called the Oak of Reformation. A formidable soldier, Dudley was the coming man. He had distinguished himself at the recent Battle of Pinkie, Somerset's attempt to aid the new Protestant Reformation in Scotland and at the same time to marry Edward VI to the infant heiress, Mary of Scotland. But if Dudley had emerged as the hero of the hour, Somerset had been humiliated. For the Scots did not like what was complained of as a 'rough wooing', and Mary was smuggled over to France to marry the dauphin instead.

Somerset not only looked foolish, he was also visibly corrupt. Although all of the Council enjoyed the proceeds from a further suppression of the chantries, the protector's share was large enough to begin building the first Italianate mansion in England, Somerset House in the Strand, which until recently was the national repository of our records of births, deaths and marriages. But it was an excuse for dismissing the protector. That same year, Somerset was ousted from the Council, and Dudley, or the Duke of Northumberland as he became, took control.

Northumberland, even more than Somerset, was the champion of the radical wing of the Church. England became a haven for the more advanced Protestant divines like Martin Bucer and Peter Martyr fleeing from the wrath of the Emperor Charles V, whose armies seemed to be on the point of suppressing the German Reformation altogether. Despite the popular reaction to the first prayer book, the English Church took an even sharper turn away from Henrician Catholicism by publishing the second prayer book in 1552 and the Forty-Two Articles of Faith a year later. In fact, for all the outrage it had caused, the first prayer book was as Catholic as its progenitor Henry VIII. But the second, though also written by Cranmer, showed just how fast Protestant intellectual thought was moving in England. The Church had swung towards the Zwinglian idea of Communion being a ceremony of commemoration rather than a Real Presence, and many important Protestants of a strongly radical tendency were appointed to key bishoprics: Nicholas Ridley, who was a convinced Zwinglian, became Bishop of London and John Hooper became Bishop of Gloucester and soon attracted attention by refusing to wear the vestments of a bishop because the ancient Church would not have insisted on them.

In July 1553 Northumberland was alarmed to see that the sixteen-year-old king's always fragile health was going downhill rapidly. He would have to act fast if he wished to preserve his power. By Henry VIII's will and by parliamentary statute the succession had been fixed on Catherine of

Aragon's daughter Princess Mary and then on Princess Elizabeth. Yet if Edward was succeeded by Princess Mary, who was well known for having the Catholic Mass celebrated in her own apartments, she would endanger the whole English Protestant Reformation. Instead, with the backing of the Archbishop of Canterbury Cranmer and the Bishop of London Nicholas Ridley, Northumberland persuaded Edward that the throne should go to the strenuously Protestant Lady Jane Grey, who as the eldest granddaughter of Henry VIII's sister Mary had the next claim

EDWARD THE SIXTH.

to the throne. Princess Elizabeth had no Catholic leanings either, but she lacked the unique qualification that Lady Jane possessed, as far as Northumberland was concerned: Lady Jane was married to his son.

In his own hand, Edward VI sketched out a new will bypassing Mary and Elizabeth. The crown was to go to Lady Jane Grey. Two days later, on the evening of 7 July, the pale young king's consumptive lungs gave out. The palace guard was doubled to make sure the news did not leak out before Northumberland could arrest Princess Mary. But somehow a messenger galloped from London to warn Mary at Hunsdon in Hertfordshire that her brother was dead and she must flee. Before the sun rose the thirty-seven-year-old Mary, with a few retainers, had reached Kenninghall in Norfolk.

In London a furious Northumberland proclaimed the gentle Lady Jane Grey queen. But her reception was less than rapturous, and she was anyway unwilling to be Northumberland's puppet. After a reign of only ten days, while men swarmed to Princess Mary's army in the eastern counties, Mary was welcomed by the rest of the Council into London. She entered the city without resistance on 3 August, riding side by side with Princess Elizabeth, and after imprisoning Lady Jane and Northumberland, became queen.

Mary I

(1553–1558)

Mary ruled for five short years before she succumbed to stomach cancer. Though dumpy and plain, the new queen combined the steely Tudor willpower with a profound Catholicism inherited from her Spanish mother. Despite all the pressures brought to bear by her father and brother, she had refused to abandon her faith, believing that it was her mission to return England to her ancient religion. In this she was actively abetted by the Spanish ambassador, who became one of her most important advisers. Directly she became queen all the Protestant bishops, Hooper, Ridley and Cranmer, were replaced by the 'Catholic' bishops of Henry VIII's reign who had meanwhile been languishing in prison.

Stephen Gardiner, who had been Bishop of Winchester since 1531, though imprisoned for two years under Edward VI, became Mary's lord chancellor and chief religious adviser. The first act of the new government's Parliament was to return religion to the state it had been in after Henry's Reformation: the Six Articles were brought back; Mass was celebrated; those members of the clergy who, like Cranmer, had married were forced to renounce their wives; Edward's bishops were imprisoned and Protestants were expelled from the country. But the queen had no plans to rest there. By the second year of her reign in November 1554, though she had at first taken the title Supreme Head of the Church, she had repealed the Reformation statutes and returned England to the Church of Rome.

The dissolution of the monasteries had secured the gentry's and the nobility's loyalty to the Henrician Reformation. Property also explained the ease with which Mary returned England to Rome. For she was enough of a Tudor pragmatist to agree that the restoration of monastery lands to the Church could be no part of the new settlement. As a result, the transformation of the country back to Roman Catholicism was achieved without incident – the roots of Protestantism in England did not lie deep at mid-century. Later that year Mary's cousin Cardinal Pole, the papal legate who had been exiled in Rome for so long, returned to England to preside over the dismantling of the Henrician Reformation. He became Archbishop of Canterbury.

Meanwhile Mary's decision in 1559 to marry her princely cousin, Charles V's son, who was to become Philip II of Spain, aroused the most vehement opposition in Parliament, Council and the country at large. But she was determined, for everything Spanish aroused her unquestioning reverence. When Ambassador Renard had suggested marriage between herself and Philip she fell into transports of excitement without ever having met her intended, and immediately gave her sacred promise that she would marry none other. There were riots and a rebellion led by Sir Thomas Wyatt, the son of the poet, whose intention was to place Princess Elizabeth on the throne.

Only Mary's prompt action in riding to the Guildhall in London and telling the crowds that she would postpone the Spanish marriage until it had been agreed by Parliament re-enlisted public support. Though Wyatt proclaimed Elizabeth's ignorance from the scaffold, Mary did not believe him. Lady Jane and Northumberland were executed and an outraged and terrified Elizabeth was taken by river to the Tower of London, from whence her mother had never returned alive. Here she famously refused to go in through the entrance known as Traitor's Gate and, sitting down on the flagstones, declined to move. 'Here landeth as true a subject, being prisoner, as landed at these stairs,' she said imperiously. And until the sun set and she at last consented to go in, no one dared move her.

But no evidence could be found to convict Elizabeth. She would not have been so foolish to plot openly. Her early life had made her a most circumspect and cautious personality and she had already had to throw herself on her knees and beg for her freedom when Mary's advisers, such as Bishop Gardiner, had suggested she be arrested because she might form the focus of a Protestant plot. Though Elizabeth spent a couple of grim months in prison convinced that each day would be her last – the scaffold erected to execute Lady Jane Grey remained in place – eventually she was released. She went to live quietly at Woodstock in Oxfordshire and then at Hatfield, north of London.

QUEEN MARY TUDOR.

The arrival in London of the grave Philip of Spain, with his flaxen beard and cold eyes, saw not only the return of England to the old religion but the persecution as heretics of those who refused to conform. Cardinal Pole set up a commission to inquire into heresy and soon began burning all the Edwardian bishops. First to go was John Rogers, the Canon of St Paul's, well known for helping with the translation of the Bible that Cranmer had sponsored. He was followed by Bishop Hooper of Gloucester, whose conscience had stopped him wearing vestments because St Peter would not have worn them. Taken to Smithfield in his long white shift, he was tied to a stake and logs were piled round him until only the upper half of his body could be seen. As the fire slowly consumed him, he never uttered a sound.

The three other most celebrated personalities of the early English Reformation, Cranmer, Latimer and Ridley were all taken to Oxford to be examined in their faith by the new Catholic bishops. Cranmer's trial was postponed because, having been made archbishop by the pope, his case had to be transferred to Rome. But Latimer and Ridley were condemned to death for denying Transubstantiation, the transforming of the bread and wine at Communion into the Real Body and Blood of Christ. They were trussed back to back at a stake in the town ditch at Oxford. As the flames rose and their agony began, the ever courageous Latimer said to his trembling fellow martyr Ridley, 'Play the man, brother Ridley; we shall this day light such a candle, by God's Grace, in England, as I trust shall never be put out.'

And he was right. Until the Marian martyrs, of whom 300 were burned in the next three years, Protestantism had really been confined to a tiny percentage of the country. But, influenced by the civilizing spirit of the

Bishop Nicholas Ridley and Bishop Hugh Latimer depicted in the Protestant bestseller, *Acts and Monuments*, first published in 1563 by John Foxe which became known as *Foxe's Book of Martyrs*.

Cardinal Reginald Pole, Mary's cousin, who became Archbishop of Canterbury when Mary briefly returned the Church to Rome.

Renaissance, the people of England were more horrified by the burnings under Mary because of the visible human anguish it caused than they would have been in the middle ages. Moreover, the persecution of heretics was all part of the unwelcome Spanish influence under which the country had fallen since the queen's marriage. The methods of the Spanish Inquisition, which gave Spain a bad name and was soon to be described in *Foxe's Book of Martyrs*, did more to convert England to Protestantism than all the efforts of the Protestant divines. The queen herself became known as Bloody Mary.

Cranmer too soon met his death by burning. For all his great literary gifts, the former archbishop had never been a very strong character and he was now an old man. After five months of imprisonment, his spirit was broken. He agreed to recant and at Cardinal Pole's suggestion put his name to papers describing himself as the author of all the evils which had fallen on the nation since Henry VIII. But as one of the chief architects of the Protestant Reformation Cranmer was such a major figure that Cardinal Pole and Queen Mary required a very public renunciation from him. It was arranged that this would take place before a large audience in St Mary's Church at Oxford.

To everyone's surprise, at the pulpit Cranmer suddenly showed a courage no one had known he possessed. In a firm voice he denounced the pope as anti-Christ and his doctrine as false. Angry Catholics removed him before he could finish speaking and hurried him to the stake outside. But even then he outwitted them. For Cranmer thrust his right hand into the fire saying loudly, 'It was that unworthy hand which offended by writing lies and recanting, therefore it must burn first.'

Although it was popularly believed that it was her Spanish advisers who were chiefly responsible for the burnings, in fact Mary herself derived enormous satisfaction from them. Never in rude health, and usually having a poor appetite, she would eat a heartier dinner after a burning had taken place. The emotional gratification that she took from persecuting heretics was one of the few she obtained. Quite soon after the marriage Philip removed himself back to his own kingdom and visited his English wife only periodically when he needed money for the war against France.

The Martyrdom of Dr Thomas Cranmer. Into the flames he first thrust the hand which had signed his recantation from Protestantism.

Marian martyrs burning.

The Martyrs' Memorial, Oxford.

The struggle of Valois versus Habsburg, of Henry II of France against Charles V and then Philip II took many surprising shapes and forms. Not the least of these was when Philip forced Mary to declare war on France, and English troops took part in the assault which won the Battle of St Quentin. But like everything to do with Mary the affair ended in disaster. In 1558 in a tit-for-tat action the French high command attacked England's last possession in France, the port and staple town of Calais. Though its governor had repeatedly warned that he did not possess enough food or soldiers to defend his position Mary's government misunderstood how urgent the situation was.

When reinforcements finally arrived, it was too late. The war was extremely unpopular and the antipathy towards Philip and Mary herself meant that Parliament was no longer the obedient tool of the crown. It refused to vote supplies. The government could raise money only by forced loans and illegal customs duties. News of the fall of Calais burst upon England like a thunderclap; it was the *coup de grâce* for Mary's already poor health. She had miscarried one child. Now she lay dying of a stomach tumour which for many months she had pitifully believed to be a pregnancy. Loathed by her people, her husband far from her side, shortly before she passed away the unhappy queen uttered the immortal words: 'When I die the word "Calais" will be found engraved on my heart.' A few hours later on that same day, 17 November, died the other great defender of the ancient faith, Cardinal Pole.

Meanwhile messengers had galloped to Hatfield, where the twenty-five-year-old Elizabeth was living, conscious that with her sister dying childless she was the future queen. The learned Elizabeth was reading the classics under an oak tree when the messengers arrived and hailed her as their sovereign. Then she said very slowly in Latin, 'This is the Lord's doing and it is marvellous in our eyes.' As was remarked at the time, it was a good sign for a queen to be reading books instead of burning them, and so it proved.

Elizabeth I
(1558–1603)

The clever, slender young woman who took over the English throne in 1558 had not kept her head on her shoulders through all her vicissitudes without it having a deep effect on her character. When at the London pageant for her coronation the figure of Old Father Time passed by, she was heard by people standing near her to murmur with wonder, 'And Time has brought me hither.' Elizabeth's insecure and troubled early life had created a consummate pragmatist, who had a great deal in common with her grandfather Henry VII. Like him she was thrifty to the point of miserliness when it came to spending money. This was fortunate as the country she inherited had been almost bankrupted by Philip's war. Unlike her father she was reluctant to go to war partly because of the expense, partly because she was so cautious that she was reluctant to commit herself to one side or the other. She rarely moved in a straightforward fashion but dilly-dallied on foreign policy – to the despair of her ministers.

The new queen's experience of religious extremism in her brother's and sister's reigns had left her with a great dislike of such emotions and a natural tolerance. Soon after her accession she announced she 'would make no windows in men's souls', and for the first decade or so of her life she was content for a secret Catholicism to go on as long as the outward forms of Protestantism were observed.

Queen Elizabeth inherited the Tudor common touch and charm that her brother and sister had so signally lacked, as well as the strong personality which had kept England at the feet of her father. She had his formidable intellect, his warmth and his striking wit. She had none of her mother's dark colouring, having pale Tudor skin, red hair and an imperious hooked nose. Like Henry VIII she believed in showing herself to the country and staying with the gentry and nobility who upheld the Tudor state, hence the very many houses whose grandest bedrooms bear the legend 'Queen Elizabeth slept here'. Like Henry VIII too she held a very splendid court, full of balls, masques and intrigues, at which the most dazzlingly dressed figure and the most spirited dancer was herself.

She was just as capable as her father at bending Parliament to her will

Traitor's Gate on the Thames at the Tower of London which Elizabeth famously refused to go through.

and she never failed to get the supplies she asked for. Though constantly urged by her Council and Parliament to marry and ensure a Protestant succession she never did. She was perhaps finally wedded to her country. As she said in her Golden Speech when she had been forty-three years on the throne, 'Though God has raised me high, yet this I count the glory of my crown, that I have reigned with your loves. And though you have had, and may have, many mightier and wiser princes sitting in this seat; yet you never had, nor shall have, any that will love you better.'

Queen Elizabeth the Great presided over a unique moment in English history. Her seamen sailed round the world and kept the seas free for Protestantism by defeating the Spanish Armada. Her playhouses saw productions of some of the greatest drama the world has ever known, the plays of William Shakespeare. And at a time when the wars of religion were creating bitter civil conflicts all over Europe, the middle way she followed helped Protestantism to take peaceful root. While so many monarchs met deaths by assassination, Elizabeth survived.

The queen was extremely vain, a characteristic she inherited from her coquettish mother; from her father she got a love of regal splendour. To the end of her life she delighted in court revels and fabulously expensive dresses, whose fashions became more and more exaggerated as the century wore on. Frilled ruffs, vast hairdos, jewels by the yard, banquets and male favourites were the hallmarks of her reign, and she soon acquired the nickname Gloriana. Ambassadors who did not know her regarded as frivolous her obsession with dancing and with young men – favourites like Robert Dudley, Earl of Leicester, Sir Christopher Hatton and

The Tower of London.

Elizabeth I.

finally the Earl of Essex. They did not see the dedicated and Machiavellian stateswoman closeted with master strategists like Sir Francis Walsingham and plotting how to keep Philip of Spain at bay. They failed to take seriously a woman whose criteria for selecting civil servants was so disinterested that she chose the great statesman William Cecil as her chief minister or principal secretary of state because she believed 'that you will not be corrupted with any manner of gift, and that you will be faithful to the state, and that without respect of my private will you will give me that counsel you think best'. Unlike those of her father, her ministers left her service only if death removed them. Cecil was at her side for forty years.

The new queen's most pressing problem was the English Church, now rejoined to Rome. As a highly accomplished daughter of the New Learning who spoke fluent Latin and French and read Greek, Elizabeth possessed religious sympathies that were advanced Protestant, those of the second Edwardian prayer book. She did not believe in the Real Presence, as she made clear soon after her accession by leaving Mass when the Communion wafer was elevated. But her intention was to return the Church to that of her father's less controversial Reformation, which did not offend Catholics. But a huge problem faced her, namely personnel. The old Henrician Protestants were dead, the clergy in charge were Catholic and the men required to run the Elizabethan Church could only be the

Calvin, the French theologian living in Geneva who influenced many English exiles during Mary's reign.

Protestants who had fled abroad, the Marian exiles.

The Marian exiles were just the sort of religious extremists towards whom the queen felt a natural antipathy. Far from being the polished courtiers her feminine nature delighted in, they were rough and ready, deliberately eschewing good manners in favour of sincerity. Many of them had been profoundly influenced by Jean Calvin in Geneva, one of the main centres for Protestant refugees. Calvin's study of the Bible had convinced him that hierarchy was wrong and he rejected much of the Church's supervision of religion: there should be no official prayer book, and churches should be run by small groups of ministers or presbyters. He rejected even the few sacraments Luther had accepted, for he had worked out a theory of predestination – men and women were either damned or saved. What mattered was the moral purity of the elect (as the saved were known). Rather than in acts of worship their religion was to be expressed in the moral purity of their daily life, in conduct and clothing (from this would derive their name of Puritans). With the new queen a Protestant, the Marian exiles had returned to England full of high hopes of significantly reforming the Church of England along Calvinist lines.

But this autonomous and democratic kind of religion could not have appealed less to Elizabeth. As her father's daughter she believed that the state control of religion was necessary for an orderly country and she spent much of her reign combating Puritanism, with only moderately successful results. She was personally affronted by their leading spokesman, the savage propagandist John Knox, whose notorious pamphlet *First Blast of the Trumpet against the Monstrous Regiment of Women* attacked women rulers. She banned him from London, so he found his way to Scotland and founded the Calvinist Reformation in Scotland. Like most Puritans the strength of Knox's religious convictions meant he was no respecter of persons, even of royalty. Elizabeth found this intolerable.

John Knox, Calvinist religious leader of the Scottish Reformation.

Nevertheless the Marian exiles were all the clergy the queen had to work with. Fortunately the Dean of Lincoln, Matthew Parker, whom Elizabeth made Archbishop of Canterbury, was a man after her own heart. The scholarly Parker, who had also been her mother

Anne Boleyn's personal chaplain, had managed to remain in England during Mary's reign and so had not come under any extremist influences abroad. Like the queen he believed in the Church's regulation of religion. He thought it more important to please the majority of English people who were still attached to old forms, whether in rituals of worship or vestments. Thanks to Parker and the queen's genius for compromise and harmonization, the 1559 Acts of Supremacy and Uniformity, whereby the English Church once more cut its links with the papacy, appeared to be all things to all men. Although the Elizabethan settlement really took for its essentials the second prayer book of Edward VI, its Communion seemed both to celebrate a Real Presence and to be a commemorative act. The new Church thus offended as few Catholics as possible, in order to unite England behind the queen. Elizabeth declared herself more modestly to be the Church's supreme governor instead of supreme head, in order to leave her ecclesiastics free to determine affairs of the Church. And to make sure the Puritan clergy toed the line, Archbishop Parker set up the Court of Ecclesiastical Commission to enforce the Elizabethan settlement in every parish.

Archbishop Matthew Parker, Elizabeth's first Archbishop of Canterbury. He had been Anne Boleyn's chaplain.

In the early part of her reign Elizabeth's moderation paid off. She had little trouble from English Catholics or the Catholic clergy, most of whom became priests in the Church of England. It was the former Marian exiles whose behaviour continued to anger her. Initially she was in too weak a position to protest when many of them refused to adopt signs of popish 'superstition' such as wearing surplices or making the sign of the cross. But seven years after her accession in 1565 the queen and Parker felt strong enough to move against the Puritans. Parker's 'Advertisements' were given to the clergy. These were guidelines enforcing observance of the prayer book and the wearing of surplices, which resulted in about thirty clergymen losing their livings.

With this action the way became clearer for the Puritans. Most of them had believed optimistically that the Elizabethan settlement was only a beginning. Now it was clear that as far as the queen was concerned it was intended to be the end. From then on there were constant attacks against Church government from the Puritans, taking their stand on the New Testament. Since there were no bishops in the New Testament, went one argument, there should be none in the Elizabethan Church. With the death of Parker in 1575 the queen found herself more isolated than she had supposed. Many MPs and many of her civil servants, especially those who worked for Cecil's colleague, her other royal secretary Sir Francis Walsingham, had become increasingly attracted to the aims of the Puritan clergy. They disapproved of the Ecclesiastical Commission which was compared even by the faithful William Cecil, or Lord Burghley as he had become, to the Spanish Inquisition in its ruthless methods and lack of interest in a fair trial.

Archbishop John Whitgift, Elizabeth's Archbishop of Canterbury, from 1583 until her death, foe of the Puritans.

The appalled queen suddenly found that her new Archbishop of Canterbury Edmund Grindal was in sympathy with what is known as the 'prophesyings' movement, the increasingly popular Bible self-help groups run by the Puritan clergy to which the laity were invited. As they often resulted in criticism of the Church, Elizabeth believed they should be suppressed. Grindal believed they should merely be regulated. When the archbishop, greatly daring, refused to suppress them he was suspended for five years. In 1583 his place as Archbishop of Canterbury was taken by John Whitgift. The small, dark and ferocious Archbishop Whitgift was as much a Calvinist as Grindal, but, for him, where Puritan ideas conflicted with a settled order of doctrine the law of the land should prevail. With Whitgift in charge, pursuit of the Puritans became much more effective. No fewer than 200 clergymen lost their livings when all those suspected of being Puritans were hauled up before the Court of Ecclesiastical Commission to swear to a new Act of Six Articles emphasizing the Royal Supremacy in religious affairs. By the end of her reign as Elizabeth became increasingly severe in her treatment of dissenters, the death penalty or exile was the punishment for all those who would not attend the Anglican Church.

Henry VIII's equivocation about the Mass had kept the Catholic powers out of England. Elizabeth's equally careful footwork with the religious settlement, her stern line against Calvinists and her warm reception of France and Spain for the first twelve years of her reign also kept England free from invasion. In fact, so mixed were the signals coming from the queen that her widowed brother-in-law Philip II believed he could marry her – as did various other Catholics such as Archduke Charles of Austria, the future Henry III of France and his younger brother the Duke of Anjou. Thanks to Elizabeth's caution over the settlement, during the first decade of her reign when her title could have been in dispute, and Philip of Spain could have invaded to aid English Catholics, no Catholic plots erupted. On the whole Catholics paid their fines, did not attend Anglican services and had Mass said quietly in their own homes.

But towards the end of the decade the situation changed, for a number of reasons, and the chief enemy to the Elizabethan state became Catholicism. For the next twenty years Elizabeth and Protestant England found themselves under serious threat. This was the consequence of the arrival in England of Elizabeth's first cousin once removed, Mary Queen of Scots, a Catholic who as Henry VIII's great-niece had a claim to the English throne, being next in blood.

When Elizabeth had expelled John Knox from England and he had taken his fiery energies north to Scotland, the religious revolt he inspired among the Scottish Protestant nobles, the Lords of the Congregation as they called themselves, turned into a patriotic war to rid Scotland of the French Catholic regent Mary of Guise, mother of Mary Queen of Scots. Though Elizabeth disliked helping rebels, on her Council's advice in 1560 she had despatched troops to aid the Scots against the French government. On the death of Mary of Guise what was in effect a Calvinist Scottish republic had been created by the Lords of the Congregation: a new Scots Parliament renounced the pope and a General Assembly was created, the chief council of the Presbyterian Church. Undeterred by this Calvinist seizure of power, a year later the daughter of James V – recently widowed by the death of Francis II of France – landed in Scotland to claim her kingdom as Mary Queen of Scots.

Mary Queen of Scots was a great beauty, tall and fascinating. But in contrast to her cousin Elizabeth she possessed almost no political skill or feel for statecraft and had a foolishly headstrong and passionate character. At first, however, her charm won over the Protestant lords ruling Scotland. She made no attempt to drive out the Calvinist religion now established there or to reconvert the country. But she did insist on hearing her own Mass in her private apartments, thereby incurring the wrath of John Knox, who publicly preached in Edinburgh that one of the queen's Masses was 'more fearful to me than ten thousand armed enemies'. But Mary emphasized to her Catholic contacts abroad, especially Philip of Spain and her Guise uncles, that now was not the moment to invade Scotland and attempt a reconversion. She allowed her half-brother the Earl of Moray, an illegitimate son of James V, to continue to govern Scotland.

In fact to begin with Mary Queen of Scots' only ill-judged action was her bid to be declared the childless Elizabeth's heir. But Elizabeth, who was irritated by reports of her cousin's glamour, and her Council were adamant that her claim should not be acknowledged. The pope had never authorized Henry VIII's marriage to Anne Boleyn, so to believing Catholics Elizabeth was not the legitimate ruler of England. The true claim was that of Mary Queen of Scots. As a Catholic, Mary might well become a rallying point for Catholics in England – as indeed she eventually proved to be.

As long as Mary remained a widow, all went well. But in 1565 she fell in love with Lord Darnley and determined to marry him, thus enraging both Moray and Elizabeth, for Henry Darnley was the grandson of Margaret Tudor, Henry VIII's sister, a relationship that would strengthen Mary Queen of Scots' own claim. Moreover, Darnley was one of the leaders of the English Catholics. Elizabeth and Cecil issued a declaration that the marriage would be 'perilous to the amity between the queens and both realms', and provided a safe haven in Newcastle for Moray and the other Protestant lords. They had revolted against the marriage and, after a short civil war in which Mary and Darnley triumphed, were expelled from Scotland. The marriage went ahead as planned.

Only a few months were needed for Mary to find out the quality of the man she had married. She began to detest him, as he was weak, cruel and a drunk. Moreover the twisted and treacherous Darnley had no intention of merely being a consort of the queen. He decided to make a bid for the crown himself, with the support of the queen's enemies, Moray and the Protestant lords in England. In a hideous plot which may have been intended to make the pregnant queen miscarry, her private secretary, the Italian David Rizzio, was murdered before her eyes in March 1566 at Holyrood Palace in Edinburgh by twenty heavily armed men. These were no common assassins. They included not only important nobles but the queen's husband himself. Somehow, despite her horror, Mary Queen of Scots managed to keep a cool head and persuade Darnley to abandon his fellow plotters. Once again the conspirators were expelled from the country. Meanwhile Mary seems to have begun planning her revenge, having conceived a passion for the dashing James Hepburn, Earl of Bothwell.

Bothwell was an unscrupulous border lord who was to become her third husband. There seems little doubt that Mary was involved in the explosion at a house south of Edinburgh called Kirk O' Field which killed Darnley, though it was masterminded by Bothwell. Before long, however, the Scottish lords who had been Bothwell's allies turned on him in fury. Moray and the Lords of the Congregation then returned from exile and at knifepoint forced the queen to renounce the throne in favour of her thirteen-month-old son James (whose father was Lord Darnley). In 1568, she escaped and fled in a humble fishing boat to England, determined to throw herself on her cousin Elizabeth's mercy.

Mary Queen of Scots' arrival in England put Elizabeth and Cecil in an extremely difficult position. If she remained in the country, she could still be a focus for Catholic plots. On the other hand it would be foolish to allow her to depart for France where she might raise troops to assert her claim to the English crown. Faced with this conundrum, Elizabeth elected to play for time. She announced an investigation into Mary's connection with Darnley's murder. This allowed her to keep the queen in captivity indefinitely.

In England the Queen of Scots indeed became a magnet for Catholic conspiracies, particularly after a new pope, Pius V, took up her cause in 1570, excommunicating Elizabeth and calling for her to be removed from the English throne. Twelve months after Mary's arrival in England there had been an ill-thought-out rising by the northern earls, the ancient houses of Percy and Neville, on whose lands Catholicism still flourished. Even though it ended in miserable failure, thereafter a new plot was discovered almost every year for eighteen years until Mary's death. Meanwhile the fourth Duke of Norfolk, the son of the poet Earl of Surrey, was drawn into a new conspiracy headed by an Italian banker in the pay of Philip of Spain named Ridolfi. On every tide letters went to Spain from Norfolk, Ridolfi and Mary herself devising ways to seize power, backed by Spanish troops crossing from the Netherlands under the Duke of Alva.

But working with Cecil was Elizabeth's exceptional foreign minister Sir Francis Walsingham. A combative Puritan Walsingham was not only waging a war against England's enemies; he considered himself to be fighting a global battle against Catholicism. Like a great spider he sat at the centre of an amazingly complicated and secret espionage system which covered the whole of Europe. His network of spies soon obtained enough evidence to have Norfolk arrested and executed for treason in 1572. Though the House of Commons demanded the Queen of Scots' head as well, Elizabeth held them off. For another fifteen years the prematurely ageing Mary lived in Staffordshire at Tutbury Castle never quite losing hope – especially when Moray was assassinated – that she would be returned to her throne. It was not to be.

Mary Queen of Scots' imprisonment in England coincided with a resurgence of Roman Catholicism, what is known as the Counter-Reformation. Rejecting attempts to come to an accommodation with Protestantism, Catholicism reorganized itself. The Jesuit order was founded expressly by St Ignatius Loyola to attack the new faith in Protestant countries. Following his example, a Lancashire Catholic named William Allen established a seminary at Douai in Philip II's territories in the Netherlands to send back priests to England to revive the Catholic religion. They were to promote an uprising of English Catholics in conjunction with a Spanish invasion, which Allen and his followers saw as the only solution.

From the 1570s onwards the priests from Douai started to flood back secretly into England as missionaries, hiding in special rooms called priest-holes, constructed for them in English country houses Although to celebrate the Mass and thus deny the queen's supremacy was treasonous, until the 1570s the letter of the law tended not to be enforced. But the arrival of the seminary priests, and the Jesuits' success in prodding Catholic consciences awake, suddenly posed a genuine threat to English security.

There began an unspoken hostility between England and Spain which in episode after episode nudged both countries nearer to open conflict. Since Elizabeth wished to avoid going to war at all costs and Philip had plans to invade only when the time was right, England remained at peace until 1587. But if the queen refused publicly to acknowledge Spain as the enemy, her seamen had no qualms about doing so. The English Channel and the oceans of the New World became the two countries' unofficial battleground, where Englishmen enriched themselves and did their bit for Protestantism by attacking any Spanish ship that hove into view.

By the late sixteenth century Englishmen had recovered all the zest for maritime adventure they had lost since the time of their Viking forebears. The discovery of the New World kindled a taste for exploration among

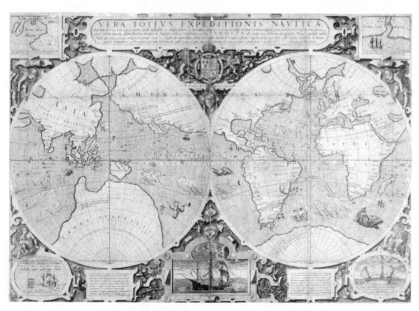

Map of Drake's voyage round the world.

English merchants everywhere. The Company of Merchant Adventurers headed by Sebastian Cabot, the son of the John Cabot who discovered Labrador, had for some time been breaking into new markets in the Baltic.

But the most celebrated of all these explorers in their time were the Elizabethan adventurers and master mariners Francis Drake and John Hawkins, who combined their voyages of discovery with terrorizing the Spanish Main. Nowadays Drake's cousin Jack Hawkins is held in low esteem as he was the founder of the English slave trade, supplying Africans to labour in the tropical heat of the West Indies and South America – a terrible traffic in human cargo which was to make so much money for him and other English merchants over the next 200 years.

Francis Drake was Elizabethan England's greatest popular hero. He was also the English seaman most feared by the King of Spain for his bravado and his burning commitment to Protestantism. Drake came from a strongly Protestant Devon family and dedicated his every waking moment to making trouble for the Spanish. Any Spanish shipping that ventured into the Channel, even if it were carrying Spanish grandees, was considered fair game. In 1572, granted a privateering commission (which licensed him to make private war against the Spanish), Drake embarked on an expedition to seize the bullion of the Spanish fleet, and landed at Panama. Having got a glimpse from there of an unknown ocean, the Pacific, he became obsessed with sailing into that sea. It was all part of the national campaign to beat the Spanish at their game of controlling the New World. Five years later he set off again from Plymouth with five ships in which the queen and much of the court had shares.

Following Magellan's route of fifty years before, Drake sailed down the east coast of South America plundering Spanish shipping as he went and braving immense storms, one of which lasted fifty-two days. He finally got through the turbulent straits at the foot of South America which Magellan had discovered, and then navigated northwards up the length of South and Central America, hugging its west coast. But where Magellan had turned west and cut through the Pacific Ocean to die in the Philippines, Drake carried on all the way up to California and landed at San Francisco, a Spanish settlement, which he renamed Drake's Bay. He attacked the Spanish treasure ship called the *Cacafuego*, seized jewels and silver worth millions today and returned home in triumph, only the second seaman since Magellan to circumnavigate the globe. He was to be knighted ostentatiously by the queen on the deck of his own ship, the *Golden Hind*.

Elizabeth had no scruples about benefiting from plundered Spanish bullion. She had enough piratical spirit in her to take shares in many of Drake's expeditions, to refuse to hand him over to the Spanish authorities as they frequently demanded and in effect to treat Spain as the enemy. But as yet she had no wish to take on a man as wealthy and powerful as Philip of Spain, who had the silver of the Americas at his back and who in 1580 would add Portugal to his dominions.

Thus on the official level Elizabeth was still keen to appear in a placatory light to Philip of Spain, even when in the momentous year 1572 the cause of Protestantism seemed to require its champions to stand up and be counted. Shortly after the Ridolfi plot, the hatred the Netherlanders felt for the Spanish occupying army of General Alva erupted in revolt. To the astonishment of Europe, under the leadership of William of Orange the seven courageous northern Protestant provinces threw off the iron hand of Spain, their overlord since the Emperor Charles V received them as part of his inheritance through his Burgundian grandmother. Goaded beyond endurance by the bloody executions of their leaders, the destruction of their ancient political liberties and the torture of the Inquisition, they called themselves the United Provinces. Only the ten provinces of the Catholic south – which approximates to the area of modern-day Belgium – stayed loyal to Spain and became known as the Spanish Netherlands. In France, by contrast, things went less well for the Protestants. On 24 August, the Feast of St Bartholomew, all the Huguenots (Protestants) assembled in Paris for the wedding of their leader Henry of Navarre to the French king's sister were murdered in their beds, possibly by order of Catherine de Medici, the queen mother. It seemed that the aggressive Counter-Reformation might triumph at last in France.

The plight of these beleaguered Protestants aroused the strongest feelings in England, particularly in the royal Council. But Elizabeth would not permit her ministers to rush to the aid of the Protestant cause in Holland when there was a likelihood of it creating war with Spain, a Spain strengthened by the triumph of Catholicism in France. For all her own Protestant sympathies and enjoyment of Drake's antics at Spain's expense, her innate caution would not allow England to go in for heroics. The massacre of the Huguenots made her all the more keen to settle with Philip and begin trading again with the Netherlands.

But Elizabeth was prepared to send aid for the Huguenots who had been forced to take refuge in the massive fortress of La Rochelle on the Atlantic coast. Now that there was a real likelihood of the ultra-Catholic or Guise party triumphing in France and allying with Spain to invade England, it made sense to distract the French by forcing them to deal with a serious revolt at home. Elizabeth therefore secretly despatched arms and ships to help the people at La Rochelle.

Nevertheless, though the queen was anxious to stop England being dragged into a religious war, battle lines along a Protestant–Catholic axis were increasingly being drawn in Europe. With the accession of a new ultra-Catholic king Henry III in 1574, France began edging towards an alliance with Spain that ten years later was an accomplished fact. Only the threat of English and German Protestant troops being sent to the Huguenots under the Prince of Condé slowed down the process by which France was succumbing to the Counter-Reformation.

The arrival of a more successful commander in the Netherlands, the Duke of Parma, gave rise to fears by 1579 that the north would soon be subdued, and to rumours that the soldiers gathering there from Spain would be used to invade England. Fear that the Spanish presence would impede access to Antwerp, England's largest trading centre, made it imperative to seek a stronger alliance with France. There was no better way to secure it than by the queen's marriage.

An elaborate pavane of two years' duration ensued between the fifty-year-old Elizabeth and the younger brother of Henry III, the Duke of Anjou, which many hoped would result in her marrying at last. For twenty-five years Elizabeth had held off against all the gentlemen of the English court – such as Robert Earl of Leicester, who won her heart and was said to have killed his wife for her – just as she had resisted the repeated requests from the House of Commons for her to marry. Anjou, who was twenty years younger than Elizabeth, became the queen's 'little frog' and the object of many endearments. But he was a poor soldier who made a mess of an attempt (with English money and French troops) to aid the seven northern provinces, which continued to hold out against Spain. Like all the queen's marriage projects it came to nothing, and Anjou returned to France. But at least he was a bulwark of Protestantism in the face of a French government growing daily more pro-Spanish.

By 1585 the gloves were off between England and Spain. No one, apart from the queen, was in much doubt that it would soon be war. Spain was now set on invading England by the back door, from both Ireland and Scotland. In 1579 Spanish soldiers, Spanish money and Spanish priests had been sent over to Munster in Ireland to fan the embers of a Fitzgerald rebellion and turn it into a national conflagration. The revolt was savagely suppressed and the old Fitzgerald lands were 'planted', as the term then was, with

Elizabethan poet Edmund Spenser.

Elizabethan adventurers like the poet Edmund Spenser, author of *The Faerie Queen*. A prolonged campaign to turn Scotland Catholic was only just averted by making her king James VI the English government's pensioner and ally, and reminding him that he was Elizabeth's heir presumptive.

Events now moved fast. In 1583 diplomatic relations between Spain and England were cut, when the Spanish ambassador Mendoza was expelled from London after he was revealed as the author of the Throckmorton Plot to assassinate Elizabeth and replace her with Mary Queen of Scots. In retaliation, Philip seized all English shipping in his ports. Drake and Martin Frobisher, at the queen's express command, set off with thirty ships to take her revenge. Sailing to the West Indies they attacked the Spanish fleet, burned the important city of San Domingo and returned with their plunder to England. Once again the silver bullion being carried by the Spanish fleet failed to reach the Netherlands, so once again Spanish troops there could not be paid. Instead the silver docked in England.

In 1584, the threats against the queen's life brought about the Bond of Association, a document devised by Cecil and Walsingham. Aimed at Mary Queen of Scots and her son James VI, it declared that anyone on whose behalf Elizabeth's death was procured would themselves be put to death. The Bond was endorsed by the entire Council, and was enthusiastically signed by thousands of Englishmen. Soon afterwards, Parliament passed an act making it illegal for any Jesuits or seminary priests to come to England. The international situation had already darkened with the assassination of the Netherlands' leader William of Orange and the Spanish seizure of Antwerp under the generalship of the Duke of Parma. In France Henry III's government was now controlled by the ultra-Catholic Guise faction, who seemed keen that their country should become little more than an outpost of Spain.

At last the queen was persuaded to yield to Cecil's entreaties to help the Dutch, as there was no longer any chance of the French going to their rescue – though she persisted in maintaining the fiction that she was not at war with Spain. The Netherlands campaign, under the inept leadership of the Earl of Leicester, was unmemorable, except for the gallant death of the poet Sir Philip Sidney. At the siege of Zutphen he famously gave his last cup of water to a dying soldier, saying, 'Thy need is greater than mine.'

Then in 1586 came the crisis Elizabeth had dreaded. Walsingham's spies had found frequent links between Mary Queen of Scots and Spanish plotters but had never been able to make out a case against her. Now a conspiracy involving an impressionable young Catholic named Anthony Babington from Derbyshire, who like many others had fallen under the spell of the romantic Queen of Scots, and a seminary priest named John

Ballard proved her undoing. Mary, believing the channel through which the letters went was impregnable, was indiscreet enough to put in writing what could be read as her approval of the assassination of Elizabeth. At last Walsingham had the evidence he needed. Even Elizabeth agreed that Mary would have to be tried for treason.

The English government was gambling that the fragility of James VI's hold on his throne and his allowance from the English government would discourage him from invading England on his mother's behalf. And indeed the trial took place without incident at Fotheringhay Castle near Peterborough in October 1586. Although Mary refused to respond to the charges on the grounds that as Queen of Scotland she was not Elizabeth's subject, she was condemned to death for treason. She had become too dangerous to live, but her cousin still would not sign her death warrant.

Eventually, in February 1587, Elizabeth relented. But, though she had signed, she would not allow the death warrant to be sent to Fotheringhay. She became completely hysterical, with the result that members of the Council were forced to take matters into their own hands. Queen Elizabeth's private secretary William Davison was told to take the warrant on their authority to Fotheringhay, and the Scottish queen was executed in the Great Hall there, having been denied the comforts of her own religion. Instead, while the Protestant Dean of Peterborough prayed noisily, the queen read from her own prayer book. Then, holding a crucifix in her hand, she mounted the scaffold, which all through the previous night she had heard being built, and leaned her once elegant but now stout frame across the block.

When Elizabeth was told that Mary was dead, she went into deepest mourning for what she said was not of her making. It was put out that she had wept in agony when she heard the news, and perhaps she had. In her fury, the luckless Davison was made a scapegoat and dismissed from government service. Nevertheless, every personal article of clothing which had belonged to the late Queen of Scots was burned or destroyed so that nothing should survive that could become a memento or holy relic for Catholics.

The execution of the Queen of Scots was the last straw for Philip II. Now that Mary was dead there was no danger of France being drawn into conflict on behalf of her former queen. England would be his alone for the taking. William Allen, founder of the Douai seminary and by now a cardinal, assured Philip that a Spanish invasion would be greeted with an uprising against Elizabeth by English Catholics. In 1587 the alarming news spread that all the wealth of Spain was going towards preparing what her leaders called 'the invincible Armada' to invade England. Philip claimed the English throne as the nearest rightful descendant of John of Gaunt.

But things did not go quite as planned. Francis Drake led a daring raid on the harbour of Cadiz and burned, sank or captured 10,000 tons of shipping. What he called 'singeing the King of Spain's beard' delayed the Armada for a year while new ships were built. Philip's other important miscalculation was to assume that Cardinal Allen had been correct in his belief that all English Catholics were waiting for the day when the Spanish would arrive to save them. In fact, the death of Mary Queen of Scots had assured their loyalty to Elizabeth. A Spaniard as an English king instead of the popular Gloriana was not an attractive idea. Elizabeth herself refused to approve the Council's insulting plan to disarm the Catholics, and Lord Howard of Effingham, a prominent Catholic related to Norfolk, found his religion no bar to commanding the fleet as its lord high admiral.

For the next year England was absorbed in war preparations. Unlike Spain, she had no standing army and had to rely on county militias whose training was organized by each lord lieutenant, an office invented at the time of Edward VI. But England's military weakness meant she had to rely on repelling the invasion at sea. That was where the main battle should take place. The navy, which ever since Henry VIII had been run professionally, now came into its own under the direction of Jack Hawkins. The old pirate used his practical expertise to build ships that were technically in advance of those of the Spanish. The new vessels were deliberately built as fighting machines, compact and low in the water, able to swing round quickly after knocking holes in the sides of the high Spanish ships.

By the early summer of 1588, the English horizon in the south-west was being scanned daily for the moment when the first pinnaces of the Spanish fleet would be seen emerging from the Bay of Biscay. But nothing happened before mid-July, for though the Armada first set sail in May it was blown back to Portugal by poor weather. A further two months had to be spent in refitting. Characteristically the queen, despite her Council's disapproval, had by August moved the court down to Tilbury where a training camp for the land army had been established. It was commanded by her favourite, Robert Leicester, despite his poor showing in the Netherlands. At Tilbury she lived in a white tent among the troops, wearing a metal breastplate. Here, at the height of the conflict, she would make one of her greatest and most inspiring speeches to the assembled soldiers sitting on the ground. Unlike politicians today with their army of speechwriters, every word was written by Elizabeth herself.

'Let tyrants fear!' she said.

I have always so behaved myself, that under God, I have placed my chiefest strength and safeguard in the loyal hearts and goodwill of all my subjects; and therefore I am come amongst you to live or die amongst you all, to lay down for God and for my kingdom and my people, my honour and blood, even in the dust. I know I have the body but of a weak and feeble woman; but I have the heart and stomach of a king, and of a king of England too, and think foul scorn that Parma or Spain or any prince of Europe should dare to invade the borders of my realm.

Although for many nights English lookouts had been posted next to the unlit beacons built on every cliff and prominent hill along the south coast to give warning of the invasion, it was not until 19 July that they were set alight. On that day a Scottish pirate named Fleming saw the first of the 136 ships of the Armada entering the Channel. He sailed east as fast as possible to Plymouth to tell the fleet that there were Spanish ships off the Lizard peninsula, near Land's End. Drake had been playing a game of bowls with Lord Howard when the momentous news was given to them. He now put a restraining hand on the admiral's arm, for Howard had been about to give the signal to launch the fleet. 'We have time to finish our game of bowls,' said Drake calmly. Howard complied. In contrast to the commander of the Spanish fleet, the Duke of Medina Sidonia, who had no knowledge of ships or sea-fighting yet was the absolute general of the Armada, Lord Howard was happy to leave tactics to Drake and his experienced fellow seamen.

It was not until dusk that the signal was given. The Spaniards were rather puzzled by the English response. Instead of launching an attack from Plymouth, Howard and Drake allowed the Armada to sweep majestically on up the Channel. Only then did they set off in pursuit. One eyewitness described the Armada as being like a half-moon in front, the horns stretching out over seven miles. Drake's plan was to force the enemy to keep going by staying behind the Spanish Armada and firing at it. He intended to use the wind, which was in the south-west, as a weapon against the Spanish. So the English fleet, with Howard in the first ship, Drake in the second, Hawkins in the third and Frobisher in the fourth, hung on to the Armada's tail all the way up the Channel. While they could stop or go on at will, the Spaniards were unable to turn on their pursuers.

To the English people watching from the shore it was an alarming scene. The Channel was filled with huge Spanish ships heading, it seemed, inexorably for Flanders to take the Duke of Parma's 26,000 men across to England. But that crucial rendezvous never took place. When the Spanish fleet paused to take on supplies and anchor at Calais Roads in the Straits of Dover off Gravelines on the night of 7–8 August, Drake saw his chance. With the same speed of thought he had shown at Cadiz he drove in fireships among them in the night, so alarming the Spaniards that they abandoned their anchorage. While the Armada was still in a state of confusion the English attacked it in a battle which lasted nine hours. The combination of the English fleet blocking the Channel behind them and the wind still blowing from the south-west meant all Medina Sidonia's ideas of meeting Parma and escorting his army across the Channel vanished into the summer air. The only way for the Armada to escape the English fleet and get home was to flee north round the coast of Scotland.

Terrible gales pursued the Spanish and blew them off course on to the

English defeat the Spanish Armada, 1588.

coast of Norway or wrecked them on the rocky shores of Scotland and Ireland. Some 2,000 corpses were counted on the beach of Sligo Bay alone. Out of the 136 ships of what had once been called the Invincible Armada, only 53 limped home. Elizabeth caused a commemorative medal to be struck. It read, 'God blew and they were scattered.'

Parma had never rated the chances of the expedition very highly. Dutch rebels controlled the coastal waters off Flanders, so his soldiers could never have got past them. Later historians have believed that the odds were against the Spanish succeeding so far from home when they had none of the supply lines for food and ammunition that the English ships could call on. Nevertheless the Armada seemed a very great danger at the time and the delivery of England extremely providential. Certainly the defeat of the Spanish Armada was a massive blow to Spain and the Counter-Reformation. It preserved Protestant England and the Protestant United Provinces, which by 1588 had become the Dutch Republic, thus halving the Spanish Netherlands. By the end of the century, Catholicism – even in France – no longer possessed the threateningly pro-Spanish dimension it once had. Under the first Bourbon king Henry IV, the former Henry of Navarre, French Catholicism became more liberal and tolerant. Henry IV was a Protestant who on his accession had converted to Catholicism in order to unite the country, uttering the cynical quip, 'Paris was worth a Mass.' He protected Protestantism through the Edict of Nantes and closely allied himself with Elizabeth against Spain.

There were two more Armadas in 1596 and 1597, the first of which was destroyed in Cadiz harbour by Lord Howard and Elizabeth's new favourite Robert Devereux, Earl of Essex, Leicester's stepson. Neither was on the scale of that of 1588, and both were equally unsuccessful. But by the end of the century the English sallies into Spanish territory were not the triumphs of yesteryear. In 1591 an expedition to the Azores became famous in the annals of maritime history for the last stand of the *Revenge* under the Cornishman Sir Richard Grenville. He was defeated by the Spanish navy after almost twenty-four hours of battle. Like the queen herself, her celebrated seamen Drake and Hawkins were growing old, and they died together at sea in 1595 after a last attempt to seize Spanish treasure.

Though many of the queen's favourite gallants were now dead, Gloriana herself refused to accept the passage of time. When she was nearly seventy she conceived a last great passion, for the Earl of Essex. The thirty-three-year-old's exploits at Cadiz had made him the hero of the hour, and thanks to his relationship with the queen, he had become one of the most powerful men in the country. Elizabeth was said to be completely infatuated with him, allowing him all kinds of liberties, including quarrelling with her, which had never been granted to any other of her courtiers.

Essex's ambitions were limitless. He was especially keen to dislodge Burghley's son Sir Robert Cecil from the cherished position to which he had succeeded in the queen's counsels. Essex may in fact have been aiming to marry the queen. Whatever the truth, when she sent him to Ireland in 1599 to put down the uprising of Hugh O'Neill, Earl of Tyrone, there was gossip that he intended to seize the throne by turning his Irish troops on the queen herself. Mysterious meetings with Tyrone after a very unsuccessful campaign added grist to the rumour mill. When Essex abandoned his post in Ireland and suddenly appeared one morning in the queen's bedroom at her palace of Nonsuch before she was up, Elizabeth herself believed it was the beginning of a coup. She was only half dressed, and had not had time to put on the huge red wig which took years off her age or the white lead make-up that set her features in a youthful mask. Wisps of her grey hair were hanging down. In a mixture of fury and fear she banished Essex from court.

Essex began to keep wilder and wilder company, and in February 1601 he staged a revolt in London which, though intended to remove the Cecils from power and reinstate Essex himself at the queen's side, seemed merely treasonous. He was tried and executed that same month. There is a story that Essex from the Tower despatched a great ruby ring the queen had given him in happier times to ask her to relent. But he sent it via the Countess of Nottingham and she never handed it on. Two years later when the countess was dying the queen came to visit her and the countess confessed what she had done. The queen clutched at her heart as if it would break and ran out of the room crying, 'God may forgive you, but I never can.' This may be an old fairy tale, but it is certainly true that no more than a month after the countess's death the queen herself also passed away. In any case as her friends died out Elizabeth had fallen into permanently low spirits. She did not have the same rapport with her new ministers as she had had with her old, not even with Cecil's son Robert. She was increasingly depressed as she was left alone in old age: 'Now the wit of the fox is everywhere on foot, so as hardly a faithful or virtuous man may be found,' she remarked mournfully to one courtier.

Elizabeth had shown her father's genius for charming the Commons, and her own civil servants had Cromwell's aptitude for managing Parliaments: Sir Robert Cecil insisted on sitting in the House of Commons to control it better and many new boroughs were created to return Elizabeth's supporters. But by the end of her life the queen no longer had the energy to be amused as she once had been by the Commons' outspokenness. A bitterness was growing up between her and the now large numbers of Puritan MPs whose persecution by the Elizabethan Church was unremitting. That old parsimoniousness came into its own: she spent little so as not to have to call Parliament. Nevertheless, unlike her successors, Elizabeth always knew when to give in to the Commons. In 1601 she appeared to be about to abandon the monopolies system, after years of complaints in the Commons. A monopoly allowed the holder to set the price of a particular product – Essex had been the holder of the sweet-wines monopoly until it was removed from him after his disgrace. Monopolies were an excellent way of rewarding favourites and courtiers, but they weighed very heavily on ordinary people. But when she heard one MP say

Sir Walter Raleigh, Elizabethan colonist executed by James I.

The Indian Village of Secoton, painted by John White in 1585 when he visited it with Sir Richard Grenville.

there would soon be a monopoly in bread, with her usual sparkle she told the Commons how much she owed them for keeping her in touch with her kingdom and promised to abolish the system.

And a very glorious kingdom it was in many ways. The explorer Sir Walter Raleigh had founded the first English settlement in America, which he called Virginia in honour of the Virgin Queen. The charming and poetic Raleigh had first come to Elizabeth's attention when he spread his cloak beneath her feet to save her embroidered shoes from a puddle. He soon became one of her intimate circle, falling from favour only when she discovered he had married without her permission. Raleigh introduced two new plants to this country, the potato and tobacco, which were cultivated by the redskinned men he had encountered in America. But while the potato thrived, particularly in Ireland where because it was cheap and easy to grow it became the poor man's food, the English climate was too wet and cold for tobacco. Nevertheless Sir Walter established a popular taste for it and, as the colony of Virginia developed, tobacco became one of its principal exports. Expanding the nation's consciousness was not without its risks: when Raleigh first put tobacco in a pipe and lit it as he had seen the 'redskins' do, his servant threw a bucket of water over him thinking he was on fire.

From 1576 England had its first purpose-built theatre in Halliwell Street, Shoreditch, in London, east of the City boundary on the north bank of the Thames. It had been opened by an actor and manager called James Burbage. When Burbage died in 1597, his sons Cuthbert and Richard (a famous actor and friend of Shakespeare) moved the entire building upriver to Bankside, Southwark, where it was rebuilt as the Globe. Having a proper theatre to work in had an electrifying effect on the volume of plays written. A host of young men like Christopher Marlowe, whose first play *Tamburlaine the Great* was performed in 1587, Ben Jonson and William Shakespeare were inspired by the open-air theatre to make London a capital for drama. By the mid-1590s Londoners had thrilled to such favourites of our day as *The Two Gentlemen of Verona, Love's Labour's Lost, The Taming of the Shrew, A Midsummer Night's Dream* and *Romeo and Juliet*. Such was Shakespeare's success that the son of a glover from Stratford upon Avon in Warwickshire became part of the court as a groom of the chamber. In his many history plays Shakespeare was inspired by the historical chronicles collected by the printer Raphael Holinshed and perhaps by the works of the antiquarian William Camden, to become the Tudors' bard. Blackening the Yorkists with plays like *Richard III* played an important part in Tudor propaganda. From Cranmer onwards the English language was being fashioned into a newly expressive instrument. The King James Bible, begun the year after Elizabeth's death, is a

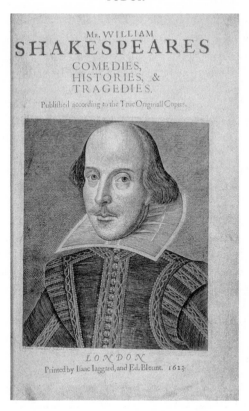

Title page of the First Folio, the collected plays of William Shakespeare, 1623.

monument to a period which saw an astonishing literary flowering and ended with the Metaphysical poets.

By February 1603 the great queen who had presided over almost half a century of excitement and expansion was fading fast. She remained in her apartments, without eating or sleeping, and refused to change her clothes or go to bed. Day after day she sat utterly silent, with her finger in her mouth, on cushions scattered round her bedchamber. When the diminutive Cecil said with tears in his eyes, 'Madam, you must to bed,' she suddenly stirred and said, 'Little man! little man! Your father would have known that "must" is not a word we use to princes.' But a few hours later she at last consented to be put into the carved bed, behind whose hangings she tossed and turned during her final hours. On 23 March she could no longer speak. As her favourite Archbishop Whitgift prayed on beside her, she drifted into unconsciousness and died at about two o'clock the following morning.

Elizabeth had always refused to name her heir, but Sir Robert Cecil announced that she had indicated it was to be James VI; he had a chain of horses waiting every ten miles so that his trusted messenger Sir Robert Carey could convey the news all the way to Scotland so that the succession might be ensured as swiftly and as safely as possible. Sixty-two hours later, James VI knew that he had become James I of England, and began to make his way south. The Elizabethan age was over. A troubled era awaited England when all the contradictions the queen had managed to reconcile by her powerful personality would break into open warfare. Nevertheless at the beginning of the seventeenth century England seemed in good shape: Ireland was subdued, another Spanish attempt to invade England through Ireland had been defeated by Lord Mountjoy at the Battle of Kinsale in 1600, and Protestantism was gaining hold in Wales after the first translation of the Bible into Welsh by William Morgan, Bishop of Asaph. The accession of James I and VI to the English throne achieved what centuries of English monarchs had sought but had never achieved: the whole island was united under a single king. More importantly in the sea of troubles beyond England, he was a Protestant king.

STUART

James I

(1603–1625)

From the death of Elizabeth in 1603 until 1714, England was nominally ruled by the Scottish dynasty, of whom James I was the first king. By the end of that era she had become the largest trading and colonizing nation in the world. Her dauntless countrymen, who had been great seamen in Elizabeth's reign, turned into colonists under the Stuarts. They settled the greater part of the east coast of North America and most of the West Indies, and had trading stations from west Africa to India. As this notable expansion in trade began to enrich the non-noble or middling classes, the financiers, the merchants, the businessmen and the lawyers, inevitably it enhanced the House of Commons' sense of its own power. Conscious of the wealth they commanded, these classes desired more of a hand in government. Yet this conflicted with the new dynasty's profound belief that Parliament, the law and the Church should be subservient to the crown.

During eighty years of convulsion and upheaval, driven by religious conviction, Englishmen struggled to decide whether the king's will should be supreme or Parliament's. It took a bloody civil war, a republican experiment after the execution of one king, then the deposition of another, to settle the question permanently in Parliament's favour. From William and Mary onwards the line of succession passed into the gift of Parliament, and Protestantism became an unconditional qualification of the English monarchy. By the end of the seventeenth century Protestantism had become synonymous with the rule of Parliament and liberty, while Catholicism was identified with tyranny and royal absolutism.

But in the early days of James I's reign there were few indications of the conflict that awaited his descendants. The arrival of the House of Stuart on the English throne unified the kingdom as never before. Thanks to the recently completed Tudor conquest of Ireland, James I was king of the western island in fact as well as in name, which his predecessors had never been. Like Elizabeth, he benefited from the good advice of Robert Cecil (created Earl of Salisbury in 1605), and he persisted with most of the old queen's policies. But there was one considerable difference: James, who

JAMES THE FIRST.

liked to think of himself as a great peacemaker, ended the war with Spain as soon as he came to the throne.

In many ways James's greatest problem was that he was Scottish, and the Scots had been the traditional English enemy since time immemorial. He was a tactless Scottish king at that, too ready to offer niggling criticisms of his magnificent predecessor though he had depended on her pension for the previous quarter-century. James's sensible idea to unify Scotland and England into one kingdom – Great Britain as he called it – by having one Parliament and one legal system was treated with derision by the English Parliament. Despite efforts to do so under Cromwell, it was not achieved until a hundred years later, in the reign of Queen Anne. All that James was able to effect in his lifetime was that every Scots man and woman born after he ascended the throne became English citizens; he also invented a flag for the unified country called the Union Jack – the crosses of St George and St Andrew combined.

Despite the smooth Salisbury's best efforts, James's promotion of Scottish rights got him off on the wrong foot with the court and the country. So did the very obvious way he reserved his closest friendships for a gaggle of Scottish favourites who made it clear that they were looking forward to plucking the rich southern goose for all it was worth. In spite of his erudition James's attitude to his new country was perhaps not much more sophisticated than that of a Scots border raider looking south and spying the rich lands of the English. On his way south James had already shown his lack of interest in English customs by hanging a thief without trial by jury.

The English, who were used to Elizabeth's commanding, glamorous and autocratic court, were moreover embarrassed by the informal and undignified ways of the Scottish king. Though he was the only child of the beautiful Queen of Scots and the elegant Lord Darnley, James I was not such a perfect physical specimen. Once-popular descriptions of his grotesque appearance and personal habits – a tendency to dribble because his tongue was too long, greasy hands because his skin was too delicate to wash – have been exposed as satire. But in the seventeenth century, when a king was supposed to be a warlike and masculine figure, his new subjects were contemptuous of James having his doublet and breeches specially padded against daggers because he was so fearful of being assassinated, and they were scandalized by his habit of always having good-looking young men about him. A weakness in his legs from childhood rickets meant he liked to lean on other men's arms, and this only increased his reputation for effeminacy.

Although initially the English were predisposed in favour of a man as ruler, and one with a large number of children, James I was incapable of making the effort to endear himself to his new people. Everything he did annoyed the English, especially his refusal to attempt to learn or understand their customs. They also detested his self-important habit of lecturing all and sundry – he went so far as to describe himself as 'the great schoolmaster of the whole land'.

Unlike the usurper Tudors, the Stuarts were highly conscious of their hereditary right to rule, their family having already been kings of Scotland for over two centuries. But James I combined scholarship with kingship, and was an immensely erudite author. His particular interest in theology drew him to many excited conclusions about the nature of royal government, which he published at length in books and pamphlets in the course of his reign. According to the 'Divine Right of Kings', a doctrine James had deduced for himself, the fact that God had provided kings to act as His representatives on earth entitled them to control every institution in the kingdom from the laws to Parliament. There was no place for Parliament in James's scheme of things unless it was totally subservient to the king. A king, James earnestly told the House of Commons in one of his many lectures to that body, 'is the supremest thing upon earth: for kings are not only God's lieutenants upon earth and sit upon God's throne, but even by God himself they are called Gods'.

James tended to dilate on this idea at every opportunity, whether at court or to Parliament, in his irritating Scottish accent. He had it promoted in Sunday sermons through the English Church. Unfortunately it clashed with the reality of life in England, which the Scottish king was loath to understand. Although the autocratic and God-like Tudors clearly believed in something along the lines of Divine Right, they had been far too cunning to put it into words, or to do anything without appearing to consult Parliament. The learned James strangely lacked the Tudor shrewdness for seeing what was under his nose. Welcome or not, the Tudors had acknowledged that during the previous three centuries Parliament had become something like the partner of the king. Thanks to its control of money bills the king could not govern without it. In return MPs expected to have their say on most matters in the kingdom – where, as they would tell the disbelieving James, there was a tradition of free speech. They had grown used to debating foreign policy, which fortunately in Elizabeth's reign had largely jibed with their deeply Protestant patriotism, and to running affairs in the Commons with little interference from the king.

But James refused to see their point of view. From the beginning to the end of his reign he managed to offend and be offended every time he met MPs. The boldness of their demands amazed him and affronted the royal dignity which he was determined to uphold. For unlike Scotland, where he had been at the mercy of the Kirk (the Church) and the powerful Scots nobles who had kidnapped him twice, England had a reputation for strong monarchs. He spent a good deal of time complaining about the House of Commons to anyone who would listen, not least the delighted Spanish ambassador. The highly educated James persisted in addressing MPs in a condescending fashion as if they were his children, and his inability to see any point of view other than his own truly merited the French king Henry IV's description of him as 'the wisest fool in Christendom'.

James I's reign was almost immediately marked by drama and discontent. There were two factions at court, one led by Robert Cecil, the other by the great Elizabethan gallant, explorer and poet Sir Walter Raleigh. Raleigh found himself a casualty of James's favouring Cecil when he was removed from his prestigious position as Captain of the Guard. In the heady atmosphere of the new regime the impulsive and now embittered Raleigh was drawn into a conspiracy known as the Main Plot, to abduct Cecil.

No sooner had the Main Plot been discovered than the Bye Plot emerged. Wilder spirits among the Catholics, who were disappointed that the son of the martyred Mary Queen of Scots had not immediately suspended the draconian Elizabethan penal laws against them, planned to kidnap James and replace him on the throne with a Catholic cousin. With the uncovering of this plot, Catholics were treated even worse than before. While Raleigh himself was condemned to a life in the Tower for the next thirteen years (where he wrote A History of the World and much poetry), the very Puritan House of Commons enforced the penalties against Catholics to a level which brought them to despair.

Henceforth if any Catholic fell behind in paying the monthly fine of twenty pounds for not attending Protestant services, they incurred the crippling penalty of forfeiting two-thirds of their property. As the fines worked out at £240 a year, which was beyond the reach of men in respectable but moderate circumstances, quite soon the ordinary Catholic was ruined. A real element of persecution came into play, and there were night-time searches of private houses by armed soldiers looking for priests. The Church of England clergy became spies in their own parishes, required to denounce to the authorities all those who were not attending Protestant service on Sunday in their local church. A final insult awaited Catholics when they were refused burial in Protestant graveyards.

Even the wealthier Catholics had their lives destroyed for their faith.

Protestant bishops were bound to excommunicate prominent Catholics in their dioceses and then certify their names in Chancery, which prevented Catholics from leaving money to relatives by deed or will. To add to the Catholics' terrors, rumours were circulating that in the next Parliament measures would be taken to ensure the total extirpation of their faith. Hostile statements from the king and the fierce language of the Bishop of London in a sermon at St Paul's Cross seemed proof to the exhausted Catholics that the rumours were true. It also convinced the extremists among them that something would have to be done. They decided that their best hope was to blow up the Puritan Houses of Parliament on 5 November 1605 when the king would open Parliament for that term. Having kidnapped the king's daughter Princess Elizabeth, they would proclaim her queen on condition that the Roman Catholic religion was restored.

The leader of the plot was a Warwickshire gentleman named Robert Catesby, but the man who laid the gunpowder trail in the cellars of the Houses of Parliament on the night of 4 November was Guy Fawkes, a soldier of fortune who had fought in the Netherlands. From his name derives the tradition of giving 'a penny for the old guy', and it is he who is burned in effigy every 5 November. Fawkes was discovered crouching by the barrels of gunpowder with his dark lantern – one of the Catholic peers, Lord Mounteagle, having warned Salisbury, his conscience stricken by the thought of his fellow Catholic peers being blown up. It has since become part of the tradition of the Opening of Parliament for Beefeaters to conduct a ceremonial search of the cellars.

Appalled by the near miss, the government acted with great swiftness and savagery. In order to get to the bottom of the conspiracy, the authorities arrested any Catholic they had suspicions of, without troubling to obtain proof of their involvement. Guy Fawkes himself was hideously tortured and the Catholic community was scoured from top to bottom. In fact the whole country, including ordinary Catholics, was thrown into a state of shock by the sheer enormity of the assassination attempt. This was reflected in Shakespeare's play *Macbeth*, written during the plot's aftermath and performed six months later, which reverberates with the horror of an attack on the Lord's Anointed. The government was particularly keen to get its hands on the Jesuits, who ever since their formation had been regarded as dangerous enemies of the English state. The authorities moved to arrest three prominent Jesuits who were important leaders of the Catholic community, Father Gerard, Father Garnet and Father Greenway.

Although Father Gerard and Father Greenway escaped to the continent, Father Garnet managed only to get to a house called Hindlip near

Worcester which belonged to Thomas Habington, brother-in-law of Lord Mounteagle. There he lived in fear and trembling, sending protestations of innocence to Cecil, hiding in one of the many priest-holes constructed a generation before by a Catholic carpenter sworn to secrecy. Despite Mrs Habington's brave attempts to mislead local magistrates who had been tipped off that he was in their vicinity, Father Garnet was found lying in a tiny chamber carved out under the hearth of a fireplace.

As a result of the Gunpowder Plot, all Catholics had become deeply unpopular. But with the arrest and interrogation of Father Garnet the idea that Catholics were natural traitors took a much stronger grip on the English imagination, and proved hard to eradicate. Loyalty to foreigners, whether Philip of Spain or the pope, had put a question mark over the Catholic community ever since England turned Protestant. When it emerged that Garnet had actually known about the plan to blow up Parliament because under the seal of the confessional another priest had told him of Catesby's own confession three months earlier, public opinion turned even more dramatically against Catholics, many of whom decided to seek a less hostile environment on the continent.

New laws forbade Catholics to appear at court or to dwell within ten miles of the boundaries of London. They could not move more than five miles from home without a special licence which had to be signed by four neighbouring magistrates. A career in the professions was barred to them – there could be no Catholic doctors, surgeons, lawyers, executors, guardians, judges or members of any town corporation. To remain a Catholic meant in effect renouncing society or refusing to be part of it – hence the word 'recusant' used of old Catholic families (from the Latin verb *recusare*, which means to refuse). And those recusant families clung on somehow to their religion, but in the process became very poor and unworldly and remained so for over two centuries, until the Catholic Emancipation Act in 1829.

Enormous fines were imposed if a child was not baptized into the Protestant faith within a month of its birth. James's royal favourites and the Exchequer soon got in the habit of exploiting Catholic recusant estates as a useful source of income, eagerly enforcing sequestration of two-thirds of their property for non-payment of fines. That worldlywise king Henry IV warned James I from across the Channel that religion was 'a flame which burns with increasing fierceness in proportion to the violence used to extinguish it', and that such severe laws would lay him open to worse plots. But, strange to say, it did not. Catholics, perhaps because their religion encouraged them to turn the other cheek, sank meekly into second-class citizenship.

In fact it was from the Puritans that James had most to fear. Extremely well represented in the unruly House of Commons, they had the boldness to accost the new king on his journey south from Scotland to take up his new position, presenting what is called the Millenary Petition because it was signed by a thousand Puritans. This requested the king to end the Elizabethan oppression of their beliefs through the enforcement of uniformity and to make changes to the prayer book. Confident of his ability to debate with them and pleased with his theological learning James promised that the next year there would be a conference to debate all these issues. But when the meeting took place at Hampton Court the Puritan divines realized they had picked the wrong audience. Despite or perhaps because of his fierce Scots Presbyterian background, the new king was just as much the enemy of all attempts to introduce the Presbyterian system (from 'presbyter', the Greek for elder) to England as Elizabeth had been. In fact James was mightily in favour of bishops as a prop of royal authority, and had every intention of reintroducing them to Scotland. As he remarked to the divines, 'Scottish Presbytery agreeth as well with monarchy as God with the devil.' He would put it even more pithily in his summing up of the High Church position: 'No bishop, no king.'

The best the Puritans got out of the king was the decision to undertake a new translation of the Bible. In 1611 the beautiful Authorized Version, the product of forty-seven scholars, which we know as the King James Bible became the universally preferred version in Protestant services and

The Jerusalem Chamber at Westminster Abbey where part of the King James Authorized Version of the Bible was written.

Protestant homes. Using much of William Tyndale's wording, it is a remarkable piece of scholarship, and remains one of the masterpieces of English literature, its phrasing having had an incalculable effect on the English language.

To all the Puritans' pleas for a more solemn way of life, especially on the Sabbath, the king made it clear that this was not what he had in mind for England. Indeed under him the Church of England began to take on a distinctly conservative tinge, especially when Richard Bancroft became Archbishop of Canterbury after Whitgift's death. But the greatest exponent of movement back towards the Catholicism of Henry VIII's time was William Laud, who became Bishop of London, and at last in 1633, under James's son Charles I, Archbishop of Canterbury.

PURITAN COSTUMES.

Thanks to Laud's influence the Church of England revolted against the overwhelming Calvinism of the Puritans. Instead it adopted the ideas of a Dutch professor named Arminius which stressed its fellowship with the ancient Church at Rome. Over the next twenty years as the battle for authority was waged between Parliament and king, Puritans tended to gravitate towards joining the House of Commons and pressing for their rights there, while the Church of England became the leading supporter of royal autocracy. Led by their bishops, parish priests preached that it was wrong to resist a ruler who was appointed by God and above the law. Thus religious and constitutional issues became completely interwoven as the Stuart kings made a habit of overriding the law of the land and ruling without Parliament.

It was really only around the time of Salisbury's death in 1612 that James's autocratic tendencies came more and more to the fore and his struggle to extend his power at the expense of Parliamentary liberties began in earnest. There had been some acrimonious skirmishes earlier in the reign: James was angered and amazed by Parliament's refusal in 1607 to give Scotsmen the full rights of Englishmen or to agree to freedom of trade between the two countries. He was affronted when the Commons told him in no uncertain terms that his insufficiently Protestant foreign policy and his peace with Spain dismayed them, a peace made more suspect by his wife Anne of Denmark's known Catholicism. James's attempt to interfere in the election in Buckinghamshire of a felon named Shirley on the ground that all privileges derived from the king was successfully resisted. The Commons sent him such a vehement and furious petition insisting that its ancient liberties such as the right to free election had nothing to do with the royal power and were the longstanding birthright of the English people that he backed off. Under Elizabeth the Commons would never have dared address the monarch in this fashion, but James's being a foreigner gave it a chance to assert itself, and indeed at first it attributed his behaviour to his ignorance of the way the country worked.

But seven years into his reign the king was no longer so foreign and he was much less timorous. By 1610 he had had enough of Parliament's hectoring him, and was determined to raise his income. Following a decision in the courts that it was legal for the king to change the rates of customs charges without reference to Parliament, James took the opportunity to issue a whole new slew of taxes on his own authority. And when there was an outcry from the Commons he simply closed Parliament down. It would become the pattern in the reigns of both James and his son Charles to live by raising money outside Parliament so as not to have to deal with the Commons. In 1614 James tried to manage it through what were called 'Undertakers', MPs who would attempt to influence votes on the king's behalf, but this 'Addled Parliament' was so enraged by the Undertakers and recalcitrant in its attitudes that he dissolved it after three weeks. For most of the next eleven years he ruled without Parliament.

Nevertheless, the king could not rule without money. At first he resorted to bribing gentlemen to become baronets if they gave him a thousand pounds; if they paid 10,000 pounds they could become lords. But his extravagant lifestyle forced him into more desperate courses. When the Spanish ambassador Gondomar dangled the prospect of a six-figure marriage dowry if James's second son Charles married a Spanish infanta, the king became increasingly fixated on the thought of the great dowry which would get him the income to enable him never to call Parliament again – and he grew obsessed with developing a foreign policy to please Spain. The death of his elder son, the talented, deeply Protestant and popular Prince Henry, in the same year that Salisbury died, removed a last restraining influence on the king, for the new Prince of Wales, Prince Charles, was shy and retiring, and spoke with a stammer. Disregarding the fervent anti-Spanish feeling in England, James allowed Gondomar to become one of his most influential advisers.

For all his pomposity, James was also frivolous and rather lazy. He preferred to spend most of his time hunting and, after Salisbury's death, left government business in the hands of a stream of inappropriate favourites like Robert Ker, Viscount Rochester. Ker was a handsome aristocrat chosen like all James's favourites for his looks rather than his grasp of English foreign policy. Leading a hermetically sealed existence at the court, the Earl of Somerset (as he became in 1613) saw nothing wrong with the growth of Spanish power at court and in fact encouraged it. Somerset and his notorious wife Frances soon involved James in scandal when they were both tried in the House of Lords for the murder of Sir Thomas Overbury. Though both were found guilty and condemned to death, even greater odium was incurred when the king used his royal powers to pardon and free them.

The sense that English standards were being unacceptably lowered and corrupted was reinforced when in 1616 the lord chief justice of the Court of Common Pleas, Sir Edward Coke, was dismissed for trying to prevent the king from interfering in law cases. According to James, divine right entitled him to suspend the law when it suited him. He was backed up by his lord chancellor, the ambitious Sir Francis Bacon, who believed that judges should be the supporters of the royal prerogative or will. But Coke, who was immensely influential among lawyers and MPs both in his lifetime and after, had arrived at the conclusion from his study of jurisprudence that even the king should be subject to the common law.

The last nail in the coffin of James's reputation was the execution in 1618 of the Elizabethan hero Sir Walter Raleigh on trumped-up charges relating to the Main Plot of fifteen years before. The real reason Raleigh, the last relic of the golden years of Elizabethan England, was executed was to please Spain. To quench James's thirst for gold Raleigh had been released from the Tower to search for the treasure said to be at the bottom of a lake in the fabled land of El Dorado, somewhere in Guiana, and the old Elizabethan had been unable to resist burning a Spanish settlement that was blocking his route. It was now evident that the king would do anything to placate the Spanish. English policy seemed to be in the hands of the Spanish ambassador.

How harmful this was was thrown into relief at the outset of the Thirty Years War, which began in 1618. James's son-in-law Frederick, the Elector Palatine of the Rhine in Germany and a notable Protestant, was offered the crown of Protestant Bohemia (today's Czech Republic) in place of the Catholic Habsburg overlord the emperor Ferdinand II. At the battle of the White Mountain in 1620 Frederick and the Bohemians were defeated, and with the Spanish having invaded the Palatinate, he and James's daughter Elizabeth now found themselves without a home. Their plight aroused enormous popular interest in England. By 1622 the Commons was formally petitioning for war with Spain, for a Protestant marriage to be arranged for Prince Charles, and for further penal laws to be imposed on Catholics. In spite of all these straws in the wind, James remained so anxious to ally himself with wealthy Spain and arrange the ever tantalizing Spanish marriage for which he had sacrificed Raleigh that he continued to negotiate with Gondomar. He believed that only by such means could the Spanish be persuaded to withdraw from the Palatinate and restore Frederick to his throne.

George Villiers, Duke of Buckingham, the unpopular favourite of both James and his son Charles I.

Meanwhile accurate rumours began to circulate that the price to be paid for the Spanish infanta was the conversion of England by the back door: the conditions laid down by Spain were that the marriage was to be no hole-and-corner affair. It had to have the approval of Parliament, and the penal laws against Catholics had to have been suspended for three years before it could take place. All the children of the marriage were to be brought up as Catholics, and their Catholicism would not interfere with their right to the throne.

Public feeling deepened against the king with the rise of his new favourite, the vain and frivolous Duke of Buckingham, whose notoriety eclipsed even that of the Somersets and whose willingness to accept bribes became a byword. By the end of James's reign the all-controlling Buckingham seemed to be the real ruler of England, not least because he was coming to have just as great an influence over the future king Charles I as over his father. Undeterred by the popular hostility to the Spanish marriage, in 1623 Buckingham and Charles set off in disguise on a madcap romantic adventure to speed up negotiations which had been hovering in the balance for eight years and bring back the Spanish infanta. But neither the glamorous Buckingham nor the small, nervous Charles had any success in Madrid. There were just more delays while the stiff Spanish court made it clear that it was displeased by the lack of formality of the young Stuart and his friend and laid down further conditions for the Catholic education of the royal children and the composition of the infanta's personal household: a bishop and no fewer than twenty priests were to be constantly in attendance.

In the end the marriage came to nothing, owing to the predicament of Charles's sister Elizabeth (known as the Winter Queen after her brief seasonal reign in Bohemia). Although James clearly could not quite bring himself to sacrifice the Spanish marriage for his daughter's happiness, his son Charles could. When the Prince of Wales finally asked point-blank whether Spain would fight the emperor Ferdinand to restore the Palatinate, and was given the answer no, Charles lost his temper. To the great relief of the English public he sailed home without the infanta, and now that diplomacy had failed was furiously determined on war to save his sister.

The House of Commons, which had been dreading the Spanish match for years, fearing that it would spell the end to Protestantism both in England and abroad, delightedly voted supplies. An alliance against Spain was made with France, for Cardinal Richelieu, Louis XIII's chief adviser, had ambitions to see his country advance at the expense of the Habsburg influence in Spain and Austria. Instead of the infanta the Prince of Wales was engaged to Henrietta Maria, the French king's sister, who like the king was small, but gay and spirited.

Nevertheless, the attempts to send help to the Palatinate in 1624 were unsuccessful. The expedition did not go well, even with French help under the leadership of the German soldier of fortune Count Mansfeld. It was poorly prepared, without proper quartermastering, so that food supplies and clothing were inadequate and thousands of soldiers died without even fighting. Its failure seemed of a piece with the general hopelessness of the administration and with its poor calibre, given that government positions were secured by bribes to Buckingham. The Commons longed to call the gorgeous favourite before them to account for his actions, but he was untouchable.

Instead James I's reign drew to an end with further quarrels: the Commons once more demanded a check to the monopoly system, which in the licensing of public houses was becoming a serious source of income for royal courtiers. The Commons also impeached the lord chancellor Sir Francis Bacon for taking bribes. Bacon admitted the offences, resigned and was imprisoned, only to be released by James – who, whatever his failings as a king, was kind to his friends. The king died in March 1625, leaving the Commons determined to remove Buckingham from power.

Not all was gloom, though, for the new king. The crown might be beleaguered in Parliament but by the beginning of Charles I's reign English rule extended firmly over lands which had been mere spaces on Elizabethan maps. And for the first time, under the rule of Charles Blount, Ireland had a peace that held, aided by a series of strategically sited forts from Sligo Bay in the north-west to Carrick Fergus on Belfast Loch. Blount, who was rewarded with the title Earl of Mountjoy, took over from Essex as lord deputy in Ireland in 1600 and, once Hugh O'Neill, Earl of Tyrone and Hugh O'Donnell, Earl of Tyrconnell had been forced to seek refuge in France – in what is known as the Flight of the Earls – the real subjugation of Ireland began. In 1610 Tyrone's lands were divided among mainly Scots Presbyterian settlers as a Protestant garrison in what is called the Ulster

Plantation, confirming Mountjoy's thoroughgoing conquest of the country. They were given the fertile eastern parts, while the barren and wild north-west was all that was allowed to the native inhabitants. The new settlers were bitterly resented by the old Irish and the Norman Irish; relations between the new Ulstermen and the old would be the source of much trouble right down to the present day.

Elizabeth I would have known about the East India Company now flourishing on the west coast of India because, like the trading stations on the west coast of Africa in Gambia and Sierra Leone, it had been founded in her reign. In 1600 the Company had set out to take a share in the spice trade in the East Indies or Malay Archipelago. The Dutch had arrived five years earlier and were the area's dominant presence, having seized most of the old Portuguese settlements as part of their war with Spain, so the English chose to concentrate on the mainland of India. Thanks to the good relations achieved by the diplomat Sir Thomas Rowe with the Moghal emperor, who ruled most of India by 1612, the East India Company had concessions in southern India at Surat and Madras and was setting up factories (the seventeenth-century term for trading posts). Such small beginnings were the starting point for the British Empire in India.

But the most striking developments of all in James's reign were the English settlements planted in America after the disappointments of Raleigh's colony at Roanoke in Virginia. Urged on by the popularizing writings of Richard Hakluyt, especially his book relating Elizabethan voyages of discovery, *Principal Navigations, Voiages and Discoveries of the English Nation*, England woke up to the possibilities of the New World, which was already resounding to Spanish, French and Dutch accents. Most of the English settlers in the first part of the seventeenth century were Puritans, who founded the group of colonies several hundred miles north of Virginia known collectively as New England, where they could worship after their own fashion.

A group of Separatists from Scrooby in Nottinghamshire began the settlement of New England when they set sail in the *Mayflower* and founded Plymouth colony in 1620. In the decade preceding the Civil War, perhaps as many as 5,000 Englishmen and women a year emigrated to Plymouth's neighbouring colony of Massachusetts, established in 1629 by a group of Puritan lawyers led by John Winthrop as a reaction against the increasingly ferocious measures taken by Charles I and Archbishop Laud to wipe Puritan practice from the face of England. Other colonies along the eastern seaboard followed during Charles's reign, including Vermont, Connecticut and Rhode Island. The penalties against Catholics inspired Lord Baltimore to establish the Catholic colony of Maryland in 1632 just north of Virginia, named in honour of Charles I's wife Queen Henrietta

Maria. While the northerners depended on exporting fish and skins for their livelihood, the southerners soon depended on importing African slaves from the English traders on the west coast to work their large tobacco and cotton plantations, since like the Spanish they believed their European constitutions prevented them from labouring in the humid heat.

A Virginian ship washed up on an island began the settlement of the Bermudas in 1609 and many islands in the Caribbean followed. There too the English settlers began to import African slaves to work their plantations. Since the ancient Greeks, honey had been used for sweetening, but the discovery of sugar cane and its superior taste resulted in the Caribbean specializing in cultivating it. The slave trade begun by Jack Hawkins developed into a longstanding and degrading institution. Manufactures from England such as textiles were sold to west Africa in exchange for slaves, who were then transported in the dangerously unhealthy confines of slave ships to the West Indies and the southern colonies such as Virginia. To pay for the slaves sugar, cotton and tobacco were sent back to England's most important ports, Bristol and Liverpool. Many respectable English merchant families made their fortunes in this convenient triangular trade.

But though all these developments were changing the lives of the English – so that by the end of the century Englishwomen in the most obscure parts of the country could sweeten their new drink, tea, with West Indian sugar while their husbands and brothers smoked pipes of American tobacco – the new king had immediate problems close at hand. Though Charles I disliked Parliament as much as his father had done, he was at its mercy, for he needed supplies to pay for the continuing war against Spain.

Charles I

(1625-1649)

Divine Right (1625-1642)

Charles I was grave, slow in thought and, owing to a speech impediment, no less slow in conversation. Though he lacked his father's great intellect, he had a wonderful eye and was a connoisseur of the arts. Thanks to him the royal family began a collection of works by superb contemporary painters such as the Dutchman Peter Paul Rubens, whom Charles commissioned to execute the magnificent vision of James I on the ceiling of the Banqueting Hall at Whitehall. Charles also acquired old master pictures like the Raphael and Leonardo cartoons now at Windsor and in the National Gallery. He was the patron of the Italianate architect Inigo Jones, who built the exquisitely simple Queen's House at Greenwich and many other beautiful classical buildings. Jones introduced the Palladian style of architecture into England, with transforming effects on the country houses of the era – Wilton, near Salisbury, with its double cube room, is the most famous example.

Jones also designed many masques for Henrietta Maria to act in. The French queen, who was small and childlike, delighted in acting for the king with her ladies. These Renaissance inventions were fantastic court entertainments, almost like plays, with elaborate costumes, and with lines usually written by the playwright Ben Jonson. Despite growing Puritan disapproval of play-acting, vehemently expressed in sermons and pamphlets, Charles's court was famous for its amateur theatricals. These masques tended to have for their theme the divine majesty of the king, which had a special appeal to Charles as he was intensely religious. He became close friends with the

Charles I's wife, Queen Henrietta Maria, daughter of Henry IV of France.

rising star of the Church of England William Laud, and appointed him Bishop of London in 1628 and Archbishop of Canterbury in 1633. Laud reinforced Charles's sense of the monarch as the Lord's Anointed, whose views could not be questioned, and he even went down to the Houses of Parliament to put this view across during Charles's first Parliament.

This Parliament, no less than those of James I, was turbulent and contentious. The antagonism between king and Commons continued into Charles's reign without a break. On behalf of his sister Elizabeth, Charles had agreed to fund a new military expedition by his uncle King Christian of Denmark against the Catholic League in Germany. But though he expected to be granted supplies for a popular war, the Commons was in a very belligerent mood and refused to grant the new king customs duties for life as was traditional at the beginning of a new reign – they would be for one year only. MPs also demanded that Buckingham be sacked, suggesting that Charles look back to the wise behaviour of Elizabeth, who had relied on the advice of a council rather than the rule of favourites. Though Charles dismissed Parliament for its insulting behaviour, he soon had to recall it because of increasing foreign difficulties. A quarrel over the treatment of the Huguenots in France meant that Charles was also at war with his French brother-in-law Louis XIII, who had been England's ally against the Habsburgs.

The atmosphere at his second Parliament was extremely frosty. At Buckingham's suggestion, the noisier and more critical MPs like the former chief justice Sir Edward Coke and the Yorkshire landowner Sir Thomas Wentworth were made sheriffs by royal command, which meant that they could no longer attend the Commons. But gagging them made no difference to the temper of the House; it was now led by a gifted orator, the Cornish baronet Sir John Eliot. The Commons continued to call for Buckingham's impeachment, so Charles actually went down to Westminster to berate MPs for questioning his servants, particularly one who was so close to him. Once again Charles dismissed Parliament, warning MPs that whether it was called at all was entirely up to him, and he further antagonized them by temporarily imprisoning Eliot. Meanwhile Charles's inability to manage Parliament prevented England from committing troops to Christian of Denmark against the German Catholics, with the result that Christian and his army had been comprehensively defeated.

But Charles was obstinately determined not to be beaten by the Commons. More sensible rulers would have been forced by his dire financial and political situation to retreat from any warlike activities. Egged on by the high-handed and arrogant Buckingham, Charles instead cranked up the hostilities with France to a higher level by going to the rescue of the rebellious Huguenots at western France's port of La Rochelle.

Since Parliament had been dissolved, he decided to resort to yet another unparliamentary tax to raise money for the wars. The method he used was a forced loan, imposed on all those liable to pay tax. Hundreds of the most respectable citizens throughout the country, men of wealth and position, went to prison rather than submit. Within weeks came a legal challenge from five knights of the shire. In what is known as Darnell's case, they demanded to know of what crime they were accused, asking to be released through the well-known common law writ or process of habeas corpus. Habeas corpus forced anyone holding any prisoner to produce him in front of a judge and describe his offence; if the judge did not accept that the alleged offence was a crime, the prisoner had to be released. But although the judges in Darnell's case ruled in favour of returning the knights to prison, the only reason given for their incarceration was that it was the king's command, which in itself seemed a poor reason and a tyrannical precedent.

Nevertheless, even with the forced loans there were still insufficient funds for the war against Louis XIII, and in 1628 Charles was once again forced to recall Parliament. The Commons was determined to make it clear to the king that he could not carry on in the way he had been. The more extreme members presented the king with a very strongly worded denunciation of his policies in a protest entitled the Petition of Right. Masterminded by the MPs Sir Edward Coke, Sir John Eliot and the country landowner John Pym, it is generally considered by historians to be one of the most significant constitutional documents of English history. The Petition of Right informed Charles just what the law was regarding 'the rights and liberties of the subject', and demanded an end to what its authors described as all the king's illegal innovations. If the king would not assent to the Petition, the Commons said they would impeach Buckingham. This threat secured the royal assent, and in return Charles got the supplies he had asked for.

These were the mere opening shots in what became constant warfare. Buckingham, now Lord High Admiral of England, was never brought before the Commons. Later that year, to immense popular delight, he was murdered in Portsmouth by a Puritan madman while supervising ships to go to the aid of La Rochelle. But the House of Commons was not done yet. In its next session in 1629 it launched yet another assault upon the king. This time it attacked his religious advisers, Sir John Eliot producing a bill that condemned anyone who allowed Arminianism or any innovations in religion (meaning Roman Catholicism), or paid customs dues without Parliament's permission.

Under Laud's influence the Church of England had become completely identified with Charles's political policies. From every pulpit Anglican priests preached Divine Right and the duty of non-resistance to the king. Moreover the thoroughgoing way in which Laud was restoring the Church's ceremonies to the rituals of Henry VIII's time (what is now known as High Church), such as bowing at the name of Jesus, convinced most Puritans that he was on the point of returning England to Rome. In fact Laud had no such intention. But his hatred of Puritans and his unqualified support for a king who to contemporary eyes was a tyrant aroused the widespread conviction that the-soon-to-be-reintroduced Roman Catholicism would be the natural handmaiden of absolutism and oppression. These fears were exacerbated by rumours that the price of Henrietta Maria's marriage had been a promise to suspend the penal laws against Catholics. This had indeed been the case, though that secret part of the marriage treaty had not been fulfilled. Meanwhile Henrietta Maria's habit of openly worshipping at her own Roman Catholic chapel within the Palace of Whitehall did nothing to calm the situation.

When Charles heard that, despite his assenting to the Petition of Right, the debates at Westminster were getting completely out of hand, and that Laud, his new Bishop of London, was being attacked as a traitor, he sent a message from Whitehall to order the speaker of the House of Commons to halt the proceedings. But the Commons shut the door in the face of the king's messenger. Astonishingly, instead of the MPs leaving the chamber as the speaker had been trying to get them to do, two strong young MPs Holles and Valentine got the speaker by the arms and held him down in his chair while the House voted through Eliot's motions. By the time the king's troops arrived from Whitehall to break down the doors, it was too late.

The motion had been passed. But as a result of this behaviour Parliament was once again dissolved. Sir John Eliot was imprisoned in the Tower of London where he died three years later, his poor treatment having fatally aggravated his consumption.

In the fight between Parliament and the king, the gloves were now well and truly off. For eleven years, up to 1640, Charles managed to rule without calling Parliament. After his past errors he had enough common sense to realize that he could not both govern without Parliament and carry on two wars abroad. He therefore made peace with both France and Spain and utterly

William Laud, Archbishop of Canterbury under Charles I before the Civil War.

abandoned his sister, brother-in-law and the Protestant cause on the continent, where the immensely bloody Thirty Years War continued to rage until 1648.

The king's chief advisers in this period were Bishop Laud (Archbishop of Canterbury from 1633) and Sir Thomas Wentworth. The immensely efficient and hardworking Wentworth had been offended by what he considered to be the revolutionary new rights the Commons was claiming over the king. With his advice Charles began to rule through the prerogative courts, where the conventions of the common law were not observed, such as the Court of Star Chamber, the Council of the North (which functioned as a sort of northern Star Chamber) and the Court of High Commission, which Laud used vigorously to enforce uniformity in the Church against the Puritan clergy.

Laud was determined to wipe out Puritanism. It was, he said prophetically, 'a wolf held by the ears' waiting only to spring. During his Primacy he and his supporters visited every single diocese in England to test the parish clergy's beliefs and their use of ritual. Where the clergy failed they were sent before the Court of High Commission to be imprisoned and savagely punished – and savage was the only word to describe their treatment. William Prynne, a Puritan lawyer and the author of *Histriomax*, a book that attacked play-acting as immoral – which was seen as a thinly veiled attack on the queen – was tortured, branded with hot irons and had his ears cut off. It was during these years that perhaps 30,000 Puritans, confronted by such treatment and being unable to worship as they pleased, emigrated with their families to the freedom of America.

Laud and Wentworth, who were intimate friends, both believed that what England needed were effective reforms in every department of state. They called their attempt to bring greater efficiency to Church and state 'thorough' government. Wentworth, who had tried out 'thorough' as president of the Council of the North, was sent to Ireland to bring order to the country and implement Laud's obedience to episcopal rule there. His strongarm tactics were just as unpopular as Laud's, and he managed to alienate every faction in the country.

The absence of Parliament and the oppression of the Church bred an atmosphere of the greatest dissatisfaction in England, her inhabitants being unused to having no voice in the nation's affairs. English monarchs had always needed the goodwill of the local landowners and merchants to act as unpaid judges and magistrates and help keep order in the countryside, but now in the 1630s the machinery of government began to break down as many of the gentry refused to serve Charles I.

Furthermore, as the years went by, it looked as if Parliament might remain in abeyance indefinitely. Charles proved superb at finding obscure laws that could be revived to provide substitute taxes, such as the feudal relic that any man owning over a certain acreage without being dubbed a knight could be fined. Reasons were found to return some of the old pre-Reformation Church lands to the king, enraging not a few landowners, as did extending the royal forest and subsuming valuable land. Charles craftily increased the customs duties of tonnage and poundage, though Parliament had granted him these taxes only for the first year of his reign.

It was not until 1634 that the king revived the old ship money levy. In theory this ancient right was levied on all maritime towns and ports to build more ships in time of danger. Certainly the Royal Navy did need to build more ships to protect England against the increasingly hostile Dutch navy, but on the whole this tax was raised only during wartime, and England was not at war. The seaport towns, their merchants and corporations, nonetheless paid up without a murmur, but the following year, when the king extended ship money to inland districts, it became clear that this was tax by the back door.

A wealthy Buckinghamshire landowner named John Hampden, who was an old friend of Sir John Eliot as well as a former MP, refused to pay ship money, and in 1638 his case was brought before the courts. Although the ship money was pronounced perfectly legal by the judiciary, Hampden's case and Hampden himself sharpened the mounting anger against the king's government. It was not, however, in England but in Scotland that the discontent was to first manifest itself in revolution.

The home of John Hampden, leader of the Parliamentary opposition to Charles I.

Most unwisely, though inevitably in view of 'thorough', Charles and Laud had turned their attention to reforming religious practices in Scotland and bringing them into line with England's. They decided that the Scots would benefit from a new prayer book, even though the Scots were just like the English Puritans in that they preferred to invent prayers as they went along. A storm now burst about their ears. At the first reading of the new prayer book at St Giles in Edinburgh there was very nearly a riot when the service began. A footstool was hurled at the Dean of St Giles by a woman named Jenny Geddes, who became a national heroine, and the sedate streets of Edinburgh became the scene of wild civil disorder which spread throughout Scotland. In March 1638 most of the nation signed a document called the National Covenant which bound all its signatories to defend the true reformed religion based on interpretation of the Gospel and to resist papistry.

St Giles's Cathedral, Edinburgh, where the Scottish rebellion against Charles I began, after the reading of the new prayer book in 1637.

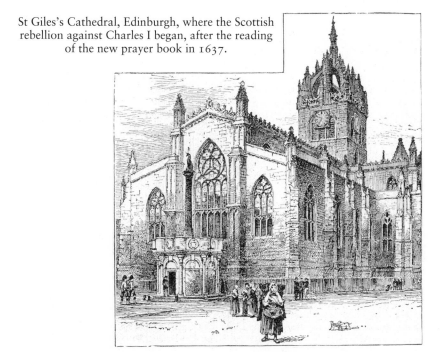

Angry messages flew back and forth across the border from a newly created committee of prominent Scotsmen led by the Earl of Argyll and the Earl of Montrose. Known as the Tables it became in effect the government of Scotland, committed to protecting Scots Presbyterianism. Although Charles now withdrew the prayer book, it was too late. A General Assembly of the Church had met at Glasgow, abolished the bishops whom

James had introduced and Charles had reinforced, and declared that the king had no right to interfere in the Church of Scotland. It paid no attention to Charles's order from London that the Assembly was to dissolve itself.

A more sensible king would have backed off at this point but Charles was infuriated by the challenge to the royal authority by Scottish subjects. To him there was no question but that he must go to war against the Scots, and the standoff between himself and the Scots in the summer of 1639 is called the First Bishops' War. But since he had no army and no Parliament to raise money for one, he could only appeal to the ancient hatred of the English for the Scots, and the angry mood the English were in meant he raised very few that way. He was rapidly forced to make peace, and by the Treaty of Berwick he allowed a free parliament and General Assembly of the Church to thrash out their discontents.

But when it became clear that the Scots still had no intention of deviating from their course of maintaining the Covenant, abolishing the prayer book and getting rid of the bishops, for Charles the issue meant war. He dissolved their gatherings and recalled Wentworth (newly created Earl of Strafford) from Ireland. Strafford nobly lent the king a great deal of money of his own and managed to convince him that the only way he could raise enough money to fight the Scots was by recalling Parliament. In April 1640 the first Parliament for eleven years came together. Charles had hoped to use the Scottish threat of invasion to make MPs do his bidding. But having been denied free speech for so long, the Commons was not in the mood for obedience. Strafford counselled the king to listen to its demands and, in particular, to end ship money. But after three weeks Charles dismissed what is known as the Short Parliament and began the Second Bishops' War.

Without the money from Parliament to raise a proper army, the king had to rely on borrowing more money from friends. The Second Bishops' War ended in a rout, with the Scots army camped in the northern English counties as far south as Newcastle. With general disaffection throughout England, the king was eventually forced to make a very expensive truce with the Scots. He had to pay them the then enormous sum of £25,000, and to summon a new Parliament to meet on 3 November 1640.

The Long Parliament as it was called would endure in various guises for the next twenty years. Given the continued presence of the Scots army in Northumberland and Durham – with which it is almost certain Pym was secretly in communication – the king was powerless. Unless he made concessions to Parliament and thus could raise money for an army to drive out the Scots, they would advance further into England. In the first session both the pillars of Charles's government, Strafford and Laud, were arrested for treason and impeached – Laud was accused of conspiring illegally to return the Church of England to Rome and Strafford of plotting to overthrow Parliamentary government.

While the Lords hesitated over whether Strafford could really be said to have committed treason when treason was a crime against the king and Strafford was the king's faithful minister, the Commons saw that the trial might end in Strafford being released and the slippery king get away again. One of the more violent Puritans, Sir Arthur Hazelrigg, jumped to his feet and demanded a Bill of Attainder against Strafford – in other words, that he be condemned to death without trial. Although the Lords hesitated again, the discovery of an apparent plot by the king and queen to ask the northern army to save Strafford hastened his end. Hysteria was rising uncontrollably in London, encouraged by Pym. He announced that Queen Henrietta Maria had sent for French soldiers who would shortly be landing at Portsmouth.

Throughout the proceedings against him Strafford had kept his head,

urging the king to counter-attack by impeaching the Puritan leaders for their treasonous letters to the Scots Covenanters. But the king was apparently paralysed by the awfulness of his predicament. He sat watching Strafford's trial, staring vacantly into space for much of the time, his face working nervously. Beside him was his son, the ten-year-old Prince of Wales. As the City of London trained armed bands for the coming crisis, and Parliament passed the Attainder against Strafford, Charles hesitated.

He alone could have saved his devoted servant from these trumped-up charges by refusing to sign the bill. Perhaps he should have done so, because he had constantly assured Strafford that he should have no fear, that he would never be executed because the king would protect him. Ever

Thomas Wentworth, Earl of Strafford, with Laud one of Charles I's chief supporters, who was impeached and executed in 1641 by order of the Commons.

the good servant, Strafford wrote to the king saying that he would willingly forgive him for his death, 'if it leads to better times'. Secretly he never really thought it would come to it. But with violent men patrolling the streets and fears for his wife and children, Charles made his decision. He threw Strafford to the lions. The king had already offered never to employ Strafford in a confidential capacity again and had even suggested life imprisonment, but now he signed the Attainder.

Charles never forgave himself for it and believed that his subsequent ill luck was the result of his betrayal. He even sent the young Prince of Wales with a message down to Westminster after he had signed the Attainder, pleading for Strafford's life. But it was too late. Strafford shook his head with disbelief when he heard that he was to die. As he went out to his execution at Tower Hill on 12 May 1641, he was heard to say, 'Put not your trust in princes.' Imprisoned in the Tower Archbishop Laud heard the drum roll and then the sudden thud as Strafford was beheaded in front of 200,000 people. He wrote bitterly that Charles was a prince 'who knew not how to be or to be made great'. But as one contemptuous Puritan remarked brutally, 'Stone dead hath no fellow,' and that summed up the reactions of the Puritans in the House of Commons.

Robbed of his two chief counsellors, the king had to rely on the bad advice of the politically inept Queen Henrietta Maria. As a foreigner she was incapable of appreciating that the Long Parliament was becoming the senior partner in government throughout 1641. Now that Strafford was dead and Laud as good as, the Commons concentrated on destroying all the instruments of government Charles had used during what was described as the eleven-year tyranny. The judges who in 1629 had pronounced forced loans to be legal were committed for trial. All the king's methods of raising taxes without Parliament such as ship money, tonnage and poundage were pronounced illegal and unconstitutional. All the prerogative courts were destroyed, the Star Chamber, the Council of the North and the hated Court of High Commission. Prynne was released, without his ears but otherwise hale and hearty. By the Triennial Act, it was ordered that no more than three years should elapse between Parliaments and elections were to be held whether the king had summoned Parliament or not.

However, when by the Root and Branch Bill the Commons set about removing the bishops from the Church of England and substituting in their place a Presbyterian system of Church government consisting of lay elders, a royalist party began to emerge, led by the lawyer Edward Hyde (the future historian Lord Clarendon) and Lucius Cary, Viscount Falkland. Now that Charles's worst abuses of power had been removed, the more moderate members of Parliament did not want what was becoming a revolution to be taken any further. The royalist party were offended by the Puritans' hatred of tradition, their joylessness and their contempt for anything elaborate, whether it was clothes, manners, books or religion. Of course the Puritan party numbered great poets and thinkers among them, such as John Milton, arguably England's greatest poet. But a considerable proportion were also uneducated people who feared what they could not understand. English people who valued their cultural heritage became uneasy that much that was of value built up over many centuries could be destroyed by destructive zealots.

But, despite the development of a royal party in Parliament, it was rapidly becoming evident that Charles had no real interest in ruling through Parliament and observing the rules of the game. During the Parliamentary recess in the summer of 1641 he rushed off to Scotland, intending to persuade the Scots and their army to come in on his side and mount a coup in England. But he fell foul of infighting among the Scottish nobility, and succeeded only in increasing suspicion of himself even among the royalists.

Then the real crisis began. With Strafford dead, the Catholic Irish realized that the time was ripe for a rebellion and massacred the Protestant settlers in Northern Ireland. On 23 November 1641 the dispossessed landowners, the Norman Irish and the ancient Celtic Irish, turned on the English colonists, driving them off their lands and destroying the system of 'thorough' in Ireland. Although the numbers killed were exaggerated thanks to anti-Catholic hysteria, the Parliamentary party interpreted the rising as the first action of an Irish Catholic army about to invade England on behalf of the king.

The Irish rebellion raised the stakes of the game at Westminster considerably. An army now had to be mustered to put it down, and that army could not be allowed to fall into the wrong hands – that is, used against the Parliamentarians by the king. Vicious rumours were sweeping the capital: not only had the king and queen inspired the massacre, but the foreign queen was in touch with Catholic powers abroad. She was said to have authorized them to send armies to invade England and crush Protestantism. In an atmosphere of acute tension and distrust Parliament, led by Pym, agitated for further revolutionary changes. To rally his followers against Hyde's and Falkland's royalist party, that same November Pym issued the Grand Remonstrance, which listed all Charles I's crimes to date and accused him of a 'malignant design to subvert the fundamental laws and principles of government'. The document went on to demand the power to vet the king's ministers and to call for a Presbyterian Church settlement.

Fortunately for Charles, like the Root and Branch Bill the Grand Remonstrance gained him more friends. The royalist or constitutional party now consisted of almost half of the Commons. At the end of November 1641 the Grand Remonstrance was passed in the House of Commons by a mere eleven votes and was probably far too revolutionary to get through the Lords. But at the beginning of January 1642 Charles spoilt all by trying to arrest the most prominent members of the Parliamentary party – five MPs (Pym, Hampden, Holles, Hazelrigg and

Strode) and Lord Mandeville. Evidently the leopard had not changed his spots. Charles had not really repented his bad old ways and had become over-confident again when he saw that support for him against the extremism of Pym was growing.

In fairness to Charles, Pym was hardly playing strictly by the constitutional rule book himself. A rowdy mob was permanently in attendance outside the Houses of Parliament menacing anyone who was not for Pym. Pym was unwilling to restore safety to the streets because the pressure of the mob would help him achieve his aims. Charles had been secretly warned that Parliament was about to impeach Queen Henrietta Maria for inciting the Irish massacre and conspiring against the people. Where there was impeachment there might well be attainder. That is why on 3 January 1642 Charles struck first. He accused the five MPs and Lord Mandeville of high treason. But neither House of Parliament would arrest them, claiming that the king was encroaching on their privileges. When she heard this, Henrietta Maria is supposed to have shouted at her husband, 'Go, you coward, and pull these rogues out by the ears, or never see my face more.' But when Charles broke all precedent and marched to Parliament with several hundred soldiers to arrest them, he found, as he said, that 'all the birds were flown'. They had escaped to the walled City of London where they were protected by citizen train-bands and sailors from the port.

The train-bands then moved to surround Parliament, so that within a week the five MPs had returned to their seats in the Commons. On 10 January, having learned that the Commons was about to arrest the queen for treason, Charles and the royal family abandoned the royal palace of Whitehall and fled like thieves in the night to Hampton Court, to Windsor, to Canterbury and finally to the port of Dover. The king would not be seen at Whitehall again until another January seven years later when he stepped out from the Banqueting Hall to be executed.

From Dover on 23 February Queen Henrietta Maria left the country, taking with her the magnificent crown jewels which she intended to pawn in Holland to pay for an army to rescue her husband. With her was her eldest daughter, the Princess Mary, who had been married by proxy to the important Dutch ruler William II of Orange the year before. They were to seek refuge with her husband. Meanwhile Charles set about rallying support in the country, for clearly there was to be no going back.

War was declared six months later on 22 August. In the intervening months Charles had made some attempts to achieve consensus with Parliament – he had even signed a bill removing bishops from the House of Lords. The Militia Bill, which was to remove royal control of the army, and the Nineteen Propositions, which sought to restrict royal power so that the king would be ruler in name only, were the last straw. Charles saw that the only way to save his throne was by war. But his attempts to seize a great cache of arms stored at Hull and to commandeer the fleet both failed: the fleet was thoroughly pro-Parliament, as was the governor of Hull.

Charles meanwhile retreated north to York, and in June sent out directions to all his loyal supporters and friends across England to call out their local militia on his behalf. In the north and west men armed themselves as they had never done before and came out for the king. But all over the south and east an equal number of men, such as the MP Oliver Cromwell, a Cambridge squire who would have left England for America had not the Grand Remonstrance passed, also called their horses in from the plough and armed themselves to the teeth.

On 11 July the Houses of Parliament announced that Charles had begun the war, and a month later declared that all men who served the king were traitors. On 22 August, watched by his young sons Charles and James in their children's armour (Charles II's can still be seen in the Tower of London) the king unfurled the royal standard before the walls of Nottingham Castle. The Civil War had begun at last.

The Dutch artist Van Dyck, who became Charles I's court painter just as Holbein had been Henry VIII's, has left us with a vivid record of the major personalities of the court. With their colourful silk clothes, their lacy collars, their feathered hats and their charming lovelocks as their long, curling hair was called, they cannot help making a somewhat less serious impression than the Parliamentarians: they were not called Cavaliers for nothing. By the time the Civil War broke out, the extremism of the Puritans had ensured that Strafford and Laud were not the only high-minded, hardworking men to have supported Charles. Nevertheless a sort of artistic truth is to be found in the striking contrast between paintings of the two sides, court and Parliament. There is an absence of ornamentation about the Parliamentarians' clothing and appearance – the dark cloth, the plain collars and the short hair cropped under a pudding basin that gave them the name Roundheads. And there is a terrible purposefulness in the portraits of Oliver Cromwell, Sir Ralph Hopton and General Ireton. Plain was their appearance, plain was their talk, and unlike the Cavaliers they had been in deadly earnest from the beginning, not just now when it was really too late.

Civil War (1642–1649)

From the very first luck seemed to be against the king. The royal standard with its prancing golden lions rampant blew down outside Nottingham Castle as soon as it had been put up, to everyone's secret dismay. But before long the king's men were too busy with preparations – unrolling maps, arranging for ammunition, calculating food and supply lines – to think about this bad omen. Nevertheless the news that the navy and the City of London had declared for Parliament could not be anything other than worrying. In the end those two factors would give the Puritans an outstanding advantage: thanks to the navy, the Parliamentary forces could move their troops far more quickly to trouble spots than the royalists could. The king's soldiers had to go everywhere overland. The seaports too were an important part of the resistance to the king and prevented his troops from using their harbours. Mastery of the City meant that Parliament controlled the money supply from customs and trade. In the long run it would be extremely difficult for the king to pay for extra supplies of weapons or troops from abroad. Nevertheless just as the House of Commons at the outbreak of war had been evenly divided between the royalists and the Parliamentarians, so too was the country. The conflict would be very long drawn out.

For the Civil War turned into two linked civil wars. The first, which took place from 1642 to 1646, can be described in simple terms as the king versus the radicals – in other words, the half of Parliament led by Pym. In the course of the war, however, the aims of Parliament changed. The

1643: destruction of the Cheapside Cross (one of the Eleanor Crosses) during the first part of the Civil War.

Parliamentary army itself became a separate revolutionary movement determined to resist the return of Charles I, who by then had drawn the Scots and most Parliamentary MPs on to his side. There was thus a second civil war in 1648 in which the army was triumphant. Parliament would be emasculated, the king executed, and a Commonwealth replaced the monarchy. After military triumphs against royalist armies raised in Ireland and Scotland, where the Presbyterians had crowned the Prince of Wales Charles II, the army leader Oliver Cromwell became lord protector – in effect a republican dictator. Seven years later in 1660 after the Commonwealth had degenerated into a new sort of tyranny under which Parliament was as powerless as it had been during the 1630s, the constitutional wheel came full circle: Charles II was restored to the throne by one of the republic's ruling generals, George Monck.

When the First Civil War began in 1642, England more or less divided along the same geographical fault-line that it had done during the Wars of the Roses. The north, Wales, the south-west and the more rural parts were for the king, while London, the east, the south and the south-east, where there was a greater concentration of towns and commercial wealth, tended to support the Parliamentary cause. Within these categories there were of course exceptions. Inside generally royalist areas, the clothing towns – for example, in the West Riding of Yorkshire or in Somerset – would contain pockets of Parliamentary supporters, for almost all people who made their living by trade were Parliamentarians. The two universities, Oxford and Cambridge, were for the king, and had begun melting down their college silver to pay for arms (though Oliver Cromwell, as the local MP for Huntingdon, put a stop to that in Cambridge).

For the first two years of the war the king's strategic aim was to reach London. He never got nearer than Turnham Green in Hammersmith, right at the beginning of the war. Then the sheer size of the London train-bands which had made such a nuisance of themselves outside Parliament under the Puritan Earl of Essex, Elizabeth's favourite's son, made Charles turn about and head for Oxford. Thanks to its enthusiasm for the still-imprisoned Laud, Oxford was vehemently pro-royalist, and the king made his headquarters there for the rest of the war. By and large the campaigns of 1643 were favourable to the royalist party. The king's dashing nephew Prince Rupert, the son of the Elector Palatine and the Winter Queen, captured Parliamentary Bristol. Having defeated Lord Fairfax and his son Sir Thomas Fairfax at Adwalton Moor near Bradford, the Earl of Newcastle held all Yorkshire for the king except for Hull. Cornwall and Devon and the south-west up to Devizes in Wiltshire were royalist. The king's men were further encouraged by the early deaths of two of their most inspiring opponents: Hampden died at Chalgrove Field in a battle

Lucius Carey, Lord Falkland, who became one of the leaders of the royalist constitutionalist party in the face of religious extremism.

with Prince Rupert, and Pym of cancer.

However, Plymouth, Hull and Gloucester were all serious threats to the royalists' ability to maintain their position. Meanwhile one of Pym's last actions had been to weight the scales of the war further in Parliament's favour when he added the Scottish armies to Parliament's cause. By an agreement of September 1643 known as the Solemn League and Covenant, in return for establishing Presbyterianism in England the Scots came in on Parliament's side and lent it 20,000 men.

Charles too was looking for outside help. By an agreement with the Irish Catholic rebels called the Cessation, which meant he would cease to prosecute them, he had the help of an army from Ireland. But this also only confirmed the king's reputation as a man determined to restore papistry in England through the hated Irish Catholics.

But the Scots army was a much more soldierly affair. After it joined the Parliamentary side, the tide of victory started to turn in the rebels' favour. In July 1644, once the Scots had fought their way south to join up with the Fairfaxes in Yorkshire, one of the most important battles of the war took place. The king's best generals, his nephew Prince Rupert and the Earl of Newcastle, were conclusively defeated at the Battle of Marston Moor. Hitherto Prince Rupert's great weapon, his cavalry charge, had been irresistible. Now, however, he came up against the Eastern Association army, which had already covered itself with glory at Hull. These troops, raised from the eastern counties of Essex, Cambridgeshire, Norfolk and Suffolk, were very strongly Puritan – many of the emigrants to America had come from the same region.

The Eastern Association had gained a great reputation for their zeal and discipline. They were a new kind of Puritan soldier who sang hymns as they marched,

Prince Rupert of the Rhine. Charles I's nephew and a superb cavalry commander.

Sir Thomas Fairfax, the lord general of the New Model Army, takes possession of
royalist Colchester during the second part of the Civil War, 1648.

who frowned on drinking, but who were as ferocious with the pike as any
soldier fuelled on spirits. The most important figure in the Association was
the profoundly religious Oliver Cromwell, the burly MP, who quite
unexpectedly, since he had never been a soldier, was coming to the fore as
a result of his exceptional military talent. In the first year of the war he had
been so impressed by Prince Rupert's use of cavalry at the Battle of Edgehill
that he started training his own mounted troops. By Marston Moor the
eastern counties cavalry were as proficient in the saddle as Prince Rupert's
men, and much more disciplined. In the end, that discipline, and the
bravery of the Scots, turned the battle, and the royalists were routed.
Cromwell said afterwards that 'God made them as stubble to our swords.'
From that day forward the man who is also known as Old Noll for his
large, potato-like nose would be christened Ironsides because no one could
get through the iron sides of him and his men.

Losing Marston Moor meant that the royalist cause lost control of the
north. Though the south-west continued to be held by the king's generals,
the defeated royalist army remained stationed in the midlands for the first
half of 1645. Charles's plan was that it should join up with royalist troops
recently raised by the Marquis of Montrose from the Highlands of
Scotland. In an extremely surprising turn of events, Montrose, who had
been one of the leading spirits of the Covenanters, turned against his

Calvinist allies and backed the royal cause. He hoped the chastened king could be brought to act in a more restrained and constitutional manner.

That same year Montrose swept through Scotland in a series of stunning victories and soon controlled almost the whole country. It was a feat made more remarkable by the fact that at the beginning of the campaign his cavalry had consisted of only three horses, and his army had comprised undisciplined Highland clans whose leisure time was passed by feuding with one another. But the combination of Montrose's noble and inspiring personality and the clans' traditional loathing of the Campbells, whose chief Argyll was the head of the Covenanters, had welded them into an unstoppably ferocious fighting force.

In the Parliamentary camp, meanwhile, the knowledge that the war was still not won was making its leaders reconsider the way their army was organized. Just as Parliament had been divided on the question how far they should go in rebelling against the king, the Parliamentary leaders themselves were also becoming divided about their cause. Despite their importance in the earlier constitutional battle between Parliament and King, figures like the Earl of Manchester (formerly Lord Mandeville) and Essex had become rather afraid of making all-out war on the king. Manchester had been heard to say that he thought the war would never be ended by the sword, only by discussion. Furthermore, he warned, 'If we should beat the king ninety nine times and he beat us once we should all be hanged.'

These more moderate thinkers within the Parliamentary cause, who had a majority in the House of Commons, became known as the Presbyterian party when the question of what to do about the Church of England established a fault-line through which political divisions emerged. Their willingness to impose Presbyterianism on England through the Church, spoke of a respect for hierarchy that was opposed by the more radical Parliamentarians, the Puritan Independents who believed in religious toleration and whose leader in the Commons was Oliver Cromwell. Though the Independents were a minority party among MPs, most of the army was of their religious persuasion. The Independents tended to be more exaltedly religious men, belonging to the Independent religious sects and impelled by simple religious imperatives. They despised the Presbyterians' softening attitude and believed that command should be taken away from people who were not prepared to go for outright victory over a wicked king.

After some adroit manoeuvring behind the scenes by Cromwell, in February 1645 the Self-Denying Ordinance deprived all members of the Houses of Parliament of their commands – only Cromwell himself was excepted in recognition of his remarkable skills as a general. Manchester and Essex were forced to retire and the Parliamentary forces were now called the New Model Army, controlled by Cromwell as lieutenant-general of cavalry under Sir Thomas Fairfax, who became commander-in-chief. The New Model Army was intensely religious, as the Eastern Association had been, and hero-worshipped Cromwell. As a sign that extremists among the Parliamentary forces were seizing power, Laud was at last executed.

Despite Montrose's victories in Scotland, the year 1645 proved decisive for the Parliamentary armies. In June at the Battle of Naseby in Northamptonshire the king's army was even more conclusively trounced than it had been at Marston Moor. After a tremendous initial charge whose impetus completely broke up the left wing of the New Model Army under Henry Ireton, Prince Rupert never followed through. He indulgently allowed his cavalry to vanish from the battlefield to pillage the Parliamentary baggage train. In his absence Cromwell's soldiers cleaned up. As the royalists fled, they left behind not only most of their arms cache but Charles I's secret papers. These revealed that, in order to entice the Irish Catholic army to England, the king had promised to suspend the anti-Catholic laws; he was also plotting to pay for foreign troops to invade England, which his son Charles had left the country to arrange. This only confirmed the Parliamentarians' darkest fears of a future England oppressed by absolutism and sinful Catholicism.

A Parliamentary soldier.

In September 1645 the king's last hope of aid from the northern Scots died when Montrose was comprehensively defeated at Selkirk by the veteran Scots general David Leslie. Though the personal valour of Montrose's Highland troops was incomparable, they did not understand the need to remain as an army at harvest time. Around August many melted away back to their glens. Meanwhile Montrose's attempt to rally the Lowlands foundered on the Lowlanders' Presbyterian hatred for Charles's Irish Catholic allies. Montrose escaped to the continent, while that same month Charles's last army outside Cornwall was defeated at Rowton Heath near Chester.

At the beginning of 1646 the king's army even lost its hold on the west when Truro, the capital of Cornwall, surrendered to its besiegers. Thereafter the writing was on the wall. In May, as town after town fell and the Roundheads began to approach the royalist headquarters, Charles left Oxford and rode north to surrender to the Covenanter Scots camped at Newark. They took him on to Newcastle. Finally, in June, Oxford was captured by the Parliamentarians and the First Civil War was over.

Charles had chosen to give himself up to the Scots because there was a possibility that they might back him against the English. Tensions had not abated between the factions into which the Parliamentary cause had divided. Indeed the split between the Presbyterians and the army had become so serious that the Presbyterian MPs sent their own representatives hurrying north to negotiate separately with the king and the Scots against the army. They suggested that the king should be returned to power under certain conditions, the so-called Propositions of Newcastle: Presbyterianism would become the established Church, Parliament would control the army and the fleet for twenty years, and there would be strict enforcement of the laws against Catholics. But these were the very conditions that Charles had rejected before the war, and in the end he could not bring himself to accept them. In January 1647, in return for £400,000 owed to them in army back-pay, the king was handed over to Parliament by his Scots jailers and then conveyed to Holmby House in Northamptonshire. The Scots now journeyed north back to their own country, leaving the army, which increasingly looked to Cromwell as its leader, to continue its struggle for power with the Presbyterians.

During the first six months of 1647, while the king remained at Holmby House, the antagonism between the army and the Presbyterians intensified. The Independents' or soldiers' influence in Parliament was increasing and the Presbyterian MPs were very alarmed at the way the army had become a political force and saw a future for itself as part of the government. They had expected that once the war was over it would disperse and leave them to rule. The Presbyterians decided to strike first. If they could disband the New Model Army, then the threat from its men would disappear. The Presbyterians made the mistake of not paying its wages first – in the case of the cavalry these were ten months in arrears. The army simply refused to disband. Instead it mutinied and elected its own political council, on which Cromwell was the leading light.

By June 1647 Cromwell with his usual tactical genius saw that he would have to seize the most important piece on the chessboard: the king. He despatched Cornet Joyce to Holmby House to capture Charles for the army and take him to the old Tudor palace of Hampton Court. The army meanwhile marched to London and expelled eleven Presbyterian MPs from Parliament, thus proving itself just as much an enemy to Parliamentary privilege as Charles had been. Its leaders now offered the king their own Heads of Proposals. These were rather reasonable: Charles could return to the throne so long as Parliament met every two years; bishops could be restored so long as no one had to obey them; and the prayer book could be reintroduced so long as its prayers were not compulsory.

But these straightforward men with their straightforward ideas were

346

dealing with the wrong man. Convinced after the expulsion of the Presbyterians from Parliament that internecine war was about to erupt between the two Parliamentary sides, Charles simultaneously entered into secret negotiations with the Scots and the English Presbyterian party, believing he could bargain with them from a stronger position after the army's offer. He escaped to the Isle of Wight and, though he was captured and held in Carisbrooke Castle, still contrived to send secret messages to the Scots and negotiate with them.

At Carisbrooke the devious Charles managed to sign the Engagement, a single treaty with the more moderate Covenanters under the Marquis of Hamilton, who had deserted Argyll. Under the Engagement, Charles finally agreed to establish Presbyterianism in England, but to suppress all heretical sects – which included all the sects gathered under the banner of the Independents – as soon as a Scots army had invaded England and set up a new Parliament. By 1648 a combination of the Presbyterians' fear of the extreme sectarians in the army, the king's intrigues and the news that a Scots army would come to their rescue had welded the English Presbyterians, the royalists and the Presbyterian Scots together to make common cause.

The Second Civil War began with risings in Kent and Essex in June, and in South Wales in July. The Thirty Years War had just ended with the Treaty of Westphalia, so the king had a hope of Catholic continental troops coming to his aid. But Fairfax defeated the Kent rebels and Cromwell, having crushed the rising in Wales, went on to destroy the small and inadequate Scots army at Preston. The Essex royalists surrendered a fortnight later, at the end of August 1648. And though the Second Civil War was now over, the danger to the Parliamentary cause had not evaporated. As a sign of the pro-royalist mood in the country, no fewer than nine ships of the fleet suddenly changed sides and sailed to Holland to join the Prince of Wales.

Ominously the new crisis made the army turn violently against the king, in the belief that he could never be trusted again. Disgusted with the king's lack of plain dealing, it published a declaration stating that it was its duty 'to call Charles Stuart, that man of blood, to an account for the blood he had shed, and the mischief he had done to his utmost against the Lord's cause and people in these poor nations'. It had had enough of delay and negotiation, and events were moving towards an uncontrollable finish. Forcibly removing Charles from the Isle of Wight, where he had had considerable freedom of movement, the army imprisoned him under twenty-four-hour guard in Hurst Castle in Hampshire, before transferring him three weeks later to Windsor. Then on 6 December 1648, in what is called Pride's Purge, 143 Presbyterian MPs were ejected from the Commons

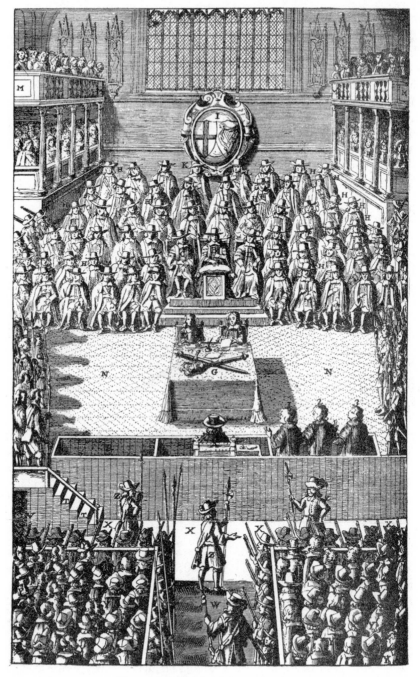

The trial of Charles I, January 1649.

by troops under Colonel Thomas Pride. The remaining members, forming the Rump Parliament, were Independents, supporters of Oliver Cromwell and the army.

The army now insisted that the king be brought to trial. Though the House of Lords refused to countenance such a step, a *soi-ditant* High Court of Justice was created by a vote of the House of Commons. It consisted of 135 commissioners, few of whom were lawyers, none of whom were judges, and a lowly provincial lawyer named John Bradshaw was elected president. On 20 January 1649 King Charles stood trial beneath the hammer beams of Westminster Hall where his distant ancestors had once dispensed justice. Beyond the little world of Westminster the rest of England was stunned by the army's presumption.

Though he might have lost his kingdom, Charles had not lost his wits. In a loud voice, his stammer for once not detectable, he asked by what authority he had been brought to the bar, for no authority existed in England to try a king. 'By the authority of the people of England,' Bradshaw replied. But Charles would not answer to the charges of an unconstitutional court and refused to say anything throughout the rest of the trial. His son the Prince of Wales, who had wept uncontrollably in Holland when he heard what was happening, now sent a piece of blank paper to the Rump, declaring that he would put his signature to any demand if his father's life was spared. But it was to no avail.

The 'court' continued to hear the evidence against the king. As nothing was said in his defence, it was shown that the king had made war on his people, had raised troops against Parliament and had been a 'tyrant, traitor, murderer, and public enemy to the good people of this nation'. He was therefore sentenced to death by having his head severed from his body.

The death warrant was signed by only 59 of the 135 commissioners. The rest had slunk away, reluctant to set their names to a document of such dubious legality. Thus Charles I was condemned to death by a minority of the court, which had been established by a minority of the House of Commons, indeed by an illegal remnant thereof, and without the concurrence of the House of Lords.

Unexpectedly, in the face of death Charles I showed a strength and dignity nobody knew he possessed. As one writer put it, 'Nothing in his life became him like the leaving it.' On 30 January the king was executed outside Banqueting House in Whitehall, which Inigo Jones had built for his father James I. When he stepped on to the scaffold, a small figure dressed all in black, Charles was quite composed; he had spent the last days of his life praying with the Bishop of London, William Juxon. Because it was such bitter weather he wore two shirts, so that a shiver of cold would not be mistaken for one of fear. All round Whitehall, steel-helmeted men on horseback kept the crowds at bay. But there were hundreds and thousands of people nevertheless. When the head with its long, black, flowing locks was severed from the body, a terrible cry went up from the crowd like a soul in pain.

A witness noted in his diary, 'The blow I saw given, and can truly say  with a sad heart, at the instant whereof, I remember well, there was such a groan by the thousands then present as I never heard before and desire I may never hear again.' As the masked executioner held up the dripping head and said, 'Behold the traitor Charles Stuart,' there was no shout of triumph, only the sound of smothered weeping. Realizing that all had not gone to plan, the army now hustled the people out of Whitehall. The body was removed for embalming before it was taken to Windsor. St George's Chapel would be its final resting place.

There is a story, which has the ring of truth, that on the night of the king's execution, while the body was still lying at Whitehall, a hooded figure approached. Looking at the royal corpse, he muttered with some regret, 'Cruel necessity.' It has always been believed that this was Oliver Cromwell.

Death transformed the foolish, treacherous king into a martyr, and a book which was said to comprise his last prayers and meditations, the *Eikon Basilike* ('The Royal Image') became a bestseller in England and Europe. The poet John Milton was forced to mount a very unsuccessful public relations exercise against it, and put out a booklet showing why it was always lawful to put tyrants to death. The poet Andrew Marvell, a partisan of Cromwell's, was so impressed by the way the king had died that he immortalized it in verse:

> He nothing common did, or mean,
> Upon that memorable scene:
> But, with his keener eye
> The Axe's edge did try:
>
> Nor call'd the Gods with vulgar spite
> To vindicate his helpless Right
> But bow'd his comely head
> Down, as upon a bed.

The Commonwealth and Protectorate
(1649–1660)

England was now declared to be a republic or Commonwealth. Despite the existence of the Prince of Wales the monarchy was abolished, as was the House of Lords. Only the House of Commons remained unaltered since Pride's Purge. For the present, while the new order shook down, it was still the old Rump Parliament. Its MPs selected forty-one men to be members of a Council of State. The regicide Bradshaw was president and the poet John Milton was Latin secretary, the equivalent of foreign secretary today, for all diplomatic correspondence was written in Latin. Though Oliver Cromwell was one of the new regime's most important figures, his role continued to be lieutenant-general of cavalry, and as yet subordinate to Fairfax. Their military skills were needed immediately, for danger threatened the young republic at home and overseas.

On the one hand the martyrdom of Charles I had considerably revived royalist feeling. Abroad such was the revulsion at the spilling of royal blood that in Holland and Spain England's ambassadors were both assassinated. At the same time within the army itself the widespread Leveller sect (among the more extreme of the Independents) was not content with the political settlement. Its members wished to go much further than keeping the old Rump Parliament for they believed in universal male suffrage – they had plans to allow the vote for all men regardless of their wealth, and to abolish personal property. They therefore mutinied, threatening to attack Parliament and force free elections. Cromwell, believing that this was the beginning of anarchy, decided that the Levellers had to be put down. 'Break them in pieces. If you do not break them, they will break you,' he said to the Council. He and Fairfax crushed the rebellion by arresting its leaders at dead of night in Burford, Oxfordshire.

Even more alarming to the life of the young republic was the situation in Scotland and Ireland. Both countries had thrown off English rule. The execution of Charles I caused more problems than it solved. It rallied the royalist Presbyterian forces in Scotland, where the Prince of Wales was immediately proclaimed King Charles II. In Ireland a powerful army of Protestant royalists and Catholic lords arose under James Butler, Marquis

351

of Ormonde. Ireland was the threat which needed dealing with most urgently, for the Prince of Wales and Prince Rupert – now commanding the royalist fleet – were on their way there to join Ormonde and encourage the royalist cause.

OLIVER CROMWELL.

Accordingly Cromwell, as the army's greatest soldier, set off for Ireland where he proceeded to lay siege to two of the most important royalist garrisons, Drogheda and Wexford, in September and October 1649. Since they would not surrender, once he had captured the towns he put the entire garrison to the sword, an act which was undoubtedly brutal but not illegitimate by seventeenth-century rules of siege. He justified his conduct by saying that he hoped that thereby less blood would be spilt in the rest of Ireland, whose inhabitants would submit more readily if they knew he would show no mercy.

By 1650 the reconquest was complete. Once more Ireland was reconstructed along inimical English lines; this time her land was redistributed among Cromwellian soldiers, a new English garrison to subdue the natives. The Irish had the choice of renouncing their Catholicism or being resettled beyond the Shannon in the moorland of Connaught – hence the expression 'to hell or Connaught'. To this day the name of Cromwell is pronounced with peculiar loathing by the southern Irish.

Cromwell was next needed in Scotland. By July 1650 the Prince of Wales was at the head of an army of Covenanters. Although Charles was almost powerless and Scotland continued to be ruled by the Scots nobles under Argyll, the threat of a Stuart in that country was too great to be ignored. Cromwell's initial invasion was a failure as the Scots were masters of never actually giving battle, and the weather, hunger and sickness started to eat into the English numbers. But on 3 September Cromwell won one of his greatest victories at the Battle of Dunbar against his former colleague David Leslie. Soon after Edinburgh and the Lowlands were controlled by the English occupying army. By now Cromwell was commander-in-chief of the army, for Fairfax – who since Charles I's trial had been uneasy about the direction the army was taking – had resigned.

The following year the hard-pressed Covenanters crowned the Prince of Wales Charles II of Scotland at Scone, the ancient coronation seat of the Scottish kings. In August they invaded England, hoping that a crowned king might rally royalists to their cause. But after less than a month's campaigning, on the anniversary of Dunbar, 3 September 1651, Cromwell defeated Charles at the Battle of Worcester. Even the wily Argyll was

Archibald Campbell, 8th Earl and 1st Marquis of Argyll, leader of the
Covenanters who crowned Charles II in Scotland. Painting by David Scougall.

forced to agree to Cromwell's terms: Scotland became a commonwealth
like England, the Scottish Parliament was abolished, the Presbyterians lost
their Assembly. Instead freedom of worship for all Puritans was
guaranteed and so was free trade between the two commonwealths.

Charles himself managed to escape to France after a great many
astonishing adventures which have passed into folklore. After some valiant
hand-to-hand fighting in the streets of Worcester, when he was heard to
shout that he had only one life to lose, he was forced to linger in the west
midlands. There he hid in the priest-holes of friendly recusant houses such as
Moseley Old Hall near Wolverhampton and Boscobel House in Shropshire,
since the army was guarding all the bridges over the Severn to prevent his
escape from Welsh ports. His most celebrated hiding place, after soldiers
began to search Boscobel House itself, was up the huge oak tree behind it,
along with another royalist on the run with him. All day long the Roundhead
soldiers tramped about beneath – it never occurred to them to look above
their heads where the two rebels clung to the oak's leafy branches.

The future Charles II hiding up an oak tree after the battle of Worcester, 1651.

After Boscobel, in order to get to the coast the future king had to be disguised as a manservant. Eventually he was smuggled out of the country at four in the morning in a fishing boat from Shoreham in west Sussex. The government had put up notices offering a reward of a thousand pounds to anyone who could give information on the whereabouts of 'Charles Stuart, son of the Late Tyrant'. As Charles was exceptionally recognizable we must conclude that many people did know who he was but elected to keep his secret. It was an indication of the royalist sentiment that was beginning to return under the new tyranny of Parliament. Nine years later it would restore Charles to his father's throne.

But if peace in the three former kingdoms had been established for the moment by Cromwell's crushing victories, the infant republic continued to be regarded with considerable hostility abroad. In the case of Holland this led to the First Dutch War (1652–4). There were many similarities in outlook between what were now two Calvinist republics. Protestantism had drawn them together against the Catholic powers in Elizabeth's time, but trade rivalry in the East Indies and Dutch sympathy with the royal cause made relations unfriendly. It needed only a spark to start a war. It was provided in 1651 when the Rump Parliament tried to transfer some of the lucrative Dutch carrying trade into English hands by means of a new Navigation Act. It forbade the importation into England or the English colonies of goods that were carried in any ships other than those of their country of origin. The Dutch were infuriated that the English Commonwealth should benefit from one of their most profitable businesses.

The First Dutch War took place entirely at sea. In theory the Commonwealth was in no position to fight, let alone win, because it had no proper navy. But a Somerset Puritan named Robert Blake, who had captured Taunton from the royalists, turned out to be as good a 'general at sea' as on land, and trounced Holland despite her maritime expertise. The greatest English seaman until Nelson, Admiral Blake triumphed against the leading Dutch seaman Van Tromp, whom he defeated off the Texel in 1653. With the Treaty of Westminster the following year, English supremacy over the North Sea was established, the Dutch promised not to aid the royalists and the English carrying trade began its lucrative growth.

The crisis of the Dutch War failed to heal the splits that were appearing once again in the government of the republic. For some time many in the army had nursed a mounting hostility to the self-satisfied Rump MPs, many of whom had held their seats for almost fifteen years. Army leaders believed that it was time for the Rump to dissolve itself, allowing fairer elections that would produce a House of Commons that was more representative of the English nation. But the Rump MPs were very comfortable as things were, and in April 1653, far from agreeing to a free election, they began to put through an act to prolong their existence. Cromwell took action.

Bursting into the Commons with his soldiers, Cromwell told them, 'It is not fit that you should sit here any longer!' He began to throw the MPs out, including the speaker, whom soldiers pulled down from his chair by his gown. Then, though an MP named Thomas Harrison warned him that what he was doing was very dangerous, he ordered his men to remove the golden mace, symbol of the speaker, the authority of the House of Commons. 'Take away this bauble,' said Cromwell bleakly.

Cromwell was now the supreme power in the land, a military dictator who believed God had given him a superior knowledge of what was right for the country. He had not lost faith in Parliament as an institution – after all, he had fought for the Parliamentary cause with every atom of his being. It was just a question of finding the *right* kind of Parliament. Over the next few years he would experiment with a variety of national gatherings, for he remained anxious not to abandon the Parliamentary principle. But he was nearly always disappointed. His guiding principle was that England should be ruled by a community of the righteous. In his first attempt at constructing a Parliament to his liking, which became known as the Little Parliament, Cromwell decided that a quick way of ensuring that only the godly were elected was for the candidates to be selected by their local Independent church. So stringent were the criteria they had to comply with – these embraced the number of times the candidate prayed each day, for example – that in the whole of England only 139 really God-fearing men could be found who were worthy to be MPs.

A typical member, who gave the Parliament its nickname, the Barebones Parliament, was an Anabaptist preacher and leatherseller called Praisegod Barbon or Barebones. Unfortunately holiness did not guarantee intelligence. Within eight months, by December 1653, the Little Parliament of unworldly saints who wanted to abolish whatever they could get their hands on – lawyers, priests, government – were seen by Cromwell to be completely unworkable. They were dismissed.

To take its place the army's Council of Officers instead proposed an Instrument of Government, England's first written constitution. It provided for a 400-seat unicameral Parliament – a new House of Commons to which for the first time MPs would be elected from Scotland and Ireland. But while the House of Lords remained abolished, a lord protector, Cromwell himself, was to rule the country with the aid of the Council of State. As soon as Parliament met in September 1654 its members began to make difficulties, especially the more extreme republicans who disapproved of the king-like role of lord protector. Four months later, in January 1655, Cromwell dissolved it as peremptorily as any Stuart king had done.

A royalist rising in Wiltshire under Colonel Penruddock brought more trouble, and Cromwell used it as an excuse to impose martial law, dividing England into eleven districts run by major-generals. This, historians believe, was perhaps the single most important factor in turning the country's thoughts towards a restoration of the monarchy. For, although most people would have encountered something of the Puritan way of life, this was their first experience of a daily existence entirely ordered on Puritan lines, and they loathed it. Used to considering themselves a free people, the English found the restriction of personal liberty which the Puritan code involved unbearable. Fines were imposed for swearing, for sporting activities, for gambling and for drunkenness. The Puritans had already shut all the theatres, but now pubs and inns were closed down if the local major-general considered there were too many in one district. Any judge who attempted to query the new martial laws was removed from office, and, though Parliament was in abeyance, taxes were raised without its permission. Had it not been for the threat presented by the army, the people would probably have risen in revolt.

But Cromwell also had many admirable qualities. Just as he was a magnificent general, he was an outstanding statesman who served English interests well. In many ways he lacked personal ambition, and was driven instead by his sense of God's will. Righteousness prompted him to rebel against Charles I, and a desire to impose further righteousness on the people of England, since they could not work it out for themselves, turned him into a dictator. In many respects Cromwell was wise and liberal. Although Roman Catholics and High Anglicans remained outside the fold, a preacher of any persuasion – from Baptist to Presbyterian to Independent – could hold a living in the Church of England. And Cromwell, like all Puritans, was positively philo-Semitic because of his interest in the Bible. Although there probably had always been small unofficial Jewish communities living in London, it was Cromwell who in 1656 invited the Jews to return, though it was not until 1664 that Edward I's legislation was reversed. So it was that the Jewish community began to re-establish itself in England, bringing immense wealth, culture and useful continental contacts for the Cromwellian government.

The advancement of British interests and influence abroad was vigorously pursued by Cromwell. After the Dutch War he attempted a Protestant foreign policy of which Walsingham would have approved – not least in his use of Louis XIV to put pressure on the Duke of Savoy to prevent the further slaughter of the duke's Protestant subjects, whose bones 'scattered on the Alpine mountains cold' were the subject of one of Milton's best known sonnets. By the mid-seventeenth century, however, Protestantism was no longer an automatic link between countries. Though Cromwell made treaties with Sweden and Denmark, trade rather than religious conviction was the driving force. Far more important in the European scheme of things was the fierce rivalry between Spain and France, directed by Cardinal Mazarin on behalf of the ambitious boy-king Louis XIV.

By the end of the century, the France of Louis XIV would turn out to be the great impediment to European freedom. But Cromwell was born a hundred years earlier, at the end of Elizabeth's reign in 1599. His worldview was Elizabethan: for him Spain as the champion of Catholicism would always be the main threat to England, particularly as she was the obstacle to further English expansion in the New World. In 1655, now formally allied to France (an alliance which had driven Prince Charles Stuart from the country), England declared war on Spain after Philip IV refused to allow religious toleration to English traders in the Spanish colonies and free trade in the West Indies.

The island of Jamaica was captured by Sir William Penn and Robert Venables in the first year of the war, and before long had developed into an important British colony. In 1657 the Spanish treasure fleet was seized at Santa Cruz in Tenerife and brought home, covering Admiral Blake with glory (Blake, however, died at sea on the return voyage and was buried in Westminster Abbey). The last part of the war saw the English fighting beside the French against Spain. One consequence of this was that, after victory in the Battle of the Dunes, Dunkirk was occupied by the English. Thanks to English aid, Spain was comprehensively defeated by France. In the long run this would raise problems for England and Europe, for it was yet another step towards France's plans of world domination which by 1689 England was forced to form a coalition to curtail.

In 1656 Cromwell tried restoring Parliament again, bringing the rule of the hated major-generals to an end. However, at least a hundred of the new MPs turned out to hold extreme republican views. As a result they were barred from entering the Commons by Cromwell's soldiers, whereupon in protest another fifty refused to attend Parliament. Thus the new House of Commons was less representative of the will of the people than ever.

In 1657, after a failed assassination attempt on Cromwell by the Leveller Colonel Saxby, the new Commons attempted to return to something similar to the English constitution as it had been before the Civil Wars. This they outlined in their Humble Petition and Advice, in which they entreated Cromwell to become king and asked for the House of Lords to be revived, though it was to be called the Other House, and consist of life peers nominated by the lord protector. The immense disapproval this would have brought on him from his old comrades-in-arms dissuaded Cromwell from taking the title of king, but in all other respects he was quite king-like. Indeed, as if he had established a hereditary monarchy his son was to be lord protector after him. When Cromwell died of a fever on 3 September 1658, the anniversary of the victories of Dunbar and Worcester, worn out by the strains of office, the Protectorate passed to his elder son Richard Cromwell.

But the new Cromwell was not at all the same thing as the old, and his Protectorate lasted only eight months. Richard Cromwell was a pleasant country gentleman who had none of his father's energy. He was not even a Puritan. Immediately upon his accession all the disagreements between extremists in the army and Parliament burst into renewed life, now that his father was no longer there to suppress them. The army insisted that its commander general Charles Fleetwood, who was married to Cromwell's daughter Bridget (Ireton having died), should have special powers independent of the protector and the Commons. Squabbles between Richard Cromwell and the army weakened the regime and in April 1659 the generals forced him to dissolve Parliament. Shortly afterwards, the younger Cromwell resigned the Protectorate. He retired to his country estates, leaving the army to rule alone.

A period of very unsatisfactory chaos followed: the army leaders could agree on nothing except to bring back the Rump, the Independent MPs left in the Commons after Pride's Purge, who had been expelled by Cromwell in 1653. They considered the most recent Cromwellian Parliament to be yes-men and not radical enough. When it became evident that the government in London was losing control, there was a Presbyterian rising in Cheshire which was suppressed by one of the army generals, John Lambert. On his return to London Lambert expelled the Rump again, but on Boxing Day the growing confusion throughout England forced the army to recall the Rump once more.

These events were observed from Scotland with increasing impatience by General Monck, where he was part of the occupying army. A professional soldier who had fought for the royal cause until his capture in 1644, Monck had come to the conclusion that a monarchy with its powers severely curtailed was what the country needed if order was to be restored. A famously silent man, he gave little indication of his intentions as he began to march on London as the beginning of January 1660. But something of his ideas began to leak out. Increasing numbers of people joined his army as it came south, including many disenchanted Presbyterians and Parliamentary leaders of the First Civil War such as Sir Thomas Fairfax. Once in London Monck announced that he wished to summon a free Parliament. He insisted that the Rump recall the Presbyterian MPs who had been removed at Pride's Purge. This gave the Presbyterians a majority over the Rump, and they voted that the Long Parliament first summoned in 1640 must finally end.

General George Monck who restored the monarchy in 1660.

Monck, who had been made commander-in-chief of the army, having refused the office of protector, had been in communication with Prince Charles Stuart in exile in Holland. On Monck's advice Charles issued a proclamation of his future intentions on 4 April. Known as the Declaration of Breda it promised a general pardon to those who had acted against the crown, stated that Parliament would decide all issues of importance and announced that Charles wished to allow 'liberty to tender consciences' in matters of religion as long as they did not disturb the kingdom. Meanwhile the free Parliament – known as a Convention because no royal person had summoned it – of Lords and Commons was called, to which were returned a great many royalists and Presbyterians. The Convention, having voted in favour of the motion that the government of England ought to be by king, Lords and Commons, invited Prince Charles Stuart to return as king.

On 29 May, his thirtieth birthday, the dark and charming Prince of Wales arrived in London to be crowned King Charles II.

Charles II
(1660–1685)

The return of the handsome Prince of Wales was greeted with frank rejoicing after the misery into which the Commonwealth had degenerated. It was expressed in the cheering crowds that waited for his arrival and lined his entire route from Dover to London. Nevertheless as his ship – called the *Naseby* after the great Parliamentary victory, now tactfully renamed the *Royal Charles* – crossed the sea, Prince Charles told Samuel Pepys the diarist, who was one of the officials accompanying the royal family's return, that he could not rid his mind of his last time in England, when he had been a wanted man with a price on his head. How unlike this return in triumph! As he neared London Charles said, with the sardonic humour which exile had encouraged, that it must be entirely his fault that he had stayed away so long – he had yet to meet anyone 'who did not protest that he had ever wished for his return'.

And indeed since the settlement made at the Restoration dissolved all the acts of the republican government, and Charles II's reign was said to date from the death of his father in 1649, it was as if the Interregnum had never been. Nevertheless, whatever the political compromises, the new king was a very human being who was hardly going to forget the treatment his family had endured. Beneath Charles's affable manner there was a steely resolve never, as he put it, 'to go on his travels again'. He would adopt whatever means he could to accomplish that for himself and his relations.

Despite the celebrations, the tensions between the Presbyterians who had brought back the king and the royalists themselves were unresolved. Indeed they coloured the rest of the reign, for the forces represented by the Parliamentary rebels did not vanish with the Restoration. The Puritan Revolution might have gone too far, but the Civil War had been an expression of an uncontainable feeling. The new monarchy was immeasurably enhanced by Charles's personal popularity – he had not, however, restored himself. Those who had brought him back, the great lords, the MPs, the merchants, the lawyers, had fought that war for Parliamentary rights and were never going to allow a return to the times of Charles I. When they found out that beneath his airy charm the new king

believed just as much in royal power as his
father and grandfather had, a new struggle
began between king and Parliament. It was
spearheaded by the former Cromwellian
politician Anthony Ashley Cooper, created
Lord Ashley in 1661 and later Earl of
Shaftesbury, whose followers became
known as the Whigs.

At first, however, Charles II's autocratic
instincts were constrained by his pre-
carious position and by his former adviser
in exile, the lawyer Edward Hyde. The
father-in-law of Charles's brother James,
Duke of York, who had married his

CHARLES THE SECOND.

daughter Anne, Hyde was now raised to the peerage as the Earl of
Clarendon and became lord chancellor. Edward Hyde had been one of the
leaders of the opposition in Charles I's time; as a result the Restoration
monarchy began life shorn of the worst excesses of that reign. Most of the
acts of the Long Parliament before the war which Charles I had agreed to
remained on the statute book, while the instruments of Stuart despotism –
the Star Chamber, the Court of High Commission, the Council of the North
– remained in the dustbin of history. Ship money and any taxes raised
without Parliament's consent continued to be illegal, and the Triennial Act
stipulating that Parliament must convene every three years was reinstated.
All the ancient feudal levies to the king were finally abolished and Charles
was granted £1,200,000 a year for the rest of his life.

Pudgy, faithful and now over fifty, which was twenty years older than
most of the king's circle, Clarendon was old-fashioned and pompous, but
he had been in exile with the royal family for years, sharing their greatest
tribulations, and Charles listened to him. They shared a desire to make the
new monarchy secure by settling it on the widest foundations, an objective
endangered most conspicuously by the monarchy's natural supporters, the
Anglican Cavaliers. Though the first measure of the Restoration
Convention was the Act of Indemnity and Oblivion, which covered
everything done during the Civil War, once the Convention had given way
to the overwhelmingly Cavalier Parliament the act was to some extent
ignored. Thirteen expendable former members of the Commonwealth
government were executed. Cromwell's corpse and those of two other
regicides, his son-in-law Henry Ireton and John Bradshaw, were dug up
and hanged. The Cavaliers were also determined to scupper the king's
efforts to include the Puritans within a broad new Church of England.

The Anglican Cavaliers loathed the Independents and Presbyterians who had ruled England during the Commonwealth. They might not be able to take their revenge on the chief men of the Commonwealth, many of whom now held important positions at the court of Charles II, but they could take their revenge on their co-religionists. They were convinced that all Baptists, Presbyterians and Independents were instinctive republicans, that given half a chance their meeting places would once again be seedbeds of revolution, as they had been before the Civil War. The Cavaliers' one aim was to cut the ground from under the Puritans' feet so that they should not be allowed to get a hold anywhere in England, whether it was in the corporations (or boroughs) which returned members of Parliament or among the clergy.

Charles II's attempt to achieve a new Church settlement informed by the Puritan leaders, whose views were canvassed for the 1662 prayer book, foundered on a disastrous combination of Anglican obduracy and the Puritans' refusal to compromise over bishops. Instead, a series of acts unfairly known as the Clarendon Code brought back the High Anglicanism of Laud as the official national religion, to be enforced in every branch of the English state structure. The Corporation Act of December 1661 required all town officials to swear to renounce the Covenant, take the Anglican Communion and obey the king. Bishops were restored to the Church and to the House of Lords. The Fourth Act of Uniformity in 1662 ordered all clergymen who refused to use the prayer book, who had not been ordained by a bishop and who would not renounce the Covenant to lose their livings. At this, a phenomenal 2,000 clergymen resigned from the Church of England.

Previously, under the Commonwealth the different Puritan sects – the Independents, Baptists, Presbyterians and two new ones that sprang up in the 1650s, the Quakers (so called because they quaked at the spirit within them) and Socinians (who became known as Unitarians) – had regarded themselves as members of the Church of England. No longer. From the Clarendon Code dates the tradition of Dissent, or Nonconformity as it became known in the nineteenth century. With the departure of its most fervent ministers, much of the vigour and strength of religious feeling went outside the Church of England, accounting for its decline in the eighteenth century. The Methodism of John Wesley would be needed to revive its spiritual passion.

Just as the forces that had provoked the Civil War were still present in Charles II's government, albeit in diluted form, the more powerful ideas of Puritanism did not disappear, they simply went underground. The Clarendon Code had the effect of dividing England into two nations, one official, the other unofficial. Unable to participate in public life for the next 150 years and educated at their own high-minded academies, the Dissenters developed a mental independence that gave them a healthy lack of respect for the powers that be. The Puritanism which still existed within the Dissenters became an underground spring that infused the national life in the most curious and vital way. In the Nonconformist consciences it continued to be a force for reform and social change.

There was an initial flurry of prosecutions of Dissenters, as the Conventicle Act of 1664 prevented more than four people assembling to worship without the Anglican prayer book – the writer John Bunyan, who was minister of a flock of Baptists in Bedfordshire, spent twelve years in prison, during which he wrote one of the masterpieces of English literature, *Pilgrim's Progress*. But as time wore on the Clarendon Code was not always observed, as there were no church courts to ensure enforcement. In 1689 an Act of Toleration modified the laws, allowing Dissenters to worship in peace, and the Five Mile Act of 1665 which forbade all dissenting clergymen to come within five miles of a corporate town or their old living soon lapsed. Meanwhile energetic men prevented from becoming sheriffs, MPs, judges or even university students devoted themselves to practical activities like banking and manufacturing.

Compared to the rest of Europe, England was extremely liberal, introducing religious tolerance a century before most European countries – in France Louis XIV would soon revoke the 1598 Edict of Nantes which permitted Protestant worship and political freedom. This tolerance owed a great deal to the gracious character of Charles II, who had originally wished to grant 'liberty to tender consciences'. He had suffered too much at the hands of the religiously inclined (hence his celebrated quip, 'Presbyterianism is no religion for a gentleman') to like bigotry in any form. He even gave permission to the Quakers under William Penn, son of the Cromwellian admiral, to set up Pennsylvania in America as a proprietary colony so that they could worship unmolested. At their first meeting, this grave, good man would not remove his hat in Charles's presence because he disapproved of kings. Thereupon Charles removed his own, saying it was the custom that *one* of them should be bare-headed.

The new king was immensely popular. He possessed a zest for enjoyment – he was nicknamed the Merry Monarch – which mirrored his subjects' yearning for a return to normality after the stern Puritan experiment. He led the way in a riot of parties, dancing and dissipation, consorting with actresses who were mistresses and mistresses who became duchesses. Restoration comedy by writers like Vanbrugh express the spirit of the age: amoral and lascivious. Throughout England games, festivals, gaiety, maypoles and Christmas all returned, for Christmas under the Commonwealth had been a day of fasting to atone for past sins.

Charles II made yacht racing into a national sport, pitting his skills as a yachtsman against his brother the Duke of York. He also made horse racing at Newmarket into a fashionable activity, which is why it is often called the sport of kings. He loved the company of jockeys and was frequently observed chatting to them. Wherever he went he was followed by the little dogs with plumed ears and tails, which have ever since been known as King Charles spaniels. The sentimental English were entranced by the king's informality. Unlike his stately father, he was always accessible and friendly, generally being the first to wave when people recognized him walking in Windsor Great Park.

England, with its play-acting traditions established so strongly for over a century, had keenly missed the theatre, shut down by the Puritans. Now the gregarious king was to be seen almost every night at playhouses such as the Theatre Royal Drury Lane, and at the new Italian musical genre called the opera. An orange-seller and actress called Nell Gwynne became one of his favourite mistresses. In the new air of freedom women like Aphra Behn became playwrights, for the Puritans had stressed the role of women as submissive to their husbands. The country was swept by mockery of the Puritans in poems like *Hudibras* by Samuel Butler which concerned the adventures of a Presbyterian knight, and satirical comedies of the sophisticated new manners like William Wycherley's *The Country Wife*.

The poet John Dryden who had celebrated Charles II's return in his poem *Astraea Redux* was appointed poet laureate. Music, which had also been discouraged under the Cromwellians, was renewed in churches all over England. The new court painter Sir Peter Lely captured the risqué flavour of the Restoration,

Published by Harrison & Co. Aug. 1. 179.

Restoration poet laureate and playwright John Dryden.

in the revealing dresses of the heavy-lidded beauties like Barbara Villiers, Lady Castlemaine, and Louise Duchess of Portsmouth who presided over the court. Almost all of them bore bastard children by Charles II, who was happy to recognize them as his own since his wife Catherine of Braganza was unable to conceive. Almost all of the sons were created dukes, with the result that many English dukes today descend from what used to be called the wrong side of the blanket.

WHITEHALL IN THE SEVENTEENTH CENTURY.

Even before the Restoration, seventeenth-century England had seen a host of important new scientific discoveries thanks to the liberating effect on thought of the Renaissance and Reformation. Science, which had been dead since the classical Greeks, revived mightily and in countless ways invisibly touched and improved the nation's life. Farming techniques copied from the Dutch reclaimed land in the fens and East Anglia. By the 1670s new methods improved yields so much that the English were for the first time able to export corn. Before the Civil War Charles I's doctor William Harvey had demonstrated the circulation of the blood as well as how embryos develop in the womb. By the middle of the century it had become a tradition in London for men interested in experimental science to have meetings together in what was called the 'invisible college', and in 1662 the distinguished members of this 'invisible college' were incorporated into the Royal Society, helped by a grant from Charles II. The lively and intellectually curious new king had scientific interests throughout his life, himself performing experiments as a hobby – though he mocked the Royal Society members for seeming to do nothing but weigh air. In fact the weighing of air by Robert Boyle as a means of discovering the properties of gases and his invention of an air pump was the starting point for one of the transforming inventions of the modern world, the steam engine, developed by the Englishman Thomas Newcomen in 1712.

Perhaps the most celebrated Fellow of the Royal Society was the extraordinary mathematics professor Isaac Newton, born in 1642. He revolutionized the laws of physical science, which had long rested on Aristotelian calculations, when he worked out the rules of gravity after observing an apple drop to the ground. Newton's work held good for the next 200 years. As the poet Alexander Pope would wittily put it:

Nature and Nature's Laws lay hid in Night.
God said, *Let Newton be!* and all was Light!

English architecture, which had seen no important new public buildings during the twenty years of the Interregnum, began to celebrate the lush forms of the baroque: Christopher Wren, another Fellow, soon to be famous for rebuilding St Paul's, designed the Sheldonian Theatre in Oxford. Meanwhile a convivial and courteous public life began to flourish in the new coffee and chocolate houses of London and the greater provincial cities which contrasted favourably with the boisterous character of public houses and inns. Coffee, chocolate and tea were fashionable new imports into England that attested to the exponential growth in English trade from Africa to Malaysia.

Rump and Protectorate innovations considered to be of value, such as the Navigation Act of 1651, were re-enacted by the Cavalier Parliament to give them greater legal force, but the Cromwellian Union of England, Scotland and Ireland was repealed and their abolished local Parliaments were reinstated. In Scotland, however, the Covenanter movement had been a national phenomenon which was far more universal than its Puritan equivalent in England. Not only did widespread local rebellions greet the return of bishops and the tightening of English control over the Kirk, but thousands of Covenanters who refused to worship other than after their own fashion were imprisoned or killed for their beliefs and their leader Argyll was executed.

In contrast to Scotland, in religious matters the majority of the Irish fared quite well, owing to Charles's sympathy for Roman Catholicism. Catholics had fought for him and hidden him, while his wife, his mother and his favourite mistress were all Catholics. Under Charles's lord lieutenant in Ireland, the Earl of Ormonde (created duke in 1661), the Mass was once more unofficially allowed to be heard. It was in Ireland that one of the great problems of the Restoration, how and to whom should confiscated estates be restored, was shown in its purest form. Despite their huge sacrifices for Charles's father, most of the Catholic Irish royalists never received back a penny for the estates seized as punishment by Cromwell and redistributed to his soldiers – who formed too convenient a new addition to the Protestant garrison in Ireland to be disturbed.

It was with his leanings to Catholicism that Charles II would come most perilously into conflict with the nation he had been recalled to rule. His sympathy for the French Catholic king and rumoured secret dealings began to inflame the old Puritan party, who were already angered by the Anglican settlement of the Church. Under the former Cromwellian Lord Ashley, a Parliamentarian in the mould of Hampden and Pym, a bitter Parliamentary opposition to Charles II was created. For, at the Restoration, Catholicism represented to the English psyche as strongly as ever the tyranny and absolutism that Parliament had fought two civil wars to overcome.

Since the early days of Cromwell, English foreign policy had been to back France against Spain in the struggle for mastery in Europe. The Restoration government merely continued that theme, helped by the intimacy between the two sovereigns. Charles II was not just closely related to the French king Louis XIV – they were first cousins – he had also spent a great deal of time at his court during the Interregnum. He saw Louis as a real friend to whom he could turn in times of trouble. It was Louis, keen to draw England more tightly into his net of alliances against Spain, who had arranged the marriage of Charles to Catherine of Braganza, sister of the King of Portugal.

This marriage was extremely fortunate for the burgeoning English trade with India for it brought England the port of Bombay in India, as well as Tangier in Africa. Bombay soon became the East India Company's most lucrative place of trade, its acquisition marking the real beginning of the British Empire in India. Nevertheless, the Portuguese marriage had contemporary significance because it was a hit against Spain. Portugal had only just become independent again after three-quarters of a century under Spanish rule, thanks to French aid and French soldiers. When Charles II sold Dunkirk back to France to please Louis in 1662, it seemed to reflect the unwelcome and growing influence that the French king had over his cousin. It began to be said that England was the tool of France.

By the mid-1660s, after five short years, the honeymoon between Charles II and Parliament had ended. An interminable and unsuccessful Second Dutch War, the unceasingly scandalous and expensive royal mistresses – all of whom seemed to be ladies-in-waiting to the queen – and the corruption and extravagance of the court were proving increasingly unpopular, their enormous costs prompting questions in the House of Commons. The king had also begun to show tendencies that reminded Parliament all too unhappily of his ancestors, when he attempted without success to declare an Act of Indulgence to counteract the Act of Uniformity. He wanted Parliament to pass the measure to 'enable him to exercise with a more universal satisfaction that power of dispensing which he conceived to be inherent in him'. Since the king's inability to suspend or dispense with the law had been one of the rallying cries that began Parliament's resistance to Charles I, this was hardly promising.

In 1665 the Black Death returned to England – this time known as the Great Plague – and killed 70,000 people. It was followed the next year by the Great Fire of London, which in five days burned down half the city and no fewer than eighty-nine parish churches, as well as old St Paul's. In the face of these great natural catastrophes, many contemporaries abandoned their recently acquired habits of scientific reasoning and concluded that the two events represented the judgement of God on an immoral people.

Once more, as it had during the Black Death, the terrible cry of 'Bring out your dead!' was heard, though this time medical advances counselled isolation and the marking of plague houses with a red cross. In an effort to prevent themselves breathing in the germs which were believed to carry the bubonic plague, the well-to-do carried little bunches of flowers in which to bury their noses. From this custom dates the macabre nursery rhyme (sneezing was one of the symptoms of the disease):

Ring a ring a roses
Pocket full of posies
Atishoo, atishoo
We all fall down.

PLAGUE PITS AT FINSBURY.

The Great Fire of London, 2–6 September 1666.

As before, the Great Plague was carried by the black rat, now proliferating thanks to the dramatic growth of the Port of London made necessary by the inflow of produce from the colonies.

Such was the fear of papists that the Great Fire, which started in a baker's shop on Pudding Lane, was widely assumed to be the work of Roman Catholics. Charles II and the Duke of York endeared themselves to the city by taking a hands-on role in helping to extinguish the flames. It was the duke who put an end to the blaze, using gunpowder to blow up houses and make a gap the fire could not pass over.

But it was not enough to revive the royal popularity that had prevailed at the time of the Restoration in 1660. The openly Catholic leanings of the court aroused mounting suspicion, greatly aggravated by rumours that the Duke of York, next in line to the throne, was in the process of converting.

If the Plague and the Fire seemed a judgement on a corrupt court said to be in the pocket of the French, the final straw came in 1667. Having blockaded the Thames, the Dutch had the effrontery to sail up the Medway and capture some of the best English warships. As if that was not bad enough, Louis XIV – the supposed friend of England – suddenly switched sides and backed the Dutch. He was alarmed by the rapid growth of English colonies when his ultimate plan was for France to replace the Spanish Empire as a worldwide power. All was chaos and confusion, and England now faced two formidable enemies. Some sort of scapegoat was needed to deflect the anger rising in Parliament against the king. The chosen figure was the architect of Charles II's return, his faithful servant Lord Clarendon.

Although Clarendon was the father of the Duke of York's wife and grandfather of the two heiresses to the throne, Princess Mary and Princess Anne, he was unpopular at court as he disdained to hide his disapproval of its louche behaviour. Moreover, having been the king's tutor once he could not break himself of the habit of treating his former pupil as if he were still a schoolboy. Nevertheless he was a loyal servant, whose veneration for the House of Stuart was such that he had opposed the marriage of his daughter, as a mere commoner, to the Duke of York. But, like his father, Charles II had a ruthless side. He did not hesitate to throw his servant to the House of Commons. Unlike his father, though, Charles had the goodness of heart to warn Clarendon of his impending fate so that he should not be imprisoned or executed but could escape to France. There he died after completing his magisterial account of the Civil War, *The History of the Great Rebellion*.

The Second Dutch War had grown out of rivalry between the Dutch and the English in North America. As well as expanding south – the large new colony of Carolina had been established in 1663, like its capital Charleston

WILLIAM PENN.

William Penn, the Quaker founder of
Pennsylvania.

named for the king – English settlers began to fill up the land between Maryland and the states of New England, which the Dutch considered to be their own territory. Stalemate in the war led to a new peace signed at Breda which gave the old Dutch colony of New Amsterdam to the English, who were commanded by the Duke of York. It was renamed New York in his honour, though its largest island retained its Dutch name, Manhattan. Acquiring New York was crucial for the string of British colonies running along the eastern coast of America. New Amsterdam had prevented a continuity of national settlement between northern New England and the south; now that it had changed hands, the land began to fill up with English settlers.

These colonial successes made Louis XIV more anxious than ever to ensure that England was contained within his net of alliances. To his annoyance, the disparate collection of new ministers who had masterminded the fall of Clarendon were united by their distrust of French ambition. Known as the Cabal from the acronym made by the first letters of their name Lords Clifford, Ashley, Buckingham (the son of Charles I's favourite), Arlington and Lauderdale, they made a new Protestant alliance with Holland and Sweden. This Triple Alliance temporarily halted Louis in his tracks, forcing him to withdraw from his campaign to overrun the Spanish Netherlands on behalf of his wife, sister of the King of Spain.

The displeased Sun King therefore changed tack. Feelers were once more put out to Charles via his sister Minette, the Duchess of Orléans, who was married to Louis' brother, known as Monsieur. By 1670, when the two monarchs signed the Treaty of Dover, Louis XIV had lured Charles and England back into his camp: they were now committed to go to war with him against Holland, in return for a stretch of the Dutch coast and the island of Walcheren, near the mouth of the Scheldt.

There was a secret clause in the treaty, however, which was to have enormous costs. For Louis the price was the massive sum of £160,000 a year to be paid secretly to his cousin to make Charles independent of an increasingly restive and unbiddable Parliament. For Charles it was much greater. He sacrificed the last shreds of confidence that the English nation had in the Stuarts as kings. For by the secret clause, which Charles revealed only to the Catholics Arlington and Clifford, the English king was to declare himself a Catholic 'as soon as the welfare of the realm would permit', and Louis was to earmark 6,000 French soldiers to help turn England Catholic.

This was extraordinarily risky behaviour on the part of Charles. Lord Shaftesbury (as Anthony Ashley Cooper became in 1672), who was the leading political personality of the day and Charles's current lord chancellor, was already very doubtful about the king. As an intemperate ex-Cromwellian, indeed a former member of the religious Barebones Parliament, he was waiting to pounce on any tyrannous royal behaviour. For Shaftesbury, an ambitious, passionate, ruthless character and a vituperative orator, the king was back on sufferance.

As with many of his followers, Shaftesbury's visceral hatred of absolutism and Catholicism, incarnate in the figure of the continental tyrant Louis XIV, had been forged by the great political struggles of the previous half-century. Intellectual justification for the need for continuous revolt was provided by his friend and personal physician, the political philosopher John Locke, whose contract theory of civil government would inspire the American colonies to rebel a hundred years later. Shaftesbury's followers, the Puritan or country party as they were known in contrast to Charles II's court party, had many links to Dissent and its manufacturing interests. The Dissenters saw not only a threat to freedom of thought but a customs threat to English trade in the stranglehold the bellicose Louis XIV had over so many continental ports.

If Shaftesbury and others had begun to pick up rumours about the secret clause, their suspicions were exacerbated just before the war began against the Dutch. In 1672, as a first step in the implementation of the secret clause, Charles issued a Declaration of Indulgence. Without Parliament's approval he suspended all the penal laws against Roman Catholics and Dissenters, exhibiting that old Stuart tendency to dispense with

Parliamentary procedures which the country had fought a war to stop. The House of Commons was so outraged that in February 1673 it refused to vote supplies until the Declaration of Indulgence was withdrawn. The following month Charles gave in and withdrew the Indulgence. But, though the Commons voted supplies for the war, it also quickly passed a Test Act to root out Catholics. The Test Act required all office holders to swear that they rejected the doctrines of the Roman Church and to prove that they had recently received Anglican Communion. Charles angrily prorogued Parliament, but the damage was done. For the Duke of York, the future James II, was obliged to resign as lord high admiral. Arlington and Clifford had to go too.

These resignations were followed a few months later by Shaftesbury's dismissal as lord chancellor. For the rest of Charles II's reign the country was racked by a long-drawn-out struggle between the cadaverous Shaftesbury, whose opposition party stood for limiting the king's power, and Charles II and his court party. From the end of 1673 the king's party were led by the Cavalier Anglican Thomas Osborne, like Shaftesbury a skilled Commons organizer who did not scruple to buy support when all else failed, and was said to set aside £20,000 a year from customs receipts to bribe MPs. Created Earl of Danby, Osborne was as determined to uphold the royal prerogative and eradicate Dissent as Shaftesbury was to pursue the will of Parliament and establish toleration. Thus for the first time in English history there emerged two distinct parties in the House of Commons, from which derive our present-day two-party system.

Under pressure from the increasingly anti-French House of Commons Charles was forced to make peace with Holland in 1674 and the Third Dutch War came to an end. As early as 1677 Danby, Charles II's new chief minister after the demise of the Cabal, was raising an English army to help the Dutch and arranging the marriage of James's daughter Princess Mary, heiress presumptive to the English throne because Charles II was childless, to Charles's nephew William III of Orange, stadholder of the Netherlands. The marriage took place in November. Louis XIV was incandescent at the way Charles had failed to prevent Danby returning to the principles of the Triple Alliance, because he had been sending his cousin further enormous secret subsidies in return for the promise that England would make no alliance with a foreign power without France's permission.

By now Louis had had enough – his policy of bribing Charles had got nowhere. He decided to turn his attentions to the opposition under Shaftesbury and bribe them instead. This of course could not have been more dangerous to Charles II. Louis revealed to Shaftesbury the second and third secret agreements Charles had signed to prorogue or adjourn Parliament at the French king's bidding for £100,000 a time to prevent

Parliament declaring war on France. In July 1678, stymied by Danby's threat of an English army defending Holland, Louis made peace with the Treaty of Nijmegen and not long afterwards revealed to Shaftesbury a fourth secret treaty, under which Charles had been paid to withdraw from the Dutch alliance and which had been written out in the reluctant Danby's hand.

From August 1678 events were anyway moving in Shaftesbury's favour with the discovery of the supposed Popish Plot. Titus Oates, a moonfaced rogue clergyman, announced that there was a secret plot afoot for Catholics with French aid to embark on a massacre of Protestants, including the king and the Duke of York. Since the Duke of York was already a Catholic and the king could not have been more friendly to Roman Catholics, this was palpable nonsense. But the strange death of the examining magistrate Sir Edmund Berry Godfrey fired the ever smouldering embers of anti-Catholicism into furious life and it swept the country. Innocent Catholics were tried and found guilty on no evidence at all, and Shaftesbury saw his chance. He exploited fears that Protestantism was under threat to get Danby impeached for his activities as the king's emissary to Louis, activities proven by his handwriting. In January 1679 Charles was forced to dissolve Parliament and call new elections to save Danby and to prevent himself being attacked on his French policy.

However, the new Parliament which met in March was extremely hostile to Catholicism and to the Duke of York. Shaftesbury began to bay for the blood of the openly Catholic duke and for his exclusion from the throne. Defiantly, Charles dissolved Parliament and called fresh elections again in the hope of getting a better House, which would vote against Shaftesbury's Exclusion Bill. On its last day Shaftesbury got the Habeas Corpus Act passed which prevented the crown from delaying trials and imprisoning without cause.

Nevertheless, Charles was so alarmed by the new House of Commons that he refused to allow it to sit. The backers of the Exclusion Bill, Shaftesbury's followers, petitioned the king to allow Parliament to meet. Their country party became known as the Petitioners, and soon they got the nickname the Whiggamores or Whigs because the Scots Covenanters with their Petition of 1638 had been called Whiggamores. Meanwhile the court party, formerly led by the imprisoned Danby, who expressed their abhorrence of Shaftesbury's attempt to interfere with the royal prerogative, began to be known as Tories (from 'Toraidhe'), which was the nickname used of Catholic rebels in Ireland.

Parliament was champing at the bit, but the king continued to refuse to allow it to assemble. The situation in London began to turn distinctly nasty; there were mutterings about a new civil war. Rebellion broke out in both eastern and western Scotland when the Covenanters, who had been persecuted for almost twenty years, rose up and murdered the pro-English Archbishop Sharp near St Andrews. They were led by the son of the Argyll who had led the first Covenanters. Shaftesbury by now had plans, which were being widely discussed, for Charles's illegitimate son, the showy and shallow Duke of Monmouth, to succeed as king instead of the Catholic James. Shaftesbury manoeuvred to get Monmouth sent north to put the Covenanters' rising down, so that he might cover himself in glory. Monmouth did just that, defeating the Covenanters at the Battle of Bothwell Bridge near Glasgow, and they were then brutally punished by the Duke of York whom Charles had sent north to get out of harm's way. Argyll was exiled from Scotland.

Meanwhile Charles played a waiting game. It was not until October 1680 that Parliament was permitted to assemble, whereupon the Exclusion Bill passed in the Commons. The succession was saved by the Lords, which rejected the bill when Lord Halifax convinced his fellow peers that it was better to be like him, neither a Whig nor a Tory but a Trimmer between the two.

Nevertheless, what is known as the Exclusion Crisis had not gone away. To prevent the emergence of a figurehead for the Whig cause Charles had sent Monmouth out of the country. Encouraged by the feeling of moderation in the air now that the reaction to the Popish Plot had died down, in January 1681 he dissolved Parliament and called a new one to meet in Oxford. There Shaftesbury would not have the sort of influence he did in London thanks to the London mob and a gang of apprentices called the Whiteboys. As Pym had done, he used this threat of street violence to intimidate MPs. The king meanwhile coolly began to negotiate with Louis once more for further income to save him from having to call Parliament again.

When Parliament met in Oxford in late March, so defiant were the Whigs and so belligerent was their mood that they attended with armed soldiers – as did the king. For a moment England again trembled on the brink of civil war. And once again the cry went up in the Oxford Parliament to exclude the Duke of York from the throne, even though the Royal Council was now suggesting a regency during his lifetime: Princess Mary would rule for him followed by Anne.

When the Whigs refused to accept this, Charles cunningly dissolved Parliament one last time – he never called a Parliament again. There was a real possibility that, had Parliament remained sitting, a new civil war would have begun or a Whig revolution have taken place. But the Whig leaders had lost their chance. Without a Parliament to attend, MPs drifted away, and the moment had passed. Two months later Shaftesbury was hauled before a Grand Jury in London for inciting revolution, but the Londoners trying him were all Whigs and the charges were dismissed. Amid great rejoicing, Shaftesbury was released. He fled to the Hague in Holland with Monmouth, but died there in poor health a few weeks later.

What was called the Tory reaction then began. It was aided by the discovery of the Rye House Plot in 1683, a conspiracy by a handful of Whig extremists, most of whom were former Cromwellian soldiers, to assassinate Charles as he rode past an inn named Rye House on the road between London and Newmarket. Even though the plot was the work of fanatics, Charles used it as an excuse to overthrow the last of the Whig leaders. On very flimsy grounds he executed two aristocrats from distinguished families, Lord Russell and Algernon Sidney, neither of whom were probably involved with the plot but who had been among the chief movers in the Exclusion Crisis.

Sidney, who had served on Cromwell's Council of State, was killed for having in his possession papers supporting tyrannicide, while Russell died for refusing to agree that it was wrong to resist tyranny. These doctrines were the essence of what the Civil War had been fought for, and were considered reasonable ideas by many aristocratic Whig families who had fought for the Puritan Parliamentary cause. Thus Charles II by the end of his reign had considerably alienated many magnates as well as MPs. Sidney and Russell were seen by the Whigs as martyrs to the cause of civil liberty. As will be seen, their relations were only temporarily quiescent. They would take their revenge in the next reign.

For the last two years of his life the king was triumphant. In the period known as his despotism, he set out to remodel the machinery by which Parliament was elected, in order to give the Tories a majority. He recalled all the royal charters of town corporations, which were where the Whig strength lay (the Tories were in the counties), and restored them only after a new corporation of Tories had been nominated to take the place of the old. He even invented a royal right of confirming all elections to the corporations. No one dared gainsay him. All the plots and death threats against him had given him a new popularity. James, Duke of York was restored to the Privy Council and to the Admiralty in defiance of the Test Act; Dissenters and Whigs were imprisoned, and Danby released.

In a final climax to Charles's sweeping the board, he failed to summon Parliament – in contravention of the Triennial Act of 1641, which laid down that Parliament had to be called every three years. Warning bells began to ring, even for his supporters. Halifax was especially disappointed by the king.

However, the strain of asserting himself, and of conducting his energetic love life, finally told: the king was quite unexpectedly laid low by a stroke in February 1685, aged only fifty-eight. While he lingered, apologizing with his usual elegant wit for being 'an unconscionable time dying', Father Huddleston, a Catholic priest who had been present in one of the Catholic houses when Charles was on the run after the Battle of Worcester, was smuggled in up the backstairs of the Palace of Whitehall. Brought by the Duke of York, he gave the king the Last Rites according to the Catholic faith. From being a homeless exile Charles II had come home in triumph, and he now died in his own splendid bed, incontrovertibly a powerful monarch. His last words characteristically did not concern affairs of state. 'Let not poor Nelly starve,' he said, and then expired.

Despite the arbitrary style of his last years, Charles II's reign had seen the beginning of the two-party system and the further development of Parliamentary government. Danby's impeachment had finally established the responsibility of ministers to Parliament. By a mixture of tolerance and laziness Charles managed to heal the terrible wounds of the Civil War, and that was no mean feat. However, despite the growth of the colonies, his reign was not very illustrious. Charles's links to France meant that by her inaction England helped the spread of a power which posed a genuine threat to the religious and civil liberty of Europe. His reign, which had begun in hope, ended in the triumph at home of a cynical absolutism not unlike that practised by the Sun King himself. It would lead to a new revolution to curb the Stuart kings' power once and for all.

The younger Buckingham made up a verse which delighted Charles II:

> We have a pretty, witty king,
> Whose word no one relies on,
> Who never said a foolish thing
> Nor ever did a wise one.

Three hundred years later, that still seems to be the last word.

James II
(1685–1688)

The Tory reaction enabled James II to become king without a murmur of protest. Parliament voted him the enormous sum of £1,900,000 a year for life, which gives a good indication of how popular he was. But though he was brave and hard working and led a quiet private life with his second wife, the Catholic Mary of Modena, James was almost as disastrous a king as his father Charles I, from whom he inherited some unfortunate character traits, being both obstinate and extraordinarily unrealistic. During James's reign all the anxieties about papistry and absolutism that had amounted to a call to arms for seventeenth-century Englishmen once more came to the fore. He owed his accession to the support of the Anglican Tory party. The moment he made it clear that he planned to turn England into a Catholic country, and a Catholic country that fulfilled everyone's worst fears, his cause was lost.

James indicated the way he was heading right at the beginning of his reign, but such was the feeling against the Whigs that at first it made no difference. Though he was crowned in Westminster Abbey by the Archbishop of Canterbury William Sancroft under the Protestant Rite, on the second Sunday of the new reign the king attended Mass openly at Whitehall, with the chapel doors pushed wide so that all could see what he was doing. Pro-Catholic measures followed, including a warning to the bishops that the king would not have the clergy preaching against the dangers of papistry. And although he did not need the money, James II too became Louis XIV's pensioner, for the Sun King hoped to repeat his trick of neutralizing Britain for the coming struggle.

By the summer of 1685 the Whig exiles in Holland were in despair. The Duke of Monmouth and the Earl of Argyll decided to try and raise a revolution before James became too entrenched. Argyll crossed to Scotland to his own lands, while Monmouth went to the west country, where he proclaimed himself the lawful son of Charles II and the real king of England. Both risings failed, Monmouth being defeated and captured at the Battle of Sedgemoor in the New Forest. Hundreds of Monmouth's supporters were executed (most of them hung, drawn and quartered) in the

James II.

famously punitive Bloody Assizes, presided over by the lord chief justice Judge Jeffreys. Hundreds more were sentenced to transportation to the West Indies.

James seized the opportunity Monmouth's rebellion offered to create a Catholic standing army loyal only to him. Using the excuse that the militia was not good enough, he raised new regiments officered by Roman Catholics to protect him against what appeared to be incipient revolution, and would not disband them. By October 1685 the king's army of 16,000 men was exercising menacingly just outside London on Hounslow Heath. With this large force at his disposal James was in a better position to see his wishes carried out in Parliament. He asked for the Test Act to be abolished, for he saw no reason why his fellow Catholics should be prevented from holding office. But Parliament refused, believing that with a Roman Catholic king it was more important than ever that the Test Act remained in place. When MPs denounced his use of dispensing powers to appoint Catholic officers, James prorogued his one and only Parliament. He also dismissed all his Tory ministers except for the cynical and unprincipled opportunist Robert Spencer, Earl of Sunderland, who quickly converted to Catholicism.

Over the next two years matters went from bad to worse. In July 1686 James illegally established a Court of Ecclesiastical Commission presided over by his new lord chancellor Jeffreys, the Hanging Judge, which was to suppress clerical opposition and Romanize the Church. Henry Compton, the outspoken Bishop of London who protested against this, was suspended by the king. Judges installed during the triumph of Charles II declared that James had the power to dispense with the law if he wished and appoint Roman Catholics to state office. In case after case the king took enthusiastic advantage of this ruling, filling Oxford and Cambridge with Catholics and

James Scott, Duke of Monmouth, the illegitimate son of Charles II, whose 1685 rebellion claimed the throne for himself against the Catholic James II.

introducing four Catholic peers into the Privy Council. In April 1687 by a Declaration of Indulgence James suspended all laws against Catholics and Dissenters, hoping to win some of the Dissenters on to his side. But, although the Dissenters had been persecuted by the Anglican Church, they infinitely preferred Protestantism to Catholicism and were not wooed.

There was now a general feeling in the air that matters were approaching a crisis. Senior Tories like Danby now united with the exiled Whigs and conspired to find a new ruler. The obvious choice was Princess Mary, the heir to the throne, a staunch Protestant who was married to William III of Orange. Through a variety of means William, a valiant foe of Louis XIV, had made his opposition to the repeal of the Test Act and to the defeat of Protestantism quite clear. Meetings with the Dutch ambassador started secret negotiations for the Stadholder to come and save England from James II. The sense that Protestantism was in danger had been amplified by the arrival in England of the French Protestants, the Huguenots, 400,000 of whom had been expelled from France by Louis XIV over the previous two years, following his revocation of his ancestor's Edict of Nantes. All over England people thrilled with horror as French exiles told of their hideous experiences at the hands of the Catholic Louis, and the spectre of their own houses being demolished and churches burned began to hang over the nation.

In June 1688 events started moving towards their climax. The catalyst came with James's second Declaration of Indulgence. This was to be read in all churches on the first two Sundays of that month. At this the Archbishop of Canterbury, William Sancroft, the saintly and easygoing old man who had crowned James king, could bear it no longer. With six other bishops, he petitioned the king not to make the clergy break the law. Infuriated when the majority of the clergy duly refused to read the Declaration from the pulpit, James charged the bishops with seditious libel and sent them to the Tower. Scandalized, the English were convinced that their Protestant institutions and liberties were about to be overturned. As the bishops approached the Tower in their barge, crowds gathered to watch and shouted for their blessing.

Archbishop of Canterbury, William Sancroft, one of the seven bishops tried for resisting James II's attempts to strengthen royal power and return England to Catholicism.

Princess Anne wrote to her sister Mary

in Holland that 'things are come to that pass now, that if they go on much longer, I believe no Protestant will be able to live'. She added, 'I am resolved to undergo anything rather than change my religion; nay if it come to that, I had rather live on alms than change.' The spectacle of such key establishment figures as six English bishops on trial was an affront to the English way of life. Nevertheless the country stayed reasonably calm because James's two daughters remained staunch Protestants. There was no reason to doubt that in due course a Protestant queen would reverse her father's acts.

But now, to add urgency to their deliberations, Mary of Modena, James II's second wife whose previous children had died in infancy, gave birth to a son, a new Prince of Wales. The prospect of another Catholic king to follow his ageing father was insupportable. The almost miraculous birth after a long gap aroused a great deal of suspicion about the origins of the baby – a rumour went round that it had been smuggled into Mary's bedroom in a warming pan. (As a consequence of this damaging uncertainty, until quite recently the home secretary has had to be in the vicinity of the birth of the heir to the throne, in order to certify that the infant was not a substitute.)

There was no time to lose. On 30 June, the day a London jury acquitted the bishops to wild rejoicings, a fateful letter was taken to William of Orange, inviting him to save England from tyranny and Roman Catholicism. He would have to bring an army strong enough to oppose James and secure elections to a free Parliament. It was signed by seven men of all political persuasions and from different parts of the kingdom. They had thousands more at their back, in the armed forces, in the shires, in the Church, in the absent Parliament, all united by their belief that the liberties guaranteed by English Protestantism were in danger of vanishing altogether under James. Among the signatories were the Tory leader Danby, once the Whigs' most bitter enemy; Compton, the suspended Bishop of London; a Russell and a Sidney, both of whom were closely related to the Whig martyrs of Charles II's reign; and the wealthy Whig magnate the Earl of Devonshire, who was related to the Russells by marriage.

William III had dedicated his life to preserving his country from the French – he could not ignore an invitation which would add England to the coalition against Louis XIV. What was later described as a Protestant east wind blew William and his fleet down the Channel past where James had the English fleet waiting for him, so that not a shot was fired against the future king.

William of Orange landed at Torbay in Devon on the symbolically Protestant date of 5 November, the day the Catholic plot to blow up the Houses of Parliament had been discovered. From Torbay the stadholder marched unopposed through the west of England towards the capital. He had a large army with him of 15,000 men – about 4,000 of whom were English soldiers lent to the Dutch. Fortunately almost all England, from the lords lieutenant down to the armed services, were in agreement with his coming, 'to give assistance this year sufficient for a relief under these circumstances which have now been represented', in the words of the note which invited him. All the western grandees came out to meet him as he headed for London, and the crowds swelled behind him.

James rallied his army to meet William at Salisbury, but so many troops deserted that he dared not fight, and William proceeded slowly on to London. Even James's most beloved soldier, John Churchill, who had been a member of his household for twenty years, abandoned him and joined William. So did his daughter Princess Anne. There was hardly any resistance at all, which is why 1688 is referred to as the bloodless revolution. The queen and the infant Prince of Wales, James Edward Stuart, were despatched to France. Having left a letter on his dressing table, reproaching his country for forsaking him, the king realized that the game was up. He threw the great seal of office into the Thames to make it difficult for the regime to sign any official documents and tried to follow his wife and son over to France. Embarrassingly, he was brought back by two English fishermen who had recognized him, but was then allowed to depart in peace by William.

James's flight cleared up a good many issues. The free election could be held without bloodshed, as there would be no clash of troops. The City of London, which was fast dissolving into chaos, was restored to order by William's troops. In January 1689 the writs were sent out summoning a Parliament, which as at the Restoration was called a Convention, its purpose being to draw up the new royal settlement. There was a fundamental problem, however. Both Tories and Whigs had joined together in calling for the assistance of William of Orange, but their ultimate objectives were very different. The Tories still believed in the divine right of kings and wished to establish a regency: James II could remain king in name while Mary with William's aid governed in fact. But the Whigs, as befitted their revolutionary origins, wished to abolish Divine Right once and for all. Their aim was to emphasize that the crown was subordinate to Parliamentary authority.

But a regency would make James II and his son a perpetual rallying point for the disaffected. After much argument the Convention Parliament voted through the motion that by leaving for France James had abdicated and the throne was simply declared vacant. It issued a Declaration of Rights outlining James's illegal acts; in order not to offend the Tories or Churchmen, no blame was attached to the king himself but was attributed to his ministers.

Declaration of Rights, February 1689, made by Parliament when it offered William and Mary the throne.

Meanwhile the problem of the Tories' theoretical anxieties about who should and who should not assume the throne were swept aside when William of Orange declared tersely that he had not come to England 'to be his wife's gentleman usher'. He would either be joint sovereign with her or he was going home to Holland. As the last thing anyone wanted now that William had arrived was for him to leave again, it was quickly agreed that he and his wife should be joint sovereigns. On 23 February William and Princess Mary accepted the throne they had been offered by Parliament and signed the Declaration of Rights.

This was the grand finale in the great drama of the struggle between the Stuart kings and Parliament which had taken centre stage for so much of the seventeenth century. It laid the ground rules for the British constitutional monarchy. The Glorious Revolution of 1688, as it was ever after apotheosized, secured English Protestantism, which was now identified with the rights and liberties of the people against the attacks of a despotic Catholic king. Although two Stuarts still sat on the English throne, the monarchy not only had been created by Parliament but was responsible to it. The revolution marked the ultimate supremacy of Parliament over the Stuart belief that the royal prerogative was above the law. The king was at last no more than an official of the state who could be dismissed by the state. Divine Right, though still hankered after by the Tories, had been destroyed as a political concept. Parliament had triumphed over the crown.

William and Mary

(1689–1702)

William III was small, asthmatic, dark, almost hunchbacked and unprepossessing in the flesh. But although paintings flatter him, mainly by depicting him on a rearing horse in the heat of battle, they truthfully convey his heroic essence. After Louis XIV William was the single most important individual on the late-seventeenth-century European political stage. For thirty years his tireless activities held back the tide of French domination. His life of struggle, and the treachery he had observed in the highest places – including on the part of his uncle Charles II, who had proposed dividing his nephew's homeland between himself and Louis XIV – made him highly secretive. He trusted no one other than his small Dutch inner circle. Among them his only real intimate was the Dutch courtier William Bentinck, one of the chief negotiators with the Whigs before the Glorious Revolution. Bentinck was created Duke of Portland by William, with whom he had been friends since boyhood. His devotion to the king was such that when smallpox struck the royal household, killing Queen Mary, Bentinck took upon himself all the most onerous duties of nursing William.

Even after thirteen years in England William's dependence on his Dutch intimates was undiminished, so that by the end of his life there was considerable English resentment of this foreign influence. His tendency to keep his cards close to his chest was understandable in view of the two-faced behaviour of many of the English. A great many of them, even the Duke of Shrewsbury – one of the immortal seven who had invited him to succeed James II – brazenly hedged their bets from the moment William became king and corresponded with the king-in-exile James II at St Germain in Paris. The truth was that, though the revolutionary settlement was destined to endure, at its beginning no one could predict that it would. Even the heiresses to the throne, Queen Mary and the future Queen Anne, continued to have pangs of guilt about usurping their father and their half-brother. Throughout William's reign Princess Anne wrote to her father clandestinely.

Moreover, despite all they owed to William, the senior bishops in the Church of England were very ungrateful. Now that Protestantism stood in

no danger, the Archbishop of Canterbury, William Sancroft, and the Bishop of Bath and Wells allowed themselves the luxury of refusing to take a new oath of allegiance to William and Mary on the ground that they were not the rightful heirs. Since there had to be an archbishop who recognized the new monarchs, the non-juring (or swearing) Sancroft was replaced as the Primate of All England by the low-church John Tillotson. Though the

The Glorious Revolution: William III, Prince of Orange, arriving at Brixham, Torbay, Devon, 5 November 1688, to accept the English invitation to save the country from James II's tyranny.

Non-Jurors party of the Church proved to be small and insignificant, much of the clergy and indeed many of the Tories remained secretly wedded to the cause of James II. Known as Jacobites (after the Latin form of James,

'Jacobus'), they found it impossible to abandon their allegiance to the divinely ordained Stuart line of kings, for all James's unsatisfactory religious beliefs.

The Anglican clergy's behaviour was also a reaction to William III's Dutch Calvinism (it was much the same as Presbyterianism). From the beginning of his reign it had been clear that the new king's sympathies were with establishing a broader Church through a Comprehension Act. But, though this was defeated and the penal code against the Roman Catholics remained, the 1689 Toleration Act officially recognized the principle that people should be allowed to practise their religions in ways other than those of the state Church. It permitted Protestant Dissenters to have their own dedicated buildings so long as they believed in the Trinity. In fact, as a result of the act, with the exception of Roman Catholicism toleration of every religion became the custom in England. Even Unitarians worshipped in their plain rooms undisturbed.

The English were also increasingly keen to make sure that the Dutch king understood that he was the servant of the House of Commons. Thus instead of Parliament granting an income for life, William and Mary received a sum that was renewed on an annual basis. Likewise, though the king could keep a standing army, he had to apply to Parliament each year for it. Both these acts had the effect of ensuring that Parliament met each year.

After Whitehall was destroyed by fire on the night of 4–5 January 1698, William spent a good deal of time with his fair, handsome wife at the newly built Kensington Palace, which they preferred to Hampton Court, even though Christopher Wren had improved it for them. And as a modern residence in the countryside near the hamlet of Kensington, it made a pleasant contrast to the dirty old Palace of Whitehall which sprawled everywhere and which had become such a den of iniquity under Mary's uncle, Charles II. Queen Mary's unaffected manner endeared her to her fellow countrymen, and she introduced them to the Dutch tulip, to paintings of Dutch seascapes, to blue and white china, and to building in brick after the Dutch fashion. Neat geometric Dutch gardens, using topiary and water features which were so popular in Holland, became all the rage. The royal couple's garden may be seen at Kensington Palace beside the orangery, another novelty which Queen Mary brought to England and which enabled her to grow ornamental oranges in honour of William of Orange.

Calling a halt to Louis XIV's territorial aggrandizement had been William III's great mission for almost all his adult life. He was not really interested in the English crown except as a means of bringing England's considerable weight on board the coalition against France. Fortunately this war was in England's interests. King William's War began in 1689 in Ireland, where William's father-in-law James II had landed at Kinsale with a small French army. (It is therefore sometimes also known as the War of the English Succession.) Being largely Catholic most of the country supported James's cause, but that did not mean that Ireland was pro-English. The opposite was true. Their ultimate objective was not so much to put James back on the throne of his forefathers as to assert Irish independence and drive the hated Scots and English settlers out of the lands they considered with some justice to have been stolen from them. To this end they began to burn the settlers' cattle and homes over their heads, forcing them to barricade themselves into the cities of Londonderry and Enniskillen. But no amount of brutality could break the Protestants' nerve, nor could a diet of only rats and cats as their food ran out. Londonderry held firm until June 1689, when a fleet from England arrived on Lough Foyle, and the siege, like that of Enniskillen, was raised. Thanks to these and other successes, the north of Ireland was made secure for William. James was forced to meet his son-in-law at the River Boyne, two miles above Drogheda, in July 1690.

Announcing that he had not come to Ireland to let the grass grow under his feet, William III drew up his army the other side of the River Boyne from James. All William's soldiers wore an orange sash, the colour of the House of Orange. (Such sashes may be seen to this day on Protestant Ulstermen during what is known as the marching season in July, when they commemorate their victories under 'King Billy'.) Though William was gravely wounded in the shoulder by one of the cannon balls James's troops sent over, he remained impassive and, crossing the river, his forces soon put James to flight.

William was very generous with his terms. By the Treaty of Limerick all Irish soldiers could either disband, enlist under William or follow their leader the Earl of Lucan to France. But the treaty also permitted the Roman Catholics 'such privileges in the exercise of their religion as were consistent with the law or as they had enjoyed in the days of Charles II'. William allowed no fewer than 11,000 Irishmen to depart for France. They became the celebrated Irish soldiers known as the Wild Geese who would be the backbone of many a royal continental regiment and stalwarts of the Stuart cause. But the Protestant Irish who had seized control of Parliament were less forgiving. The violent deeds of the past century were too recent to forget, so the religious toleration the treaty guaranteed was never ratified. In fact a new penal code was enforced against the Catholics which was more disabling than before.

Although Ireland had been subdued the day before the Battle of the Boyne, the French Admiral Tourville had won such a crushing victory over the Dutch and English fleets at Beachy Head that for two years England was at the mercy of a French invasion. Fortunately when the fighting between the French and English moved from Ireland to the Netherlands, and the English armies under William began to hold down the French, the threat never materialized. And after the English victory at the Battle of La Hogue in 1692 English ships once again controlled the Channel.

But William and Mary's sovereignty still had to be enforced in Scotland. As befitted the home of Scottish kings, the cause of the Stuarts continued to have immense emotional appeal there, particularly among the Catholic Highlanders, and would do so for the next fifty years. As keen Presbyterians, the Lowlanders on the other hand had every reason to dislike James II, and a Convention of the Scottish estates formally offered William and Mary the crown. But a breakaway group was formed when the Scottish Kirk abolished bishops once more, and a new Church full of exiled bishops, the Episcopalians, became a source of Jacobitism. Its members, together with the Highland clans under John Graham, Viscount Dundee (a cousin of the great Marquis of Montrose), rose in a pro-Stuart rebellion at the end of 1689, only to fade away when Dundee was killed at the Pass of Killiecrankie.

Once the rebels were back in their shielings, the government in London decided that the Highland clans must finally be brought to heel. Their chiefs were the key: they had complete control over their clans, which they treated like an enormous family – in fact in Gaelic the word clan means children. If all the chiefs were made to swear an oath of loyalty to William and Mary it would be binding on the whole clan and put an end to further insurrections.

The last day for taking the oath was New Year's Day 1692. However, on that date, one clan chief still had not made his vow, and that was the head of the Macdonalds of Glencoe. For whatever reason, the Mac Ian as he was known only reached the English garrison at Inverary on 6 January. He had exceeded the deadline by just five days, and that during a traditional holiday period when little business was transacted. But the Lowland authorities were fed up with the wild ways of the Highlanders and were itching to punish their lawlessness. John Dalrymple, the Master of Stair, who was William's vindictive and self-important minister for Scottish affairs, wrote to London, demanding that an example be made of the clan. He said it was necessary for 'the vindication of public justice to extirpate that set of thieves'. William himself signed the order commanding the Macdonalds to be rooted out, but Dalrymple's was the sinister hand that added the note that the 'affair should be secret and sudden'. The soldiers 'were not to trouble the government with prisoners'.

Dalrymple's henchman Argyll put the affair into the hands of his clansmen, the Campbells, enabling them to use legal means to avenge themselves on their hereditary enemies, the Macdonalds. On 1 February 120 Campbells disguised as government soldiers arrived somewhat mysteriously in the desolate valley of Glencoe and billeted themselves on the Macdonalds. Their orders were to secure all the exits out of the valley and in a few days' time to kill all its inhabitants, even the children. Meanwhile the Campbells relied on the ancient laws of Highland hospitality to ensure that they themselves came to no harm. On 13 February banked turf fires provided the only dim light for a cold-blooded atrocity. As the Macdonalds slept peacefully under their green plaids, the Campbells rose up and butchered thirty-eight of the people who had been their hosts for almost a fortnight.

Three-quarters of the Macdonalds, mainly women, managed to escape, warned by the Campbells' use of the gun instead of the silent bayonet. Nevertheless very many of them perished with their tiny children amid the cruel February snows as they fled in their thin nightclothes. Almost miraculously, though, those Macdonald women who did escape mostly turned out to be pregnant with boys. Several months later many young Macdonalds came into the world to revive their clan. This evil deed blackened the name of the Campbells for generations and caused such a scandal that it finished the Master of Stair's career, forcing him to retire from William's government.

Once Scotland and Ireland were subdued the king could give all his attention to the fighting in the Netherlands. In 1695 his perseverance paid off at last when he captured the border fortress of Namur and finally put a stop to the expansion of French territory. By 1697 Louis had accepted that it was checkmate, at least temporarily, and the two sides signed the Peace of Ryswick. Louis withdrew his support of James II, recognized William as King of England and returned all of his conquests since 1678, except for Strasbourg and Landau. With the Treaty of Ryswick William had for the first time dented Louis' ambitions, an achievement he owed to England's participation in the war.

One of the reasons for England's success was that the country now had very deep pockets from which to fund the war, on account of the founding of the Bank of England in 1694. This was the brainchild of the ingenious financier and Whig politician Charles Montagu, chancellor of the Exchequer and another of the seven who had signed the invitation to William of Orange to become King of England. King William's War was much more expensive than any other previous conflicts for the numbers it put into the field and because of how long it lasted. The feeding and clothing of thousands of soldiers abroad for eight years ultimately cost £40 million. The usual way of paying for wars had been through the land tax, a charge by the acre on those who owned land. Not only was this immensely unpopular with Tory squires, who tended to be land rich and cash poor, but it soon became clear that it was impossible to fund such a large-scale war as this through taxation.

Charles Montagu hit upon the idea of a permanent loan to the government. Previously the Treasury had relied on short-term loans from the goldsmiths, the chief government lending agents, which had to be paid back immediately and were extremely expensive. This time the money was to be lent by the public, and in less than a fortnight the required sum, to be known as the National Debt, had been raised and was to be loaned to the government on a permanent basis. This would yield for its lenders – wealthy City people and some ordinary merchants – an annual return of 8 per cent interest, which the government was to pay through taxation.

The Bank of England began to issue notes within a few years of its founding and became a deposit bank. It was one of the most important pillars of the new monarchy because it tied the propertied classes to the revolutionary settlement. If James II were restored, it was hardly likely that he was going to repay the money the Whig Bank owed to its investors. In the same period, around the mid-1690s, Lloyd's coffee house became the best place in London to find insurance for ships and cargo. Lloyd's reputation would grow over the next 300 years to become the premier insurance market in the world.

But the same year the Bank of England was founded, in the middle of the war, Queen Mary died of the smallpox epidemic. William was heartbroken and had to be carried fainting from her deathbed. He was prostrate with grief for weeks afterwards, unable to prevent himself from breaking down when he received Parliament's message of sympathy at her loss. In his wife's memory he commissioned Christopher Wren to remodel Greenwich Palace as a naval hospital, and on his own deathbed it would be discovered that he wore a miniature painting of her next to his heart.

Her death unleashed a good many forces that had been held in check – Mary at least had been James II's daughter. There was a rash of assassination attempts against the man the Jacobites considered to be an illegitimate king, and the Commons thought it necessary to draw up a second Bond of Association, as in Elizabeth's day, to protect him and the Protestant succession.

Grief drew William and his sister-in-law Princess Anne back together. They had become estranged owing to William's suspicions about John Churchill's loyalties to James II, which had got Churchill, now Earl of Marlborough, dismissed from the army in 1692 and sent to the Tower. Since he and his wife Sarah were Princess Anne's closest friends, a great coldness had grown up between the two sisters by the time of Queen

Mary's death. But Anne presently began to act as her brother-in-law's hostess, and relations became more cordial between William and Marlborough, who would carry on the fight against France after the king's death.

As the century neared its end, William, whose health had never been good, had become exhausted by military campaigning and by his constant shuttle diplomacy. He had begun his reign with a mixed ministry of Tories and Whigs in a bid to unite the nation, but the effect of the Jacobite plots (whose authors were all Tories) and of the Tory dislike of the war was that a decade later his ministers were all Whigs, a ministry that came to be known as the Junto. The Tories objected to the expense of a long land war and of a large permanent army, which they said was thoroughly unEnglish. In contrast the Whigs, with their commercial interests, continued strenuously to support the war as the only way to keep continental ports free from the French. To the Tories William now seemed emphatically to be a Whig king. A third Triennial Act was passed, which closed the loopholes which Charles II had exploited, and prevented any Parliament lasting longer than three years. His progressive ideas allowed the Licensing Act to lapse in 1695, which meant that newspapers could no longer be censored by the government. In combination with the Toleration Act, this enhanced the sense that England was an extraordinarily free country compared to the rest of western Europe. By the 1720s the political philosopher Montesquieu would describe the English constitution as one of the wonders of the world. The most thriving, creative and impertinent press in the world had been given the conditions in which it could flourish, an extra watchdog to safeguard the liberties of the English.

At the 1698 general election, however, with the country tired after nine years of war, the Tories under Robert Harley (after whom Harley Street is named) won a majority in the House of Commons, forcing William to dismiss the Whigs and cut back the army to a mere 7,000 troops. This turned out to be premature, however, for in 1700 an extremely important event took place that altered the balance of power in Europe: the ailing, childless King of Spain Charles II passed away.

The question of what should happen to the vast Spanish Empire had been hanging over Europe for decades since it had become clear that Charles II would never produce an heir. Until he died, in theory there were three candidates for the throne of Spain, two of whom were unwelcome to England and Holland. One was the dauphin or heir to the French throne, whose mother was Charles II's sister, the other was the Archduke Joseph, heir to the Habsburgs, whose mother was another of Charles II's sisters. Should either of these men succeed they would enlarge their own territories far beyond what was consistent with the balance of power. France or

Austria would become significantly top-heavy if either acquired not just Spain, but ten provinces in the Netherlands, the Duchy of Milan, Mallorca, Mexico (which then included California and much of Texas), all of South America except Brazil and Guiana, Cuba, Trinidad and other parts of the West Indies and the Philippines, not to mention the silver and gold mines of the Spanish Empire.

Ever since the Treaty of Ryswick William of Orange had been negotiating with the emperor and Louis XIV to find an equitable way of making sure that the enormous Spanish Empire should not be left to either power. The upshot was a Secret Partition Treaty in 1698, by which the main powers, the empire, France and England, agreed that on the death of Charles II a third heir, the empress's grandson, who was the Electoral Prince of Bavaria, would become the new King of Spain. The unexpected death of the electoral prince the following year scuppered that plan, and a Second Secret Partition Treaty was drawn up in March 1700 whereby the emperor's second son, the Archduke Charles, would become king.

But this neat solution failed to take the ideas of Charles II into account. When he died in October 1700, it was discovered that he had left the whole Spanish Empire to his great-nephew, Louis XIV's grandson Philip of Anjou. Philip was despatched south to become Philip V of Spain, and a new war, the War of the Spanish Succession, broke out. French troops began to invade the Spanish Netherlands, occupying its barrier fortresses and ports.

It was a major setback for William III. All he had battled for, in his determination to restrict the power of Louis XIV, had been swept away. Meanwhile in his unwieldy adopted country the Tory reaction was in full throttle. The Tories would not vote a penny for supplies for the new war. In their view the government should focus on the pending English succession crisis not the Spanish, after the death in July of Princess Anne's only surviving child, the eleven-year-old Duke of Gloucester. The Tory Parliament was determined to drive home the point that England was not the servant of the Dutch king but the other way round. Its attitude to William became positively insulting when it asked the king to exclude all foreigners from the Privy Council and passed a series of acts to limit his powers still further by preventing foreigners from holding office or sitting in Parliament. MPs even attempted to circumscribe the king's freedom of movement by stopping him from leaving England without the permission of Parliament. William threatened to abdicate and return to Holland, but he was persuaded to remain and the legislation continued. Though he had made no attempt to interfere with the judiciary, a new statute prevented judges being removed except by act of Parliament, and in 1701 the Act of Settlement was passed which removed the crown from James II and his

Catholic family, and stipulated that if William and Anne died without heirs it should pass to Sophia, Electress of Hanover, the Protestant granddaughter of James I, daughter of Elizabeth of Bohemia, the Winter Queen, and her heirs. The act also laid down that all future kings and queens must be members of the Church of England, a requirement that remains valid to this day.

In the autumn of 1701, however, the ostrich-like Tories were forced to take their heads out of the sand and wake up to the reality of Louis XIV's intentions. On 6 September, when James II drew his last breath at St Germain, Louis broke the Treaty of Ryswick – by which he had acknowledged William III as the rightful King of England – and instead recognized James II's son, known to history as the Old Pretender, as James III.

Louis had made a major miscalculation. The idea that the King of France should decide who was the King of England brought Tory and Whig together to vote for war. To William's relief England threw herself into a new Grand Alliance of the English, the Dutch and the Habsburg Empire. William recalled his Whig ministers and began to increase the army once more. There was nothing he liked better, he said, than war. As the new year got under way, he was eagerly anticipating the campaign. But it was not to be. Out riding one misty morning at Hampton Court on 20 February 1702 his horse tripped over a molehill and the king fell, badly breaking his collarbone. For anyone in a less run-down state of health than William, the break would have been unimportant. But the stress of being his own chief minister in Holland and England, and a life of unrelenting toil, led to his death on 8 March. Even though the Jacobites at home and abroad toasted 'the little gentleman in black velvet' who had brought about his death, the crown went not to the Pretender but to Princess Anne.

Anne
(1702–1714)

Queen Anne was the last of the Stuarts to sit on the English throne. She was a dumpy, badly educated little woman, but her Englishness and sociable nature made a pleasant contrast to her cold and difficult brother-in-law. Her keen interest in the Church of England ensured that many potential Jacobites among the clergy or the Tories saved any further plotting for after her death. The new queen was supremely unathletic, indeed immobile, suffering from gout so badly that she is the only monarch who has ever had to be carried to her coronation. But paradoxically it was during Anne's reign that the genius of her intimate friend Marlborough made England renowned for her military prowess, as the queen presided over victories which smashed to smithereens the hitherto unbreakable power of Louis XIV. Thanks to Marlborough's triumphs, England acquired the territories which constituted her first empire and transformed her into a formidable international presence.

Anne's reign not only coincided with the whole of the twelve-year War of the Spanish Succession. It was also the beginning of a century whose most prominent characteristic was its cult of reason. England's Glorious Revolution, when a mystical notion of Divine Right gave way to government by contract, had been a significant herald of this cultural change. The European phenomenon of the Enlightenment, as infatuation with logic was called, encouraged the belief that every problem, political, philosophical, practical, could yield to the application of reason. Only after the French Revolution revealed that reason could also have its dark side when taken to extremes did the fixation on logic begin to fade.

But such issues were far above the head of Queen Anne, who did not cultivate the company of thinkers. Simple domestic pleasures – card games, visiting gardens and intimate friendships – were her preoccupying interests. In 1702 her best friends were still John Marlborough and his wife, the imperious Sarah Jennings, who had dominated her since their schooldays. But it was extremely fortunate that Marlborough in effect now became ruler of England, for Anne's reign opened with the country in serious danger. It would be Marlborough whose gifts as a military

QUEEN ANNE.

OB. 1714

FROM THE ORIGINAL BY KNELLER IN THE COLLECTION OF
THE R⁺ HON⁺ᵉ THE EARL OF EGREMONT.

strategist saved England from a French-controlled puppet king. For while the French and the allies were roughly equal in number; Louis' army was the greatest fighting machine the world had seen for centuries, honed in battle over forty years. On William's death Marlborough not only took over the Dutch king's role as commander-in-chief of the Anglo-Dutch army, but also assumed William's all-consuming mission to destroy the French.

At stake was more than just the question of who dominated Europe. If Louis were to overrun Holland, as looked more than likely since the Spanish Netherlands to the south were now completely under French control, an invasion of England to put his Catholic candidate James III on the throne might be only days away. That would be the end of the Protestant monarchy, and of all the rights and freedoms the Glorious Revolution had enshrined.

Though England had at last produced a general in Marlborough skilful enough to defeat the Sun King, to begin with things did not look at all promising. Marlborough was considered to be one of the best staff officers in the English army, but he still had a reputation for being unscrupulous, over-ambitious and untrustworthy.

Worse still, at the start of 1704 the situation suddenly became desperate. The Elector of Bavaria declared himself for Louis and his grandson Philip V and allowed French troops into his country, thus opening up to them the valley of the Danube and the road to Vienna. With the aid of the Bavarians, the French were sweeping all before them so completely that they were seriously threatening to take the emperor Leopold I prisoner. If that happened Louis would have won, because the English and Dutch could not have carried on the war without the empire's soldiers.

Half the emperor's army, which should have been fighting the French, was putting down a revolt in his possessions in Hungary. The French were poised to capture Vienna and claim victory. From every quarter their armies were streaming, getting ready with the Bavarians for their last push. It seemed that nothing and nobody could prevent the fall of Vienna, for in the days before troop trains the 250 miles separating it from the rest of the allied army in Holland seemed insuperable: the Anglo-Dutch troops would not be able to get there in time.

Against this background of fearful anticipation, while Louis dallied in the great rooms of Versailles supremely confident of victory, Marlborough decided with the unexpected flair of genius to rush his army the 250 miles across Europe. His plan was to reach the French in Bavaria and defeat them before they got to Austria, and that is what he did.

Marlborough had two great problems. First of all, the key element of his plan was surprise. Not a word of where he was going could be allowed to leak out or the French would assemble a larger army in Bavaria to meet him. Therefore no one other than Prince Eugene of Savoy, his trusted opposite number, commander-in-chief of the emperor's army, was allowed to know about it. For this reason, to escape the notice of French agents and also the summer heat, Marlborough's army marched during the night and early morning, from three a.m. to nine. But Marlborough also had to keep his destination a secret from the Dutch, because they would have refused to allow him to leave their frontier undefended. Both the French and Dutch therefore believed that Marlborough was off to attack Lorraine or Alsace – until he turned east away from the Rhine, and they realized he was making for Bavaria.

Marlborough's journey was a breathtaking feat of organization. At each halt, fresh horses, food and guns met the troops whose morale was thereby maintained at a high level, and a new pair of boots awaited every soldier at Heidelberg. In similar fashion to Henry V, Marlborough was popular because he always looked after his men. Unlike many generals, he always led personally from the front, and he was well known, again unlike so many of his more callous contemporary commanders, for loathing unnecessary bloodshed. Moreover he never fought a battle unless he believed he could win it.

Marlborough's rendezvous with Prince Eugene and the Emperor Leopold's forces was across from the little village of Blindheim (Blenheim) on the upper Danube in Bavaria. All at once the French had to rush their troops there, forced to turn their attention away from capturing Vienna in order to prevent the allies from overrunning Bavaria. As the French looked across at the English in their distinctive red and white coats, massing more and more thickly in the marshy ground surrounding a little stream called the Nebel, the turn of events must have been alarming. The English were supposed to be by the North Sea in Holland, sixty days' march away according to conventional calculations. Yet here they were in the heart of Bavaria menacing them with their drums and their bloodthirsty roars.

Never had more hung on a battle for the allied commanders. For Marlborough it was the fate of England, for Prince Eugene it was that of his master the emperor. By 12 August the two greatest soldiers of their day, Prince Eugene, tiny, erect and exquisitely dressed, Marlborough always rather untidy and black with dirt from his forced march, had finished their earnest conference in a small white tent. Surprise had been the theme of this operation and now they decided to attack at dawn. The French still outnumbered the allies by 8,000 men. But by the suddenness of their onslaught and superior tactics the allies broke through the enemy lines to the central command post, causing the Elector of Bavaria to flee. The day was theirs. Twenty-three thousand French soldiers died and the allied forces took 15,000 prisoners. Marshal Tallard had to surrender too. For twenty years the French had been unconquerable in pitched battle; at Blenheim their reputation for invincibility was destroyed.

Marlborough, with his habitual casualness, scribbled a message of victory in pencil on the back of a restaurant bill and sent it to his wife, who like the rest of England was waiting anxiously for news. It took eight days for the news to reach London, but when it became known that Marlborough had defeated the Sun King and had prevented what everyone considered to be the imminent invasion of England, the country went wild with joy. Printers' presses were besieged with orders for facsimile copies of his note. So great a victory was it deemed to be that a special service was held at the new St Paul's built by Sir Christopher Wren and an enormous sum of money (plus a dukedom) was voted to Marlborough by Parliament. In gratitude Anne also gave him much of the land where the medieval royal palace of Woodstock had formerly stood in Oxfordshire, and the architect Vanbrugh was commissioned to design a palace worthy of the nation's saviour. It was called Blenheim.

This great victory had a beneficial effect in respect of Scotland. Anglo-Scottish relations had been in poor shape since the disastrous attempt by Scots to launch their own colonization programme at Darien in Panama in the time of William and Mary. The Darien scheme had been their answer to the English Navigation Laws which prevented Scots from trading with English colonies, but the lives of all the settlers were lost either to disease or to Spanish hostilities, as the Spaniards considered it to be their territory. The failure of the English government and the English colonies to send supplies to the ill-fated colonial experiment, or to do anything to help the Scots against the Spanish, left a residue of extreme ill-will. The Scots had duly taken their revenge in 1704. The external danger which England faced from Louis XIV obliged Queen Anne to agree to the Bill of Security, under which the Scottish crown would be given to a separate Protestant candidate unless Anne's successor on the English throne devolved his or her powers to executives from the Scottish Parliament.

The idea of another king in the north made Westminster distinctly uneasy: James III had only to convert to Protestantism and the Bill of Security would offer an opening for his return. But in the wake of Blenheim and the capture of Gibraltar by Admiral Rooke in 1705 the English government felt strong enough to raise the stakes with Scotland. Unless the Scots accepted the very beneficial proposals for Union now set out, and abandoned their plans for a separate monarchy, every native of Scotland settled in England or serving in the armed forces would be seized and held in prison as an alien. After Christmas 1705, what was more, no Scottish goods, manufactures or livestock would be allowed into England.

Just to show they were in earnest the government began massing on the borders of Scotland troops that were no longer required to be at the ready against Louis XIV. Ruin faced the Scots, but wealth and prosperity awaited them if they would surrender their ancient independence. There was little choice. An agreement was hammered out, formalized in October 1707 in the Act of Union, providing for one united Parliament and for taxation and

Blenheim Palace's tapestry of the Battle of Malplaquet, 11 September 1709, Marlborough's bloodiest victory during the War of the Spanish Succession.

coinage to be the same in both countries. The Scots obtained forty-five seats in the House of Commons at Westminster and sixteen seats in the House of Lords. They were permitted to maintain their separate legal system and the Presbyterian Church of Scotland, which the coronation oath would require the monarch to defend. Henceforth the prospect of lucrative trade with the colonies was open to all Scottish manufacturers. In the event the inhospitable nature of their own country, their gritty national character and their appetite for hard work meant that for the Scots the chief attraction of the English colonies was as places to emigrate to. Scots men and Scots women played a role out of all proportion to their numbers in constructing the British Empire.

From 1707 onwards, England, Scotland and Wales were known as Great Britain, and James I's Union Jack, composed of the combined crosses of St George and St Andrew, finally became the national flag. Anne thus became the first Queen of Great Britain. But the extreme distaste with which the majority of the Scots viewed the Union is indicated by the fact that during the next forty years Scottish Protestants did nothing to stop two attempts by Catholic Highlanders to put Catholic Pretenders on the English throne.

The years which followed Blenheim were marked by a string of astonishing victories for Marlborough and Prince Eugene – Ramillies, Oudenarde and Turin. The Sun King's grip on Europe was steadily weakened, almost all the Spanish Netherlands were taken over by the allies, and the French were driven out of Italy, enabling Leopold's son the Archduke Charles to be established in Milan and Naples. The harrying of Louis' grandson Philip V continued so successfully that Barcelona was captured, followed by Madrid, and the archduke was then proclaimed Charles III of Spain by the allied armies – only for the Spanish to beat the allies at the Battle of Almanza in 1707 and restore Philip to the throne. In 1711 the unexpected death of Charles's brother, the new emperor Joseph I, made the archduke the emperor Charles VI. The allies were now far less eager to see Charles made King of Spain, as they had no wish for the Habsburg Empire to combine with the Spanish. As a result the fighting dragged on with little enthusiasm.

At the beginning of Anne's reign a Tory government had been in office under Marlborough, with his close friend the Cornish politician Sidney Godolphin as lord treasurer, who was in charge of finding the money for the war, and Daniel Finch, Earl of Nottingham, a typical Tory High Churchman, as secretary of state. As the conflict continued, Godolphin and Marlborough found themselves increasingly alienated from their own party and moving closer to the Whigs because of their deeper commitment to the hostilities. To keep the Whigs onside, Marlborough and Godolphin found themselves beating off High Tory attempts to end the loophole allowing Dissenters to hold office by occasionally taking communion in the Anglican Church. But when they prevented a Bill against Occasional Conformity passing, Nottingham and his supporters angrily withdrew from government. While the Tories increasingly made 'the Church in danger' their rallying cry – playing on the fears of the Tory queen – Marlborough found it much simpler to govern with Whig ministers who never criticized the war. This earned him the undying hatred of his old party. They watched and waited and sharpened their knives, but as yet they could do nothing.

However, while more peers from the former Whig Junto joined Marlborough's government, and newer Whigs like an able young squire from Norfolk named Robert Walpole sifted documents in government ministries, the foundations of their power were being undermined both at home and abroad. The victory of Malplaquet in 1709, which cost the lives of 20,000 Englishmen, aroused no enthusiasm and the war became distinctly unpopular. Marlborough, the man commonly believed to have saved the nation, most unfairly acquired the nickname 'the butcher'. Still more unfairly, the queen herself soon turned against the Marlboroughs.

Throughout her reign Anne had lavished titles, jewels and houses on her beloved Marlboroughs, including the special honour of a lodge at Windsor. Sarah Marlborough, given the very powerful positions of keeper of the privy purse and mistress of the robes, had in her arrogant way considered them only her due. And for about six or seven years this way of life continued much as before. The Marlboroughs in their secret code were known as Mr and Mrs Freeman, while Anne and her husband Prince George of Denmark were called the Morleys. But the Duchess of Marlborough evidently began to tire of having to be continually at the beck and call of the demanding queen, whose martyrdom to gout and dropsy meant she could scarcely perform the simplest task for herself.

Sarah was delighted when a cousin of hers, Mrs Abigail Masham, who had become one of the queen's chief waiting women, did so well with Anne that she began to accompany her everywhere. The duchess encouraged Mrs Masham to take her place at court functions, and more importantly at the many tête-a-tetes the queen liked to enjoy with her ladies-in-waiting. Sarah, an impatient character, had had quite enough over the previous twenty years of comforting and being Anne's best friend and counsellor. The queen would use any excuse to follow Sarah to Windsor – she had no pride where her favourite was concerned.

But Abigail Masham was not the innocent creature she appeared. Not only was she Sarah Marlborough's cousin, she was also related to the Tory leader Robert Harley, with whom she was in cahoots. Quite soon Mrs Masham, who had specific instructions from Harley on how to poison the queen's mind against the Whigs, began to oust the duchess from Anne's affections. But when it was Mrs Masham to whom the queen turned for comfort over the death of her beloved husband Prince George, the duchess's jealous rage knew no bounds. Although Prince George was the brother of the King of Denmark, he had been looked upon with amused contempt by his royal relations. His painstaking hobby of making model ships in little closets all over the royal palaces was seen as no occupation for a grown man. Charles II had set the tone for the way he was treated at court by remarking, 'I have tried him drunk and tried him sober, and there is nothing in him.' His wife, however, adored him.

Sarah now banned Abigail from the queen's side just when she was prostrate with grief. Indeed she spent so much time and ink insulting the new favourite and quarrelling with Anne that the queen even wrote to Marlborough himself to beg him to ask Sarah to behave with a little more dignity and to see that her 'tattling voice' would soon make them both the 'jest of the town'.

Incredible as it was to seasoned court observers, Marlborough's own relationship with the queen, thanks to his wife's uncontrolled behaviour, was waning fast. Outside the royal apartments the Whigs feared with good reason that Abigail's whisperings were eating away at their government as well as at Marlborough's position.

Tory High Churchman Henry Sacheverell, whose 1709 impeachment for saying the Church was in danger under the Whigs brought a Tory government to power.

The government actually fell as a result of the Whigs' ill-thought-out prosecution of a Dr Sacheverell, a High Tory preacher whose sermons had attacked Dissenters, the Whigs and the Revolution settlement as pernicious to the Anglican Church. The queen took the keenest possible interest in the trial. Most unusually she attended it in person and was extremely offended by the Whig prosecuting counsel's speeches, which confirmed her view that the Whigs had little or no respect for the monarchy. Nor did the country at large care for the idea of Sacheverell being prosecuted in a country which prided itself on free speech – it smacked of the sort of tyranny the Whigs said they were battling in the war against Louis XIV.

By the time of the October election in 1711 Mrs Masham and Harley had so prevailed upon the queen that she had already dismissed most of the Whigs from government, even her old friend Godolphin, and replaced them with Tories. Victory at the polls under the banner of 'The Church in danger' confirmed that the Tories were now in power. Duchess Sarah had already been removed from her offices, for the queen could bear her rages and ungovernable behaviour no longer. But Anne showed herself once again the weak character she was when that same year she sacked the greatest servant of her reign, the Duke of Marlborough, from all his posts pending investigation of Tory charges of peculation or embezzlement. Though the charges were easily rebutted, Marlborough had had enough. Scarcely on speaking terms with his wife, wounded by the way he had been betrayed by the queen, he no longer wished to remain in England. He went abroad, never having lived at the magnificent palace built by the nation to commemorate his great victory. His bitterness was completed by the queen's refusal to grant him a last audience.

The game was at last in the hands of the Tories, led by Harley, a clever, dark, secretive little man. They were determined to end the war. The Jacobite second Duke of Ormonde was appointed commander-in-chief and in 1712 he obeyed the secret orders not to fight of the conniving Tory secretary of state Henry St John. This disgraceful campaign resulted in the defeat of Prince Eugene and the emperor Charles VI. All further help was withdrawn from both the Austrian and Dutch armies to force them to the peace table, while the essence of the English peace was separately and dishonourably obtained with France behind their backs.

Though Louis XIV remarked that 'The affair of displacing the Duke of Marlborough will do all for us we desire,' in fact with the Treaty of Utrecht in 1713 the Tories concluded the negotiations for an extremely profitable peace. The Whigs made a great deal of the Tories' shabby treatment of Britain's former allies but there was nothing they could do. Harley had been wounded by a would-be assassin, so the negotiating team in Paris was led by Henry St John, who became Viscount Bolingbroke that year. Bolingbroke, the best orator in the Commons and a completely unprincipled politician, nevertheless laid the basis for the future British Empire in the agreement he wrung out of the French.

By obtaining Newfoundland, the Hudson Bay territories and the former French colony of Acadie (newly named Nova Scotia in honour of the Scottish Union), Britain challenged France for dominance in North America. As well as thereby gaining a very strong naval position in the New World, Britain got Gibraltar and Minorca, which made her a powerful new presence in the Mediterranean. These colonies and possessions doubled her maritime trade, so that, having completely taken over the Dutch carrying business during the past half-century of sporadic war, she was on her way to becoming the chief trading nation in Europe. In the southern hemisphere, she added the island of St Kitt's to her West Indies possessions, and obtained a share in the shameful but lucrative slave trade with the Spanish colonies, known as the Asiento, as well as the right to send one ship a year of manufactured goods to South America.

The Treaty of Utrecht also tried to ensure that the crowns of France and Spain, so close in blood, could never be united. Austria under the emperor Charles VI received most of Spain's former external European possessions – the Spanish Netherlands, Milan, Naples and Sardinia – while the Dutch now had the right to garrison principal frontier towns such as Namur against the French. The dukedom of Savoy became a kingdom and acquired Sicily, while the principality of Brandenburg became the kingdom of Prussia – her rise to prominence in Germany as Austria's rival would form one of the dominant themes of the next two centuries. The treaty thus to a very large extent dictated the balance of power in Europe until the end of the eighteenth century. Nevertheless the era was to be dogged by international wars as Spain attempted to get back her former territories. For her part, France in her new race against Britain for colonies and trade would turn to what was known as the 'family compact' between the two Bourbon sovereigns.

The Treaty of Utrecht forced a by now very aged Louis XIV once more to recognize the Protestant Succession in England, which left the throne after Anne to the Electress of Hanover's heirs. But despite having played such an important role in the negotiation of the treaty, the scheming Bolingbroke had already made up his mind that he preferred the pretender to a foreign king. It was well known that there was no future for the Tories under George of Hanover. As one of the emperor's best generals, George remained extremely angry about the Tories' betrayal of the allies and had become closely connected to the Whigs. And it would be the Elector George the Tories would be dealing with, because it was clear that, like Anne, his eighty-three-year-old mother the Electress Sophia was not long for this world. Knowing therefore that the minute Queen Anne died they would fall from power, many other Tories were now openly leaning towards the pretender. Even while Bolingbroke had been in Paris negotiating the peace, he had also been in contact with Jacobite agents.

So cautious and careful were the actions of the Tory ministers that it is very hard to establish what sort of plot was being hatched, who was in on it, indeed whether there really was a concrete plot at all. Nevertheless, what does seem to have happened is that messages were sent by the Tories to the pretender in France, suggesting some kind of uprising when the queen died. But, though the Whigs were out of power, they had not lost their political nous. They prompted the ambassador of Hanover to apply to the House of Lords for George, the electress's son, to take up his seat in the House as Duke of Cambridge. Thus he would be in England in case of any attempts at a *coup d'état*. Anne, however, was so infuriated by discussion about the future heir, because of its painful associations with the death of her son, the Duke of Gloucester, that she sent a venomous letter to the Electress Sophia denying George permission to come over. This was said to have brought on the electress's final illness. She collapsed and died in the Herrenhausen gardens just seven weeks before Queen Anne, leaving George in direct line of succession.

Matters were moving fast in favour of the Jacobites and the pretender, and Anne did nothing to stop this because she could not bring herself to come out against her half-brother. At the bottom of her heart she also believed in the hereditary principle. A split had developed between Harley (now the Earl of Oxford) and Bolingbroke over the Schism Bill, which sought to prevent Dissenters educating their children in their own schools, Oxford himself being a Nonconformist. But the underlying cause was that ultimately Oxford supported the Hanoverians while Bolingbroke was a Jacobite. Mrs Masham thought she sensed a sinking ship and deserted her cousin for Bolingbroke's side. After a long, unseemly altercation between the two men in front of the dying queen, Anne dismissed Oxford and made Bolingbroke head of the government. The Jacobites felt that victory was practically within their grasp.

But just as Bolingbroke, now effectively prime minister, was perfecting his plans for revolution, they were ruined by the swollen, dropsical queen. Three days later, on 30 July, she had an apoplectic fit. It was clear that she could die at any moment. While Bolingbroke hesitated, for he needed a few more weeks to be utterly ready, the three Whig dukes of Somerset, Argyll and Shrewsbury seized the reins of government. As Bolingbroke's supporter Jonathan Swift put it bitterly, 'Fortune withered before she grew ripe.' While Anne lay dying and only semi-conscious in her great carved bed, she was persuaded to gasp out the name of Shrewsbury as lord treasurer.

Published by Harrison & Co May 1. 1793.

LORD BOLINGBROKE.

Henry St John, Viscount Bolingbroke, Tory Jacobite plotter who attempted to prevent the Hanovarian succession in 1714 on the death of Queen Anne.

With that authority, the minute Anne had breathed her last on 1 August 1714, the Whig dukes were able to proclaim the Elector of Hanover as King George I, having already called out the militia in the City of London and sealed all the ports. Bolingbroke allowed himself one rueful comment: 'In six weeks more we should have put things in such a condition that there would have been nothing to fear. But Oxford was removed on Tuesday; the queen died on Sunday! What a world is this, and how does fortune banter us!'

Thanks to the Whigs' presence of mind, the transfer of power from the government of Queen Anne to King George went perfectly smoothly. It was said that 'not a mouse had stirred against him in England, Ireland or Scotland'. So quiet was the country that the new king, the first of the

Hanoverian monarchs, did not appear in England until 18 September – almost two months after Anne's death. With his arrival the Tories would go into the wilderness for half a century, and England would be governed by a Whig oligarchy under the nominal authority of German kings.

The bitter politics of the last Stuart's reign had coincided with a new literary flowering. The fierce pamphleteering during the Civil War and the relaxation of censorship at the end of the seventeenth century had together honed a wonderfully sharp instrument in English prose. Some of the most striking invective and dazzling satire England has ever known was written in an eminently direct and natural fashion by writers such as Jonathan Swift and Daniel Defoe. Geniuses like Vanbrugh and Hawksmoor thrust up the houses of the wealthy in a striking baroque, not least that of Castle Howard, but the most memorable architecture of Queen Anne's reign, as befits its mild namesake, was a homely and restful doll's-house style, much influenced by the use of red brick in Holland. Also notable in Anne's time were the fifty new churches she commissioned.

Anne's simplicity, her gentle nature, her piety and the sad history of her seventeen children dying without reaching adolescence encouraged people to take her to their hearts. Her Englishness, which she had stressed in her first speech to Parliament, was a blessed relief after thirteen years of a Dutch king. It would be looked back on nostalgically during the reigns of the German Georges who followed her.

HANOVERIAN

George I

(1714–1727)

George I was fifty-four years old when he became King of Great Britain. Inevitably he was always more interested in Hanover in northern Germany, where he had lived all his life and ruled as an absolute autocrat, than in Britain, where he was constantly troubled by the vociferous House of Commons. Hanover, which was smaller than Wales, had only very recently been admitted to the first rank of German states when its ruler became one of the electors of the Holy Roman Empire. As such, it was considered somewhere of no importance by the English, whose country for three centuries at least had been one of the leading players on the European stage and was now poised for imperial grandeur. But the new king was Hanovercentric in the extreme. He saw everything from a Hanoverian point of view and thus considered it a great honour for Great Britain to be united to Hanover. This would also be the attitude of his son George II. The far sighted warned that England would be dragged into continental wars for Hanover's aggrandizement which were none of her business, that Hanover and her separate foreign policy might become the tail that wagged the dog. Nevertheless these were problems which had to be set aside as lesser evils than having a Catholic on the throne.

The English in 1714 were therefore forced to behave as if they had buried their xenophobic tendencies. A large turnout of the aristocracy in the Painted Hall at Greenwich welcomed the new king and his strange retinue of Turkish body servants captured at the siege of Vienna. With him were his very many Hanoverian ministers gabbling away in a foreign language. Those who spoke English had made it known in their slightly crude way that they were all looking forward to increasing their fortunes at the wealthy English court. For their part the English courtiers made jokes behind their hands about the very long, unpronounceable names of the Germans, which were generally held to sound like bad fits of coughing.

Though outwardly polite, the English political classes were fairly contemptuous of the German king – for he was a king not by Divine Right or by the Grace of God as the old phrase had it, but most definitely by act of Parliament and on Whig revolutionary principles. George I had been called to the throne by Parliament; if he failed to do his job right – for the moment at least, when he had no support in the country – he could equally be returned to Hanover. Furthermore the new king had no personal qualities to capture his volatile subjects' hearts and minds. He had inherited nothing of the Stuart charisma that had periodically shown itself through the generations, whether in Mary Queen of Scots or Charles II. It was hard to believe that he was the nephew of the legendary Prince Rupert of the Rhine.

George I was a German Brunswick through and through. He was small, pop-eyed and jowly, and his methodical German ways extended even to his dealings with his mistresses. There were two of them, both Hanoverian. One was hugely fat, the other thin and super-stitious. The English rapidly christened them the Elephant and the Maypole. Both passed every other night with the king, on a strictly rotating basis. Whichever mistress it was, the evening always passed in exactly the same way. A frugal supper having been consumed by just the two of them, they would play cards and listen to music. Then the king would begin his interminable cutting out of little silhouettes made of paper. The English thought he was insufferably dull, and his mistresses so ugly that they could see no point in his having them.

George I, the great-grandson of James I and first Hanoverian King of Great Britain and Ireland. He was the Elector of Hanover, brought to the throne by the 1701 Act of Settlement which created the Protestant Hanoverian Succession and passed over the Stuart dynasty.

Furthermore George I had a mon-strously vindictive side. He shut up his wife Sophia Dorothea of Celle for thirty years in virtually solitary confinement to teach her a terrible lesson for having an affair with the dashing Count Königsmark. It was said that he had had Königsmark killed and his body cut up and buried beneath the floorboards of his wife's dressing room for daring to make love to her. What is known for sure is that Königsmark was never seen again after he left his mistress one morning. The next day Sophia Dorothea found herself locked up in the castle of Ahlden, with only the swans on the surrounding grey waters for amusement. Her terrified ladies-in-waiting were informed that she was never to leave the castle until the day she was carried out in a coffin. Her little son, the future George II, was only nine when Sophia Dorothea was wrenched from the bosom of her family for daring to do what her husband openly did himself. When George was older, he tried to swim the moat to see his mother, but he was fished out by guards before he got very far. As a result the Prince of Wales regarded his father with loathing.

The new king could not be faulted for extravagance. He spent no money on public buildings or on living in great state, unlike his Whig ministers who built palaces for themselves, decorated by the finest craftsmen of the day. And though he famously said, 'I hate all Boets and Bainters,' he did not hate musicians. He brought Handel to this country from Hanover, where he was Kapellmeister, to become the royal court musician. In London Handel wrote much of his most celebrated work, including his *Water Music*, which was first performed at a concert on the Thames in front of George I's royal barge, and the *Messiah*.

George was too interested in Hanoverian affairs to address himself to English politics. He was unable to understand much English and having to discuss government business in Cabinet with his ministers in poor French and worse Latin was an effort he did not care to repeat very often. Frequently absent in the beloved homeland for up to half the year, he left the country to be ruled by the Cabinet. As a result Cabinet government, or government by ministers rather than by the monarch, which had been developing very fast under Anne, rushed forward in leaps and bounds under George I and George II. George I did not realize that into the deft hands of the Whig chiefs, the heads of those grand landed aristocratic families who had been accruing power since the Revolution, he was delivering privileges which even under Anne had been the prerogative of the monarch. Thus it was the Whigs who now determined the composition of the ministries, who decided when the Parliamentary session should end and who distributed the vast panoply of lucrative offices at the disposal of the crown which ensured men's loyalty.

It was not until the era of George I's grandson, George III, who was born in England, that the Hanoverians became wise to what was going on. George III took it upon himself to claw back the crown patronage appropriated by the Whig grandees, but for two generations, during the reigns of his father and grandfather, they controlled everything in the name of the king. The Whig oligarchy thus remained in power from 1714 to 1760, an astonishing forty-seven years. For all that time the Tories were in the wilderness, heavily tainted with Jacobitism by their Stuart sympathies and by the conduct of their leader Bolingbroke, who on George I's accession had fled to become the Pretender's chief adviser.

More than ever, it was the House of Commons within Parliament which mattered. The two great figures of this period, Sir Robert Walpole and

William Pitt, owed their prominence to their mastery of it. Walpole, a twenty-stone Norfolk squire, controlled its members by straightforward bribery, while the slender, sarcastic Pitt made them do his bidding by outstanding oratory. Both of them accepted peerages and moved from the Commons to the Upper House only when they recognized that their time had come. For under the first two Georges, the tendency that had been developing from Charles II onwards became a fully fledged political principle: the country was governed by the Cabinet via the system of party government which had been growing up over the previous two reigns. In other words, the Cabinet, consisting of the king's ministers with seats in either the Lords or Commons, had to belong to the party which had a majority in the Commons.

George I's frequent absences in Hanover led to another important constitutional development: during his reign there first grew up what became known as the office of prime minister. This was the chief executive who could take decisions in the king's absence. For twenty years, George's reign and that of his son George II were stamped with the imprint of the extraordinary prime minister who carved out this office, Sir Robert Walpole. Hated by many of his contemporaries for his greed, his cynicism and his astonishingly widespread system of bribery and corruption, Walpole nevertheless succeeded in his objective of establishing a climate of peace and stability within which the fragile new Hanoverian dynasty could grow. Convinced that the Stuarts would always seize the chance to take the side of Britain's enemy in wartime and achieve a restoration by the back door, he became notorious for his refusal to go to war. He therefore skilfully if unscrupulously skirted attempts to bring Great Britain on her allies' side to honour treaty commitments. He kept peace with France for twenty years and charmed the Tory squires into becoming Whig supporters by the low taxation that flowed from avoiding foreign wars. Thanks to Walpole's shrewdness and careful nurturing, the Hanoverian dynasty pushed deep roots into British soil.

Nevertheless, in many households throughout the country there remained an emotional attachment to the Stuarts as the rightful dynasty. Tory squires would make secret toasts to James II's son, 'the king over the water', by passing their wine over a glass of water. Walpole, the consummate realist, was anxious to ensure that that remained the limit of their physical activity; he believed that if he tolerated this form of Jacobitism he would slowly reconcile England to the Hanoverians.

Even so, less than a year after George I arrived in England Jacobitism flared into a dangerous rising known as the Fifteen. By late spring 1715, there was an ominous mood in the country which in the summer turned into riots, with mobs calling for 'James III and No Pretender'. In September it burst into open rebellion at Braemar in Scotland under the Earl of Mar, when he raised the standard for James III and VIII.

As well as Anglican squires who could not overcome their instinctive dislike of a foreign king, the Stuart cause flourished among recusant Catholic families as a result of the Stuarts' loyalty to the ancient faith. Such families were better able to cling to their forbidden religion in out-of-the-way places than in central England, so Jacobitism was strong in the west and north of England. But the greatest concentration of Jacobites was in Scotland, where a significant number of both Lowland and Highland lords were for once united against the Hanoverian king and yearned for the ancient House of Stuart. To all these parties the Jacobites in France began sending messages, concealed in gloves, sewn up in coat linings, instructing them to be ready to fight for their rightful king when he landed on his own soil – which they promised would be soon. It was in Scotland that the Jacobite plotters under Bolingbroke decided the uprising should begin.

But nothing in the ill-fated rising of the Fifteen went according to plan. Most calamitous of all, the French troops promised by Louis XIV never materialized. With appalling timing – or what might be called the blessing of history on the Hanoverians, like the Protestant east wind of William III – five days before the Earl of Mar raised the Stuart standard, the Sun King died. The French government was now headed by the pro-Hanoverian regent, the Duke of Orleans, who put paid to all hopes for troops to back the pretender. Mar was thus stranded in Scotland, having raised the Highlands, but quite unsure of what he should do next. He needed military support in England, but this grew less and less likely. In the face of the Jacobite threat a Riot Act had been passed, enabling magistrates to arrest any gathering of twelve or more people if they failed to disperse after a proclamation ordering them to do so had been read out. The government used it to the hilt to arrest many of the southern ringleaders.

But by November after the Battle of Sheriffmuir near Stirling, fought between Mar's 10,000 men and the government's 35,000, it became clear that George was in little danger. Apart from being outnumbered, Mar was a feeble general who retreated when his soldiers believed that one last charge would have won the day. Too late in December 1715 did the pretender arrive, but his own person did nothing to raise his armies' spirits, for he was a very solemn, tall, white-faced young man with none of the Stuart magic expected from the legendary king over the water. The refined, French-educated pretender was in turn horrified by the appearance of his most fervent supporters, the Highlanders. To him they were filthy savages, with whom he could scarcely bring himself to converse.

Perhaps the pretender could have achieved something if he had marched south, but Mar gave the order to retreat north to Perth after Sheriffmuir, and after that the Fifteen was lost. On 16 January 1716 the rebels melted back north, and on 4 February Mar and the prince abandoned their romantic followers. They took a boat for France, leaving the leaders of the northern English and southern Scottish rebellion, Lords Derwentwater, Kenmure, Nithsdale and others, to be beheaded.

The whole episode had been so mismanaged that the government granted a general amnesty, and the Scots were scarcely punished at all. But the English Catholic lords like Lord Nithsdale were viewed as a potentially serious threat, and the government and George I decided to make a proper example of them.

There was still enough anti-Hanoverian feeling in England for many people to feel that it was quite monstrous that Englishmen should be executed by a German king who had only recently arrived in the country. George increased his unpopularity when it was announced that he intended to hold a ball on the night before the beheadings. Fortunately for Lord Nithsdale, his wife was a woman of spirit who was not going to stand by and see her husband executed for an affair of honour which she believed most English people should have been involved in anyway. She had seen the king at a dance a few nights previously, and, greatly daring, had bearded him in a small anteroom. Unable to control her tears at the thought of her husband in the Tower of London with only days to live, she had fallen on her knees before the king. 'Spare his life, Sire,' she cried, 'and he will become the most loyal of your servants.' But the king brutally pushed her aside and ordered his guards to throw her out.

This story, which quickly made the rounds of the court, was regarded as outrageous, that an Englishwoman and the wife of a great English landowner should be treated so by a mere Hanoverian. There was considerable sympathy and delight when it was heard that the enterprising Lady Nithsdale, not a whit discomfited by her ordeal, had picked herself up, wiped her tears away and hotfooted it to the Tower. With her ladies' maid, and another woman, she had persuaded a guard who was softer-hearted than the king to let her in to say her goodbyes to her husband. The guard, made jolly with port that she had thoughtfully brought with her, scarcely noticed that when the attractive Lady Nithsdale left, she actually had three female companions with her rather than the two with whom she had arrived. As dawn broke, the sleeping figure of Lord Nithsdale was revealed to be a mere bundle of rags. Thanks to his wife's daring, that evening he was drinking wine in the sweet air of France, while the heads of his unluckier companions were no longer attached to their bodies.

Though the Old Pretender remained alive he now had to find a safe berth other than his old home, France. The regent Orleans with an ailing boy-king Louis XV on his hands and with designs on the throne himself was anxious to have the Hanoverian government as his ally. If Louis XV died he would need English backing to claim the French throne, against its nearest heir the French King of Spain, Philip V. And in fact it was in Spain that the pretender found a warmer reception for his cause. It tallied perfectly with the Spanish chief minister Cardinal Alberoni's burning desire to resurrect Spain's former prestige as a world power which had been destroyed by the Treaty of Utrecht. The pretender was Spain's chance to get her revenge on the English.

At the battle of Cape Passaro in 1718 the English had once again stymied Spain's plans for supremacy in the Mediterranean, where her soldiers had seized Sardinia and Sicily, by defeating the Spanish fleet. Alberoni was so angry about Cape Passaro that he retaliated by taking up the cause of the pretender. He interested King Charles XII of Sweden in the plot, who was furious with George I for buying the ex-Swedish duchies of Bremen and Verden from Denmark. Charles XII was one of the greatest generals of the age, and if he had appeared in the Highlands at the head of an army the Hanoverians would really have had something to fear. But once again destiny seemed determined to keep George on the throne, because Charles XII died quite suddenly before this new plan got off the drawing board. Alberoni's last attempt to put the pretender on the throne was in 1719 when 5,000 men under the command of Ormonde sailed for Scotland, but only 300 men reached her shores and they were soon defeated at Glenshiel.

The scare the Fifteen had produced resulted in a flurry of legislation to stabilize matters by strengthening the government. The Septennial Act increased the Whigs' hold on power by providing that henceforth elections were to be called every seven years instead of every three; it lasted until 1911. One of George I's principle secretaries of state, General Stanhope, veteran of the last war, by contriving a new Quadruple Alliance of France, England, Holland and the emperor Charles VI forced Spain to the peace table. Removal of the troublesome Alberoni was one condition England laid down. Without Alberoni's patronage the pretender was once again condemned to roam Europe, looking in his usual rather half-hearted fashion for sponsors for his great enterprise. He at least had the consolation of having recently fathered a little boy, Prince Charles Edward, so the Stuart direct line would continue.

George I's first government had originally been made up of a mixture of old Junto Whigs like Marlborough's son-in-law the Earl of Sunderland and the brave and distinguished Stanhope. Stanhope, his aide John Carteret and Sunderland were the sort of Whigs William III would have recognized, ones who believed in the need for England to play her role in Europe. But the government also included a new generation of Whig statesmen, of whom the most important were Lord Townshend and his brother-in-law

Sir Robert Walpole, who was then chancellor of the Exchequer, and they split with Stanhope over continental involvement. In many ways these two men were more like Tories than Whigs, given that their priority was to put the country's finances on a sounder basis by avoiding wars and foreign entanglements of all kinds. After their break with Stanhope, who was now in effect chief minister, they retreated to their estates in Norfolk to bide their time. Any free hours they had in London were now passed at Leicester House, the home of the Prince of Wales, as they were building an opposition round the 'reversionary interest', as the party of the heir to the throne was known. It was not to be long before they were recalled by George I.

Whatever Stanhope's diplomatic gifts, in many areas his government was unsatisfactory. But it was above all in financial matters that the administration was to come a cropper, for the bluff ex-soldier did not exercise sufficient control over his ministers, and in 1720 the crisis of the South Sea Bubble burst. This was a financial scandal of great magnitude, a side-effect of ministers' new-found enthusiasm for getting people to buy shares in government enterprises to pay for public borrowing. Inspired by the Whig Bank of England's success in paying for the wars in 1711 under Harley, the Tories founded the South Sea Company to take over £900,000 of the National Debt in return for a monopoly of all the trade to South America granted to England at Utrecht.

The company was a joint-stock company: that is, people invested money and received a good dividend in return. Its directors aspired to manage the whole of the National Debt, which stood at the then enormous sum of £52 million, thanks to the cost of the French wars. With commissions it was a lucrative business and in 1720, by bribing government ministers, the South Sea Company was given permission by Parliament to take over half of it. The directors of the company proceeded to enrich themselves by persuading government stockholders that they would do better to exchange their state bonds for South Sea stock.

The combination of advertisements promising an opportunity to make enormous profits in the South Sea Company compared to government stock and of government ministers themselves backing the South Sea stock proved irresistible. The price of the shares skyrocketed, and everyone from dustmen, shopkeepers and chambermaids to merchants and MPs bought some. People behaved quite crazily: many of them borrowed the value of their house and belongings together and then bought shares with the borrowed money. Very few resisted the temptation to make so much apparently easy money, though the ageing Duchess of Marlborough said publicly she believed that 'This Bubble will soon burst.'

By the winter of 1721 South Sea shares were yielding an astonishing thousand-pound dividend. But the company started to issue writs against other companies which were trying to cash in on its success, and this had a catastrophic effect on the market. For what happened was that confidence was lost in all ventures, especially the South Sea Company. The market crashed, so did share prices. With the collapse of the South Sea Bubble, people were wiped out overnight; hundreds of thousands of people faced bankruptcy. Panic and distrust of the government swept the country, particularly when it emerged that government ministers had accepted bribes to promote the shares. One minister committed suicide, and the chancellor of the Exchequer, John Aislabie, was thrown out of the House of Commons for corruption. Stanhope died of a heart attack from the stress, while Sunderland was under investigation. The whole of England was verging on hysteria.

Meanwhile, in Norfolk, the ex-chancellor Robert Walpole continued calmly to run his estate and get on with his own business. Pleasant echoes

Sir Robert Walpole, all-powerful Whig prime minister to the new dynasty, later 1st Earl of Orford. Bust by John Michael Rysbrack.

of what was becoming an increasingly deafening chorus of demands that he should be brought back to rescue the government reached his sylvan retreat by every mail. Every newspaper called for him to save the nation. Walpole was the man who had spoken out about the dangers of the mania for speculation. He had 'bottom'; he was a sensible politician with a real grasp of finances. Sunderland bowed to the inevitable, and on the back of the South Sea Bubble Walpole rose to supreme power. He was asked to take over the reins of government, and from then on he conducted himself brilliantly.

Sir Robert, as he soon became, abandoned the court of the Prince of Wales without a backward glance. With his brother-in-law Townshend he restored confidence to the country and sorted out the government finances. For the rest of George I's reign there was peace at home and abroad. The economy made a rapid recovery, helped by the new trading opportunities opened up by Utrecht. One of Walpole's greatest clevernesses was to make it very easy as time went on for most Englishmen to become Whigs. By the mid-century the number of Tories in the House of Commons had been reduced to sixty. Walpole even managed to placate the die-hard Tories by leaving the Church settlement unaltered – one of his favourite mottoes was 'If it's quiet, don't disturb it.' Though he personally believed in freedom of religion, he saw no point in upsetting the High Church elements by removing the Test and Corporation Acts which other Whigs had openly pledged to abolish. Equally he saw no reason why Nonconformists should suffer from civil disabilities, so every year he passed an Act of Indemnity for everyone who had violated the Test Act, enabling Dissenters too to hold office. This was a typical piece of subtle Walpolean compromise: it didn't quite please everyone, but it pleased everyone enough for it to work.

Under the managing influence of such a clever, worldly man, the urge to restore the Stuarts died out quite rapidly. Though it remained a dangerous buried coal, it would require a great deal of activity to blow it back to life. How unvital it appeared is indicated by the fact that Francis Atterbury, Bishop of Rochester, was not executed in the wake of an abortive Jacobite conspiracy but merely banished. Even Bolingbroke was allowed back into the country, though he was banned from the House of Lords.

With the kingdom in such capable hands it was much easier for George I to spend several months each year out of the country relaxing at his old court of Herrenhausen, which he found far more appealing than anything London could offer. In 1727, when the first Hanoverian king died from a massive stroke at Osnabrück in Hanover, England remained quiet and peaceful and no Jacobite rising disturbed the straightforward and easy transfer of power from father to son. It was the middle of the night when Walpole brought the new king the news that his father was dead. It must have been a curious scene. Walpole, who was by now extremely large, had to lower himself with some difficulty to his knees to hail his new sovereign. George II, half asleep and pulling his breeches on, said crossly, 'Dat is von big lie.' He had consistently been denied any responsibility by his father, who had always refused to make him regent in his frequent absences, and he could not believe that he was now to be king.

Even the slick and imperturbable Walpole suffered a few days' anxiety that George II would dismiss him from office, as he had hated his father so much and saw Walpole as his father's man. In fact George offered the job to a nonentity named Sir Spencer Compton, but his sensible wife Caroline of Ansbach, who was a close friend of Walpole, managed to convince him that it was in his best interests to keep Sir Robert as prime minister. George II was crowned with Walpole stage-managing everything in his usual competent way.

The old king was buried in Hanover. No one mourned him very much, except the 'Maypole', now Duchess of Kendal. She had been very worried about his health ever since news had come that Sophia Dorothea, the unfortunate prisoner at Ahlden, had died. It had been prophesied by a fortune-teller that the king would pass away within a year of his wife, and as a result the duchess had been terrified by every omen. But though she was overcome with grief she was said to have a new consolation at her villa at Isleworth. A large black raven had flown into her house shortly after the king passed away and she became convinced that it contained his soul. Many stories circulated of how she could be seen curtseying to the raven and listening deferentially to its croaks – until she died not long after of a wasting disease.

George II

(1727–1760)

In most ways George II was a far nicer man than his father; like George I he was a brave soldier, but taller and better looking. He spoke better English too, sometimes acting as his father's interpreter with the English ministers. The first two Georges took such a close interest in the British army that it was the one institution that experienced some attempts at reform in an era very careless about public services. Discipline was improved, and the system of outfitting was overhauled. Commendably George II did not approve of the English practice of purchasing commissions, believing that the holding of a command should be merited. The success of British arms during the Seven Years War of 1756–63 which sealed the First British Empire was due in no small part to the Hanoverian influence.

One of the first things George II did when he became king aged forty-four was, rather touchingly, to put a portrait of his unhappy mother on display. (No one knew he had secretly always carried a miniature of her in his pocket, which he liked to take out and gaze at when he was alone.) The new king's experience of England so far had been punctuated by humiliating rows between himself and his father. They culminated in George I threatening to have the then Prince of Wales arrested at his first son's christening. Fortunately a great deal of soft pedalling by the prince's clever, flirtatious wife Caroline of Ansbach managed to avert this.

Caroline of Ansbach had not been at all in awe of her late father-in-law, but she could see that she and her husband had far more to gain if he ate his pride and was on speaking terms with his father than if he was at daggers drawn. Blonde with a magnificent embonpoint and intellectual tastes (she corresponded with the leading philosophers of the day for amusement) Queen Caroline enjoyed ruling George II. She even tolerated his apparently insatiable appetite for mistresses – English ones, she opined, at least would teach him better English. Throughout her husband's reign she continued to urge him to entrust himself utterly to the suave Walpole's wisdom. For his part Walpole commented pleasantly, 'I have the right sow by the ear.'

But, despite his own suffering at his father's hands, George II's atrocious relations with his own son and heir Frederick, the new Prince of Wales, who arrived from Hanover to live in England aged twenty-one in 1728, were no less a source of scandal. That intimate observer of the Georgian era Horace Walpole, Robert's son, remarked that 'it was something in the blood' which prevented the Hanoverians from getting on with their heirs. After a quarrel with his parents, Frederick, or 'Poor Fred' as he was generally known, actually carried his wife out of their palace while she was in the middle of labour, to prevent his first child, Princess Augusta, being born near the hated pair.

Just as before, the opposition of out-of-office Whigs and Tories soon began to gather at the court of the new Prince of Wales at Leicester House. By the mid-1730s Frederick, Prince of Wales was its official sponsor. This had the beneficial effect of creating the 'loyal opposition' which of course was loyal, after its fashion, to the new dynasty, though its antics drove Walpole mad with rage. And antics they were, ranging from endless satires to plays and cartoons that poked fun at the prime minister. The truth was that, by unscrupulous use of spies and corruption, by both charming and browbeating the decent, straightforward, new king and his worldly wife, the quick-witted and cunning Walpole had absolute control of the country, just as he had under George I. What was new and admirable about Walpole (though there was much to appal) was that he valued peace and the wealth and progress it created, when most other European statesmen of the eighteenth century were interested only in the easy glory of war.

Sir Robert Walpole was one of the most talented managers of Parliament that England has ever seen, and he was as greedy for power and wealth as his huge girth and many houses (including the nonpareil Houghton, his country house) suggest. His two chief henchmen were the Pelham brothers, one of whom, Thomas, Duke of Newcastle, was the most talented fixer of elections in the history of Parliament. An apparently hesitant, scurrying figure, who looked, one wit said, as if he had lost half an hour somewhere and was busy looking for it for the rest of the day, the duke was a very shrewd judge of men, unequalled in the black arts of power-broking and using the government machinery for patronage. Like his master Walpole, Newcastle believed that 'Every man has his price, it is only a matter of determining it.'

Walpole decided that the only surefire way to keep the Whigs in power and the Stuarts out was to use bribery to secure the adherence of the political and official class of both parties, whether it was by places in ministries or lord lieutenantships or the bench or money itself. MPs used to come to his office to receive handouts in gold. For all its corruption, this system brought real tranquillity to a potentially unstable country whose ruling dynasty had been introduced not much more than a decade before. And Walpole controlled it all with unprecedented efficiency. Nothing could be done, at least at the beginning of his rule, to prevent him driving whatever bills he wanted through the Parliament he handled so exquisitely.

But Walpole also pleased the Whigs' natural constituency, the merchants and financiers, with his wholesale reform of the tax system. He was not just the hearty, hunting-mad squire who preferred to be in the saddle for eighteen hours a day, as his supporters liked to portray him. He was a real product of the Enlightenment. Though a coarse man, he was also a coldly intelligent one, convinced that any problem could be solved by the application of reason. It was practically a religion with him to get rid of the bumbling methods of the past, the red tape stifling the new businesses, and to apply scientific analysis to trade and industry and the reform of the tax structure. He and his officials in the ministries, who were frequently distinguished Fellows of the Royal Society, were obsessed by the new science of statistics.

In order to promote England's manufactures and foreign trade, booming since Utrecht, Parliament was persuaded to abolish many of the import duties on raw materials as well as almost all export duties. What the Treasury lost at source it would gain in personal taxation. In other words, the government would reap more revenue from the pockets of the energetic businessmen who were causing fabulous wealth to flow into the country. Trade was growing dramatically more than it ever had before and changing society in the process.

The people with money were no longer the landed gentry, whose money came from farming. In the England of the 1730s wealth was moving to the City, to the traders, to the enterprising merchants arranging deals abroad, as evidenced by the massive increase in shipping. But though wealth was shifting into the hands of the merchants who were creating it, the tax structure reflected the past: the bulk of the money raised by the Treasury still came from the land tax, which fell heavily on the gentry, whereas merchants tended to live in cities and have their wealth in cash. Walpole changed all that. Though he belonged to the Whig party, his family background was that of the naturally Tory small-landowner class – many of his friends and many of his friends' fathers had been ruined by the land tax, which had quadrupled as a result of the French wars. He now shifted the tax burden to the new wealthy. His sympathy for his fellow squires, the Tory backwoodsmen, was another factor damping down their desire for a Stuart on the throne again, as they saw how good Walpole was for their interests.

Commercially and financially Hanoverian England could not have been flourishing more vigorously. At the same time, with the amoral prime

Bishop Joseph Butler, the influential theologian and moral philosopher, whose 1736 *Analogy of Religion Natural and Revealed* defended revealed religion against the Deists.

minister to set the tone, the country slipped into a period remarkable for the corruption of its public officials. The Church of England gave no lead: it was becoming a respectable occupation for the brother of the local squire, and very squirelike and unpriestlike the parson became in his comfortable Georgian rectory. It was only towards the middle of the eighteenth century that Methodism revived the religious zeal of the past. The lord chancellor Lord Macclesfield was even tried for selling judicial appointments. Many justices of the peace were connected to the criminal underworld by a kickback system, or were involved in the smuggling business which was sometimes arranged by entire villages. At Porthgwarra near Land's End in Cornwall the deep tracks of a permanent pulley system may still be seen today where the best local families, and the worst, connived to outwit Customs.

Because there seemed no end to this system, a system without shame, the only recourse of the opposition was to satire. When one of George I's mistresses sold the right to create a new copper coinage for Ireland to a highly unsuitable businessman named Wood, Dean Swift responded with *The Drapier's Letters* (1724). George II's court was clearly the thieves' kitchen in John Gay's *The Beggar's Opera*, with Walpole as its chief character MacHeath, the swaggering highwayman. Very sharp practice was the rule of this infinitely hard-edged, commercial, godless and ruthless age, so similar to our own, where the only sin was failure, and success was worshipped.

Without wars to fight and blessed with low taxation, the British concentrated on domestic trade by improving the country's communications. The enthusiasm for building canals, which would see 3,000 miles cut into the country by the end of the eighteenth

George Whitefield, evangelical preacher who inspired John Wesley and helped begin the eighteenth-century religious revival.

century, had started by 1720. Stone roads were laid. Travel through the country became much faster, increasing profits for both merchants and farmers able to sell to a bigger market. For the aspirant middle classes, the successful tradesmen moving away from living over the shop, whose burgeoning wealth meant their wives had servants and were freed from household drudgery, the first circulating library was opened in Edinburgh by Allan Ramsay in 1726. Its imitators that sprang up nationwide soon featured that celebration of middle-class life, the novel, as it began to emerge under Fielding and the bookseller Samuel Richardson. The middle classes had the money to attend to their health, and at the same time indulge their new *amour propre* by rubbing shoulders with national leaders of fashion in the pump rooms of Bath. Bath's regular crescents and squares were built on Enlightenment principles with bigger windows to let in the light and closer attention to hygiene. But despite these material improvements for the fortunate, even to its contemporaries the age of Walpole appeared a sleazy period for manners and morals. Its crudity and cruelty were epitomized in the work of William Hogarth, notably in *The Rake's Progress*, painted between 1733 and 1735.

John Wesley, the founder of Methodism.

Against such a background, it was remarkable that those who were uncorrupt and disinterested continued to flourish at all. For more high-minded currents did exist in Walpole's England. The spirit of philanthropy was represented by the Tory James Oglethorpe who in 1732 founded Georgia as a new colony in America for people released from debtors' prison. The Wesley brothers began to revitalize the Church of England in the late 1730s, in a movement known as Methodism. Their charismatic preaching, devotional faith and infectious enthusiasm provided comfort for many like the poor whose lives on earth were very harsh, and who were not served well by a Church which had lost much of its mission.

One member of the opposition determined to resist the snares of the Walpolean system was the extraordinary young MP William Pitt, the other dominant figure of the reign of George II. By the mid-1730s the theatrical Pitt had made a name for himself as an exceptional speaker. Despite the little that has survived of his speeches in an era before shorthand or television or radio, he is considered by historians, as he was by his contemporaries, to have been the greatest orator the House of Commons has ever produced. He was part of the opposition to Walpole who called themselves Patriots and claimed the moral high ground in the face of his cynicism. Unlike the Stuarts, Walpole never tried to avoid Parliament – indeed the Parliamentary system developed to an unparalleled extent under him. Nevertheless his use of bribery and corruption was believed by the Patriots to have ushered in a new kind of tyranny.

Walpole called them contemptuously the 'Patriot boys', with all that that suggests of juvenile and foolish behaviour. But by the mid-1730s they consisted of the most impressive of the Whigs – William Pulteney, Carteret, the diplomat and wit Lord Chesterfield, the aristocrat Grenville brothers and their brother-in-law William Pitt himself. Pitt's maiden speech attacking jobbery in the government was so striking that Walpole had his army pension removed, in hopes that he would be muzzled. But Pitt was not at all embarrassed by financial hardship. He drove around town in a shabby old carriage, publicly proclaiming his poverty in pointed contrast to the ostentation of Walpole's wealthy placemen. He became the scourge of Walpolean sleaze, denouncing corruption, placemen and yes-men.

Walpole's talent for hogging the limelight ensured that for the next decade there were constant defections of the more talented members of government to the opposition. The prime minister ultimately preferred to have all the glory himself. He soon drove out from the Cabinet any MP with too independent a voice, like the talented foreign policy expert Carteret, whose command of German was so good that there had been a real risk he might supplant Walpole in George II's counsels. Many others, like Pulteney, left because they disapproved of Walpole's foreign policy, which was predicated on friendship with France even if that meant ignoring treaty violations. In 1730 Townshend, who as Walpole remarked had previously been the 'senior partner' in their relationship, found the going too hard against the ambitious Walpole and retired from government to experiment with his cattle on his country estates. 'Turnip' Townshend made his name for posterity by discovering the value of turnips as a winter feed.

Chief among the mischief-makers of the mixed opposition of Tories and disaffected Whigs was the ex-Jacobite Bolingbroke, whose shenanigans continued to be tolerated by the unruffled Walpole. The minute Walpole had allowed him back into the country Bolingbroke had begun his scurrilous polemical magazine the *Craftsman*. Dedicated to insulting Walpole, the 'man of craft', it called on all patriots to establish higher standards in public life, and was intended to revive the Tory party and make them fit for office. Bolingbroke's booklet *On the Idea of a Patriot King* was eagerly embraced by the heir to the throne, Frederick, Prince of Wales, the idealistic young man with intellectual tastes who headed the

Patriot movement. In fact Poor Fred never became king, predeceasing his son, the future George III, after succumbing to pneumonia in 1751. But that son, having absorbed all these ideas, saw himself as the Patriot king, and from 1760 onwards would try and replace aristocratic Whig power with the 'King's party'.

Balked of power, deprived of action, the opposition through the *Craftsman* had their revenge on Walpole by taunting him with insults and obscene cartoons. Though he was always trying to have the printers and editors thrown into prison for abuse and slander, they usually managed to find some sympathetic judge who released them. Walpole was so infuriated by *The Beggar's Opera* and a profusion of theatrical farces about him, many by the novelist Henry Fielding, that he passed the Licensing Act in 1737. This made the lord chamberlain the censor of the British theatre, without whose licence plays could not be performed. That role was not abolished until 1968.

Walpole was not only the first head of the government to be called prime minister, he was also the first prime minister to live at 10 Downing Street. Its spare, unostentatious elegance is symbolic of the power of the Whig oligarchy: George II might wear a crown and live in a palace, but the real power was exercised behind the façade of what looked like a quiet gentleman's townhouse. It resembled a large number of housing developments being built all over Georgian London, still to be seen today in Bloomsbury and Islington. They were lived in by a remarkably successful upper class of Georgian gentlemen and their wives, whom foreign observers thought remarkably caste-free. The English aristocracy intermarried uninhibitedly with wealthy City families in a way that was unimaginable on the continent.

The first real check to Walpole, the English Colossus (one of the many nicknames by which the omnipotent prime minister was sourly known), took place in 1733 when he attempted to stymie the flourishing smuggling industry. There was no point trying to increase the customs duties paid when goods entered Britain, as that was where the smuggling came into play. Having no little experience of illegally imported French brandy himself, Walpole saw that the only solution was to tax the article at retail level and transfer tobacco and wine from Customs to Excise.

Ever since it had first been invented by the Long Parliament, Excise had had a bad name because of the brutality of the Excisemen. It was entirely up to them to decide what tax was to be paid, and they collected it with menaces immediately after they had made their inspection. All over the country angry Englishmen and women cried that it would be bread and cheese next if the government was starting to tax wine and tobacco. English liberty was at stake. The opposition, with its obscene and savage cartoons in the *Craftsman*, had primed its audiences well.

There was a very ugly mood in the capital not only among the poor, but in the city itself. A mob surrounded the House of Commons to make sure that the bill did not go through, and burned Walpole and Queen Caroline in effigy. Walpole himself made a humiliating escape through the back door of a coffee house. When he saw his majority sink to sixteen on the second reading, he withdrew the bill: the consummate pragmatist had seen the writing on the wall. He would not spill blood to get taxes, he said. Walpole continued in power for another nine years after this, but his monolithic state began to crumble.

The rock upon which Walpole actually foundered was the very policy that had made him so successful: his avoidance of war. Maintaining friendly relations with France and Spain for eighteen years despite some provocation had made the country prosperous, won elections and kept the Stuarts out. But by the late 1730s all the merchants and businessmen in the City of London who had been Walpole's greatest supporters believed that what was needed against Spain was not peace but war.

Britain's trading success in the South American markets – a Spanish preserve since Cortes – opened up by Utrecht had infuriated the Spanish. Although technically the English were allowed to send one ship a year to trade at the great market of Porto Bello, which was the entrepôt for South America, in practice the ship was accompanied by a great many other less official ships, which reloaded the one ship as she emptied. With the British government turning a blind eye to its nationals' illicit behaviour at Porto Bello, the Spaniards' only recourse was to carry out forced searches on all British shipping, since every British vessel was suspected of smuggling.

The English newspapers outdid one another with lurid accounts of Englishmen in Spanish jails suffering tortures worse than those inflicted by the Spanish Inquisition for simply plying their trade. By the late 1730s the Spanish coastguards' habit of stopping and searching in an aggressive and violent fashion had become a silent war between the two countries. British businessmen believed that it needed to be recognized as such.

They no longer wanted adroit avoidance of hostilities – they were champing at the bit to use war to break into new markets, to get into South America and import her gold and silver. The City of London and the opposition saw the hidden hand of France behind the Spanish attacks on English shipping; they were sure that Walpole was being bamboozled by France, that what England was facing was not so much rivalry with Spain as a battle for trade and colonial supremacy with France. Walpole's foreign policy was also alienating his master George II, because it had greatly weakened Austria. Like his father, as an elector of the Holy Roman Empire George II was loyal to the emperor in Vienna and believed that Austria must always be backed to limit the power of France. Then in 1737 Queen Caroline died. She had been Walpole's greatest supporter, and from her death he had more difficulty in clinging to power. The tide was running against him.

By contrast, Pitt in his daring, his brilliance and his arrogance encapsulated the mood of British merchants. War against France at the beginning of the century had won Britain the trading supremacy conferred by Utrecht. War with Spain was necessary now. When in 1739 Walpole would have been happy to accept Spain's offer of compensation, put forward in the Convention of Pardo, for rough handling of British seamen, Pitt swayed the House of Commons against him. There could be no more half-measures. Quivering, slender, furious and dressed in his customary black Pitt told the House from the opposition benches that the Convention of Pardo was 'a surrender of the rights and trade of England to the mercy of plenipotentiaries'. The complaints of England's despairing merchants were the voice of England condemning Walpole's policy of peace at any cost. 'If that voice were ignored,' he warned in a sibilant whisper, 'it would be at the government's peril; it *must* and should be listened to.'

He sat down to a storm of applause, which was echoed next day in every newspaper. The Duchess of Marlborough let it be known that she had left Pitt a legacy in her will to point up Walpole's pusillanimity and show that Pitt was her husband's natural successor. In 1739 Walpole reluctantly opened hostilities in the war which is known as the War of Jenkins' Ear. Britain's ostensible *casus belli* was that one of her nationals, a Captain Jenkins, had had his ear cut off during a search when his ship was sailing through Spanish waters. But that had been back in 1731. It was simply an excuse.

Despite the great national excitement, the war did not open well. Though Porto Bello was captured, with the loss of only seven men, the few skirmishes were completely indecisive. In the middle of all this, a general election fell. Walpole scraped back into office, but it was with a very small majority. He was soon defeated on a vote of no confidence and in 1742 he retired. Much of his administration remained, including the Pelham brothers, but the foreign policy expert Lord Carteret, who had long languished in opposition, returned to power for two years under Prime Minister Spencer Compton (now Earl of Wilmington), propelled by his knowledge of continental affairs. For Carteret's rise and Walpole's fall were both the effect of a new war which had begun on the continent in 1740, the War of the Austrian Succession.

This soon superseded the War of Jenkins' Ear. It had opened with the upstart kingdom of Prussia's outrageous seizure of mighty Austria's duchies of Silesia. Prussia was then a struggling north German state, but her soldiers and military traditions were shortly to become the wonder of Europe. Austria, however, was the home of the Habsburg emperor, whose dynasty had dominated the German-speaking lands of the continent for the past 300 years.

The figure behind the capture of Silesia was the twenty-four-year-old Frederick II of Prussia, whose father had died only a few months earlier. He had taken swift advantage of the accession of the young and inexperienced Maria Theresa to her father Charles VI's hereditary dominions to rush his troops into the duchies of Silesia to the south of Prussia, claiming them as his own. He followed this up by defeating the Austrians at the Battle of Mollwitz. It was a fantastic humiliation for Maria Theresa and Austria, the great Habsburg power, to be defeated by the House of Brandenburg. Though all the emperor's allies had signed the Pragmatic Sanction, a treaty which announced the indivisibility of all the Austrian possessions left to Maria Theresa, Prussia had no intention of honouring it.

Where Prussia led, other states followed. France and Bavaria, which had much to gain from dismembering the Austrian Empire, signed an alliance with Prussia. Maria Theresa rode to Hungary and rallied the Hungarians to her side, but the situation looked bleak for her. The whole German continent was in uproar, while the remnants of Austrian power in Milan were now harassed by Spain and Sardinia. For the first time in three centuries the electors had chosen as Holy Roman Emperor a candidate who was not a member of the House of Habsburg, preferring the Elector Charles of Bavaria whose armies were running amok all over Maria Theresa's lands.

Both George II and the foreign secretary Lord Carteret agreed that this time treaty obligations to Austria should be fulfilled now that there was no Walpole to prevent it. Large subsidies were paid to Austria to help her hire troops to defend herself. A spate of negotiations by Carteret, the most gifted diplomat of his generation, removed Prussia from the war. He persuaded Maria Theresa to let Frederick keep Silesia. In return Frederick guaranteed George's precious Hanover against the French. George himself, who was an ex-professional soldier, in person led a large army consisting of English, Hanoverian and Hessian troops to the Low Countries to attack the French and keep them away from the main theatre of war in the imperial lands. Wearing a yellow sash over his armour, the colours of Hanover, the king was victorious at the Battle of Dettingen in 1743. But it could no longer be disguised that everything that Walpole had feared had come to pass. Britain and France were once more at war, with all the expense and disruption which that entailed.

Dettingen did a great deal of good for George II's reputation in England

– though some courtiers had to stifle yawns at his hundredth retelling of the battle. In the short term the French were frightened back across the Rhine. But over the next two years things began to look quite shaky for the Hanoverians. Walpole had said privately to friends when Britain exploded with patriotic pride as the war against Spain opened, 'They are ringing their bells now, but they will soon be wringing their hands.' He was right. French spies had reported to their government that there was still a lot of support for the Jacobite cause in England. Once again, as Walpole had always predicted they would, the French prepared to invade England and spark off a general rising to divert her from the Austrian War.

Their plans were defeated in 1744 by a great storm. Only tempestuous winds, what Pitt called 'those ancient and unsubsidized allies of England', prevented a French army landing on Britain's coast. It was to have had the son of the pretender, Prince Charles Edward Stuart, known as the Young Pretender, at its head. But French military success in the next year, 1745 – the swingeing French victory over George II's second son the Duke of Cumberland at Fontenoy, when the Dutch ran away and the British and Hanoverians were hopelessly outnumbered – prompted the French to concentrate their efforts in the Low Countries and to abandon the plan to conquer England and restore the Stuart line.

But their supposed puppet candidate, the twenty-five-year-old Prince Charles Edward, was not so easily put off. He was as spirited and courageous as his father had been sad and uninspiring. With Britain distracted by war it seemed the optimum moment to win back his ancestral lands. So began the Forty-five rebellion. With only seven men but 1,500 muskets, twenty small cannon, ammunition and 1,800 broadswords clanking in the hold, the prince landed at Moidart on the west coast of Scotland in late July 1745. He at last exerted in his handsome person the extraordinary Stuart charm that always cast such an ill-fated spell over its audience.

Prince Charles Edward Stuart, known as 'Bonnie Prince Charlie' and the 'Young Pretender', because he was the grandson of King James II. His Jacobite army invaded England in 1745, but was turned back at Derby.

Many Highlanders doubted the wisdom of the enterprise without French backing, but the government in England took the threat extremely seriously. There was concern at the highest levels about whether there were enough guards to defend the royal palaces. The prime minister, Henry Pelham, who had taken over from Wilmington and Carteret because of the poor progress of the war, anxiously sent word to George II that he must return from Hanover. There seemed to be a level of disaffection among the people which might be turned into hostility towards German George and a welcome for the Young Pretender.

Bonnie Prince Charlie, as he was becoming known, seemed to have luck on his side. By the end of September he had taken both Perth and Edinburgh, and had inflicted a comprehensive defeat on the English general Sir John Cope at the Battle of Prestonpans outside the latter city. Until Prestonpans there had been a debate within the government whether the situation really merited recalling the troops from the Austrian Netherlands. Now it was deemed a first-class emergency. The British army would have to be back in London to defend the capital before Bonnie Prince Charlie got there.

Meanwhile many of the prince's advisers urged him to declare Scotland's independence, to wait for the arrival of reinforcements from France and reorganize his troops. But, carried away with his own success, the prince could think only of London. Avoiding Newcastle and General George Wade, Charles made for Carlisle. On 14 November it surrendered. Two weeks later the Scots entered Manchester. However, all was not well. Huge numbers of Highlanders, homesick away from their native glens, had deserted between Edinburgh and Carlisle. The English Jacobites, such as the Duke of Beaufort and Sir Watkin Wynn, refused to rise in the south because there was no French invasion to back them up.

Though the rebellion was doomed, it did not seem so when the tartan army streamed into Derby, only 127 miles from London. Even though government forces were closing in from behind, there was now just one army between Bonnie Prince Charlie and the capital, and the crown. So desperate did the situation seem, with reports of the Highlanders having their broadswords sharpened at a blacksmiths in Derby, that there was a run on the Bank of England. George II put all his treasures on a yacht in case he had to flee to Hanover.

It all changed at Derby. The prince was for pressing on to London. Who knew what would happen if there was a pitched battle with George II? But his advisers convinced him to retreat: Scots and Irish soldiers in the service of the French king had arrived in Scotland, and they preferred to regroup and launch another assault on England the following year. Meanwhile Wade and the Duke of Cumberland were getting far too close behind him. Cumberland was in Staffordshire. The rebels therefore limped back towards the northern port of Inverness on the Moray Firth, where reinforcements were believed to be awaiting them. But the Scottish army was running out of steam, money and arms, while Cumberland's men were having new boots and good food sent up to them from boats which landed daily on the Scottish coast. Even the Highlanders, austere though their lifestyle was, were completely exhausted by the time they faced Cumberland's men on Drumossie Moor at Culloden in April 1746. It was a cold windswept plain above Inverness, with no natural advantages for the defenders and a very poor place to give battle. It was Bonnie Prince Charlie's choice. His military advisers tried to dissuade him, but he paid no attention.

Though the celebrated, bloodcurdling whoops of the Highlanders were only a faint echo of the sounds which had terrified the people of Derby, the kilted warriors still managed to break two regiments of Cumberland's front line. But after that it was a massacre. Culloden was a battle decided by firepower. The well-fed, well-armed redcoats who outnumbered the Jacobites by 3,000 men destroyed the clans. Those who were alive fled, hobbling along secret ways across the mountains to the west coast and then on to fishing boats to France. Back at the battlefield Cumberland gave orders for the wounded rebels still lying on the field to be bayoneted to death, earning himself the name of Butcher.

The prince himself made for the Western Isles and would have been captured on South Uist had he not been rescued by a brave local lady named Flora Macdonald. She dressed him up as her maid, and very peculiar he looked too, because like his great-uncle Charles II he was exceptionally tall. For five months Prince Charles Edward wandered the west of Scotland like his followers, trying to evade the government soldiers. In an orgy of revenge, to terrorize the locals into betraying Bonnie Prince Charlie's hiding place, the soldiers raped their women, took their cattle, destroyed their humble dwelling places, burned their lands, and broke their ploughs, with the result that many of these crofters died from exposure and famine. To the English government's fury, although the reward on Bonnie Prince Charlie's head was £30,000, not one of the Highlanders betrayed him.

At last Charles managed to find a boat willing to take him back to France via Skye, and he bade a grateful farewell to Flora. The famous song 'Speed bonnie boat, like a bird on the wing, over the sea to Skye, carry the lad that's born to be king over the sea to Skye' refers to this moment. But the prince, who was emphatically not born to be king, would live on for another forty-two years until he died at last in 1788 in Rome. By then a sad drunkard, full of fond reminiscences of his adventures, he was a curiosity to travellers doing the Grand Tour. But in his gross, swollen features the observer could see no trace of the youth who had fired a nation to arms.

Old age was something few of Prince Charles's followers lived to enjoy. This time, as far as the Hanoverian government was concerned, the Jacobites had come far too close for comfort. Severe measures were taken

Thus to expire be still the Rebells Fate While endless Honours on brave WILLIAM waits.

Published according to Act of Parliament Sept. 29th 1746. by ye Proprietor R. Forrest &c. Sold at ye Plume of Feathers in Windmill Street, S. James's London, prob. by whom may be had a curious Print of ye Duke for a Watch-Case.

William Augustus, Duke of Cumberland, second son of George II. He was called Butcher Cumberland for his treatment of the Jacobites after he defeated them at the Battle of Culloden, which ended the '45 rebellion. The print shows a dying Highlander in the tartan, which along with all other Highland customs, were forbidden after the '45.

to deal with them and make sure such a threat never arose again. The Highland way of life was proscribed. The wearing of tartan to mark clan memberships was forbidden; the chiefs' important hereditary sheriffdoms and jurisdictions which had made them a law unto themselves were abolished. No Highlander was allowed to carry or own a sword, small arms or rifle, and where there was even the remotest suspicion that they had been Jacobites they were thrown off their land. Although some of these holdings were returned forty years later, that did not help those who lost their homes and had to rely on the goodwill of relatives for their daily bread. The leaders were all executed on Tower Hill, including the wily old Lord Lovat. He had hedged his bets, pretending to be loyal to King George II while sending his son to fight for the prince. Though he was eighty-three years old, Lovat managed to escape to a mountain cave in a glen leading to the west coast before he was betrayed.

But though the last of the Stuart threats to the Hanoverians had been conclusively dealt with, abroad the war went on. Though the Austrian Netherlands had been completely overrun by the French, they had not succeeded in breaching the United Provinces defences. At the same time, under Admirals Anson and Hawke Britain had regained supremacy of the seas. The French lost Cape Breton, the eastern tip of Canada, and its capital Louisburg to Britain; they had been captured by the American colonists. By now it was clear that the two chief protagonists of the War of the Austrian Succession were France and Britain, with Maria Theresa's Austria playing a poor third and minor role. In all this the war with Spain had been forgotten. In fact the Treaty of Aix-la-Chapelle, which at last ended the war in April 1748, did not even mention the original cause of the War of Jenkins' Ear, the Spanish right to search British boats.

The treaty restored most of Austria's territories to Maria Theresa. Nevertheless the empress was outraged by the way she had been treated. Frederick of Prussia kept her Silesian duchies, while Sardinia took some of the Milanese, and she had to give Parma to the King of Spain's younger son. Though the war had been fought on her behalf, Austria had come off worst of all the countries.

Prime Minister Henry Pelham presided over a country growing ever more prosperous. The Old Pretender was expelled from France, whose rulers once again recognized the Protestant Succession. The Battle of Culloden had truly ended the threat of the old dynasty supplanting the new. When the Old Pretender died in 1766 even the pope did not hail the once bonnie prince as King Charles III. By his tact Pelham held together the old coalition of the Whigs as before. His premiership saw Britain in 1752 adopt the improved Gregorian calendar and lose eleven days in the process. The calendar had been calculated in the sixteenth century by Pope Gregory XIII, to correct errors in the old Julian calendar – it had taken Britain only one and a half centuries to join the rest of western Europe.

But if the Protestant Hanoverian dynasty and thus Parliament and the Revolutionary Settlement were at last secure – the next Hanoverian would have an English accent and pride himself on being British – the threat from France had not vanished. The rivalry was intensifying in two different arenas: among the trading posts of the two great powers in India, several oceans away, and in the colonies of North America. In the coming world war France and Britain would battle it out for colonial supremacy – and Britain, though she was a quarter the size of France, would emerge the victor. By the end of the Seven Years War she would control immense territories on two of the seven continents, and have become an empire encircling the globe.

While Pelham's government cut back the army for peacetime conditions, in India the struggle continued between France and Britain to fill the power vacuum caused by the death of Aurangzeb, the last Mogul emperor of India, some forty years before. Previously the European settlements which had been founded round the coast of India since the sixteenth century had been no more than trading stations within the local rulers' territories. The companies which went out to India saw themselves as merchants only. They were not *conquistadores*, a role which would in any case have been impossible under Mogul rule.

Under the auspices of the East India Company, the English settled at Madras on the south-east coast, at Bombay and at Calcutta, which was founded at the end of the seventeenth century as Fort William, beside a branch of the Ganges. Interspersed with these English 'factories' or trading stations were those of other nations: the French in particular had factories at Pondicherry in the south near Madras, and in the north-east near Calcutta they founded another one named Chandernagore. But by the 1740s the many warring Indian principalities into which the Mogul Empire had disintegrated had become a battleground for English and French influence. The Marquis de Dupleix, the French governor-general, had embarked on a programme of training the local Indian peoples, who were known as sepoys. Dupleix's schemes for a few French leaders with guns and money gradually to dominate India's immense continent was about to bear fruit. His candidate for the nawabship of the vast Karnatic region of southern India, which contained both Madras and Pondicherry, was poised to take the throne. Most of southern India would now be in effect a French colony.

At the same time the enormous, unpopulated tracts of virgin land in North America lying to the west of the eastern seaboard became another flashpoint between France and England. From 1749 onwards the French built forts along the Rivers Ohio and Mississippi and the Great Lakes, to pen in the English colonists and prevent new settlers moving west into the empty prairies beyond the Ohio Valley. When Pelham died unexpectedly in 1754, the covert enmity between the French and English settlers in North America had just erupted into a frontier war. The Virginians, led by Major George Washington, a young Virginian plantation-owner, tried to destroy Fort Duquesne. It was the opening move in their campaign to prevent the French putting limits to their expansion.

Over the next two years the fighting grew so furious that it became clear that it would have to receive official recognition from the two mother countries, and reinforcements were sent out by Britain and France, before war was declared once more in May 1756. In India, too, the undeclared race to control the great subcontinent was given official sanction by the French and English governments. There British morale had been hugely improved since 1751 by the astounding exploits of a former clerk of the East India Company called Robert Clive. Clive had foiled Dupleix's attempt to control the Karnatic by capturing its capital, Arcot. He had had no military training whatsoever, but he was a voracious reader who spent all his spare time learning about battle tactics, and from Arcot onwards he put his studies to amazing effect. Clive had audacity, charisma and strategic judgement in equal quantities. With only 200 British soldiers, many of whom were raw recruits just arrived from England, and 300 sepoys, he gave such heart to his troops that they marched fearlessly into enemy country and captured Arcot without losing a man.

Although General Dupleix returned with massive Indian and French reinforcements to besiege Arcot, under Clive's indomitable leadership, the British and their sepoy allies kept the army of 3,000 men at bay for fifty days. In the end Dupleix had to retire, because Clive's men simply refused to give in. Notably heroic was the behaviour of the sepoys, who declined to drink any of the last supplies of water, believing that Europeans had more need of it than they. The siege of Arcot passed into legend. Dupleix was disgraced and left for France, and Britain controlled most of the Karnatic.

Not only was Britain at war in India and America, she had also begun very unsuccessful hostilities in Europe. The three wars together are known as the Seven Years War. The underlying cause of the European war was Maria Theresa's continued obsession with the duchies of Silesia. Outraged at the way she had been treated by her former ally England, in order to retrieve the duchies from Frederick II she allied herself with her old enemy France, as well as with Russia and the Elector of Saxony. Although George II disapproved of his aggressive nephew Frederick, he saw intense danger in the new line-up of Catholic powers on the continent. Accordingly, in January 1756 the king agreed to a defensive alliance between Great Britain and Prussia.

But the dynamic Frederick the Great, as he became known, was not going to wait to be attacked by the great powers now surrounding him. In August 1756, he once again started a war in Europe. He invaded Saxony, seized the war-plans detailing Prussia's dismemberment and published them in the newspapers as justification for his own behaviour. As Prussia, Britain's only ally, struggled against the invading armies of France,

Austria, Saxony and Russia, bad news came from every part of the globe. Though Clive in India followed up Arcot with a series of victories, the situation seemed to be turning in favour of the French; the same was true in America. News had just arrived of the tragedy of the Black Hole of Calcutta, in Bengal in north-east India: the Nawab of Bengal, Siraj-ud-Daula, one of the chief allies of the French, had overrun the English trading post and shut up its defenders in a tiny jail. One hundred and forty-seven prisoners had died of suffocation overnight. In America the French forts on the St Lawrence and Ohio were holding the line against the English colonists, and inflicting serious damage on them.

In Europe the situation was yet more alarming. Hanover had been overrun: the king's second son, the Duke of Cumberland, had been forced to sign the Capitulation of Klosterzeven, handing over George II's beloved electorate to the French. The French fleet had triumphed over the English navy, traditionally its superior. It had captured Minorca, the best harbour in the Mediterranean, owing to the incompetence of Admiral Byng, who had been sent with a fleet to relieve it. Though Byng was the son of the man who had won the great victory of Cape Passaro, he was cast from a less glorious mould. Flushed with success, the French were now mustering boats at the Pas de Calais to invade England. The country was on the brink of catastrophe, and no one seemed able to take control, as the government had been riven by faction ever since the death of the tactful Henry Pelham in 1754.

The new prime minister was his brother Thomas Pelham, Duke of Newcastle. Despite his reputation for being the great fixer of elections, Newcastle did not have his brother Henry's social gifts and could do nothing to smooth relations among the Whigs. His rudderless government drifted hopelessly from crisis to crisis, with the whole previously secure basis for British life unravelling. The country was thrown into what can only be described as a blind panic: the City of London and many other cities sent deputations to the king begging him to do something about Britain's grave lack of defences. The government, desperate to be seen in control and to find a scapegoat for their hopelessness, had Admiral Byng shot on the quarterdeck of his own ship. As Voltaire said dryly, it was 'pour encourager les autres'.

There was just one man who the nation believed could save them, and that was the universally popular Pitt. As Dr Johnson observed, while Walpole was 'a minister given by the king to the people', Pitt was the 'minister given by the people to the king'. Pitt had been harping on for twenty years about the need to increase the numbers and training of the militia at home and to stop relying on German mercenaries. But he was still only a minor minister and, as far as the king was concerned, one who had irredeemably blotted his copybook by his past attacks on British involvement in the War of the Austrian Succession. Pitt's Parliamentary speeches decrying money spent on continental quarrels had guaranteed his sovereign's unrelenting hatred. 'It is now too apparent that this great, this powerful, this formidable kingdom is considered only as a province of a despicable electorate,' Pitt had memorably said, and George II could not forget it.

Pitt never bothered to dress up his contempt for George II's Hanoverian commitments nor to conceal his belief that Britain should be absolved from having any part in them. The taxpayers' money would be much better employed on defending the American colonists from the French. Pitt had been furious when the war against Spain had been superseded by the War of the Austrian Succession. Britain's war should be on the sea, traditionally her most successful element, and the battles fought for trade.

Despite the almost insuperable enmity of the king, it began to be clear as the government's reputation disintegrated that only Pitt could restore its authority. Pitt alone, the Great Commoner, as he was nicknamed for calling ministers to account in the House of Commons, still possessed a reputation, as he had done since he first denounced Walpolean jobbery and sleaze. Though cities all over the country were calling for Pitt, still the king hesitated. He gave in only when his sensible mistress Lady Yarmouth, on whom the sight of mobs drilling in London had a chilling effect, said that he must choose Pitt or lose his throne. Pitt's terms were quite unpalatable to George – he insisted that he personally be responsible for policy – but the resignation of Newcastle over Minorca in 1756 forced the king's hand. The Duke of Devonshire took over the government, but it was Pitt who in effect became head of it.

Though Pitt's weakness was that he did not command a sufficiently large faction in the House of Commons, as Newcastle did, his strength was the overwhelming personal support for him in the country at large. He had complete confidence in himself and in his ability to breathe that confidence back into the nation. 'I know that I can save the country and that no one else can,' he said.

Unlike the rest of the government, Pitt had a comprehensive plan for the war. For the previous eight years he had been paymaster-general under Henry Pelham, because the king would not have him as war minister. Traditionally this post was a way, as Walpole expressed it, of 'putting a little fat on your bones': in other words, the paymaster-general made money by creaming a percentage off each government transaction. But Pitt had refused to take anything other than a ministerial salary. Instead he used the office to accrue information about British trade and settlement abroad. Everything he read over those eight obscure years consolidated his beliefs about the need for war with France to defend Britain's trade.

If Walpole was the great eighteenth-century minister for peace, Pitt was the great minister for war. In his breadth of knowledge, his daring and his success, he is comparable only to leaders on the scale of Marlborough or Churchill. It was Pitt's vision that pulled a triumphant war effort out of a country which had forgotten how to fight after years of reliance on German mercenaries. Pitt breathed new life into services that had decayed under Walpole's placemen in ministries, whose neglect long after he was gone had left Britain's ships rotting at quaysides.

A Bill for a National Militia was passed to raise soldiers to defend the country against the French invasion and beef up the numbers of an army which was pitifully small compared to the French, thanks to the British fear of a standing army in peacetime. Pitt ignored question-marks over the Scots' loyalty in order to take advantage of the fact that they were the best natural soldiers in the country and raised two Highland regiments. He believed that, if their native aggression was given an outlet against Britain's enemies, it would prevent a repeat of the Forty-five. These new troops should be used to assault the coast of France to distract the French from their fierce attacks on Prussia. Prussia herself was to be given an enormous subsidy for troops, as well as a British army in Hanover to protect her from the French. Under the generalship of Frederick the Great, Prussia was the one power which could keep the French at bay and the only German state worth subsidizing.

However, one of the army's most senior commanders, the Duke of Cumberland, was, like his father the king, allergic to Pitt. When told that he was to take the orders of a man who had spent twenty years insulting the sacred name of Hanover, he refused to serve under him. This gave George II the excuse he needed to get rid of Pitt, whom he continued to loathe. But when the king attempted to form a ministry without either Pitt or Newcastle, he found that it was impossible, for the one was supported by the voice of the people and the other by a majority in the House of Commons. As George prevaricated for eleven weeks, from all over Britain the most important corporations sent Pitt boxes of gold as symbols of their support.

In the end the king bowed to the inevitable. Pitt was back in, with Newcastle running the House of Commons for him with his patronage and his majority. Technically Newcastle was prime minister and Pitt secretary of state, but the real prime minister who took all the decisions (frequently over the heads of the chiefs of staff) was the Great Commoner himself. It was not a moment too soon for Pitt to return to the helm. Finally his plans began to pay off. The King of Prussia rewarded Pitt's faith in him when he heroically defeated the assembled might of those European colossuses the

French and the Austrians, and held off the Russians. Ferdinand of Brunswick, meanwhile, in charge of the allied forces in Hanover, protected his western flank. To those who now complained about the vast expense of the German continental campaign, Pitt replied that it was for once justified: the French had to be tied down in Europe so that they could not send too many troops to America and India. 'I will conquer America for you in Germany,' he told the House of Commons.

Pitt believed that with sufficient encouragement Britain's much larger colonial population in America could even the odds vis-à-vis France, which was four times her size and whose army was in mint condition. In order to drive the French off the North American continent, every colony should be organized for total war. All the state assemblies from Georgia to New England would be encouraged to raise their own militias and send men to fight. Tactfully Pitt gave high commands to American soldiers, though they had had none of the professional military training of the British. A propaganda campaign was launched at the American colonies to create a spirit of mutual endeavour between them and the mother country, without which Pitt knew the war would be lost – hitherto the colonies had considered themselves to be quite unconnected to one another.

In 1758 Pitt sent out a bold new American expedition of huge dimensions and astonishing ambition. It was a three-pronged attack on Canada, France's largest settlement, centring on Quebec. Pitt believed that once Quebec was captured, Canada would fall to the English, and French power in North America would collapse. British and American troops were to come from New York in the south, the west and the east, the latter via a seaborne landing. The eastern expedition was intended to recapture Louisbourg, the strategically important capital of Cape Breton Island, and the western operation was to take back Fort Duquesne as Braddock had failed to do. Meanwhile, under Lord Abercromby, the British were to advance up the Hudson river from New York and destroy all the French forts guarding the route north.

To the surprise of many senior military staff, the task was entrusted to the command of young officers. But they were men in whom Pitt had seen leadership qualities – an ability to think the unthinkable and improvise under fire. All the officers he plucked out to command expeditions turned out to be superb generals. And they were inspired by Pitt himself. He imbued them with his own sense of purpose, of fighting for the Protestant free world. Louisbourg, the gateway to the St Lawrence, was captured that year against all the odds, chiefly because of Brigadier Wolfe's bravery in establishing a beachhead under fire. From then on British arms triumphed. Fort Duquesne, the site of Braddock's ambush, which would have been the key link between the French colonies in the south and

Canada, was taken by John Forbes in a single assault and renamed Pittsburg. Meanwhile Colonel Bradstreet, a celebrated New Englander soldier who was known for his rapport with the Indians, captured the important Fort Frontenac. From then on the forts on Lake Ontario fell one after another, until the capture of Fort Niagara brought the Great Lakes under British control.

But the most astonishing feat of arms in the American campaign was the capture of Quebec by the thirty-three-year-old Wolfe, now a general. Letters detailing the British plans of attack for Canada had been stolen, so the Marquis de Montcalm, the gifted French commander, had enough time to move troops down to Quebec from Montreal further upriver. The city was bristling with guns and soldiers when the British arrived. Worse still, by the time the superb sailors among Wolfe's team had picked their way up an often dangerously shallow river (they included James Cook, soon to become famous for his discoveries in the South Seas), Montcalm and his men had positioned themselves quite perfectly above them. Quebec was built on a headland known as the Heights of Abraham, and French troops were disposed round the citadel guarding every approach.

The only possible way into the city was therefore up the sheer cliffs rising from the St Lawrence to the Heights of Abraham. These great escarpments of chalk loomed impregnably above the British. Even if they could be climbed, and in any case there seemed nowhere to land from the river below, the French would be able to pick them off as they ascended. No one even considered the possibility of getting enough men up the cliffs to fight a battle, certainly not the 5,000 British soldiers whose tents sprawled as far as the eye could see on the south bank of the St Lawrence.

The rest of the summer of 1759 was spent by the British gazing at the city as it sparkled tantalizingly above them. The situation in their camps was made more gloomy because General Wolfe was coughing blood incessantly into a bowl by his bed, a victim of consumption. It had become clear to many from his emaciated looks and hacking cough that he was not long for this world. For most of that summer, his brigadiers were near despair, as day after day passed and Wolfe could not emerge from his tent. The season was ticking on. Autumn would soon arrive and once the St Lawrence froze all plans would have to be postponed until the following year when spring melted it again. The men could not be left indefinitely outside Quebec.

The few orders Wolfe did give seemed to make no difference. The canny Montcalm would not be lured out of his eyrie to protect the villages surrounding Quebec which Wolfe ordered his men to attack. The bombardment of Quebec from below had no effect. An attempt to storm Montcalm's camp had been hopeless. Wolfe became so ill that he could

The Taking of Quebec, 1759. Under the command of General James Wolfe, in the middle of the night, British troops scaled the cliffs leading to the Heights of Abraham where Quebec stood. Shortly after, the French were driven out of Canada.

scarcely lift his head, and he asked his seconds-in-command to draw up their own plans.

Then at the end of the long hot summer, when for a short time the consumption went into remission, the old Wolfe showed himself. He had

444

an audacious plan, a gambler's plan, the sort of plan that Pitt banked on his commanders having as a last resort. On a trip along the St Lawrence, Wolfe had noticed a tiny inlet the river had carved into the cliffs; he believed that if his soldiers could land there at night, they could scale the cliffs under cover of darkness and surprise the French in the morning.

At dead of night, Wolfe led the 5,000 British and American soldiers with blackened faces silently downriver in rowing boats till they were opposite the Heights of Abraham. As he was borne along the treacherous river whose rocks and shoals made it a hazard to all but Quebeçois, Wolfe softly read out his favourite poem, *Elegy Written in a Country Churchyard* by Thomas Gray, published only a few years before, a copy of which his fiancée had just sent out to him from England. His thin face, touched by moonlight, seemed to wear a beatific expression as he murmured the sonorous words whose Romantic, melancholic spirit echoed his own. As the mysterious cliffs loomed up ahead and the men rested on their muffled oars, Wolfe closed the book. 'Well, gentlemen,' he said, 'I had rather have written that poem than take Quebec.' But then he leaped overboard, into the swirling St Lawrence, and ran ahead of them until his was only one of the many tiny figures on the vast cliff face pulling themselves up by ropes.

When dawn rose over Quebec, Montcalm awoke to see on the plain behind him, above the cliffs said to be unclimbable, row after row of British redcoats. They were in battle array and far outnumbered the French, whose sentries' mangled bodies bestrewed the cliffs or floated in the river below. It was a breathtaking, almost impossible, feat, to have put thousands of men on top of a cliff overnight, but Wolfe had done it.

In a few hours it was all over; Quebec was taken by the British and Americans, who had fought like devils under Wolfe's inspired leadership. Despite being hit by three musket balls, Wolfe allowed his wounds only to be hastily dressed before he encouraged the line to make the final charge that ensured victory, a victory achieved with just one cannon and no cavalry against an enemy armed to the teeth. As the smoke of battle cleared, and he was fainting from loss of blood, Wolfe saw that the French retreat had been cut off as he had directed. The next minute he was dead. Montcalm, too, died from wounds received that day.

Although the actual surrender of Canada to the British crown would not take place for another year, by holding Quebec and thus commanding the St Lawrence waterway, the British prevented the new French commander from bringing his troops up to relieve Montreal. When reports of Wolfe's gallant death reached England, George II was so inspired by the story that he commissioned Benjamin West to paint a narrative picture of the dying Wolfe which may be seen today in the National Portrait Gallery.

As Pitt had vowed, with the exception of Louisiana in the south the French had been wiped from the face of North America. Their plan of linking Canada and Louisiana and preventing the English colonists from expanding west was in ashes. The extraordinary effort Pitt had exhorted from the colonists with every last drop of his being had come good when they had fought together in the first imperial war. In what became known as the year of victories, 1759, from all parts of the globe came nothing but encouraging news: Britain had captured important French settlements on

Robert Clive and Mir Jaffier after the Battle of Plassey, 1757. Plassey was one of Clive's most important victories. It secured British rule over Bengal, and formed the basis for the British Empire in India. He was aided by Mir Jaffier, the commander of the army of the Nawab of Bengal who came over to the British.

the island of Goree off west Africa and in Senegal itself. The capture of Guadeloupe, one of the West Indian sugar islands, which had been attacked when the British failed to take Martinique, raised Pitt's reputation to new heights among his fellow countrymen, as well as bringing £400,000 in income in one year alone. In India under the extraordinary Clive there had been a series of victories, which as in North America had driven the French off the Indian subcontinent. Most important was the Battle of Plassey in 1757, which secured the large area of Bengal in the north-west as a British dependency ruled on behalf of Britain by a new nawab, Mir Jaffier. Sent there from the south, with 2,000 British troops and 5,000 sepoys, Clive destroyed the 40,000-strong army of France's ally Siraj-ud-Daula.

Like Wolfe's triumph on the Heights of Abraham, Plassey determined the shape of the future. Adding Bengal to the Karnatic made Britain the most powerful European presence in India; those territories became the basis for the British Empire in India. Though Clive retired to England on grounds of ill-health, his work was continued by Colonel Eyre Coote, who had been at Plassey and who had a unique relationship with the sepoys. By 1761 after decisive victories against the French at Wandewash and Pondicherry, Coote had extirpated the last of French influence in southern India. In Europe too the year 1759 drew to a triumphant close for Britain, bringing nothing but victories: Ferdinand of Brunswick relieved Hanover by drawing the French army into a successful ambush at Minden.

Even the threat of a new French invasion of Britain was foiled by the exceptional bravery of Admiral Hawke, Pitt's favourite admiral. Transport ships to take French soldiers across the Channel had collected at the mouth of the Seine. Their advance was to be covered by the Brest fleet, so the best chance of preventing it was to destroy the fleet which was anchored below Finisterre, on France's Atlantic coast, in Quiberon Bay. Distance, and the appalling November weather, would have stopped most men from putting to sea, let alone sailing for the Bay of Biscay, but Hawke was not to be deterred. Though driving rain rendered visibility nil, and massive waves were breaking across the decks, he ordered his pilot to rush into the shallow waters of Quiberon Bay. Its rocks stuck up like needles and the long suck and swell of water presaged disaster for any ship not already at anchor. But it was there that the Brest fleet was drawn up. And it was there that Hawke shouted in words that became legendary, 'Lay me alongside the *Soleil Royale*!' The valiant British navy followed Hawke straight into the middle of the French ships and sank them, losing only forty men.

Lost in admiration at the change in Britain's fortunes under Pitt, Frederick the Great proclaimed that 'England was a long time in labour, but at last she has brought forth a man.' The Prussian king himself was almost as popular in England as Pitt, as may be seen from the number of pubs still named the King of Prussia. But in the middle of all these victories in 1760, when England's reputation had never been higher, George II died suddenly, aged seventy-seven. The throne now passed to his grandson George III. By the end of his reign George II had grown quite fond of the man who had expanded his dominions beyond recognition. Now in 1760, despite all he had done for Britain, Pitt was vulnerable to being toppled by a new court.

George III

(1760–1820)

Patriot King (1760–1793)

Unfortunately the hero that Britain had at last brought forth to the admiration of Frederick II was not to the taste of the new king George III. Handsome and blond, a devoted husband to Princess Charlotte Mecklenberg-Strelitz who bore him fifteen children – all but one in Buckingham House, which he purchased as a family home in 1761 – the twenty-two-year-old George had his own ideas of heroics. The conspicuous part was to be played by himself. He was enormously influenced by Bolingbroke's writings on the ideal of the Patriot King, whose every virtue he hoped to embody. The Patriot King had as one of its particular tenets that the king should choose his ministers from the best men of all the parties. Parties led to faction, which destroyed the nation; they should be replaced by the lofty figure of the Patriot King from whom all goodness would spring.

Of a pious nature, with a rather slow and limited intellectual capacity, but with firm opinions once he had formed them, George III had a passionate distrust of the dirty arts of politicians – especially those of the great Pitt. He had complete faith in his own ability to cleanse the Augean stable of Whig patronage which had run the country since 1714. In fact, considering the formidable men ranged against him, George would be remarkably successful over the next twelve years. Blessed with a will of iron and considerable cunning, he clawed back the patronage of the crown from the Whigs and substituted his supporters, known as the King's Friends, in the Houses of Parliament. For all his youthful ideas he soon became as adept as Walpole at using pensions to create placemen.

But by doing so George put himself on a collision course with his fellow countrymen. To British politicians of the 1760s the idea that the king should control the legislature, that is Parliament, through his Friends, was anathema. It was an article of post-revolutionary faith that there should be checks and balances in the constitution, otherwise there was a real danger of arbitrary power. The first twenty years of George III's enormously long reign (it lasted for nearly sixty years, though he was incapacitated for his last decade) were therefore disturbed by a new struggle between Parliament and king which was expressed at its most extreme by the radical politician John Wilkes. But those two decades also saw a war to the death between the American colonies and Britain because the king refused to acknowledge America's own Parliamentary traditions.

The legal rights and liberties of the citizen were the outstanding universal phenomenon of the second half of the eighteenth century. The spirit of the time in George III's domains was against him. Where he viewed his role as the unifying Patriot King, on both sides of the Atlantic his reign was seen as conflicting with the rights won a century before. The interfering king was destroying liberty, which – like reason – was becoming the buzzword of the age.

George III's reign coincided with the coming to fruition of ideas emanating from the mid-eighteenth-century Enlightenment movement in France, a system of beliefs which spread like wildfire. These ideas were popularized by the French philosophers of the time (for France ever since Louis XIV had been the cultural centre of Europe) in their hugely influential *Encyclopédie*, first published in 1751. Organized by the philosopher Denis Diderot and containing articles by political theorists such as Montesquieu and philosophers such as Voltaire and Rousseau, the *Encyclopédie* aimed at nothing less than explaining the universe. Its founders' optimistic notion was that, if the *Encyclopédie* contained explanations for everything, progress would result as knowledge advanced. Newton's discovery of the physical laws of the universe, which he began to publish from the 1680s on, the Swedish botanist Linnaeus' classification of the natural world into species in 1737 and the scientific discoveries which proliferated in the first half of the eighteenth century convinced them that the intellectual laws of the universe could be determined by the application of human intelligence.

The most striking feature of the Enlightenment was its followers' belief in the benevolent power of man's reason. If every aspect of human life – institutions, laws, beliefs – were subjected to reason, man would be inspired to improve it. Its next most important aspect was that the laws which the Enlightenment philosophers, not least Jean-Jacques Rousseau, postulated about the universe by and large moved most of them away from conservative forms of government like monarchies towards the concepts of human rights and equality. Many of the political ideas that inspired the Encyclopédistes came from England. John Locke was hailed by them as one of their own, and Montesquieu cited the separation of powers in England as the model for rational government. Tradition was regarded as being almost as bad as superstition, which in the Christian Churches had been responsible for so many deaths the century before. Deism went in tandem with the Enlightenment, the belief that there was a God but that its or his laws were to be known not through established religions like Judaism or Christianity, but by discovering certain common principles. As with a scientific experiment, every belief was to be questioned and, if it was found wanting in the light of reason, abandoned.

For reason, it was believed, led to virtue. The effect that these ideas had on the world are impossible to underestimate. It was only when the French Revolution had run its course and thrown out every piece of irrational human custom in its pursuit of rational virtue that disenchantment with reason and experiment set in. But until 1789 the western world was awash with all kinds of people tearing down the old in the search of the new. The ideas the Encyclopédistes promoted, of political freedom, of social justice, of equality, would prove so powerful that they moved men to fight wars, to pull down palaces, to create a new world.

Nevertheless the compelling, the intoxicating brilliance of the Encyclopédistes' writing was such that philosophical ideas of reform – and philosophers themselves – became the fashion even among the most conservative monarchies of Europe. If Caroline of Ansbach had corresponded with philosophers twenty years before, in the mid-eighteenth century autocratic monarchs like Catherine the Great of Russia, Frederick the Great of Prussia and Joseph II of Austria were so influenced by philosophical ideas that they wanted to put them into practice. They prided themselves on being enlightened, as did people from all walks of life all over the world. From such a standpoint eventually flowed the reform movements in England at the end of the century, which demanded religious toleration, an end to slavery, prison reform, parliamentary reform, trade reform and constitutional reform.

In his own way the young George III represented something of the spirit of the age that was determined to sweep away the old and the outworn. He believed in restoring virtue to the country. Unfortunately, when he was a little boy his autocratic mother, who had been brought up as a princess at the despotic court of a small German state and was horrified by the impudence of the English Parliament, was always saying to him, 'George, be a king.' He never forgot her advice. But his interpretation of kingship not only conflicted dramatically with the English political tradition. It also led him into conflict with the Whig leaders of his reign, the Earl of Shelburne and the Marquis of Rockingham.

In the atmosphere of the Enlightenment they prided themselves more than ever on being the keepers of the flame of freedom, as true heirs to the Revolutionary Settlement. And they kept up the Whig reputation for being in contact with advanced thought. Just as Locke had been doctor to the first Whig Lord Shaftesbury, the scientist and dissenter who discovered oxygen Joseph Priestley was Lord Shelburne's librarian, responsible for much advanced rationalist thought percolating into Whig ruling circles. The stage of George III's reign was thus set for repeated confrontation.

George III remained under the influence not only of his mother Augusta, Princess of Wales, but also of his former tutor Lord Bute, a tall, vain Scotsman, said to be her lover, who was known for priding himself on his good legs. Bute was loathed by most people, partly because he was Scots (the Scots were still very unpopular) and partly because of his passion for intrigue and secret plots. But he did have the sensible idea of getting the new king off to a good start by emphasizing how English he was compared to his great-grandfather and grandfather, George I and George II. George III made a famous speech from the throne in the perfect English accent derived from a childhood spent at Kew, which began, 'Born and bred in this country I glory in the name of Briton.' Nevertheless, though he might be regarded with sentimental enthusiasm after such a start, by the easily moved public, to the political classes (that is, the great Whig network spread so effectively throughout the country) George seemed a dangerous new phenomenon.

Emotional and affectionate, the young George III put his faith in those he loved, chief of whom was the Tory Bute, who had been his tutor ever since his father, Poor Fred, died when George was twelve. The pompous Bute was appointed secretary of state by the king and thrust into Pitt's administration. George did not appreciate that Pitt should be given free rein, while Pitt himself, as a consummate autocrat – Horace Walpole said that he wanted the crown and sceptre and nothing less – was furious that the Cabinet had to have Bute on board representing the king and putting obstacles in his path. Pitt was insulted when Bute wanted George III in his coronation speech to call the war 'bloody and expensive'; he insisted that it be changed to 'just and necessary'. Undermined in his own Cabinet and prevented from declaring pre-emptive war on Spain, France's ally, Pitt resigned in October 1761. Bute was left to face renewed hostilities with Spain in December (though it brought Britain Hanava and Manila) and to manage the peace which all sides were wearily coming to believe was necessary.

The Treaty of Paris, signed in February 1763, brought to an end the Seven Years War, but despite Pitt's entreaties no mention was made by Bute of Britain's magnificent ally Frederick the Great, who had fought so bravely on her behalf. Bute followed up this ungrateful behaviour by withdrawing without warning the subsidy Frederick had come to depend on. In a sad turnaround the King of Prussia, who had helped to win the war which had left Britain the world's top trading nation, became her implacable enemy.

Pitt denounced the peace, which he said was 'as stained as Utrecht', but just as at Utrecht the gains to Britain from the Seven Years War were immense. Bute's offensive behaviour certainly left Britain most ominously without a friend in Europe, with Prussia feeling as betrayed as Austria had been, but the British part of North America now extended to the Mississippi. What had become the only French colony in North America, Louisiana, was now worth so little to France that she soon sold it to Spain, in 1762. As a result of giving Havana and Manila back to Spain in return for Florida, the whole of the American eastern seaboard was now in the hands of British colonists, as of course was the vast formerly French settlement of Canada. In addition all the French and Spanish American possessions in the southern part of North America to the east of the Mississippi, with the exception of the town and island of New Orleans, became British too.

Minorca was given back to Britain. In the West Indies Britain kept Grenada and the Grenadines, Tobago, St Vincent and Dominica, but restored Martinique, Guadeloupe and St Lucia to the French. In India all the gains made since 1748 were confirmed. In west Africa the French were handed back Goree, while Britain kept Senegal. In central America Britain obtained the right to cut and trade in Honduras logwood, which would eventually result in protectorate status. Though the French lost Cape Breton by the Peace of Paris, they were still allowed to use the great fisheries round Newfoundland which they had traditionally shared with the British for over a hundred years.

Meanwhile, within Great Britain, the king was starting as he meant to go on. When continuous disagreements with Bute had forced the other pillar of the government, the chief of the great Whig connection the Duke of Newcastle, to resign in May 1762, George III seized the opportunity to dismiss all his followers and dependants. Not only was any Whig who had voted against the treaty in the Houses of Parliament thrown out, so also were Newcastle's most modest clients such as excisemen. With a quill pen the king personally ran through the name of the Duke of Devonshire on the list of members of the Privy Council, while three of the greatest magnates of the Whig party, Newcastle, Rockingham and the Duke of Grafton, were dismissed as lords lieutenant.

This wholesale sacking of the Whigs was known to their sarcastic contemporaries as 'the massacre of the Pelhamite Innocents'. The Whigs were truly amazed by the speed and venom with which the young king had struck. As a result the great Whig connection, or 'old corps' Whigs, for the first time in two generations broke up into small rival groups, of which the most important were those headed by Pitt and Rockingham. But, just as the king desired, some Whigs began to desert their party and move towards the idea of becoming King's Friends.

The elegant Bute soon found the rough and tumble of politics too much for him. He preferred, as he put it, to be 'a private man at the side of the King', so he retired while nevertheless continuing to make trouble by advising George informally – or from behind the curtain, as was said at the time. Yet the country still had to be governed. Since George III was only at the beginning of his drive to dispose of the Whigs, he was forced to call upon the competent but unimaginative Whig George Grenville, who headed one of the smaller Whig factions, to lead the government. Grenville, who was Pitt's brother-in-law (though he had quarrelled with him), had few manners and was constantly rude to the king. He was also immediately faced by trouble. At home, the increasingly outrageous newspaper put out by the daring MP John Wilkes, and its insulting criticisms of the king, had to be suppressed once and for all. In America, when Grenville asked the colonists to help pay for the enormously expensive war by a new levy, the stamp tax, to be imposed on every legal document, his request was met by rioting.

Grenville saw no reason why the burden of the colonies' defence should fall on the English taxpayer alone. And perhaps if they had been asked to consider the request in their assemblies the Americans would have returned a favourable answer. The problem was the peremptory way in which the

Engraved by Ridley

ADAM SMITH L.L.D.

The economist Adam Smith, author of *The Wealth of Nations*, 1776. His theories of the importance of free trade dominated 19th-century Britain.

tax was demanded. The American colonists had a very proud parliamentary tradition of their own in their assemblies. Following the example of their English cousins in the seventeenth century, they held to the belief that they could not be taxed without their consent. Since they were not represented in the British Parliament as they had elected none of its members, the British Parliament had no right to tax them. The passing of the Stamp Act in 1765 in the Parliament at Westminster, but not in their own parliaments and state assemblies, resulted in uproar and riots driven by a slogan which seventeenth-century Englishmen would have understood: 'No taxation without representation'. Six of the thirteen colonies' governments made formal protests.

As a patriotic duty Americans refused to accept the stamped paper sent over from England, and boycotted British manufactures. British manufacturers who relied on the vast American trade started to go bankrupt, and amid the chaos, alarmed by such fury, Grenville resigned. The Stamp Act was repealed in 1766 by Grenville's successor, the Marquis of Rockingham. Grenville had been no less thoroughly defeated at home by the antics of the libertarian Wilkes, a member of the debauched Hell-Fire Club.

Ever since the accession of George III, Wilkes's newspaper the *North Briton* – so-called in mock-honour of Bute's antecedents – had specialized in attacking the king's rule. The removal of the 'old corps' Whigs (with secret encouragement from his confrères) had been portrayed as another royal attack on liberty. Wilkes and his paper already had a reputation for scurrility, but in issue No. 45 of April 1763, he went too far when he alleged that the king's speech to Parliament included a lie. Grenville, who was a lawyer himself, was determined that the recalcitrant Wilkes should feel the full force of the law. He had Wilkes and the printers of the *North Briton* tried and imprisoned for having had anything to do with the production of the paper, through the unspecific catch-all mechanism known as the general warrant. But Grenville was made to look foolish by an unsympathetic judiciary. On appeal, Chief Justice Charles Pratt released Wilkes by ruling general warrants illegal.

The squinting, licentious Wilkes was already a popular hero among high-spirited and sophisticated Londoners who themselves had long enjoyed a reputation for disliking restraint of all kinds. Wilkes's imprisonment was worked up into the issue of the right of the citizen to publish the truth and Pratt's judgement was represented as a blow for liberty. Wilkes sued the government for his arrest and was given damages by the ecstatically partisan London jury. The House of Commons nevertheless expelled him, and because he risked arrest once more for an obscene poem, he was forced to flee for France. But this was only the beginning of his career as the self-appointed gadfly of the state. Often on the run Wilkes had enough of the popular vote behind him to be re-elected to Parliament, to be made an alderman of the City of London and finally to become mayor. He began to campaign for freedom of all kinds, but particularly for press freedom and American rights – a campaign which for the next ten years convulsed the colonies with violence.

For the sake of some governmental stability, George had asked Lord Rockingham to take office as prime minister because he had assumed the leadership of the largest Whig faction, which contained many of the 'old corps' Whigs – that is, the old Newcastle or Pelhamite Whig connection. Rockingham (whose secretary, the Irishman Edmund Burke, was to become the supreme thinker of the Whig party) had a great deal more common sense than Grenville. But thanks to the king's activities behind the scenes, and those of the King's Friends whom he imposed upon the ministry, the Rockingham government could not last. Though the Duke of Newcastle was a member of the government as lord privy seal, he was too old and unwell to be of much use, while Pitt – who was temperamentally unsuited to playing a supporting role – refused to shore up the ministry. It was thus to Pitt once more and his small band of followers that George III turned to form a government in 1766, in hopes of a smoother time ahead since Pitt himself had now professed contempt for the party system.

In theory Pitt might have ameliorated the continuing poor relations with America. He had persuaded Rockingham to repeal the stamp tax by pointing out how foolish it was to threaten the trade with the American colonies, worth £2 million a year, for the peppercorn rate of stamp duty, which might bring in one-tenth of that revenue. In his view Britain might have a moral right to tax the colonies, but she had no legal right. However, Pitt now fell ill and was obliged to take a prolonged leave of absence, while refusing to resign as prime minister. This left his rash chancellor Charles Townshend to rush into more taxation of the American colonies, since the problem of the unresolved war debts had not gone away. Townshend hoped he had found a way round the dispute by imposing customs duties, which after all were indirect taxes on tea, glass, paper and other essentials, but the Americans saw through this. Their response was more rioting.

Moreover, even before Pitt had what seems to have been some kind of a nervous breakdown, his government was not at all the same as his old ministry. In his pride and grandeur he had accepted the earldom of Chatham. In effect, though, this was the equivalent of being 'kicked upstairs'. As he now had to sit in the House of Lords, he could no longer employ his formidable powers of rhetoric to control the House of Commons. And since he would not have one party, the Chatham administration was made up of an unworkable ragbag of men of opposing views. Edmund Burke would memorably describe it as 'such a piece of

Tomb of William Pitt the Elder, Earl of Chatham, Westminster Abbey. It celebrates his conduct of the Seven Years War which hugely expanded the British Empire.

mosaic, such a tessellated pavement without cement, patriots and courtiers, king's friends and republicans, Whigs and Tories, that it was indeed a curious show, but unsafe to touch and unsure to walk on'. Chatham was far too grand to try and wield this mass of warring factions into a workable whole, and it became beset by internal problems when Townshend died unexpectedly. The severity of Chatham's illness at last compelled him to resign in October 1768.

Then Wilkes returned to London from abroad to make mischief. Despite being imprisoned once more on the outstanding charge of his obscene poetry, he got himself elected MP for Middlesex where his depiction of the corruption in Parliament gained him a willing audience. Chatham's first lord of the Treasury, the Duke of Grafton, now took over as prime minister, and his government made the House of Commons refuse to accept Wilkes's election and keep him in prison. Wilkes decried this as further evidence of a conspiracy against liberty, and rioting began outside his prison in Southwark in 1768. The following year he was re-elected and expelled three times. Re-elected one more time, his seat went to his defeated opponent.

By 1770 Grafton had had enough. He had battled against attacks in the House of Lords by a revived Chatham, roused by the imprisonment of Wilkes, which he too saw as an issue of liberty, but he was soon defeated, resigning after two years under the stress of it all. Since all the Whig factions were by now in a profound state of disarray and disagreement with one another, Grafton's ministry gave way to one consisting entirely of the King's Friends under Lord North. The son of the Jacobite Earl of Guildford, North was a witty, cherubic and deceptively sleepy-looking man with the sort of emollient skills needed to hold a government together. At last the king had triumphed. Though North was the first Tory to hold office in two generations, the real point about him was that he had risen to power as a King's Friend. For twelve years Britain got ministerial stability under this affable man, who understood that his hold on power depended on his accepting that the real chief minister was the king.

Unfortunately these years coincided with increasing restiveness in America. English goods were being simultaneously boycotted by all the colonies, while mobs roamed the streets of Massachusetts led by masked men called the Sons of Liberty, who tarred and feathered anyone not in agreement with them. The Massachusetts Parliament debated what form a protest to the British government should take which would deny Britain's right to make laws for or to tax the colonies. This was a revolt fast developing into revolution.

There were now 10,000 British soldiers in Massachusetts, for Grafton had sent out 2,000 more to Boston, and every day the Boston mob spent hours taunting the troops; tempers were at breaking point. On 2 March 1770, seven British soldiers separated from the rest of their regiment were backed into a corner by an enraged mob advancing down one of Boston's boulevards, hurling abuse and stones. Fearing for their lives, the soldiers fired into the crowd and killed five men. This was immediately seized on by American agitators as a 'massacre' and they demanded nothing less than that all British soldiers should leave the colonies.

George III could not view the colonists' actions with tolerance; it was not in his nature. They were rebellious subjects whose ideas should not even be listened to, but must be destroyed. Yet the people whose views the king had no patience for were highly sophisticated men and women with their own political traditions who, just as much as their cousins across the Atlantic, had been profoundly influenced by the ideas of John Locke, especially in his sanctioning of rebellion against unjust rulers. In the years since the founding of the American colonies (in the case of Virginia and New England, well over a hundred years before), their own institutions had grown up which were completely independent of and far more real to them than what went on 3,000 miles away at Westminster. Many of the colonists were as practised in debating in their own assemblies as any MP. Well educated at their excellent new universities of Harvard and Yale, they were growing ever more impatient with the mother country. By a strange irony of history, the supreme sacrifice Pitt had demanded of the Americans, the propaganda he had bombarded them with in order to make the colonies see the French as their enemy, had given the thirteen colonies much more of a sense of common destiny than ever before.

But ever since George III had come to the throne and started taking his kingdom in hand there had been other more immediate reasons for friction. The mercantile system, under which the colonies were to import British manufactures but make nothing themselves, infuriated the Americans. They wished to build up their home manufacturing base, but were forbidden to do so by law. Under the old Whigs the colonies had been pretty much left

View of Billingsgate Market.

to themselves to run things, but George III had insisted on a much more rigorous observance of the mercantile system. The illegal trade with other parts of Europe and other colonies to which everyone had turned a blind eye was curbed, and customs duties at colonial ports were raised.

At first North tried to be conciliatory to the colonists. He repealed all the taxes except for the one on tea, which was only three pence per pound, and removed the soldiers from Boston. He promised that the British government would not try and raise any more taxes in America, but at the same time, because the king insisted, he weakly said that the tax on tea would nevertheless remain as a matter of principle. The 298 chests of British tea that arrived in Boston Harbour in December 1773 provided too good a symbol of British oppression for an increasingly important circle of American agitators to miss. In what has become known to history as the Boston Tea Party, a group of patriotic young Americans dressed as Mohawk Indians climbed aboard ships in the harbour and emptied all the tea into the water. All patriotic Americans from then on refused to drink tea.

Lord North and George III reacted with intemperate fury. They attempted to punish the Bostonians as if they were children by withdrawing all responsibility from them by means of the Coercive Acts (known to the Americans as the Intolerable Acts). In 1774 the agitators were sent to England for trial, the Massachusetts charter of government was suspended and the colony was henceforth to be ruled directly from Britain. To add insult to injury the port of Boston was closed until compensation had been paid to the tea-merchants. The British government was so ignorant of what effect these draconian measures were going to have on the American colonies that it never considered that the Americans would rather fight than put up with them. The renowned Virginian orator Patrick Henry spoke for all Americans when he said, 'Give me liberty, or give me death!'

At Westminster, unlike the rest of Britain which was outraged by the impudence of the Americans, Chatham, his followers and the Rockinghamite Whigs, all opposed the Coercive Acts and called on the government to give in and save the empire. They persuaded North to offer a get-out clause: if the colonies made a grant towards the expense of the war they would not be taxed. But it was to no avail. Events in America were achieving their own rolling momentum. When the British commander General Gage, who had replaced the governor at Boston, tried to carry out his orders to dissolve the Massachusetts Parliament, the Bostonians simply reassembled at Concord, a few miles to the west.

Realizing that the moment had come for real defiance of the mother country, the people of Massachusetts organized their militia into a company called the Minute Men, because they could be called out at one minute's notice. They also started to pile up guns in their clapboard houses. When Gage sent troops to seize the rebels' military stores in April 1775, they were attacked at Lexington and 270 British soldiers were killed. The shot fired then has been called one that 'echoed round the world', for that was the beginning of the American Wars of Independence.

The Americans then went on the offensive. They drew themselves up on Bunker Hill overlooking Boston Harbour and there at first they kept Gage at bay. All the colonies joined Massachusetts and declared war on Britain, whose legal dependants they had been only a few months before. They appointed George Washington, the hero of the Seven Years War, their commander-in-chief. He was sent up to Massachusetts to co-ordinate the war effort there. In Britain the government grasped that the situation in America was much more serious than had been thought and despatched General Sir William Howe across the Atlantic to Boston to take over from Gage because he was a veteran of the Seven Years War and therefore knew the American terrain well.

Washington was an inspired choice of leader. Not only was he famous in the colonies for his bravery, but having served with British soldiers he understood the enemy's strengths and weaknesses and knew that the British redcoat was vulnerable to the unexpected ambushes and sudden skirmishes in which the colonial militia excelled. But he had a great deal to accomplish before his citizen soldiers were ready to fight. Though the Americans' outstanding merit was that unlike the British they were fighting for a cause they were prepared to die for, they would be at a disadvantage if they met the redcoats in pitched battle. Enthusiasm and passion would not always carry the day over formal training. Thanks to the passivity of General Howe, who sat at Boston doing nothing all winter, Washington was able to take advantage of those few vital months to drill his troops into disciplined regiments. In 1776 he and his army seized Dorchester Heights, which commanded Boston. Instead of doing battle Howe withdrew to Brooklyn in New York, leaving Washington in possession of one of America's largest ports.

Once in New York Howe began recruiting as many men as he could find. But since few Americans would fight in the British army he was driven to using the colonists' enemy, the Indians, and importing 18,000 Hessians to fight against the Americans. These things further alienated the Americans, especially as the German mercenaries' behaviour was very brutal indeed.

On 4 July 1776, the date which America's national holiday memorializes, the colonists sitting in Congress in Philadelphia issued the celebrated Declaration of Independence, calling the colonies the 'free and independent States of America'. Written by Washington's fellow Virginian planter

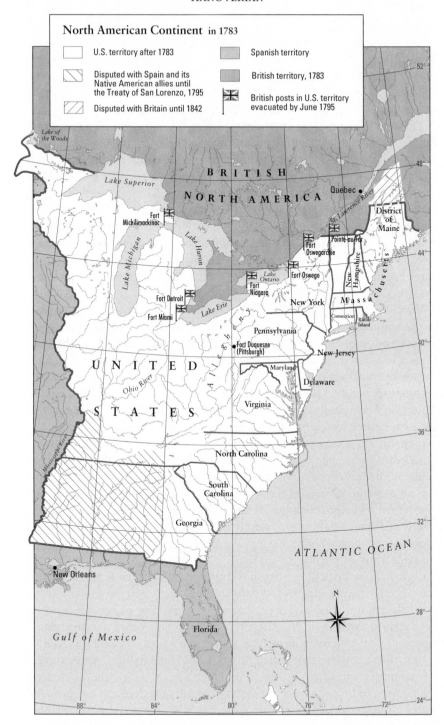

North American Continent in 1783

☐ U.S. territory after 1783

▨ Disputed with Spain and its
Native American allies until
the Treaty of San Lorenzo, 1795

▨ Disputed with Britain until 1842

☐ Spanish territory

■ British territory, 1783

✠ British posts in U.S. territory
evacuated by June 1795

Lake of
the Woods

B R I T I S H

N O R T H   A M E R I C A

Quebec ●

Lake Superior

Fort ✠
Michilimackinac

Lake Michigan

Lake Huron

St. Lawrence River

District
of
Maine

✠ Pointe-au-Fer
Fort ✠
Oswegatchie

Fort Detroit ✠

Lake Erie

Fort Miami ✠

Lake Ontario
Fort
Niagara

✠ Fort Oswego

New
Hampshire

Massachusetts

New York

U N I T E D

Ohio River

Allegheny

● Fort Duquesne
(Pittsburgh)

Pennsylvania

Connecticut
Rhode
Island

Massachusetts

New Jersey

S T A T E S

Mississippi River

Maryland

Delaware

Virginia

North Carolina

South
Carolina

Georgia

● New Orleans

Florida

A T L A N T I C   O C E A N

N

Gulf of Mexico

52°

48°

44°

40°

36°

32°

28°

24°

88°   84°   80°   76°   72°

Thomas Jefferson, the Declaration burned with the spirit of the Enlightenment. Most ringing of all its utterances was the phrase 'we hold these truths to be self-evident, that all men are created equal, that they are endowed by their creator with certain inalienable rights, that among these are life, liberty and the pursuit of happiness'. George III was denounced for his 'history of repeated injuries and usurpations', and condemned as 'unfit to be the ruler of a free people'.

Meanwhile to the surprise of the British, a series of military successes for the colonial Americans now ensued. Washington, who marched down from Boston to force the British out of New York, had been defeated, and forced to retreat to Philadelphia. But the British masterplan of an army under General Burgoyne arriving from Canada to join Howe and drive Washington into the south in order to separate New England from the rest of the colonies was humiliatingly defeated. In 1777 at Saratoga on the Hudson river, Burgoyne had to surrender with all his soldiers to the American General Gates.

Saratoga was the turning point for the colonists. Until then the other European powers had not thought it worth their while intervening in the conflict. They had assumed the Americans stood no chance of success against the victor of the Seven Years War. But not only did Saratoga revitalize American morale. More importantly it secured French troops and a French fleet as France officially recognized the colonists' independence and formed an alliance with America. In 1778 the young Marquis de Lafayette arrived as commander of the French forces which were to fight side by side with the Americans against the British. The end of the war effectively came when the British under General Cornwallis surrendered at Yorktown in Virginia in 1781. They had been defeated by a combined operation: a blockade by Admiral de Grasse's French fleet from the sea and a land-siege by General Greene.

But Britain was still fighting a new world war, against the Spanish now as well as the French. In 1779 Spain had followed the lead of her Bourbon relation and attacked the British. A year later so did Holland, brought in by Britain's insulting adherence to the Law of Neutrals, by which Dutch ships carrying (say) French goods were liable to be seized by the British. Further hostility to Britain on similar grounds came from an alliance, the Armed Neutrality of the North, formed by the neutral powers Russia, Denmark and Sweden. They would not allow Britain to stop their ships carrying goods for her enemies. During the war Britain temporarily lost command of the sea: Minorca was seized, Gibraltar was besieged and most of the British West Indies were occupied by the French.

Across the globe Britain's enemies seized the opportunity offered by the American War to attack her. In India the French attempted to return to their old position of superiority: the Maratha warriors were incited to war against the English and were on the point of overwhelming Bombay, the Sultan of Mysore, Haidar Ali,waged war all over the Karnatic and the French temporarily seized control of the Indian Ocean.

Fortunately for Britain the old hero of the Seven Years War in India, Sir Eyre Coote, was still alive. He completely destroyed the forces of the Sultan of Mysore, while the governor-general of India, Warren Hastings, made a name for himself when he showed great presence of mind in sending troops from Bengal to relieve Bombay. Once Yorktown had fallen, the French attempted to seize Jamaica. They were defeated near Dominica by Admiral Rodney, who restored British naval supremacy. In Ireland a gifted barrister turned politician named Henry Grattan raised what was in effect a substantial army of hundreds of thousands of Protestant volunteers, supposedly to defend Ireland. Backed up by the threat these men represented, a convention met in 1782 at Dungannon – copying the Congress of Philadelphia – and unilaterally declared legislative independence from England.

After Saratoga, although the British government finally offered to repeal all the acts passed for the American colonies since 1763, the Americans were no longer prepared to accept any role for British Parliamentary statutes. In early 1782 Britain at last formally accepted that the Americans were not to be subdued by force and recognized American independence. Soon afterwards, peace was made with the rest of Europe. In September 1783 by the Treaty of Versailles Britain retained Gibraltar, though Spain received back Florida once more together with Minorca, and France was given Tobago, Goree and Senegal.

In Britain events had not stood still during the war. With the issue of liberty dominating the arguments of the day, the 1770s saw Granville Sharp begin the anti-slavery movement, launching a campaign that led to a legal judgement of 1772 which forbade slavery in England. Giving reasons for his decision to free James Sommersett, a black slave brought to London by a West Indian plantation-owner, the judge declared that 'no law of England allowed so high an act of dominion as slavery'. Sharp was helped by a former African slave, Olaudah Equiano, born around 1745, who was sold to a Royal Navy officer. After fighting in Canada and the Mediterranean, Equiano, who was one of about 30,000 black people living in England in the late eighteenth century and who settled in Bristol, wrote an influential first hand description of slavery. He became much in demand to give lecture tours for the growing number of abolition committees.

The poor progress of the war contrasted dramatically with the triumphs achieved during the Seven Years War over the same ground and radicalized the British public's assessment of the government, adding to the widespread conviction of corruption in high places. The Americans were not alone in believing that they were not properly represented in Parliament. The loss of the American colonies, the failure of the war and the temporary loss to the French of control of the high seas (an American privateer named Paul Jones had created mayhem by attacking British seaside towns) made many more doubt the efficacy of the prevailing political system. Mass meetings were held throughout the country to demand the reforms in Parliamentary representation for which Chatham and Wilkes had been campaigning for the previous decade.

The most striking was the 'out of doors' petition movement begun by highly respectable Yorkshiremen. Lawyers, farmers and gentry demanded another hundred country seats to reflect population changes and rid Britain of corruption and the useless placemen round the king who they believed were responsible for the war going so badly. The Great Yorkshire Petition presented in 1780 was copied by twenty-four other counties. In Parliament it was represented by Edmund Burke's 1780 Civil List Bill which pledged to investigate who was receiving government pensions.

Britain was undergoing tremendous change and dislocation imposed by the agricultural and industrial revolutions. Throughout the eighteenth century, new techniques of husbandry using drainage, new grasses, fertilizer and crop rotation invented by among others Jethro Tull and Walpole's brother-in-law Townshend, and later popularized by Thomas Coke and Arthur Young, had been transforming farming by providing hugely improved yields. George III himself, 'Farmer George' as he was nicknamed, was fascinated by his own farm at Windsor and wrote on agricultural topics under a *nom de plume*. The new farming needed larger farms of 200 acres or more if they were to succeed, and as information about these methods spread, so the rate of enclosure of the common land quickened – a process that reached its peak in the first half of George's reign as some two million acres were enclosed by countless private acts of Parliament. The English countryside, from being mainly ribbon strips of smallholdings, became a place of extensive fields surrounded by hedgerows.

As improvements in farming practice created regional unemployment during these years, particularly in the midlands, textile manufacturing piecework at home offered another way of earning money. The full industrial revolution did not get under way until the mid-1780s when Edmund Cartwright's power loom, combined with James Watt's double-acting steam engine, transformed the British cotton industry almost overnight. From 1764 with James Hargreaves's invention of the Spinning Jenny, which adapted John Kay's Flying Shuttle of the 1730s to a multi-spindle system, cotton manufacture was becoming a far more profitable business. Then Richard Arkwright's invention of the waterframe, which used water to run the spinning machine far more speedily than the hand loom, not only moved work out of the home in the early 1770s into cotton mills, it attracted the new landless labourers north to the Pennines. For centuries the rushing waters of the Pennines had provided natural sites for the water mills of the woollen industry, and it was there that cotton manufacture took off.

The well-to-do could not be wholly disconnected from the anger over enclosures that was often taking the form of riots, nor did many of them want to. For the way the educated thought about the less fortunate was changing, from the anti-slavery movement to the new concern for the treatment of prisoners expressed in 1777 when John Howard wrote his *State of the Prisons in England and Wales*. But they were not only influenced by the rational thought of the Enlightenment, which in England (propelled by Jeremy Bentham, a barrister and philosopher) was moving towards Utilitarianism – the novel belief that government should be directed towards the greatest happiness of the greatest number. They were also affected by the great religious revival movement begun by the Wesley brothers and the preacher George Whitefield, which from the late 1770s swept the Church of England, creating the Methodist Church.

In the space of thirty years the influential Evangelical movement, as their followers who remained within the Church of England were known, would transform the manners and mores of Britain. The Evangelicals concluded that the people of Britain were very nearly as much in need of missions as those natives in foreign lands who were sent Bibles and clergymen by the growing number of religious societies. The national mood was slowly shifting towards a greater seriousness, the sort of mood that is thought of as Victorian. Piety and hard work were becoming the watchwords of England. They were the values of the inventive middle-class manufacturers, whose factories were poised to make Britain into an industrial giant.

To George III's anger the loss of the American colonies caused Lord North to resign, and forced the king to bring back the 'old corps' Whigs he detested under Lord Rockingham. But it was a short-lived government. The MP John Dunning's critical motion 'that the influence of the Crown has increased, is increasing and ought to be diminished' was the last gasp of a dying breed. Legislative independence for Ireland was passed by Parliament – the Dublin Parliament was led by Henry Grattan – while Burke's Civil List Act responding to the out-of-doors agitation removed some of the crown's sinecures and pensions which the Whigs abhorred and excluded government contractors from becoming MPs. But the political scene was altering. The old-style Whig leaders of aristocratic birth, progressive thought and libertarian morals ranged against the king were out of kilter with the new mood. After France had entered the war, feeling hardened against the Whigs as a group, their support for the Americans now seeming especially unpatriotic. They were epitomized by the swashbuckling Charles James Fox, the most famous Whig of his generation, who had helped revive the party during North's administration and was now one of Rockingham's secretaries of state. But it would be Fox's great rival, Chatham's son William Pitt the Younger, who caught the respectable tone of the age and became prime minister, while Fox's unscrupulous behaviour brought the Whigs into further disrepute.

Ideologically Fox had a great deal in common with the young Pitt, who was ten years his junior. They both believed in religious tolerance, the reform of government abuses and parliamentary reform. Pitt, like Fox, was a superb orator, with gifts he had inherited from his father, his first speech in the House of Commons prompting Burke to remark that Pitt was not 'merely a chip off the old block but the old block himself'. The differences between Fox and Pitt were really temperamental, but Pitt was made for the new age. He was far more circumspect and middle class in his attitudes, controlled where Fox was impulsive, and pragmatic where Fox was courageous but unrestrained.

The great-grandson of Charles II by his mistress Louise de Kerouaille, Charles James Fox was the second son of the daughter of the Duke of Richmond. His father, the wily politician Henry Fox, had made a fortune out of the Seven Years War as paymaster-general in the way that Chatham had disdained. Fox was said to be losing his father's ill-gotten gains more quickly than they had been made, at all-night gaming, the great vice of the period, which saw hundreds of thousands of pounds staked on a throw at the green-baize gaming tables of clubs like White's or on the horses. Fox's irregular life never stopped him making a dazzling speech in the House of Commons after a night without any sleep. To his admirers this was true glamour.

However, Fox's whole radical style of politics – such as stirring up the London mob to intimidate the House of Commons, which was one of his set pieces – was going out of fashion. Ever since the summer of 1780, when the Gordon Riots against a new relief act for Roman Catholics had ruined half of London in three days of uncontrollable violence, out-of-doors agitation had been deeply discredited. The petitioning of Parliament by the half-mad Protestant fanatic Lord George Gordon, with 'No Popery' as its slogan, had made the streets literally run with blood. Catholic chapels were burned, prisons were opened and many killed. Ministers seemed paralysed, and it was George III who saved the day by ordering troops to fire on the rioters. These events had frightened off the middle classes, who preferred to remain unenfranchised – in the event, until 1832 – than be associated with mob disorder.

On the unexpected death of Rockingam in July 1782, the intellectually gifted but unpopular Lord Shelburne became prime minister, only for Fox, who had been fighting with Shelburne, to destroy the ministry by resigning (though he was Foreign Secretary) taking the 160 Rockinghamite or 'old corps' Whigs with him. Shelburne, left high and dry, was forced to govern with the King's Friends and his little group of Chathamite Whigs – among whom remained the twenty-three-year-old Pitt, who became chancellor of the Exchequer. Though he had spent the previous twelve years tormenting Prime Minister North over the prosecution of the American War, Fox's only route to power again was to join forces with the Tories. Together he and North would have enough MPs to form a government. By April 1783, in a cynical power-play that scandalized the electorate, the Fox–North axis forced Shelburne out before he had seen through the treaty to end the war. Under a nominal prime minister, the Duke of Portland, Fox's and North's coalition government took office. North, following an apparently amazing conversion, announced that 'The appearance of power is all that a king in this country can have.'

But, just as before, George III was not to be underestimated. He now loathed the treacherous North only slightly less than Fox, who he believed with considerable justification was leading his son the Prince of Wales into bad ways. One observer watching the burly Fox swagger across the floor at Buckingham House to kiss George's hand as a sign of taking office, remarked that the king looked like a furious horse who 'turned back his ears and eyes' as if he was about to throw the new minister. George not only defeated Fox's attempt to increase the prince's allowance but managed to get the whole administration ejected over Fox's India Bill. This proposed that, instead of a governor-general, India should be ruled by seven commissioners appointed directly by Parliament.

Fox's reputation for untrustworthiness and his large majority in the House of Commons led to the general assumption that his aim was to secure Indian patronage for himself and his friends. This was greatly resented on the ground that it infringed. the East India Company's chartered rights, while the King's Friends considered it an attack on the royal prerogative. The king was heard to mutter that if the India Bill passed he would take the crown off his head and put it on Mr Fox's untidy black locks, while the cartoonists contented themselves with drawings of Carlo (Charles) Khan riding into London on an elephant and taking all before him. The hitherto impassioned belief that the crown's influence should be limited had passed its high-water mark. What was far more pressing was that Fox and his followers should be restrained.

While the affable, black-browed Fox relaxed after effortlessly piloting the bill through the Commons, George III put his own sly plan of attack into action. He instructed a young peer named Lord Thurlow to take a visiting card to all the members of the House of Lords dining before the vote, on which he had menacingly inscribed in his own handwriting the words: 'Whoever votes for the India Bill is not only not the King's friend, but would be considered by the King his enemy.' The Lords' role in the eighteenth century was as the king's advisers and, because George III had been lavish with his creations, they were mainly supporters of his, if not actually King's Friends. The king's enmity was something no eighteenth-century peer desired. They defeated the bill.

That same night, 18 December, the king sent for Fox to demand the seals of office. He had a new candidate ready for supreme responsibility, the twenty-four-year-old William Pitt, the youngest prime minister in history. Twice previously the king had secretly approached the virtuous and hardworking Pitt, for all his youth, to see if he would take office at a time when Shelburne could not control the House of Commons and opposition to the American Peace Treaty was threatening its progress. On both occasions Pitt had declined, feeling that he would not himself be able to control the House. The determined king did not give up easily. He kept coming back to Pitt, and eventually by taking soundings persuaded him he should have a go at being prime minister and see whether office did not eventually bring MPs over to him.

To jeers of derision, and the taunt 'A kingdom entrusted to a schoolboy's care', the tall slender young man took over the government. He refused to call an election, relying for his power entirely on the support of the king, and slowly the Tories in the House of Commons began to abandon North for him, not least because he was unsullied by compromise. Pitt was a very different man from Lord Chatham, cool where his father was passionate, happy to be a member of a team where Chatham had to dominate, simple where his father had preferred the grand style. And he was a consummate party politician, where his father had been a statesman and virtuoso war-leader. But it was no longer possible to talk with the same certainty of Whigs and Tories. Many of the old Whig aristocratic families had cut their connection with the party, which was itself continuing to decline in popularity. In the first election Pitt dared call, in March 1784, as many as 160 of Fox's Whigs lost their seats – Fox's Martyrs as they were humorously known. The Pitt government, which Fox had contemptuously termed a 'mince-pie administration' because he did not believe it could outlast the Christmas season in which it began, endured for seventeen years.

After the election Pitt was in a uniquely powerful position: he had not only the country behind him, but the two Houses of Parliament and, most crucially, the king. He was powerful as no one had been since the days of Walpole. An eminently sensible and worldly man who believed that those with wealth should be involved in politics and have a proper stake in the country, Pitt filled the House of Lords with a new Tory aristocracy which became as powerful as the old Whig revolutionary families. But though he was now at the head of the Tories, he did not forget his liberal origins as a reforming Whig, and put an end once and for all to the dubious methods by which government had been carried out for almost a century, by reforming the audit of public accounts. Like his father, Pitt refused to take the additional income from obscure sinecures, 'perks', which so many other politicians in office lived off.

Despite British mastery of the seas, it was rumoured that in peacetime things had got pretty slack with the navy, that there was not a single ship which could set sail and not need to call in for repairs. The dockyards were said to be slow and incompetent at their work. The sensible Admiral Howe, a reformer after Pitt's own heart, was made first lord of the Admiralty. In five years the fleet was up to speed again, with ninety ships of the line ready to sail to whatever ocean required their presence.

Though Pitt was now head of the Tory party, he continued to be a disciple of the radical economist Adam Smith, who had formed part of Shelburne's team of advisers. Smith, whom Pitt would continue to consult, had written a seminal work, *The Wealth of Nations* (1776), that turned on its head the mercantile protectionist orthodoxy to which all European colonial powers of the time subscribed. His argument was that low duties and freer trade between nations would dramatically increase their wealth. Pitt's attempts to free Irish trade from the restrictions imposed on her by English manufacturers met with shortsighted obstructions thanks to the clout of Lancashire businessmen, but his imaginative treaty with France created the lowest possible duties between the two countries. He hoped trade would encourage peace between the ancient enemies. As a painstaking financier who believed in fiscal probity, Pitt also established a sinking fund to pay off the National Debt, which after two world wars had reached £250 million, and reduced the duty on a large number of items such as tobacco, spirits and tea. It was the resulting cheapness of tea that encouraged the British to become a nation of tea drinkers, and to favour 'the cups that cheer but not inebriate', as one of the period's most characteristic poets, the Evangelical William Cowper, would write.

To some extent Pitt's zeal was shackled by his dependence on the support of the king and the King's Friends. He was a consummately practical politician who more than most believed that politics was the art of the possible. Although, true to his origins, he introduced a Reform Bill on coming to power, his motion to purchase some corrupt boroughs and redistribute their seats failed. When he saw how unpopular this measure was in the House of Commons, he simply abandoned it. Likewise, despite his belief in religious toleration, he would not lend his official backing to a series of attempts to repeal the Test and Corporation Acts between 1788 and 1791. The importance of the sugar industry to the economy and the lobbying of the powerful West Indian interests also stalled the abolition of the slave trade, but at least progress to that end was being made.

Pitt was fortunate that the beginning of his premiership coincided with that astonishing moment in the industrial revolution when James Watt's perfected steam engine allowed mass machine production of textiles and iron and steel. Although Britain had developed manufacturing processes throughout the century in tools, textiles and pottery the introduction of Watt's steam engine in the early 1780s changed the speed of production exponentially. In the space of a few years Britain could produce all kinds of goods from cotton sheets to machine tools ten times more quickly and ten times more cheaply than any other country in the world. For all Pitt's reforms, without the wealth created by the industrial revolution the country would have been bankrupted by war and by the ten-year boycott by America of English goods.

In only one area did Pitt win less than golden opinions from contemporaries and that was the trial of the former governor-general of India, Warren Hastings, which arose out of Pitt's 1784 act to regulate Indian affairs. Pitt's reforms, while not going so far as Fox's, gave the East India Company a government-run Board of Control, a new department of state. Its president was to be a member of the British Cabinet whose role was to supervise any political decisions of the company with regard to the Indian territories. The British government would also have a veto over the company's choice of governor-general, though the company's commercial policy was to remain unrestricted.

In the course of investigating the East India Company's affairs, poisonous reports from his rivals prompted questions over Hastings's conduct. Hastings was an extraordinarily able and constructive administrator, but his rooting out of corruption within the East India Company itself had aroused hostility, while his high-handed ways of doing business made him a great many enemies. Eventually he was impeached for extorting money, for corruption and for the murder of a witness against him. Most of the charges turned out to be untrue, and after what was then the longest trial in history, lasting for over seven years, he was acquitted – though he had been utterly ruined in the process. His friends blamed Pitt for not preventing the impeachment, but Pitt felt that the British government could not be seen to condone Hastings's actions or stand behind a man against whom there were so many adverse rumours. As a result of the trial a much higher code of conduct was demanded of the British Indian civil servant as a caste.

Thanks to Pitt's ceaseless work, England looked as if she faced the last decade of the century in tolerably good and modern shape in both her internal structures and her external relations. She had also added a new colony to her empire. The continent of Australia was founded in 1788 as a penal colony when the English government established a convict settlement to make up for the loss of America as a home for prisoners whose sentences had been commuted to transportation. The explorer Captain James Cook, who had discovered New Zealand and the eastern coast of Australia on his voyages in the 1770s, had reported that Botany Bay would make a favourable place for a settlement. In January 1788, when the settlement of Sydney (named after the then home secretary) was founded, convicts were taken from their temporary prison hulks on the Thames to start a new life a world away. By 1830, over 50,000 convicts had arrived. Soon afterwards the state governments ended the practice, and Australia in the 1850s was instead flooded with gold prospectors and sheep farmers attracted by the wide open spaces. Australia's neighbour New Zealand was to remain unsettled by the English until 1839, when Edward Gibbon Wakefield's New Zealand Company began colonization.

In foreign relations, as with everything else, Pitt was careful and sensible. He retrieved the alliance with Prussia as well as the age-old one with Holland lost during the American War of Independence. He was the first European statesman to recognize the potential danger the formerly sleeping giant Russia posed, now that she was becoming more involved in European affairs. The sturdy network of alliances ended England's dangerous isolation which had been hers for far too long after the American War. Those foreign friends would be much needed in the turbulent years to come, as the hidden pressures boiling away under France's glittering surface were soon to break out like a volcano, showering destruction far beyond its own circumference.

But in 1788, as a portent that trouble could erupt out of nowhere, George III suddenly lost his wits and became a violent maniac. He got out of his carriage while driving at Windsor, approached a tree, gripped its lower branches as if shaking it by the hand, and carried on a long conversation with it in the belief that it was the King of Prussia. His agitated wife Queen Charlotte eventually managed to lure him back into the carriage. But the king was so ill and strange on the night of 6 November that the two eldest princes, the Prince of Wales and the Duke of York, together with his doctors and his equerries, had to spend the night in the room next to his bedroom for fear of what he would do next. All night long he ran up and down the draughty corridors of Windsor Castle, gibbering, unreachable, a hopeless lunatic. The queen was too frightened of him to share a room with him any longer, and the king's footmen were so exhausted by his behaviour, because he needed so little sleep, that one named Fortnum had to leave for the sake of his health. He started a food emporium in Piccadilly.

It now appears likely that what looked like mental illness was actually a manifestation of a disease called porphyria, nevertheless there was absolute consternation in the higher echelons of government, for the way was open to a regency in the person of the wild and extravagant Prince of Wales, or Prinny as he was known. Campaigned for in Parliament by Fox who at last saw his chance to become prime minister, the post fondly predicted for him since his earliest and very precocious youth, it seemed as if England would be turned over to the irresponsible rule of the twenty-six-year-old heir to the throne. Like his champion Fox, the Prince of Wales was not only a gambler, but he was a declared bankrupt. He had also contracted a secret marriage, to a Roman Catholic no less, a Mrs Fitzherbert, in defiance of George III's 1772 Royal Marriages Act which still prevents his descendants marrying without the monarch's permission. While Prinny and his brothers amused their friends and scandalized their acquaintances performing imitations of George III's nightly doings, in the House of Commons Pitt duelled with Fox to prevent an automatic regency passing immediately to the Prince of Wales.

Pitt insisted that only Parliament could appoint a regent and that Parliament must investigate how to proceed. In a great scene in the House of Commons, Pitt won the debate. Behaving outrageously as usual, Fox announced to his stunned audience that since the king was 'legally dead' there was no need of precedents. What mattered was not what a Parliamentary committee thought but that there was in the kingdom a person different from everyone else in the kingdom – an heir apparent of full age and capacity to exercise the royal power with an automatic right to the throne. At this Pitt was heard to laugh and say, 'By God, I'll unWhig that gentleman for the rest of his life.'

Fox had entirely contradicted the great founding principle of the Whig revolution. The Whigs by offering the crown to William III had ended the hereditary succession by Divine Right and changed it into an institution dependent on the will of Parliament, Pitt said. Fox's argument was destroyed and George III remained king. While Parliament was setting up the regency the king recovered, greatly to the nation's relief. The fact that he was spending hours of the day trussed up in a straitjacket to stop him damaging himself and others was kept from the country, though there had been alarming and widespread rumours. Hale and hearty once again, though more than a little shaken, the king returned from Kew where he had been kept under the not very tender ministrations of Dr Willis. This episode, when Pitt's loyalty and quick wits had saved the day, deepened the relationship between prime minister and sovereign. It was another king however, just across the Channel in France, whose fate began to influence Britain's future when in 1789 the French Revolution began.

The French Revolution was one of the seminal occurrences of the last 200-odd years, and its reverberations continue to make themselves felt. Most of the governments of the world at the outset of the twenty-first century reflect in some form a belief in mass democracy. The French Revolution was the first experiment in that form of government. It began with an attempt by the French king Louis XVI to raise money by calling a meeting of his Parliament, the Estates-General, which had not met since the early seventeenth century. That was the fuse which set off the long-delayed explosion. By 1789 the French state was bankrupt, because of the wars it had waged unceasingly for a hundred years. The only way to tap new resources on the level required, economists realized, was to change the bizarre tax system in France. Almost unreformed since the middle ages, the fiscal structure contained privileged exemptions for the wealthy, the nobility and the Church, who paid almost no taxes at all. The greatest impositions, such as the notorious salt tax, fell on the poorest, as did the main levy, the land tax.

Tax exemptions tied in with other gross inequalities. Unlike the English, who for many centuries had been equal before the law, the French nobility had legal privileges. Their monarch, even so, was an absolute one. His word literally was the law since a letter from the king, the *lettre de cachet*, was enough to send anyone to jail for the rest of their life without trial or explanation. The French people had no recourse to Parliament to withhold monies from the king to combat this absolute style of monarchy. Though French philosophers had a tremendous effect on the rest of Europe, none of their ideas were practised in their own country. Frenchmen and women now passionately wanted to order their society along more sensible, rational lines.

At long last the first meeting of the Estates-General since 1614 was called at Versailles in order to raise taxes. What the king had not appreciated was how widespread and urgent was the French people's desire for reform. With the force of a dam breaking, they created a new body called the National Assembly, the French nobility themselves voted to jettison their ancient privileges and together they proclaimed a brand new constitution based on the Assembly's Declaration of the Rights of Man on 26 August 1789. This was influenced by the American Declaration of Independence, with its insistence on liberty, equality and man's natural rights, which had enthused the Marquis de Lafayette, one of the revolution's early leaders. But above all it was coloured by that classic Enlightenment document, the *Social Contract* of Jean Jacques Rousseau. Like Locke, Rousseau held that government was a contract between the people and their rulers, though most crucial to the course of the Revolution was his belief in what he called the General Will of the People.

But who was to identify this was precisely the problem. From the first, the French Revolution was accompanied by mob violence. So strong were English feelings about ending tyranny that the storming of the Bastille prison on 14 July 1789, notorious as a symbol of the *ancien régime* and the *lettres de cachet*, that Fox spoke for many when he hailed it as the greatest event 'that ever happened in the world, and how much the best!' The young poet William Wordsworth would reflect the feelings of a host of other young Romantics when he exclaimed that it was 'bliss' to be alive at such a time in the history of the world. Most English people felt a natural sympathy for the cause of individual freedom; they rejoiced that liberty was flourishing in a land which since the days of Louis XIV had been a byword for repression.

But the Declaration of the Rights of Man was followed by more extreme behaviour when a mob forced the king and queen out of the Palace of Versailles and took them back to Paris and to what was captivity in all but name. Lafayette had to raise a regiment of middle-class national guards to restore order to a Paris where the army had looked on as the mob rampaged. When the new Constituent Assembly made Louis XVI a constitutional monarch, Pitt and the English government remained sympathetic to this curtailment of the tyranny of the absolutist Bourbon dynasty. A French constitutional monarchy would give the two nations facing one another across the Channel more in common. But what began with noble speeches about universal rights soon degenerated into terror and mob rule.

In October 1790 by every boat refugees of the wealthier sort began to flee France with only the clothes they stood up in, warning that there was no making terms with the revolutionaries. They revealed how the furious peasants were paying no heed to what lawyers were doing in Paris – whether it was separating powers or establishing the rule of law and the rights of the individual. Centuries of being treated like beasts had at last provoked them and their Parisian counterparts, the Sansculottes, into behaving like beasts. The starving peasantry had started to go berserk: they were burning the châteaux where their forefathers had worked since time immemorial. They were looting castles, seizing gold, killing their masters indiscriminately, regardless of how well they had been treated.

In Paris the constitutional monarchy with an Assembly became a revolutionary government which was continuously reinventing itself, but which ultimately depended on violence. Though Louis XVI remained king in name, by 1792 he, the queen and their two children had been made prisoners, and their friends feared the worst. As one observer related there soon became 'reason to fear that the Revolution, like Saturn, might devour in turn each of her children'.

As the Revolution raged on, idealistically attempting to put right centuries of wrongs, disestablishing the Church, then getting rid of God and putting the more logical Cult of the Supreme Being in His place, renaming the months in a more descriptive way, no leader of the Assembly ever lasted for very long. After a few months he was always arrested for undefined crimes against 'the People'. The real power in Paris was in the radical political association called the Jacobin Club. There the most advanced revolutionary thinkers, such as Danton, Marat and Robespierre, hammered out a Republic of Virtue which aimed to destroy all human traditions which got in the way of logic and their interpretation of the Will of the People. These leaders were fast becoming dictators under the cloak of the great revolutionary slogan 'Liberty, equality, fraternity'.

Of all the English contemporaries the reaction of Edmund Burke, mentor of the Rockingham Whigs, was both the most pessimistic and the most accurate. He who had been such a supporter of liberty in the past turned into a Conservative overnight. His famous book *Reflections on the Revolution in France*, written only a year after the storming of the Bastille, presciently foretold chaos. Then, he wrote, 'Some popular general will establish a military dictatorship in place of anarchy.' The appalled Burke now believed that it was not possible for mankind to tear up the past: human institutions needed to develop slowly. So strong were his views that, to Fox's anguish, he publicly repudiated his old friend in the House of Commons.

The French revolutionaries' treatment of the royal family plunged Europe into war. Queen Marie Antoinette was the aunt of the Habsburg emperor and when the news got abroad that the king and queen were prisoners Austrian and Prussian troops commanded by the Duke of Brunswick were moved across the frontier to save them. But the mob responded to this threat to the Revolution with the September Massacres, a mindless slaughter of prisoners. In three days the people of Paris killed 6,000 royalist prisoners, bursting into the jails and murdering them where they stood. The heads of ordinary criminals joined those of friends of the royal family on pikes, to be paraded through the streets. All that autumn of 1792 the sound of the tocsin called the city and the citizens to arms. To shouts of 'À la lanterne!', which meant string them up on the streetlamps, the citizens of Paris complied.

And then, to the horror of Europe, when the revolutionary committees summoned every French citizen to join the army in a *levée en masse*, this revolutionary army managed to defeat the Prussians. This news had an effect similar to the British defeat at Saratoga. It had never been imagined that raw recruits, untrained and untried in battle, though 50,000 strong and burning with desire to protect their homeland, would defeat the renowned Prussian troops at the Battle of Valmy. But they had, and they had driven them back across the French frontier.

In response to the foreigners' invasion, the revolutionaries announced that the monarchy no longer existed. In its place a republic was declared. Then, in October, the Revolution which Mirabeau and Robespierre had vowed would not be exported, crossed the frontier. Fighting battle after battle the *levée en masse* streamed across the continent, seizing several German towns, then Basel in Switzerland where they proclaimed another republic. Finally, having inflicted a humiliating defeat on the Austrians at the Battle of Jemappes, the French took Brussels and Antwerp. If the ragged masses who died in droves for their country were alarming – when one lay down another twenty patriots sprang up behind him – still more frightening to the governments of Europe were the Decrees of November 1792, which announced that the French armies would help all people wanting to recover their liberty. The thirty-one-year-old Madame Roland, the wife of one of the Assembly's deputies, executed for no apparent reason, summed up the bewilderment of her contemporaries at what was happening to them with the words she uttered on the scaffold: 'Oh Liberty! What crimes are committed in thy name!'

Only a year before, Pitt had cut taxes and reduced British expenditure on arms because he was optimistic about the new constitutional French monarchy. He still thought Europe had never had more reason to expect peace. But events now followed one another so rapidly that even he was unprepared. In January 1793 the French king had received a hasty trial by committee, which bore no relation to a proper legal process. He was executed by that perfect eighteenth-century invention, the logical and efficient guillotine, which made executions faster and more humane.

News of Louis XVI's execution was greeted with widespread revulsion in Britain. The British government's reaction was immediate. To their surprise, the suave French ambassador Chauvelin and the special envoy, the elegant Bishop Talleyrand, the future prince, were told in no uncertain terms to leave the country within the week. In the House of Commons Pitt publicly deplored the fate of the king as an outrage against religion, justice and humanity. Unlike Britain, he said, where no man was too rich or too grand to be above the reach of the laws, and no man was so poor or unimportant as to escape their protection, the death of Louis XVI showed that in France neither applied.

Pitt still refused to go to war immediately, as Burke urged him to. He could not see it as part of the British government's job to launch a moral crusade purely on the ground that the French were 'the enemies of God and man', even though he felt it to be true. But he gave the French a stern warning. If France wanted to remain at peace with England, he told the

William Pitt the Younger addressing the House of Commons on the French declaration of war, 1793.

Commons, she must show that she had renounced aggression and was going to stay within her borders, 'without insulting other governments, without disturbing their tranquillity, without violating their rights. And unless she consent to these terms, whatever may be our wishes for peace, the final issue must be war.' Unlike his father Chatham, Pitt the Younger believed in peace. But it had to be a peace that was real and solid, consistent with the interests of Britain and the general security of Europe.

It had been growing fairly inevitable that Britain would go to war. The Revolution's foreign policy threatened monarchies all over Europe by its mere existence. However, it was only after the revolutionaries had declared that 'the Laws of Nature' meant the important Scheldt estuary was open to all shipping that Britain was forced into the conflict. France had threatened the neutrality of Holland, which Britain was bound by treaty to defend. There was nothing for it. Reluctantly Pitt steeled himself to put an end to the peace and progress that he had pursued for ten years.

But Pitt was pre-empted. The same day that he was speaking in the House of Commons, the men battling for power within France agreed to declare war on England and Holland. It was a war that would engulf Europe for the next twenty-three years and would not end until the Battle of Waterloo.

The French Revolutionary and Napoleonic Wars
(1793–1815)

During the next two decades of almost continuous war with France, the tolerant political climate of Great Britain underwent a dramatic change. Pitt had originally declared that this was not to be a war against 'armed opinions'. It was to protect British commerce, which was threatened by French ships on the Scheldt. However, it soon became clear that fighting 'armed opinions' had to be its objective, since the French government had vowed to help all nations which rose against their rulers. Just as 'Jacobite' had been a catch-all phrase in England denoting an enemy of the state for half the eighteenth century, so the revolutionary 'Jacobin' was to be in that century's last decade and the first decades of the nineteenth.

Only a few years after celebrating the Glorious Revolution's hundredth anniversary, for the English the word 'revolution' had taken on the most fearful connotations. Apart from a short-lived ministry of 1806–7 during which they abolished slavery, the Whigs and their ideas were as firmly out of office and out of fashion as the Tories had been for two generations. Political conservatism was in vogue, and more to the point was in office. In the face of war and the threat to British institutions posed by sympathizers with the French Revolution, the rational liberal convictions of Pitt and of most of the political classes vanished so absolutely that it was hard to recognize the former friend of reform in the young prime minister.

Even before the war Pitt had become alarmed by support for the Revolution. When a pamphlet entitled *The Rights of Man*, written by the radical Tom Paine and proposing an English republic, sold 200,000 copies in 1792, all further 'seditious writing' was forbidden by law. Paine was prosecuted and had to flee to France, escaping arrest by an hour thanks to a warning from the poet William Blake, who had had a prophetic dream about him. He was later elected to the French Convention. Once war commenced, a regime of complete repression was instituted. Pitt closed down the enthusiastic Corresponding Societies which had sprung up all over the country since the Revolution as a means of obtaining information about the great political experiment in France. In the new mood of suspicion most political clubs were considered nests of revolutionaries. If they would not abolish themselves, their members were imprisoned.

To make the authorities' work easier, in May 1794, habeas corpus, the foundation stone of English liberties, was suspended. This measure, which allowed the government to hold citizens in prison indefinitely while they were investigated for unspecified crimes, was opposed by only thirty-nine votes in the House of Commons. Moreover, contact with France was forbidden as a treasonable act punishable by death. Had it not been for the example set by Fox's continuing brave outspokenness, in which he was followed by his nephew Lord Holland, the playwright Richard Sheridan and the young nobleman Charles Grey, it might not have been opposed at all. Many Whigs were becoming increasingly uneasy about their leaders' opposition to the war. By July 1794 a large number of them, headed by the Duke of Portland and Edmund Burke, had crossed the floor to join Pitt's Tory party.

The war against Revolutionary France opened with Britain as a partner in the First Coalition, formed as a result of Pitt's efforts in 1793 and including Holland, Spain, Austria, Prussia, Portugal and Sardinia. Britain's allotted role was to concentrate on what she did best, which meant exploiting her large fleet. She was the only European country not to have conscription – indeed her army's very existence had to be approved by Parliament every year. The fleet, on the other hand, was that of a powerful maritime nation, and was successfully used to preserve the sea routes and seize enemy colonies. The route to India was saved when in 1795 the British captured the Cape of Good Hope from Dutch settlers. In India itself at Seringapatam prompt action by the governor, Marquis Wellesley, brother of the future Duke of Wellington, prevented Tipoo Sahib endangering the colony by stirring up trouble on behalf of the French. But the effect of concentrating on the colonies was that Britain's interventions by her army in Europe were too limited to be successful. Attempts to bring aid to the pockets of French royalist resistance in the Vendée in the west and to Toulon in the south were failures, while an army to the Austrian Netherlands under the Duke of York was run out of the country.

What Britain could do, however, thanks to the trade surpluses now mounting in the Treasury, was to pay for the armies on the continent after the fashion of Pitt the Elder. She had reached this position thanks to the application of Watt's steam engine, which propelled British industrial development into a different league from other European countries. The strength of the British fleet meant that British manufacturing exports and imports of raw materials from the colonies were almost unaffected by the war, while British manufactures were stimulated by the demand for materials from uniforms to tents to cannon balls. In an already reactive and practical industrial culture, a shortage of labour drove the ironmasters and factory owners, who were daily pushing invention forward in their factories, to greater heights of mechanization.

Since the Austrian armies alone consisted of perhaps 300,000 highly professional soldiers, Britain and her allies believed that the combination of so many countries against a rabble would prove irresistible, that France would soon be defeated and forced to retreat behind her old frontiers. But the French Revolutionary Wars showed that the world had reached a new stage. Fighting a war was no longer just a question of military science.

Beliefs too could provide a secret weapon. Wherever France's Armies of the Republic marched, their call for 'Liberty, equality, fraternity' found an emotional response from those living under more repressive regimes, and they were welcomed as liberators. Nor did the amateur leadership in the French military matter at all. The armies under the ex-lawyer Lazare Carnot were honed into a magnificent new fighting machine. Where they were not magnificent, their enormous numbers as 'the nation in arms' made up for their defects, and they swept all before them. In 1794 the French humiliatingly drove out the Austrians from the Netherlands and severed the Habsburgs' 300-year link with that country for ever.

And the efficiency of the coalition armies on the continent was undermined by the fact that Britain's main allies, Austria and Prussia, were far more interested in carving up the weakened kingdom of Poland with Russia than in eradicating the threat the French armies posed to the world order. After two years of war Prussia made peace with France, abandoning the coalition in order to finish off the partition of Poland (Russia, Austria and Prussia vowing to extinguish the name of Poland), while a mere two alarming encounters with the French armies had been enough to persuade Spain to ally with France. In addition, Holland had become a French puppet-state, the Batavian Republic. But Pitt had high hopes of the Austrian army, which still held Italy, for it was the largest in the world. Pitt also had information that after four years of war not only were the French armies suffering from exhaustion and lack of supplies, but the inexperienced government in Paris was running out of money. A peace might be arranged. But these were not conventional times. By October 1797, in an astonishing, almost miraculous campaign in Italy under a young Corsican general named Napoleon Bonaparte, the French had expelled the Austrian army from Italy and changed the shape of the war.

The British had first encountered Napoleon Bonaparte at the beginning of the war in 1793 when the masterly tactics of the twenty-three-year-old had defeated the British fleet's attempt to help the royalist resistance in the south of France by seizing Toulon. Napoleon was a small, thin, sallow-skinned, shabbily dressed artillery officer affectionately known to his men as the Little Corporal. After the Italian campaign he captured the world's imagination as one of history's greatest generals. Bonaparte began to be compared to Caesar and Alexander the Great rolled into one; and he certainly shared their dreams of conquest. During the Italian campaign he had thrown the Austrian defences into chaos by the swiftness of his forays, winning a series of victories that enabled him to overrun the entire peninsula. The portrait of a long-haired, windswept Napoleon holding a standard at the Battle of Arcola as he turns to urge his men on is perhaps the best-known image of him as a young man.

By the end of the Italian campaign his men would do anything for the leader who could apparently pluck victories from the air. Wellington, Napoleon's great opponent, would say in his memoirs that he had always believed that Napoleon's presence on the battlefield was the equivalent of 40,000 men, and military historians have agreed. The reason why Napoleon succeeded when everything was against him was because his personality caused the men to march and fight harder than any could have dreamed possible.

The peace party at Paris with whom Pitt had been negotiating for the previous two years were cast aside in favour of a war party headed by Napoleon Bonaparte, who had no intention of allowing his conquests to stop at Italy. By October 1797 Italy had become a series of republics set up by Napoleon. Alarmed by the threat the French Grand Army posed to Vienna, and to preserve the Veneto for themselves, the Austrians too made peace with France. With the Treaty of Campo Formio they were out of the war. Of the theoretically invincible First Coalition, Britain was left to face Revolutionary France on her own. Italy, whose indented coast had provided harbours for the British navy, was now out of bounds, her waters swarming with French and Spanish ships. French armies were established up to the left bank of the Rhine and the Alps, on what the French government decreed to be France's 'natural frontiers'.

For Pitt and the British, the years of Napoleon's most startling triumphs, which inspired Beethoven's Eroica Symphony, were very bad years indeed. Not only did the French seem unstoppable, but since Spain's desertion Britain's independence had been seriously threatened by three fleets. The combined forces of the Spanish and the French and the Dutch had the potential to seize control of the Channel and launch invasions of both Ireland and England. In 1796 French soldiers landed at Fishguard in south Wales and there were abortive attempts at invading Britain via Ireland. Only bad weather at Christmas that year stopped French soldiers being received at Bantry Bay by an Irish independence movement. But there was still the constant danger that the inherent anti-British feeling in Ireland would always make it a landing spot for the vanguard of French invaders. There Theobald Wolfe Tone, the leader of the United Irishmen – an increasingly republican progressive reform movement, which included both Catholics and Protestants – was only waiting for propitious conditions and French soldiers to throw off British rule.

The personal bravery of Rear-Admiral Horatio Nelson at the Battle of Cape St Vincent in February 1797 prevented the Spanish fleet from seizing control of the Channel. Nevertheless for much of the ensuing year Britain continued to be threatened by three navies, a predicament made much more grave by a series of mutinies (against bad conditions) in her own fleet which left the Channel quite unguarded. Only the quick wits of Admiral Duncan saved Britain from invasion by the Dutch when the mutinies were at their height. Duncan was out at sea watching the Dutch fleet in the Texel, quite alone and without a fleet apart from two little frigates. He sent the frigates up to where they could be seen by the Dutch from the Texel estuary; for the next few weeks the frigates signalled to an imaginary fleet out of the Dutch line of vision, and the invasion plan was abandoned. Then in October Duncan destroyed the Dutch fleet at the Battle of Camperdown.

There was danger of a different kind that same year. No one had appreciated quite how expensive the war would be. Thanks to the war's monumental costs and the gold disbursed to the allied armies, and despite the trade surpluses, the Treasury was empty. The Bank of England was about to suspend payment. There was a danger of real civil disorder, as poor harvests had brought severe social distress. Fortunately Pitt persuaded the king to put his authority behind a Parliamentary bill which allowed Bank of England notes to be issued as legal tender throughout the country instead of gold. The armed forces continued to be paid in gold, but the rest of the country used banknotes until 1819. This in turn brought its own troubles: prices rose but wages followed far more slowly. With so many labourers living just above subsistence level, local authorities throughout the country started to supplement their wages out of the rates, copying what was called the Speenhamland system of poor relief begun in Berkshire in 1795. As a result farmers saw no reason to put up their labourers' wages, which thus remained static for twenty years.

By 1798 Pitt was forced to introduce a rising scale of income tax to help pay for the war. It was based on the simple principle that taxing the rich at a higher rate would raise more money; it proved extremely unpopular with them, especially because the war showed no sign of ending. Pitt's attempts to bring the French government to the peace table, by returning France's captured West Indian colonies with a £400,000 bribe, had been rejected. The French had no need of money after Bonaparte's looting of Italy: all her treasures whether in gold or Old Masters were being dragged on baggage trains into France. And the French had no intention of moving out of the Netherlands, which was Britain's precondition for peace. Elated by Bonaparte's victories the French government was happily contemplating other campaigns – invading Egypt and Syria, perhaps Turkey and India, to make a new empire in the east.

But it was in that year, 1798, that the balance of the French Revolutionary Wars began to tip in Britain's favour. Nelson was in the grip of a deep conviction that the continental alliances on which Pitt had spent so much energy generally turned out to be useless. He believed that only British sea-power could save Europe from French domination. Thanks to him it did. When he heard that Napoleon with a flotilla of ships had managed to slip out of Toulon and capture Malta, one of the best harbours in the eastern Mediterranean, he became intuitively convinced that the Corsican must be heading for Egypt and possibly India. In this he was quite right, though it was a closely guarded secret even from the French ships' captains themselves. As the weather changed to the luxuriant warmth of the Middle East, Nelson followed grimly behind on what he was sure was Napoleon's trail. Without permission from his commanding officer he continued to sail east, severely hampered by the loss of his frigates during a storm – because in the days before radio these scouting ships, known as 'the eyes of the sea', would have been miles ahead searching for information. For the rest of the voyage Nelson was completely blind as far as long-distance scouting was concerned.

Extraordinarily enough, Nelson and the English fleet actually overtook the French ships during the night of 22–23 June. But because he had no frigates he never realized what had happened; the French fleet seemed simply to have vanished. While Nelson sailed fruitlessly round the eastern Mediterranean, the French war plan went like clockwork. By the end of July the loss of India loomed as Napoleon led his army south across the desert, defeated the rulers of Egypt, the Mamelukes, in the Battle of the Pyramids and captured Cairo. At last Nelson stumbled on a clue to where the French fleet had hidden itself. French ships were seen off Crete steering south-east, and on the morning of 1 August Nelson was back at Alexandria once more, to find his first instinct had been right all along. The French fleet was anchored in the crucially important Aboukir Bay, five miles east of Alexandria at the mouth of the Nile river.

Without pausing for even a moment, even though it was dusk, Nelson sailed straight in and attacked the enemy. The French, who had first sighted the English fleet in the far distance at two o'clock in the afternoon, were astonished that Nelson had made no preliminary skirmishes and by his lack of orthodoxy in choosing to give battle at six in the evening, since night-fighting was notoriously difficult. Theoretically the French fleet under Admiral Brueys was in a very good position at Aboukir Bay because Brueys had mounted batteries on the shore, but their range turned out to be too short. Brueys' second big mistake – but he was ignorant of Nelson's talent for spotting a vulnerable point which to others seemed nothing of the kind – was to have ordered his ships to be anchored far enough apart to give his ships room to swing round. Nelson suddenly realized that, if there was room for an enemy ship to swing, there was room enough for British ships and their uniquely skilled sailors to anchor alongside.

After a long night illuminated by a massive explosion and by burning ships, Nelson had captured or killed 9,000 men. But he had not only destroyed French naval power in the Mediterranean. Horatio Nelson's outstanding and unexpected victory against the French navy at the Battle of the Nile literally changed the course of the war. French plans were checked for the first time in five years. The British gained control of the eastern Mediterranean while the French army, with the best general it possessed, was left stranded in Egypt, having never received the reinforcements it was relying on, the soldiers on board ship in Aboukir Bay. But above all the Battle of the Nile gave heart to Britain's former allies, such as Austria. Up to now they had all accepted defeat. Now they tore up their peace treaties, enabling Pitt to form the Second Coalition of Britain, Austria, Russia, Naples and Turkey, and renew the war by land. Egypt became France's firm enemy as a result of her treatment by Napoleon and Britain's firm friend, while any ideas Napoleon had of starting a war in India had become pipe dreams. He was now in the middle of extremely hostile enemy territory surrounded by angry Turks and Egyptians. Nelson summed it all up when he said laconically, 'Their army is in a scrape and will not get out of it.'

When the news of the destruction of the French fleet at Aboukir Bay reached England two months later on 2 October the country went wild with joy. After five years of inexorable French military success the British could scarcely believe that at last they had dealt a serious blow to the enemy. Nelson was the hero of the hour, inspiring public prints and cartoons as adoring as Napoleon's in France. Lively, immensely charming and very patriotic, Nelson displayed genius and daring in a string of triumphs at sea between 1797 and 1805 which established the British maritime supremacy that would last for a hundred years. He had been in the navy since he was twelve and had often been wounded – he had only one arm (the other had been amputated) and one good eye (the other could only distinguish between light and dark). A small man, his clothes always looked too big for him – the future King William IV said that he was 'the merest boy of a Captain that I ever saw' – he was adored by his men.

Typically Bonaparte refused to admit that the Battle of the Nile was a defeat. The Army of Egypt was told in one of his most grandiloquent speeches that it must go on and accomplish great new things. But for once he had taken on more than he bargained for. The Sultan of Turkey, refusing to lie down under the French invasion, despatched two armies against Napoleon, and on 22 August 1799 the Little Corporal saw that the time was ripe for him to return to Paris before the disastrous Egypt campaign became known. Effectively deserting his troops, he sailed secretly from Alexandria on a small frigate to mount the coup which overturned the French government, the Directory, and enabled him that November to become France's principal ruling consul, a virtual dictator. A year later, when Sir Ralph Abercromby landed in Egypt and defeated the French at the Battle of Alexandria, the last wraiths of their hoped-for eastern empire melted away.

The Austrians now drove the French out of Germany. The Russians under the leadership of the remarkable Russian General Suvorov began to force the French to retire up the Italian peninsula, back the way they had come. The French were also attacked in Switzerland and Holland. But after a good start the Second Coalition did not realize its early promise. Led by poor commanders the English were pushed out of Holland and Pitt's attention was distracted by a rebellion that blew up in Ireland at the end of 1798. In Switzerland the French defeated the Russians at Zurich before Suvorov could get there.

The rebellion in Ireland was a revival of the one that had failed the year before for lack of French and Dutch troops. Revolutionary ideas had increased the already strongly anti-British tendencies in Ireland. The Irish anyway had little regard for a British king, and when they saw the French throwing off their monarch they were encouraged to do the same. Their excuse was Pitt's Catholic Relief measures, which were felt not to have gone far enough. In 1792 and 1793 Pitt had agreed that as a concession to the large number of Irish Roman Catholics, in Ireland Catholics should be allowed to sit on juries and vote in elections even if they could not stand for Parliament themselves. But eventually the hot-headed Wolfe Tone abandoned hopes of internal reform and concluded that revolution was the only answer. The British navy guarded the Channel and Irish Sea so efficiently, however, that what had been intended to be an Irish uprising backed by French military support turned into a civil war. Members of the newly formed extreme Presbyterian Orange Lodges in Ulster, named in remembrance of William of Orange, fought bitterly against the United Irishmen and their largely Catholic following. Despite strong support in Wexford the revolt failed, so that by the time French troops had managed to sneak across to Ireland's west coast they were too late.

The need for a proper solution to the Irish problem had become acute, particularly now that Napoleon had escaped from Egypt and was directing French military operations. To Lord Cornwallis, the former general of the English army in America sent over to keep peace between the warring factions as lord lieutenant, the Irish appeared congenitally incapable of seeing one another's point of view. He told Pitt that Ireland could be ruled only by a neutral government which had none of the Irish prejudices and hatreds. Rule from Westminster was the only way of escaping the implacable antagonisms of Irish internal politics.

But short of main force how could Pitt get the Dublin Parliament to vote for its own destruction? Not only was its existence a matter of national pride, but it was such a nest of entrenched interests. Pitt's solution was what he viewed as an extremely generous offer: Ireland should have one hundred seats in the Parliament at Westminster, and would thus play a part in decision-making way above her power and importance in the world. Free trade was to be established between Ireland and England. But it was the carefully designed package of bribes for the greedy and unpatriotic Dublin borough-mongers which got them to abolish the Dublin Parliament and their independence for the sum of £7,500 per seat. As for national acceptance of the Union, Pitt understood that the only way to win over the Irish and make them loyal to England was by courting the Catholics. The Act of Union between Britain and Ireland was predicated on its being accompanied by Catholic Emancipation for the Irish. Roman Catholics were to be admitted to Parliament and have their disabilities removed.

What Pitt had left out of the equation was the ailing king. George III took his coronation oath very seriously. As a Protestant monarch, he believed that it would be dereliction of his sacred royal duty if he allowed the remedial measures for the Catholics to go before Parliament. Despite all the arguments put to him, he held to his idea that allowing Catholic Emancipation would violate his promise to uphold the Protestant religion. 'None of your Scotch metaphysics,' he said to Pitt's friend the Scots politician Henry Dundas, when the latter tried to persuade him otherwise.

The Act of Union of 1800 thoroughly tied Ireland to Great Britain, temporarily at least. The first United Parliament sat in February 1801 and contained within it one hundred Irish members of Parliament, twenty-eight Irish peers and four Irish bishops. But it had a dramatic consequence: it caused Pitt's resignation. Pitt felt he could not stay in office as the failure to introduce Emancipation made it look as if he had deceived the Irish Catholics to get their support. Since any mention of the Catholics wound the king's nerves up to an alarming pitch, it was better if his prime minister resigned. Addington, the inconspicuous Speaker of the House of Commons, took his place.

Throughout the year 1800 the Second Coalition was on the retreat. Russia and her huge armies had already pulled out of the alliance; the new tsar Paul wished to be the chief arbiter in making peace with Britain and thereby gain Napoleon's gratitude. Tsar Paul, exploiting resentment of British naval policy on enemy goods, began to create an armed Northern League of former neutral countries, whose Danish navy posed a real danger to British defences. Then, in a typical feat of daring, Napoleon took his army straight over the Alps through the snow to attack the Austrians, crossing the Great St Bernard Pass to fall on the Austrians' rear where they were besieging Genoa. By December the Austrians had been driven back down the Danube. Terrified that Vienna would be Bonaparte's next target, in February 1801 they signed the peace treaty of Lunéville and withdrew from the coalition. Once more the British were left to face the French alone, and they had to do so under Addington, who had little executive sense.

Nevertheless by 1801 the tsar's plans to create a dangerous Northern League had been thwarted by Nelson. The slaughter at the Battle of Copenhagen in April when the British sank the Danish fleet was so terrible and the two navies so evenly matched that Admiral Parker started signalling to Nelson to 'leave off action'. But Nelson believing, accurately as it turned out, that he could bring the Danes to their knees, put his telescope to his blinded eye so that he could not see his commander's signal. He continued fighting until the Danes accepted his offer of a truce. The Northern League's most fearsome weapon, the Danish navy, was now out of the picture, and the League was soon broken up by the assassination of Tsar Paul.

Thus by 1802 Great Britain and France were level pegging, and a peace between the two nations was successfully negotiated: Great Britain could not hurt France by land, and France could not hurt Britain by sea. Both nations were utterly weary of war and in March that year the Treaty of Amiens was signed, which accepted the stalemate between the two countries. Britain agreed to recognize the French Republic and to give back all the colonies she had taken from France, apart from Trinidad and Ceylon. Malta was to be returned to the Knights of St John, who were to be under the protection of the tsar.

But the Peace of Amiens was not a peace so much as a truce, which Napoleon made use of to regroup his forces. He illegally annexed Piedmont and Elba to France, moved troops into Switzerland and was still occupying Holland. When in response the British refused to surrender Malta to a Russian protectorate, because of the growing rapprochement between France and Russia, hostilities resumed. But the nature of the conflict had changed. Not only are the wars which raged once more from 1803 to 1815 called the Napoleonic Wars, but the spirit of them was different.

The French revolutionary armies had invaded monarchist countries as an act of self-defence to prevent their enemies crushing the Revolution and restoring the royal family. But, though Napoleon's armies still claimed that they were recovering the liberty of the people from medieval laws, the Napoleonic Wars were old-fashioned wars of conquest. Bonaparte had drawn the Revolution in France firmly to a close. Not content to merely be military dictator as the first consul for life, in 1804 Napoleon crowned himself emperor in the presence of the pope, and six months later made himself King of Italy.

Britain was the most substantial threat to France's new ruler. Just as she had resisted the French revolutionary armies, Britain steadfastly resisted the extension of the Napoleonic Empire. Bonaparte or 'Boney' was contemptuously regarded as a new embodiment of the French tyranny and absolutism the British were used to combating. In the coming war Britain would not only be Napoleon's chief opponent, but often his only opponent. For his part Napoleon had become obsessed with the idea of humbling the British. During the peace his consular agents had been involved in unobtrusive espionage, taking country walks whose subsidiary intention was to spy out good landing places.

But now the gloves were off. Much of the original attraction of the French Revolution for radical thinkers in this country had died out when Bonaparte had abandoned its republican forms and made a Concordat with the pope. But even if some, like Fox, continued to be attracted by the great ideals of the Revolution, all arguments were irrelevant from June 1803. For Napoleon had begun massing an enormous army of 150,000 soldiers to invade England. While he stirred up revolts simultaneously in Ireland and India (the latter being put down by a superior young officer named Sir Arthur Wellesley) the camp at Boulogne on the north-east coast of France had already accumulated 90,000 Frenchmen and the flat-bottomed boats required for the operation. The emperor was waiting for the moment when the tides and winds would converge to carry what was known as the Army of England over the Channel to conquer the recalcitrant islanders. Napoleon had even had a medal made bearing the legend 'Struck in England 1804'.

When news of this build-up of troops across the Channel, with soldiers practising disembarkation techniques, reached England, the people became seriously alarmed. An invasion might only be days away, for even in the early nineteenth century the Channel took just hours to cross. At this crisis the British longed for the return of Pitt's safe pair of hands, or as the politician George Canning called him in a piece of light verse, 'the Pilot that weathered the storm'. Not only was the new prime minister Addington a complete nonentity but he had a poor grasp of foreign affairs and had even begun reducing the navy to save money. As another of Canning's jingles put it:

> Pitt is to Addington
> As London is to Paddington.

By May 1804 not even George III could keep Addington in power. Pitt returned having promised never again to mention Catholic Emancipation to the king for fear that it would bring on his madness. Once more it was up to Pitt to plan the new war against Napoleon and hope that somehow he could persuade another coalition to materialize. Unlike Addington, during the peace Pitt had not been won over by Napoleon's protestations of friendship. Convinced that war would recur soon, he had thrown himself into organizing the drilling on the south coast of the enthusiastic volunteer movement which was to provide 300,000 soldiers for the British army. He also supervised the building of those huge, round, windowless Martello towers you can still see today that were to serve as coastal defences. But after a year of the Grand Army sitting on the coast waiting for the best moment to cross the Channel, Napoleon realized that he might be waiting until Doomsday. The Channel was too well guarded by the British fleet. It would have to be overwhelmed by superior force. Napoleon therefore forced Charles IV of Spain to enlarge his fleet and join with the French to overcome the British once and for all. When British secret service agents reported this, Pitt declared war on Spain in December 1804.

Despite the overwhelming numbers against them, the British had one advantage on their side. The French navy after the Revolution was never up to the standard of the pre-revolutionary service; in a technical profession lack of technique counted badly against it. This also meant that Nelson could take risks he might not necessarily have got away with under the French *ancien régime*, for one of his characteristics was his ability to react to situations without scouring the rule book. But he also had extraordinary captains. Unlike the British army, where until the late nineteenth century officers could buy their rank, the king's ships were considered far too valuable to be trusted to amateurs. Learning how to sail a ship to the exacting standards of the Royal Navy took a long time. Commanders at sea could not be anything other than excellent seamen, and there was a very strict order of training. Officers started as a midshipman, as Nelson did aged twelve on a battleship, and worked their way up.

Napoleon's plan depended on the French navy joining up with the Spanish in a union of the fleets. But for the first half of 1805 the French naval ports of Toulon on the Mediterranean and Brest on the Atlantic were so closely barricaded in by British ships that the French fleets could not get out. But then in the summer the French had a bit of luck. A storm allowed Admiral Villeneuve and the Mediterranean fleet to escape from Toulon where Nelson was blockading him and join up with the Spanish fleet at Cadiz. The first part of the union of the fleets had been accomplished. The French and Spanish navies raced for the safety of the West Indies with Nelson in hot pursuit. But, to Nelson's frustration, the minute that Villeneuve heard of his arrival in American waters, he rushed back to Europe hoping to free the French navy at Brest.

On 22 July the combined fleets of France and Spain arrived off Cape

Finisterre at the north-west corner of Spain. It was the watching brief of Sir Robert Calder, who was patrolling the harbour of Ferrol. Calder had only fifteen ships of the line, while the French and Spanish had twenty-five. Nevertheless, knowing what the enemy vessels portended, the daring Calder attacked the combined fleet and captured two of their ships. But the overall consequence was better than that. For Villeneuve was so unnerved by the English ferocity that he whisked the Spanish ships out of Ferrol, made south for the safety of Cadiz, and ruined Napoleon's plans. If the combined fleets had instead sailed north they might have seized control of the Channel there and then, and overseen the safe crossing to England of the immense French army. But they did not, and England was safe for the time being.

Pitt had meanwhile managed to conjure up a new alliance against Napoleon, the Third Coalition, consisting of Austria, Russia and Sweden, which had become more wary of the Little Corporal's intentions. After Villeneuve's failure Napoleon had decided to cut his losses. The troops from the Channel ports were hurried to south Germany to fight Austria before she could get ready. But Napoleon's plan to control the Channel had not gone away. It could easily be resurrected. In the late summer of 1805 Pitt believed that destroying the combined enemy fleet sheltering down at Cadiz remained the most crucial task of the war. The situation was desperate, and it required desperate solutions. Admiral St Vincent had written after the Battle of Copenhagen, 'All agree there is but one Nelson.' It was Nelson that Pitt called in to see him at Downing Street to entrust him with an extraordinarily important task.

For this courageous man held the fate of Britain and the free world in his hand. On land in 1805 Napoleon was unbeatable; if the threatening allied fleet were not destroyed, he might be unbeatable on sea as well. Then the invasion of England would be assured. This was Britain's very last chance to continue to survive against Napoleon. As Nelson left Portsmouth on 14 September on board the *Victory* people knelt on the shore and prayed.

Although Nelson reached Cadiz at the end of the month, it took three weeks to lure Admiral Villeneuve out to give battle at Cape Trafalgar. On 21 October Nelson went up on to the *Victory*'s poop having visited every deck to boost morale. He was wearing the dress uniform of a vice-admiral of the White Squadron of the Fleet, to which he had been appointed in 1804. In the view of his friend and flag-captain Thomas Hardy this made him too conspicuous, but Nelson felt that it was important that his men should be able to see him. Looking out over the dark sea, which was a mass of fluttering white sails, he said, 'I'll amuse the fleet with a signal,' and asked for the message 'England confides [meaning 'trusts'] that every man will do his duty' to be run up. But since a flag for 'confides' did not exist, the word 'expects' was used instead. Then the battle began.

Nelson had twenty-seven ships to Villeneuve's thirty-three. His plan was to use his three biggest ships, the *Victory*, *Neptune* and *Temeraire*, 'like a spear to break the enemy line', the great Nelsonian innovation. He and Vice-Admiral Collingwood were leading two lines of fourteen and thirteen ships spaced about a mile apart. They would bear down at right angles on the two enemy lines and cut them in three, to create maximum confusion. This they proceeded to do at considerable cost to themselves.

Two hours after the battle began, a French sniper perched in the rigging of the *Redoubtable* picked Nelson off from about forty feet away. As he fell to the deck bleeding fatally all over his white uniform, Nelson cried, 'They have done for me at last, Hardy. My backbone is shot through.' Hardy carried the greatest seaman of the age, perhaps of any age, down to the surgeon's cabin, while Nelson concealed his face with a handkerchief so the men would not see the agony he was in. For four hours the admiral lay dying amid the din and smoke of battle. But by 4.30 in the afternoon his strategy had worked and the battle had been won. Of the thirty-three enemy ships, only eleven returned to Cadiz. As his ship's log reported, when the victory had been reported to Lord Nelson, 'He then died of his wound.' His last words, as a weeping Hardy held the little body in his arms, were 'Kiss me, Hardy. Now I am satisfied. Thank God, I have done my duty.'

At one o'clock in the morning of 6 November 1805 the Admiralty received the news of Trafalgar, and by two in the morning Pitt knew. That restrained man was so stirred up that he, who could always put his head on the pillow and sleep, for once could not do so. Throughout Britain, people wept when they heard the news of Nelson's death. Even the London mob, who usually celebrated victories with fires along the Thames and frenzied toasts, were silent from grief.

And the British could not have been in direr need of victory, especially one that secured control of the seas. Only three days before, Napoleon, moving faster than had been thought possible, with a Grand Army of 190,000 men, had forced the Austrian army to surrender at Ulm. Three days after the news of Trafalgar had roused the nation from gloom, Pitt attended the annual banquet at the Guildhall. His popularity in the country was such, after the great victory against Boney, that his carriage was unhitched from its horses and drawn to the dinner by cheering crowds. At the end of the evening the lord mayor proposed the health of 'the Saviour of Europe'. Pitt responded with one of his most quoted and briefest speeches: 'I return you many thanks for the honour you have done me, but Europe is not to be saved by any single man. England has saved herself by her exertions, and will, I trust, save Europe by her example.' The young soldier who had done so well in the fight against the powerful Maratha chiefs in India was present. Arthur Wellesley, the future Duke of Wellington, said of Pitt's speech, 'He was scarcely up two minutes; yet nothing could be more perfect.'

But though Pitt was in good form that night, in reality his health was breaking under the strain of overwork and the increasingly depressing news from the continent. Little more than a month later, amid the snow of Austerlitz, on 2 December Napoleon utterly routed the Austrians and Russians. The resulting Peace of Pressburg gave France back control over Italy and most of Germany. So many of the hereditary Habsburg lands were redistributed to the smaller German principalities that the Holy Roman Empire became an archaic concept and the last Holy Roman Emperor Francis abdicated on 6 August 1806. The new German states were organized into the Confederation of the Rhine, headed by Napoleon himself. Not only was he formally recognized as King of Italy, but he made all his brothers kings. The Bourbons were evicted from Naples in favour of Joseph Bonaparte, Louis was placed on the throne of Holland and Jérôme became King of Westphalia, at whose heart were George III's hereditary Hanoverian lands.

Except for England, almost the whole of Europe from the south of Spain to the borders of Russia was now controlled by Napoleon, and within the year Prussia and Russia would be entirely defeated. Pitt himself, passing a map of Europe in the company of his niece Lady Hester Stanhope, gloomily told her to roll it up, because it would not be wanted for the next ten years. Pitt himself would not live to see them. His doctors sent him to Bath for the waters, but it did no good for a constitution shattered by exhaustion and poisoned by the port which doctors then prescribed as a cure-all. Instead of relaxing he was feverishly working at new permutations of alliances – would Prussia help? – but without success. He gave the dreaded order to withdraw the British army from northern Europe. Then the dying man sank into a fever of delirium. He called 'Hear! hear!' to imaginary debates in the House of Commons, and kept summoning his messenger to ask how the wind blew. If the wind was in the east the news travelled faster. Then just before he died on 23 January 1806, Pitt suddenly shouted in a voice of agony that his cousin watching by the bed could never forget, 'Oh, my country! how I leave my country!' He was only forty-six.

In England there was a sense of loss almost as if the sun had fallen from the sky. For more than twenty years Pitt had presided over the British government. For most of that time he had been considered an inspiring figure, whether as the personification of virtue when he was a young reformer, or more recently as the man whose prompt actions had saved Britain from revolution and French invasion. To millions of people the solitary figure of Pitt, the 'watchman on the lonely tower' as Sir Walter Scott called him after his death, often seemed to be all that stood between them and Napoleon. Every morning in Downing Street, he had been at his post in his severe black coat, methodically plotting the course of Napoleon's latest troop movements and the latest engagements in all the different countries of Europe. He had been consumed by a patriotism which left no time for any other life than the late hours at the House of Commons. A sickly frame could not endure it for ever. And perhaps, as was said at the time, the news of Austerlitz was a blow from which he never recovered. Fox, who was himself to die later in the year, turned pale when he heard the news, and exclaimed that there was 'something missing in the world'.

Meanwhile, just as Pitt had predicted, the map of Europe continued to be redrawn by Napoleon. On 14 October 1806 at Jena he destroyed even Prussia's crack troops in a resounding victory and went on to occupy Berlin. Of the Third Coalition, only Britain and Russia now remained in the field. And by June 1807 it was only Britain. For after Russian troops had been beaten by Napoleon on their own borders at the Battle of Friedland, Russia decided to submit to France. At the Treaty of Tilsit of 1807 on a raft in the middle of the River Niemen, the Russian emperor agreed to Napoleon's plan to parcel out Europe between them into zones of eastern and western influence. Russia was at liberty to help herself to Finland, Sweden and Turkey as long as she recognized that the rest of Europe was Napoleon's, including the French-controlled Grand Duchy of Warsaw. Russia also agreed to join the Continental System, a comprehensive blockade which Napoleon had imposed against all English goods to try and starve Britain into surrender.

Under this policy, Britain was forbidden to export any of her goods to any of the ports of Napoleon's satellites, and by now that meant all the ports on the continent. All British shipping of whatever kind was to be seized, as was the shipping of any country which had used British ports. Defiantly, Lord Grenville – the new Whig prime minister, who took office because there was no natural Tory successor to Pitt – had retaliated by issuing Orders in Council which denied the freedom of the seas to any of Napoleon's allies. Thanks to Nelson's victory at Trafalgar it was really the French who were in a state of blockade. And in order to prevent the Danish fleet being pressed into service against her, Britain simply seized it. Nevertheless, these were desperate days. If help did not come soon from somewhere on the continent, to start a fightback against Napoleon, the British Isles might be starved into leading the half-life of a Napoleonic satellite.

Funeral procession of Pitt's rival, Charles James Fox.

This was anyway not a glorious era for the country. The dying Charles James Fox's efforts got a bill passed in 1807 which made Britain the earliest European country to outlaw the slave trade, but Britons themselves were experiencing a different kind of slavery in the early factories. The unrelenting war effort and fear of revolution meant that there was neither the time nor the political will for social reforms. One year after the Whigs had formed a government they were turned out by George III for trying to give English Catholic officers rights equal to their Irish comrades. Henceforth the king would have only Tory governments, in which after Pitt's death the reactionary or Ultra wing of the party predominated. MPs like Sir Francis Burdett, Sir Samuel Romilly, Samuel Whitbread and Henry Brougham, known as Radicals, were lone voices in Parliament drawing attention to the need for less savage laws, better treatment of the poor, and shorter and more representative Parliaments. They were a new generation of brave and unpopular politicians following in the footsteps of Fox and his nephew Lord Holland. The difference was that they were not connected to the great Whig aristocratic families. The Radical movement's supporters were found in the large towns and among intellectuals who had been

William Wilberforce, Evangelical MP whose campaigns to abolish the slave trade triumphed in 1807, though he died before slavery throughout Britain and the empire was outlawed in 1833.

members of the Corresponding Societies until they were made illegal.

But there was one area of the Tory government's policy that was dazzlingly successful. The decision to send a small army to the Iberian Peninsula in 1808 and support the resistance against the French there turned the tide against Napoleon and led eventually to his downfall. The theoretically straightforward little war in the peninsula, which the emperor dismissed as the Spanish Ulcer, became a cancer that destroyed the Napoleonic Empire. Until 1808 Bonaparte had been content to leave his southern neighbours as cowed allies. But the obstinate Portuguese refused to join in the Continental System against the British, with whom they had a long history of favoured trading status. Though the Spanish king Charles IV helped Napoleon capture Portugal, while the British evacuated the Portuguese government in warships, the emperor soon perceived that the warring Spanish Bourbon dynasty might be neatly replaced by his own brother Joseph, currently the King of Naples. In so doing Napoleon created his own Achilles' heel. Passionately proud of their history, scornful of the French peoples living north of them, the Spanish were not having any Frenchman on their throne. Like all other European nations the Spaniards were defeated in pitched battle by Napoleon. But, unlike the other peoples of Europe who were crushed by Napoleon, Spain refused to accept the French occupation.

A series of spontaneous risings swept the peninsula. Though it was occupied by the cream of the French armies under General Junot, the bare rocky country would not be subdued. Spanish guerrilla armies hidden all over the hills breathed defiance at Napoleon. The new King of Spain, Joseph Bonaparte, was forced humiliatingly to abandon the Spanish capital, Madrid, and to retreat with the French army to Bayonne, on the other side of the Spanish border. Meanwhile a self-appointed provisional government hidden in the Asturian Mountains of northern Spain sent a message to London asking for help. From this tiny foothold began the climb-back which would result in victory on the battlefield of Waterloo. In 1808, however, that was a happy outcome which could scarcely have been predicted.

The man put in charge of the peninsular expedition, Sir Arthur Wellesley, was a lieutenant-general in the British army, fresh from glory in India. Pitt had admired him for the way he 'states every difficulty before he undertakes any service, but none after he has undertaken it'. Wellesley was now landed with a small force in Portugal and kicked off the Peninsular Wars with a flourish at Vimeiro when he defeated General Junot, whose troops outnumbered his by three to one. But the incompetence and shortsightedness of two more senior British generals who arrived immediately after the battle enabled Junot apparently to recover, and despite Wellesley's victory an armistice was agreed in the form of the infamous Convention of Cintra. This allowed the French to evacuate Portugal with all their troops and arms and the gold they had looted from Portuguese churches, all of which were conveyed to France courtesy of the British navy at considerable expense. All those evacuated troops could of course be used against Britain in the near future.

The stupidity of these arrangements created a scandal in Britain, and Wellesley was the only commander to escape with his reputation. On the other hand, at least Cintra left Portugal free of all French soldiers, and thus made it a very good starting point for British operations against Napoleon in Spain. For there, at the end of 1808, the emperor himself arrived in his magnificent travelling Berlin carriage with his solid-gold campaigning dinner service. He was stung to the quick that the backward Spanish peasantry were defying the master of Europe. By 4 December he had defeated the Spanish forces and the French tricolore was once more flying over occupied Madrid.

As Wellesley was still in London giving evidence into the inquiry into the Cintra débâcle, the new commander of the British forces in Portugal was the affable and popular General Sir John Moore. He had just crossed into Spain to join up with the Spanish armies when he heard the news of their defeat. He was then at Salamanca, horribly near Napoleon and with insufficient troops to fight him. He courageously decided to draw the emperor north by threatening his communications with France. This would keep him away from the Spanish army, which was fleeing south to recover its strength.

Moore's tactics worked. Napoleon went north towards Burgos, leaving the Spanish to regroup in the south, but Moore had to beat a rapid retreat over the bleak mountains of the Asturias in the raw Spanish winter, pursued by the furious emperor's forces. He managed to get his men to Corunna in the north-west corner of Spain, where he had been promised that transport ships would be waiting to take him and his men back to England. But to their dismay there was nothing at the fortified town except sullen grey waves, while at their heels was Marshal Soult, one of Napoleon's most gifted generals. It was then that Moore managed to rally his exhausted, mutinous, demoralized men to make a stand. Though the transports finally arrived and the British sent Soult packing, Moore himself died in the mêlée, and was buried hastily at dead of night outside Corunna's walls with bayonets for spades. Moore's legendary courage and daring inspired the famous poem 'The Burial of Sir John Moore at Corunna', which begins so evocatively:

> Not a drum was heard, not a funeral note,
> As his corse to the rampart we hurried;
> not a soldier discharged his farewell shot
> O'er the grave where our hero we buried.

The arrival from Corunna of the piteous, emaciated British soldiers, who had almost perished as a result of administrative bungling, as well as the shame of Cintra, increased the unpopularity of the government at home. Headed by the Duke of Portland, one of the former Whigs sufficiently alarmed at the beginning of the French Revolution to join Pitt as a Tory, the administration was proving hopelessly incompetent, as disaster after disaster piled on Portland's head. George III's second son the Duke of York, who had shown himself an able administrator as commander-in-chief of the army, was forced to resign when his ex-mistress Mary Ann Clark (an ancestress of the writer Daphne du Maurier) revealed that she had used her favours to get commissions for wealthy friends.

Next came further military catastrophe at Walcheren, where the British had sent an invasion force to capture Antwerp in a bid to distract Napoleon and help Austria, which had once more declared war against France. For a moment in 1809, the Spanish risings had engendered the idea that the rest of occupied Europe would manage to throw off the Napoleonic yoke. The emperor had abandoned his pursuit of Moore to rush off to fight Austria, and it looked as if some of the German principalities would join her. But thanks to lack of co-ordination between the naval and military arms and poor reconnaissance the British forces never got nearer than Flushing and had to return home without striking a blow. Four thousand men died of fever that July at Walcheren, a small island in Zeeland above Antwerp. Meanwhile Austria had been shown by Napoleon's decisive victory over her at Wagram in the same month how unwise it was to raise a finger against her overlord. She made peace and provided Napoleon with a second wife, the youthful Archduchess Marie

Louise. By a strange turn of the wheel of historical fortune, she was the great-niece of Marie Antoinette.

Military failure, reports of improper use of influence during the election, a scandalous duel between Canning, now foreign secretary, and the war and colonial secretary Viscount Castlereagh, and his own poor health brought about Portland's resignation as premier. He was replaced by the former chancellor of the Exchequer, the right-wing Tory Spencer Perceval, who proved as unmemorable as Portland, and the trade slump continued. The Whig opposition, who had close links to manufacturers keen for the war to end, continued to attack the government for wasting money on the Peninsular War. But the one good thing about the Tory government was that it refused to abandon the peninsula. Indeed the only bright spot amid widespread gloom were Wellesley's sustained military successes in Portugal.

At his own insistence Wellesley had been back on the peninsula since April 1809, having impressed upon his fellow Anglo-Irishman Castlereagh the urgency of his mission there. He was convinced that Portugal could still be defended with only 20,000 British troops and 4,000 cavalry alongside a newly recruited Portuguese army, while the Spanish guerrillas tied down the French in their own country. He believed that the peninsula was especially important as a theatre of war because it showed the other European nations that their French oppressor was not invincible. Vimeiro had emphasized that the Napoleonic column, that massive and alarming spectacle of moving soldiery and glinting metal, sixty men deep, which had evolved out of the overwhelming numbers of the untrained French citizen-army, could be outmanoeuvred. In terms of firepower most of the men were actually useless while in column formation, because those in the middle were never able to fire for fear of hitting their comrades. The Napoleonic column that had spread fear through Europe could be defeated if a thin line of infantry – thin because it was only two men deep to enable every man to fire – directed musket fire at it. This would be the pattern over and over again in encounters between Napoleon's armies and Wellington's.

Wellesley believed that it was essential to maintain the friendship of the Portuguese people. On landing he issued the strictest orders to his soldiers. It was absolutely forbidden to requisition anything from the locals or to lay hands on the female population. The Protestant British, who tended to deride what to them seemed the more superstitious elements of Roman Catholicism, were to be respectful of the Portuguese people's religion. Anyone who laid a finger on a woman or stole a chicken was to be hanged. Wellesley's measures were harsh but effective. The Portuguese, who scarcely had enough food for themselves, were particularly grateful for his orders. The disciplined behaviour of the British troops was a pleasing change from the pillage and looting of the French soldiers.

Wellesley forged the 20,000 men he had brought to the peninsula into a superior military instrument. But Portugal was once again threatened with invasion by the French from two directions. The odds were greatly against the English, and Wellesley chose to give battle only when he knew he could win, because, he said, 'As this is the last army England has got we must take care of it.' Though there were terrible losses of life, Wellesley pursued the French out of Portugal to Talavera, halfway across Spain, but after inflicting a crushing defeat there on Soult with the help of 30,000 Spanish troops, he decided that the British army's position in Spain was untenable and retreated back to Portugal. His men now had to be even more carefully preserved because the French had put 200,000 soldiers into the peninsula. To this end Wellesley, now created Viscount Wellington of Talavera, constructed the strategical masterpiece known as the Lines of Torres Vedras. It was to be a lair in which Wellington's army – the British troops and 25,000 Portuguese soldiers – would hole up over the winter.

The Lines of Torres Vedras – 'old towers' in Portuguese – were actually a series of more than a hundred forts complete with redoubts, ditches and earthworks north of the city of Lisbon. Wellington's army would be able to keep a steady holding pattern until hunger supplemented by ambushes drove the French out of Portugal. The fortifications were thrown up in such secrecy that the French had absolutely no idea of their existence. It was not until what was intended to be the French army of occupation under General Masséna got to within two days' march of the Lines in the autumn of 1810 that they realized they could go no further. The whole British army had vanished into the hillside. Wellington had meanwhile given orders to the reluctant but nobly self-sacrificing Portuguese farmers to lay waste all the country around Torres Vedras and bring all their provisions and livestock within the Lines. He intended to hold out there indefinitely until starvation forced the French army to go away.

The British supply boats that he had waiting offshore permitted Wellington to sit out the winter of 1810–11 with his men. Outside Torres Vedras the French army under General Masséna prowled and ultimately starved, thanks to their policy of depending on the local produce. In the end, after waiting from October to March, in the course of which 30,000 French troops died, Masséna and his men were forced to abandon Portugal. In 1811 Wellington began his campaign to drive the French out of Spain. In that same year the Prince of Wales at last became regent, his father George III having been diagnosed as incurably mad. Although he had allied himself with the Whigs since his youth, the new prince regent was obliged to accept a Tory government, and the Peninsular War therefore continued unimpeded.

By April 1812 all four of the most important fortresses of Spain – Ciudad Rodrigo and Almeida in the north, and Badajos and Elvas to the south – had fallen into British hands. But they had only done so after a series of sieges whose huge fatalities required gallant self-sacrifice on the part of the British soldiers. At Badajos Wellington wept at the appalling waste of life when the storming of an incomplete breech required his men to use the bodies of dead colleagues as bridges. Nevertheless his object had been attained: the road to Spain lay open, and, beginning with a magnificent victory at Salamanca, he began to achieve his aim of forcing the French out of the south of Spain and keeping them out.

Wellington's influence in the corridors of power over the war's strategy was now unexpectedly helped by the tragic death in May of the prime minister Spencer Perceval. After Perceval had been shot by a crazed businessman named Bellingham in the lobby of the House of Commons, the new prime minister Lord Liverpool made Wellington's old ally Castlereagh foreign secretary. Meanwhile events in another part of Europe were aiding the allies. It was in 1812 that Napoleon finally overplayed his hand. He had parted company with the Russians over who should have Constantinople (modern Istanbul) and, believing that they were about to ally themselves with Britain as they were allowing British goods into their ports, in June he made the outstanding error of invading Russia.

His best soldiers were withdrawn from Spain to fight the new Russian foe, and were replaced by raw recruits. But not only was Napoleon badly overstretched. On its home territory the awakening colossus straddling the continents of Europe and Asia, which stretched from Poland in the west to China in the east, was too gigantic an enemy even for Napoleon. The 600,000 French soldiers he poured into Russia counted for nothing in its vast empty spaces. Like France herself, Russia was the nation in arms; and just as the French nation in arms in 1793 had proved too much for Europe, the Russian nation in arms was too much for Napoleon.

By 19 October Napoleon decided to abandon his attempt to conquer Russia, whose patriotic inhabitants were so determined to defeat him that they had burned their own capital, Moscow. It was far more important to return to his own empire, which he had been out of contact with for too long. The long and dreadful retreat from Moscow began. The ravenous once Grand Army broke up under the combined onslaught of hunger, the Cossacks and what Napoleon's renowned general Marshal Ney called General Winter. Thousands of Frenchmen were abandoned to their fate. They died where they lay. Too weak to move they were buried alive in the snow or became the food of wolves. Those who did not die – and the dead numbered a staggering 170,000 – made their way home often barefoot and without overcoats.

Unlike Wellington who provided for his men with meticulous care and invented the rubber boot which bears his name, Napoleon did not look after his soldiers. As Wellington said, 'No man ever lost more armies than he did.' Wherever he was, and in whatever circumstances, even if his men were starving, his aides were under orders to make sure that the ultimate luxury of white bread was available for the emperor.

Meanwhile, encouraged by the humiliation of Napoleon's retreat from Moscow, the Prussians, Swedes and Austrians once more declared war on Napoleon, their soldiers paid for by British subsidies. Now that their ranks no longer consisted solely of patriotic Frenchmen, the emperor's armies had lost some of the vigour and *esprit de corps* which had won the breathtaking campaigns of the past. Soldiers from Italy and the German Confederation of the Rhine made up much of their numbers. The Napoleonic Empire was beginning to pull apart under its own contradictions.

Against the inferior recruits in the French army in Spain, Wellington's already triumphant campaign turned into a rout. By 1813 after a superb set of flanking movements he controlled the whole of the peninsula, and had pressed the French right back to the Pyrenees. Then in October of that year in central Europe the allies won a decisive victory. At the Battle of Leipzig the troops of Austria, Russia, Prussia and Sweden threw Napoleon and 190,000 French soldiers back across the Rhine. By January 1814 all the German states had risen against Napoleon, impelled by a proud new sense of German nationalism. Having defeated Soult, Wellington crossed the Pyrenees to join the invasion of France as allied soldiers advanced from all directions. By the end of March Tsar Alexander I was in Paris along with leaders of the other victorious nations, while Napoleon himself was forced to abdicate and retire to the Italian island of Elba.

The more far-sighted pointed out that Napoleon was far too near Italy for safety, and that the people of France should be consulted on the question of what sort of ruler they wished for. But the victors were too frightened of another French Revolution rocking their own thrones to do anything but immediately reimpose the Bourbon monarchy in the shape of Louis XVIII, younger brother of Louis XVI. Deliberations about the future shape of Europe were referred to a Congress at Vienna. But into the peacemaking – conducted in a self-conscious return to the style of the pre-war era by aristocratic diplomats in between glittering balls – broke hideous news. There was no point in continuing: Napoleon had escaped from Elba. The Hundred Days of his last campaign had begun.

He was on his way from the south back up to Paris with an army of his veterans which was snowballing by the hour. Marshal Ney, who had been sent to capture Napoleon and had vowed to bring him back in a cage, instead had joined his old comrade once more. The fat and unpopular Louis XVIII made no attempt to rally the French people. They scarcely knew him, as he had spent the war in England. All too mindful of his elder brother's dreadful fate, he quickly got out of the country in an undignified scramble. Europe was back at war again.

It was decided that each great power should provide 150,000 men against Napoleon. The British forces under Wellington, who was by now not only a duke but commander-in-chief, were deputed with the Prussians under Field Marshal Blücher to defend the southern Netherlands north-east of the French border. It was there that Napoleon decided he should strike. He needed a conclusive engagement to defeat that section of the allied armies to enable him to link up with his followers at Antwerp before Russia and Austria had time to invade from the east. The Battle of Waterloo turned out to be conclusive in another way. It was the final end of the man Wellington called 'the great disturber of Europe'. But the situation was not straightforward. The victory of Waterloo was far from predictable. As Wellington, the Iron Duke, would himself say later, it was 'a damned nice thing – the closest-run thing you ever saw in your life'.

Wellington's best, most highly disciplined peninsular veterans were far away in America. They had been sent there for a new Anglo-American war which had broken out in June 1812 over the carrying trade. What he was left with was a force he described as 'an infamous army' – 27,000 raw recruits most of whom had never held a gun in their lives. 'I don't know what effect these men will have on the enemy,' he remarked, 'but by God they frighten me.' Moreover it was the emperor himself who was advancing out from France on 12 June 1815 with his most devoted partisans, veterans of twenty-two years' campaigning.

Wellington himself had come to the conclusion that Napoleon would need to strike quickly before the Prussian and British armies could work out their strategy, but he had no idea just how soon that would be. Absolute success and the complete defeat of Napoleon would depend on the arrival of 30,000 Prussians under Blücher, to bring the combined Anglo-Dutch forces up to about 65,000, still 5,000 lighter than the French. But the two armies were a considerable distance from one another. Wellington and the Anglo-Dutch army were in the main path of the emperor's advance, and in the event the Prussians very nearly never turned up to help them. For Napoleon's intelligence was excellent as usual. He decided that the Prussians must be attacked first at Ligny and put out of action before he dealt with the Anglo-Dutch forces.

As a result of Napoleon's secrecy and swiftness it was not until the afternoon of 15 June that Wellington discovered that his opponent had crossed the French border and was at Charleroi with 70,000 men. 'Napoleon has humbugged me,' said the furious duke. Not only were the Prussians being attacked at Ligny, but 1,500 French skirmishers had attacked an outlying Dutch division at Quatre Bras. This meant that the French were advancing up the highway to Brussels and were only twenty miles away.

Wellington now ordered his army forward to concentrate at the cross-roads of Quatre Bras in order to divert Ney from Blücher and the Prussians at Ligny. Though there was an inconclusive draw between the two sides at Quatre Bras, by the end of the day Wellington had succeeded in his limited objective: the British had prevented the French getting any nearer Brussels. Meanwhile the Prussians had retreated eighteen miles from Ligny to Wavre, which was due east of Waterloo.

When the Prussian retreat became known, Wellington decided that Waterloo was where he should fall back to. He would make his stand there and hope that the Prussians would somehow come to his aid. The area crossed the highroad between Napoleon's troops at Charleroi and allied headquarters at Brussels. It was bordered by the little village of Waterloo in the north, now on the outskirts of modern Brussels, and the Château de Hougoumont to the south with the farmhouse of La Haye Sainte in the middle. Wellington had had his engineers survey the ground for the past week for the maximum advantage. Every building, every peculiar feature of the landscape, had to be adapted for defensive purposes.

In the middle of the night Wellington got word from the seventy-two-year-old Blücher, who had been seriously wounded at Ligny, that even if the old general had to be tied to his horse he would personally lead out his troops against Napoleon's right wing the next day. As 18 June dawned, there was a terrific downpour, so often the prelude to victory for Wellington. The soldiers awoke to find themselves in a sea of mud, but were soon up and about preparing for battle in their red coats. Everywhere rode the duke in his cocked hat and civilian clothes, which he found more comfortable than regimentals, raising everyone's morale by his phlegmatic and indefatigable presence.

Napoleon, for his part, rose late. He shared none of his generals' fears about the British infantry or the battle itself, for he believed that the Prussians had been too badly mauled by Ligny to be able to join up with the British. Nor did he rate his opposite number. Rather curiously, considering the havoc Wellington had inflicted on his armies, Napoleon dismissed him as a 'bad general'. He took his time waiting for the ground to dry out for better use of his cavalry. That was another mistake, for every hour that passed gave the Prussians more time to come to the aid of the

Anglo-Dutch, hours during which Wellington was seen surreptitiously looking at his watch and wondering where they were.

The Battle of Waterloo began with an attack by the French on the Château de Hougoumont. Though it was set on fire, the British held it all day, protecting Wellington's right as well as preventing the French advance up the highway to Brussels. The French fruitlessly used up troops trying to

The end of Napoleon comes after his 100 days. The Battle of Waterloo, near Brussels, 18 June 1815.

capture it, but they never did. Meanwhile the battle raged as again and again the French columns assailed the British positions without success. The British were very carefully arranged in squares by Wellington. Drilled in preceding months by their sergeant majors, the novice infantrymen had quickly learned the 'steadiness' under fire that according to the duke made the British the best soldiers in the world. They could not have had more need of it. For against their squares came first the fearsome French infantry columns and then for two hours the French cavalry. 'This is hard pounding, gentlemen,' said Wellington at one point, 'try who can pound the longest.'

But each British soldier, as taught, continued calmly to take aim and fire, and then kneel and let the man behind him, whose gun was cocked, take aim and fire in his turn, as the first lot cleaned their guns and loaded once more. The French cavalry with their glittering cuirasses and high plumed helmets, galloped round and round the squares trying to put an end to the steady firing by breaking them up and finding a way through the troops. But nothing could shake the steady British line, though they could scarcely see in the smoke and scarcely hear in the din. All the while the beautiful French horses and their superb riders crashed one by one into the mud – looking, as Wellington later remembered, like so many up-ended turtles. But the squares held. Later when he examined the battlefield with its awful debris the duke found a whole square of men who had died in formation rather than let the French pass. When Wellington had been asked if he could defeat Napoleon, he had pointed at a redcoated infantryman and said, 'It all depends on him.' His confidence had been well placed.

Nevertheless, it had not been until mid-afternoon that Wellington got sight of tiny flickering troop movements in the woods in the far distance to the east. These were the first signs of the Prussians whose horses and guns he had been anxiously watching for since daybreak. At six o'clock in the evening La Haye Sainte, the farmhouse holding the centre, fell to the French. It was then that Napoleon tried to drive in Wellington's line between the farmhouse and Hougoumont. But the French were held off by the 52nd Regiment, whose attack on the left flank of the French ended in the use of bayonets. Just before sundown Napoleon sent in his elite Imperial Guard. But even they were beaten off by the allied infantry. For the first time ever the most legendary warriors in Europe broke ranks and abandoned the battlefield.

And then, just before eight o'clock with only about half an hour of daylight remaining, the Prussians at last arrived. Blücher was more dead than alive, but he had not failed his allies. Here he was, his long white moustache black with dust, but as energetic as ever, able to deploy his army to chase the French back into France. From beneath his tree, mounted on his chestnut mare Copenhagen, veteran of so many battles, Wellington waved his hat three times towards the French. The British could go forward at last. 'In for a penny, in for a pound!' he shouted. Up to the ridge came line after line of scarlet-clad infantrymen, charging on to pursue the terrified French. It was the end. Napoleon fled for Paris, where he immediately abdicated in favour of his son, the King of Rome, hoping that the child could become King of France in his stead. A short time later he was safely isolated in mid-Atlantic on the island of St Helena, borne there by the Royal Navy frigate HMS *Bellerophon*. He had thrown himself on the mercy of the prince regent and the English, who, he said, were the most generous of the allies. He died on St Helena six years later.

Radical Agitation (1815–1820)

The Battle of Waterloo rid the world of the menace to peace that Napoleon represented so long as he was free. But the widespread support his Hundred Days had received in France ensured that the peace settlement made in 1815 was far more punitive than had been first envisaged. Although France's borders reverted to those of the pre-revolutionary period, a humiliating army of occupation was put into northern France for five years, paid for by the French and commanded by Wellington, who also became Britain's ambassador to Paris. To underline the fact that Napoleon was no longer the master of Europe, all the treasures he and his soldiers had looted from round the world, such as the four horses of St Mark's in Venice and sumptuous paintings from the Vatican, were returned to their rightful owners. So furious were the Parisians at this, for they now considered that the loot belonged to them, that the works of art were taken away at dead of night to avoid rioting.

All round France, which had terrorized Europe for a generation, her neighbours were strengthened to prevent her breaking out again. The former Austrian Netherlands (Belgium) were joined to Holland under a prince of the House of Orange to give France a more formidable presence on her north-east frontier. Further south her eastern border was more strongly defined by consolidating the 300 pre-war principalities into a German Confederation of thirty-nine states. Within the Confederation Prussia was reinforced by the addition of two-fifths of the former kingdom of Saxony and territory in the Rhineland. Such an entity would make the French think twice before they tried to expand their borders again.

For similar reasons the mountain kingdom of Piedmont was also enlarged. Norway was taken away from the Danes, who had been allies of Napoleon until very recently, and combined in one kingdom with Sweden. South of the Alps, though most of her princes were restored to the *status quo ante*, Italy was back firmly under the protection of Austria. Russia, the new player in European power politics whose giant armies overshadowed the Congress, used the peace settlement to expand westward. The conference agreed to her demand to include the so-called independent kingdom of Poland in her empire; it was the price to be paid for Russian aid in the war.

The political thrust of the post-1815 settlement was thus strongly conservative, and where it did not interfere with the imperial ambitions of the great powers, it was legitimist – that is, it restored the ruling families who had been in power before the French Revolutionary Wars. As Lord Castlereagh, the British foreign secretary in charge of the peace negotiations put it, 'We want disciplined force under sovereigns we can trust.' The problem was that the conservative statesmen running the Congress, particularly the Austrian chancellor Prince Metternich, were so determined to bury the dangerous ideas which the French Revolution had set free in the world that they completely ignored the wishes of the native populations.

For all the conservative aims of the peace, the history of the next hundred years was to be the working out of the effects of the French Revolution as the Poles, the Italians and the Germans revolted against the settlement. The French Revolutionary ideals resurfaced in powerful offspring, liberalism and nationalism, that were not confined to Europe. Further wars and revolutionary convulsions produced a unified Italy, a unified Germany and conflagration in the decaying Ottoman Empire. England herself, whose Parliament already had a version of democracy in place, by expanding the suffrage over the next hundred years did just enough to prevent her own revolutions. There were sufficient far-sighted members of both Houses to see what had to be changed to fit the post-revolutionary age. Parliament itself could provide the safety valve so lacking on the continent. Nevertheless it was a bumpy ride.

Though Britain's conference negotiators were the Ultra or extreme Tory Anglo-Irish aristocrats Lord Castlereagh and the Duke of Wellington, their sense of what a Parliamentary democracy would not tolerate made Britain a leavening liberal presence among the repressive eastern European powers. Britain refused to join a new international organization to police Europe, an anti-democratic straitjacket called the Holy Alliance and proposed by the excitable Tsar Alexander I. It would permit the great powers to intervene in one another's affairs if they thought that Christianity, peace or justice were threatened, or, more bluntly, if the government became too liberal for their liking. Given her representative system of government Castlereagh and Wellington knew that Britain would never countenance the powers interfering by force in a country's internal affairs. On Holy Alliance principles, one of the first places to be invaded might be Britain.

What Britain could agree to was practical and pragmatic. In order to keep the peace in Europe and prevent another Napoleon ever arising, the victorious great powers, Britain, Russia, Austria and Prussia, formed a Quadruple Alliance to stop by armed intervention any aggression by France which would alter the Congress of Vienna settlement. Castlereagh had been sufficiently impressed by the recent co-operation between the powers to believe that a permanent system of conferences, like the Congress of Vienna, which he called the Concert of Europe, was a good way of hammering out issues before anyone resorted to war. By the second Congress in 1818, France had finished paying her war indemnity early, so Castlereagh got her occupying army withdrawn and France herself welcomed back into the fold of great powers. He believed that this would ensure Europe's future stability, for if France continued to be a European pariah it would make her disruptive and dangerous.

However, the Congress system which Castlereagh had such hopes for was hijacked by the Holy Alliance and Britain pretty well withdrew from it. The next few years were dogged by uprisings and demands for more liberal rule in Spain, Portugal, Naples and Piedmont. By 1820 the Congresses were issuing claims that they had the right to put down revolutions in foreign countries as well as clamping down on the press and on liberal teachers in the German universities. As a result Britain no longer attended in an official capacity, sending observers to Congress meetings rather than ambassadors. Britain, said Castlereagh, whose own king was the product of a revolution, could not logically 'deny to other countries the same right of changing their government' by similar revolutions. Thus by the 1820s Britain was once more the friend of constitutional change abroad, as she had been before the French Revolution.

As befitted the nation over which shone the glory of Waterloo and the honour of removing the menace of Napoleon, and which had financed a great deal of the war, Britain did extremely well out of the peace. After Trafalgar she had seized the opportunity to rid herself of any rivals at sea, and she remained the dominant country in the carrying trade. She now usefully expanded her trading bases throughout the world, adding Malta, the Ionian Islands, the small island of Heligoland off the coast of Hanover and some important former French West Indian islands – St Lucia, Tobago and Mauritius – to her colonial possessions. The route to India was safeguarded by her continuing to hold the Cape of Good Hope, which she had captured from the Dutch, as well as Ceylon (now Sri Lanka), at the foot of India. Britain's naval and commercial supremacy was confirmed.

Thanks to the British delegation the 1815 Peace Treaty contained within it a clause condemning slavery, in the face of Spanish and Portuguese protests. The efficient mobilization of British public opinion by the Anti-Slavery Society made it impossible for Castlereagh to draw up a treaty determining the shape of post-war Europe without registering a protest at the continued reliance of European economies on slave labour. By 1817, in return for £70,000, Portugal and Spain had both abolished their slave trade. The Netherlands had outlawed it the year before, and it continued to be outlawed in all French territories, as it had been by the French revolutionary government in 1793.

What has been called Britain's second Hundred Years War ended with France most conclusively beaten. In the new century Russia was the power whose activities Britain regarded with the most suspicion. But now that peace was established the government's most pressing problem was the domestic situation. The severe hardship and dislocation caused by twenty years of war combined with the industrial revolution was tearing the country apart. What was happening at home needed urgent attention and bold surgery. But surgery in the shape of Parliamentary reform, which the starving working class and the disfranchised middle classes were united in calling for, the Tories were most reluctant to grant.

The British government's sympathy for liberal movements abroad did not extend to democratic campaigns at home. The end of the war had given these campaigns new impetus for it exacerbated the already miserable living conditions of the working classes. Even during the war the Radical and democratic electoral movements had grown hugely because the galloping pace of increased mechanization had caused a steady stream of people to be laid off from their jobs. Social distress convinced them they required a voice in Parliament to make the government more responsive to their needs. In Parliament reform was called for by Radical MPs such as Henry Brougham the legal reformer and Sir Francis Burdett and their allies, the greatly reduced Whigs, including Lord John Russell and Lord Grey.

From 1811, the year the Prince of Wales became regent, there was rioting among labourers in Yorkshire, Lancashire and Nottingham in protest against the use of improved textile machinery in place of hand labour. At times hardship had been so acute that the poor had to sell their household furniture for food. Many of them, like the Luddites, skilled stocking-makers in Nottingham under the leadership of Ned Ludd, smashed the machinery that was making them redundant, for Pitt's Combination Acts had prevented any bargaining with their masters. In 1813 seventeen of them had been executed for their protests.

In 1815 their situation was made worse by 200,000 ex-soldiers flooding home to seek jobs, as well as the abrupt closing of the factories that during the war had produced uniforms, tents and armaments. British textile industries were badly affected by the swift post-war revival of manufacturing on the continent. As for farming, agricultural wages were still being kept low by the impact of the Speenhamland system of support from the rates. Even outside agriculture wages had remained unchanged since the war began. Prices, however, had risen 200 per cent, more in the case of bread due to a recent run of poor harvests and the high cost of cultivating moorland during the war. In the days before enclosures when factory workers had been subsistence farmers, the price of bread would never have affected them, but now they were no longer in a position to grow their own food. What was needed was cheaper food.

For manufacturers the solution was simple. They imported cheap foreign wheat to feed their workers. But the landowners believed that was ruining British farmers. Without thought for interests other than their own, and with astonishing insensitivity, in 1815 their Tory representatives in the Commons and Lords passed a new Corn Law. Henceforth foreign corn could be imported only if the price of wheat rose to a certain level, eighty shillings a bushel. In 1815 when the Corn Law Bill was passing through Parliament there were furious riots round the Houses of Parliament as starving workers tried to use physical force to get MPs to vote against the bill, which they had no other means of resisting.

Lord Liverpool's government, in particular the alarmist home secretary Addington (the former prime minister, who was now Lord Sidmouth), didn't see that the hungry people smashing machinery or taking to the streets had no other means of redress. They believed that these outbreaks marked the beginning of Britain's own long-deferred revolution. The period between 1815 and 1822 was unprecedented for protests against the government and the savagery of official reaction. One of the chief hindrances to dealing intelligently with the post-war social and economic dislocation was the government's identification of any demands by the working man with the Jacobinism which had destroyed the property-owning classes in France.

The government panicked. Laws were passed which punished machine-breaking with the death sentence. As the Romantic poet Lord Byron said in an angry speech to his fellow peers in the House of Lords, a life was now valued at less than a stocking frame. Since no police force existed, Sidmouth used spies to try and round up the ringleaders. Instead these spies acted as *agents provocateurs*, deliberately inciting isolated pockets of the most disaffected workers to overthrow the government and encourage mob violence when what most of the protesters actually wanted was specific reforms within the system. For the miracle was that despite the widespread misery there was no real uprising by the British people. Most people believed in the ability of Parliament to right their wrongs. They marched and attended meetings to discuss Parliamentary reform addressed by Radicals like the most famous journalist of his generation, William Cobbett, and by speakers like Henry 'Orator' Hunt. Though the government might see Hunt as a dangerous agitator, like Cobbett he agitated for reforms through Parliament.

Unfortunately in December 1816 at a vast Parliamentary-reform gathering at Spa Fields in Clerkenwell organized by the Radicals, the machinations of Sidmouth's agents and extremist elements ensured that all the worse suspicions of the government were confirmed. The meeting was taken over by the Spenceans, the revolutionary followers of Thomas Spence who believed all land should be nationalized. What had been intended as a peaceful demonstration turned into a riot. Some of the demonstrators were flying the *tricolore* and wearing the Caps of Liberty which had been so prominent during the massacres in Revolutionary

France. Calling for a Committee of Public Safety they began to march east to seize the Tower of London, but were broken up at the Royal Exchange in the City.

Similar disturbances, none of them serious, continued throughout 1817. Then, for a year, good harvests and cheaper bread calmed the country. But in 1819 the combination of bad harvests, which once again meant that people couldn't feed themselves, and the failure of the Radical Sir Francis Burdett's bill in favour of universal manhood suffrage, caused violent episodes to start up again. Still the government refused to see the agitation for Parliamentary reform for what it was. Tragically when an enormous and peaceful demonstration in favour of reform took place on the outskirts of Manchester at St Peter's Fields, in August 1819, it was treated as the beginning of the uprising.

Because the Radicals abhorred violence and wanted to distance themselves from people like the Spenceans, no one was allowed to carry anything which might possibly be interpreted as a weapon. The authorities were to have no excuse to claim provocation. The presence of women, children and indeed babies in the crowd was intended to show once and for all that these were demonstrators who believed in peaceful ways. As they came on with hand-painted banners waving above them to ask for the reform of the Corn Laws, votes for everyone and the representation of their areas in Parliament the only danger they posed was in their numbers. They were 40,000 strong. Nevertheless the atmosphere was friendly and orderly; the mothers had provisions for their families in their covered baskets.

The meeting had been approved by local magistrates, but they had since lost their nerve. At St Peter's Fields, therefore, were drawn up large numbers of yeomen cavalry, some of whom had been at Waterloo. Their behaviour now was far from distinguished. When the Radical speaker Henry Hunt got to the platform, he saw that magistrates were there waiting for him. In order to prevent any trouble he said that he was quite willing to be arrested. But the magistrates insisted that he speak. Halfway through his address, however, they sent soldiers in to arrest him. Not unnaturally the crowd disliked this. As with indignant cries they tried to stop Hunt being dragged off, the magistrates told the waiting cavalry to charge into the crowd.

Into the mass of wives and babies and banners rode the soldiers. Hewing and hacking with their sabres, their horses' enormous hooves tossing children into the air, they killed eleven people, including a child, and badly injured 400 more. The disgusted nation gave the event the sarcastic nickname 'Peterloo'. From every section of society a torrent of indignation poured out against the oppressive Tory government. The son of the MP for Horsham, Percy Bysshe Shelley, wrote a powerful poem *The Mask of*

Anarchy, advising the victims of the government to shake off their chains. 'You are many, they are few,' he told them.

The Tory government followed Peterloo with the repressive Six Acts. These made it almost impossible to hold outdoor meetings, tried to destroy the Radical press by extending stamp duties to all kinds of journals which put most of them beyond the reach of the working man, widened magistrates' powers to search private property for seditious literature and got rid of jury trials in certain cases. Thwarted by such methods Radical agitation died down. Only the discovery of the Cato Street Conspiracy in 1820, a plot to assassinate the Cabinet organized by a Spencean named Thistlewood who intended to set up a provisional government, did a little to convince public opinion that perhaps behind the reformers a hideous revolutionary conspiracy really had been lurking.

The Radical movement's imagination was soon caught by the plight of the prince regent's wife, Caroline of Brunswick. For in 1820 George III died. The virtuous young king of golden hair and iron will had long ago declined into a hopeless lunatic at Windsor, his hair long and white. Despite his condition the nation genuinely mourned a man who had been such a familiar figure for so long – he had reigned for fifty-nine years – and was known for his unassuming and simple ways and his exemplarily uxorious relationship with Queen Charlotte. The sybaritic and sophisticated prince regent at last became king as George IV after a regency of nine years.

George IV
(1820–1830)

George IV was renowned for his exquisite and exotic taste, his knowledge of the arts and a set which was as fast-living and grand as his father's court had been homely. On his accession to the throne in 1820 he toured his dominions, winning huge acclaim in Scotland. The visit was masterminded by the highly influential novelist Sir Walter Scott, whose popular historical works like *Rob Roy* had completely rehabilitated the treacherous Scots as noble and magnificent savages. George IV was cast into ecstasies by tartan. Tartan everything – trews, curtain material and little boxes – became all the rage, with the wild romantic Highlands replacing the Lake District as a popular destination for the feeling and artistic. As prince regent, George and his architect John Nash had made the little seaside village of Brighthelmstone in East Sussex into the smart resort of Brighton. Even today Nash's rich neo-classical style determines much of London's character – he designed Regent Street, Carlton House Terrace, Trafalgar Square, Marble Arch, St James's Park, and, by doubling Buckingham House in size, Buckingham Palace. But Nash abandoned that style to build Prinny a fabulous palace, the fairytale Brighton Pavilion whose onion domes seem stolen from the shores of the Bosphorus.

The prince recent had lived at Brighton until his father's death with his highly respectable Roman Catholic mistress Mrs Fitzherbert. As we have seen, to assuage her principles when he was Prince of Wales he had taken part in a marriage ceremony with her, though as he had not asked his father's permission it was invalidated by the Royal Marriages Act of 1772, and there was therefore no danger of a Catholic heir succeeding to the throne.

In 1795 the extravagant prince was forced to marry his first cousin Caroline of Brunswick on the understanding that Parliament would exonerate his colossal debts and increase his Civil List income. But he found her so unattractive that he left her three days after his only child Princess Charlotte was born. He took mistresses, and even for a period resumed living with Mrs Fitzherbert, all the while showing great hostility to his wife. As a result the Princess of Wales indulged her taste for louche

EUROPEAN MAGAZINE.

M.rs FITZHERBERT.

Published by J Sewell Cornhill 1794.

Mrs Fitzherbert, mistress of the Prince Regent. He secretly and illicitly
married her in 1785.

company, a taste which eventually led to rumours that she had had a child
out of wedlock. By 1806 the prince had forced the government of the day

to launch an investigation into her behaviour in order to get rid of her. This was called the Delicate Investigation. Her husband said that her house at Blackheath had become the centre of much scurrilous rumour, though no more scurrilous than that surrounding the Prince of Wales himself. But nothing much could be found to justify divorce proceedings, and the princess eventually went abroad, wandering from watering hole to watering hole with a further series of not very distinguished admirers.

The death of his father persuaded George IV, who had quite lost his handsome looks and had become extremely obese despite miracles of corseting, that it was the moment to rid himself of Queen Caroline once and for all. But his wife had other plans. As soon as her father-in-law died, she came rushing back to England to demand that she be crowned beside her husband and that her name be reinstated in the list of members of the royal family who were prayed for in church every Sunday (the king had had it removed). But George would not be dissuaded from a divorce. To achieve this there had to be a trial of the queen before Parliament. The feeble behaviour of the government, which did nothing to stop the trial for fear of the king replacing it with a Whig administration, added to the people's contempt for the Tories. The ill-treated queen, who seemed a symbol of their own repression, became immensely popular.

A Bill of Pains and Penalties, which was in effect a divorce bill, was brought before the House of Lords. The queen's alleged lovers and members of her retinue, who were mainly Italian, were cross-examined in public about her private life. Caroline was defended by the most brilliant lawyer of his time, Henry Brougham, the Radical MP who was a fervent supporter of all the great causes of the day – legal and parliamentary reform and religious emancipation. Thanks to his advocacy the trial of Queen Caroline ended in fiasco for the government, making them more loathed than ever. The divorce bill was only just carried through the Lords, but was passed by so few votes (nine) that it was never introduced into the House of Commons.

Though she had been informed that she was to play no part in the ceremony, the poor queen insisted on attending George IV's coronation at Westminster Abbey in July 1821. After being refused admittance to the Abbey, she moved on to Westminster Hall, where the royal party was gathered, and beat her fists on the doors until she had to be removed. It was no way to treat anyone, let alone a granddaughter of George II and the estranged wife of a king. Less than three weeks later Queen Caroline died at Hammersmith, perhaps of a stomach disorder, her condition probably aggravated by the humiliating way she had been treated.

Although the government under Lord Liverpool was afterwards notorious for being the most repressive for a century, within it were the seeds of change. The Cato Street Conspiracy proved to be the point when fear of revolution in Britain reached its climax. After it, a new more progressive era in Britain began, heralded by the death in 1822 of Viscount Castlereagh, the inspiration of the more conservative section of the party. Without Castlereagh, the only way Lord Liverpool could survive as leader was by giving office to the more liberal section of the Tory party, who were more influenced by manufacturers than by landowners. Indeed one of them, the new home secretary Robert Peel, sprang from the recently established manufacturing aristocracy. He was the grandson of a Lancashire weaver who had made a fortune.

The leader of the liberal Tories, George Canning, who was in favour of Catholic Emancipation, became foreign secretary, while at the Board of Trade was William Huskisson, another disciple of Pitt who was convinced that free trade was the answer to the world's ills. A more humane influence could now be felt at the heart of government, though Parliamentary reform continued to be evaded. Canning believed that prosperity would be the salvation of Britain and would do away with the need for it. And prosperity he, Huskisson and Frederick Robinson, the chancellor of the Exchequer, believed would come if Britain could be freed from as much protectionism as the country would bear.

The energetic voices of the manufacturers of Birmingham and Manchester, with whom the Canningite Tories were in close touch, convinced Huskisson to reduce the duty on a great number of raw materials, making it much cheaper to manufacture goods, while the duty on manufactured goods themselves was also reduced. Huskisson ended the mercantile system and the disputes over the carrying trade which had been the cause of such trouble between Britain and other countries, most recently the United States (the Anglo-American War of 1812–15 had ended in compromise, though not before British forces had captured Washington DC and set fire to the White House). Britain was now such a successful trading nation that she could do away with these remnants of a bygone age. Under the new system of 'reciprocity' Huskisson's legislation permitted treaties with foreign countries in the carrying trade which would allow their ships to use British harbours and vice versa.

But perhaps the most important figure in Liverpool's government was the home secretary Robert Peel, the shy, stiff redhead who had taken over from Sidmouth in 1822. Britain's social fabric was damaged almost to the point of no return, and many abuses needed radical redress. Peel was a man of conservative views, but an active conscience allied to a strong sense of justice meant that under his leadership the Home Office became an agency for social reform. Like most reformers of the first half of the nineteenth century, Peel was heavily influenced by the Utilitarian ideas of the English

Enlightenment philosopher Jeremy Bentham. Encapsulated in the proposition that the aim of government should be to achieve 'the greatest happiness of the greatest number', Bentham's thinking had a revolutionary effect on the British.

The very fact that the hours worked in the new mills had been questioned since the first Factory Act in 1802 was a sign of a more humanitarian mood – no one had previously tried to limit the hours men worked. A new Factory Act in 1819 which prevented children under nine years old working in cotton mills showed that there continued to be widespread support for state intervention in certain social issues. Then, from 1822, within Britain that spirit of progressive reform knocked off course by the French Revolution reasserted itself at government level. Advised by the pioneers of criminal law and prison reform Sir James Mackintosh, the Quaker Elizabeth Fry and John Howard, Peel did much to improve prison conditions. With the employment of trained staff, prisoners were treated better and the idea of rehabilitating them to fit them for a new life outside jail began to take hold. The use of iron fetters, so much in evidence even today in twenty-first-century American prisons, was forbidden unless it had the consent of a judge.

A harsh penal code had been the eighteenth century's legacy to the nineteenth. Above all there were 200 felonies for which the penalty was death. Although execution for pickpocketing had been abolished in 1808, shoplifting continued to be a capital offence. But since so many unimportant crimes received the death penalty most London juries on principle refused ever to convict. In 1823, hoping that juries would enforce the law if the sentences were more appropriate, Peel halved the number of such crimes and reduced legal material which had been accumulating since the thirteenth century to a few comprehensible statutes.

Next it was the turn of the working man to be treated as a human being. In 1824, after pressure from the Radicals, Peel took the great step forward of repealing the Combination Acts and restoring trade unions. Now employees could act collectively to raise their wages or to petition for shorter hours. Peel had none of the Tory Ultras' fear of the workers because he knew them from his father's textile mills. He believed that they had rights. 'Men who have no property except their manual skill and strength', he said, 'ought to be allowed to confer together, if they think fit, for the purpose of determining at what rate they will sell their property.'

Behind the figures and research which convinced Peel and Huskisson that trade unions would not wreck trade was a tailor with a shop in the Charing Cross Road named Francis Place. But Place was no ordinary tailor. He was a Parliamentary lobbyist who was passionate about the extension of the franchise and whose shop became a research library and meeting place for the Radical movement. Like William Cobbett, he was convinced that the way to salvation for the working classes was through Parliament rather than revolution.

In 1826 when a new trade depression swept across England, Peel – against the wishes of many Tories – passed an emergency law allowing some cheap foreign wheat to come on to the market. He was accused of bowing to the mob, but he believed it was more important to assuage distress temporarily, so that the poor were not also starving as they contended with unemployment. His forethought prevented a famine as there was a bad harvest that autumn to add to everyone's problems. Peel refused to view outbreaks of violence as an attempt to overthrow government. He was sympathetic to what he saw as a problem which was 'fundamentally one of human suffering'.

In 1829 Peel established the first Metropolitan Police Force, set up by Parliament with a commissioner at Scotland Yard directly responsible to the Home Office. He had been convinced by James Mackintosh, and by his own experience with a policing experiment as a young chief secretary in Ireland, that punishment was not a deterrent. A proper organization dedicated to preventing crime was the way forward. The success of the Metropolitan Police Force soon encouraged its imitation across the country, for crime figures were rising in the new industrial towns. Previously maintaining law and order in England had depended on the amateur talents of nightwatchmen, parish constables and the threat of coming up against the magistrate. But what worked in small villages where everybody knew one another was no longer feasible in crowded conurbations with shifting populations. By not arming the police, Peel silenced the old objections to a professional police force becoming the instruments of tyranny they were held to be abroad. The police were forbidden to act as spies like Sidmouth's old network of *agents provocateurs* who had caused so much misery in the past. The new constables became so popular that they got the nickname they retained until very recently of Peelers and Bobbies, after their creator Robert Peel.

And abroad George Canning, the new foreign secretary, reclaimed Britain's old role as the foe of absolutism among the nations striving to be free. The son of an actress, Canning had a gift for the dramatic gesture which had been lacking in the austere Castlereagh. Britain stopped sending even observers to Congress meetings because, Canning said, the British people did not like 'their representative communing in secret with despotic powers'. In 1826, the British fleet frightened off the Congress powers in the shape of Spain and France as they set about invading Portugal to stop King John granting his country a liberal constitution. Ever since the Peninsular War, Spain had been in awe of British military power, and as soon as

Canning showed he meant business by sending 4,500 troops to Lisbon conveyed by a large British fleet the Spanish retreated. Portugal was allowed to have her constitution.

In 1823 in defiance of the rest of the powers Canning recognized the independence of the South American colonies which had revolted against Spain. Not only did he threaten to use the Royal Navy, which was undefeated since Trafalgar, against any power that tried to recapture them for Spain, he enlisted the aid of the youthful United States of America, prodding President Monroe into declaring that South America was a sphere of interest to be treated as her own backyard. The so-called Monroe Doctrine stated that the United States would treat any European attempt to colonize the American continent or interfere with any of its countries or regimes as an act of war. In a memorable phrase Canning proclaimed, 'I called the New World into existence to redress the balance of the Old.' Recognizing the independence of the new republics of Buenos Aires, Colombia and Mexico made George IV so angry that he refused to read out the news to Parliament, pretending that he had lost his false teeth. Underlying Canning's heroics was trade. For 300 years British merchants had tried to penetrate the old Spanish stamping ground of South America. Now they had independence the ex-Spanish colonies were enjoying a lucrative trade with British merchants which Canning was determined to preserve.

Although the Concert of Europe was almost dead as a system of political co-operation, it lasted just long enough for Canning to achieve independence for Greece from the Ottoman Empire. It was with the Greek revolt against Turkish rule in 1821 that the first manifestation arose of what would be one of the great problems of the nineteenth century. Known to British diplomats as the Eastern Question, the issue was how far Russia should be allowed to expand into the power vacuum left by the declining Ottoman or Turkish Empire which stretched from the Balkans to Persia (Iran). Since the late eighteenth century the British had been alarmed by Russian ambitions to expand southwards, whether west into the Balkans or east into Persia, which directly threatened the route to India. Despite disapproval of Turkish rule which had given the country a bad name for centuries, the British Foreign Office believed that the Ottoman Empire was a bulwark against Russia. It had to be defended in its entirety because otherwise it would disintegrate.

The Greek Wars of Independence offered just the chance to move south that Russia desired, for Greece had warm-water ports and an outlet on to the trading lake of the Mediterranean. By treaty with Turkey Russia had some notional rights to defend the Christian populations of the Muslim Ottoman Empire. Russian interest in the fate of the Greeks had been quickened by the personality of the new tsar Nicholas I, who acceded to the throne in the autumn of 1825. He was keenly religious, and the Greeks who belonged to the Orthodox Church were not only useful potential empire material but his co-religionists. Posing as the champions of their Orthodox co-religionists the Russians might take over the Greek peninsula. This Canning was determined to prevent.

But though Britain's official aim was to prop up the ailing Turkish Empire, as it would be for the next fifty years, in the case of the Greek Wars British public opinion and Canning were fervently on the side of the Greeks. Every cultivated Englishman in the early nineteenth century was classically educated, and Latin and Greek philosophy and literature were the main subjects at university. When the Greek war broke out, it immediately attracted a host of British volunteer fighters paid for by Philhellenic societies which had sprung up everywhere. Among them was the living embodiment of Romanticism, Lord Byron.

In 1827 after five years of war the Ottoman forces were joined by Egyptian troops and began to overrun Greece. Although Britain was officially neutral, British public opinion – outraged by Turkish massacres of Greeks – demanded in no uncertain terms that the government do something. As a responsive and modern politician Canning saw that he could not ignore this upsurge of feeling. He came to the conclusion that, if Russia was going to intervene, in this instance the best hope for the future was to work alongside her, in the old Concert of Europe. With the backing of France and Russia, he negotiated a deal that in reality obtained freedom for Greece from the murderous Turks while it nominally prevented the dismantling of an important section of the Ottoman Empire. Remaining in theory a part of the empire and having to pay Turkish taxes, Greece would in practice have self-government.

In 1827 Lord Liverpool had a stroke, and Canning took over as prime minister. However, the enlightened Canning believed in Catholic Emancipation and this prompted all members of the government who were against it – led by Wellington and Peel – to resign, because they believed it would be the end of the Union with Ireland. Canning was in any case never popular among many of the Tories, who tended to think he was too clever by half, and in order to carry on in government he was forced to bring into his Cabinet some Whigs, who had been a negligible force in politics for twenty years, headed by the youthful Lord John Russell. The price of their support was a bill that repealed the Test and Corporation Acts against Nonconformists.

But by 1828 the gifted Canning was dead, after a long period of very poor health. His place as prime minister was briefly taken by Frederick Robinson, the former chancellor of the Exchequer, now Lord Goderich.

But in January 1828 Goderich had to resign because his Cabinet could not agree over the navy's sinking of the Egyptian and Turkish fleet at the Battle of Navarino in support of the Greeks, Vice-Admiral Codrington having acted on his own initiative. George IV offered the premiership to the Duke of Wellington, who violently disapproved of this destruction of Turkish ships that could be useful in the future against the Russians. Wellington created a government of some liberal followers of Canning's, such as Viscount Palmerston and Huskisson, and brought back the Tories who had resigned over Catholic Emancipation, including Peel.

Exceptional soldier though he was, Wellington was no diplomat and he quickly undid Canning's delicate footwork in the east. Canning's aim had been to contain the Russians by forcing them to act in concert, but when Wellington apologized to the Turks for the Battle of Navarino the Russians were disgusted that the allies had not finished off the job and invaded Turkey in 1828. The conservative Wellington's fear of revolution made him the enemy of any kind of independence struggles. But he now saw that it was better to make sure that Greek independence was real independence with international guarantees, otherwise Russia would make Greece part of her own empire. He therefore led the way to a tripartite agreement between Britain, France and Russia which enabled Greece to become free in 1829. It was the first blow in the dismembering of what was to be called the Sick Man of Europe, but there was nothing else for it.

Meanwhile at home the liberal wing of the Tory party found the Iron duke too reactionary for them to stomach. He treated them like subalterns whose role was to get on with obeying his orders. Soon after the repeal of the Test and Corporation Acts all the liberals such as Huskisson, William Lamb (the future Lord Melbourne) and Palmerston resigned. Wellington was left to govern with Peel and the Ultra Tories. The repeal of the Test and Corporation Acts had been a sign of a growing desire to end religious discrimination, even if thanks to Walpole the Test Acts were honoured in the breach. Within the year a daring election campaign in Ireland forced Wellington to bring in Catholic Emancipation.

For some time a number of politicians had believed that Catholic Emancipation would have to take place. But the several bills introduced to give the Catholics the vote had been rejected by the House of Lords, a number of whose members had Irish estates. As there were very few Catholics in Britain by now, its importance lay in its application to Ireland. Pitt had given Irish Catholics the vote at the end of the eighteenth century, but as George III had prevented total Emancipation Catholics still could not hold any official positions. They might no longer be penalized for practising their religion, but they could not be magistrates, judges, county sheriffs or members of Parliament.

Politicians like Canning had believed that the only way to bring order to a country with a stupendous murder rate was to give the Catholics more of a stake in running it. With proper responsibilities, the Catholic community might give their backing to law-enforcement, but, excluded from power, they saw the magistracy as part of an alien system administered by the Protestant ascendancy. The problem was that most Irish Catholics were against the Union and were increasingly in favour of repealing it so that they could govern themselves.

By the late 1820s the Catholics in Ireland had become much more militant. This was partly the effect of a new kind of patriotic priest turned out at Maynooth in Kildare ever since the Napoleonic Wars had cut off the Irish from their usual seminaries on the continent. The anger and resentment which in the past had been damped down by an apolitical clergy were also being stirred up by a well-off barrister named Daniel O'Connell. A speaker of genius in a country renowned for persuasive tongues, he soon became, in the old cliché, the uncrowned King of Ireland.

O'Connell set out to create a situation in which it would be impossible to refuse the Catholics the vote. His organization, the Catholic Board, was publicized from every Catholic pulpit, becoming an extremely powerful pressure group which was funded by a 'Catholic rent' of a penny each month and orchestrated continuous agitation for Catholic Emancipation. When the Catholic Board was banned, as it had all the hallmarks of a political organization, O'Connell and his friends simply revived it under a different name, the Catholic Association.

Thanks to the work of the priests and O'Connell, at the next election in 1828 the forty-shilling Roman Catholic freeholders in the counties (the property qualification entitling them to vote) had the courage to rebel against their powerful Protestant landlords. They voted instead for Catholic candidates fielded by the Catholic Association. It had always been theoretically possible for Catholics to stand for Parliament, as long as they took the oath of supremacy when elected. Of course in practice it never happened because swearing in that way would mean denying their faith and acknowledging that the British monarch was head of the Church. But, argued O'Connell, who was to know whether the elected MP would or would not take the oath? He was gambling on the expectation that, once a Catholic had been elected to Parliament, it would be extremely embarrassing for the English if they were to prevent him taking his seat. After all, Parliament's refusal to allow the legally elected John Wilkes to take his seat had created an uproar sixty years before.

To the government's consternation O'Connell was returned as the MP for Clare, by an overwhelming majority. The Catholic Association warned that at the next election it would send back not just one but sixty Roman

Catholic MPs. The system was in deadlock. Wellington was certain that Ireland would erupt in civil war if O'Connell was not allowed to take his seat at Westminster. Although only a year before the duke and Peel had both resigned office rather than serve under the pro-Emancipation Canning, Wellington now accepted that he had been outwitted – he had to support Catholic Emancipation and bow to *force majeure*. Wellington's prestige as an upholder of the Protestant establishment and as an Irish Protestant grandee convinced the king that Emancipation had to be granted. Extremely reluctantly, for like his father he believed that his coronation vows bound him to uphold the Protestant religion, George IV agreed. O'Connell's effrontery had won the day.

From 1829 onwards Roman Catholics could sit in Parliament, though they still could not become lord chancellor or prime minister. Wellington would not allow O'Connell to take his seat in the House of Commons this time round, however, as the Catholic Relief Act had not been passed when he was elected. To get his revenge Wellington also dramatically increased the property qualifications for freeholders to £10 a year, putting the vote out of reach of many of the peasants and small farmers who had returned O'Connell. Nevertheless quite enough supporters remained to get O'Connell returned as MP at the next election.

But not only did Catholic Emancipation mark the beginning of the end of the old establishment, it marked the end of Tory rule. The Ultra Tories were furious with Wellington because of what they considered his betrayal, and in 1830 they stabbed him in the back by voting with the Whigs to remove him and Peel from government. Their actions brought a Whig government to power for the first time since 1807.

William IV
(1830–1837)

The gathering sense in England in 1830 of the old order passing away was enhanced on 26 June by the death of George IV. The First Gentleman of Europe, as he was known, had epitomized the glittering rule of the aristocracy. A few months later the opening of the first long-distance steam railway line between Manchester and Liverpool was another indication that a clean break was about to be made with the past. The railway project was considered so exciting that the opening ceremony was attended by most of the Cabinet, including the prime minister the Duke of Wellington. They watched George Stevenson's celebrated steam engine, the *Rocket*, inaugurate the line.

But England was not only about to be transformed by the different pace of rail travel. Her population in the next decades would have gadgets their ancestors could not have dreamed of. They would soon be using the electric telegraph, invented by the Englishmen Charles Wheatstone and William Cooke, and enjoying what its English pioneers William Fox-Talbot and J. B. Reade called the photograph, but which was known in France as the daguerreotype. In the first steamships they would be crossing the Atlantic in ten days rather than the three months it took by sail. They began to have the sort of plumbing not seen in England since the Romans, to the great benefit of their health. They read by the gas light created by William Murdock at Watt's steam-engine factory in the late eighteenth century which had become commonplace in towns. And, now that they didn't have to strain their eyes by candlelight, they devoured vast three-decker novels by popular writers such as Charles Dickens, who would become the figures of the age, as well as its harshest critics.

With all these changes went a dramatic alteration in the governing of Britain. The dynamic commercial classes responsible for her newfound wealth would no longer be denied a share in guiding her destiny. In 1832, despite opposition from Wellington and much of the aristocracy, the Reform Bill delayed for forty years was passed. It had been accompanied by unprecedented middle-class demonstrations directed by Radical political activists and the reanimated spectre of revolution. What's more,

Isambard Kingdom Brunel, one of the greatest Victorian engineers. He built
Paddington station, the Clifton suspension bridge at Bristol and railways in India.

there would be two more Reform Bills later in the century which extended
the franchise further than that of any other European country. Only ninety
years later every adult male, regardless of what he owned, would have the
vote.

It was the beginning of a seismic shift in political consciousness. The
population was no longer divided into gentry, lawyers, merchants, a few
educators and farmers, as it had been for hundreds of years. There were

many thousands of professionals participating in the new occupations thrust up by the ever increasing permutations of the industrial revolution. They were boiler makers, machine-tool makers and, as the steam age took hold, engineers of every description, from mining to civil. They might not have had what was considered to be a gentleman's education based on the classics, but they were full of self-confidence, and highly opinionated. There were too many without a vote in the giant new conurbations of Sheffield, Birmingham and Leeds to find it amusing that the rotten borough of Old Sarum had seven electors who between them returned two members of Parliament – though the 'town' consisted of no more than a ruined castle on a hill.

The principal towns were beginning to build populations of hundreds and thousands of people. The great leaps forward in the iron and steel industry made throughout the eighteenth century by generations of inventive ironmasters like the Darby family, who discovered that pit coal could smelt iron more effectively than charcoal, moved the iron trade permanently from the Weald of Sussex to the north. Towns like Derby, Birmingham, Sheffield and Glasgow which had a history of metalworking – small manufactured iron and steel items of all descriptions, from hooks and eyes to weapons – grew exponentially, boosted by the demands made by the war.

The political will for reform became inexorable. The Tories under Wellington returned to power in the new Parliament in August 1830 to mark the accession of George III's third son, the sixty-five-year-old Duke of Clarence, as William IV. George IV's only child, the virtuous Princess Charlotte, of whom much had been expected as she little resembled her raffish parents, had died at seventeen. But this Parliament was full of men who had been elected on the reform ticket. All over Europe the post-war attempts at reaction and repression had come to an end. A spirit of violent, visionary nationalism swept her populations, expressed in plays, operas and poetry. Revolutions broke out in France, Belgium, the southern provinces of the Netherlands, Poland, Italy and parts of northern Germany.

Even though the Polish and Italian revolts were suppressed by their Russian and Austrian masters, in France and Belgium the middle-class liberals triumphed. Charles X, the reactionary Bourbon French king, brother to both the ill-fated Louis XVI and Louis XVIII, who had tried to restrict the power of the emerging middle classes and the press, was overthrown. In his place was installed a cousin, the son of Philippe Egalité, as a king on constitutional lines restricted by Parliament. He became King Louis-Philippe, known as the citizen-king. Belgium successfully separated herself from Holland and became an independent kingdom.

The success of liberalism abroad made pro-reformers feel all the more strongly that they should not give up in Britain. Queen Caroline's legal champion, the Radical Henry Brougham, showed the way opinion was flowing when he managed to get elected to one of the Yorkshire seats. For an outsider to be elected to a celebratedly xenophobic county was a sign of the desperation among its inhabitants that there should be a voice in Parliament for the huge industrial conurbations like Leeds, Sheffield and Huddersfield. It had become simply intolerable that not one of their inhabitants, however wealthy and important, had a vote between them.

Yet in the new Parliament's first session the Iron Duke made it clear that as long as he was in power the people could wait for ever before they could participate in Parliament. When the veteran Whig reformer Lord Grey said he favoured change, Wellington responded that the Parliamentary system was so perfect that he could not imagine how a better one could be devised. It was the final straw for what was left of the liberal Tories. Abandoning party loyalty they voted with the Whigs to turn Wellington out of office, and Earl Grey formed the first Whig government in over twenty years.

Grey was not a frightening figure for people fearful that Britain was about to have her own revolution. He was a member of the House of Lords with large landed estates. But he had fought for parliamentary reform all his political life and it was appropriate that he should be the prime minister to take the country into a different epoch. He had waited many decades for this moment and under him a memorably reforming ministry came to power. It consisted of Whigs, a sprinkling of Radical or extremist Whig MPs like Henry Brougham, who became lord chancellor, and liberal Tories. Among the Canningite Tories who joined the ministry were Palmerston and Lord Melbourne.

Grey himself had been born in 1764, but most of his colleagues were young men determined to modernize the voting system – England was the Mother of Parliaments (in John Bright's phrase of a generation later) and it was important to stop the model for all forward-looking countries becoming a laughing stock to its own citizens. On 31 March 1831 Lord John Russell, the young Whig who had successfully taken the Test and Corporation Acts off the statute book and opened state offices up to non-Anglicans, moved a first reading of a Reform Bill in the House of Commons. The reforms were sweeping: 168 members of Parliament were to lose their seats, sixty boroughs were to be removed. All boroughs with fewer than 2,000 inhabitants were to be disenfranchised and the thirty boroughs with fewer than 4,000 inhabitants were to lose a member. All the seats liberated by these measures were to be given to the unrepresented cities like Manchester, Leeds, Birmingham and Sheffield, to new London boroughs and to the large under-represented counties like Yorkshire.

To the existing electoral roll of 400,000 voters Russell had added around a quarter of a million adult males, not all of whom owned their own homes. It was a daring stroke. For previously only property-holders had been deemed responsible enough to vote – though a large property qualification remained necessary to stand for Parliament. By extending the franchise in towns to households which paid an annual rent of £10 Russell gave the vote to the middle classes, to shopkeepers, small businessmen, engineers, teachers. It was the end of Parliament as the exclusive fiefdom of the landed interest.

In the counties where the franchise had always been more democratic – freeholders whose property was worth only forty shillings a year had been allowed to vote – some of the more well-to-do tenant farmers were brought into the franchise, though there were still no poor working-class voters: thus £10 a year copyholders and leaseholders for twenty-one years or more to the value of £50 got the vote. From now on there was to be an electoral register, which would be proof enough of a man's right to vote, and the actual voting, or poll, instead of stretching over weeks (which gave much leeway for abuse), was to take place in towns over the course of one day, and in the country over two, because distances were greater.

The Reform Bill passed its second reading in the Commons by just one vote. The looks on the faces of the amazed Tories were compared by an onlooker to those of the damned. But the Tories were not beaten yet. They managed to defeat the bill in committee – the stage in the passing of an act by Parliament when it is scrutinized in detail. The government resigned and called a general election.

In effect a referendum, the Reform Bill election took place amid scenes of tremendous excitement. A great many reformers were returned to Parliament. In Birmingham, under the direction of the Radical campaigner Thomas Attwood, soon to be MP for the city, a huge number of citizens joined the organization called the Political Union, which Attwood had created to persuade existing voters to support pro-reform candidates in the election. Backed by the rallying cry 'The Bill, the whole Bill and nothing but the Bill', the Reform Bill now passed without too much difficulty through the House of Commons. But in October 1831 the House of Lords, true to its nature as a conservative landowning body, threw it out. Rioting broke out all over the country. Peers and bishops were attacked in the streets; in Bristol the bishop's palace was fired. Nottingham Castle was razed to the ground because it belonged to the Duke of Newcastle. In many towns and cities the army had to be called out to restore order.

But much more alarming than the mob excesses was the rebellion of the middle classes. All across Britain, in town after town, her most respectable citizens – lawyers, teachers, doctors, the backbone of the country – rushed to join the Radicals' newly formed Political Unions, copied from Birmingham, to signal their outrage at the vote being withheld from them. Their self-proclaimed object was 'to defend the king and his ministers against borough mongers'. In Birmingham, where the church bells were specially muffled and tolled day and night to show the city's fury, the 150,000 members of the Political Union announced that they were ready to march on London. As had happened under James II in the face of his attempt to turn the country Catholic, the British started to refuse to operate the great voluntary system of local government service on which the country's wellbeing and orderliness depended. They would not act as JPs or as sheriffs. Courts could not sit. The public-service ethos which is an inestimable part of the fabric of Britain was effectively being suspended. It began to be disturbingly clear that the country was in real danger of falling apart if something was not done to appease the reformers.

Against this background the Whigs created a third version of the Reform Bill in December 1831. It got through the Commons and then through the Lords, because many peers, alarmed by what was happening in the country at large, were starting to see that the Reform Bill was unstoppable. But it was stymied at committee stage at the end of April 1832 when a number of peers tried to prevent some of the provisions being debated. Worse still the affable king refused to rescue Lord Grey, declining his request to create fifty new Whig peers to override the Tory majority in the Lords.

As the third of the many sons of George III, William IV had grown up believing himself to be of little consequence, as indeed he had been until his elder brother the Duke of York, the heir presumptive, died in 1827. As Duke of Clarence he had enjoyed a very cosy family life in Richmond, where he lived until 1811 with a jolly actress widow named Mrs Jordan, by whom he had ten children all without benefit of marriage. In 1818 he was persuaded to marry a more suitable royal personage, Princess Adelaide Saxe-Meiningen. She produced two daughters, but unfortunately they did not have the health of his illegitimate family, and died young. Having been educated at sea for the most part, very far from the grandeur of court ceremonial, William IV seemed completely unpretentious, with the decidedly unregal rolling gait of a sailor. After he became king he continued his amiable habit of giving lifts to friends in the street and, despite his new royal status he always moved up to give them room. Known as Silly Billy, supposedly behind his back, he is said to have muttered at his coronation, 'Who's the Silly Billy now?'

While the Reform Bill had been going through Parliament, the bluff, pop-eyed king had become extremely agitated and soon lost all his earlier democratic feeling. Grey had no option but to resign. Wellington was once more sent for and invited by the king to be prime minister, for William believed that the duke would manage to get through a modified and acceptable version of the bill.

The feeling in the country by now was at fever pitch. The Duke of Wellington, who fifteen years before had been venerated as the saviour of the nation, was the most unpopular figure in the country. His old home Apsley House at Hyde Park Gate still bears the iron shutters it was thought necessary to fit to his windows against the mob. When it was known that Wellington was trying to form an administration, in what are known as the Days of May giant placards appeared all over London with the slogan 'Go for gold and stop the Duke!' Obediently, in Manchester and Birmingham people started to take their money out of their accounts to destabilize the currency. The Political Unions advocated withholding taxes from the government. There is no doubt that had the duke been able to form a government there would have been civil war. The whole system was in a state of collapse; the middle-class Political Unions were drilling in companies, bringing in men with military training to organize them.

In the face of such civil disorder, just as with Catholic Emancipation Wellington had the sense to realize that he had to bow to the will of the people. He gave up trying to form a government and, in a tense interview with the king at Windsor, told him to recall Earl Grey and accept the bill. To preserve the monarchy from the indignity of being forced to create peers against the king's will, and save the peerage from being devalued, Wellington cajoled so many of his friends not to vote that on 4 June 1832 the bill went through the House of Lords with a large majority.

The first reformed Parliament sat in 1833. Strangely and symbolically a year later the old House of Commons burned down. On its site arose the magnificent pseudo-Gothic pile we see today, designed by Charles Barry. Its medieval air rightly reminds us of Parliament's origins at the end of the thirteenth century. Nonetheless, the reformed House of Commons had a new and modern spirit. Power had finally passed away from the few whose ancestors had entitled them to shields and quarterings. The new MPs were commercially minded, progressive and urban. Even so, the gentry and aristocracy still had an inbuilt majority in the House of Lords and remained the leaders of the county constituencies for many years to come.

What was immediately expressed by the House of Commons was what had become the most fervent belief of the newly enfranchised, religious middle classes: the wickedness of slavery. The trade had been abolished in 1807, but slavery itself had not come to an end – indeed it continued to underpin the economy of the West Indies. One of the Grey government's first actions was to outlaw slavery throughout the British Empire, and the planters were compensated financially with the colossal sum of £20 million between them. William Wilberforce, the father of the anti-slavery movement, died that very year on the point of seeing his great work come to fruition.

The spirit of the new Whig administration was to seek improvement and change, and many of the MPs wanted it to mark the end of aristocratic *laissez-faire* and the beginning of interventionist government. A large number of commissions were set up by Lord Grey to investigate the state of the country – whether in schools, factories, the Church or local government – and identify areas where it could be improved. And on paper the Whig reforms were impressive. This Parliament was responsible for the beginnings of a national system of education. Funds for school buildings were granted to the two Church organizations, the Anglican National Society and the Nonconformist British and Foreign School Society, which were the chief providers of schooling for the poor. By 1839 there was an Education Department for the control of elementary education.

Under pressure from the Radicals and the Ten-Hour Movement, committees of local citizens dedicated to limiting the hours worked in factories, a new Factory Act was passed in 1833 which extended the cotton-mill legislation of 1819 and applied its provisions to all other textile factories. Children under the age of nine were not to be employed in any of them; a distinction was made between children, aged nine to thirteen, who were allowed to work nine hours a day, and young persons, aged thirteen to eighteen, who were allowed to work twelve hours. Employees under the age of thirteen had to spend half their hours being educated, by tutors to be provided by the mill-owners. And by creating a paid governmental factory inspectorate, the Whigs ensured compliance with the health and safety regulations in buildings in relation to ventilation and moving machinery.

One of the most urgent problems facing the Whig government was the agricultural depression, which had not let up since 1815, and the acute rural poverty that manifested itself in incessant rioting. Hayricks were burnt; threshing machines were sneaked out of farm buildings at night and attacked with hammers. But although the Whigs believed in rationalization and modernization, they dealt as savagely with the disturbances as the Ultra Tories. Nine men and boys were hung for burning farmers' ricks, while many continued to be sent overseas to the penal colony of Australia. Nevertheless under the energetic direction of reformers such as the strenuous and controversial Sir Edwin Chadwick, whose innovative inquiries into the health of the working man transformed public health, the Whigs launched a commission to investigate the widespread discontent.

In the commission's view the operation of poor relief was to blame. The Speenhamland system of supplementing agricultural wages from the rates which so many counties had adopted during the Napoleonic Wars had made the rates so burdensome that many farmers could not afford to keep their own land. An already distressing situation had begun to spiral out of control when farmers lowered wages as well as laying off labourers, and the local magistrates attempted to reduce the mountain of taxation by capping the poor relief. In 1834 the old Poor Law, which dated back to the reign of Elizabeth, was abolished. By the new Poor Law, assistance out of the rates (what would today be called unemployment benefit) could be doled out only to the 'aged or infirm'. Any healthy man or woman who was sufficiently 'able-bodied' to work but needed assistance from the parish rates had to live in the workhouse, a large local institution set up to house the indigent. The new system also standardized the administration of the Poor Law, which had varied from parish to parish, and made it easier to look after vagrants and orphaned children. By removing the agricultural subsidy, in the long term the Poor Law forced farmers to put up wages.

In December 1834, however, the king suddenly felt that he had had enough of all this busybodying. He was sick of the Whigs' progressive ideas, mainly because they showed no respect for the Church of England. Melbourne, the new leader of the Whigs – for Grey had retired in protest against a new Coercion Bill to limit crime in Ireland – had just reduced the number of Irish Protestant bishops by ten. Parliament might have acquired a far greater middle-class component, but William IV used the royal prerogative to dismiss the Whigs for meddling with the Church. He made Sir Robert Peel prime minister in the hope of some respectable Tory policies.

In fact Peel was attempting to form a different Tory party, one with liberal leanings. He wanted to change it from a party of protectionist landowners to one that could represent manufacturers as well. If the Tories were to survive, Peel believed, they would have to reach out to where the new power lay, to middle-class opinion. It would take him the best part of ten years to rebuilt support in the country for the Tories, or Conservatives as he now called them. They were conservative because they wished to conserve the best ancient institutions, but they also looked to the future. At the next election, however, the Tories were still in a minority in the Commons, so the Whigs under Lord Melbourne returned.

As William Lamb, Lord Melbourne had been married to the notorious Lady Caroline Lamb of Byronic fame. Brought up among the racy Whig hostesses of the late eighteenth century, for his aunt was Georgiana, Duchess of Devonshire, he was in some ways an anachronism. He was concerned with the old abstract Whig ideas of liberty but not much with improving the conditions of working men, from whose predicaments he was in every way quite insulated. Nevertheless the detached and intellectual Melbourne was a modernizer, and a series of innovative acts improved the nation's efficiency.

The Municipal Reform Act of 1835 removed control of the towns from secretive, self-perpetuating oligarchies and gave it to the middle classes, just as the Great Reform Act had done with Parliament. In the pursuit of religious freedom, the Whigs continued to cut back the Church of England's hold over the country's institutions. In England and Wales the thousand-year-old custom of the local vicar being entitled to the tithe or tenth of his neighbours' earnings was abolished. From 1836 marriages could be solemnized in Nonconformist chapels. Though religious tests would not be abolished at the ancient universities of Oxford and Cambridge until 1871, in 1836 the University of London was founded in order to grant degrees without them. Now Nonconformists, Catholics and Jews could study in England instead of being forced to go to Scotland or the continent. Stamp duties on newspapers were reduced to a penny. The first compulsory civil registration of births, deaths and marriages took place in 1837, supplementing the parish registers invented in 1538 by Thomas Cromwell. In 1839, thanks to the efforts of Rowland Hill, the penny postage was adopted: any letter could be carried for a penny to every part of the British Isles.

House of Correction in Coldbath Fields, Islington, London. One of many prisons extended in the mid-19th century, after transportation ended and new methods of punishment were required.

But despite these modernizing laws, much anguish pulsated beneath the surface. The 1834 Poor Law was disastrous in the short run. *Oliver Twist*, which Dickens wrote three years after the new system began, exposed workhouses as places of institutionalized cruelty whose inmates were treated like prisoners though their only crime was poverty. Every little bit of individuality, every bright touch, whether it was just a bunch of daisies in a jar or a treasured knitted shawl, was banned. Meals were taken in silence; couples were split up from one another and from their children; and all slept in dormitories. Workhouses survived until the early twentieth century when the 1906–14 Liberal government introduced old age pensions, national insurance and unemployment benefit.

As for the factory legislation, it might have improved conditions, but the reformer and philanthropist Lord Shaftesbury revealed that Britain had no reason to feel proud of herself when there were five- and six-year-olds working down the mines. By allowing the evangelical Shaftesbury to lead an investigation into factories, the Whig government unleashed the whirlwind. Though he had been the driving force behind the 1833 Factory Act, he was not satisfied with it, and decided to broaden his remit into investigating coalmines. His reports into what he found there reduced some MPs to tears when extracts were read to the House of Commons in 1840.

Shaftesbury's 'blue books', the reports to Parliament of the Royal Commission on Children's Employment in Mines and Manufactures, sent a shudder through Britain. In unemotive, official language which made its subject matter all the more chilling, they detailed how six-year-olds spent twelve hours a day under the earth harnessed to trucks of coal, dragging

Children working underground in the mining industry. This print was one of the pictures illustrating Lord Ashley's 1842 report to Parliament. The children are on hands and knees hauling a laden wagon through a low gallery.

them along tunnels knee-deep in water, while their mothers heaved coal on their heads up to the top of the mine. That was how Britain was obtaining the coal which made her 'the workshop of the world'.

The result was the 1842 Mines Act, which ended the employment of women and girls and boys under ten in the pits, and the Second Factory Act of 1844, which reduced the hours women worked to twelve and children to six and a half hours a day – though children were now allowed to be employed from the age of eight. Still shocking to our eyes, it was a great step forward to contemporary opinion. Friendless and parentless apprentices, and young boys of ten or more whose parents needed their money, continued to be sent down the mines for thirty years to come. Their tiny, blackened, undersized figures for some reason did not evoke the same pity and fury among MPs that their sisters did. The ten-hour day Shaftesbury campaigned for so tirelessly remained out of reach for years, defeated by economists' predictions about a fall in manufacturing, a loss of markets and wages, and by the power of the manufacturers. Though the ten-and-a-half-hour day came in in 1850, it was not until 1874 that the ten-hour day was at last made the legal maximum.

Sir Edwin Chadwick's *Report on the Sanitary Condition of the Labouring Population of Great Britain* in 1842 revealed the filthy urban slums so many Britons were living in, which had been thrown up cheaply everywhere round the textile mills and coalmines. Factory workers lived like animals, herded indecently ten to a room. The new streets were built so quickly, and there were so many of them, that the sewerage practice of the old midden heaps which had been acceptable in small numbers in a village or hamlet became positively hazardous in the new towns.

Textile workers suffered from lung diseases brought on by inhaling cotton fumes in ill-ventilated buildings. The fires and smoke belching out from the factory chimneys besides which they lived darkened the skies for miles around. Natural sunlight rarely penetrated, and life was carried on in a perpetual sulphurous glow to the sound of machines pounding night and day. Even at midday it felt like midnight. The striking change from the 'green and pleasant land' which the mystical poet William Blake had known as a boy had made him wonder two generations before whether a better, more Christian life could ever take hold again in the face of the new capitalism. Blake had been considered a dangerous radical in his time, but his views were becoming mainstream.

Now that people knew more about the hell-like misery so many workers endured in the 'satanic mills', the industrialization process which had been hailed with such excitement as the beginning of the modern age began to be questioned. In 1844 the son of a German cotton manufacturer Friedrich Engels, in a striking indictment of the industrial process, delineated the lives of the poor in Manchester in his book *The Condition of the English Working Class*. The suffering that Engels saw convinced him that only revolutionary change would stop the masses from being exploited by their masters. Robert Owen, the son-in-law of Arkwright's partner, as long ago as 1799 had made his mills at New Lanark in Scotland co-operative, with the profits being shared among the workers. Though the experiment failed, Owen was so disillusioned by the toll that the industrial revolution was taking on people's lives that he concluded trade unions were the only answer.

J. M. W. Turner would be one of the last important artists to celebrate the power and glamour of steam in his painting *Rain, Steam and Speed* in 1844. By 1848, obeying the precepts of the century's most influential art critic John Ruskin, the Pre-Raphaelite Brotherhood of painters would self-consciously hark back to the world portrayed by fourteenth-century Italian painters as a revolt against their own time. A misty medievalism became the mode as artists and intellectuals retreated from machines and modernization. By the last quarter of the nineteenth century William Morris had created the utopian Arts and Crafts movement, which celebrated both the individual artistry of the traditional craftsman over the machine made and a revivified idea of the community.

Dickens's *Oliver Twist* was the first of a series of socially concerned novels which drastically changed the sensibility of the reading public. Instead of thrilling to the popular so-called 'silver spoon' romances of high life, as they had been wont to do, readers were brought face to face with the meaning of rank poverty. The miseries of the age were publicized through the circulating libraries. By the late 1840s novelists like Mrs Gaskell and Charles Kingsley with *Mary Barton* and *Alton Lock* had begun to rouse the British public to the same kind of anger about the lives of the poor and children in factories that they had felt about slavery. An informed public became a concerned public in nineteenth-century England. It was a uniquely high-minded period, where the national discourse was led by politicians, reformers and writers whose unquenchable desire to change the world for the better had a contagious effect. Lord Shaftesbury's indignant revelations were the beginning of what became an ineluctable belief that it was morally wrong to wear out children in factories; by the end of the century compulsory elementary education at last brought child labour to a close.

But, despite a new awareness of the human cost of their prosperity, the British also revelled in their dramatic success abroad under the confident touch of the Melbourne government's swaggering foreign secretary. This was Henry Temple, the third Viscount Palmerston, the racehorse-owning epitome of John Bull, who was in fact an Irish peer and thus allowed to sit in the House of Commons. The pugnacious Palmerston held up a flattering self-image to the British. The eloquent champion of liberalism and constitutionalism, he supported the lawful queens of Portugal and Spain and sent packing the reactionary pretenders to their thrones, Don Miguel and Don Carlos. He safeguarded Belgium from the Dutch king's attacks and guaranteed her neutrality. Thanks to the fiery 'Pam', constitutional rule remained firmly established not only in the Iberian Peninsula but in all western Europe, in the teeth of opposition from the absolutist monarchies of Russia, Prussia and Austria.

At the same time Palmerston had no scruples about toppling sovereigns if they didn't suit British interests, or using force to support British trade. The term 'gunship diplomacy' was invented for him. In 1838 fears about the danger to the north-west frontier of the Indian Empire presented by Russian intrigues in Afghanistan set off the First Afghan War. The British sent an expedition to replace the apparently pro-Russian Amir of Afghanistan Dost Mahomed with a British puppet. It was followed by the First China War a year later, when the Chinese destroyed contraband British opium belonging to British traders and closed their ports to the lethal but lucrative crop being pushed by Indian and British merchants.

It was a war easily won by Britain and the powerful Royal Navy. By the Treaty of Nanking in 1842, five Chinese ports were to be opened to British goods with tariffs which did not spoil British trade, while British traders were not to be subject to Chinese laws. In addition Britain became the owner of the island of Hong Kong in perpetuity, and of neighbouring Kowloon twenty years later. By 1898 the Crown Colony of Hong Kong also included the adjoining New Territories, acquired on a ninety-nine-year lease to Britain, expiring in June 1997. In the twentieth century Hong Kong would become the source of vast trading wealth. Although high-minded MPs like W. E. Gladstone objected to forcing the Chinese to import opium against their will, Palmerston ignored him, arguing that it was the local Chinese gangs controlling the local opium traffic that did not want the drug in China, not the Chinese people.

In 1839 Palmerston responded to the French-inspired revolt of the Pasha of Egypt, Mehemet Ali, against the Ottoman Empire and Egypt's invasion of Syria by the swift despatch of the Royal Navy to Acre. With the added threat of the allied armies of Russia, Austria and Prussia the following year, the pasha was stopped dead in his tracks. Since the cornerstone of nineteenth-century British foreign policy was to maintain the Ottoman Empire in its entirety as a bulwark against Russia, Mehemet Ali's rebellion could not be countenanced. Nor could France's attempts to extend her influence in the Middle East. Both were quelled when Mehemet Ali submitted to the Turkish sultan in return for his rule in Egypt being made hereditary. And in a deft move at the peace conference which followed in London in 1841, Palmerston got the Bosphorus closed to all warships, including Russia's. For ever since 1833, in return for aiding the Turks during an earlier revolt of Mehemet Ali, a worrying closeness had developed between the sultan and the tsar, and Russian ships had been freely issuing out of the Black Sea.

Palmerston's bluff and rather brutal character appealed to the British. He was admired for the way his common sense prevented him getting too carried away by lost causes. It was his view that Britain had no eternal enemies or allies, only eternal interests which it was her duty to follow. Palmerston was debonair, xenophobic and famous for his love affairs, even being cited in a divorce case in his late seventies. He detested pomposity. There was one person, however, who did not share the widespread adulation of Pam, or Lord Cupid as he was also known. That was the new monarch, Queen Victoria, who succeeded to the throne in 1837. Strong-minded, modest and soon to be happily married, over the next thirty years she would be increasingly offended by his high-handed ways and his Regency-rake lovelife.

Victoria

(1837–1901)

Corn Laws and Irish Famine (1837–1854)

Victoria was the eighteen-year-old niece of William IV. On the king's death in June the throne passed to her as the only child of his next brother, the Duke of Kent, who had died when Victoria was eight months old. In contrast to the dissolute court life of her uncles, Victoria had been brought up extremely quietly at Kensington Palace by her widowed mother, Princess Victoria of Saxe-Coburg-Gotha. Thanks to her German mother's serious nature the new queen had a strong sense of duty. She was to transform the monarchy into an object of great pride and affection after it had fallen into disrepute. Her reign, which ended sixty-four years later at the beginning of the next century, would be one of the most glorious, and the longest, in Britain's history. At her accession Hanover became separated from the English crown because the so-called Salic Law operated to bar women from the throne. Victoria's uncle, the Duke of Cumberland, became King of Hanover instead.

Until she married in 1840, Victoria was innocently infatuated with her first prime minister, the suave Lord Melbourne, on whom she entirely depended for comfort and information in her new position. She was a naïve young girl, as was emphasized by the long hair falling over her dressing gown when she greeted the Archbishop of Canterbury and the lord chamberlain on their arrival at Kensington Palace at five in the morning, straight from William IV's deathbed. But, although she still slept in her mother's room, Queen Victoria's Journal reveals a determined character with a profound sense of what was owed the country: 'I am very young and perhaps in many, though not in all things inexperienced, but I am sure, that very few have more real goodwill and more real desire to do what is fit and right than I have.' The coronation took place in June 1838.

But, though Lord Melbourne had the favour of the queen, by the end of the 1830s he was running out of support in the country. Palmerston's skilful footwork all over the globe had helped British interests to flourish as never before, but he was a very expensive foreign secretary. Britain was going into a slump which was hitting the working classes especially hard now that support from the rates had been withdrawn. By the early 1840s, the Hungry Forties as they were known, unemployment in northern textile towns was so bad that the poor in cities like Leeds were living on money raised by local citizens. The workhouses couldn't contain them. In one town, 17,000 people were reported as starving to death. The lacklustre Whig government's only solution to reining in the deficit occasioned by Palmerston's adventures was to pile on indirect taxation. That took the price of living through the roof. Melbourne had quite the wrong temperament to be prime minister at this critical moment. Under his leadership the Whigs' reforming zeal was slowing to a halt.

The Radicals, whose organizations had done so much to get the Reform Bill passed, were extremely dissatisfied. It had become clear that most of the Whigs saw the bill as the end of franchise reform rather than a starting point. They had little time for working-class organizations and were fearful of the potential power of the trade unions. In particular they were alarmed by Robert Owen's plan for a Grand National Consolidated Trades Union to represent all the trades and craft unions in one body to make them a more formidable force. In 1834 six agricultural labourers from Dorset were sentenced to transportation to Australia, the so-called Tolpuddle Martyrs, for the 'crime' of being seen taking secret oaths. Because their Friendly Society of Agricultural Labourers was affiliated to Owen's, their harmless actions were assumed to have revolutionary significance. Despite the furore in the country provoked by the sentence, Melbourne who was then home secretary refused to commute it, though after two years' lobbying the Martyrs were at last released.

Because there was no will for reform within Parliament, Radical MPs became involved in an out-of-doors lobbying movement. In 1838 a former Irish MP called Feargus O'Connor and a mechanic named William Lovett founded the London Workingmen's Association to obtain what the Reform Bill had failed to achieve. Lovett drew up a petition consisting of six demands for constitutional reform which was presented to Parliament by Thomas Attwood, the Radical MP and founder of the Birmingham Political Union. It was known as the People's Charter and its supporters were called the Chartists. The Charter insisted that there should be no property qualification for the suffrage: every man over twenty-one years of age, regardless of his wealth, should have the vote. MPs should be paid for their services, otherwise only those with independent fortunes could afford to stand for election. The vote should be secret, to make it harder to threaten voters. Constituencies should be of equal worth. Lastly the Charter demanded annual Parliaments. These would give MPs less independence and oblige them to listen to their electors.

Within seventy years other than annual parliaments all the Charter's points would have been complied with. But in the 1830s and 1840s the Chartists encountered great opposition, not least because a section of their membership advocated violent revolution. In 1839 the branch known as the Physical Force Party planned a general insurrection, to be initiated by the seizure of the town hall at Newport in South Wales – only for the mayor and his supporters to defend it with such vigour that they prevented the Chartists from storming it. The rising never took place, and its leaders were transported to Australia. Though the majority of Chartists were in favour of using peaceful constitutional means to achieve their goals, they were tainted by the Newport affair. Acute distress inevitably meant that among Chartist members were machine-breakers and mill-burners, so a reputation as dangerous revolutionaries always hung over them. For ten years from 1838 the Chartists held huge, alarming rallies to try and persuade Parliament to agree to their aims, but without success.

Monster demonstrations and marches were not just employed by the Chartists, however. The most powerful and best-organized pressure group of the period was the Anti-Corn Law League, another out-of-doors movement, founded in 1838, which began to march on a daily basis in a campaign for the repeal of the laws against importing cheap corn. The poor suffered terribly through the late 1830s. Unemployment enabled employers to keep wages low, and the continued Tory majority in the House of Lords and the power of the landed interest kept the price of bread out of the reach of the impoverished. Until the corn laws were finally repealed in 1846 to feed an Ireland facing starvation after the failure of the potato crop, the League's agitation to get rid of this last bastion of landed privilege was as violent as that of the Chartists. But it was much more effective, because among its supporters were the wealthy, respectable manufacturers of Yorkshire and Lancashire.

The Anti-Corn Law League was headed by two superb orators – Richard Cobden, a calico printer, and John Bright, a Quaker manufacturer, both of whom became Radical MPs in the 1840s. Bright made formidable political capital out of Biblical references and the Lord's Prayer. It was a sin, Bright said in a hundred speeches, a hundred newspaper articles, to stop the poor being able to eat their daily bread – a resonant phrase which was hard to counter. He cast the mantle of a religious crusade over the Anti-Corn Law League's campaign for cheap bread. By public meetings and by making great use of the penny postage – the new campaigning technique – the League eventually created the same sort of groundswell which had brought about the Great Reform Bill, and it soon developed into support for free trade. If cheap foreign corn were imported, the country it came from would allow Britain to export there, thus establishing a new market for her finished goods. Meanwhile, in a desperate attempt to curb the soaring

National Debt, the Whigs sought to raise money by adding more and more import taxes to foodstuffs, a policy which neither raised money nor allowed the poor to eat.

A sign of the dissatisfaction with life at home can be detected in the expanding number of colonies settled by the British in this period. The year 1836 saw South Australia colonized and its capital Adelaide named after the wife of William IV, and three years later New Zealand was settled by Gibbon Wakefield. In South Africa the British were a growing presence. The original European settlers of Cape Colony, the Boers were antagonized by the abolition of slavery in the British Empire in 1834, because they depended on slavery for their farming, and the following year most of them began the Great Trek northwards out of Cape Colony to create the Republic of Natal on the north-east coast of South Africa. But the vigorous British settlers pursued them and took over Natal in 1843. In 1854 the Boers moved further north to create two more Boer republics, the Orange River Free State and the Transvaal, and there they were left in peace.

After the American rebellion, the British ruling authorities had no great expectations that colonies would remain tightly bound to the motherland. After a rebellion in 1837 by the French in Lower Canada against the English in the Upper Province, Canada was allowed self-government three years later, with an executive ministry directly accountable to the Canadian Parliament. This would form the basis for self-government in most of the colonies. In 1850 representative government would be given to South Australia, Victoria and Tasmania – just before the discovery of gold in Victoria caused a rapid increase in the Australian population.

In contrast to these advances, the home country herself was beginning to look ungovernable. The one hope for some kind of reconciliation between all the warring factions and for bringing the reform movement back to Parliament was provided by the impressive Sir Robert Peel, with whom most of the Radicals were now voting. In 1839 Melbourne's majority fell to five and he resigned, leaving it to Peel to form a government. But the young queen caused a constitutional crisis when she refused to dismiss her Whig ladies-in-waiting. Under previous administrations the members of the royal household had tended to belong to the governing party, and they would resign when their party lost power. But to a queen who was scarcely more than a girl her ladies (who were part of the Melbourne set) were not just political symbols – they had become her intimate confidantes. Though Melbourne had quite properly advised her that she must have Conservative ladies-in-waiting, as Peel had requested, the young queen dug in her heels. She found Peel cold, awkward and stiff, a depressing contrast to the dashing gaiety of Lord Melbourne. The affair became known as the Bedchamber Crisis. Absurdly, as neither side would give way, and Peel insisted on Tory ladies-in-waiting, Melbourne and the Whigs resumed office again – as it was said, 'behind the petticoats of the Ladies of the Bedchamber'.

But it was not for much longer. A combination of fears about the Whigs' budget, which in a last-ditch attempt to curb the deficit had taken a step in the direction of free trade, and Peel's support in the country enabled the Tory leader in 1841 to force an election and win a massive victory. Victoria had meanwhile married her first cousin Prince Albert, the younger son of the Duke of Saxe-Coburg-Gotha, whose calm, pious, loving nature and guidance greatly benefited his wife. One consequence was that the need for Lord Melbourne and the Whig ladies was removed. Prince Albert had studied British history and was anxious to be worthy of the position he found himself in. He had ambitions to do something for the arts, of which he was a considerable dilettante, and he got on well with Peel, for he shared his moral earnestness and exalted sense of public duty.

Peel himself and his fellow MPs, like the gifted W. E. Gladstone, the son of a Liverpool merchant, who became president of the Board of Trade, had been moving in the direction of free trade themselves, and Peel's government decided to try a cunning experiment. Peel's daring stroke was to bring back the abhorred income tax, invented to bear the burden of the Napoleonic Wars. Now its purpose was to lessen the burden of indirect taxation on the poor. By restoring income tax, though only as a three-year experiment, Peel and Gladstone believed that the tariff could be lowered on many ordinary items, including corn. Instead the money the deficit required would be raised from the comfortably off, who would scarcely feel it. Peel reduced or removed duties on over 600 consumer goods and raw materials, budgeting for a loss of £2 million which would be made up by the reintroduction of income tax. With income tax rated at sevenpence in the pound, and by exempting those whose annual incomes were less than £150 – which meant the majority of people, since a curate earned only £100 – the government would be left with a surplus of £500,000 to help reduce the deficit. Though the situation continued to be grave, gradually over the next few years prices began to come down to a more acceptable level.

To all aspects of government Peel's businesslike mind brought sensible management. With his Bank Charter Act the money supply was stabilized. The entitlement of the many small private banks to issue notes above the actual reserves they held had led in the past few decades to a harmful series of failures. Such issuing was now forbidden. The late 1830s and 1840s was the time when the British railway experiment took off and to some extent alleviated unemployment in the textile industries. Lines crisscrossed the length and breadth of the country, much of it financed by share issues to speculation-crazy private citizens. The restriction of credit by the Bank Charter Act damped down the economy just when it was threatening to overheat.

Lord Aberdeen was Peel's foreign minister. He made a dramatic contrast to Palmerston, aiming at peace abroad as part of the administration's attempts to keep its costs down. War was expensive and did not allow tax cuts. The Afghan War had cost £15 million as well as thousands of British lives when the government was being suffocated by a £7 million deficit. It had also been quite pointless. In 1841, ignoring the British puppet, the tribesmen of Afghanistan rose up, massacred many of the British and put the amir Dost Mahomed back on his throne. Worse still, though a safe-conduct was given to the British troops to allow them to evacuate the country and return to India, they were ambushed as they tramped back through the mountains. Out of 15,000 troops only one man, a Dr Brydon, made it back alive over the Khyber Pass, the gateway to British India. The new governor-general of India Lord Ellenborough furiously ordered the Afghan capital Kabul to be sacked as punishment.

After this disastrous episode, Aberdeen and Peel were opposed to further expansion on the Indian subcontinent. They did not share Palmerston's fear of Russia and were alarmed at the way Ellenborough in 1843 rushed into annexing for security reasons the province of Sind, which bordered the Bombay Presidency. Nevertheless the territory ruled by the British continued to grow. In 1845 the British humiliation at the hands of the Afghans encouraged the Sikhs of the independent Punjab to the north to launch their own attack, only for the Punjab to be reduced to a protectorate under the Maharajah Dhulip Singh.

Unlike Palmerston, who was distrustful of French ambitions, Aberdeen desired friendly relations with France. Queen Victoria and Prince Albert were twice guests of Louis-Philippe at his court at Eu. There the royal pair were introduced to the French court painter Franz Winterhalter, who would execute a series of charming portraits memorializing them and their large family. Louis-Philippe returned the compliment and visited them at Windsor. Friendly relations developed into an *entente*, a diplomatic understanding between two powers. Lord Aberdeen's mild manner resolved by diplomacy boundary problems for Canada created by the movement west of the growing population of the United States. At issue were the north-west coast where Vancouver is situated on the Pacific and the boundary between Canada and Maine.

President Polk had just been elected in America on the ticket of 'fifty-four fifty or fight', a policy to extend the state of Oregon to the line of latitude of 54.50 degrees, right up to the boundary of the Russian territory of Alaska. Peel and Aberdeen were determined that the American border should begin lower down at the 49th parallel, otherwise Canada would have no outlet on to the Pacific. Polk did not fight, and the 49th parallel was established as the boundary between America and Canada, except for a small dip south to include Vancouver Island. A treaty negotiated by Castlereagh which had abolished navies and military establishments on the Great Lakes remained in place, symbolizing trustful relations between the two powers.

Despite the fundamental surgery of Peel's first budget the unrest continued, and the Anti-Corn Law League continued to lobby for total repeal. Peel was disgusted at how far the League was prepared to go in its irresponsible use of orators to inflame opinion, but secretly – like many of his more liberal colleagues – he had been converted. Cheap foreign corn seemed the only way to solve the problem of feeding the starving unemployed in textile towns. Overseas powers were simply not producing enough to be able to threaten British farmers with exporting enormous amounts of cheap wheat.

Since the effect of lowering corn duties in 1842 had not been to reduce agricultural workers' wages, by 1843 Peel had real anxieties about whether he could continue to be in favour of the corn laws. He believed that successful farming would ultimately depend on better ways of farming, not on protection. The unending, increasing and organized level of anger against the corn laws might come to threaten the landed classes and indeed the whole country. Peel was perpetually frightened of a revolution. That year his private secretary Edward Drummond was mistaken for Peel himself and assassinated by a madman named Daniel Macnaghten while riding in a royal procession in the prime minister's carriage (Peel was with the queen).

In all probability Peel would have reformed the corn laws sooner rather than later. All his budgets were nudging towards free trade. But in response a violent and irresponsible pressure group dedicated to protection, popularly known as the anti-Anti-Corn Law League, was set up by the Ultra wing of the Tory party, whose members had been opposed to Peel ever since he betrayed them with Catholic Emancipation and feared that the days of protecting estates based on wheat farming were numbered. In the 1830s they had created the nostalgic Young England movement within the Tory party centred around a mystical and probably mythical idea of the aristocracy. The anti-Anti-Corn Law League was headed by the gifted young speaker Benjamin Disraeli, a cultivated, flamboyant novelist and the first British MP of Jewish extraction, and by the horse-mad Lord George Bentinck, son of the Duke of Portland.

As the traditional supporters of the Church of England, the Ultra Tories were alarmed by Peel's determination to lessen the grievances of the

Catholics in Ireland by increasing the state grant to the Catholic Maynooth College. This was a time when the Tories' worst fears about the dangers of Catholic Emancipation were being realized. For in 1845 John Newman, the influential leader of the Anglican High Church or Oxford movement, which emphasized the Church's links to the ancient pre-Reformation Church, caused absolute consternation when he became a Roman Catholic. Disestablishmentarianism, the ending of the Church of England's official position, seemed to be in the air. Only the year before 500 ministers and many of their congregations had broken away from the Church of Scotland to form the more democratic Free Presbyterian Church of Scotland, known as the Wee Frees after their opening prayer 'We the Free Church of Scotland'.

Bentinck and Disraeli forgot Peel's resurrection of the Tory party. They remembered only what they considered to be his numerous betrayals of it. Night after night Disraeli, who wore weird and wonderful clothing in the House of Commons, strange cloaks in yellow, black and orange, disloyally directed exquisitely turned jibes at his party's leader. In one of his best taunts, he said that Peel had found the Whigs bathing and run away with their clothes.

But Peel was not only having to deal with enmity in his own party in Parliament and outside it, where he was burned in effigy by the Anti-Corn Law League. In Ireland in 1843 Daniel O'Connell, backed by an organization which looked back to 1798 and called itself Young Ireland, announced that this was to be Repeal Year. To crowded meetings held at some of the most historic places in Ireland, including Tara, home of the old High Kings of Ireland, O'Connell said he was aiming for three million members, a repeal warden in each parish and a national convention to rid Ireland of what he called the 'Saxon'.

Alarmed by the possibility of a fresh Irish triumph after O'Connell's adroit tactics during the campaign for Catholic Emancipation, Peel banned the meetings. O'Connell had to choose between obeying the law and creating an armed insurrection for which he had neither the temperament nor the inclination. When his followers found that he had no intention of fighting, the enthusiasm which had propelled the movement forward shrivelled and died. The English government nonetheless foolishly decided to prosecute O'Connell for high treason, on the ground that it had to make an example of him. But the House of Lords set the conviction aside and three years later, on a pilgrimage to Rome, O'Connell died, a broken man.

Perturbed by the level of anti-Union feeling, the exceptionally high murder rate and the general dissatisfaction in Ireland, Peel sought help from education. Despite Catholic Emancipation all the most influential jobs continued to go to the Protestants, as they were far better educated than the Catholics. In 1845 Peel founded the Queen's College at Belfast, Cork and Galway in order that Catholics and Protestants might receive a secular university education side by side. He hoped to remove any rational grounds for discrimination against the Catholics. But like most things which the far-sighted Peel did that were just and constructive, it earned him tremendous unpopularity. Many Catholics as well as Protestants thought that the new colleges would be godless institutions.

But a terrible catastrophe was about to take place in Ireland which ensured that, despite Peel's best intentions, hatred and resentment were to be the chief emotions felt by the Irish towards England for a century and a half. For in 1846 a disease of the potato destroyed what had become the Irish peasantry's only food crop. Thanks to the historical evil of a large number of English absentee landlords, almost no Irish peasant owned his own land. The scientific farming that had transformed England in the eighteenth century had never existed in Ireland, where anyone who attempted to make improvements in their methods of farming would have their rents raised by the agents. The only way for the Irish peasant to make money – and the peasantry comprised three-quarters of the population – was to sublet part of their land to another family and get a cash rent. As a result they had to feed themselves off a very small amount of soil.

The Irish had discovered that the crop which required the least soil for cultivation was the potato. Out of a population of eight million, four

Famine burial in Ireland. A million people died in the famine of 1846/47 after the failure of the potato crop which was their staple diet.

million people were by 1845 living on potatoes alone. It was not a balanced diet, but it was adequate if the crop was good. That summer an American fungal disease known as the potato blight appeared in Europe. It turned every potato to slime in the ground. The wet weather that summer was especially conducive to the spread of the disease. In August Peel, nervous of the implications, demanded weekly reports from the constabulary on the state of the crop and sent scientists over to investigate. By October the report from the Lord Lieutenant of Ireland was clear. The potato crop had been pretty well destroyed throughout the country. Half the population of Ireland were faced with complete starvation, four million people who rushed from potato plant to potato plant hoping that the stench rising from the fields did not mean all of the potatoes were rotten. But there was not much chance of beating a disease carried on the wind and worsened by the rain.

At a Cabinet meeting on 6 November Peel declared that on the evidence he already had it was necessary to open the ports to cheap grain from abroad at a reduced emergency tariff and put a new Corn Bill through Parliament. But only three of his ministers would back him. The others did not believe in the emergency and preferred to wait for the end of the month when the two scientists Lyon Playfair and Professor Lindley would have finished their report. Even when the report came in, the Tory party would not back the repeal of the bread tax. Peel resigned, but when the Whig Lord John Russell attempted and failed to form a ministry to repeal the corn laws, Peel nobly took back his resignation and formed a government again solely for that purpose. The repeal of the corn laws in May 1846 was finally carried by the Free Traders, who were Peel's supporters in the party (they became known as the Peelites), together with Russell's Whigs. But Peel himself was forced out as Tory leader and the party split into Peelites and Protectionists. Headed by Disraeli, the Protectionists attacked Peel in the most wounding manner as a traitor to his party. But in his last speech as prime minister Peel insisted that he had not betrayed any conservative principles. He had simply done what he came into Parliament to do, which was to show that 'the legislature was animated with a sincere desire to frame its legislation upon the principles of equity and justice'.

But the Irish did not see the Westminster government that way. Though the Archbishop of Dublin asked prayers to be said in every Catholic church for God's mercy, there was to be no mercy. The devastating figure of one million Irish people died in one year alone, between 1846 and 1847, and another million would die over the next three years; those who did not die of starvation were carried off by mortal illnesses brought on by malnutrition. For the sacred nineteenth-century laws of political economy decreed that corn could not be delivered free to the population. It could only be put into government depots and paid out in return for labour. This bureaucratic approach was useless during an emergency. It took months, hundreds of thousands of deaths and the example of private charities physically taking provisions to the people for the British government to see that in an emergency there was no room for economic laws. The only way to get food to the starving was to deliver it to the people directly in a vast relief effort.

The Irish famine was the greatest social disaster to befall any European state in the nineteenth century. But the new Whig government that took over from Peel, led by Lord John Russell, proved inadequate to the task. By the Soup Kitchen Act of 1847 Parliament finally voted £10 million to help Ireland. Thus more than three million men, women and children received food from the soup kitchens. But the humanitarian aid ceased long before it should have done. At the end of 1847 the British government decided that the Irish should thenceforth be supported by their local parish unions. Yet, with the economy destroyed, there were no rates to pay for that support. The official British view was that if any further help was given to the Irish it would make them too dependent on government aid. It was the same mindset which had turned workhouses into forbidding places to keep the poor out of them.

Most landlords behaved with astonishing callousness. Far from being appalled by the sight of men, women and children dying around them, their agents only registered missing rents. What was of concern to themselves and their employers was that the cottar system of farming – the smallholder with a couple of fields – was proving unprofitable. A ruthless series of evictions began. At mid-century it was averaging almost 20,000 families per year, as landlords incorporated many smallholdings into larger ones on English lines. A constant kind of guerrilla warfare against landlords was the response of those who remained. In 1848 there was another failed attempt at rebellion under the Young Ireland movement, which had been resurrected under a man named Smith O'Brien. But the most frequent reaction of the Irish to their homeland's ills was to abandon her.

Sure that things would never get better in their lifetime, during the course of the next fifty years one million Irishmen and women bitterly made their way to the friendlier shores of the United States of America. They settled predominantly on the eastern seaboard, particularly around Boston. As important as their pitifully scant belongings was the loathing they carried in their hearts for the English. It was sealed in blood by the famine, and persists among their descendants even today. The treatment of the Irish during the famine by the English is taught in some American schools as an act of genocide, the deliberate murder of a people.

But in Britain herself the mid-century was faced with confidence and self-belief. After the repeal of the corn laws the Tory Protectionists were led by the Earl of Derby, after Lord George Bentinck's death in 1848, and by Disraeli. With Peel's death out riding in 1850, leadership of the forty Free Traders known as Peelites was taken over by Lord Aberdeen, the former foreign secretary. Despite their small numbers the Peelites had a great deal of weight in the House of Commons as they contained some of the ablest men in Parliament, such as Gladstone and Sidney Herbert. They frequently voted with the Whigs and Radicals, and would gradually over the next twenty years merge to form the Liberal party.

By 1852 free trade had so much been proved to be the most profitable way for Britain to function that it became national policy for all the parties; protectionism was quietly abandoned by Derby and Disraeli. The repeal of the corn laws had not destroyed British farming. Labourers had not been thrown out of work nor cornfields abandoned, as had been feared. It was only in the last quarter of the nineteenth century that surplus wheat from the North American prairies ruined prices in Britain. The price of corn had not dropped as dramatically in 1846 as the Anti-Corn Law League had expected, but that was because the cost of all commodities rose over the next ten years, and repeal acted to offset that rise in the case of corn.

Britain in the period 1846 to 1852 was peaceful compared to the previous decade. It was felt that a great social injustice had been removed in the tax on bread. Times were more prosperous, and there were fewer people out of work. Thanks to Shaftesbury's continued work, factory legislation regulated most places of manufacture – the bleaching and dyeing industries, the lace factories the match factories, the Potteries – the result of a slew of commissions to investigate the physical conditions in which children were employed. In the Potteries six-year-old children were found to be working fifteen hours a day. Inspectors made dreadful discoveries in match factories: there women developed a disease called 'phossy jaw' caused by phosphorus, which rotted away their faces.

In 1848 under the Public Health Act backed by Lord Shaftesbury, Sir Edwin Chadwick set up the Board of Health, which had powers to overrule local authorities. Towns thrust up by the industrial revolution were forced to put in proper buried sewerage systems, replacing the shallow troughs which had run down streets since the middle ages. Life expectancy in such towns, which had been up to 50 per cent less than in the countryside, rose dramatically as a result. Shaftesbury also helped abolish the practice of putting small boys up chimneys to sweep them, though it was not until 1875 that the system finally ceased when a sweep's licence became conditional on his not having broken any of the laws on employing children. Public opinion was marshalled against such practices by Charles

Kingsley's novel *The Water Babies*, published in 1863. As Lunacy Commissioner, Shaftesbury exposed the treatment of the insane in institutions. Until his intervention many of the mentally ill spent their already unhappy lives chained to their beds in darkness.

Even 1848, the year of revolutions on the continent, passed in Britain without much notice. Although the presentation of what turned out to be the Chartists' last petition was treated as if Napoleon was about to invade, with the eighty-year-old Duke of Wellington in charge of London's defences and with cannon on every bridge, the expected mass demonstration never materialized. The petition was brought quietly to Downing Street in a cab. Although it was mocked when some of its signatures were found to be false (the Duke of Wellington, Mr Punch and Queen Victoria were all inscribed several times), it was an impressive demonstration of working-class British people's faith in Parliament, even though they were excluded from it.

It was an era when the popular writer Samuel Smiles's doctrine of 'self-help' became a watchword. The Friendly Societies started up just before mid-century, inviting workers to make a weekly payment as an insurance against illness or unemployment, and providing an income if those eventualities occurred. Some of the trade unions provided similar benefits to their members. The Co-op, still to be seen on certain high streets today, also sprang into being. It began with individuals getting together in a co-operative venture to buy foodstuffs in bulk – that is, at wholesale prices. As the years went by, Co-ops set up normal shops where food was sold at ordinary prices; the profit at the end of the year was divided between all the members of the co-operative.

At mid-century Britain was reaching the peak of her prosperity as leader of the industrial revolution. Her extraordinary success in international markets, particularly those of South America and India, encouraged Russell boldly to repeal what was left of the Navigation Acts. No country could stand comparison with Britain in cheap manufactured goods. The British carrying trade with the rest of the world was no longer to be restricted to designated countries – any country's ship could carry British goods, and could man it with sailors of any nationality. This increased the volume of shipping available to British merchants and manufacturers. By 1850 a quarter of the world's trade was going through British ports.

It was a measure of Britain's overweening self-confidence that Palmerston, Russell's foreign secretary, threatened to bombard Athens in 1847 when the Greek government refused to compensate a Gibraltarian merchant named Don Pacifico, whose house had been destroyed by riots. This sort of behaviour disgusted the Peelites and their allies the Radicals. To Palmerston and his followers, however, the British Empire had become like the Roman Empire of old; as Palmerston himself put it in one of his most grandiloquent speeches, 'The Roman, in days of old, held himself free from indignity, when he could say, *Civis Romanus sum*; so also a British subject, in whatever land he may be, shall feel confident that the watchful eye and the strong arm of England shall protect him against injustice and wrong.'

In 1851, to symbolize what was hoped would be an era of peace and progress, Prince Albert organized the Great Exhibition to put on show the best goods the world could manufacture. Expected to be the first of many such international gatherings, it took place in Hyde Park in a specially built glass and iron structure designed by Joseph Paxton and nicknamed the Crystal Palace. Visitors came via cheap excursion tickets on the new railways. The Great Exhibition was visual proof that the British led the world in the superiority, the variety and the cheapness of their manufactures, 90 per cent of which were now exported. Out of it came the Victoria and Albert Museum, to provide a place of permanent exhibition for the arts and manufactures. Visitors to the Crystal Palace, like the

INTERIOR OF THE GREAT EXHIBITION.

The Great Exhibition of 1851 organized by Prince Albert to show off the superior British goods which made her 'the Workshop of the World'.

novelist Charlotte Brontë, who remained enthralled by the Duke of Wellington, were able to spot him still strolling briskly about. His death in September 1852 marked the end of a triumphant era for the British that had begun with Waterloo.

Prosperity bred a new confidence everywhere, which in the female sex appeared as rebellion. Women, the silent majority who for centuries had been considered mentally and physically the weaker sex, suddenly became more visible. They wrote defiantly of subjects which hitherto they had been considered too ladylike to address. They refused to accept the limited role of virtuous wife and mother which British nineteenth-century society was keen to promote. The Woman Question, what was appropriate for women, became the subject of furious debate. By 1851 there were the first shoots of feminist organizations such as the Sheffield Women's Political Association, which was set up to demand the vote.

The first novels of the Brontë sisters appeared in an extraordinary year, 1847–8. The Brontës outraged convention with their passion, their honesty and their realism, and so did writers like Elizabeth Barrett Browning, Mrs Gaskell and Harriet Martineau. Queen's College school was set up in Harley Street in 1848, where it remains today, to equip women for the professional life many were demanding. There began to be a rash of schools for women, such as North London Collegiate (1853) and Cheltenham Ladies' College (1858), founded by the redoubtable Frances Buss and Dorothea Beale. From there in theory it was a short step to demanding university degrees and the vote, though neither were granted until the second decade of the next century.

Britain congratulated herself on feeling scarcely a tremor during the revolutions of 1848, a consequence of her foresight in accepting social and Parliamentary reform before it was forced on her. Her stability and tolerance turned her into a magnet for political refugees, as she is today. In London salons at any one time might be encountered the exiled French citizen king Louis-Philippe, the architect of conservative reaction Metternich, as well as innumerable Italian revolutionary patriots in exile. In fact, so confident was Britain, so liberal in her thought, so unthreatened by inimical views, that within her ample bosom she even found room to shelter the sworn enemy of her capitalist way of life, Karl Marx.

Expelled from Paris and Brussels for his *Communist Manifesto* of 1848 (the first draft was written by Friedrich Engels), for forty years Marx laboured freely in the British Museum, employing statistics supplied by Engels, to provide a recipe for progress. They attacked capitalism, religion and culture and looked forward to what they believed would be the last stage of an inevitable historical process: after a dictatorship of the proletariat there would be a withering away of the state, and an idyll where all property would be owned communally. Their beliefs, which are also known as scientific socialism, would have a profound and often invigorating effect on politics for the next 150 years.

But in 1853 Marx and Engels were relatively unknown figures. The Radicals were still dedicated to the franchise reform. The chancellor of the Exchequer W. E. Gladstone's intellectual obsessions were focused on producing both the conditions for free trade, which Richard Cobden continued to promote as the answer to the world's ills, and the low taxation which he himself believed necessary for creating a self-reliant working man. In 1853 with his first budget Gladstone reduced duty on imports to the lowest levels ever seen, and announced that he intended steadily to reduce income tax until its complete abolition in 1860. Once the new scale of duties took effect and stimulated consumption, income tax would no longer be necessary. Gladstone's budget expressed his confidence in Britain's power as top trading nation and her ability to keep peace in the world. He also cut back on the army, for he felt no war threatened. As a fervent Christian he believed that most wars were morally wrong anyway, and that a Christian with money in his pocket would do more good than the government.

In India Britain directly governed an enormous part of the territories of the subcontinent. The empire stretched from Sind in the west to the southern tip of Burma in the Far East, where the ill-treatment of British merchants in Rangoon resulted in the annexation of Pegu in 1852; the Second Sikh War of 1848–9 led to Britain's outright annexation of the Punjab. Yet the next two decades would reveal Britain's rule in the east to be fragile, expose the state of her army as deplorable, and demonstrate that she was no longer the arbiter of international events. For on the continent France and the emerging countries of Italy and Germany were determined to destroy the 1815 Vienna peace settlement and remodel the map of Europe to their own liking, with incalculable results.

Palmerstonian Aggression (1854–1868)

The next twenty years of English life took place against an unprecedented amount of war and frontier alteration on the continent of Europe as the will to unify Italy and Germany became unstoppable. By 1871 these two countries were no longer mere 'geographical expressions' but nations united by political institutions, headed by a single ruler. The unification of Italy under the constitutional King of Sardinia-Piedmont had been passionately desired by the three leading liberal British statesmen of the period, Palmerston, Lord John Russell and Gladstone. Nevertheless the last pieces of the jigsaw of the Italian peninsula were fitted into place only with the aid of the militaristic Prussian state. Her own pursuit of German unification meant attacking her neighbours: first Denmark, then her fellow German Austria, finally France.

Prussia's chancellor Otto von Bismarck had told his fellow countrymen that 'the great questions of our time will not be decided by speeches and majority decisions' but 'by blood and iron'. And by 1871 the world order was utterly changed, signified by the Prussian king being crowned German emperor at the Palace of Versailles. Built by Louis XIV, it had symbolized the power of French civilization. Now the German presence there emphasized the humbling of French pride and the destruction of France's Second Empire. Prussia's superior army and lack of scruple about the use of force made her the dominant power on the continent. And a united Germany, under the aegis of the war-hungry Prussian state, became the unexpected big player on the world scene. Britain, one of the most active guarantors of the post-Waterloo settlement, had been confined to the sidelines, unable to influence most of these events or to rescue the balance of power.

From 1871 until the First World War broke out in 1914, the aggressive nature of the Prussian state alarmed contemporaries, but without a continental army there was little Britain could have done on her own to resist Prussia's rise to power, with so many other European states bent on change. Her distrust of a new Napoleon across the Channel made the help of a French army out of the question. For in the 1850s and 1860s, though Russian expansion in Asia continued to be the threat to India, the real menace as far as the British were concerned was Napoleon's unpredictable nephew Prince Louis Napoleon.

Prince Louis Napoleon – who had been elected president in 1848 but wished to prolong his term of office – seized power in 1851 on a programme to alter the humiliating frontiers of 1815 to France's advantage, and a year later proclaimed himself the Emperor Napoleon III (his first cousin the King of Rome should have been Napoleon II). A restless dreamer, an idealist and by the end of his reign a seriously ill man, the new

Napoleon was a catalyst of change in Europe, seeking glory in war and ready to exploit any situation to enhance his popularity with his people and restore France to the world status from which he believed she had been demoted. Although Napoleon III would periodically be Britain's ally – indeed he had spent a period of exile in London, when he had enrolled as a special constable – the news that there was a new Napoleon in power across the Channel created a volunteer movement as it had in the days of Pitt the Younger. Throughout his twenty-year reign there were war scares in England when 150,000 men would drill on the south coast – commemorated in Tennyson's poem 'Riflemen form!'

Palmerston, Lord John Russell's foreign secretary, at first welcomed Napoleon III's coup. His liberal sympathies had prompted him to react with delight to the 1848 revolutions all over Europe, but when what had been constitution-making turned to fighting in the streets, he became seriously alarmed. He thought that the danger of real revolution was so great that it was better for France to be ruled by military despotism. Without the authority of the queen or the prime minister, Palmerston gave official recognition to Louis Napoleon's coup. But Queen Victoria and Russell had had enough of Palmerston's idiosyncratic and impetuous behaviour, and he was sacked. Furious, he decided to take his revenge by bringing down the government over a bill to strengthen the militia against the Napoleonic threat. Since Palmerston could not form a government on his own, the Tory Protectionists under Lord Derby as prime minister and with Disraeli as chancellor of the Exchequer came in. But, though Disraeli made the Tories abandon protection, the Peelites continued to be close to the Whigs, and neither could do much with Palmerston outside their tent.

At the end of 1852 the Whigs and Peelites put the government in the minority and the Tories resigned. Like musical chairs, a new coalition of Peelites and Whigs headed by Lord Aberdeen took its place. Gladstone returned to the Treasury, Lord John Russell became leader of the House of Commons, and Palmerston was reinstated in the government, this time as home secretary. But though he might be at the Home Office Palmerston's presence gave martial vigour to the administration. In 1853 when the Russians invaded two Ottoman provinces on the Danube and sank the Turkish fleet, Britain responded with war. The Eastern Question had once more taken centre stage, though the war itself was to be fought on the south coast of Russia where the Crimean Peninsula juts into the Black Sea.

The background to the conflict was quite straightforward. For a long time the Russian tsar Nicholas I had been seeking to pre-empt what he considered to be the inevitable break-up of the Turkish Empire by dividing it among the great powers. The feeble nature of Ottoman rule even before mid-century had convinced him that the empire should be parcelled out sooner rather than later. This would prevent the chaos of an uncontrolled disintegration and the creation of independent Balkan nation states. Ever since Greece had won her independence, the peoples of Bulgaria, Albania, Serbia and Macedonia had been stirred by the idea of governing themselves.

As long as Russian influence remained paramount at Constantinople, the tsar was prepared to leave the Turkish Empire alone. But in 1852 it seemed that the French were replacing the Russians as most favoured nation. For Louis Napoleon's ambassador to Turkey persuaded the sultan that henceforth Latin monks in Jerusalem should hold the key to Christ's tomb, the Holy Sepulchre, instead of Greek Orthodox monks. This was intended to endear Napoleon's regime to the French clergy.

The 'affair of monks', as it was known, plunged Europe into war. To the Russians, for Latin monks to hold the keys to the Holy Sepulchre was no different from having French warships in the Dardanelles. What the tsar and his advisers did not want was control of their Turkish neighbour to fall into the hands of France. This was what prompted the Russian invasion in 1853 of the Danubian principalities of Wallachia and Moldavia (modern Romania). The Russians then refused to leave unless the Turks announced that the Greeks were the custodians of the Holy Sepulchre. When the Russians sank the Turkish fleet at Sinope on the Black Sea on 30 November the British were hot for war against the threatening Russian bear. With Palmerston always distrustful of Russian intentions, an alliance was made with the new Bonaparte emperor, who welcomed the end to France's quarantine after Waterloo.

In January 1854 the French and British fleets, which were already at anchor off Constantinople after the Russian invasion of the Danubian provinces, sailed up the Bosphorus and into the Black Sea. There they would land troops to destroy the Russian military installation at Sebastopol in the Crimea and weaken Russia so thoroughly that she would not try to seize Turkish territory again, while another British fleet would go north to Kronstadt on the Baltic coast, the Russian equivalent of Portsmouth.

From start to finish the operation was a disaster. The British troops were equipped neither for the Russian winter nor for a long siege. It had been incorrectly assumed in England that capturing Sebastopol could be achieved in six weeks. It took a year. Autumn storms wrecked almost every ship carrying food supplies and warm clothing across the Black Sea. Such clothing as did eventually arrive was often inappropriate or unwearable owing to the carelessness of the quartermaster's agents – there were, for example, 5,000 left boots because they had not been paired before they left. The conditions of the peninsula are memorialized in the word 'balaclava'. Our modern article of clothing derives its name from the battle named after the nearest Russian town to Sebastopol. The cold was so intense and the British so badly equipped that the men had to put stockings over their faces and cut the eye and mouth holes out. The Crimean War is also infamous for the Charge of the Light Brigade. Immortalized in the poem by the poet laureate of the day Alfred, Lord Tennyson, 600 British cavalrymen led by Lord Cardigan rode two miles up 'the valley of death' straight into the firing line of the Russian guns – the result of the subordinate officer Lord Lucan's misunderstanding of an order, and only a third of them returned alive. Marshal Bosquet, a French general who witnessed the charge, exclaimed disbelievingly, 'C'est magnifique, mais ce n'est pas la guerre.'

Fortunately those British soldiers did not suffer wholly in vain, for there was another, more influential witness at the scene of this crime of ineptitude. The correspondent of the London *Times*, W. H. Russell, called their masters to account and showed the nineteenth century that the pen really could be mightier than the sword. Russell was the first of a different breed, a war correspondent. Although most armies had endured suffering, it was the first time that a nation's public had been made vividly aware of it. The humming wires of the telegraph had shrunk the world. Via Vienna initially and then from the new telegraph office at Constantinople, Russell sent back daily despatches reporting on the course of the war.

Above all, Russell attacked the absurd deference to regulations laid down in London and the failure of the army chiefs to adapt to circumstances. Soldiers were falling ill because of their poor diet. They could have been eating rice, which was easily available locally as it was the mainstay of the Turkish diet, but they were prevented from doing so – because rice was not the standard issue as laid down in the regulations. Bales of urgently needed supplies could not be unpacked unless a board was called – a board being six designated men required to note the contents of the bales as they were unpacked to prevent thieving. Due to the chaos and confusion of the war, bales of winter uniforms or dressings would languish for weeks unopened because enough members of a board could rarely be found at the same time. Meanwhile the troops in the field missed the winter coats waiting at the quayside, and the wounds of the sick worsened without the clean lint trussed up in the bales.

But Russell's daring criticism had done its bit. The often lazy and somnolent genie of British public opinion, so powerful when awake, awoke now. The hopelessness of Aberdeen as a war leader and the need for a masterly and decisive character like Palmerston was signalled when the House of Commons voted in favour of a Royal Commission to investigate the way the war was being handled in the Crimea. Aberdeen treated this as a vote of no confidence, and resigned. Palmerston took over as prime minister.

But before the Aberdeen government fell in 1855, the war minister Sidney Herbert had redeemed himself a little. He had asked his friend, the wealthy thirty-four-year-old Miss Florence Nightingale, who ran a nursing home in Harley Street, to go out to Scutari to visit the British hospital on the Turkish side of the Black Sea opposite Constantinople, and find out what was going wrong with the nursing. For until Florence Nightingale started managing the hospital, more men were dying at the Barrack Hospital at Scutari than in the field hospitals. The mortality rate was running at almost 50 per cent of the hospital population. For more to survive lying on frozen ground with a thin bell tent above them than in a large hospital suggested that there was something very badly amiss. Florence Nightingale was the one person Herbert thought might make a difference to the unhappy situation by sheer force of personality, and he was right. Her time at Scutari was as important to the success of the war as Palmerston's taking over the running of it.

To Miss Nightingale, as she tripped round the wards in her neat white apron, one of the most obvious problems was immediately apparent. Wherever she went, wounded men were lying alongside open sewers breathing in infection. The conditions were worse than those of a prison. She was also appalled by the attitude of the officers to their men. She and her thirty nurses could not believe that their simple requests, such as the removal of the men from the area of the sewage, frequent disposal of waste, clean pyjamas, a monumental quantity of lint and properly cooked meat, were seen as 'spoiling the brutes'. She noted caustically that Lord Stratford de Redcliffe, the influential ambassador to the Ottoman court, for many years had twenty-seven servants all to himself. The hospital was in full view of his palace on the Bosphorus. But, to her amazement and indignation, he offered no help at all to the British citizens he represented, even though 'the British army was perishing within sight of his windows'.

Fortunately Palmerston listened to Florence Nightingale. The British steam engine was harnessed to help the British army. A railway was quickly built between the harbour and the siege camp at Sebastopol, for ferrying supplies efficiently and the wounded comfortably. Soyer, the sought-after chef of the Reform Club, volunteered his services in the Crimea to develop delicate food for convalescents. Under a regime of tender loving care where they were treated as human beings, the soldiers began to recover in the hospital where previously they had tended to die.

Florence Nightingale never used the word 'germ' – in fact the concept of germs would not be known for over a decade, when it was discovered by Joseph Lister, the inventor of antiseptics. But she had an intuitive sense of bacteria, or dirt as she called it, passing from one person to another. In the case of the seriously ill, she noted, this could be fatal. By forcing the orderlies and her nurses to wash their hands between examinations, she caused the rate of infection to drop dramatically. Before the invention of antibiotics, this was almost miraculous. Thanks to elementary hygiene rules, Florence Nightingale defeated something that could destroy an army – disease.

The Royal Commissioners investigating what went wrong in the Crimea had nothing but the highest praise for Miss Nightingale, who had become known as the Lady with the Lamp (owing to her habit of wandering softly about the beds by night holding a small lamp). From the end of the Crimean War nursing became an admired profession under the strict rules she had set out. Previously the nurses used in hospitals had simply been pairs of hands, and tended to be ex-prostitutes retrieved by clergymen from a life on the streets.

For all Florence Nightingale's dedicated work, of the 25,000 British soldiers in the Crimea, no fewer than 10,000 either lost their lives or were shipped home to England as invalids. Despite brave fighting by the British, it was the valorous French army (to whose numbers were added 15,000 Sardinian soldiers to ensure that the Italian question got a mention at the peace table) who were chiefly responsible for the fall of Sebastopol. By 1856 the war had drifted to a close, with both sides eager for peace; the Russians were particularly anxious to see the back of the British fleet which still surrounded the naval base at Kronstadt. The Treaty of Paris, signed that year, satisfied the French and English and humiliated the Russians by neutralizing the Black Sea. The demilitarization of the Black Sea proved unenforceable after 1871, however, when Russia seized the opportunity presented by war between France and Germany to abrogate the treaty unilaterally. By the 1890s the Russian fleet was one of the strongest in the world and Sebastopol had been rebuilt. Nevertheless, by insisting that Turkey put her house in order in her treatment of Christians, the treaty gave Russia less excuse to interfere in her internal affairs and rendered the continued upholding of the Ottoman Empire a more respectable aim of British diplomats.

The British military establishment proved almost as impervious to reform as the Ottoman Empire. Despite the scandal over the conduct of the Crimean War and despite the Royal Commission's findings, only a few of its recommendations were implemented. It would take more than fifteen years and the defeat of the French army by the Prussians to make Britain sufficiently exercised about the state of her own army to revise her defences in a thorough fashion.

Since 1855 Palmerston had been prime minister at the head of a Whig government, and so he remained – apart from a Tory interlude, a second Derby–Disraeli ministry in 1858–9 – for the next ten years until his death. In foreign affairs he was progressive, a Whig or – as the Whig–Peelite coalition was increasingly becoming known – a Liberal, the friend of constitutional governments and exiled Italian patriots. But, where domestic affairs were concerned, Palmerston's reforming instincts had come to a full stop. As he would say in the early 1860s, when he was being pressed for educational and franchise reforms, 'There is really nothing to be done. We cannot go on adding to the statute book *ad infinitum*.' Until he died, therefore, the Liberal party was unable to follow its true path. It was kept in a conservative straitjacket.

Palmerston was soon occupied with another war, defending British interests in China. Despite the concessions made after the first China War, China remained reluctant to open herself up to trade with the west, a trade Britain was most eager to pursue. She would not even allow a British embassy on Chinese soil. When the Chinese authorities imprisoned the crew of an English ship named the *Arrow* for suspected piracy, it was the excuse for war. By 1860, after the capture of key forts in the Peiho river and the burning down of the emperor's summer palace as revenge for the murder of unarmed westerners, Palmerston had opened the major Chinese ports up to British custom and established diplomatic relations. In 1857 Richard Cobden, the veteran Radical, had put down a motion of censure against Palmerston's aggression, and Palmerston went to the country. But his actions towards China were completely approved and he was returned with a majority of eighty-five seats.

With Britain remaining in such a bellicose mood the news of mutiny in India in 1857 broke like a thunderclap. A series of revolts and massacres by Indian troops threatened British rule as well as the lives of British men and women besieged in Cawnpore and Lucknow. Worse still, at that precise moment the British army in India was denuded of British troops, most of them having been diverted to the Crimea, China and Iran. For the seizure of Herat in Afghanistan by Russia's allies, the Iranians, was believed to threaten the north-west frontier to India. The British army in India therefore consisted mainly of sepoys. The mutiny broke out at Meerut and spread all over northern and central India, but it was the East India Company's Bengal army that was most strongly affected. The immediate cause was a change in weaponry, to the new Enfield rifle, an effect of the Crimean War. The Enfield rifled musket had been observed to be superior to the old smooth bore. A mischievous rumour swept the ranks that the tallow used to grease the cartridges was made with a mixture of cow and pig fat. This disgusted and offended at one stroke both the Hindus and the Muslims who now made up most of the army of India: Hindus believe that the cow is a sacred animal, whereas Muslims believe that to touch a pig will defile them. Both therefore refused to handle the cartridges, because, in order to use them, the soldier had to bite off one end.

But its underlying cause was the drastic westernization process India had been undergoing for the previous twelve years. The last governor-general but one, the Marquis of Dalhousie, was a keen modernizer in the tradition of his predecessor Lord William Bentinck, who believed it was his duty to open India up to progress. Bentinck had destroyed the Indian custom of suttee in the 1830s – the burning of widows on their husbands' funeral pyres – and eradicated the Thugees, a caste of hereditary murderers whose religion in the service of the goddess Kali directed them to wander around the country strangling their victims. Dalhousie stepped up missionary activity as another means of spreading western civilization among the Indians. He brought the telegraph to the country, built proper roads, tackled education, created irrigation systems, constructed industrial ports and above all introduced the railway to India. Though Dalhousie had many admirable objectives and a vision of what could be achieved in India, his programme failed in one major respect. He did not take Indian sensibilities into account.

For Hindu Indians, the majority of the population, the railway did not represent progress as it did in Europe. In India the railway was seen as an attack on the caste system, as different castes would have to travel in the same compartments. In 1856 Dalhousie's successor Lord Canning further outraged Indian notions, especially among the Brahmins in the Indian army, when he made altered conditions of service apply. Henceforth Indian troops had to go abroad as part of their service contract. It was another opportunity for the caste miscegenation forbidden by the Hindu religion.

Above all Dalhousie had angered Indians with the amount of territory he had added to British India by what he called his doctrine of lapse. As well as Burma – by the Second Burmese War in 1852, Lower Burma and the important trading station of Rangoon were annexed – British India obtained Sattara in 1848, Nagpore in 1853 and Jhansi in 1854. These were three hereditary lands of the Maratha warriors that Dalhousie took over on the grounds that each of the rulers lacked a direct descendant. Hindu policy in these circumstances was to adopt a male heir, but the governor-general would not have that. He maintained that the sovereignty of a nation 'lapsed' to the paramount power – the British government – in default of the natural heirs of a ruling family. Power could not pass to the adopted sons without the consent of the governor-general, and that Dalhousie would never grant.

By the 1850s no Indian ruling family of a dependent state, however princely, felt secure with Dalhousie, who had enormously extended the boundaries of British India. The final straw was the annexation of the powerful kingdom of Oude in 1856, again because there was no male heir of the body. To British eyes the administration of Oude was despicably corrupt and cruel, since the bulk of the massive taxes fell on the miserable poor, but its annexation enraged the kinsmen of the late ruler. Dalhousie himself had noted with concern that there was a great deal of unrest among the Brahmins of the Bengal army, a high proportion of whom had been recruited from Oude. A strange prophecy was circulating that a hundred years from Clive's victory at Plassey in 1757 the British would be driven out of India. When stories of the abysmal performance of the British army in the Crimea started to reach India, it encouraged the Indian troops to revolt.

The spark for mutiny was the Enfield rifles and their supposedly sacrilegious cartridges handed out to the Indian troops at Bengal. But though the tallow was withdrawn it was not soon enough to stop wild rumours sweeping the country that it marked the start of an attempt to destroy the caste system and the Hindu and Muslim faiths, and to convert India to Christianity. Panic spread throughout the country and the revolt began. The Indian Mutiny was the worst crisis the British Empire had encountered since the Napoleonic Wars. Much of India joined the rebels, leaving isolated garrisons like Cawnpore and Lucknow in British hands. But eventually, after a long siege, the British garrison at Cawnpore under Sir Hugh Wheeler was forced to surrender.

Unfortunately the siege of Cawnpore was led by a vengeful victim of Dalhousie's lapse policy called Nana Sahib, the adopted son of the last Peishwah of Poona. Nana Sahib tricked the British garrison into letting their wives and children go by granting them a safe-conduct pass. Then, before the eyes of their husbands and fathers, as the party of women and children began sailing away downriver Nana Sahib's soldiers opened fire on them.

Those who escaped death were dragged bleeding and terrified to a local palace and locked up. There, five of Nana Sahib's men hacked them to death and threw their limbs, large and small, down the well of Cawnpore. When news of Cawnpore reached England from the three men who managed to escape it poisoned the attitude of the new British garrisons towards the Indians for a generation. The rage of the English soldiers when they discovered the remains of their comrades' wives and children down the well of Cawnpore led to equally barbarous scenes of retaliation upon the Indian population – some were tied to cannons and blown up – which could likewise not be forgotten by their Indian victims.

At Lucknow, the garrison managed to hold out until help arrived with General Havelock, who had come from the Punjab. Britain had annexed the Punjab and its subject province Kashmir in north-west India only eight years before after two strenuous wars against the Sikhs, a very martial people. However, British treatment of the Punjab was very different from that of Oude and the other disaffected areas thanks to its administration by the Lawrence brothers Henry and John. The Lawrences, who had spent most of their adult lives bound up with Indian affairs, respected and admired Indian culture and deplored Dalhousie's doctrine of lapse. The regime they created in the Punjab, which the Sikhs found acceptable, ensured that it stayed loyal to Britain. In fact the military traditions of the Sikhs and the fearless soldiers they produced became a crucial element in the maintenance of the empire – never more so than at the time of the Mutiny.

Confident that the Punjab would not rise, a force was collected of partly British and partly Sikh soldiers which marched south from the Punjab to recapture Delhi, while others sailed along the Ganges to relieve the weakened defenders of Lucknow. Fortunately for the British, most of Bombay, Madras and Lower Bengal did not join the rebellion, and most independent local leaders such as the princes of Holkar and Sindhia remained allies of the British. Fortunately, too, a detachment of soldiers on its way to the Second China War could be diverted to India instead.

The Indian Mutiny dramatically demonstrated that it was absurd for most of the enormous subcontinent of India to be governed by what was essentially a commercial company, even if there was a Cabinet representative to oversee its affairs. A Conservative government, the second Derby–Disraeli administration, was now in power, Palmerston having been briefly thrown out of office in February 1858. The India Bill which dissolved the East India Company after it had ruled India for 101 years had the assent of both parties. It transferred the government of British India to the crown, which was represented by a secretary of state for India, and an expert council replaced the old Board of Control which had been composed of directors of the company. In India itself, a viceroy replaced the governor-general, and all the former presidencies such as Bombay and Madras were henceforth subordinate to his rule. The company's army became conjoined with the British army. The son of Prime Minister George Canning, Lord 'Clemency' Canning, who had acted with aplomb during the Mutiny and insisted that most of the rebels be treated leniently, became the first viceroy.

But the minority Derby and Disraeli government was driven from power in 1859, and Palmerston came back for his second period as prime minister. Although it was called a Whig–Peelite coalition it was in effect the first administration of what by 1865 was becoming known as the Liberal party. A few days before Palmerston took office, at a meeting at Willis's

Rooms in London on 6 June 1859 some 300 Whigs, Peelites and Radicals had pledged themselves to work as one against Derby and Disraeli. For many years they had supported one another on the issues where they had ideas in common, such as representative government and free trade. Now there was fusion, though the tension between the disparate elements continued under Palmerston, since their leader shared none of the commitment to a wider franchise and social progress that would be an increasingly dominant theme for the new party.

In fact, regardless of party, there was a widespread consciousness among much of the House of Commons of the changing times. Dissenters or Nonconformists, whose numbers at mid-century in some cities rivalled those of the Anglicans, would make up much of the Liberal party's supporters. It was no longer appropriate for Britain to continue to be confined within the Anglican settlement of two centuries ago. A less exclusive mood was emerging in the country. Under the Tories in 1858 a Jewish Disability Act allowing non-Christian jurors to become MPs allowed the Jewish Lionel de Rothschild to take the seat in the House of Commons he had won in 1847. In the same year the Property Qualification Act laid down that for the first time MPs did not have to be men of wealth.

William Ewart Gladstone, chancellor of the Exchequer from 1859 onwards, was one of the leaders of the progressive section of the Liberals. He clashed frequently with Palmerston, who was almost a quarter of a century older. While Gladstone's whole life was a voyage of intellectual exploration, Palmerston's ideas were immovable. He could not understand Gladstone's palpably growing confidence in the perfectibility of man and democratic ideas. Gladstone was increasingly disquieted that lack of money prevented some people from voting. It offended his Christian conscience, which led him to regard all men as equal. He would soon be making speeches in favour of universal suffrage and Parliamentary reform, though Palmerston had given strict orders that all attempts at expanding the franchise were to be shot down. Palmerston even tried to stop Gladstone's bill to reduce duty on newspapers to make them cheaper and more accessible to the working man, and sided with the House of Lords when it tried to throw it out. But Gladstone triumphed by wrapping the bill up in the budget. As a money bill, constitutionally it could not be touched by the Lords.

The natural scientist Charles Darwin's *Origin of Species*, published in 1859, whose theories about evolution were popularized as 'the survival of the fittest', increased Britons' belief in their civilization. So did writers like Lord Macaulay, the dramatic historian whose 'Whiggish' view of the unending progress of English history was the required reading of the day. Although the Indian Mutiny implied that the fruits of Victorian civilization might be less valued by other nations, the patriotic mission to impart material achievements to less fortunate peoples did not cease.

British penetration into central Africa in the 1850s reinforced the country's sense of superiority. Africa's impenetrable equatorial interior had defied Europeans since Roman times. At the end of the eighteenth century a young surgeon named Mungo Park had died in his attempt to follow the uncharted Niger river to its source during his intrepid solo journey into the Gambia, and no Briton had ventured there since. Tropical disease and the lack of maps made any expedition potentially suicidal. But in the 1850s, 1860s and 1870s missionaries like David Livingstone and British explorers like Sir Richard Burton and J. H. Speke at last mapped out Africa's geographical contours. The invention and widespread use of steamships facilitated travel to Africa, while breakthroughs in medicine made it possible to survive.

There had been considerable missionary activity in southern Africa, working from the Cape northwards, ever since the British had captured it during the Napoleonic Wars, and it was their activities which reawakened interest in equatorial Africa. David Livingstone, a former mill hand from Lanarkshire in Scotland, was the most celebrated missionary of Victorian England. He became a national hero and was given a state funeral at Westminster Abbey in 1874. His statue, with its peaked tropical cap, located outside the Royal Geographical Society headquarters opposite Hyde Park, reminds us that he was also one of the nineteenth century's most important explorers.

Having enterprisingly taken a short course in medicine because he believed it would be of use to him, but with no special knowledge of Africa, Livingstone had been sent to Bechuanaland (now Botswana) by the London Missionary Society in 1840. From there he travelled north on foot into the unknown. Using beads to barter for food, armed with his Bible and a gun, he spent the next thirty years crossing and recrossing parts of east-central Africa where no European had been before to bring her Christianity and to denounce slavery. Whereas malaria and other tropical diseases had put paid to earlier European adventurers, Livingstone's survival was ensured by his pioneering use of quinine.

He still suffered endlessly from malaria, but the quinine enabled him to stay alive, and he refused to give up his mission. Like all missionary endeavours it was kept going purely by public subscription. And on those journeys of conversion Livingstone was the first European to discover Lake Ngami, the Victoria Falls, the Zambezi valley, Lake Nyasa and the River Luabala, which turned out to be the mighty River Congo.

From 1865 to 1871 Livingstone vanished in the jungles of Africa. Such was the world's anxiety about the whereabouts of this amazing man that the journalist and explorer H. M. Stanley was sent out by the *New York Herald* to look for him. Alone on the shores of Lake Tanganyika Stanley spotted an elderly white man and it was then that he hailed him with the immortal words, 'Dr Livingstone I presume?'

Livingstone had been intent on finding the source of the Nile, the river which flows from south to north. This had become an obsession for the Victorians, and was a mystery unsolved since Herodotus. Rumours emanating from Egyptian explorers and missionaries, and from Livingstone himself, suggesting that the source lay in the great lakes rather than in Herodotus' four fountains at the heart of Africa, sent a number of British expeditions to Africa in the 1850s. The most talked about was that of the flamboyant Arabist Sir Richard Burton, who had entered the Holy City of Mecca in disguise, and the explorer and soldier John Hanning Speke. Together they discovered Lake Tanganyika in 1858. But it was Speke who courageously travelled on alone to find where the Nile river rises out of a great lake he named Victoria in 1862, in honour of the queen. As he made his way down waters unmapped by Europeans, Speke came upon the explorer Sir Samuel Baker, who was slowly making his way up the Nile, charting it as he went. In fact the various sources of the Nile continued to be disputed, so that in 1864 Baker would discover another source, Lake Nyanza, which he called Lake Albert in honour of the prince consort.

By 1864, however, Prince Albert had been dead for three years. In 1861, at the age of forty-two, the prince consort had fallen victim to typhoid, scourge of rich and poor before the arrival of proper sewage disposal. Queen Victoria had always been obsessed with the unhealthy and ancient nature of the drains at Windsor, and had been putting in new ones when her husband became ill. After a locum doctor's initial failure to diagnose typhoid, nothing could save him. Once widowed, Prince Albert's adoring wife, mother of nine children, became a recluse, quite unable to appear at any state occasions so terrible was her grief. Colossal new buildings in London, the Albert Hall and the Albert Memorial opposite one another in Kensington, provided public expression of her unhappiness. The monarchy became extremely unpopular as the queen, soon known as the Widow of Windsor, withdrew from public life to live in the deepest seclusion. Ever after she blamed the Prince of Wales, the future Edward VII, for his father's death, because she believed that Prince Albert had caught the fatal disease while visiting him.

Queen Victoria's ten-year period of mourning coincided with a low in Britain's external relations, when the ageing Palmerston lost his touch. He became preoccupied with the danger posed by Napoleon III to British security and – as Prince Albert's death had removed a very useful source of information about German affairs – failed to understand the significance of what was going on in Prussia, where in September 1862 Bismarck had become first minister.

Palmerston had looked with the strongest approval on the Italian wars of unification, which began in April 1859, soon after the end of the Indian Mutiny. England preserved a decisive and helpful neutrality. The three most important members of the government, Palmerston, his foreign secretary Lord John Russell and Gladstone his chancellor of the Exchequer, had the greatest sympathy with the Italian cause – the Risorgimento or rebirth – as did most of the *bien pensant*, educated, anti-papal middle classes, for Britain had long been a home from home to Italian nationalist exiles. In 1861 the first Italian Parliament proclaimed Victor Emmanuel king of a unified Italy.

The Italian wars of liberation had begun after a secret deal between Napoleon III and the Italian nationalist leader Count Camillo Cavour that they should attack Austria together and drive her out of Italy. When it emerged that the price for the emperor's help in Italy was the lands of Savoy and Nice, which brought the French frontier in the south up to the Alpine passes, Palmerston never trusted the French leader again. It confirmed the British belief that Napoleon III was a warmonger who would do anything to enlarge France's territories. The final insult came in 1859 when the French engineer Ferdinand De Lesseps in a moment of inspiration began building the Suez Canal – a passage by water across Egypt from the Mediterranean through to the Red Sea. Palmerston believed it was intended to threaten the British Empire in India.

So Britain began to draw apart from France, just when she might have begun to need an ally on the continent, though relations between Italy and England remained warm for over half a century. By 1859, the war scares which had alarmed Britain throughout Napoleon III's reign brought about a Royal Commission to look into British defences. It pronounced them inadequate. Napoleon not only had a fleet of steam-powered boats, he was said to be building a huge naval base at Cherbourg just across the Channel. From there would he not one day try launching an invasion of England from Boulogne, just as his uncle had planned?

Demands for the expenditure needed to put Britain on a war footing led to endless rows between Palmerston and Gladstone. Fortifying Portsmouth and Plymouth in the manner Palmerston required would involve drastically raising the taxation that Gladstone tried every year to reduce, morally convinced as he was of the wickedness of war. With Gladstone's encouragement, in 1860 the Radical Richard Cobden brought about the Franco-British commercial treaty reducing tariffs between the two countries, as part of their commitment to the doctrine of free trade which both men believed was the most enduring way of maintaining peace. But distrust of France continued.

In 1861 the American Civil War broke out when Abraham Lincoln became president on an anti-slavery ticket. The Southern states' wealth depended on a slave economy if they were to run their cotton and tobacco plantations at profit, so Lincoln's arrival in the White House prompted them to announce that they would exercise their right to secede from the Union, forming the Confederate States under the presidency of Jefferson Davis. But the Northerners refused to allow this to happen. When the Southerners tried to seize Fort Sumter near Charleston, the capital of South Carolina, civil war erupted. Despite their abhorrence of slavery, the majority of the British were sympathetic to the South. Gladstone, who was convinced of each nation's right to self-determination, said that Jefferson Davis had created a nation, and Palmerston himself preferred the gentlemanly ways of the South and their aristocratic society to the crude energy of the Northern Yankee. Nevertheless it would have been a great mistake for Britain to take sides and be drawn into the war. Palmerston successfully insisted that Britain remained neutral.

In northern England, however, manufacturers wanted the government to lift the Northerners' blockade of the Southerners' shipping. This was preventing the Southerners' exporting their cotton, on which much of Lancashire's multi-million-pound industry was based. However, even if Britain had succeeded in lifting the blockade, the partial ruin of the Lancashire cotton industry would still have taken place, for the men and women who worked the machines announced a boycott of all Southern cotton on the ground that they did not want to support the cause of slavery. The result was a million people in Lancashire living on the rates, a situation a hundred times more pitiful than the Hungry Forties. Nevertheless, the principled operatives continued to insist that they would rather starve than support slavery. As a result of the war, Egypt soon became preferred as one of the chief sources of cotton for British manufacturing, all the more so after it was occupied by British forces in 1882.

The American Civil War came to an end after four years of fighting in 1865. The North had won under the military genius of Ulysses S. Grant, helped by their greater wealth, their industrial economy and a larger population which triumphed over the agrarian and less populated South. Their swift action in creating a powerful navy to paralyse the Southerners' principal exports of cotton and tobacco was also decisive. In the course of the war all black slaves were declared to be free.

Napoleon III used the United States' civil war to venture into what America by the Monroe Doctrine defined as her sphere of influence. Mexico was a part of the 'back yard' she considered a no-go area for the European powers. But war-torn America was too preoccupied to object when alongside a British force sent to demand the repayment of a debt owed to foreign bondholders came a French expedition to make the bankrupt Mexico a client state of France. Napoleon III thus turned the younger brother of the Habsburg emperor Franz Joseph I into the Emperor Maximilian of Mexico. However, with the end of the American Civil War in 1865 the Americans were able to force Napoleon to withdraw his soldiers and abandon the so-called emperor to be executed by the Mexicans.

The Mexican adventure confirmed Napoleon's reputation for reckless meddling. But it was his European activities the British worried about. British diplomats were convinced that the emperor's policy was to move the French frontier up to the Rhine, as indeed it was. Despite the favoured-nation status France and Britain now had with one another, the threat this would pose to Belgium, always Britain's first priority for her security, increasingly entailed ruling out any thought of alliance with Napoleon. In 1863 the evident discontent of the Poles, who had rebelled against their Russian overlords, and the claim by the North German Confederation to the Danish duchies of Schleswig and Holstein, gave Napoleon the opportunity to propose a European Congress so that all the post-1815 boundaries could be looked at afresh. The British made it abundantly clear that they had no interest in what they believed would be an excuse for France to shift her own boundaries.

But, in the case of Schleswig and Holstein, Britain suddenly needed an ally. Encouraged by Prussia, the North German Confederation was not frightened off by Palmerston's command to leave the duchies alone – he had completely underestimated the force of German nationalism. In 1863 the new King of Denmark inherited his throne through the female line. The duchies recognized inheritance only through the male line. Thus the way was open for a German heir. When the King of Denmark promulgated a new constitution which incorporated the more Danish duchy, Schleswig, wholly into Denmark, Austria and Prussia acting for the German Confederation threatened the Danes with war if they would not give up the duchies altogether.

To Palmerston the idea of the Confederation of German states, new-comers in the power games of Europe, deciding who the territories of the ancient Danish monarchy belonged to was preposterous. But he no longer had the grip on current events that had made him such a force to be reckoned with in the past. The septuagenarian Palmerston had first become an MP as long ago as 1809. He had no idea of the significance of Bismarck and the series of wars he had planned to weld the German states into one united Germany, nor of the overwhelming German desire to achieve this. When to Palmerston's amazement in February 1864 Prussian and Austrian troops called Britain's bluff and invaded Schleswig–Holstein, seizing the duchies from Denmark, there was nothing he could do.

Palmerston had assumed that the Germans would be frightened off by his warning that the Danes would not be fighting alone. His gallantry was inspired by the marriage of the Prince of Wales to the exquisite Danish princess Alexandra that very year. When the Austro-Prussian preparations for war continued, approaches to Napoleon for an army elicited the information that Bismarck had promised France compensation on the Rhine if she stayed neutral over the Danish provinces. But Schleswig–Holstein could not be saved by the British navy alone. After all Palmerston's bluster, the Danes had to fight on their own.

Britain's international reputation, already low after the Crimea, sank lower still. By now Palmerston and Russell were looking increasingly foolish. Queen Victoria called them 'two dreadful old men'. Lord Derby described their ineffectual posturings over first Poland, when they had fruitlessly demanded a say in the treatment of the Poles, and then Denmark as a policy of 'meddle and muddle'.

With Britain a spent force and France compliant, to the surprise of the duchies' inhabitants, not to say the German Confederation and the German Prince Frederick of Augustenberg in whose name the Austrians and Prussians were fighting for the duchies, Schleswig was annexed to Prussia, and Holstein to Austria.

After Schleswig–Holstein, even German liberals began to support Bismarck. They saw the truth of his harsh words about the military means needed to unite Germany. In 1866 the promise of the Austrian-held Veneto to Italy and the Rhine provinces to the emperor Napoleon III prepared the way for a new war. Bismarck had bought off the Russians by supporting them against the Polish rebellion in 1863, and waited for what he called the favourable moment. Now Prussia could be sure of no stab in the back from the east from Russia when she attacked Austria to seize the leadership of the North German Confederation for herself. With Russia and France both neutral, Prussia and Italy attacked Austria together, on the specious pretext of the administration of Holstein.

In three weeks, to the watching world's amazement, the Austrian army had been defeated by the Prussians, by their superb soldiers, their disciplined tactics and their new needle guns, at the Battle of Königgrätz, or Sadowa as it is known in England, in July 1866. Austria was expelled from the North German Confederation and the Veneto was duly ceded to Italy. But when Napoleon III called in the great prize he believed that he had been bribed with, the shifting of the French frontier to the edge of the Rhine provinces above Alsace–Lorraine, Bismarck made it brutally plain that he had been playing with Napoleon's dreams. It was out of the question.

But Palmerston was not there to see this astonishing manifestation of Prussian military aggression which turned the world upside down. Lord Cupid had died after a good breakfast of mutton chops a day short of his eighty-first birthday in October 1865. Despite recent mistakes he remained beloved of the Victorian public, his robust tendency to refuse to toe the diplomatic line when natural justice was at stake always sure to stir British emotions. Lord John Russell briefly became prime minister again. His thoughts continued to revolve round broadening the franchise. The reformers among the Liberals were now in the ascendant, but there were still enough of Palmerston's supporters to join the Tories and bring down a new Reform Bill and Russell's ministry in 1866. Derby became prime minister and Russell retired as leader of the Liberals, his place being taken by Gladstone.

In the event, by a strange turnaround, thanks to the canny Disraeli it was the Tory government which brought in the Second Reform Bill of 1867. Disraeli had been exasperated by his party's exclusion from power for twenty years. A new clamour for franchise reform had started up, and by the autumn of 1866 there were riots in Hyde Park, with crowds shouting 'For Gladstone and liberty'. Disraeli had persuaded the Conservatives that unless something was done to gratify working men's desires for a democratic Parliament they faced the possibility of real disorder. It was clear that the Tories did not appeal to middle-class opinion, but they might achieve an upsurge in support if the potentially vast working-class constituency was given the vote.

Although some of the Tory grandees like Lord Cranborne (the future prime minister Lord Salisbury) handed in their resignations in 1867, the age of middle-class democracy begun by the Great Reform Bill now came to an end. Disraeli 'dished the Whigs', as he put it, by introducing household suffrage in the towns. Even lodgers got the vote as long as they paid £10 a year in rent and lived in the same rooms for a year (it was £12 a year in the counties). Lord Derby called it 'a leap in the dark': who knew what government would be voted for by a new kind of voter, whose lack of education made educational reforms more pressing than ever? Accompanying the bill extending the suffrage was a Distribution of Seats Bill – eleven obsolete boroughs were disenfranchised, and thirty-five others having fewer than 10,000 inhabitants gave up one member, freeing up MPs for towns whose populations had grown and counties whose populations were also increasing.

By the Reform Act of 1867 Disraeli brought in an innovative dimension of working-class support for the Tories which he would foster by a striking foreign policy, his 'forward' attitude to the empire and important social reforms. His tough stance as a negotiator where Britain's interests were at stake was sharply defined against the approach of the Gladstonian Liberal party, which was committed to an ethical foreign policy, international standards of morality and the rights of small nations.

In the late 1860s Britain got her first taste of the Irish militancy that would bedevil British politics for the next fifty-five years. The previous decade had seen the founding in the United States of the Fenians, an Irish secret society devoted to establishing a republic in Ireland, and with the end of the American Civil War many Irishmen took their military experience to their native land. In 1867 they tried an uprising. When that failed they moved on to mainland Britain, where a series of outrages culminated in the blowing up of a wall of Clerkenwell Prison. Gladstone believed that that was what he called the chapel bell, ringing to declare that his mission was to pacify Ireland.

Solving the Irish question would be the consuming ambition of the second half of Gladstone's career. Appropriately it was Ireland that in 1868 brought down the Tory government (now led by Disraeli owing to Derby's ill-health). The Tories traditionally were the party of the established Church. Even Disraeli could not change that. So when Gladstone took up the cause of disestablishing the Protestant Church in Ireland as a way of pleasing the Irish population, the Conservatives had to oppose it. Disraeli's government fell as the Commons, by a huge majority, voted for Gladstone's proposals. At the 1868 election the newly enfranchised electorate ungratefully gave Disraeli only 265 seats and 393 to Gladstone, who thus formed the first Liberal ministry.

The sixty-four-year-old Disraeli retreated to lick his party's wounds and reorganize it by creating the Conservative Central Office. His poetic, elegant and slender person, with its thin, witty face surrounded still by long, lustrous black lovelocks, was replaced at the government despatch box by the frequently anguished, almost superhumanly strong Gladstone.

Gladstone and Disraeli (1868–1886)

William Ewart Gladstone's vigorous first ministry began in 1868. For the first time the aristocratic Whigs were no longer in a majority in the Liberal party and the Radicals and Nonconformists were to the fore. Gladstone presided over the sort of reforming government which had not been seen since Grey and Peel and which produced the beginnings of the modern Britain we take for granted today, committed to a meritocratic democracy. Both the civil service and the army were thrown open to competition. In 1870 an exam system was instituted for the civil service, while in the army from 1871 commanding rank was no longer to be achieved by purchasing a commission.

Ever since the Crimean War the disgraceful performance of the army had convinced many that it should be reformed from top to toe and purged of its aristocratic commanding officers. But it was extremely hard to persuade the army itself of this, particularly as the Duke of Wellington continued to be held up as a vindication of the system. Edward Cardwell, the new secretary for war, believed that this was not only unfair, but in the light of the behaviour of Lords Lucan and Cardigan in the Crimea positively dangerous. Moreover the menace of Prussian arms had now reached France, just across the Channel, where the destruction of the French army in a matter of days had given the question of army reforms additional urgency.

There was furious opposition to Cardwell. The House of Lords threw out the bill to protect its own. But Gladstone was not going to be thwarted. He ingeniously made Queen Victoria cancel the royal warrant which authorized the purchase of commissions. The system of buying promotion was at an end. Short service was introduced, and the militia and volunteers were integrated with the commissioned forces. Cardwell also destroyed the division of command which had plagued both the Napoleonic and the Crimean Wars – between Horse Guards, where the commander-in-chief's department was based, and the War Office. The commander-in-chief, a post which had usually been held by a royal duke not necessarily on the side of the elected government, was made subordinate to the secretary for war, who had to be a member of the ruling party.

The legalization of trade unions in 1871 accompanied the broadening of the franchise, the Trade Union Act recognizing their status as friendly societies. From 1872 the Secret Ballot Act ensured that voters could no longer be intimidated – perhaps by an aggressive candidate – as they spoke their votes to the teller. From now on the vote was an anonymous piece of paper placed in the ballot box. Women still did not have the vote, but the old pseudo-scientific prejudices about women's brains being inferior to men's, and the debates about women's capabilities which had occupied so much newspaper print for the previous forty years, were dying down. Though they could not take degrees, by 1872 women started being accepted at Cambridge, with two female halls of residence, Girton and Newnham. The London Medical School for Women was established in 1875, and Oxford followed in 1878 with Lady Margaret Hall and Somerville.

At Oxbridge women no longer met only members of the Church of England. For by at last abolishing the University Test Act in 1871 under pressure from the Nonconformists the Liberals opened the ancient universities to all the intellectual talent in the kingdom, even if they were Jews, Roman Catholics or Nonconformists. Until that date non-Anglicans had been prevented from studying at Oxford or Cambridge, if they could not take an oath of allegiance to the monarch as head of the Church of England.

And as part of these changing mores the position of women continued to improve throughout the rest of the century. Though they were hardly a minority in the country, women had begun the nineteenth century not only socially but legally inferior to men. Married women could not be represented separately from their husbands in the law courts until 1857. The influential philosopher John Stuart Mill's 1869 publication *The Subjection of Women* both reflected advanced thought and did much to raise the consciousness of his era about how women were oppressed. Enlarging the franchise on such a wide scale brought up the question of female suffrage. In 1865 Mill, who was the Radical MP for Westminster, proposed the vote for women, eloquently advocating the equality of women to men in an amendment to the Second Reform Bill. Though it was defeated, female suffrage societies began to spring up in the major cities.

In 1869 the Liberal government gave women the right to vote in municipal elections; from 1870 women could vote in school board elections and be elected to the boards, while by 1894 women played a more visible role in local government, as they were allowed to serve on urban and district councils. In 1873 the humane Custody of Infants Acts ensured that all women could have access to their children in the event of divorce or separation, a right previously denied them and the cause of much anguish.

From the 1870s to the end of the century a mass of case law was built up to support women as independent beings with separate and equal rights. In 1882 the Married Women's Property Act at last put an end to the husband's legal right to all his wife's earnings. Although in practice suspicious fathers and brothers, or clever women like Charlotte Brontë, had always found ways round this by creating trusts to which only they had access, it was a significant development.

Education was also fundamentally reformed. In 1870 the Cabinet minister W. E. Forster, a former Quaker married to the daughter of Dr Arnold who had revitalized Rugby School with an ethos of public service, carried an Elementary Education Act through the Commons. This created the first national system, making education available to all children from the age of five to thirteen. Any local district could elect a school board which would have the power to levy a rate and then spend it either on schools already existing in their area or on building new schools. Although the boards were given powers to enforce attendance up to the age of thirteen, it was not until 1880 that elementary education was made legally compulsory, and it was not until 1891 that this became meaningful when a new Education Act made it free.

The period after the Second Reform Bill is often seen as marking the transition from the rule of the middle classes to a wider democracy. But the universal feature of late-Victorian Britain was the proliferation of a self-improving middle-class high culture. It is glimpsed in the imposing civic buildings of Liverpool and Manchester – the concert halls, the orchestras, the art galleries, the public parks and the free public libraries begun by the American millionaire philanthropist Andrew Carnegie in 1880. The Victorians loved joining things and they loved building things.

Since 1845 there had been the university boat race between Oxford and Cambridge, since 1863 a Football Association. In 1864 the first county cricket match had been held. The youthful cricketer W. G. Grace had played for the MCC and was soon to have the sort of following that top sports stars have today. The railways and the introduction of three national Bank Holidays in 1871 contributed to increasing the British fascination with competitive sports – in the same year the Rugby Football Union was founded. In 1873 the first lawn tennis club was established, and the neo-Gothic Natural History Museum finished. Easily mistaken for a cathedral, the museum towered over South Kensington and provided a home for the curious specimens being sent back to Britain by her explorers.

For those with literary tastes, by the 1870s there was a different spirit abroad. Charles Dickens, whose skewering of social wrongs had epitomized the early Victorians, died in 1870 with his last novel *The Mystery of Edwin Drood* unfinished. Now that the state had been mobilized to address social problems, and organizations like the Salvation Army set up, the novel could concentrate on the emotions and moral dilemmas, as in George Eliot's *Middlemarch* and Thomas Hardy's first novel *Under the Greenwood Tree*, both published in 1872. Hardy's background as the son of a stonemason signified that the novel was beginning to encompass a hitherto unrepresented section of society. The king of poetic enchantment continued to be Alfred, Lord Tennyson, the Poet Laureate. The first

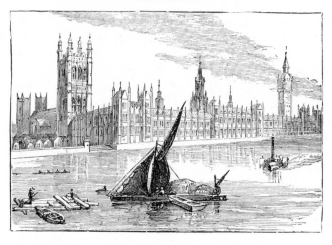

The new Houses of Parliament whose architect was Sir Charles Barry. The building was begun in 1836, finished in 1868.

generation of children had been thrilled by an Oxford mathematics don Charles Dodgson who under the pen name Lewis Carroll wrote *Alice's Adventures in Wonderland* in 1865. He followed it up in 1871 with *Through the Looking Glass*. Though still in deepest mourning Queen Victoria had become an author herself, publishing the bestselling *Leaves from the Journal of Our Life in the Highlands* in 1868, the same year that Wilkie Collins published *The Moonstone*.

As modernizers, the Liberals approached with some impatience the way justice was dispensed. Its obscure and dusty traditions drastically needed reorganizing and rationalizing. The complex of law courts in the Strand,

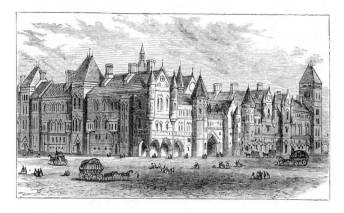

The Royal Courts of Justice in the Strand, built after the 1873 Liberal government Judicature Act.

known as the Royal Courts of Justice, between Lincoln's Inn and the Temple was built in the 1870s to house all the civil courts. Henceforth they were to be administered together under one roof. The very gradual development of English law over the centuries from the old Curia Regis of the various courts – Exchequer, Common Pleas, King's Bench and Chancery – had resulted in overlaps and unhelpful demarcations. All the courts were now brought together to form divisions of one Supreme Court of Judicature.

With the Nonconformist element so strongly represented in the government a fresh approach could be found towards Ireland, increasingly a sore in the body politic. The 1869 Church Disestablishment Act removed the insulting title of official state Church from the minority Protestant Church of Ireland. Even in the north it had next to no membership other than its clergymen, for most Ulstermen were Presbyterians. The Irish Church became a free Episcopal Church and its bishops no longer sat in the House of Lords.

But as far as the majority of the Irish were concerned the important issue was the land. Other than in the north with its linen and ship-building industries, farming provided the only employment in Ireland. Depopulation after the famine had brought in a series of landlords attracted by cheap land, but they proved as ruthless as the old, and only a little more scientific. Gladstone's first Irish Land Act in 1870 attempted to put right the many grievances of the Irish tenant farmer, by compelling landlords to compensate tenants for evictions if they had made improvements in their holdings. A system of loans was instituted to enable tenants to purchase land.

But though the Liberal government might congratulate itself on being such an effective new broom, its reforms had taken place against a menacing background. It was at last plain after the Franco-Prussian War of 1870–1 that the balance of power had tilted away from France and Britain. For 400 years the British had viewed the French with wariness if not enmity. At the Battle of Sedan in September 1870, when the North German Confederation took a Bonaparte emperor prisoner as well as the astounding number of 104,000 of his soldiers, the French became pitiable victims.

In continued pursuit of his ambition to unite the remaining southern German states under Prussia, Bismarck tricked the French into beginning the Franco-Prussian War on the basis of their objections to the German Hohenzollern candidate for the Spanish throne. Napoleon III needed a war to revive his flagging popularity. But though it emerged that he had intended to move the French frontier into Belgium and that he still had hopes of the Rhine provinces, the cumulative impression of Prussian savagery and French weakness left Europe gasping. The price of peace was the surrender to Germany of the French lands of Lorraine and Alsace and payment of an indemnity 'for causing the war' of £200 million to Germany. A German garrison would be maintained on French soil until it was paid. France took ten years to recover her strength as an international force, and for the first time the British began to envisage Germany as the enemy. Real fear of Prussian soldiers forced the British army to agree to the much needed reforms outlined above.

But Britain remained neutral over the Franco-Prussian War. She was not in the mood nor had she the strength to interfere in the continent of Europe when attacks on the old balance of power became regular events. British statesman were conscious of how foolish the British lion had looked roaring over Schleswig–Holstein when it had no teeth. When in 1871, seeing the French disorder, the Russians abrogated the peace treaty that had ended the Crimean War and remilitarized the Black Sea, Britain accepted that there was nothing she could do.

In the mysterious way of electorates, a subtle discontent began. The man in the street felt that Britain had been worsted by the Russians over the Black Sea. There was also a dawning realization that, though Britain dominated world shipping, her share of manufacturing was beginning to decline from the high-water mark of twenty years before. Gladstone had also agreed to have an arbitrator appointed over claims by the United States that she should be compensated for the destruction of Northern shipping during the Civil War by the Confederates' British-built *Alabama*. When news broke that the arbitrator had decided that Britain should pay the colossal sum of £3 million to the United States, it was greeted with stupefaction. It was not so many years since Palmerston had laid down the rule that Britain's natural mode of expression was gunboat diplomacy. The *Alabama* affair added to the British public's impression that Mr Gladstone was unable to stand up for Britain's interests abroad, whatever good he did at home. Did being Liberal-minded also make you feeble-minded?

By 1874 the British public had had enough of being improved. With the reorganization of the Conservative party by Disraeli, the Tory machine became a formidable weapon at elections. The dazzling Disraeli attacked Gladstone and the Liberals as not being patriotic enough, comparing the Cabinet seated on the front bench opposite him to a range of exhausted volcanoes. He played on the fears of the well-to-do. How would their sons get into the civil service or the army now that the old routes of patronage were gone? Among the less progressive there was a feeling of the world changing too much and too fast for them.

Gladstone's 1872 Licensing Act, which shortened the hours of drinking, annoyed everyone who enjoyed passing time at their local. He himself told his brother after his defeat at the next election that he had been 'borne down in a torrent of gin and beer'. That election came in 1874: Gladstone dissolved Parliament with the manifesto promise to abolish income tax, but Disraeli became prime minister for the second time, and remained so until 1880. Gladstone for his part announced moodily that he was leaving the Liberal party and Parliament, so that he might have 'an interval between Parliament and the grave'. In fact he would be prime minister for three more terms, which fortunately for her the queen lacked the prescience to see.

Disraeli was ecstatic – he was back at 'the top of the greasy pole' as he had put it in 1868. The queen was very pleased too. Gladstone had lectured her during private visits as if she were a 'public meeting'. Much to her annoyance he was always trying to involve the Prince of Wales in state business. Disraeli the literary man treated her as if she was a character from an old romance. She was 'the Faery' to him, as he constantly told her, and she loved it. They exchanged literary gossip – 'we authors, ma'am', said Disraeli the distinguished novelist tactfully, as Queen Victoria was very proud of her journal's publishing success.

Disraeli ended a ten-year period of great unpopularity for the monarchy since Prince Albert's death, during which republican movements had mushroomed, by getting Victoria to appear in public after years of seclusion. Soon Disraeli was allowed to sit in the royal presence whereas Gladstone had always had to stand. He was also permitted to write to the queen in the first person, instead of referring to himself as 'the prime minister'. He amused her, yet he was profound and sentimental by turns. He did not frighten her with dour democratic thunderings. Being with Disraeli was as intoxicating as drinking champagne, and he enjoyed a good deal of that too.

Above all Disraeli deliberately expanded the British Empire. Like most other politicians of his era, Disraeli had previously believed the colonies to be a millstone round the British government's neck, but he changed his mind. He began instead to be excited by the idea of Britain as an imperial country with an imperial destiny, publicly regretting that the grants of self-government to colonies like Canada had not been accompanied by measures for an imperial tariff, and keen to see a federation of the Dutch and British colonies in South Africa. Disraeli added to the queen's royal titles and her glamour by making her the Queen Empress of India in 1876 and had her proclaimed in this new style at Delhi. By far his most important achievement, however, was securing the Suez Canal for Britain.

The Suez Canal was the fast route to India. When it opened in 1869 it cut the distance from Britain to India by about six weeks and thousands of miles, for its waterway was a short cut between the Mediterranean and the Red Sea. For the British, with their huge, distant Indian Empire, its strategic value was even more important than its commercial. In the event of another Indian Mutiny or of invasion of the subcontinent by Russia, the Suez Canal could carry reinforcements far more quickly than the old route down the Cape. If the British controlled it, they controlled the gateway to their eastern empire.

Disraeli was at his best in foreign affairs. For him, secret deals and backstairs arrangements were the breath of life. When in the autumn of 1875 he heard a rumour from one of his sources that the Khedive of Egypt was about to go bankrupt and that his shares in the Suez Canal were up for grabs, or more importantly were on the point of being grabbed by a French syndicate, he had no time to lose.

Parliament was still in recess and could not grant the money immediately. It might take months to debate such a purchase and give its approval. In a typically dashing move, Disraeli approached the Rothschild banking family, whose liquidity was such that they had often produced the cash to pay the troops during the Napoleonic Wars when the government was running short. The prime minister's private secretary Montague Corry was sent to the Rothschild bank headquarters at New Court. Ushered into Baron Rothschild's presence Corry told him that the prime minister needed the then colossal sum of £4 million (worth about a billion pounds in today's money). 'When?' asked Lord Rothschild, without much excitement. 'Tomorrow,' said Corry. Rothschild was picking at a plate of lustrous muscatel grapes on a silver-gilt stand. He took another grape and, having ruminated thoughtfully, spat out the skin. 'What is your security?' he asked. 'The British government,' said Corry. 'You shall have it,' said Rothschild.

With the Rothschild loan, Disraeli bought 40 per cent of the shares in the Suez Canal, making Britain the largest single shareholder in the company. It was a stunning coup. Disraeli sent a dramatic note to the queen telling her about the Suez Canal. 'It's yours,' he wrote, as if the Canal were a personal gift.

Disraeli's prime ministership also saw a great deal done in the way of domestic legislation. Like Peel, he believed the Conservatives must continue to remake the alliance between the commercial and landed interests in the country if they wanted to be a viable party. Since their enfranchisement in 1867 those commercial interests now had to include the working classes. There had to be social reform if what Disraeli called Tory Democracy was to be properly cemented. His government set out to improve the lot of the poor. Where Gladstone was more interested in bettering men's souls, Disraeli addressed himself to their material needs.

Thanks to the outstanding Tory home secretary Richard Cross, in 1875 the Tories passed an enormous amount of practical social legislation. The Artisans Dwellings Act enabled local authorities to sweep away slums and replace them with healthy housing. In Birmingham in particular, under the Radical mayor Joseph Chamberlain, the unhealthy slums which had grown up round sites of manufacture were levelled to the ground and modern housing constructed in their stead. Legislation removed the last legal remnants restricting the trade unions when the Conspiracy and Protection of Property Act legalized peaceful picketing.

Disraeli's chance to perform on the world stage came in 1875, a year after he had become prime minister, with the revival of the Eastern Question – that is, the question of what was to become of the Ottoman Empire. But this time it was the Eastern Question influenced by the unifications of Italy and Germany. More than ever the peoples of the Balkans felt the same nationalist stirrings for their own states, while Austria – now that she had been deprived of her territory in Italy – looked to make it up in the Balkans.

In 1875 there was a series of risings by the inhabitants of Bosnia and Herzegovina against their savage Turkish overlords which were brutally put down, despite protests from the great powers. These were followed by revolts among the Bulgarians, Serbians and Montenegrins. In the case of the Serbians and Montenegrins they were sufficiently well armed to begin a war against Turkey in June 1876. But so successful were the Turkish armies against them that Russia felt the need to back the Christian rebels. By 1878 the Russians were at Adrianople (modern Edirne), and thus threatening Constantinople.

The need to protect Turkey became pressing. But at the end of June 1876 the general British acquiescence to the policy of supporting Turkey had vanished, as the *Daily News* started to publish reports from its own correspondent of the appalling massacres taking place in Bulgaria. Just as during the Greek Wars of Independence, a wave of indignation swept the now enormous British newspaper-reading public. How could Britain, which prided herself on being the friend of liberty, the foe of slavery, the home of justice, the refuge of oppressed exiles, be the ally of such people? Was she not sullied by her association with barbarism?

Over one weekend Gladstone poured out one of the best-known political pamphlets ever written, *The Bulgarian Horrors and the Question of the East*. (Disraeli muttered that of all the Bulgarian Horrors it was the greatest.) Selling 200,000 copies in a month, in thundering phrases it called for the Turks to leave Bulgaria forthwith: 'Their Zaptiehs and their Mudits, their Bimbashis and their Yuzbashis, their Kaimakams and their Pashas, one and all, bag and baggage, shall I hope clear out from the province they have desolated and profaned.' Turkey should not be allowed by the authority of the European powers to renew her charter for ruling Bulgaria.

At a great public meeting at Blackheath Gladstone called for the liberation of all the miserable provinces rebelling against Turkey. He was back in politics. The best resistance to Russia would come not from propping up the odious Turks but by reinforcing the strength and freedom of those countries which had to resist her. The solution to the Eastern Question, said Gladstone, was 'to place a living barrier between Russia and Turkey'.

Disraeli had no sympathy for this moral earnestness. He was incapable of taking the matter seriously, even though by now a government agent sent out to Turkey had confirmed the worst of the reports and hundreds of thousands of British people believed that it was shameful for Britain to have an ally like Turkey. Disraeli felt that morals were not part of alliances; he had no moral objection to an alliance with Turkey. To the last he thought that some of the massacres were made up, the 'babble of coffee houses'. But, with Gladstone at the head of the campaign, the country became fixated on the atrocities. Even so, Gladstone's speeches incensed the queen – she began to consider him a half-mad firebrand.

With extraordinary fickleness, however, public opinion suddenly swung round in favour of Turkey after her general of genius, Osman Pasha, kept the Russians at bay for five months at Plevna. The heroic deeds of Turkish defenders during the siege did much to make the British forget the Bulgarian Horrors, as did the British weakness for the underdog. They remembered that the Russian bear extending its great shadow over Asia, threatening India, was the real enemy. A rumour even started that Gladstone was a Russian agent. In December 1877 Osman surrendered, Plevna fell, and at the end of January 1878 the Russian General Skobelev reached Adrianople. Surely Britain now had to make a move or the Russians would be at Constantinople, and unlikely ever to want to move out.

Fortunately for Disraeli, Britain was now violently pro-Turk and anti-Russian: Russia had captured the whole of Armenia and huge swathes of Turkish Asia, arousing alarm right across Europe. Passions were running very high. Gladstone was booed in the street and even had his windows broken. The music-hall song –

We don't want to fight, but by Jingo if we do,
We've got the men, we've got the ships, we've got the money too,
We've fought the Bear before, and while Britons shall be true,
The Russians shall not have Constantinople

– gave its name to the militaristic sentiment of jingoism. It was sung everywhere, and it was a sentiment that became stronger and stronger towards the end of the century. The tiny queen herself was threatening abdication if the British did not go and give 'those Russians such a beating'.

On 28 January Disraeli, who had been made the Earl of Beaconsfield, obtained a £6 million grant from Parliament for war. The fleet was ordered to leave Besika Bay and move up to Constantinople. By 15 February it was in place. The Russian army was beginning to march down towards that city when the order was suddenly given to pull up. Before its eyes were the massive grey hulls of six British warships tethered like basking sharks off Prinkipo island in the Sea of Marmara, guarding the glistening minarets of Constantinople.

The Russians returned to Adrianople. Though the tsar wanted to speed on to Constantinople, his brother the Grand Duke Nicholas believed it would be madness to proceed. On 3 March, in order to consolidate their gains while still not technically at war with Britain despite those warships, Russia quickly signed a separate peace with Turkey by the Treaty of San Stefano. Disraeli's action had stopped Russia from entering Constantinople and seizing the Straits, but for how long? For ten weeks England held her breath, believing that an Anglo-Russian war could break out at any moment.

Deeply suspicious of this peace treaty, Disraeli did not stop his preparations for war. When it transpired that the treaty provided for a rearrangement of the Balkan peninsula so that it would be dominated by a 'Big Bulgaria' whose Slav population would give the Russians the preponderant influence in the Balkans, the prime minister announced that he was calling up the reserves. Two weeks later he sent 7,000 Indian troops to Malta – a sign that India had been restored to the imperial bosom. These actions convinced the Russian ambassador to London, Count Shuvalov, that the tsar could not seize Constantinople with impunity. The Russian government conceded that the great powers would have to be consulted about these changes because they affected Europe. It was agreed to call a Congress of the great powers, to take place in Berlin, capital of the dominant power of Europe, Prussia.

The Congress was hailed as Disraeli's triumph, as in many ways it was – when it was over he was offered a dukedom by Queen Victoria. Though he was so pale from the kidney disease which killed him three years later that he wore rouge to go out at night, his actions at the Congress kept the Russians up to the mark. When they tried to stop the Turks controlling the passes of Bulgaria south of the Balkans and claimed a larger area of Armenia, he revealed a secret agreement with the Sultan of Turkey: in return for guaranteeing Turkey in Asia, Britain had been allowed to occupy Cyprus. And Disraeli now gave orders for more of the fleet to move to that island. Faced with two British fleets the Russians agreed to everything.

Disraeli returned home to be acclaimed for having secured peace. By his superior poker-playing he had restored Britain to her old international position of honour: he had reduced Russian influence in the Balkans by preventing Big Bulgaria, he had secured better rights for the Christian subjects of the sultan, who were to be monitored by military consuls, he had kept the Russians out of Constantinople, and he had stopped them gaining too much of Armenia, which could have been the jumping-off ground for penetration into Asia Minor or the Persian Gulf. In any case that danger had been neutralized because Great Britain now had a base at the eastern end of the Mediterranean.

In fact the Congress was a piece of gifted stage-management, of smoke and mirrors. Most of the agreements about territory between the great powers which made the Congress go so smoothly had actually been arranged a month before. Alarmed by Disraeli's continued threat of war the Russians had agreed to divide Big Bulgaria in two. Meanwhile Britain had made a gentleman's agreement with Austria–Hungary to support her occupation of Bosnia and Herzegovina.

Despite the excitement with which it was hailed, there was nothing very lasting about the Congress of Berlin. For all Disraeli's conviction of the need to keep the Turkish Empire as a bulwark against Russia, it had been partially dismembered and small nations put in its place. Fears of Bulgaria becoming a Russian satellite proved quite illusory. Though seven years later the two Bulgarias reunited, the new nation was resistant to Russian influence and jealous of her independence. Cyprus proved to be a deadweight round the British neck, as it was soon to be superseded as a base in the eastern Mediterranean by Egypt. Moreover Britain was embarrassed by being tied to Turkey, which never kept her promises of reform. Despite the military consuls, the rulers went from bad to worse in their abuse of human rights, the best known being the Armenian massacre of 1892. In fact the most striking effect of the Russo-Turkish War and the Congress of Berlin was that Serbia felt hard done by. Like Montenegro and Romania she had won her independence, but she had a considerable grievance because Austria–Hungary had been allowed to occupy Bosnia and Herzegovina, whose populations were mainly Serbian.

Nevertheless most of Britain, with the vehement exception of Gladstone, believed that it was Disraeli's finest hour. He turned down the dukedom but accepted the Garter on condition that Salisbury, the foreign secretary, was awarded it too. Disraeli's 'forward' policy of expanding British territories in South Africa and India was far less successful, however. Although in west Africa, where Britain had had trading settlements since the eighteenth century, she had defeated the warlike Ashanti tribes on the Gold Coast in 1873, the Zulu War of 1878–9 was a public relations disaster. The Zulus, the most fearsome tribe in southern Africa, had been driven by drought into looking for other lands on which to graze their cattle. By 1877 the bankrupt Transvaal Republic had agreed to be annexed by the British in order to obtain their protection against the Zulus.

The formidable Zulu chief Cetewayo had revived the organization of the tribe on the old military basis. All the young unmarried men had to belong to regiments; removed from their families at puberty to live in barracks beside the royal kraal or palace, they were not allowed to marry until they had wet their spears with blood. When the British demanded an end to Zulu mobilization, the Zulu War began – and, despite the obvious advantages of guns over spears, at Isandhlwana a camp of British soldiers was wiped out by an impi, or Zulu army, of 20,000 men. The Zulus used the land so skilfully, moved so fast and secretly, that no one had the least idea that they were in the vicinity, until they suddenly rose out of the dust in their feathered headdresses to wreak havoc among the British. The war continued badly: Napoleon's III's son, the Prince Imperial, who had volunteered for the British army to gain experience, was killed in an ambush. Abandoned by his commanding officer, he was found dead in a pool of his own blood – though Queen Victoria, who liked the Zulus (they were brave and 'cleanly', she thought), was impressed by the way the Zulus had been so scientific in severing his arteries that he died without pain.

At Rorke's Drift, where a handful of British soldiers held out against the entire Zulu army, British honour was to some extent redeemed, and at the Battle of Ulundi the power of the Zulus was broken for many years to come. But the war had made Disraeli unpopular. It had been conducted so badly that it would have been almost comic had the thought of men being pointlessly slaughtered not also made the electorate angry; it was their sons and brothers whose lives were being thrown away so cavalierly.

Afghanistan was another scene of humiliation. Though India herself remained quiet, Russian movements in Asia took on new significance in the summer of 1878 when tension between Britain and Russia was at its height. Fears that the tsar would steal a march in Afghanistan, where the Russian ambassador was received but not the British, instigated an invasion of the country by three British armies. The amir fled, and his son Yakub Khan signed a treaty which appeared to make Afghanistan a British protectorate. But the British resident Sir Louis Cavagnari and his entire staff at the British embassy were murdered in September 1879, and the new Amir was forced to seek refuge in the British camp. A second punitive invasion of Afghanistan followed under the masterly soldier Sir Frederick Roberts, who had won the Victoria Cross for gallantry during the Indian Mutiny.

Though Roberts took Kabul successfully, deposed Yakub Khan and made an extraordinary march from Kabul to Kandahar, the murder of a

British consul and of Foreign and Colonial Office personnel and the strikingly incompetent campaign in South Africa combined to wipe the shine off Disraeli's record popularity as a general election approached in 1880. On top of that, a severe agricultural depression struck in the late 1870s. Though this was not the Conservatives' fault, it gave the impression of a government which had lost its grip.

For in 1876 the extraordinary economic boom which the British people had enjoyed since the 1840s came to a halt. Other European countries like Germany and France which had industrialized later were now drawing level with Britain. There was a slump and a flurry of bankruptcies in 1879. At the same time British grain prices collapsed. This was the result of successive bad harvests in 1875–80 which made it impossible to do without importing cheap grain, combined with the cheapness of that foreign grain suddenly available from Canada and the Midwest of America.

The tide turned against the Conservatives as thousands of farmers went to the wall. For the cheap foreign corn continued to come into the country, unhampered by protection. And Disraeli, who had pronounced protection 'dead and damned', could not bring it back. Though other European countries turned to tariffs to protect their infant industries, free trade was still an article of British nineteenth-century faith. The result was a massive flight from the land. Between 1860 and 1901, some 40 per cent of male labourers went to live in towns or emigrated, and by the beginning of the twentieth century 95 per cent of British food was imported, as it still is. The invention of refrigeration and canning processes at the end of the nineteenth century meant that cheap meat could be bought from the Argentine, where costs were lower.

Disraeli's government had also failed to manage the House of Commons. A new generation of more militant Irish Nationalist MPs who called themselves Home Rulers was obstructing business at Westminster. The bad harvests, which were even more disastrous for Ireland's rural economy than for England's, and the fact that the 1870 Land Act was only partially successful, made them determined to have a Dublin Parliament again.

There was a lot of material for Gladstone to build on and, being a virtuoso orator, he triumphed in his whirlwind Midlothian campaign across Scotland. Disraeli's foreign policy was made to look perilous and morally wrong as Gladstone denounced any alliance with the Ottomans in energetic and novel stump oratory. He took his views to the people, giving speeches that lasted for several hours, day in, day out, wherever a railway line could be found – a new form of electioneering with whistle-stop train tours across the country. Gladstone had formulated a style to appeal to the massively increased electorate. Instead of voicing the considered views of the sophisticated Victorian gentleman, Gladstone had his eye on greater popular participation and a more emotional, simplistic approach to the issues.

The campaign was enormously successful, and the election brought the Liberals in on a huge majority in 1881 – 349 Liberals were returned against 243 Conservatives. It elevated the Grand Old Man, as Gladstone was known, to a sort of superstar status. However, thanks to the secret ballot, sixty Irishmen were elected on the Home Rule ticket. That was where the future battleground lay. Meanwhile as Gladstone started to undo most of Disraeli's imperial policies, withdrawing from Afghanistan, granting independence to the Transvaal, the great man himself was dying. Queen Victoria asked if she might visit Disraeli on his sickbed, but he refused, quipping to intimates that she would only ask him to carry a message to Albert. By April 1881 he was dead. Victoria was so upset that she personally wrote out the announcement of his death in the Court Circular. Though protocol forbade the sovereign from attending a funeral (a custom Queen Elizabeth, her great-great-granddaughter, broke when she attended the funeral of Winston Churchill), Victoria sent a wreath of primroses from Osborne, with a note saying they were Disraeli's favourite flowers.

The new Liberal Parliament looked destined for even greater success than its radical predecessor of 1868. But instead of further reforms Gladstone's second government found itself bogged down by Ireland, whose Home Rulers were now headed by a ruthless master of tactics in Charles Stewart Parnell. Much of Gladstone's time was taken up in dealing with him and his terrorist allies in Ireland, while a series of untoward events in the empire lost him a great deal of popularity. Gladstone's foreign policy was coloured by his determination to destroy what he contemptuously described as 'the castle of Beaconsfieldism' – Disraeli's grandiose imperial projects. He felt strongly that the British Empire could not continue to grow nor to administer such vast swathes of the world's population and that Britain's interests were often best served by encouraging self-determination and what he called 'the healthy growth of local liberty'.

At the Battle of Majuba Hill in 1881 the First Boer War ended in the crushing defeat of the British, and Gladstone granted the Transvaal her independence once more. Now that the Zulu threat had been removed the Boers had no reason to be federated with the British. In Britain the battle was seen as a mortifying failure for the British army and for Gladstone, who, many federationists considered, should have continued to fight to keep the Transvaal within Cape Colony. In 1880 Britain withdrew from Afghanistan. British forces had helped establish Abdur Rahman on the

1886 *Vanity Fair* cartoon of some of the most important figures in Victorian politics in the Lobby of the House of Commons. It includes W. E. Gladstone, John Bright, Charles Stewart Parnell, Joe Chamberlain, Lord Randolph Churchill, Lord Hartington (later 8th Duke of Devonshire), 6th Earl Spencer and Sir William Harcourt.

throne in the hope that the widespread support for him would make Afghanistan a firm barrier between India and the Russians. When in 1885 Russian forces occupied Penjdeh within Afghanistan's borders it seemed as though Britain might be forced into war with Russia. But by submitting the problem to international arbitration – the King of Denmark ruled in favour of giving Penjdeh to Russia – war between the two powers over what had become known as the Great Game was narrowly avoided.

Nevertheless even Gladstone could not completely resist Britain's tendency to expand into new territories to protect her existing empire. Ironically it was he himself who shifted the axis of Britain's interests into the Near East when he occupied Egypt in 1882 to prevent a rebel officer from closing the Suez Canal. For the Canal had utterly changed Britain's priorities – her foreign policy had had to swing round to protect Egypt against all comers. By occupying Egypt, Gladstone set up the base camp for the creation in Africa of an extraordinary forward expansion of the British Empire, what is known as the 'new colonialism'.

As Turkey continued to disintegrate, Egypt, which was still technically part of the Ottoman Empire under a Turkish governor, had become almost entirely self-reliant. She also became increasingly important as a major part of the world's shipping now passed through the Suez Canal. But being exposed to the huge amount of new capital that flooded in destabilized her economy. In 1879, when the state was bankrupted under the rule of the unbusinesslike and extravagant khedive, Disraeli joined France in setting up a system of dual control in Egypt. This effectively put the government of the country, which was soon largely financed by British and French shareholders, into the hands of the two western powers.

In 1882 an Arab nationalist revolt broke out under an Egyptian army officer named Arabi Pasha, who seized the crucial harbour and forts of Alexandria and threatened to close the Suez Canal. With Alexandria swept by rioting, against his deepest principles Gladstone was forced to send a British army under Sir Garnet Wolseley to occupy Egypt on behalf of the Canal's creditors. The khedive and his viceroy Tewfik were reinstated. Britain was alone in this adventure as France refused to help, still exhausted by the devastation of the Franco-Prussian War and the ruinous reparations. The mighty British fleet which had ruled the waves for three-quarters of a century was sent to pound Alexandria until it capitulated. Gladstone believed that there was nothing else he could have done, but he offended all his venerable old Radical colleagues like the Quaker John Bright, who resigned from the government.

As a result of the French no-show, dual control ended. Though the khedive had been reinstated, the real rulers of Egypt were the British army and Sir Evelyn Baring, a practical and efficient financial administrator, sent out by Gladstone to supervise the way Egypt was run and return her chaotic finances to solvency. The British thus found themselves controlling Egypt almost by accident. Only Gladstone's conscience stopped outright annexation. Although the occupation was never official, in effect Egypt became part of the empire. The British army put into Egypt by Gladstone, friend of small nations struggling for birth, would remain there until 1954.

By the time Baring retired as the first Earl of Cromer in 1907, after almost forty years of his reforming activities Egypt was prosperous and thriving. But once Britain had become embroiled there other problems surfaced. At the beginning of 1880 a fanatical religious leader called the mahdi raised a revolt in the south of the country, in the Egyptian-occupied Sudan, and soon most of the area was under his sway. An English officer, Hicks Pasha, sent south with an Egyptian army to capture the mahdi, was massacred by the rebel leader and his followers, to the outrage of the London papers. This reverse was so conclusive that the government abandoned its attempt to hold the Sudan and decided to evacuate the few Egyptian garrisons that were left round Khartoum in the middle of the country.

The engineer officer chosen to evacuate the Sudan, General Gordon, was a legendary figure to the English public. Nicknamed 'Chinese' Gordon for his thirty-three victories in the service of the Chinese, as the khedive's administrator he had zealously suppressed the slave trade in the Sudan during the 1870s. In 1883, with immense pomp Cabinet ministers and the Duke of Cambridge, the commander-in-chief of the army, saw off Gordon at Charing Cross station, but once the general got to the Sudan the government refused, on grounds of cost, to give him the further troops he needed for a successful expedition. As a result Gordon became marooned in Khartoum, cut off from his headquarters in Egypt. From late March 1884 onwards, Sir Evelyn Baring begged the Cabinet to send an expeditionary force to relieve Khartoum, but ministers could not agree despite a vociferous campaign in the newspapers and in the nation at large in favour of rescuing General Gordon. Gladstone in particular worried about being dug deeper into the African continent. He was unwilling to face the fact that by occupying Egypt he had done exactly that, irreversibly.

Despite the mounting anger in Britain at leaving Gordon, the Cabinet was paralysed for four months. Not until August was Sir Garnet Wolseley sent to the Sudan. And it was not until 28 January 1885 that his deputy Sir Herbert Stewart at last arrived to rescue Gordon, having fought his way up the Nile. But Khartoum had been taken by the mahdi two days before and Gordon himself executed.

The few who survived told of how Gordon, though weak from disease and inanition because the town had run out of food (the soldiers were having to eat the horses and dogs), had impressed everyone by the way he nursed his dying men. Most were so weak that they could no longer stand upright at the palisades of the fort. But, on 26 January, the Nile waters, which had been so low that they impeded the British rescue mission coming upriver, finally receded so far that there was only a trickle of water dividing Khartoum from the mahdi. At twilight the mahdi and his hordes crossed.

Gordon refused to wall himself up in the palace and insisted on dying alongside the inhabitants of the town. He had been killed as he was coming down the steps of the palace just before dawn when the slaughter began. It was there that Sir Herbert Stewart found his headless body. Beside it was Gordon's diary: 'If the expeditionary force, and I ask for no more than two hundred men, does not come in ten days, the town may fall; and I have done my best for the honour of our country. Good-bye.' It was the general's last entry, written six weeks before in December. Soon afterwards Gordon's head was discovered in the mahdi's camp across the river from Khartoum at Omdurman, his blue eyes still half open.

When the news burst on Victorian England there was uproar. The queen herself sent three furious telegrams to the foreign secretary, the war secretary and Gladstone himself. They were deliberately written *en clair*, that is not in the usual governmental code, so that her views would be publicized as widely as possibly by being leaked to the newspapers. It was an extraordinary action. Accusing Gladstone of being directly responsible for Gordon's death, she wrote: 'These news from Khartoum are frightful, and to think that this all might have been prevented and many precious lives saved by earlier action is too frightful.' The question now was whether to avenge Khartoum or abandon the Sudan to the mahdi. It was the news that Russia had taken the Afghan town of Penjdeh and was thus threatening India's north-west frontier which made Gladstone issue the order to retreat. Fighting both Russia and the mahdi would have been too much for Britain's never large military resources.

Gladstone became immensely unpopular. His affectionate nickname the GOM, Grand Old Man, was replaced by MOG, Murderer of Gordon. He was booed when he went to the theatre. For Gordon had been exactly the sort of man that the Victorian English prided themselves on producing. Like that other Victorian hero, the African explorer and missionary Dr Livingstone, Gordon had been a good light in a naughty world, heroically spreading abroad the peculiar virtues of British civilization, godliness and dutifulness. To forsake such a man scandalized the British public and caused them to lose faith in the government.

Meanwhile if Gladstone was despised by the public at large he was also embattled within the party. One of the reasons that he had failed to rescue Gordon was that his whole being was dedicated to solving the Irish problem. Not only had civil disorder reached an alarming pitch owing to an organization recently started up by Fenian revolutionaries called the Land League, which was persuading Irish tenant farmers to refuse to pay rent. Its president, Charles Stewart Parnell, had become leader in 1880 of the Irish MPs.

The pale Anglo-Irish Parnell, a Protestant landowner from County Wicklow, was far more formidable and ruthless than Isaac Butt, the ineffectual former leader of the Irish MPs, who had also proposed self-government for the Irish within the Union. Brought up by a mother who hailed from an old American revolutionary family, he was full of visceral hatred for the English. He saw that the large number of Irish MPs the secret ballot had brought to Westminster could be used to obstruct Parliamentary business so thoroughly that Westminster might be forced to give Ireland her independence back. Meanwhile the Land League, by making Ireland ungovernable through a land war, would put pressure on Westminster to grant Parliamentary independence to Ireland.

The Land League had been set up to resist the mass evictions that the 1870s agricultural crisis was causing in Ireland. As the low prices farmers got for wheat were not enough to cover their rent, evictions spiralled into thousands every day. Once again the dreadful but commonplace Irish scenes of the old and sick lying in their beds at the roadside were to be found throughout the country. But this time there was a difference. The Land League organized mass meetings to get rents reduced to reflect the price of wheat.

For with the best intentions Gladstone's 1870 act had a fatal flaw. Although the landlord was supposed to pay compensation if he evicted a tenant, the statutory wording was that the compensation was payable only if the rent asked for was 'exorbitant'. This was designed to protect the tenant farmer against unfair price hikes. However, that was not the issue in 1880. The rents demanded by the landlords were at the usual level. It was the farmers' earnings from crops that had fallen.

The Land League was a formidable success, but it was mainly run by ex-Fenians. They made it a brutal, lawless body founded on the belief that nothing was so efficacious as the threat of force. While by day the Land League was visibly organizing the orderly mass meetings for rent reductions, by night it was a different story. The League was running a land war. Anyone suspected of paying a rent which the League considered to be too high or who had taken over a plot from the evicted would be visited at dead of night by gangs of men. Shots would be fired through their windows, or open graves dug before their doors and signed 'Captain Moonlight' in the dirt. After a year of this treatment Ireland was at the mercy of the Land League. There were areas of the country which simply could not be controlled by the British government.

The leadership of the Land League always distanced themselves officially from the violence, as did the League's president Parnell himself in Parliament. The only course of action Parnell verbally encouraged was a 'species of moral coventry'. A proclaimed enemy of the Land League should be treated 'like a leper of old' by being rigidly denied all social and commercial contact. The most celebrated victim of this treatment, Captain Boycott, was driven out of Ireland and gave his name to this activity in the word 'boycott'. In actual fact, though, the high-sounding moral coventry was generally broken by a more practical follow-up visit from Captain Moonlight and his friends.

Parnell, however, had a different agenda from most of the Land League and its Irish-American financial patrons. Most of the Americans believed with the Land League that only through violent revolution would Ireland win her independence. Parnell thought that change would come only through constitutional means. Nevertheless he could not afford to offend the League and its shadowy backers, since the whip hand he had over the British government substantially depended on being able to control them. The trouble was that the League began to believe that the chaos that it was creating was the prelude to independence. Thus when in 1881 Gladstone gave Ireland a Land Act which incorporated all the requisites long seen as the solution of the tenant farmers' difficulties, the Land League in Ireland refused to accept it. The 'Three Fs' – fixity of tenure, free sale by the tenant of his interest, and fair rents to be determined by land courts – granted by the act might kill off the desire for Home Rule. So the rural crimes did not cease; the violence continued.

Parnell could not call a halt to the lawlessness without enraging or making suspicious the men of the hillsides, whether in America or Ireland, who were willing to go only so far with constitutional channels. But Parnell the consummate political operator, though he did not believe that the revolutionaries' way could ultimately be successful, at the same time could not lose their support. He had to play both ends against the middle. He was forced to denounce Gladstone's Land Act and the government. He thus greatly enhanced his credibility among the revolutionaries who feared being sold out, especially when Gladstone sent him to jail for not halting the violence.

But though Gladstone had exasperatedly said that the 'resources of civilization were not yet exhausted', when he clapped Parnell and his supporters into Kilmainham Jail, it seemed that they were. From prison Parnell issued a defiant statement that no rent was to be paid at all. Though the Land League was proscribed by the British government, matters had now reached stalemate. As Ireland descended into frightening chaos, the pragmatic Gladstone saw that the only way of controlling the violence was through Parnell – despite the scruples of members of his Cabinet about treating with a man like Parnell, who in their opinion had blood on his hands. To the distaste of the Irish secretary W. E. Forster in particular, Gladstone started to negotiate with Parnell in prison, promising to release him if he brought Ireland under control.

Fortunately for Gladstone Parnell was ready to negotiate. In April 1882 the two reached an understanding via intermediaries which is known as the Kilmainham Treaty. Only a month later an event occurred which smashed Gladstone's policy to ruins and made most of the Liberals want as little to do with Parnell as possible. Forster had already resigned from the Cabinet in disgust, and his place as Irish secretary taken by the Whig Liberal Lord Frederick Cavendish, who was married to one of Mrs Gladstone's nieces. But his tenure was to be brief. A few days after arriving in Dublin, as he and his under-secretary Thomas Burke walked in Phoenix Park, they were attacked and hacked to death by a splinter group of Parnell's allies, the Irish Republican Brotherhood.

The Phoenix Park murders shattered the unofficial alliance between Parnell and the Liberals in favour of Home Rule. Any further concessions to Ireland were stymied; the murdered Cavendish had been the younger

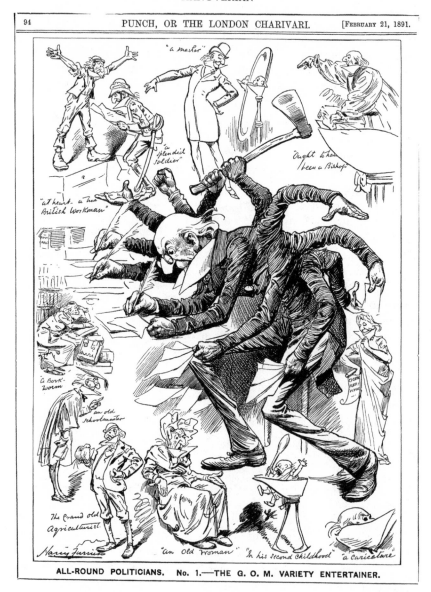

ALL-ROUND POLITICIANS.   No. 1.—THE G. O. M. VARIETY ENTERTAINER.

Punch's view of Gladstone in 1891: 'All round politicians. No. 1. The G.O.M. Variety.'

brother of Lord Hartington, who was the leader of the Whig section of the Liberal party. For fear of splitting the party, Gladstone now had to take a very hard line indeed towards Ireland. For a large number of Liberal MPs, dislike of Parnell, who made no secret of his hatred of the English, hardened into enmity, along with the most vehement conviction that Ireland should never be ruled by such a man. To the further outrage of the Liberals Parnell threw in his lot with the Conservatives by voting against Gladstone.

He caused the government to fall in June 1885 and a minority Conservative government took over under Lord Salisbury, Disraeli's foreign secretary, until an election should be held in November. Parnell, who held the same sort of secret meetings in London with the Conservatives he had had with the Liberals, believed that Salisbury if returned to office would bring in Home Rule. He therefore primed his troops on the British mainland to vote Conservative in the November election to add to the Conservative vote, while his own Irish MPs would ally themselves with Salisbury.

Meanwhile the Liberals themselves were in disarray – Gladstone's relations with his own party were fraying. The old anti-imperialist Liberals of his own generation had turned against him over Egypt. His hesitancy over further franchise reform had angered the new generation of Radicals led by the former mayor of Birmingham, the screw manufacturer Joe Chamberlain. The Radicals nevertheless pushed the 1884 Third Reform Bill through, which brought the farm worker within the franchise. When the Conservative Lords headed by Salisbury resisted the bill, to Gladstone's alarm Chamberlain responded with a campaign to discredit a class of whose power he violently disapproved. To him, a self-made man (his father had been a cobbler), the Tory Lords sitting on their ancestral acres, 'who toil not neither do they spin', had no right to interfere with a proposal to give the vote to decent working people. A series of strikingly phrased speeches calling to the country to 'Mend Them or End Them' proposed doing away with the House of Lords if it did not pass the bill. It passed, however, adding two million to the electorate of Great Britain. Its impact was magnified by a separate Redistribution of Seats Act in 1885.

At a personal level Gladstone never got on with Chamberlain. Though Gladstone himself hailed from a commercial family, his classical education put him in a different league from Chamberlain. Chamberlain, on the other hand, was angered by the way his leader played his cards so close to his chest. There were also philosophical differences. Unlike the penny-pinching Gladstone, Chamberlain and his friends saw state interference as a positive good and believed that there was great untapped potential in the colonies and the empire. But despite his ability and his influence in the country at large, Chamberlain was only president of the Board of Trade.

By the 1885 autumn election campaign, relations between Chamberlain and Gladstone were so poor that Radical Joe went out on the stump with his own 'unauthorized programme' (so called because Gladstone had not approved it) for social and agrarian reform. Each worker should have three acres and a cow. Chamberlain was a thrilling speaker and developed an immense following, particularly in the midlands. The success that the Liberals had at the polls was due to him. But the Third Reform Act had the most dramatic effect in Ireland. At the November election Parnell came back with twenty-five more Home Rulers than before. His 86 Nationalist MPs added to the 249 Conservatives gave Salisbury the majority he needed to continue in power, though the Liberals themselves had 335 members. Thanks to Parnell, Salisbury remained prime minister. But the strange alliance rapidly unravelled.

Despite Salisbury's courting of Parnell and the Irish Nationalist vote to achieve power, it went too much against the grain for the Tories to give the Irish Home Rule. There were rumours that they were about to abandon it. Meanwhile, unknown to all, by mid-December Gladstone had finally come to the decision that it was imperative that Home Rule be achieved. The strength of the Home Rule vote in Ireland in the election caused him to fear Irish secession and the possible reconquest of Ireland if a Home Rule Bill was not put through fast. Now he had heard that if the Conservatives would not do so, the Liberals must. Unfortunately Gladstone did not reveal to his shadow Cabinet his decision to throw himself behind a self-governing status for Ireland. Leaked to the newspapers on 17 December 1885 by his son Herbert Gladstone, it incensed the two key players in the power structure of the Liberal party: Joe Chamberlain was affronted at once again being kept in the dark, while Lord Hartington was incensed at the idea of giving in to terrorism.

The leak put an end to the brief Conservative government. When Salisbury announced that the Tories would not pass Home Rule, Parnell moved back into alliance with Gladstone, the minority Tory government fell and Gladstone was back in office by February 1886, having pledged to put through a Home Rule Bill for Ireland. But by the spring both Chamberlain and Hartington had not only resigned, they had crossed the floor to defeat the Home Rule Bill and their former leader from the Conservative benches. Home Rule had split the Liberal party.

With Chamberlain (denounced as 'Judas' by one Liberal MP) on his side, Salisbury defeated Gladstone's first Home Rule Bill. Ninety-three Liberals, who called themselves Liberal Unionists, joined the Conservatives. They feared that Gladstone's bill, which proposed an Irish Parliament to govern all domestic Irish affairs, would be the first step towards the break-up of the Union, because Irish MPs would no longer be represented at Westminster, which henceforth would deal with external affairs. Chamberlain in particular refused to believe that the Home Rulers really meant it when they said that Home Rule would not mean independence for Ireland.

The heated atmosphere in Parliament was added to by a member of the Conservative so-called 'ginger group', Lord Randolph Churchill, the younger son of the Duke of Marlborough. He stirred up the longstanding insecurity of the Presbyterian Ulstermen, who ever since they had been planted in Catholic Ulster in the seventeenth century had felt beleaguered. Mischievously Churchill told them they would be badly disadvantaged by a largely Catholic Dublin government. Ulstermen should do everything in their power to stop Home Rule. The slogan 'Ulster will fight and Ulster will be right' was first heard in 1886.

In June the Conservative party's ninety-three new allies stopped the bill from passing by thirty votes, and Gladstone resigned. The election of July 1886 gave the allied Liberal Unionist and Conservative parties a huge majority over the followers of Gladstone and Parnell. Their prime minister was Salisbury, whose great expertise was in the field of foreign affairs. With their Liberal Unionist allies the Tories would remain in power for most of the next twenty years.

Those twenty years were the heyday of the empire, especially in Africa where diamonds had been discovered in the 1860s and gold in the 1880s. The British presence in Africa grew so rapidly that the adventurer Cecil Rhodes dreamed of a railway on British territory between the Cape and Cairo. The two million new voters were fascinated by flamboyant figures like Rhodes, who dominated the period. Their curiosity was fed by sensationalist newspapers like George Newnes's *Titbits*, begun in 1880, the *Pall Mall Gazette* and the first mass-circulation paper, the *Daily Mail*, which went on sale in 1896.

Though the British might have obtained some of their empire in a fit of absence of mind, as was claimed a little disingenuously, for a brief period until the end of the century they suddenly exulted in it. The dedication to the cause of the empire known as imperialism was only a little short of religious fervour. It even infected the Liberals: 'The greatest secular agency for good now known to the world', Gladstone's colleague the future prime minister Lord Rosebery called it.

Imperialism and Socialism (1886–1901)

Unlike its Roman predecessors, the British Empire did not consist of contiguous territory. It was higgledy piggledy and amorphous. That was because it had been created in an *ad hoc* way over the previous 250 years by a mixture of daring adventurers, chartered companies and, very occasionally, deliberate government policy. Trade was the driving force behind the British Empire, and ever since the American colonies became independent it was the trade centred on India that controlled its direction. India was the 'jewel in the imperial crown', and protecting India was what the empire was all about.

From the beginning of the seventeenth century India had made the East India Company extremely wealthy with its spices, as well as its luxury goods of silks and printed calicoes. Two hundred years later India was the entrepôt for a very sophisticated three-cornered trade. It continued to make all concerned in it, British merchants and manufacturers, Indian merchants and maharajahs, Chinese merchants and Mandarins, and the British Treasury, very rich. After the industrial revolution Britain exported cheap finished cotton, woollen and metal goods to India, India sent some of these goods to China and China exported tea to Britain. By the mid-nineteenth century a domestic Indian cotton industry was supplying cotton for British manufacturers, as well as tea from the Indian tea plantations created for the British export market.

Britain's was never a militaristic or centrally planned empire like those of Spain and France. Nevertheless, during the eighteenth century and in the course of her duel with France for colonial supremacy in India and America, Britain used war to gain territory, and she used war to protect her commerce. Her position as the world's premier trading nation began with her gains at the Treaty of Utrecht in 1713, which she consolidated after the Napoleonic Wars. By the late nineteenth century her occupation of strategic harbours meant that safe ports for British ships were strung like a helpful safety net from the coast of China via India, through the Arabian Sea round the coast of Africa. They ran from Hong Kong, to Labuan island off North Borneo, to Aden at the entrance to the Red Sea. Keeping Ceylon after the Napoleonic Wars enabled Britain to defend India from attack from both east and west. The tea trade with China was secured in 1819 when Stamford Raffles had seized Singapore. Britain thus commanded the Straits of Malacca with what became one of the empire's most important naval bases. Her emphasis on commerce tended to ensure that the flag of official government followed unofficial traders.

The inestimable financial value of India kept even so reluctant an imperialist as Gladstone occupying Egypt to protect the Suez Canal, and it was the need to consolidate the defence of an empire centred on India that determined the government's foreign policy. Protecting India often meant extending the empire's territories. Burma, which provided India's border to the east, was annexed in 1886 as a result of fear of French activity in Indo-China. Protecting India's north-west border would have led to a protectorate over Afghanistan had her conquest not proved so elusive; it required the occupation of Baluchistan in 1876, and in 1907 the establishment of a protectorate over southern Iran. All of these moves derived from the need to control the land route to India, and that also provoked the persistent antagonism towards Russia over her own expansion into central Asia.

The empire bred its own colonial imperialists too. By 1900 Singapore, which had begun as a small island trading colony, insisted on occupying the Malay States to protect herself. In the late nineteenth century Australians and New Zealanders added about one hundred Pacific islands to their territories, such as New Guinea in 1883 and the New Hebrides in 1887. By the late 1880s South Africa, where a struggle for dominance between British and Boer had been going on for close to a century, had produced the most vocal of the colonial imperialists, an MP for Cape Colony named Cecil Rhodes. Well over six feet tall he soon became known as the Colossus, a pun on his name and on his ambitions for the British Empire.

The son of an East Anglican vicar the young Rhodes had been sent out to South Africa to cure the weak heart which eventually killed him at the age of forty-nine. Instead he made a fortune with the De Beers diamond company at Kimberley. He was patriotic to the core. His views that British territory in South Africa had to extend much further north coincided with Lord Salisbury's desire to find additional markets for British trade and to stymie German ambitions.

Rhodes was just one of the three most famous late-nineteenth-century empire-builders – the others were Sir William Mackinnon and Sir George Taubman Goldie – whose activities vastly expanded British territory in Africa. By 1900, out of thirty European protectorates in Africa fifteen were British. From the late 1880s Britain's economy was faltering under the threat of industrial competition from Germany and America. Most European countries had abandoned free trade and adopted tariffs to protect their infant chemical and electrical industries. The seeds of very widespread discontent had been sown in Britain by the depression and unemployment. Energetic, patriotic businessmen like Rhodes, Goldie and Mackinnon believed that Africa, where Britain already had a considerable presence, was the answer. Not only was Britain the occupying power in Egypt and the dominant power at the Cape, as a result of her taking the lead in the anti-slavery movement fifty years before she had ousted the

Dutch and Danish settlements on the west coast of Africa. By the mid-1870s after the defeat of the Ashantis Britain controlled the Gambia, the Gold Coast and Sierra Leone.

Much of the immense continent of Africa was empty of human habitation. It was freshly mapped by explorers and made easier to get to because of steam power; it offered markets and raw materials which were becoming scarce in Europe. Developed nations were now making their own manufactures with British machinery. Britain's falling share in world trade after a century of supremacy convinced the Conservative and Unionist governments that they should actively welcome the empire-builders' plans to extend their areas of operation. Under royal charter, specially established companies exploited the resources of and frequently ended up governing the lands whose chiefs they made agreements with. The Royal Niger Company was founded in 1886 by Goldie to consolidate Britain's already dominant position on the west coast of Africa. It extended the British territories inland from Lagos in the Gulf of Guinea to the borders of French West Africa and the German colony of Kamerun. Mackinnon's mission to end the Arab trade in slavery that Livingstone had found still flourishing on the east coast saw the beginning of British rule of the territories later known as Kenya and Uganda. The founder of the East Africa Company in 1888, Mackinnon employed H. M. Stanley to negotiate business deals with the chiefs of the Nile Lakes area. Instead of selling their people, they could be paid to have their lands mined.

The acquiring of protectorates or areas of influence in Africa by private chartered companies meant that the British government achieved foreign policy aims without despatching troops or warships. However, Britain was not alone in seeing Africa as a solution to her economic woes. By the mid-1880s her control of Egypt to secure the route to India was threatened by the penetration of Africa by other European powers determined to find their own diamond mines.

King Leopold II of Belgium made arrangements in the late 1870s with local chiefs to form a state on the Congo river, the immense river system discovered by Livingstone which bisected the African continent from east to west. Alarm at Leopold's activities resulted in a conference of the European powers at Berlin in 1884 – intended to orchestrate the peaceful division of Africa into colonies. The conference laid down rules for the claiming of territory and spheres of influence. All nations were allowed free navigation of the Congo, Zambezi and Shire rivers, while the Congo Basin formed part of the Congo Free State which became Leopold's personal fiefdom.

This set a pattern of avoidance of war, and in the next five years Lord Salisbury came to peaceful arrangements with the other European powers over the division of Africa. A private treaty with King Leopold ceded land near Lake Tanganyika to the British East Africa Company, while in 1890 Britain swapped the apparently unimportant island of Heligoland in the North Sea to Germany in return for Zanzibar and Pemba. An Anglo-French treaty defined spheres of interest in Nigeria, Zanzibar and Madagascar in 1890. In 1891 treaties with Italy and Portugal defined British and Italian Somaliland, and the extent of Portuguese and British territory.

But, despite these arrangements, Britain and the British population of Cape Town were extremely worried in 1884 when Germany joined what had become known as 'the scramble for Africa'. Convinced by her industrialists that as a united empire she should have her 'place in the sun', in the next two years Germany acquired millions of square miles to the north of the British Cape Colony, moving troops into Togo on the west coast and creating German East Africa, which reached from Lake Victoria down to the Portuguese colony of Mozambique. Most alarming of all, on the west coast of southern Africa Germany occupied the land stretching from the northern border of Cape Colony along the Orange river up to Angola, or Portuguese West Africa. It was named German South West Africa.

For three-quarters of a century Britain could have expanded into this area but had not done so. With the threat of a large German colony there in 1885, on Cecil Rhodes's advice the British government annexed Bechuanaland, the territory running north of Cape Colony between the Boer republics and German South West Africa. In the view of Rhodes and many of the Cape British, the discovery of gold in the Boer Transvaal in 1886 had wrecked the balance of power in southern Africa so that the Transvaal, with its vast income of £24 million a year flowing from the goldmines of the Rand (the massive gold-bearing ridge in the Transvaal), threatened to become more powerful than the British Cape Colony.

To tip the balance back to the Cape Colony, it was argued, a new British Empire should be constructed running north–south. There should be a forward movement up Africa. Rhodes believed that if Britain was not careful she would soon be shut in by Boer and German colonies. Germany had her eye on greater influence in South Africa and she had begun to court the Boer republics, with whom she had a natural affinity. Annexing Bechuanaland put an end to the movement of Boer settlers there, but Rhodes also believed that British territories should extend further north into Zambezia, the immense lands running up to the Belgian Congo. Rhodes's own chartered company, the British South Africa Company, was formed in 1889 to find a new Rand north of Boer territory in Zambezia. The Boers continued to be as unwilling to associate with non-Boers like

Rhodes as they had been in the days of the Great Trek half a century before. Terrified by the way their colonies, first the Cape and then Natal, had been taken over relentlessly by the British, they allowed foreigners or Uitlanders few civil rights and forced them to pay most of the taxes.

Enthusiasm for acquiring land in Africa began to snowball as the British government became influenced by the Cape imperialists, who were also the financiers of the new private companies that owned concessions in the goldmines of the Boer Transvaal. Even imperial civil servants sent out from London were infected by a patriotic sense of having to stop the Germans, the Dutch, the French, the Portuguese and the Belgians.

By 1895 the visionary Rhodes had added to the British Empire 750,000 square miles of African territory, north from the Transvaal to the Belgian Congo – the colony of Rhodesia. He became the darling of a large number of Britons and was said to be one of the richest men in the world. The mass-circulation newspapers liked nothing better than colourful tales of derring-do on the 'dark continent'; it was all part of the imperial fever which led to the dictum that 'the sun never sets on the British Empire'. As the empire now stretched through eight times zones, it was true enough.

The territory then named after Rhodes but now called Zimbabwe had been gained by a trick. Her ruler, the grand and difficult potentate King Lobengula, had been warned by the Aboriginies' Protection Society in London not to allow Rhodes anything other than the mineral rights for which he had been negotiating. But though the agreement between the two was indeed solely for mineral rights and not land rights, the summer of 1890 saw a column of handpicked Cape Colony pioneer settlers trekking into Lobengula's Mashonaland, the area south of the River Zambezi. Each had been promised a 3,000-acre farm by Rhodes, by now prime minister of the Cape Colony, in return for building a road across the country. They planted a flag at what they called Mount Hampden and even began building a city named Salisbury in honour of the British prime minister.

Though Lobengula refused to accept delivery of the charter company's shipment of rifles, to show that he repudiated the treaty, he dared not attack the settlers. After all, their superior weaponry had slaughtered his cousins the Zulus at Ulundi. Meanwhile the smoothtalking Dr Storr Jameson, Rhodes's right-hand man and the managing director of De Beers, who had negotiated the treaty with King Lobengula, continued to avow the charter company's peaceful intentions. He even relieved Lobengula's painful gout by giving him morphine injections. But Mashonaland, as some in the Colonial Office had predicted, was not a second Rand. The chartered company nearly went bankrupt paying for a police force, for a telegraph line and for a railway, while no gold showed up to finance the infrastructure. Dr Jameson, who by 1893 had become resident commissioner of the new colony, decided with Rhodes that the way out of bankruptcy would be to go further north again and annex Lobengula's other kingdom, Matabeleland. When Jameson used a border raid by Lobengula to destroy Matabeleland's army, the king took poison and was buried in an ox skin in a cave.

Matabeleland became Northern Rhodesia and was annexed to the crown. All the land and cattle of the Ndebele people were removed from them and appropriated by the company. The company's hut taxes drove the Ndebele to work as labourers since they could not pay them by selling cattle. The Ndebele, an aristocratic tribe who had always relied on servants to perform menial tasks, were forced to help build white towns or to work in the copper mines. When these proud warriors protested, they were beaten by Rhodes's men. Liberating Africa from the slave trade might have been a rallying cry in the past, but under Rhodes a new kind of servitude was taking place.

The British Liberal press was convinced of skulduggery, but doubts about Rhodes's unscrupulous methods were swept aside – the ends surely justified the means. By the late 1880s dislike and disapproval of the Colossus among the high-minded was irrelevant. 'Chartered', as shares in the British South Africa Company were known, traded for huge sums on the Stock Exchange. Influential thinkers like the Cambridge professor of modern history Sir John Seeley in his 1883 book *The Expansion of England* had already given credence to the idea of Britain's imperial mission. So did the popular novels and bestselling verse of the Bombay-born Rudyard Kipling from the mid-1880s on. However the empire was acquired, it was justified by Kipling's injunction to:

> Take up the White Man's burden –
> Send forth the best ye breed –
> Go, bind your sons to exile
> To serve your captives' need.

That was the empire's unofficial motto. The British believed they had much to be proud of when they built a church on the site of the old slave market in Zanzibar and freed the slaves winding through the forests tied to one another by wooden yokes to be shipped to Arabia. The best Victorian newcomers brought Africa the astonishing advances their century had made in medicine, education, manufactured goods and technical innovation. Christian humanitarians, often from modest backgrounds themselves, wanted to help improve the lives of people whose simple pastoral existence and superstitious beliefs appeared primitive to them.

The engineering which had changed the face of Britain changed Africa even more dramatically. Dams and bridges allowed roads to be made where no road had ever run before, across dizzying falls and gigantic rivers. British companies brought pipes for sanitation and drainage. Soon they would carry the cables for electricity for lighting, refrigeration and telephones.

Nevertheless, to the anti-imperialists in Britain much of the behaviour of empire-builders seemed like the exploitation of peoples for their cheap labour, and the theft of what was actually their property, the zinc, copper, iron ore and other valuable minerals. British soldiers might fight the Arab slave-traders who continued to prey on neighbouring African tribes, but treaties to develop the country's mineral rights were generally obtained at the point of a gun. Sir George Taubman Goldie's Royal Niger Company held a royal charter to rule all the land surrounding the Niger from the Benue to the sea, yet historically this was the land of the Benin people. These private companies, unregulated by the state, yet acting for the British Empire, had great drawbacks – as the history of the East India Company showed. Many of their number were unscrupulous entrepreneurs dedicated to nothing more philanthropic than profit margins. Nevertheless they were being allowed to rule hundreds of thousands of square miles of land, and their inhabitants.

But imperialism was overwhelmingly the mood of the age, all the more so after the celebrations for Queen Victoria's golden jubilee in 1887, which marked fifty years on the throne. When the queen processed from Buckingham Palace to Westminster Abbey attended by a great throng of representatives of all the countries and nationalities within the empire, the empire was made visible. The bestselling author H. Rider Haggard created even more of a sense of the magic and mystery of Africa with his novels *King Solomon's Mines* and *She*, published in 1886 and 1887 and still widely read today. Going out to work in the colonies, whether managing a tea plantation in India, being a district commissioner or exploring the African jungle was just what a young man of spirit might want to do. By 1907 the British Empire would occupy more than one-fifth of the world's land mass, the largest empire the world had ever seen, reaching from Canada's Hudson Bay in the frozen north to the green mountains of New Zealand in the far east.

Nevertheless, even for the most ardent imperialists there were questions that had to be asked about the empire. How large should it become, given that it was inevitably costly to administer, and for how long should it be controlled from Westminster? Moreover, there were two very specific problems with the empire, and both were to do with self-government. One was Ireland; the second was emerging as India, where the first political movement dedicated to Indian self-rule – the Indian National Congress – had begun to meet as a party.

By the late nineteenth century colonial self-government was an established fact in the case of peoples of European origin. Responsible self-government had been granted to Canada in 1840, Australia in 1856, Cape Colony in 1872 and Natal in 1892, with the British monarch's representative the high commissioner reigning but not ruling. Excluded from this were the Irish, for reasons of security, and non-European peoples whose civilizations were believed not to measure up to European standards.

Successive British governments balked at giving India self-rule. It had taken Britain long enough to give the franchise to those of her own nationals who were unpropertied and illiterate. The sense of caste made Indians seem careless of improving the education of the masses, an attitude which offended the theoretically more democratic British: a country with such widespread poverty and illiteracy was unready for democracy, for the western Parliamentary institutions which Britain believed offered the best method of ruling. As the keystone of the empire, Indian independence had to be very tightly controlled. Additional problems were created by the colour prejudice prevalent among the British population within India. In the 1880s Britons reacted with fury to the Liberal viceroy Lord Ripon's plans for judicial reform which would allow Indian judges to try Europeans.

In response the Indian Congress Party was founded in 1885, and had achieved national support by the beginning of the twentieth century. Though small measures of self-government for Indian nationals were granted during Liberal administrations by expanding the power of locally elected councils in 1892 and 1909, they were not enough. British investment and British engineers had given India 40,000 miles of canals and millions of acres of irrigation schemes. But Indian impatience with being treated like children grew. A protectionist policy against the importation of Indian textiles into Britain galvanized a Home Rule movement in 1916 under the leadership of the political activist and journalist Bal Gangadhar Tilak and the social reformer and Fabian Annie Besant.

Like India, Ireland's position within the empire was strategically too important for her to be given her freedom. While the Conservatives were in power they tried to 'Kill Home Rule with Kindness'. The Congested District Board Act of 1891 improved Irish farming methods, while various land purchase acts of the 1890s allowed more tenant farmers to buy the land they farmed with a loan from the state. The Conservatives and Unionists believed they had safely got rid of Ireland's nationalist aspirations.

In the meantime the Irish nationalists were afflicted by a series of disasters to their cause. Their leader Parnell was cleared by a Parliamentary commission in 1888 of writing forged letters which approved of the Phoenix Park murders, published by *The Times* newspaper. But when Parnell was cited in the sensational divorce case of the wife of his fellow Irish nationalist MP Captain O'Shea a year later, it destroyed his reputation and the party he had led to prominence. For this was an era when Queen Victoria would not receive divorced persons at court, and the fiercely moral Nonconformists in the Liberal party refused to have anything to do with him. Parnell was forced to resign as head of the Irish Home Rulers. He insisted on starting up his own party, but the strain of the disgrace and the campaigning was too much for him. In 1891 he departed for England on business, having told his friends in Ireland that he would be back in a week. He was, but in his coffin, dead from pneumonia aged only forty-six.

After Gladstone got his Home Rule Bill passed by the Commons but kicked out by the Lords in 1894, for a long time British politics were largely ignored by the Irish. They had lost faith in constitutional methods after the failure of two Home Rule Bills, and the Home Rulers had split into Parnellites and anti-Parnellites. Instead the ideas of Irish nationalism found their way into other areas of Irish life. An extraordinary renaissance of Irish culture took place. Scholars set out to rediscover the Irish language; schools teaching only Gaelic were opened, staffed by passionate nationalists like Padraic Pearse; Irish myths and legends inspired the poetry of William Butler Yeats, J. M. Synge and Sean O'Casey that became fuel for the fire of Irish patriotism. Paradoxically, by the early twentieth century the sense of Ireland as a separate culture and nation would build up such a head of steam that total severance from Britain proved unstoppable.

It was not until 1900 that the Irish MP John Redmond was sufficiently authoritative to reunite the Irish nationalists at Westminster and approach Home Rule by constitutional means. But in 1907 Sinn Fein, a revolutionary party standing for total independence – its name means 'ourselves alone' – was started up by the journalist Arthur Griffith and was soon attracting the support away from Home Rule. The argument had moved on a stage – Redmond had had the ground cut from beneath his feet.

Presiding over these conflicts was the bearded, bearlike and imperturbable third Marquis of Salisbury, prime minister for most of the period until 1902, when ill-health removed him from office and his nephew Arthur Balfour took over. Salisbury's bent was for foreign policy. With Europe in such a volatile state, he kept Britain out of foreign entanglements when continental states had abandoned the balance of power and were persistently forming antagonistic treaties against one another. Bismarck had tied Austria–Hungary and Russia into a complex web of alliances to protect Germany's flanks against the retaliation he believed must one day come from France.

Britain remained aloof. Salisbury believed in safety first. By refusing to make alliances with other powers Britain could not be dragged into a war that he constantly feared would break out, a war which the British people lacked both the army and the inclination to fight. It was a Canadian premier who in 1896 first used the phrase 'splendid isolation' to describe Britain under Salisbury: 'whether splendidly isolated or dangerously isolated, I will not now debate; but for my part I think splendidly isolated, because now this isolation of England comes from her superiority'.

Salisbury was splendidly isolated himself. Descended from Lord Burghley, Elizabeth I's greatest servant, he was a superior aristocrat, a remote and inaccessible figure. He spent most of his time at his stately home Hatfield House, twelve miles north of London, under whose very oaks Queen Elizabeth I had received news of her accession. The possessor of a highly cerebral intelligence, Salisbury enjoyed carrying out chemical experiments for a hobby. But he had no aptitude for personal relations and it was said that he knew the names of none of his Cabinet.

Moreover he seemed isolated from the very great social discontent of the 1880s and 1890s arising out of the worsening economic situation. In 1884 along with the Prince of Wales and Cardinal Manning Salisbury had been a member of the Royal Commission into the Housing of the Working Classes set up in response to a devastating description of life among the poor in London entitled 'Bitter Cry of Outcast London'. But, despite all the evidence he heard on the committee, only modest social reforms took place in the next fifteen years of Conservative rule, none of which did anything to help those being thrown out of work. As a natural corollary to the 1884 broadening of the franchise, the Conservatives had set up elective county councils in 1888 which theoretically removed local government from the grandees of the shires, the magistrates in quarter sessions. But most ordinary people did not have time to give to the county council, so matters continued much as before. Having the vote didn't seem to stop them living in slums, or dying of overwork, disease and simple poverty.

But just because the Conservative government lost interest in social reform after the resignation in 1886 of the only Tory democrat in the Cabinet, Lord Randolph Churchill, it did not mean that there were not plenty of people in Britain determined to effect change. Thanks to the education acts and the broadening of the franchise Britons were more politically aware and more militant. There were demonstrations by the unemployed in early 1886 which led to window-smashing in the West End. Trade unionism from being the preserve of middle-class unions like the engineers spread to unskilled industrial workers; the new unions were responsible for a series of mass strikes for higher pay and shorter hours of which the most famous was the dockers' strike in 1889. These trade unions organized on an industry-wide basis were no longer happy with the Liberals, as the old unions had been. They felt they did not adequately represent the concerns of the working man.

And progressive intellectuals were also discontented with the Liberal party after its split over Home Rule. It was becoming a party dominated by a Celtic programme of disestablishing the Welsh Church and Irish Home Rule. But because the reforming impulse was not adequately represented in party politics, it began to surface in all kinds of other places. At Oxford in the 1870s the philosopher T. H. Green, with his theory of active citizenship and the need of the classes to mingle, had a particularly strong effect on the best and the brightest spirits there. The noted university settlements in the East End of London which had begun in the 1880s – the best known is Toynbee Hall – attempted to put these ideas into practice. A law centre was set up to provide free legal advice, as it does to this day. Eager young graduates with feelings of social responsibility moved to the East End to impart their own learning to those less fortunate than themselves. From Toynbee Hall flowed the once celebrated Workers Education Association, designed to provide an adult education college and night classes for those in employment who had never had the benefit of a university education but wanted to stretch their minds.

The Toynbee Hall settlements fed into a revival of the vigorous evangelicalism that had inspired Lord Shaftesbury in his pioneering reforms of the factory laws. Ninety homes were established for destitute children in the East End by Dr Thomas Barnardo in 1870; round the same time William Booth founded the Salvation Army to do social work and rescue the wretched, the impoverished, the drunken and the sinful in the East End at large revivalist meetings. The 'Sally Army' with its 'soldiers' in black uniforms accompanied by brass bands were a familiar sight in London until the late twentieth century.

The miserable lives revealed by the strikes of industrial workers, the match girls and the dockers (who marched through London holding the fishheads which were all they could afford to eat), alarmed the social consciences of the middle class. There was a new purposefulness about the social reformers who set out to investigate the troubles of the poor. The use of scientific research and statistics to find out what was going wrong and arrive at a proper solution instead of piecemeal measures was pioneered by wealthy businessmen of conscience like the social reformer Charles Booth.

Beatrice Potter, the daughter of a rich industrialist, collected the statistics for Booth's landmark study of the poor, *Life and Labour of the People in London*; begun in 1886 it would not be finished until 1903, and became one of the most important influences on progressive thinking. It would lead to the revision of the Poor Laws and recognition of the need for old age pensions (see below).

The catalogue of monstrous facts which these studies produced reinforced a general sense of the unfairness of the present system. To many it seemed that only some form of communal ownership of the means of production or socialism would prevent the shocking human casualties which were the by-products of capitalism. A number of socialist societies grew up in the 1880s, of which by far the most influential was the Fabian Society, founded by the reformer and researcher Sidney Webb, his future wife Beatrice Potter and the playwright George Bernard Shaw. The Society was named for the Roman general Quintus Fabius who never faced the

Cartoon of a Scientific Centenary – *Punch* (1891).

superlative Carthaginian general Hannibal in battle but wore him down gradually over the duration. The Fabians intended to wear down Britain until their socialist ideas of a fairer society became accepted.

Many of these societies were influenced by Chamberlain's work in Birmingham. Such prototypes for state provision were admiringly christened 'municipal socialism' by the new socialist thinkers. But Chamberlain's radicalism was imprisoned in the Tory party, kept there by Home Rule. Even so, the Fabian Society, with its slogan 'evolution not revolution', would be instrumental in the formation of what after 1900 was called the Labour party, which was intended to represent the working man. But, by the next general election in 1892, the political system was still eight years away from the meeting at the Memorial Hall in Farringdon Street on 27 February 1900 when representatives of the Fabian Society, the Social Democratic Federation (created by a former stockbroker, H. M. Hyndman, in the 1880s) and half a million trade unionists set up the Labour Representation Committee to field candidates in the Parliamentary elections. Nevertheless the 1892 election produced some straws in the wind which suggested that the present system of parties was about to disintegrate.

Two trade unionists and the Scots ex-miner Keir Hardie were elected to Parliament. They were the tentative first attempts to create other means of representing the working man's interests than by relying on the Liberals. Their supporters had come to believe that only a political party for the trade unions would win legislation restricting the hours of manual labour. To the amazement of the silk-hatted MPs, Hardie turned up to the House of Commons wearing his working-class cloth cap as a badge of honour. Although Hardie in 1893 founded the small Independent Labour party at Bradford to fulfil such a role for the unions, when he failed to hold the seat in 1895 it proved that only a national organization could ensure continuous representation. It would take a further worsening of relations between the Conservative government and the working man as the strikes by the new unskilled trade unions became more ferocious and the legal reaction against them grew more severe to make the formation of a mass party imperative.

In 1892 a new alliance with the Irish Home Rulers enabled the depleted Liberals to become the governing party again. The election was a protest vote against the lack of social reforms by the Tories. The eighty-three-year-old Gladstone took part in no fewer than eighty-five debates and at last got Home Rule for Ireland through the Commons, only for the House of Lords to reject it. When he resigned as leader in 1894, the immensely wealthy Lord Rosebery became premier for a year. Handsome and attractive, married to a Rothschild, Rosebery did not please the rank-and-file

Liberals. He lacked both the common and the serious touch and made no attempt to acquire them – he was openly disapproved of by the still substantial Nonconformist element in the Liberal party for his frivolity in winning the Derby while prime minister not once but twice. By 1895 the Liberals were out of office again and the Conservatives and Lord Salisbury back in for another ten years on an increased wave of imperialist fervour. The Liberal administration had put through many radical changes – for one thing it had increased the democratization of local government by creating parish councils – but its programme was not exciting enough for a public thirsting for more martial triumphs. The succumbing of a section of the party under H. H. Asquith to imperialism further weakened the party's appeal for old Radicals with their long history of pacifism. Some of them were drawn to the new socialist organizations, for an important strand of socialist thought was against war.

Overall though the idea of a strong and conquering Britain was what won the public imagination and made them vote Conservative. When Salisbury returned as prime minister in 1895, imperial fever was at its height after the conquest of Lower and Upper Rhodesia. Imperialism was the dominant mood, and not just in Britain. The defeat that year of the decaying Chinese Empire by her tiny island neighbour Japan which had industrialized and modernized along western lines was the signal for Russia, Germany, France and Britain to demand spheres of influence in that empire for themselves. The Boxer Rebellion five years later resulted in the slaughter of the personnel in the European embassies' compound at Peking (Beijing). Supposedly the work of rebels, the rising was in fact aided by the Chinese government behind the scenes, but the European powers rapidly reasserted control. Even America, whose whole history had been a reaction against colonialism, succumbed to the spirit of the age and joined in carving up the undeveloped world. She declared war on Spain in 1898 and took the Spanish Empire, Guam, the Philippines, Puerto Rico and Cuba for her own. The only real success for the non-European world, which otherwise was uniformly defeated by the imperialist powers, was when the Ethiopians routed the Italians at Adowa in 1896.

Even Rudyard Kipling occasionally viewed the expanding British Empire with the melancholy of historical perspective. He wrote the poem 'Recessional' at the height of the imperial frenzy in 1897 to warn of the suddenness with which 'all our pomp of yesterday is one with Nineveh and Tyre'. But there was nothing melancholic about the ex-Liberal Joe Chamberlain, who regarded the empire's economic potential with all the enthusiasm of the screw manufacturer he had once been. Chamberlain gave up as a bad job attempting to bring both halves of the Liberal party back together, asked Salisbury for the then unimportant job of colonial secretary and took firm hold of the imperial tiller. All he could think of was that the empire which had gained three and a half million square miles in twelve years must be the solution to Britain's financial troubles. As the age of iron gave way to the age of steel, German advances in steel manufacture meant that by the mid-1890s Germany was overtaking Britain's steel production. The empire was like an undeveloped estate. If it was better managed, it could be the making of Britain – after all, its combined population was 300 million people.

Britain, Chamberlain believed, was a force for good, whose rule over the new territories of the British Empire could be justified only if she brought 'security and peace and comparative prosperity to countries that never knew these blessings before'. Under Chamberlain the Colonial Office regularized the production of tropical crops like jute, cocoa, palm oil and

Commemorative mug of Queen Victoria's Diamond Jubilee, 1897, bearing the legend 'Empire on which the sun never sets'.

coffee. In west Africa he made the government build ports and schools of medicine and sent troops to clear off marauding local tribes. He interfered in the economies of the West Indies by creating Royal Commissions to investigate the trade of the islands, some of which were facing bankruptcy since the decline of their share of the sugar industry owing to the cultivation of sugar beet in mainland Europe from the late nineteenth century. Indeed, Chamberlain let it be known that where he had once thought in terms of the nation he intended to think in terms of empire. The cautious Lord Salisbury himself even committed himself so far as to divide the world into 'living and dying' nations and emphasized 'England's . . . Imperial instincts'.

The 1887 Golden Jubilee had been marked by the first Colonial Conference of prime ministers at which Salisbury had emphasized the need of the empire for self-defence. Ten years later at the Diamond Jubilee, to mark sixty years of Queen Victoria's reign, Chamberlain tried to draw the colonies into an even closer relationship with Britain. As part of the jubilee ceremonies fifteen colonial premiers were sworn in as members of the Privy Council. At the new Colonial Conference Chamberlain attempted to create a Council of the Empire to co-ordinate defensive policy. But, although Canadians, Australians and New Zealanders took pride in belonging to the British Empire, they valued their recently achieved self-government far too much to consent to what they feared might be the thin end of a wedge of centralization. Chamberlain's invitation was politely refused.

The Diamond Jubilee was the subject of much attention both in Britain and abroad. An even larger parade of representatives of all the nationalities protected by Britain took place to mark the occasion of Queen Victoria's Diamond Jubilee than had done at the Golden Jubilee. The huge array of ships at Portsmouth reminded the world that Britain continued to rule the waves as she had done since the Battle of Trafalgar. The tiny Queen Victoria crowned by her widow's lace veil led the imperial procession through London in her open carriage. The 'Grandmother of Europe', as she was known now that so many of her children had married the heirs to European thrones, more than ever was the reassuringly human apex of the richest, most powerful, most stable empire in the world. A famous *Punch* cartoon of that era shows Britannia dancing with herself in 'splendid isolation'. Britain apparently had no need of foreign allies when she owned so much of the world. In fact the empire was heading for a fall.

With the Jameson Raid on the Transvaal Republic two years before British imperialism had begun to overreach itself. Cecil Rhodes and the Rand lords, whose engineering expertise was responsible for developing the Rand goldmines, had never ceased to resent the way they were treated by the Dutch, as it was their efforts that had made the Transvaal rich. As a boy of ten, the Transvaal's President Kruger had been part of the Great Trek away from Cape Colony to find a new promised land. He had no interest in alleviating conditions for the Uitlanders besmirching it, who were a motley crew of speculators, adventurers and camp followers. He disliked and disapproved of them quite as much as his primitive and religious fellow Boers. By 1895 affairs were at such a pitch that 35,000 Uitlanders had signed a petition asking for better treatment by the Boers, but it had been rejected. Many of the leading Uitlanders then began to plot a rising against Kruger.

With Chamberlain as colonial secretary, Britain used gunboats and soldiers in a way which had not been seen since Palmerston. Troops were sent to defeat the constant encroachments of the French into British West Africa. During his first term British battleships appeared in the Indian Ocean to force President Kruger to open the fords he had closed to prevent Uitlanders using them to avoid tax on the railways. With Chamberlain so keen to defend British interests, the inventive Cecil Rhodes, by now prime minister of the Cape, and his chief lieutenant Jameson believed they had a receptive audience for their plan to wrest control of the Transvaal and its goldfields from the Boers.

When Chamberlain was approached by Rhodes and Jameson and warned that they planned to go to the rescue of the Uitlanders with a force of about 500 men, he did not try to stop them – he may even have helped them by notifying the police of the British protectorate of Bechuanaland to join the raid. But he does not seem to have known when it would take place. Meanwhile the momentum for a rising fizzled out, partly because many of the Uitlanders were not British but German or American. By coincidence the US president S. G. Cleveland, who was facing re-election, chose this moment to threaten Britain with war over British Guiana's disputed border with Venezuela. American patriotism was running high – Cleveland talked of twisting the lion's tale.

Uitlanders did not want the raid to be a triumph for British imperialism, so their uprising never took place. Jameson and his 470 accomplices nonetheless thundered optimistically into the Transvaal. But this time he was dealing not with the more credulous warriors of the Matabele peoples but with the politically savvy Kruger, who having captured Jameson and his troops created an enormous international outcry about the attempt to take over the Transvaal. Britain responded with a whitewashing official inquiry described by the Liberal press as the 'Lying in State'. Though Chamberlain was cleared, Rhodes was forced to resign as prime minister of Cape Colony. But the British were still largely behind Jameson, whose derring-do became the subject of popular ballads, and many agreed with Chamberlain's sympathetic description of Rhodes as a 'rebel patriot'.

Anglo-German rivalry was felt more keenly round this time and was increased by a tactless telegram which the kaiser Wilhelm II, Queen Victoria's nephew, sent to President Kruger in January 1896. The kaiser congratulated Kruger on foiling the raid 'without recourse to the aid of friendly powers', which suggested that in the event of a war in South Africa the Dutch would have German arms on their side. Germany had become noticeably less friendly to the British. The two powers were rubbing up against one another in colonial and commercial rivalry round the world, with friction arising not only over South Africa but over the Middle East. Germany, intent on replacing Britain as most-favoured nation at Constantinople, used Britain's demands for reform after a new Armenian massacre by the Turks in 1898 to cement her position and obtain the rights to build a Berlin-to-Baghdad railway. France remained Britain's chief colonial rival, but she had never made the mistake of attempting to compete with the British fleet. Yet in 1897 Germany began to build a navy as big as Britain's, and when the kaiser announced that Germany's future lay on water, alarm bells began to ring within the British government. It was well known that the minuscule size of Britain's professional army required her to entrust her defence to her navy, as she had done for almost a hundred years. Germany's refusal to limit her naval expenditure while maintaining and increasing the 400,000-strong army which had mauled France in the Franco-Prussian War was an action Britain could only perceive as hostile.

Germany was replacing Russia as the power Britain felt most wary of, especially after 1890 when Russia, disturbed by the strength of the British reaction over the Penjdeh crisis, turned away from expansion in central Asia in favour of penetrating the failing Chinese Empire instead. In the mid-1890s there had been a general regrouping of alliances all round, though Britain continued to remain unallied. After the death of Kaiser Wilhelm I and the consequent fall of Bismarck, the German–Russian alliance lapsed. France, perpetually afraid of a fresh attack from Germany and desperately in need of a friend, began to court Russia. The understanding between Russia and France was symbolized when French loans were raised at the Paris Bourse for a Trans-Siberian Railway. And in 1895 their links became official. Fear of Germany had created strange bedfellows: Russia's eastern autocracy in a Dual Alliance with the volatile Third Republic of France against the Triple Alliance of Germany, Austria–Hungary and Italy. Thwarted colonial ambitions had pushed Italy on to Germany's side when France seized Tunis in northern Africa. Thus by 1895 Europe was divided into the two armed camps which were such a feature of the geopolitical world in the years before the First World War.

But uneasiness about Germany made little difference to Anglo-French colonial rivalry. In the Upper Nile at Fashoda the two countries very nearly came to blows. Though the Jameson Raid had failed, the spirit of gung-ho imperialism was flourishing more strongly than ever in England. The country now thrilled to the reconquest of the Sudan by Sir Horatio Herbert Kitchener, the commander-in-chief, or sirdar, of the Egyptian army, at the Battle of Omdurman in September 1898. British honour and the death of Gordon were avenged when Kitchener destroyed the dervish armies of the mahdi's successor, the khalifa, and retook Khartoum. The nation rejoiced even more when Kitchener faced down a small French force sent out from French West Africa to claim the Upper Nile, for France continued to be infuriated by the British control of Egypt. Straight from the heat of Omdurman Kitchener marched south to Fashoda to challenge Captain Marchand, who had hoisted the French flag. Kitchener put up the British and Egyptian flags in response and left an Egyptian force there. But though the farcical situation was worthy of the contemporary comic operas of Sir William Gilbert and Sir Arthur Sullivan, both countries were in deadly earnest. Lord Salisbury announced that Britain was prepared to open hostilities, and the Royal Navy was put on alert. But when France's new ally Russia made it very clear that she had no intention of going to war with Great Britain over somewhere in Africa, France was forced to back down.

It seemed yet another triumph for British arms, and it was in a mood of patriotic euphoria that Britain began to move towards war with the Boers. The Boers believed that the British government had been secretly behind the Jameson Raid and that there would one day be another attempt to take over the Transvaal. President Kruger's government began to stockpile arms with the enormous profits from the goldmines. Chamberlain and the rest of the Conservatives and Unionists became convinced the Boers were a threat not only to peaceful coexistence but to British supremacy at the Cape. The Jameson Raid had created race hatred between the Boers and the English settlers. After Rhodes's disgrace his government had been replaced by a Dutch ministry at the Cape sympathetic to the Boers. With some of the Boers in the Transvaal advertising themselves as liberators of the oppressed Dutch at the Cape, the possibility loomed of the colonies joining up under Dutch leadership in a Dutch United States of South Africa. There were rumours that German officers were advising the Boers. The Germans were certainly selling arms to them.

The treatment of the Uitlanders within the Boer republics worsened. There were violent clashes between Boer police and the Uitlanders, and a petition from over 20,000 workers was sent to Queen Victoria asking her to help them. The high commissioner of South Africa, Sir Alfred Milner, warned that Britain had to intervene quickly to protest about the

Uitlanders' treatment or the sight of 'thousands of British subjects kept permanently in the position of helots' would undermine faith in the British Empire. War was inevitable if Kruger would not grant the civil rights that Britain requested. There was a last conference at Bloemfontein in 1899. But the stubborn old Kruger would not betray his people and their sacred land. If the Uitlanders were given the vote, even in five years' time, they would outnumber the Boers. When Kruger could not agree, Milner broke off negotiations and went back to the Cape. The Second Boer War ensued.

Apart from Radical Liberals like the rising Welsh solicitor MP David Lloyd George and the socialists, British public opinion and press were still in the grip of military frenzy. Young men, particularly well-to-do ones, were mustard keen for the war, believing in a vague way that it would test them, that it would be good for them. Everybody imagined that the war would be short and sweet. In fact it was prolonged, very expensive and far from the walkover that Britons expected.

The Boers turned out to be superb marksmen armed with state-of-the-art European weaponry. Most of their soldiers were really just Dutch farmers, but a hard life on the veldt had left them in superb physical condition. Britain's popularity with other nations, repelled by what appeared to be bullying of the two small Boer republics by the mighty British Empire, dwindled to a dangerous low. And the Orange Free State and the Transvaal were almost a match for her. It took two and a half years, £200 million and 450,000 British soldiers to defeat 50,000 Boers. More and more volunteers were sent out by the boatload from Britain 4,000 miles away in their brand-new 'khaki' combat uniform, invented to blend into the African bush.

The Boers' fatal mistake was to attack the colony of Natal, which contained only British settlers, instead of making for the Cape where there were 30,000 Dutch. Nevertheless for much of 1899 and 1900 British troops were completely unable to relieve the siege of Ladysmith in Natal, and Mafeking in Bechuanaland on the border of the Transvaal. Under Colonel Robert Baden Powell, Mafeking held out for 217 days. (Baden Powell would later become famous as the founder of the Boy Scouts and Girl Guides movement, which trained young people in disciplined and self-reliant behaviour.) So badly did the British fare against the Boers, despite their superior numbers, that after 'black week' in December 1899, a series of massive defeats, the commander-in-chief Sir Redvers Buller was replaced by Lord Roberts. It was not until May 1900 that Mafeking was relieved by Roberts.

Ultimately the Boers were let down by their lack of military training and coherent strategy. Roberts and his second-in-command Kitchener of Khartoum managed to outflank the Boers' commander Piet Cronje. By

The Boer War: one of the blockhouses built by Kitchener to guard the railways; Howitzer gun at Balmoral camp; cricket group amongst British soldiers at Balmoral camp.

August 1900 Roberts had seized the capitals of the Boer republics Bloemfontein and Johannesburg, the main Boer armies had given up and Ladysmith had been relieved. Later that year the Transvaal and the Orange Free State were formally annexed as colonies to the British crown. A khaki election – that is, a war election, because many of the voters were still in khaki uniform – was called that year by the Conservatives, who hoped to cash in on the war's popularity.

They duly won the election, but their hold over the nation was drawing to a close. The Labour Representation Committee, prototype of the Labour party, had been created six months before in February 1900. Its candidates won only two seats in the general election, with Keir Hardie gaining one of them, and the Conservative majority was 134. But the Labour party was the rising sun, though its breakthrough would not come until the 1906 election. The long years under the Conservatives had achieved very little for many workers, as was dramatically highlighted at the beginning of the Boer War by the poor physical shape of the recruits. Shockingly, one in three of the British men who volunteered for service was found unfit for duty by the army doctors. The Tory government simply could not pay for social reforms when Chamberlain was sending British armies all over Africa, nor was there the political will.

The Boer War was continued by little groups of Boers carrying on guerrilla warfare from the hills. Lord Kitchener had taken over as commander-in-chief and in the end the Boers were defeated by his ruthless use of total war. He built blockhouses or garrison huts to guard the railways and prevent the Boers blowing them up. Much more controversially, to thwart the guerrilla tactics which made every home a potential shelter, Kitchener forced the evacuation of the Boer farms. Civilian Boers were placed in enormous concentration camps, in huts surrounded by barbed wire, a concept which was to be used with such evil effect some thirty years later in Germany.

Though it was extremely effective, such an inhumane way of proceeding created an uproar in Britain, especially when it became known that a fifth of the inmates were dying in the camps. Of the 100,000 Boers confined in them, 20,000 died. The figures were even worse for one camp, where disease and insanitary conditions killed half the Boer children interned there. It was then that the quiet new leader of the Liberals, a Glaswegian MP from a wealthy family named Sir Henry Campbell-Bannerman, forever endeared himself to the Boers and the Radical wing of his party. At a time when the national mood was blindly patriotic he dared to criticize the British army publicly by calling the concentration camps 'methods of barbarism'. A strong-minded British spinster, the fearless Miss Emily Hobhouse, led an expedition out to South Africa to find out what was going on. When she was stonewalled by the army, she took the story to the press to create more of an outcry. Chamberlain was forced to send out proper administrators for the camps to take over from the army, which had enough problems feeding itself let alone the enemy. The anti-militaristic and humanitarian spirit of England had started to reassert itself after a period of quiescence. The mushroom growth of imperialism was starting to shrivel and die as rapidly as it had sprung up.

But the Queen of England was also declining rapidly. The consummate Victorian, Gladstone, had died three years before and had been buried in Westminster Abbey after a magnificent state funeral. The old queen lived to see the first year of the twentieth century; after that her health began to falter. On 22 January 1901 she died in her eighty-second year at Osborne House on the Isle of Wight. Despite her fondness for a forthright and elderly Scots ghillie named John Brown, Victoria had never ceased mourning Prince Albert. She was buried beside him in the mausoleum at Frogmore, inside Windsor Home Park.

The Victorian age and the nineteenth century had come to an end together. When Victoria died there was not only great sorrow among her subjects but also a sense of disbelief. She had been on the throne since 1837, so that even people in their sixties had known no other monarch. She had been a fixture that seemed as permanent as the Tower of London.

SAXE-COBURG

Edward VII
(1901–1910)

The next thirteen years of life in Britain display a curious mixture of the ultra-modern existing side by side with the traditions of the past. Fifteen per cent of Britons were still employed as servants, making possible the grand lifestyle enjoyed by the well-to-do in the wake of the example set by the new monarch Edward VII. The long dresses and formal outfits we see in photographs of the Edwardians speak of an age still very different to ours. On the other hand, after the first election of Edward VII's reign, over fifty British constituencies had Labour MPs. More women had jobs than ever before as teachers and nurses and in the new profession of typist. Although they did not have the vote, a suffragette movement was beginning.

With the extraordinary Liberal landslide at the 1906 election the battles for hearts and minds waged by social reformers over the past twenty years seemed to have resulted in a great victory for humanitarianism. Ploughshares had truly become more important than swords. It was accepted that the state had a duty to care for the people in sickness and old age. By 1911 the harsh old Poor Laws had been thrown out and old age pensions and national insurance had been brought in. War went out of fashion and seemed uncivilized; it belonged to a less advanced age. Yet the period was overshadowed by an awareness of the increasing German arsenal. To defence chiefs the disarmament conferences and peace movements of the time could leave Britain disastrously vulnerable. When the period ended in the immolation of the First World War, ten million dead worldwide made a belief in progress seem like vanity.

But at the beginning of the twentieth century the omens were favourable. Telecommunications continued to shrink the globe. In 1901, after experiments conducted with the backing of the British government, the Anglo-Italian Guglielmo Marconi sent the first electro-magnetic signal across the Atlantic, from the Lizard peninsula in Cornwall to Newfoundland – Britain was linked to the North American continent by radio wave. By 1912, some 700,000 British people had telephones. Even the most distant regions of the earth, its North and South Poles, yielded up their secrets. The Briton Captain Robert Scott led his first expedition to the Antarctic in 1900–4 and discovered what he called King Edward VII's Land, while the American Admiral Robert Peary got within a hundred miles of the North Pole in 1902. London became full of motor buses. The Bakerloo and Piccadilly lines were sunk deep underground, making travel round London much faster.

Around 1905 arose the starry constellation of left-leaning intellectuals known as the Bloomsbury Group. A handful of gifted publishers, writers, artists and art historians did more to end Victorian attitudes than the death of the queen herself. Champions of the avant-garde with their art exhibitions, Roger Fry and Clive Bell introduced Britain to the conceptual revolutions taking place on the continent. Often the children of eminent Victorians – like the writer Virginia Woolf, whose father, Sir Leslie Stephen, was the founder of *The Dictionary of National Biography* – the Bloomsbury circle mercilessly deconstructed the Victorian assumptions they had grown up with. Just as the Cubists refused to go on representing the world literally, writers like Woolf challenged literary form with their fractured, allusive technique. They were mesmerized by the new science of psychoanalysis and its emphasis on the subconscious. Pioneered by Sigmund Freud it began casting its spell at the turn of the century. The importance of the instinct versus the intellect made a huge number of converts, of whom the most famous was D. H. Lawrence, a coalminer's son from Nottingham whose novel *Sons and Lovers* came out in 1913.

Presiding over these changes was the old-fashioned figure of the new king. The most abiding image of Edward VII is in the waisted Norfolk jacket he used for his favourite sport, shooting, at his unpretentious house Sandringham. The style of the Marlborough House Set, as his friends were called, harked back to the days of the prince regent. Edward revelled in meals that were not only extremely rich but involved eight to ten courses and port and cigars in profusion. But in his way he was an innovator. He made it his business to get to know people from all walks of life, including union leaders and some of the new Labour MPs. As a young man he had insisted on meeting Italian revolutionary Garibaldi when he visited Britain, to his mother's consternation. Where Queen Victoria's court had consisted of the landed aristocracy, Edward VII preferred plutocrats and Jewish financiers.

Edward's immense girth and genial presence had been a constant feature of ceremonial occasions in Britain and the empire for forty years. But Queen Victoria had prevented him from taking on any real kind of royal responsibilities and jealously guarded her powers. In fact, she disliked her eldest son, and despite protests from ministers, until he reached the age of fifty refused to allow him to read state papers. On his accession he was almost sixty. Deprived of a real role Edward had thrown himself into pleasure and did all he could to live in a way quite different to the Queen. Though the Victorian Sunday was sacred, and for many Victorians began and ended with church services, the Prince of Wales made a point of holding extravagant Sunday-night suppers. Though devoted to his beautiful and elegant wife Queen Alexandra, he had numerous mistresses, the most celebrated of whom were Mrs Alice Keppel and the Jersey actress Mrs Lillie Langtry. The subject of paintings and hundreds of society prints, Mrs Langtry was fondly known as the Jersey Lily. As Prince of Wales, Edward was cited in two divorce cases, but he shocked the manners of the day even more when it emerged that he had played the illegal game of baccarat at a house named Tranby Croft. He was called as a witness in a slander trial when Sir William Gordon Cumming sued some of his fellow gamblers at Tranby Croft for saying he was a cheat.

Once he became king, Edward VII took himself and his role far more seriously. Throughout his reign he was assiduous in maintaining peaceful relations with other European sovereigns, to many of whom he was closely related, gaining the nickname Edward the Peacemaker. His charm and extremely good French made him an important weapon to end the hostility between the two western democracies. After he had made a state visit to Paris, the final thawing out of relations between France and Britain reached a natural conclusion with the diplomatic understanding known as the Entente Cordiale in 1904. In fact ever since Fashoda a series of agreements over territories had started to lessen the hostility between Britain and France, culminating in a historic breakthrough when many old colonial disputes across the globe which went back to the early eighteenth century, including one over fishing rights off Newfoundland, were settled once and for all. France recognized Britain's occupation of Egypt unconditionally, while the British allowed the French 'a free hand in Morocco' which joined up France's north and west African imperial possessions.

This was a time of anxiety for Britain, for the Boer War had revealed her as having no friends in Europe. The early part of Edward VII's reign saw a great many attempts to improve Britain's relations with the rest of the world. Though Britain's territories had never been more widespread, the last few years had been an inglorious period, and the once magnificent isolation seemed positively irksome. To counter it, in 1902 under the new foreign secretary Lord Lansdowne, Britain made her first alliance with Japan, the rising power in the east.

Like many British politicians the king was disquieted by German intentions. His wife Alexandra, the former Danish princess who had watched with horror as Prussian troops marched into her country, regarded most

Germans with suspicion. For all Edward's desire to be a peacemaker, he greatly disliked his nephew, the rash and often scintillating know-all Kaiser Wilhelm II. The kaiser's personal diplomacy was unpredictable: he would send messages abroad or make speeches on foreign affairs without consulting ministers. Born with a withered arm, into a militaristic society which detested his mother for being English and therefore a dangerous liberal, the kaiser both admired and resented his English relations. But, though the English laughed at him and found his obsession with uniforms absurd, William was deadly serious about building a navy to rival his uncle's.

In the face of that fleet-building, Britain's greatest threat suddenly seemed to come from across the North Sea instead of from across the Channel, as it had done since the late seventeenth century. The king had strongly supported the commander of the Mediterranean fleet and future first sea lord 'Jacky' Fisher, when he had insisted that a naval base be built at Rosyth in 1903 on Britain's east coast to guard against attack from the north coast of Germany. To counter the German menace Fisher invented the huge ironclad battleship called the Dreadnought and the fast and heavily armed battle cruisers. The Dreadnought made every other warship of lower tonnage and smaller guns obsolete against it. By 1907 for the first time Britain had a General Staff; it was felt that she could no longer do without one when all the other major European powers had possessed them for the previous fifteen years.

Britain began to tie her naval security arrangements together with those of France. The Mediterranean fleet based on Malta was reduced as part of an exercise to bring more of the Royal Navy into home waters. Britain would rely on the French navy to help her patrol the Mediterranean. The two nations were to let one another in on their military secrets. There was no quicker way to draw an Entente closer together, although for fear of angering the ever touchy Germany British diplomats perpetually avoided a final commitment to France.

The last years of the Conservative government have an air of played-out exhaustion about them. Lord Salisbury resigned in July 1902 on grounds of ill-health, and was succeeded as prime minister by his nephew the gifted intellectual A. J. Balfour, formerly the chief secretary to Ireland. The Irish Land Purchase Act of the following year was the most successful attempt made by Britain to solve the Irish land problem. It put loans of £5 million a year at the disposal of tenant farmers wishing to buy out their landlords. By an annual redemption payment or mortgage, tenants would become owners of their farms after sixty-eight years. Two hundred and fifty thousand people had taken up the scheme by 1909. But, with belief in a separate Irish state gathering momentum again, the fact remained that a separate nation for the Irish was going to be a far more powerful idea than mortgages.

Balfour addressed Britain's industrial decline with a new Education Bill in 1902 which brought secondary education under control of the state and caused the building of hundreds of local grammar schools. But the problems of the poor in Britain were too immediate to be dealt with by the education of the future. An incontrovertible shock had been given to the empirically minded and practical British by the youthful science of statistics. The solid evidence of Charles Booth's figures showing the almost inevitable link between poverty and old age, published in his exhaustive *Life and Labour of the People in London* in 1903, combined with the equally influential B. Seebohm Rowntree's groundbreaking 1901 *Poverty: A Study of Town Life* in York, could not be denied. It appeared that around a third of the British people were living below what Seebohm called the poverty line.

Joe Chamberlain's faith in an ingenious new form of imperialism, an Imperial Customs Union which would have preference over the rest of the world, did not fit the mood of urgency. The Tariff Reform League – which he formed after resigning from the Colonial Office – and the import duties that would fund social programmes at home were denounced as a threat to food prices. It was Chamberlain's fate to split parties: this time it was the Conservatives' turn. Free trade was a shibboleth on which Britain had built her immense prosperity. Conservative free traders like Winston Churchill believed that an Imperial Customs Union would drastically increase the cost of living because other countries would slap on their own retaliatory import duties. The Tory free traders accordingly went over to the Liberals to campaign for the forthcoming general election under the slogan of the Big Loaf (free trade and the Liberals) against the Little Loaf (tariff reform and the Conservatives). In December 1905 the Conservative government had to resign and the Liberals under Sir Henry Campbell-Bannerman – whose moral bravery in attacking the conduct of the Boer War at the height of war fever united a party split into imperialists and anti-imperialists – returned to power. Chamberlain himself suffered a stroke the year after and had to retire from politics. The Tories had come to represent a sort of callousness. It became known that, with the high commissioner Lord Milner's acquiescence, Chinese labourers were being imported to work in the Rand goldmines on contracts that were little short of slavery. Much was made of their treatment at a time when the Labour movement was starting to feel its strength.

At the general election in June 1906 the Liberals won a landslide victory, 377 Liberal seats against only 157 Conservatives and Liberal Unionists, which gave the new government a convincing mandate from the nation to implement real social reforms. But it contained a great surprise. The number of Labour MPs had leaped from two in 1900 to fifty-three (twenty-nine for the Labour Representation Committee and twenty-four others who counted themselves Labour). The Liberals' passive acceptance of the landmark 1901 Taff Vale legal decision, which allowed a trade union to be sued for damage caused by its members during a strike, had driven the unions towards Labour. The large number of MPs fielded by the Labour Representation Committee pointed to the desire for radical change in the way that the working man was treated. After the 1906 election the twenty-nine LRC members called themselves the Labour Parliamentary party and Keir Hardie became its chairman. In fact the mood of many Liberals was very close to the new Labour party; after all, until recently the Liberals had been the party representing the working class, and in many constituencies they still were. The Liberal MP John Burns, who became minister for the Local Government Board, was the first working man to be a member of the Cabinet. A socialist engineer and trade unionist, he had been one of the chief instigators of the great strikes of the late 1880s.

The new Liberal administration contained some of the twentieth century's most outstanding politicians, future prime ministers who would steer Britain safely through the First and Second World Wars. The chancellor of the Exchequer was H. H. Asquith, a Yorkshireman and gifted Nonconformist barrister. Somewhat to the surprise of his down-to-earth relations he had married the high-spirited daughter of a chemical bleach magnate, Margot Tennant, a member of the most dashing section of Edwardian society. David Lloyd George, the solicitor known as the Welsh Wizard, was at the Board of Trade but would soon become chancellor of the Exchequer; his views were informed by personal experience of the poverty he had grown up with in the Welsh valleys as the nephew of the local cobbler. Winston Spencer Churchill, under-secretary at the Colonial Office but about to go to the Board of Trade and then to the Home Office, was the son of the Tory Democrat Lord Randolph and the American beauty Jenny Jerome. He may have been born in Blenheim Palace but he had a hatred of injustice as strong as Lloyd George's. The Northumbrian landowner Sir Edward Grey became foreign secretary, a post he would hold until after the outbreak of the First World War. In 1906, to all these men the twentieth century promised a fresh start in attempts to solve the problems that had disfigured the nineteenth.

In the case of the African colonies, as in India, most Liberal and Labour politicians believed that the British Empire was merely a trustee for the future. Britain's role was to guide them to democracy when they were ready – which meant when education had become widespread.

The black African colonies began to be governed at arm's length by Britain, the Liberals preferring to rely on local leaders and local institutions, or 'indirect rule'. British MPs formed an important part of the international mission in 1908 which investigated rumours that King Leopold had ordered massacres of African people in the Belgian Congo. When it reported that the 'mission to civilize' had resulted in the Congo becoming a private slave kingdom for Leopold, where any resistance was met by death, the king was forced to hand over its administration to the Belgian state.

As a result of Campbell-Bannerman's outspoken defence of the Boers during the war, he found their leaders easy to deal with. The Boer War peace treaty of 1902 had anyway been generous. None of the leaders was punished for going to war with Britain, and £3 million compensation was given to restart the farming destroyed by Kitchener's scorched-earth policy. The Liberal decision to grant the Boers self-government in 1907 also improved relations, although two former rebel leaders, Louis Botha and Jan Smuts, became the most important figures in the Transvaal government. In 1908 the Liberal administration invited the four South African colonies, the two Boer ex-republics and the two British, the Cape and Natal, to form a Dominion of South Africa.

However, the price of creating another Dominion, as the self-governing colonies had elected to be known since 1907, was black votes. Despite their idealism, it was a price the majority of the British government was willing to pay. When the four colonies created not a federation of colonies but a Union of South Africa in 1910, Boer ideas predominated. The old Cape Parliament had a 'colour blind' franchise, but under pressure of the Boers the new constitution of the Union included the Boers' colour bar. A deputation representing the nine million-strong black majority in South Africa led by William Schreiner, and protests from the Aboriginal Protection Society and others like the Liberal MP Sir Charles Dilke and the Labour MP Ramsay MacDonald, were ignored. The Liberal government washed its hands of the affair, on the ground that insisting on safeguards for black African rights might cause the peaceful Union process to collapse. Ministers did assure Schreiner, however, that the three black High Commission territories of Bechuanaland, Basutoland and Swaziland, which had no white population whatsoever and which were to be absorbed into the new Union, would be protected by various guarantees, and they were. But the colour bar passed. Relations with London grew much more amicable. South Africa came into the war on the side of the British Empire in 1914. Smuts, who had followed Botha as prime minister, became a member of the British War Cabinet.

Campbell-Bannerman's energy had been exhausted dealing with the aftermath of the Boer War. Some important domestic measures were passed under him, but it was not until after April 1908, when on account of Campbell-Bannerman's ill-health H. H. Asquith took over as prime minister, that the progressive wing of the party came to the fore. A flood of bills made dramatic changes to the social fabric of Britain.

Profound advances were made in the treatment of prisoners. Jail sentences were shortened. Young people under fourteen could no longer be sent to prison; instead they were held in borstals – remedial centres with educational facilities. The use of solitary confinement for all prisoners on arriving at jail was stopped, as was automatic imprisonment for non-payment of fines. The Liberal government anticipated the concerns of many penal reformers fifty years later, believing that the experience of prison was in itself harmful. Prison libraries were introduced, as well as a lecture system, to fit prisoners for the outside world to which they must in the end return. The Liberals believed that the treatment of crime and criminals was one of the real tests of civilization.

Legislation to compensate workmen for injuries received at their place of employment was finally passed in 1908. The hours to be worked in a coalmine were fixed at eight hours per day. The Trade Disputes Act of 1906 repudiated the Taff Vale case, which had forced the railway union to repay the cost of its strike in damages to the Taff Vale Railway Company. Union funds became untouchable. In 1909 a Trade Boards Act produced wage-fixing machinery to prevent sweated labour, while another act created stricter safety standards for coalmines. In 1914 the Liberals tried to reduce the number of hours of work in shops from eighty to sixty per week, but were defeated by pressure from shopkeepers. However, the government succeeded in getting one early-closing day a week, and the British tea break was enshrined in law in 1911.

The misery of seasonal unemployment was tackled by a national system of Labour Exchanges pioneered and run by a protégé of Sidney and Beatrice Webb, a young university lecturer named William Beveridge, whose special interest it was. Thirty-five years later in 1944, after a career as director of the London School of Economics, the same man would issue the Beveridge Report that gave birth to Britain's welfare state and the National Health Service, to protect the population 'from the cradle to the grave'.

But an early version of that care was given by the 1911 National Insurance Act and the Old Age Pensions Act of 1908. They were the greatest innovations of the Liberal government and they were driven through the Commons and the Lords by the energy and conviction of Lloyd George and Winston Churchill. The Old Age Pensions Act ensured that every old person had five shillings a week from the age of seventy, if he or she did not have more than eight shillings a week income from other sources. In return for a small weekly contribution by employer and employee, the National Insurance Act gave sickness benefit, free care by a doctor, and money for every week out of work. The Liberal government was on a crusade against poverty. But how was it to finance the reforms, especially as the threat from Germany was prompting a level of expenditure on both the army and navy that was unheard of in peacetime Britain?

The Liberal secretary of state for war, R. B. Haldane, who had close links with Germany, was so alarmed by the military preparations taking place there that he not only increased army spending but created the small, superbly equipped British Expeditionary Force with which Britain would help defend France against the Germans at the beginning of the First World War. The Anglo-French Entente had the effect of driving a paranoid Germany to still greater lengths to increase her navy and throw her weight around over her further colonial expansion. Germany believed that she was merely protecting her commercial interests. For France and Britain, however, she was unacceptably aggressive when in 1905, in a bid to halt the French colonization of Morocco, she threatened war if there were not a conference to discuss its future. The great-power conference at Algeçiras in Spain the following year demonstrated that Germany's rough behaviour had worked: the development of Morocco was to take place under international supervision, which would make room for German trade.

Then at the Hague Conference on Disarmament in 1907, Germany refused utterly to decrease her Dreadnought-building programme in return for reductions by the British. She was convinced that this was a cunning British gambit to make her navy less powerful. Admiral Tirpitz, head of the German navy, had been delighted that the Liberal government had lowered the amount of spending allotted by the Conservatives to Dreadnoughts in order to finance its social reforms. This had given him time to start his own programme to build Dreadnoughts, which he did with gusto.

In a world perpetually anxious about Germany it was inevitable that Britain would seek ways to protect the empire from German activities. The Entente drew her into a relationship with France's ally Russia. Once Britain's greatest enemy in central Asia, Russia had been revealed as a spent force when she was defeated by Japan in the Russo-Japanese War of 1904–5. Now it seemed far more important to achieve joint collaboration to check German penetration of the Middle East. The Anglo-Russian Convention of 1907 in theory committed Britain to nothing. It merely declared that Britain's influence was recognized as supreme in Afghanistan and southern Persia, while Russia was accepted as the dominant power in northern Persia. But the understanding between Russia and Britain increased Germany's fear of encirclement.

In 1908 the underlying tension in Europe was ratcheted up several levels when Serbia threatened to attack Austria–Hungary, and Germany retaliated by announcing that Russia would face war with her if she backed Serbia. Fearing that the Young Turk revolution at Constantinople would undermine the position she had built up over thirty years, Austria–Hungary had finally annexed the Balkan lands of Bosnia and Herzegovina, which she had occupied since 1878. But, just as the days of deference were passing in Britain, new forces were operating in relations between old empires and young upstart nations like Serbia. Austria–Hungary might think of Bosnia and Herzegovina as compensation for her lost empire in Italy and Germany, but Serbia believed she had more right to the two provinces because of their large Serb population. She was sufficiently self-confident to fight for them to create her dream of a greater Serbia, a South Slav or Yugoslav Empire, and she appealed to Russia as the special protector of the Slavic peoples to back her against Austria–Hungary.

After being so recently defeated by the Japanese, Russia was in no condition to take on Germany as well as Austria–Hungary. Austria–Hungary retained her new provinces, but that only stored up trouble for the future. Though Serbia was forced to back off, agitation about her Serb brothers in Bosnia and Herzegovina did not die away. In fact it became stronger with every passing year. The European atmosphere was not improved by an interview the kaiser gave to the London *Daily Telegraph* in which he said that most Germans detested the British and would happily go to war with them, and that he was their only friend.

In 1909, right in the middle of the crisis over the Balkans and as Britain's demands for an international conference were being ignored, came news of secret German plans for a vast increase in the size of the German navy. The German naval estimates revealed to Parliament spread panic through the country. Admiral Tirpitz had already caught up with Britain in the number of Dreadnoughts. With the new programme, he might overtake the British. Many soldiers, including Lord Roberts the commander-in-chief of the Boer War, wanted immediate conscription. The urgent need to build new Dreadnoughts was captured in the music-hall song, 'We want eight and we won't wait'. Even the Liberals, with their antipathy towards military spending, were convinced that the naval race with Germany called for more battleships to be built that year and the next.

But where was the money to come from? Not only did extra money have to be found for the ships, the new welfare provisions had to be funded too. For David Lloyd George, the chancellor of the Exchequer, the answer was a graduated income tax to get the rich to pay more. But the super-wealthy had their well-ensconced defenders in the House of Lords. Ever since the split over Irish Home Rule there had been no peers left on the Liberal side of the House. Moreover the Lords had become far too accustomed to using its Conservative majority to defeat bills sent up by the Liberal Commons.

The Liberal government's measures to promote greater fairness in British life had created a malevolent hostility in the House of Lords.

Encouraged by the fact that the last two prime ministers Salisbury and Balfour had been aristocrats, many peers felt a resurgence of the conviction that those born to wear ermine were born to the purple too. Bills to end plural voting, a new licensing bill which allowed a drinks licence to be withdrawn by the local council if it so wished, and a bill to increase the number of smallholders in Scotland, all incensed their lordships for one reason or another, and were rejected.

In 1894 Gladstone had warned the Lords when they rejected Home Rule that they were tampering with the constitution, since an unelected House was interfering with the wishes of the elected House. He had told them that they should fear for their future if they continued to thwart the democratic will. The Liberals had experienced thirty years of the Lords throwing out their measures whenever it suited them. They had had enough of their smart new twentieth-century legislation being destroyed by a group of people whom Lloyd George daringly described as being 'five hundred men, ordinary men, chosen accidentally from among the unemployed'. Should they, he asked, 'override the judgement – the deliberate judgement – of millions of people engaged in the industry which makes the wealth of this country?' Hereditary privilege was beginning to look absurd. Lloyd George decided to get rid of the powers of the Lords once and for all. He would raise the immense funds he needed by a method almost guaranteed to arouse the wrath of the Lords: a super-tax on top of income tax for higher incomes, plus a higher rate of death duty for the wealthier estates. Most infuriating of all was a tax on any unearned increase in the value of land, to be paid whenever land changed hands.

It was a tradition that only the House of Commons could alter money bills. If the Lords rejected the budget, it would be in breach of a constitutional convention. The People's Budget would be the test, as Lloyd George put it, of 'whether the country was to be governed by the King and the Peers or the King and the People'. But the House of Lords was so enraged by the budget, and by the idea of the state preparing to value every field in the country to estimate its unearned increment, that it completely lost its head. In 1909 the greatest landowners in the country still were, as they had been for centuries, the aristocracy and the landed gentry, whose relatives represented them in the House of Lords. Lloyd George's tax seemed aimed at them, the 1 per cent of the population who owned 70 per cent of the country.

Lloyd George's budget passed the Liberal House of Commons, but was thrown out by the House of Lords. The chancellor's response was to cry, 'We have got them at last!' Asquith dissolved Parliament and called a general election for January 1910 on the ground that the rights of the Commons had been usurped. The election was bitterly fought. The peers made the great mistake of taking part in it. Their collective wisdom might have been encyclopaedic and their knowledge of local affairs second to none, yet the hustings revealed the lottery of heredity at its worst. Many of the lumbering backwoodsmen appeared eccentric and selfishly concerned with their own interests.

The election, the second of Edward VII's reign, returned the Liberals to power, but the result was disappointing. The landslide had vanished. The Liberals had only three MPs more than the Unionists. To push their measures through, the Liberals were dependent on the votes of the Labour party and the Irish Nationalists. A new Home Rule Bill would be the payment demanded for the Irish Nationalists' co-operation.

The Conservative Lords suddenly agreed to pass the budget. But Asquith and Lloyd George were not put off. Asquith introduced the Parliament Bill, which strictly limited the House of Lords' powers: it should no longer be able to change or throw out a money bill; any bill which was passed by the House of Commons in three successive sessions, even if it was rejected by the Lords each time, should become law.

The Parliament Bill had only had its first reading in the Commons when the House adjourned for the Easter Break. But on 6 May 1910 the nation was abruptly distracted. Following a holiday in his favourite French resort of Biarritz, the genial Edward VII had died at Buckingham Palace after a series of heart attacks.

WINDSOR

George V

(1910-1936)

Last Years of Peace (1910-1914)

The new king, George V, was almost forty-five. As the second son of Edward VII he had pursued a career as a naval officer for fifteen years until 1892, when his elder brother, the sickly Duke of Clarence, died and he became heir to the throne. As a result of his years in the Senior Service, George V was sensible, businesslike and disciplined. He had a great sense of the empire, much of which he had visited on duty tours. To mark his becoming Emperor of India at the end of his coronation year, he gave a magnificent Durbar, or gathering, at Delhi. George's wife was Princess Mary of Teck. The granddaughter of one of George IV's brothers, the Duke of Cambridge, she had been born and brought up in England. They had six sons and daughters.

Hard-working and realistic, after his father's funeral George V called a round-table Constitutional Conference with all the party leaders to seek a consensus on what should be done about the Parliament Bill. But, with no agreement reached and reluctant to see the crown interfere in politics, the Liberals decided on a second election. George V insisted that the bill should actually be voted on by the House of Lords before Asquith called a new election, in order for the Conservative peers to propose alternative suggestions. But the king also agreed, as William IV had done in the crisis over the 1832 Reform Bill, to create around 250 peers to swing the Parliament Bill through the second chamber if the Lords rejected it.

In December 1910 the Liberal government's position was reaffirmed. The electoral result was practically unchanged: the Liberals and the Unionists had the same number of seats, 272 each, the Irish Nationalists had 84, an increase of two, while Labour's share stood at 40. The new Parliament Bill passed its third reading in the House of Commons in May 1911 to great excitement and amid ungentlemanly scenes. The son of the Marquis of Salisbury, Lord Hugh Cecil, lost control of himself and heckled the prime minister so ferociously that he had to stop speaking. In the House of Lords a 'Die-Hard' group of peers started a last-ditch movement to get the peers to refuse the bill. But by July the message had got through.

However furious the Lords might be about their ancient rights being trampled underfoot, the threat of being swamped ensured that by August 1911 enough had abstained for the bill to pass.

But there was yet more trouble for the government. An epidemic of strikes paralysed the country throughout the summer. Agitation and vituperation had surrounded the Parliament Bill. There was a feeling of alarm at the changing nature of things – not everyone in Britain was progressively minded, as the last elections had made clear. Then suddenly, at the end of June, a serious war scare began.

The German government had sent a gunboat, the *Panther*, to seize the port of Agadir in Morocco. Over the previous couple of years, German relations with Britain had improved under a new German chancellor, Bethmann-Hollweg, for he was intent on breaking up the over-cosy relationship between France, Britain and Russia. The kaiser himself had appeared to be in a more friendly mood, even visiting London in the early summer of 1911 for the unveiling of a memorial to his grandmother Queen Victoria. But, after the naval panic of 1909 and the generally threatening stance of the German government, the *Panther* could have meant anything. During the seventeen days when the German government refused to disclose its intentions, the world held its breath.

Rumours abounded that Germany was preparing for war and about to march through Belgium. Reports of the military camps in Germany, where the peacetime army approached a million men, and the increased number of German soldiers up against the Belgian frontier did nothing to dispel this. The strange elongated railway platforms, which could only have been built for troops, along the German frontier with Belgium had long been noticed by the British military. An Official Secrets Act was brought in for the first time to protect against the spying known to be going on in the dockyards and all over the country. The letters of anyone suspected of getting orders from Germany were opened.

The year 1911 saw the hottest summer for forty years. London sweltered in the heat as anxiety mounted about what Germany would do next. What did she want; did she want war? So anxious was even the pacifist Cabinet about Germany having control of a port from which her warships could raid British ships moving into the Mediterranean or across the Atlantic that it warned that Britain would go to war if the *Panther* was not removed. The Germans began to back down. They made it clear that they did not desire war with Britain or with anyone else. The *Panther* gunboat turned out to be their undiplomatic response to the French breaching the international agreement at Algeçiras that Morocco should be a free-trade area. Taking advantage of internal unrest there, the French were moving to annex the colony. Germany thought her commercial interests were being ignored by the French. The *Panther* was her way of asserting her right to interfere in Morocco if she chose.

In September, as negotiations went on with Germany, Britain was nevertheless believed to be so close to hostilities that soldiers were sent to guard the south-eastern railway lines. There was considerable anxiety about the strength of the French army, as its manpower was only three-quarters of the Germans. The once dim shape of conflict was becoming clearer. In November the Agadir crisis was over. The Germans had been given some more territory, 100,000 square miles in the Congo, so that the *Panther* could be withdrawn. But by 1912 the British military establishment had become immovably pessimistic about Germany's future intentions. Haldane, who had pushed Britain into a state of greater military preparedness with a General Staff and the British Expeditionary Force, had in 1911 insisted on a War Book being drawn up. This was a plan for each government department setting out the procedures they should follow in the event of war. Another attempt at ending the naval race between Britain and Germany by a reduction in ships had foundered. The proposed German limitations were not large enough, and they were dependent on Britain ending her Entente with France and Russia and making an alliance with Germany only. To that Sir Edward Grey, the foreign secretary, could not agree.

After Grey had turned down the German offer, the German naval estimates for 1912 were larger than ever. Britain's reaction was to remove, very ostentatiously, the whole of her magnificent battle fleet from Toulon and away from the Mediterranean. Henceforth the two navies of the Anglo-French Entente were to divide the guarding of their respective waters between them. The French were to be responsible for the Mediterranean, while the British were to protect the Channel and North Sea.

The military links between the French and English governments became soldered together. Unknown to most of the Cabinet except for the foreign secretary and the prime minister Asquith, in 1912 France and England began to share military secrets and to second staff to one another's armies.

Morally speaking there was now an alliance in all but name: an attack by Germany on France's Channel ports or her northern and western coasts must, in the French view, bring Britain into the war. But the British government nevertheless refused to make it official. British public opinion would not allow the country to fight for France if France attacked Germany first. Three-quarters of the Liberal Cabinet were pacifists who would not countenance an alliance with France, and the government continued to wish not to alarm Germany with an alliance she would perceive as aimed at her. If it did come to war, the two Entente governments would meet to hammer out what would be their next move, whether in fact they would act together. With this curious position the French had to be content. But the actions of the Liberal government spoke louder than words. Early in 1912, spurred by the Agadir crisis, Asquith set up the Invasion Committee of the Committee of Imperial Defence, which met off and on until 1914. Discussions on how to get troops to France began to absorb government attention.

The Agadir episode had been seen by other countries as a sign that force was rewarded, that aggression paid. During September 1911 when the Admiralty was quarrelling with the army about war procedure (the Admiralty wanted the army to stay offshore in boats while most of the battles were fought at sea), Italy successfully invaded Tripoli in north Africa. She had no difficulty in swiftly defeating its nominal overlord Turkey, which was racked by the chaos of a new regime. Italy's success gave hope to all the unsatisfied Balkan countries for their own war against Turkey.

Against this background of international lawlessness the peaceful fabric of British life, which had successfully survived the upheavals of the industrial revolution, frayed to breaking point. The trade unions, the suffragettes, the Conservative and Ulster Unionists, all one way and another were dissatisfied by too many or too few government reforms. Despite the Parliament Bill, many of the more recent elements in politics – the working classes, the trade unionists and the militant suffragettes – were disappointed by the slow nature of the Parliamentary process. All broke with traditional or legal methods of expressing themselves; anarchy loomed.

During 1912–14 Britain was swept by a series of national strikes that almost brought the country to her knees. Labour had lost 25 per cent of their seats at the January 1910 election. From fifty-three MPs their numbers went down to forty. It confirmed the blue-collar workers' disillusionment with Parliament as a way of addressing their concerns. The single-ballot system was weighted against a third party, which made it hard for Labour to get elected, and its supporters felt that they were not being represented in numbers proportionate to the Labour party membership. This bitterness was aggravated after 1909 when sixteen Labour MPs had to go without salaries after the Osborne case had dried up the party's funds. The Liberal-supporting railwayman W. V. Osborne had successfully challenged his trade union's compulsory levy to the Labour party, the Law Lords ruling that trade unions could no longer provide for Parliamentary representation by a compulsory levy. In 1911 the Liberals remedied this when they instituted the payment of MPs, a Chartist demand since the 1840s.

But the damage was done. The optimism which the historic number of Labour MPs in Parliament had created turned to anger when they appeared to make so little difference. Hardship remained widespread for many industrial workers. Wages had remained the same from the beginning of the century, even though prices and the cost of living had risen. People wanted instant solutions, which the threat of stoppages provided. Thanks to Labour pressure, laws relating to strike action had recently been relaxed. As a result the country was rocked by them. To the short-sighted they seemed an easier route to power than Parliament; some trade unionists came under the influence of the French Trade Union or Syndicalist movement which distrusted Parliamentary methods, preferring the strike as a method of operation. The Syndicalists looked to a Utopian future where trade unions would form the basic unit of society.

In 1910 the government reluctantly used troops against miners in the Rhondda Valley in South Wales who had attacked a pithead to get more pay. At first it sent only London policemen. The Liberals were disturbed by the thought of using soldiers in industrial disputes, believing that the owners were frequently as unreasonable as the men. But the use of troops deepened the unions' sense of grievance. During the summer of 1911, in the midst of the Agadir crisis, another rash of strikes by the seamen's, firemen's and dockers' unions brought the Port of London to a standstill until there were pay rises all round. It was followed by what was very nearly a national railway strike to protest against the deaths of two rioting dockers in Liverpool fired on by soldiers. The strike shut down most of the industrial midlands for four days. So tense was the situation, and so great was the fear of revolutionary action, that troops were brought into the centre of London. In the blistering heat their tents crowded the dried-up lawns of St James's Park, Hyde Park and Kensington Gardens, which were more usually thronged with prams. But Lloyd George was skilful in his handling of the union. The new leader of the Parliamentary Labour party, Ramsay MacDonald, joined the negotiations and the railway strike ended with no recriminations and no job losses.

Permanent machinery was set up to sort out the railwaymen's grievances. The generally sympathetic treatment the unions received helped ensure that, despite talks between the dockers, the miners and the railwaymen about a general strike, in Britain strikes never became a revolutionary instrument for social change. In 1912 after a new miners' strike for a minimum wage, when the intransigence of the owners prevented attempts to fix it mutually at local level, the Liberals passed a minimum-wage bill. By 1913 there was still less room for discontent when the government rescinded the Osborne judgement. The 1913 Trade Union Act made it legal for trade union levies to be spent on politics as long as members were canvassed for their views. Any member of a different political persuasion could decline to contribute.

The strikes petered out, but London was now subjected to an arson campaign. This was conducted by a militant branch of the suffragette movement, the Women's Social and Political Union, or WSPU, founded in 1903 when the Independent Labour party failed to include women's suffrage in their programme. It was run by the charismatic Mrs Emmeline Pankhurst and her daughters Sylvia and Christabel; Christabel had been prevented from reading for the bar, despite her law degree, because she was of the female sex.

Suffragette march in Hyde Park, 23 July 1910. It was not until 1918 that women over thirty could vote in Parliamentary elections. In 1928, the voting age for women became twenty-one, on a par with men.

The 1907 Qualification of Women Act allowed women, married or single, to be councillors, aldermen or mayors and to sit on county and borough councils, but the Parliamentary vote continued to be denied them. Thousands of women marched for the vote, but nothing was done. Mrs Pankhurst, her daughters and other suffragettes were imprisoned several times for causing public disorder when they heckled Liberal election rallies. Two attempts at franchise reform failed, the first because the Liberal government would not introduce a bill to enfranchise single women with property, as that would mean increasing the vote of the traditionally Conservative spinster. In frustration the Pankhursts decided to abandon constitutional means.

Letterboxes, a school, a railway station were set on fire. The British Museum was attacked, as was the orchid house at Kew. The suffragettes even went for the Tower of London. Across England members of the society, who numbered around 40,000 women, hoisted up the long skirts that continued to be *de rigueur* in the early twentieth century and stole out after dark to cut telephone wires. They even tied themselves to the railings of 10 Downing Street. Soon several hundred suffragettes were locked up in Holloway Women's Prison. Moreover, once the suffragettes were incarcerated they went on hunger strike. As some began to die, the anxious prison authorities turned to force feeding. But there were fears about its legality. In desperation the home secretary Reginald McKenna introduced the so-called Cat and Mouse Act, which allowed hunger strikers to be released and to be rearrested without further proceedings once they had recovered at home. One of the Pankhurst suffragettes, the forty-one-year-old Emily Davison, threw herself under George V's horse at the 1913 Derby and died from her injuries. The WSPU's extremism alienated many more moderate campaigners for women's suffrage like the veteran campaigner Emily Davies, one of the founders of Girton College, Cambridge. When Christabel Pankhurst escaped to Paris after a warrant was issued for her arrest, much of the agitation died down.

Within Britain there was a growing sense of despondency. The confidence which had been so manifest in 1906 was ebbing away, chased by vague but prevalent fears about a coming conflagration. The sinking of the *Titanic* in 1912 by an iceberg underlined the frailty even of modern man and his engineering. Even more haunting to the pre-1914 imagination was the fate of Captain Scott's expedition to the South Pole. Nature was not tamed as easily as the twentieth century thought.

At Christmas 1912 Captain Robert Scott and four others including Captain Lawrence Oates reached the South Pole, only to discover that the Norwegian Roald Amundsen had beaten them to it. When the frostbite on Oates's feet began to endanger the expedition's progress, Oates sacrificed himself for his friends by walking out of his tent into the blizzard. 'I am just going outside and may be some time,' he said. His body was never found, but his words became revered for their very British understatement. Captain Scott and the rest of the expedition failed to reach the food depot they were seeking. When an Antarctic search party at last reached them in November 1913 it was to find them dead in their tents several miles away. Beside Scott's body was the journal in which he detailed Oates's heroic end.

Even the Asquith government, which had taken power as the essence of probity and high-mindedness, was rocked by financial scandal. The telegraph signal company Marconi was awarded the contract to provide a radio service throughout the empire under the aegis of the Post Office. But in 1912 it was alleged that both the postmaster-general Herbert Samuel and the attorney-general Sir Rufus Isaacs held shares in the company and had not declared their interest. Both parties were cleared of insider dealing, Samuel outright and Isaacs because he had only bought shares from the American branch of the company after Marconi had won the contract. However, the secretary of the American company turned out to be Isaacs' brother. The suspicion that Rufus Isaacs had used his influence to secure the contract for Marconi would not go away. There was a feeling that something underhand had been going on, even if it could not quite be pinned down. The affair left a cloud over the Liberals.

Above all, Asquith was unable to control the situation in Ireland. Since 1912 when preparations for the Third Home Rule Bill began, Sir Edward Carson, the formidable solicitor-general in the last Conservative government, and the MP James Craig had assembled a private Protestant army named the Ulster Volunteers to resist Home Rule in Ulster. Now that the automatic Unionist majority in the Lords could no longer prevent Home Rule, they would put their trust in force. Andrew Bonar Law, the inexperienced leader of the Conservatives and Unionists who succeeded Balfour, encouraged this lawless behaviour. In a series of astonishing speeches, he pledged the Conservatives to defend Ulster physically against the British government if it tried to enforce Home Rule. He even went to Ireland to take the salute of the Ulster Unionist troops as they paraded.

On 28 September 1912 the whole of Belfast closed down to sign the Solemn League and Covenant to resist Home Rule. The hooting sirens of the shipyards and the machines of the factories stopped as nearly 500,000 people lined up to sign the pledge by which they refused to recognize the authority of any Home Rule Parliament. Most of Ulster seemed to be armed. Many of the men signed the pledge in their own blood.

But, although half of Ulster, the Protestants, was against Home Rule, the other half was Catholic and in favour of it. Moreover the head of the Irish Nationalist MPs, John Redmond, could not give up Ulster and Irish unity. By going for Home Rule instead of independence, Redmond had already sacrificed much. For the past few years his leadership had been challenged by Sinn Fein, the total-independence movement in Ireland, which had become notably popular in southern Ireland among blue-collar workers politicized during a series of strikes in 1912 and 1913. In Dublin an army of strikers called the Irish Volunteers had grown up under two leaders, James Connolly and James Larkin, who had none of Redmond's scruples about violence. The Irish Volunteers started drilling like the Ulster Volunteers. By 1914 they were 100,000 strong, and a third of them were in the north.

As the situation in northern and southern Ireland became more intemperate, with both sides plotting to import arms, the Home Rule Bill was passed twice by the House of Commons and thrown out twice by the House of Lords. But, by the autumn of 1913 as Home Rule came closer to implementation, the government was becoming increasingly uneasy at the idea of imposing Home Rule on Ulster. Perhaps it would be impossible to coerce Ulster; in any case it was very unLiberal to coerce anyone.

Under George V's aegis, discussions were opened between all parties at Balmoral to discuss the possibility of excluding Ulster. Redmond reluctantly agreed to partition, angering many of the Sinn Feiners and further weakening his position with the Irish Volunteers. The question was, where should the exclusion line run? The talks continued throughout the winter of 1913–14, while the two illegal armies of southern and northern Irish drilled regardless.

The apparent favouring of the Unionist side was epitomized by the government turning a blind eye to what was called the Larne gun-running in April 1914 when the Ulstermen landed 30,000 rifles and a million rounds of ammunition. The police and coastguards made no real attempt to stop the operation. But in July that year, when the Irish Volunteers landed guns at Howth near Dublin, troops were called out to stop them. Protesters threw things at troops in Dublin, provoking the soldiers to fire into the crowds, killing three and wounding forty more. This more than ever aggravated relations between Dublin and Westminster, and between Redmond and the Irish Volunteers.

Meanwhile the very loyalty of the army in Ireland had been called into question. The commander-in-chief of the army in Ireland, Sir Arthur Paget, who had strong Unionist sympathies, had chosen to ignore the tradition that the British army was apolitical and that its first duty was to obey the civilian government. In an episode known as the Curragh 'mutiny' after the area where the army was based, in March 1914 Paget told officers that he could not order those who disapproved of Home Rule, especially if their homes were in the north, to impose it on Ulster. He recommended that those who did not wish to coerce Ulster should resign from the army. No fewer than fifty officers out of seventy said they would resign if ordered north.

The secretary for war who had encouraged Paget's extraordinary dereliction of duty was sacked after this became public. Nevertheless the officers concerned could not be court-martialled, as there was an increasing anxiety at top government levels that some kind of war was not far off. The atmosphere in Europe in late May 1914 to an American observer Colonel House was 'militarism run stark mad'. The French had vastly added to their conscripts. There were constant rumours that the German army was the real force behind its country's foreign policy, that it had insisted on a war tax and had called in all foreign loans.

May and June passed. In May it seemed that a way out of the Irish impasse had been found. It was a typical piece of Lloyd George cunning: there would be an amendment to the Home Rule Bill that any county, if a majority of its voters agreed, could vote itself out of Home Rule for six years. The Nationalists concurred, but the House of Lords insisted on changing the amendment: the whole of Ulster must be excluded from Home Rule without a time limit. However, when the altered bill returned to the Commons on 14 July, the government's attention was shifting away from the passions of Ireland to the wider world.

For on 28 June the heir to the Austro-Hungarian Empire, the archduke Franz Ferdinand, had been assassinated by a Bosnian Serb in Sarajevo. Austria–Hungary had long been wanting to crush the Serbs. With her military establishment hot to strike, she was using the excuse to reach the brink of war. The question was, would she drag all the other allied nations of Europe in with her? Anxious telegrams flew between the chancelleries of Europe.

While the world once more held its breath, discussions on the Irish Home Rule Bill pressed on. The bill could not be accepted by the Commons in its amended state, but there had to be a resolution to the crisis. So uncompromising was the atmosphere that at Asquith's instigation on 18 July another round-table conference was called at Buckingham Palace. Redmond and the Nationalists accepted the exclusion of Ulster, and the Unionists agreed to Home Rule for the rest of Ireland. But the conference broke down over the counties of Fermanagh and Tyrone. With their equally mixed Catholic and Protestant populations, should they be part of northern or southern Ireland? The drilling continued in both parts of the country. Though there was as yet no civil war, the threat remained. However, the whole matter was overtaken by events in the outside world. The conference broke up without conclusion, to reconvene in the autumn. Just as its members were rising from their seats, the foreign secretary Sir Edward Grey came in, carrying the ultimatum which Austria–Hungary had sent to Serbia on 24 July. Although Serbia replied in the most abject manner, Austria–Hungary broke off relations and began to bombard her capital, Belgrade. It was the beginning of the First World War.

In September 1914, when Parliament returned after Britain had declared war in August, the position of the Irish Home Rule Bill was still fraught with confusion. The bill was meant to become law, as was a bill disestablishing the Welsh Church, because they had both successfully passed three times through the House of Commons. Although no agreement over Ulster had been reached, Asquith at first announced that the exclusion of Ulster should be added to the bill. When the Irish Home Rulers, whose seats the Liberals continued to rely on for their majority, refused to countenance this, Asquith said that the bill would have to go on to the statute book in its original form. At this the Unionists left the House of Commons in protest. Irish Home Rule and the disestablishment of the Welsh Church went on to the statute book, but with another act tacked on to them suspending both bills from coming into operation until six months after the end of the war. The issue was thus shelved.

But now we must return to the outbreak of the First World War, or the Great War as it was originally known – or, as the Fabian writer H. G. Wells and its more hopeful participants called it, the War that Will End War. Before 1914 the peace in Europe had been fragile, but it had held, partly because a great deal was done to placate Germany, partly because Germany herself refrained from hostilities. She had made herself extremely unpopular with France and Britain by continually threatening war, but she had not actually brought it about.

Despite Britain's distrust of German intentions, she continued until 1913 to try to convince Germany of her friendliness. That year another attempt had been made at calming down the atmosphere by offering a twelve-month 'naval holiday' between the two countries, but that was turned down. By 1914 Lloyd George had made the speech warning off the *Panther*, and three-quarters of the government had reverted to their old radical pacifist colours. They believed that the best hope of peace was for Britain to reduce the number of ships built.

Agreements were reached in Germany's favour about longstanding disputes over colonies in Africa, the Baghdad railway and the Persian Gulf. Despite the close relationship between the French and British military, Britain still would not enter into an official alliance with France and Russia because Grey did not want to inflame the situation with Germany. This would later be criticized on the ground that, if Britain had shown she intended to fight for France, Germany would never have gone to war.

However, in 1913 there was a tremendous upset in the Balkans which completely altered the power structure there in Russia's favour. When under Russian auspices the Balkan League Wars reduced European Turkey to a tiny corner thirty miles wide, and made Russia's influence paramount at Constantinople, some kind of war over the Balkans looked unavoidable. Kept out of central Asia and the Persian Gulf by the Entente with Britain, and out of China after her defeat by Japan in 1904, Russia had been forced back on her old stamping ground, the Balkans. She was the Slav nationalities' traditional champion. She decided to concentrate once more on her old objective of being the favoured power at Constantinople and controlling the Dardanelles, that vital conduit between her ships and ports on the Black Sea and the Aegean–Mediterranean.

But this threatened both the ambitions of Germany to expand into the

Middle East, because it put in doubt the Berlin-to-Baghdad railway which was projected to run straight through Constantinople, and the very existence of the Austro-Hungarian Empire. What made war in the near future imperative for that empire was the imminent threat to her from Serbia. In 1908 the Serbs had been prevented from attacking Austria–Hungary by Russia's weakness and Germany's strength. They had sulkily obeyed German diplomats' warning to put an end to the Serbian propaganda in government-sponsored newspapers and disarmed their gathering troops. But after Serbia's victories in 1913, which had doubled her size, all the Serb areas of the Habsburg Empire were in a fever of nationalist excitement.

It was quite evident to Austria that Serbia was no longer to be restrained by what the great powers wanted. From 1913 on, Serbian irredentism or expansionism expressed in endless newspaper articles was demanding a war to gather to the Serbian motherland the six million Serbs spread throughout the Austro-Hungarian Empire. Moreover Serbia had not only doubled in size but she had shown that her soldiers could defeat the German-trained Turkish troops, who were supposed to be the best in the Balkans. There was a real danger that in a war with the empire Serbia might win. The situation seemed so menacing that scarcely had the Balkan War peace treaties been signed than Austria–Hungary had decided that the moment had come to attack Serbia. Backed by Italy, Germany managed to restrain Austria–Hungary. The war never took place because Germany was the one ally Austria–Hungary could not move without. So, despite all the fears that Europe had about Germany, it was Germany which prevented war in 1913.

Just the same, the threat of an impending clash in the Balkans remained. Strategists in the armies of three great powers, Russia, Austria–Hungary and Germany, believed that a war for influence would come at some point. Thus when in July 1914 two Bosnian Serbs assassinated the heir to the Austro–Hungarian Empire, the archduke Ferdinand, it both seemed to be the signal that the Serbs were about to attack the empire and the perfect excuse for Austria–Hungary to fight a limited war to scotch 'the nest of vipers' – as her generals called Serbia. This time, in 1914, Germany did little to hold her back.

It was an alarming situation and desperate remedies seemed called for. Given her paranoid fears Germany could not afford to let her only ally be broken up by Serb nationalists. Many of the top generals in both the Austro-Hungarian and the German armies viewed some kind of limited preventive war in the Balkans as a solution to their difficulties, while they had the military advantage in armaments and personnel. The general European balance would be tilted against Germany and Austria–Hungary within a few years. But, for now, the army of Serbia's chief ally, Russia, was still in the throes of modernization. A group of General Staff officers within the German army did much to convince their government that this would be a good time for that limited war in order to assert German influence in the Balkans. The kaiser told the emperor Franz Joseph that Austria–Hungary had his support.

But the idea of a limited war was a chimera. Serbia's ally Russia had too much at stake not to begin her laborious process of mobilization. That decision inevitably dragged France into the war. When Russia would not cancel the orders for mobilization, Germany declared war on Russia on 1 August and on France on the 2nd. War plans drawn up in 1905 took precedence over common sense: the German plan was predicated on attacking France and defeating her within six weeks, then turning east to dispose of Russia.

After the worldwide slaughter that ensued, for the war was anything but local, some members of the pre-war German government claimed they had hoped Britain would restrain Russia from mobilizing. The British ambassador had in fact pleaded with Russia not to do so. But the complex system of alliances had a series of automatic consequences. As one writer put it, 'the guns went off by themselves'.

For Britain, declaring war was less simple. She was legally bound by treaty to defend Belgium, whose existence she had guaranteed at her birth in 1839 and reaffirmed in 1870 during the Franco-Prussian War. The Anglo-French naval arrangements which had the British guarding the Channel for both countries surely made war with Germany inevitable. But, until German troops actually advanced into Belgium, Grey was doubtful that his Cabinet and British public opinion would agree to war. The most he could tell the French ambassador was that the German fleet would not be allowed into the Channel. The army and navy nevertheless sent out their secret code and signal books to the French, albeit with an embargo on their use.

The pacifist element in Cabinet remained so powerful that when Churchill, the first lord of the Admiralty, insisted on calling out the fleet reserves, eight or nine ministers said it was unnecessary. Fortunately for Britain the maverick and impulsive genius Churchill had decided earlier in the week that the international situation looked so alarming that he should quietly send the portion of the fleet not needed to guard the Channel to hide at its 'war station' up above Britain in the secret harbour of the Orkneys, Scapa Flow. The main fleet was thus out of the way of surprise attack by German torpedoes.

Meanwhile there was no certainty about how the Belgians would respond if asked to allow German troops to pass through their country to

France. Many in the Cabinet thought Belgium might not resist. There was even a suspicion that there was a secret agreement between Belgium and Germany to allow the German armies free passage into France. Thanks to the atrocities in the Congo, Belgium's stock was not high; a secret agreement would explain why there was such a high level of German military preparations all along the Belgo-German border. Nevertheless, after much argument, a majority of the Cabinet finally agreed that violation of Belgian neutrality would bring Britain into the war.

By evening that Sunday, 2 August, war for Britain suddenly seemed very near. It was then that a twelve-hour ultimatum was handed to the Belgian government by the Germans requesting that their armies be allowed to pass through its territories into north-eastern France. But the new Belgian king Albert I was of a very different calibre to his uncle Leopold II. On Monday, 3 August the Belgians, led by their king, refused to allow the German armies in. They would fight. King Albert sent a telegram to George V personally appealing for help.

That afternoon Grey made an eloquent speech to the House of Commons which both explained Britain's legal obligations to Belgium and argued the case for intervention, for only Parliament could decide whether Britain went to war. He described the Channel guarantee to France, and requested all present to ask themselves what friendship or Entente meant when that friend was threatened by a foe like Germany. He did not believe that, even if Britain stood aside, she would be in a position after the war to undo what had happened in the course of it, to prevent the whole of western Europe falling under the domination of a single power. And he added, 'I am quite sure that our moral position would be such as to have lost us all respect.'

In the House of Commons Bonar Law and the Conservatives gave their support. John Redmond, the leader of the Irish Nationalists, also pledged his MPs to Grey. Support for war became unanimous, other than among Labour MPs, many of whom remained true to their pacifist roots. Grey had not argued the case for intervention in a spirit of enthusiasm. He believed that this war could lead to the destruction of civilization. 'The lamps are going out all over Europe; we shall not see them lit again in our lifetime,' he said that evening as he stood by the window of the Foreign Office.

The next day the order was given to mobilize the reserves. Britain still had not declared war. A twelve-hour ultimatum was given to Germany, which had invaded Belgium that morning. If Germany did not withdraw from Belgium and respect her neutrality, she would be at war with Great Britain. On the very hot night of 4 August at 11 p.m. Greenwich Mean Time, twelve o'clock in Berlin, the British ultimatum ran out. Outside the

Houses of Parliament a crowd had gathered; just before eleven it began to sing 'God Save the King'. As Big Ben tolled, the deadline expired without a single German soldier moving out of Belgium. Soon afterwards and all through the night, messages flashed halfway across the world in code telling the British Empire that it was at war with Germany.

As day broke on 5 August, thanks to Haldane the six divisions of the British Expeditionary Force under its commander-in-chief John French were ready to land in France. Fourteen territorial divisions were deputed to guard the British Isles. The immediate problem, however, was to get the six regular divisions across the Channel. This took from 9 to 22 August. For three days, when the crossing was at its height, the fleet stood guard. The operation was extremely tense, owing to fears that the troopships would be torpedoed by the Germans, but nothing happened. The Grand Fleet sailed back unscathed to its hideaway position above Britain at Scapa Flow. By the 24th British troops were in the middle of France and had begun fighting the Germans.

Lord Kitchener, the new secretary of state for war, warned against optimism. Unlike other British generals, he said that the struggle would not be over in a few weeks but might take several years. In his view the war could be won only by battles fought on land, not by seapower. A huge recruiting drive would be immediately necessary to supplement the army by half a million male volunteers. It was a mark of Liberal Britain that even in these desperate times it was believed the population would not stand for conscription.

At the outbreak of the First World War Britain faced major problems. Unlike those of the central powers, as Austria–Hungary and Germany became known, her economy was not geared for war. For this was a war that she had been conspicuously reluctant to wage and had done almost everything to avoid. Even if she recruited enough men for 'Kitchener's Army' she did not have enough guns, nor enough factories to produce guns, nor enough shells to arm them.

Today we can see that commercial and colonial rivalries created impossible stresses between the great powers and were among the most important underlying causes of the First World War. On the other hand, to those alive at the time the most striking feature about the pre-war world was the sense of menace which emanated from united Germany and her militaristic culture. Even though Austria had begun the war, Germany was assumed to be responsible. The consensus in most British households was that Germany had been wanting a war, and with the First World War she got it.

The First World War (1914–1918)

The British professional army, the highly trained 150,000-strong British Expeditionary Force (BEF), went straight to France, but the immense portion of the earth covered by the British Empire meant that British military operations took place all over the globe. Two million soldiers from the empire were occupied in what were called sideshows separate from the main action – British armies fought to take over the German colonies in Africa, and troops were poured into the Middle Eastern section of the Ottoman Empire, to protect the Suez Canal and India after Turkey had declared war on the side of the central powers in October 1914.

When the war finally ended, after four years of immense suffering, France and Britain divided between them much of the old Ottoman Empire which their armies were occupying. The British Empire was larger than ever, for Britain added Mesopotamia, renamed Iraq in 1921, and Palestine to her realms in an unofficial form of imperialism, what one historian has called the 'scramble for Turkey'. Britain for thirty years became an influential power in the Middle East. But it was an illusion. The expense of the First World War ruined British global hegemony, along with that of France, and made way for America's emergence as a superpower. The post-war settlement was really France's and Britain's last hurrah as the great imperial powers they had been for the previous 200 years. Despite Britain's celebrated naval superiority, which cast a cordon round Germany and began to starve her to death, despite the courage of the immense French armies, what finally tipped the balance and won the First World War was not those nations, but the industrial might and money of America.

The first few months of the First World War determined the shape of what became known as the western front, the location of a three-and-a-half-year campaign by British, French and British Empire troops to keep the Germans from overrunning France. As we have seen, the German military strategy, the Schlieffen Plan, was predicated on France being conquered in six weeks, before the old-fashioned Russian war machine had been completely mobilized. However, the plan, which was intended to prevent the German armies fighting a war on two fronts, was not fulfilled.

In August 1914 the immense fortresses guarding Belgium's frontier had been as much use as toy forts in stopping the German war machine. Over a million German soldiers swept through Belgium and swarmed over north-eastern France. But their progress was considerably held up at the Battle of Mons on 23 August by the BEF, which the Kaiser had called a 'contemptible little army'. And though by early September, to the horror of the inhabitants of Paris (many of whom remembered the 1870–1 Siege of Paris), the German armies were within forty miles of the French capital, the war in France was not the lightning strike and rolling up of the French

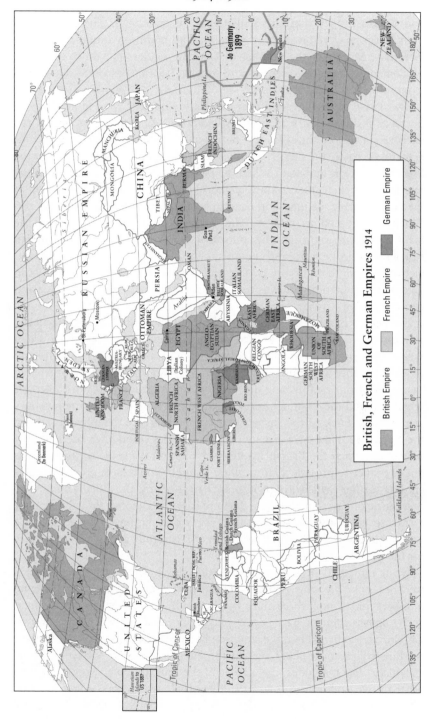

British, French and German Empires 1914

British Empire
French Empire
German Empire

and British armies that the Schlieffen Plan envisaged. The British and French troops were far more of a match than had been anticipated by the Germans. Moreover the number of German soldiers in France had been weakened by the need to send troops to what became known as the eastern front to deal with the Russians.

The Russians had invaded East Prussia before they were quite ready to do so as a diversionary tactic to help France. As a result, at one of the decisive battles of the war, the Battle of the Marne between 6 and 12 September 1914, the German armies' encircling manoeuvre to pen in the French army was defeated. When the German troops were attacked in the rear by the French chief of staff General Joffre with the BEF, the roll-up of the French armies around Paris had to be abandoned because General von Kluck was forced to retreat. The victory of the Marne wrecked the Schlieffen Plan right at the outset. Until 1917, when the Russian Revolution broke out and Lenin's new government sued for peace, Germany had to fight on two fronts, which was what she had been determined to avoid. She was never able to turn her back on France and concentrate on Russia.

Furthermore, a key ingredient of the original Schlieffen Plan had been abandoned – striking at France through Holland as well as through Belgium – which shortened the defensive line. An attack through Holland would probably have outflanked Belgian resistance and so have prevented the British from establishing defensive positions from Ypres to the coast, which secured the Channel ports for them. As it was, the German armies were pushed back to the Aisne river, and had to race the allied armies to the North Sea. Had the Germans arrived first this could have had a doubly disastrous effect: the British would have had to take some of their troops out of France to provide a Home Guard, and it would have prevented their landing further British troops in France to reinforce the allied armies. The first Battle of Ypres in Flanders, Belgium from 19 October to 11 November 1914 prevented this, at the cost of literally decimating, that is killing one in ten soldiers of the BEF, the young men so carefully groomed for warfare for the previous seven years.

What remained of both armies settled down to sit out the winter in trenches opposite one another. There they would remain in growing numbers for the next three and a half years. By the end of the war German and English soldiers had begun playing football with one another at Christmas, so surreal had the situation become. The trenches – the form of warfare which most characterized the First World War – were a visible stalemate. The two sides, the allies and the central powers, opposed each other in two continuous lines of soldiers sheltered in deep ditch dugouts. These trenches ran from the coast of Belgium, dipped south into industrial northern France and skimmed the French border with Alsace and Lorraine until they reached the frontier of Switzerland.

In December 1914 the war became real to the people of Scarborough, Whitby and Hartlepool, when they were bombarded by German warships. It was the first enemy assault on British civilians since Charles II's reign, when the Dutch fleet sailed up the Medway. By Christmas one million men of all shapes and beliefs had volunteered for the British army to defend their homeland. They were inspired by Lord Kitchener's recruiting campaign, not least the famous poster of Kitchener pointing his finger at the observer with the legend beneath, 'Your country needs YOU'.

By 1916, when conscription was brought in, as many as two and a half million Britons had volunteered to fight. After a short training in how to handle a gun they crossed the Channel to reinforce the trenches – often organized in neighbourhood battalions. For the first time ever Britain put an enormous land army into the field to prevent the Germans overrunning France. The Kitchener armies were indispensable. By the end of 1915 the old professional army, 150,000 soldiers, had been wiped out.

Over the next three years more than a million French, British and empire troops died in the trenches, often for just a few feet of land. Keeping the line steady took a terrible toll in lives. The only way the French and British could move forward and drive the Germans out, or the Germans move forward into France, was by colossal artillery barrages to clear the enemy. Then the infantry would leap out of their trenches and charge 'over the top'. The line never moved more than about twenty miles east or west, and it never really broke until 1917. It merely bulged until other men were rushed in to close the gaps.

The flower of the rising generation died and were hastily buried in the earth of Flanders. Those battlefields, or slaughterfields, destroyed many of the best and bravest who had volunteered early, unhappily for Britain in the 1920s and 1930s. The number of junior officers killed – that is, the ablest young soldiers – was especially high because so much of the action required leading from the front to take out machine-gun nests.

On the eastern front, on the other side of Europe, things did not look more promising despite the enormous numbers of Russian troops and their proverbial stoicism. The gallantry of the Russian attack on East Prussia helped save Paris and the allies, but during battles at Tannenberg at the end of August 1914, and then in early September by the Masurian Lakes, 250,000 Russians were killed. The strategy of two brilliant German officers, Generals von Hindenburg and Ludendorff, produced a triumph for their armies. Though the Russians overran the Austrian province of Galicia, by the summer of 1915 the Germans had thrown them back to the Duna river.

The Ottoman Empire had entered the war in the hope of retrieving Egypt and Cyprus from Britain. It thus posed a threat to the Suez Canal, and an additional 250,000 empire troops had to be sent to guard it. British and French troops began attacking the Turks all over their Middle Eastern empire. Indian troops provided the bulk of the soldiers for the campaign in Mesopotamia (today's Iraq) which began in 1915, though they were forced to surrender in 1916 after being besieged at Kut-el-amara on the Tigris.

In May 1915 Italy declared for the allies, after weighing up what she would get out of the war and having already had her differences with the Ottoman Empire when she seized Tripoli. She had always had close links with England and she intended after the war to consolidate her Risorgimento by taking more territory from Austria. In the secret Treaty of London of 26 April the allies had assured Italy that she would gain the southern Tyrol, the Trentino, Istria and the Dalmatian coast. Bulgaria, which might have joined the allies, came in on the German side and successfully invaded Serbia in October.

Nineteen-fifteen was not a good year for the allies. Britain, which was so entirely dependent on her colonies for food, began to have her shipping sunk by German torpedoes and submarines. Submarine warfare was a naval innovation in whose development Germany had taken the lead. The first Zeppelins, pneumatic grey airships in the sky, appeared over London in May and thereafter became one of the features of the war, attacking many British cities. A mass onslaught was carried out by fourteen German airships from the Humber to the Thames in September 1916.

There were also raids by aircraft. The first British plane had flown in 1908 and the Frenchman Louis Blériot crossed the Channel in 1909. Although it was not until the next war that the Royal Air Force was to come into its own, by 1912 its predecessor – the Royal Flying Corps – had been established, and by 1914 around 120 aircraft, divided between the army and navy, were being used for reconnaissance. In April 1918 in response to the air-raids the Royal Air Force came into existence as a separate service.

Meanwhile the British public, already appalled at losing their sons, husbands and brothers in such numbers, were scandalized when commander-in-chief of the BEF, General Sir John French, announced that his men were dying for lack of shells. This was so whipped up by the press that it came to be widely believed that it was government inefficiency that was losing the war, and the Liberal administration was forced to enter a coalition in May 1915 with the Conservatives and some Labour MPs. But with the coalition's appointment of Lloyd George as minister of munitions the production of shells increased dramatically. The energy and ingenuity of the Welsh Wizard made him the dominant figure in the government, and he soon began running the war effort more or less single-handed. In a coup effected with the help of the Conservatives he would replace Asquith as prime minister at the end of the following year.

Lloyd George's rule of thumb, as he candidly revealed, was that all generals underestimated their soldiers' needs and never ordered enough shells: one should take what the generals ordered and multiply it by three. Thanks to enterprising manufacturers, many of whom were friends of Lloyd George, munitions factories were set up all over the country. Though unionized labour was inadequate for the numbers of shells required, unions were reluctant to allow dilution – that is, to have unskilled workers brought in. But Lloyd George made a deal with the unions: for the length of the war they would accept women and unskilled workers, provided that the position returned to normal at the end of the war. He also promised to restrict profits while the war was on and union rights were temporarily in abeyance; and the unions were to participate in deciding how their industries were run via workers' committees. The trade unions thus vastly increased their role, and doubled their membership, during the war. These arrangements – what Lloyd George called 'the great charter for labour' – were a stroke of genius. He had reassured factory workers, and the resulting enthusiasm for the war and for the government had the effect of increasing productivity. The charter lessened the danger from strikes, which might have bought about Britain's defeat – for the pre-war influence of syndicalism continued, even if it was temporarily overcome by patriotism.

But, despite the increased number of shells less than a year after Ypres the Battle of Loos between 25 September and 13 October 1915 killed 50,000 British soldiers. Britain was stunned. The nation was not used to deaths on this scale. The Germans began nerve-gas warfare using mustard gas. Gas masks became a feature of the war, something else to load down the poor Tommy, as the British soldier was nicknamed. Its victims frequently had to be sent home and often became lifelong invalids racked by uncontrollable nerve-storms.

The worst setback of 1915 was the Dardanelles catastrophe. The static nature of the western front and the troubles besetting Russia's armies, which were running low in munitions and food in the early part of the year, prompted Churchill and Lloyd George to conclude that another front should be opened somewhere to break the deadlock in the west. Lloyd George had hopes of a Balkan front based on Salonika to strike north against Austria–Hungary, but it was Churchill's proposal to land in the Dardanelles on the Gallipoli Peninsula that was taken up. The expeditionary force should seize Constantinople, remove the Ottoman Empire from the war and from there run supply lines to Russia through the Black Sea.

But this ingenious attempt to break away from the stalemate of the western front was poorly executed. Mines prevented British and French warships forcing the Dardanelles, and it was decided that only by landing troops could the peninsula be taken. That operation became the province of the British army. The naval attack which could have backed up the assault was, astonishingly enough, called off – as the entire operation should have been. Since it was quite obvious to the Turks what was about to happen, they moved their guns forward on to the cliffs above the allied soldiers. The 75,000-strong force, many of whom were Australian and New Zealanders, the Anzacs, were landed at the far end of the Gallipoli Peninsula. There they stayed, unable to advance because of the Turkish gun emplacements above them. For seven months, from 25 April (later designated Anzac Day) until December, when they were at last evacuated, the soldiers were stuck at Gallipoli. Many of them never managed to get off the beach, dying there as the Turkish guns picked them off like flies. The blame for their ordeal fell on Churchill, who fell from office.

The argument was to continue throughout the war between westerners – who believed that the main war effort should be concentrated on the western front, where the war would be won after a long siege – and the easterners – who believed that the western front was taking an intolerable toll on lives with very little to show for it. The catastrophe of Gallipoli gave a great fillip to the western-fronters.

The western front remained the chief arena of the world war, to which troops from the other theatres of war, the sideshows like the Middle East, would often be seconded when major force was needed. Nevertheless, throughout the war what Lloyd George called knocking away Germany's props – her allies Bulgaria, Turkey and Austria–Hungary – continued to be almost as important a strategy. Although Lloyd George became disenchanted with Salonika, in Macedonia, as a base for the allied armies attacking Austria–Hungary on her weakest frontier from the south, he was a keen supporter of an Italian front which thrust at Austria–Hungary from the north. It would be the knocking away of the props that finally forced the German high command to accept that the central powers had lost.

But if the non-western-fronters were unpopular and Churchill's reputation was under a cloud, Lloyd George's inventive spirit continued to transform the war effort. The government became a major employer. By the end of the war the Munitions Ministry was employing three million people in the new factories. A superb state-run war economy was pouring out so many munitions that Britain could provide shells for her allies as well as for her own troops.

After Kitchener was drowned on the way to Russia in early June 1916, Lloyd George took his place as secretary for war. It was a low moment.

Kitchener's death had deeply affected British morale, and there continued to be fears about Irish stability after the failure of the Easter Rising, a republican attempt to seize power in Dublin. Ireland, always Britain's Achilles' heel, had decided to make the most of her neighbour's travails. The majority of the rebels, incluiding the Gaelic schoolteacher Padraic Pearse who had founded the Irish Volunteers, were shot. One of them, a mathematics teacher named Eamon De Valera, who went on to be the first president of the Republic of Ireland, could not be executed because he had an American passport. Sir Roger Casement, the former British consul who had landed from a submarine with German arms and German money, was tried at a summary hearing and subsequently shot. The trial dismayed many as not living up to the highest standards of British justice. On the other hand, to side with Germany was treasonous when Britain was involved in what continued to be a life-and-death struggle against the central powers.

Nineteen-sixteen was also the year of the Somme. This battle, which lasted from 1 July to 18 November, changed the British people's attitude to the war. Kitchener was not alive to see 20,000 of 'his' soldiers, who had volunteered for the war, die together in their neighbourhood battalions on the first day of the campaign. The new British commander-in-chief Sir Douglas Haig believed that he could make Britain's breakout against the German trenches across the Somme river in north-eastern France. All the powers had hoped to make 1916 the year that changed the war. The Somme campaign was intended to distract the Germans' attention from their major offensive against the French at Verdun, which had begun in February.

Verdun, south of the Ardennes, was one of the most important fortresses protecting the French frontier. It had enormous historical and patriotic resonance; the German commander General von Falkenhayn believed that the French would throw everything into defending it. Attacking Verdun would attract Frenchmen from all over the western front and the Germans would then be able to bleed France to death. Germany now perceived Britain, whose fleet was completing a blockade of German ports, as her chief enemy. Although she had abandoned the idea of invading Britain, her commanders believed that, if they could knock out France at Verdun, Britain would have lost her 'best sword' on the continent.

The Somme offensive was a disaster – the breakout never happened. Yet the offensive continued for five months, during which around 400,000 British soldiers died or were wounded. Haig did not seem to care how many there were of them. Every day from 1 July thousands of men, many of whom were inexperienced youths in their teens, were sent out of their trenches without sufficient use of artillery beforehand. They were picked

First World War, Ypres, 1917.

off by the Germans as they came. The losses were so great that the British army decided to introduce the tank as a last-chance experiment in September to flatten the German defences.

At the Somme the British wounded alone amounted to half a million. The poppies sold before Remembrance Day were chosen as a symbol of the dead because men were cut down as easily as the poppies which had first covered the Flanders fields. So complete was the slaughter of the first day of the Somme that there was no one left to dispose of the corpses. The soldiers' rotting bodies had to lie where they fell, often in no-man's land, the area between two armies – a reminder of what lay in store for those sitting in the trenches tensely waiting for the order to go. The trenches were often knee deep in water, giving rise to a disease named trench foot.

Day after day men dutifully went over the top as they were ordered, yet their deaths seemed to make no perceptible difference. A feeling of futility and anger set in against the generals who were so careless of their soldiers' lives. It proved hard to shake off, even if by 1917 it was clear that the Somme had succeeded in its objective of preventing the French war effort from collapsing and had weakened the German line. The Germans were forced to retreat to what was called the Hindenburg Line, a fortified zone behind the western front designed to halt any allied breakthrough. Nevertheless, to those who lived through the battle, it seemed that their friends had lost their lives for something as paltry as a few more miles of French land. The cost was too high. An anti-war feeling developed, in which a substantial element was hostility to Haig.

To put extra vim into the war effort, in 1916 Lloyd George cut the nation's public drinking hours. Pubs had to close at two o'clock in the afternoon, which they continued to do until the end of the century. British losses finally forced Lloyd George that year to bring in conscription. So strong was the British tradition of anti-militarism that it was not until then, two years into the war, that the authorities dared take this step, though almost every other continental government assumed that it had a right to call up its nation's citizens for the army. Again unlike anywhere else in Europe, once conscription had been introduced, against the wishes of the Liberal party, conscientious objectors were allowed to go before special tribunals and explain why they would not fight. Many of them drove ambulances as a way of contributing to the war without killing people. Conscription was part of a dawning realization that different rules applied during total war, that there was no place for British individualism, that the whole nation had to contribute to the war effort if Britain was going to win. Until that point the British had been confident that the war would end before such a move became necessary.

The superior quality of the Royal Navy, the best fleet in Europe since Cromwell, unbeatable since Trafalgar, told for the most part. In most of the battles around the globe between German and British fleets, Germany generally came off worse. However, the first big-ship encounter between the two fleets off Coronel in Chile in November 1914 was won by Germany's Pacific Squadron. This was the first British naval defeat for a hundred years and, like the bombardment of the east coast of England, greatly shocked public opinion. But the British got their revenge when Germany's Pacific Squadron was destroyed at the Battle of the Falkland Islands a few weeks later.

The two High Seas Fleets whose naval race had contributed so signally to pre-war tensions were kept out of the way until May 1916. Then, in their only engagement, they fought the Battle of Jutland. Although it confirmed British naval superiority in the North Sea this was really just a skirmish. German ships caused greater losses among the British fleet than they sustained themselves, but by the evening the German fleet was hurrying back to the Baltic. It did not venture out into the North Sea again for the rest of the war, but was kept pinned down by the threat of the British ships awaiting them.

As we have noted, the First World War saw the first use of submarines, on both sides. The Germans earned the condemnation of the world in the spring of 1915 when they began to sink ships on sight without warning, regardless of whether they were warships or unarmed vessels. The sinking of the transatlantic liner the *Lusitania* in May 1915 at the Old Head of Kinsale off Cork, with the loss of 1,201 lives, some of whom were mothers with babes in arms, created extraordinary revulsion. Many of the

Lusitania's passengers were Americans, and by chance some were friends of President Woodrow Wilson. Alarmed by an official US protest, for America was strictly neutral, Germany announced that henceforth she would attack only warships.

America remained outside the war until April 1917 when she came in on the allied side. It was just in time, for the eastern front collapsed when the Bolshevik Revolution began in Russia that autumn. There were powerful pro-German influences at work in America. As in the War of 1812, much of American opinion continued to see Britain as the enemy. Moreover, Britain's blockade of Germany violated the principle of the freedom of the seas, and Americans believed that it was typical of Britain's imperialist desire for world domination. They also objected to the British navy searching neutral ships and seizing contraband. Nevertheless, as a sign of the even-handed United States attitude to both sides, by the end of 1916 President Wilson was suggesting that he should broker a negotiated peace.

This angered the allied powers. They did not like being seen as the moral equivalent of Germany: they too wished for a negotiated peace but one based on victories over Germany. However, it was expedient to bring America's overwhelming financial and industrial weight into the war on the allies' side and to end the stalemate, so Wilson's ideas could not be treated brusquely. Discussions with the Americans about war aims had to be couched in terms that would please the then strongly anti-imperialist American people and their leaders in Congress. A doctrine of national self-determination for small countries began to be evolved which had not been the original purpose of the war at all.

The entry of America into the war on the allied side became more certain at the beginning of 1917, up to which point she had continued trying to get food to Germany via Scandinavian ports. The German high command was now desperate to take Britain out of the war and believed that it could be done by starving the British into submission. Unarmed civilian shipping was no longer to be excluded from submarine warfare; instead on 1 February 1917 a campaign of 'unrestricted submarine warfare' was begun against any vessels visiting British ports. With a hundred U-boats operating in British waters the German high command reckoned that Britain would be forced to pull out of the war after five months. In the face of this threat Lloyd George, who had become prime minister of the coalition government the previous December, once again showed his peerless executive qualities. He overrode the Admiralty and revived the convoy system which had been a feature of the Napoleonic Wars. Royal Navy destroyers accompanied merchant shipping and enough food got to Britain to keep her going despite the lethal creatures lurking off her coast.

And help was now at hand from across the Atlantic. Wilson had broken off diplomatic relations with Germany on 3 February because America could not approve unrestricted submarine warfare. And on the 23rd a telegram intercepted by British Naval Intelligence from the German foreign minister, Dr Alfred Zimmermann to the German embassy in Washington revealed that Germany was negotiating with the two threats to America's backyard, Japan and Mexico. Mexico was asked to invade the United States if the Americans declared war on Germany. Coming into the war on the allied side, as an independent or associated power, and thus not subject to allied command, was made easier for Wilson when in March the first stage of the Russian Revolution began. The reactionary tsar abdicated and was replaced by a republic which the American republic could support.

The advent of America into the war in April 1917 boosted the sinking allied morale; it also considerably shortened the length of the conflict. The British Empire's blockade of Germany was no longer being breached by America. That in the end would bring Germany to her knees, just as the prospect of unlimited manpower from North America meant that the allies must eventually defeat the central powers in the field. The arrival of 300,000 American recruits in the spring put fresh strength into the allied armed forces.

However, the second Russian Revolution of October 1917 almost undid all the advantage to the allied cause that America's entry had brought. The communist-inspired Bolshevik Revolution orchestrated by Vladimir Lenin persuaded the starving Russian soldiers to desert their theatres of war to return home from what they called the capitalist war and seek 'bread, peace and land'. The central powers therefore no longer needed half a million men stationed on the eastern front. But the Bolshevik Revolution rekindled the old revolutionary ideas which had been so prevalent in Europe before the war. Strikes increased in Britain as blue-collar workers were reminded of their historic antipathy towards their masters. In a moment of great danger for France, anti-war revolutionary propaganda and the army's carelessness with soldiers' lives in the Nivelle offensive on the Aisne in 1917 persuaded perhaps as many as 100,000 soldiers in the French army to mutiny. They were overcome only with difficulty.

Fortunately England's government was in the deft hands of Lloyd George, who with the help of the Labour MPs managed to surmount the political and industrial unrest in the country. Though there were calls for peace, and one with 'no annexations and no indemnities', the support of the trade unions – which under Lloyd George enjoyed what was in effect a partnership with government – ensured that these voices never amounted to much.

There was better news, too, from the Middle East by 1917. The Ottoman Empire fragmented rapidly under the impact of the British army based in Egypt. Jerusalem was captured under the enterprising cavalryman

General Allenby. Hussein the hereditary Grand Sharif of Mecca, a descendant of the Prophet Mohammed, had already brought the desert tribes on to the allied side with great effect, getting the Arabs to rise against their Turkish overlords whom they had detested for six centuries. The high commission at Cairo was run by scholarly and romantic orientalists. One of them, an archaeologist named T. E. Lawrence who was soon to become famous as Lawrence of Arabia, became the military adviser of Hussein's son Prince Faisal.

Lloyd George might be able to encourage the British to pull together by attending to the soldiers' needs, by promoting managerial improvement in industry, and by introducing universal suffrage in February 1918 for men over the age of nineteen and women over thirty. But the generalship of the war on the western front continued to create anxiety. The hundreds of thousands of deaths and casualties and the absence of results seemed to mean nothing to Haig. On 31 July 1917 he began another offensive in Flanders, known as Passchendaele, intended to make up for the catastrophic French campaign earlier that year and free Belgium. It lasted until 6 November and only compounded his unpopularity.

By moving north-west the British were to fight out of the Ypres triangle through Passchendaele, reach the Belgian coast and then turn on the German army. Haig had been given warnings about drainage problems in the area. He chose to ignore them. The wettest August for years turned the countryside to mud. The 'mud of Flanders' was an all-too literal expression to describe conditions which made it impossible to move forward at all. Even the new weapon, the tank, did not work. It sank. The offensive died in the mud, along with 240,000 British casualties. The pessimistic War Cabinet, whose members were anxious that there should not be a second Somme, had asked Haig to cancel the campaign if its first efforts showed no likelihood of success. But Haig persisted with the Passchendaele offensive for three long months, before he would accept that it was pointless.

There was discontent at home with food and fuel shortages; rationing would be invented in the last year of the war. The consensus in the national government was breaking down, and only Lloyd George's adroit management kept Labour in the Cabinet. The Italians were roundly defeated by their old enemy the Austrians at the Battle of Caporetto, so French and British troops had to be diverted from the western front to help them. By now Britain was blithely lending her allies huge sums of money to finance the war, and no less blithely borrowing similar quantities from America. In many countries the war effort was in danger of faltering completely. British convoys made sure the allies got food while the Germans began to starve.

The beginning of 1918 was Germany's last chance to achieve a breakout on the western front and overrun France. For three months the dice were loaded in their favour: the need for an eastern front had come to an end in March 1918 after the Treaty of Brest-Litovsk took Russia out of the war. Though units of the central powers' forces remained behind to supervise the transfer of food and oil supplies from the important Romanian oilfields, the surplus eastern front troops would reach the western front long before the American troops landed to replenish the sagging allied lines.

On 21 March 1918 German troops began a massive offensive along a huge front of four miles, almost destroying an entire British army, the Fifth, in the process. But, although the line of the western front was pushed in, gallant troops under an excellent French commander-in-chief, General Foch, who now had sole command of allied troops, rushed in to fill the gaps. Eventually in July and August a counter-offensive was begun by the British and French, whose efforts were better co-ordinated now that the two armies were united under a single command.

As the summer drew to an end, the British in the north began to push the German armies back. It was the end of trench warfare. In late September the British finally broke through the Hindenburg Line. In the Middle East Allenby's victories in Syria and Palestine continued. The British army had not only reached Mosul but was marching west towards Constantinople to be joined by troops from Aleppo. Meanwhile victories in the Balkans allowed the allies based on Salonika to fan outwards like a plume. Bulgaria had surrendered on 30 September. Allied forces reached the lower Danube, the Hungarian Plain and central Europe further west, as well as threatening Constantinople. Caught in a pincer movement the Turks signed an armistice on 30 October. That same month Austria–Hungary, which was rapidly disintegrating into ethnic groups, was defeated by Italy. She surrendered on 3 November. Germany's armies were still undefeated in the field, though they were beginning to crumple under the vigour of the American troops. But at last the German high command concluded that Germany could not continue, with her armies and people at the end of their tether. As well as being exhausted and demoralized, the German people were starving as a result of the British blockade.

On 3 October the German government had asked President Wilson to dictate the terms for peace. As the war went on, an increasing number of Social Democrats in Germany voted against the government being allowed to prosecute the war any longer. The Fourteen Points Wilson had suggested as a fair basis for peace in January were accepted by Germany on 23 October. On 7 November envoys passed through the lines to accept the armistice document from the British and French military representatives

Admiral Wemyss and General Foch who were seated together in a railway carriage. The terms required the German armies to retire behind their pre-1914 borders.

But there was now a mutiny in the German navy at Kiel that signalled the end of the old regime. In early November, imitating Russia, councils of soldiers and workmen established themselves all over northern Germany and overthrew their militaristic rulers. The kaiser fled to Holland. Despite calls for him to be hanged, the Dutch government refused to give him up. The Republic of Germany was announced in Berlin, and on 11 November, early in the morning, the new republican and socialist German government signed the armistice in the Forest of Compiègne. At the eleventh hour of the eleventh day of the eleventh month of 1918, the guns fell silent and the First World War came to an end.

After the armistice, discussions about how the world should be reconstructed in the wake of the Great War took place at the Paris Peace Conference which began in January 1919, attended by seventy delegates representing the thirty-two allied and associated powers. But drawing up the separate peace treaties for the defeated central powers was mainly the work of the Big Four, as they were known: Lloyd George for Britain, whose national coalition had been re-elected at the end of 1918, Prime Minister Clemenceau for France, Prime Minister Orlando for Italy and President Wilson.

Peacemaking and the Rise of Fascism (1918–1936)

As Sir Edward Grey had predicted, the lights of European civilization had been practically extinguished. The old pre-war European world lay in ruins. France and Belgium were devastated. Farmland everywhere was smoking or abandoned, so there was not enough food. Millions of servicemen and ex-servicemen were trying to get home, men who had lost whatever idealism had first inspired them to fight. Many of them had become fairly barbaric after what they had seen. Many of them were half starved or ill.

The Dominions had lost huge numbers of their citizens. Although no request for help from the Dominions had been made by the British government, of their own volition they had sent hundreds of thousands of men to fight. There were 60,000 Australian war dead – indeed, one in ten of Australia's total male population had been killed or wounded; and 56,700 Canadians had been killed and 150,000 seriously wounded – one in twenty of the male population.

The fields of north-eastern France and Belgium were as unusable as if they had been annexed by a foreign power. They were a kingdom of two million dead. All over Europe there was chaos. The great railway lines running across France, Italy and the Austro-Hungarian Empire which had brought soldiers so swiftly to every front were buckled and broken. The manufacturing output of everyday goods in Britain was almost nonexistent after the switch to an all-out war economy. Many of the frontiers and signposts of the continent had been changed, as territories were gained and lost by the endless tramp of different armies advancing and retreating.

Everything, not just millions of people but the familiar landmarks of the pre-1914 world, seemed to have vanished and been swallowed up in the cataclysm. The 700,000 horses Britain had imported into France had become redundant in the course of the war, which transformed tank and air warfare – they belonged to an old-fashioned, more chivalrous time. The post-war world was strange and often unnerving. Four empires came to an end as a result of the Great War, three of which had been the earth's permanent furniture for centuries: the Russian, the Ottoman, the Austro-Hungarian and the German. Before 1914 the British Empire, with its investments all over the world, had been the biggest creditor nation and the United States the biggest debtor nation. Now, it would emerge after the war, the positions had been reversed.

The Russian Empire had lost Poland, the Baltic provinces and the Ukraine, all acquired in the eighteenth century, so it no longer reached the Baltic Sea or the Black Sea and ceased to be a great power. Communist ideas and workers' councils, which had taken root in Russia, threatened revolution in many European countries, most of all in Germany and Italy where their simple solutions appealed to people exhausted by the misery of war; there was anyway a vacuum as religious belief faltered in the face of the widespread horrors. The nature of Russia's internal revolution was so antipathetic to the existing structure in the rest of the world that the Soviet government had withdrawn from the world's councils – it had no interest in participating in a world order it wished to see abolished by a universal workers' revolution. Russia had always had an enigmatic quality for the rest of Europe. When, from 1919, she developed an instrument for exporting revolution, the Communist International, or Comintern, she became a dangerous enemy.

Unfortunately for the permanence of the peacemaking process, the conflict had been too overwhelming and too many people had died for it to be arranged in the disinterested fashion it should have been. Around the world ten million soldiers had died in the Great War. Seventeen million soldiers were wounded, of whom five million would live out the rest of their lives as chronic invalids. These were numbers almost beyond the capacity of human beings to understand. The effect of losing one-third of the young men of the next European generation was as devastating demographically and psychologically as the Black Death.

There were four million European widows; in France, whose population had been hit hardest by the war, one in four children were fatherless. The period which succeeded the war could not help but be one of sorrow, suffering and pessimism. The British nurse Edith Cavell, executed by the Germans in Brussels, had become a wartime heroine to the British. Her most famous words, inscribed on the statue erected to her in London, were 'Patriotism is not enough. I must have no hatred or bitterness for anyone,' but the French had little room for anything else. Even though a government was in place in Germany which had thrown off her militaristic leaders, she was treated as if she were still ruled by Prussian autocrats and she continued to be blamed for the world catastrophe. All of this was compounded by a pandemic of the influenza known as Spanish flu. Originating in South Africa and hitting half a million German soldiers in June 1918, Spanish flu swept through the war-weakened populations killing another ten million people. It was a time of the darkest gloom.

The vindictive and punitive peace imposed on Germany by France to ensure that her old enemy could never threaten her again ruined beyond repair what before 1914 had been the dynamo of the European economy. But it also destabilized the entire structure of German civilization. As in all European countries, ordinary life in Germany was already tottering because of the hardship of the war. The Versailles Treaty with Germany, signed at the Paris Peace Conference on 28 June 1919, paved the way in the post-war period for a desperate people to seek desperate solutions.

Germany was being treated as a pariah. Economic misery and despair over her reduced status meant she soon became an aggressive pariah threatening the post-war settlement.

Unlike the reshaping of Europe in 1815, there was no equivalent of Wellington to act as a restraining influence, a statesman who had thought of the consequences of embittering Germany by her treatment. Lloyd George had won the 1918 election by talking of squeezing Germany 'until the pips squeak'. After the war Germans would become united by their belief that they had been treated unfairly at the Paris Peace Conference, and by their consequent desire for revenge. In 1815, after twenty years of French war, the allies' policy of not treating France too harshly had ensured that she could soon return to the European family of nations in a constructive spirit. That lesson was forgotten in 1919. What has to be remembered was that the French were too fearful of Germany to treat her magnanimously. They were also determined to have their pound of flesh and make the Germans feel the same pain they had inflicted on the French after the Franco-Prussian War. Twice in forty years Germany had come close to destroying France. The French aim under Clemenceau was straightforward: it was to make certain that it never could happen again. So deep was the hatred felt by France for Germany that it was believed that in order to bind the Leviathan he must be crippled first.

Germany was no longer permitted to have a navy (apart from a small surface fleet for security in the Baltic) or air force. Her army was to be the same size as Belgium's, a limit of 100,000 men, without a General Staff, to prevent German militarism becoming the threat to world peace it had been in 1914. Alsace and Lorraine were naturally enough returned to France, though for forty years they had been the centre of Germany's iron production and her new steel industry. Much of Germany's own territory was also removed from her. The Saar Basin, the centre for coal and a source of her great industrial wealth, was to be run by the League of Nations. It was to be the subject of a plebiscite in fifteen years' time when its inhabitants could choose whether to be reunited with Germany or join France. In the interim the money raised by its coal sales went to France. Although Germany kept Holstein and southern Schleswig, northern Schleswig was also to decide its future by plebiscite.

In the east, Germany lost not only three million of her population when West Prussia and Posen became part of the new Poland, whose frontiers returned to something close to what they had been in the eighteenth century before the partitions. Germany's remaining territory was also insultingly separated from East Prussia, spiritual home of the German Empire, by a strip of land known as the Polish Corridor which gave Poland access to the sea. She also lost many of her coalfields too, particularly after another plebiscite joined Upper Silesia to Poland, as well as much of her iron and steelworks. Owing to her entirely German population the port of Danzig (the Polish Gdansk) on the Baltic at the top of the Polish Corridor, was not given to Poland. However, in order for Poland's trade to continue freely Danzig was made a free city administered by the League of Nations. All in all, in Europe Germany lost about four million citizens through transfers of territory.

In fact even these measures to break up Germany did not really satisfy France's need for security. She had first demanded that her eastern frontier be advanced to the Rhine. She had to be content with a neutralized Saar Basin, the permanent demilitarization of the Rhineland – that is, all Germany to the west of the Rhine and fifty kilometres to the east of it. President Woodrow Wilson pledged that with Britain the USA would guarantee France's frontiers. As far as the Germans were concerned, the self-determination which had been one of the themes of the conference scarcely counted. But France still did not have enough.

Having been thwarted in her attempt to get the kaiser hung as a war criminal, France had to be satisfied with what appeared to be a war-guilt clause which began the reparations section of the peace treaty. This clause was intended to be a technical statement, that Germany would pay 'compensation for all damage done to the civilian population of the Allies and their property by the aggression of Germany, by land, by sea and from the air'. But it was believed for ever more to attribute the whole guilt for the war to the German people. It was another reason for Germans to be angry about the treaty – many of them considered that the allied powers had been just as much to blame for the war. 'The stab in the back' theory about the republican government started to circulate in Germany: that government, it was alleged, could never be trusted, for it had signed the treacherous peace even though the German armies had never been defeated.

The war-guilt clause would have meant that only France would obtain reparations from Germany, as most of the destructive action had taken place on her territory. Lloyd George now insisted that a clause be included covering pensions for widows and orphans of British soldiers killed in action. In 1921, after much discussion, the total cost of what Germany owed the two countries was reckoned at over £6,000 million. With all Germany's colonies also confiscated from her, so that after the war she could trade only in Europe, these reparations were beyond Germany's capacity to pay.

Nothing was discussed in person with the German delegation; they were able to raise their objections only in writing. They scarcely had time to do so – the peace treaty was more or less imposed on them. The treaty was signed in the Hall of Mirrors in the Palace of Versailles, the very room in which Germany had proclaimed her new empire to the humiliation of the French in 1871. It was now used by the French to humiliate the Germans. By the end of the next decade the view that Germany had been treated too harshly at the peace conference and deserved to have the Versailles Treaty revised had become common currency in Britain. The economist John Maynard Keynes resigned as the British Treasury's chief representative at the conference and quickly wrote *The Economic Consequences of the Peace*, in which he expressed in vigorous language his conviction that Germany had been harshly treated.

President Wilson himself optimistically believed that the League of Nations, the international body to regulate the world which was an integral part of the peace treaties, would find a way of adjusting those parts which were unworkable. No peace conference started out with more idealistic aims than that which remade Europe in 1919. Woodrow Wilson's Fourteen Points had promised a new world order based on doing away with the old patterns of secret diplomacy, arranging equality of trading conditions and providing an impartial adjustment of all colonial claims. The levelling of the pre-1914 civilization could be a positive thing if a better world was built on the ashes of the old. Most of the world's nations, including much of Germany, were dominated by a profound wish that never again should the destruction of war be allowed to ravage their lives.

Many of them, like Canada and other Dominions who were representing themselves for the first time instead of being spoken for by British imperial statesmen, came to the peace conference enthusiastically. They were inspired by Woodrow Wilson's idea of a League of Nations to outlaw war and to protect the rights of small nations. A worldwide reduction of armaments to the lowest point consistent with national safety, which would make the world 'safe for democracy' as Wilson put it, offered a chance to escape from the blind destruction of the past. The League, which Wilson spent much time and effort explaining, was to be set up in Geneva, Switzerland and every nation was invited to join and send members to its international assembly.

Wilson's novel idea, that all the peace treaties should have the League's charter as an integral and dominating part, was adopted by all the delegates. The charter was a reflection of the peace movements which had grown up during the war, as well as of the Disarmament Conferences before 1914, to find international procedures for arbitration. The powers which signed the Covenant of the League of Nations were mindful of the uncontrollable process of acceleration by which small wars could become big ones. By putting their names to the Covenant they vowed to refer their disagreements to the League for discussion before taking up arms. They also vowed to go to the aid of any fellow member which had been attacked and to act against any member which used force against the League.

It was heady stuff. The world was so exhausted by the war that none of the statesmen in Paris could imagine any country ever wanting to repeat such an experience. The dream of global peace seemed to have achieved reality. The peace conference proposed to resettle Europe along lines of self-determination to prevent the sort of quarrel the Serbs had had with the Austro-Hungarian Empire. The Habsburg Empire was already no more, and the Habsburgs were deposed after the armistice. Their immense territories were broken up into states on ethnic lines. By the Treaty of St Germain, signed with the new Austrian Republic, Austria became a small landlocked country of seven million people forbidden to join up with Germany. Bohemia, Moravia and part of northern Hungary, which were inhabited by western Slavs (the Czechs, Slovaks and Ruthenians), were united to create the Republic of Czechoslovakia. Croatia, Dalmatia, Slovenia and Bosnia-Herzegovina, inhabited by the southern Slavs, were united under Serbia to form the Kingdom of Yugoslavia. Italy, though balked of Dalmatia, obtained Trentino, Trieste, South Tyrol and Istria. Hungary, meanwhile, which lost almost three-quarters of her post-1867 kingdom – Romania acquired the whole of Transylvania – in 1920 reluctantly signed the Treaty of Trianon.

Bulgaria, as an ally of the central powers, by the Treaty of Neuilly had to cede large areas to Greece and the new Yugoslavia. The independence of Finland, and of the Baltic states of Lithuania, Latvia and Estonia was preserved. Russia meanwhile would make no peace treaty. Although initially British and French troops were sent to help the White or conservative forces within Russia against the Bolsheviks, an impasse was reached and they were evacuated.

The treaty agreeing peace with the Ottoman Empire, the Treaty of Sèvres, was not completed until 1920. It destroyed the 300-year-old Ottoman Empire, more or less expelled the Turks from Europe apart from Constantinople, made Armenia and Kurdistan independent, and removed from them Arabia, Palestine, Mesopotamia, Syria, Cyprus and what they owned in north Africa. Greece was to be given much of Asiatic Turkey behind Smyrna.

President Wilson intended that European imperialism should wither away. Former German colonies or Turkish possessions, even if they were taken over by the old imperial powers, were now to be called mandates. By an article of the Covenant of the League, the great powers like France and Britain were commanded to govern the mandates in the interests of their inhabitants until they were ready to be admitted to the League of Nations.

Thus a better world was supposed to be remodelled at the peace conference. Unfortunately, although all the peace treaties were predicated on the League of Nations, despite his enthusiasm for the new world order President Wilson had made an elementary mistake. He failed to convince Congress of the importance of the United States guaranteeing the post-war settlement, so despite his own internationalism after the war she returned to her usual isolationism. Congress rejected US participation in the League of Nations, yet the whole new settlement was based on US support for the League. Nor would America guarantee France's borders against Germany.

As for imperialism withering away, it was really lack of money as far as Britain was concerned – with the post-war slump and debts owed to America of £900 million – that in the end hurried forward the end of empire. Lord Curzon, foreign secretary from October 1919, and much of the India Office might be excited by the mandate system which gave Britain Mesopotamia and Palestine to administer as an unofficial way of extending the empire. The importance of the oil-rich Middle East had been recognized before the war and the area offered new markets now that India had her own growing manufacturing industry. With Russia locked in internal revolution, Britain had no rival in the Middle East. But a severe post-war slump prevented Britain from imposing herself on the mandated territories as she would have done in the past. The old empire itself was under attack from nationalists in India. In Ireland a war of independence against the British broke out the year after the war ended. There was a rebellion in Egypt, which had been made a British protectorate at the beginning of the war and wanted immediate independence.

Mesopotamia was in a state of revolt and despite her oilfields most members of the British government had no wish to spend money on subduing her. Though the British retained a great deal of influence, in 1921 they made her into the kingdom of Iraq. Eleven years later in 1932 the mandate ended and Iraq achieved full independence. Faisal, the son of the Hashemite Sharif Hussein, became her king as a reward for his father's help during the war. This partly offset the obligation on the British to fulfil their wartime promise of creating an independent Arab state in Syria and Palestine, as did carving the independent mandate of Jordan out of their mandate for Palestine. Faisal's brother, Hussein's other son Abdullah, became Jordan's emir. Though a British resident initially controlled both her economic and her financial policy, in 1946 the mandated territory became the Hashemite Kingdom of Jordan.

Palestine posed more of a problem because of the 1917 Balfour Declaration, which had been critical in keeping influential Jewish opinion in America onside during the war. This recognized the rights of the Jewish race to establish a national homeland in Palestine, so long as no harm was inflicted on the native Arab inhabitants. At the end of the nineteenth century, the victimization of Jews (especially in eastern Europe) had seen the growth of a powerful Zionist movement, whose objective was to establish a homeland for the Jews in their ancestral home of Palestine. In consequence, between 1882 and 1914 Palestine attracted 60,000 Jewish immigrants, bringing the Jewish population to about 85,000. The question of how many Jewish people could settle in the Jewish homeland without upsetting the lives of the 600,000 Arab Palestinians was to be the subject of much debate within the British government over the next twenty-five years. Sympathy for Jewish settlers who were attacked by Arabs wrestled with official British fears that the poorly educated Palestinians would soon be at a disadvantage in a small country with a land shortage.

The First World War had made the territorial extent of the British Empire greater than ever, but it dramatically loosened its already lax bonds. Before 1914 the imperial government was in the last resort responsible for the foreign policy of the entire empire. But by the end of the war the effect of their vast losses, their separate representation at the peace conference and their membership of the League of Nations set the Dominions on the path to real nationhood. They began to make it clear that in future wars their assistance could not be taken for granted. Separate ambassadorial representation to other countries, a lack of imperial ships to defend the empire east of Suez and a definitive Imperial Conference in 1926 resulted in the 1931 Statute of Westminster. This recognized the changed and wholly independent status of the Dominions, though they remained 'united by a common allegiance to the Crown and freely associated as members of the British Commonwealth of nations'.

But India was not part of the magic circle of the Dominions. She was very disappointed at not being rewarded as she had hoped after her efforts during the war. One and a half million Indians had fought for the empire, and India had been admitted to the Imperial Conference in 1917. Like the Dominions, India had achieved separate representation in the Assembly of the League of Nations. Many Indians, particularly Mohandas Gandhi, who had studied law in London and was a member of the Inner Temple, had believed in the liberty-loving nature of a Britain ruled by Parliament. They had assumed that India would achieve Dominion status immediately after the war. But it did not happen.

The Indian professional classes felt fobbed off by the 1919 Government of India Act which they were offered instead. It gave India a two-chambered Parliamentary system and allowed Indians to form the majority on the Central Legislative Council, but the diarchal arrangement kept law and order and taxation in the hands of non-Indians. Moreover the legislature could not remove the executive. The notorious Amritsar

Massacre in 1919, when General Dyer shot dead 379 unarmed civilians in the Punjab who were protesting against new security laws, crystallized the growing discontent with British rule. People lost faith in the Raj's promises. For the next seven years, led by Gandhi, India embarked on a new movement for independence with frequent strikes and the boycotting of British goods.

India was inspired by the empire's other 'poor relation', Ireland. In a series of dramatic moves she was casting off British authority. The harsh punishment of those Irishmen involved in the Easter Rising caused Sinn Fein and the revolutionaries to triumph over the moderate Home Rulers in the first election after the war and withdraw from Westminster. Seventy-three of them gathered in the Mansion House in Dublin and announced that they constituted an independent Irish Parliament, which they called the Dáil Éireann, meaning the Parliament of the Irish Republic. A provisional government was elected with De Valera as president. By 1919 there was all-out war between Britain and southern Ireland.

The charismatic Michael Collins, known as the 'big fella', minister of finance in the new Dáil, was southern Ireland's commander. His unorthodox army, the old National Volunteers, who wore trench coats and trilby hats, vanished into the shadows after each guerrilla exploit. His charm and his daring refusal to wear much disguise while bicycling about Dublin gave Collins the status of a folk hero. Even though 8,000 ex-soldiers were drafted in to supplement the Royal Irish Constabulary, the south of Ireland became ungovernable. Because the RIC did not have enough of their usual dark-green uniforms, the new policemen wore khaki, with the black belts and dark-green caps of the RIC. The savagery with which they hunted down the Irish guerrillas got them the caustic nickname of the Black and Tans, after a pack of hounds from County Tipperary. British politicians became sickened by what was going on in Ireland and demanded a political solution.

When Lloyd George was informed by British military chiefs that it would take a military campaign involving 100,000 men to subdue Ireland, he baulked at such an enterprise so soon after the trauma of the Great War. Money was needed to reconstruct Britain, not to fight Ireland. In 1921 the two sides began a series of negotiations. The Anglo-Irish Treaty in December resolved the Ulster Unionist problem by partitioning Ireland, turning southern Ireland into a Dominion called the Irish Free State.

But even this did not bring peace. In 1922 the Irish Civil War broke out between the pro-treaty forces headed by Michael Collins and Arthur Griffith and those like De Valera who believed that Ireland should become a republic inclusive of Ulster. As the death toll in Ireland mounted, assassinations by the newly formed military organization of the anti-treaty nationalists, the Irish Republican Army, or IRA (Collins was one of the victims), were followed by dawn executions of suspects without trial by the Irish Free State government. Eventually the cool, calculating, bespectacled De Valera, who was suspected of ordering Collins's assassination, called a halt to the anti-treaty IRA's warfare. The civil war petered out. The struggle should go forward by political means, De Valera said, though at elections he made use of terrorist pressure from the IRA to get out the vote for the rapidly enlarging Fianna Fáil republican party.

If the empire was in tumult in the early 1920s, there was much misery and dislocation in Britain herself, despite the release from war. From 1916 to 1918, when Labour seceded from the national government, Britain had continued to be ruled nominally by the coalition of three parties, though in reality the controlling figure was the amazingly energetic Lloyd George. Parliament should have been dissolved in 1916 but as an election in wartime would have been impossible, acts had been passed from time to time prolonging its life, and thus the life of the coalition. In 1918 Lloyd George and Bonar Law, the leader of the Conservatives, saw no reason not to carry on as before. They agreed that the task of returning Britain to a peacetime existence also deserved government by consensus. In the coupon election of 1918 (so called because Lloyd George and Bonar Law had written a letter or coupon asking the parties not to oppose one another) the coalition – now the 335 coalition Conservatives and 133 coalition Liberals – was successfully returned. The new government lasted until 1922. The electorate had trebled again as a result of the 1918 Electoral Reform Act. If he wanted to be prime minister again, Lloyd George had to fulfil his election promise to make Britain 'a land fit for heroes to live in'.

With such an enlarged electorate, many of whom were working class, numerous measures for social reform were required. The reforms Lloyd George promised were even more sweeping than those achieved before the war. The state would pay for housing, what were called council houses, to replace the slums that still disfigured towns. By the Unemployment Insurance Act of 1920 all workers were entitled to benefit for fifteen weeks as long as they had paid twelve weeks' contributions. But soon many of the measures – including a new Education Act in 1918 which was intended to increase teachers' salaries, provide for the compulsory attendance at school of children up to fourteen and establish continuation schools for boys and girls up to eighteen – proved impossible to implement. They were too great an expense for a country still getting back on her feet. The boom the war caused in munitions and a resurgence of the textile trade after the war were followed by a slump in 1921. There were two million people out of work. Domestic service, which had been an immense source of employment before the war, had almost vanished as few people could afford to employ servants any more. Before 1914 even the most meagre households with pretensions to being middle-class had some kind of help.

Britain did not have the severe problems suffered by some European countries. Germany lacked half her heavy industry and was bent under the huge weight of reparations. France was only beginning to rebuild her agriculture and industry, and she had to do that with almost a third of her manpower missing. Strikes had crippled Italy to the point where she feared a communist workers' takeover. In 1922 terrified of revolutionary chaos Italy abandoned Parliamentary democracy for one-party or totalitarian rule at the hands of violent ex-servicemen in the Fascist party under their leader Benito Mussolini. Parliamentary government had been discredited by a peace settlement which brought her none of the colonies she desired in Africa to add to Libya, and gave much of what she had been promised by the Treaty of London to Yugoslavia. Named after the *fasces* or bundle of twigs that Roman senators carried as a symbol of their authority, the intensely nationalistic fascists were anti-capitalistic and anti-clerical, but also abhorred socialism and communism. Awash with comforting and simplistic slogans in the nihilistic post-war atmosphere, paying lipservice to the certainties of monarchy and Church, the fascists' squads of paramilitaries restored order, purpose and international prestige to an extremely unstable country. The consequence was that by the end of the decade the Fascist party had become completely entwined with all Italian institutions, from social clubs to town councils.

But though the British might be free to take their usual pleasure in expressing their political opinions, the country was deeply burdened by America's insistence on being repaid her war loans immediately. Britain had financed much of the war for her European allies, but she had not demanded prompt payment of her debts, because most European countries were in no position to comply. Hampered by shortage of money, diminished populations and the need to work on the ruined land to make it fit for cultivation, the European economies were only slowly getting back to pre-war production levels.

In Britain the coal and cotton export markets collapsed. The business-man Sir Ernest Geddes, appointed to work out where the government could save money, and known as the Geddes Axe, hacked back many of Lloyd George's promises. 'A land fit for heroes' became an ironic saying. The general post-war discontent manifested itself in strikes and lockouts. In industries where she had led the world, Britain was falling behind because she had not invested in new machinery. Nevertheless she remained the world's leading shipbuilder for another forty years, as befitted a country whose navy had been the best in the world for over a century.

But even that bit of glory had come to an end. The Washington Naval

Agreement at the end of 1921 was a sign of the changing times when Britain agreed to parity with America in warships. She could no longer afford to build the ships or bases to defend the empire in its entirety. For the next twenty years Singapore, which was meant to be a great defensive naval base for the empire east of Suez, was not fortified properly or supplied with an adequate number of ships to defend herself.

All of the Royal Navy's ships were built in Britain, where her welders and engineers had an expertise envied by all other advanced countries. However, especially on what became known as 'red' Clydeside near Glasgow, the home of so much of Britain's shipbuilding since the nineteenth century, a fiery love of striking and militant socialist trade unionism proved fatal to the industry. A smaller navy, and the strikes which lost the yards business, combined to put shipbuilding in Britain into continuous decline.

Lloyd George lived on until 1945, but by 1922 his political day was drawing to a close amid a great deal of bitterness. He had been absent too much in Paris at the peace conference trying to hold back the French, and the Conservatives were beginning to chafe under his grip. He had split the Liberal party when he ousted Asquith, so he had few followers there. His reputation began to be harmed by tales about his honours list, about how as in the days of James I a baronetcy was to be had for £10,000, a peerage for £50,000 and so on. In the grim atmosphere of the slump tongues wagged about how well his entrepreneurial friends had done out of the war. Moreover, many Conservatives did not like the way Lloyd George had relinquished southern Ireland.

Lloyd George's fall was engineered by the 'knights of the shires', as Tory backbenchers have often been known, over the Chanak Crisis. They were worried that Lloyd George was about to resume the war against Turkey, whose republican government under Mustapha Kemal had refused to accept the peace treaty which gave Greece Smyrna. In a revolt in October 1922 they voted at the Carlton Club to resume independence as Conservatives. As Kemal's victorious army advanced towards the Dardanelles, where a neutral zone had been created, the danger of a collision with the British garrison at Chanak was averted only by the tact of General Charles Harington. The Treaty of Lausanne in July 1923 restored to Turkey at the expense of Greece much of the European territory of which she was to have been deprived.

The Chanak Crisis was the final nail in Lloyd George's coffin. He resigned, the coalition ended and the Conservative leader Bonar Law briefly formed a Conservative ministry from 1922 to 1923 until ill-health forced him to retire. The genial pipe-smoking iron manufacturer Stanley Baldwin, the epitome of British pragmatism, became prime minister for a year. He made the mistake of abandoning free trade at the December 1923 election which he had called to shore up his position, hoping that tariff reform would help the disastrous level of unemployment. But although the Conservatives returned to power as the party with the largest number of seats in the House of Commons, and Baldwin remained prime minister, he lacked a majority. With a puff of ancient free trade breath, the fading Liberals reunited under Asquith joined with the Labour party to extinguish tariff reform by a vote of no confidence. As the largest of the opposition parties, Labour was then asked by George V to form a minority government pending a general election. On 23 January 1924 Ramsay MacDonald, the illegitimate son of a Scottish farmworker, was sworn in as leader of the first Labour government. He became foreign secretary as well as prime minister.

The excitement within the Labour party at achieving office for the first time after the disappointments of the post-war period was tremendous, though the government lasted for only eight months. Being dependent on the Liberals to remain in power, the Labour government could not bring in some of its more extreme ideas, such as taking key industries into state ownership, as Clause 4 of their 1917 manifesto demanded, or 'the gradual building up of a new social order' by wealth redistribution, as their constitution decreed. In the privacy of his diary George V wondered what his grandmother Queen Victoria would have thought of a government whose members were 'all socialists', but he believed that they should 'be given a chance'.

Nonetheless, the conservatively minded feared the Labour government as if it were the prelude to a Bolshevik Revolution. In the recent past, Labour councils such as Clydeside and the London Borough of Poplar had flown the red flag of revolution. Under the high-minded idealist George Lansbury, who in the 1930s briefly became leader of the Labour party, Poplar Council became a byword for the defiance of central government by local authorities. Poplar Labour councillors were frequently imprisoned or otherwise in trouble for refusing, because theirs was a poor council, to pay as much as rich local authorities towards the upkeep of the London County Council. They made a habit of paying out more poor relief than their rates afforded.

In fact the short-lived Labour minority government was decent, sensible and constructive. Its members were anxious to prove themselves trustworthy and responsible custodians of government. Such policies as they implemented in their eight months were for the most part a continuation of Lloyd George's. Many of the Labour party's leaders, including home secretary Arthur Henderson, were vehemently opposed to the tyranny and ideology of the communist system in Russia, which some of them had seen at first hand. They were determined that Britain with her Parliamentary democracy should not adopt anything like it. Labour constantly refused to allow the few thousand members of the British Communist party (founded in 1920) to link up with Labour. Communists were not permitted to be Labour candidates or even to be members of the Labour party.

With the former professions of ministers ranging from engine-driving to furnace-stoking, their principal aim was to raise the expectations of the working class. A new Education Bill made a first tier of secondary education the right of the many instead of the preserve of the few who could afford private education. It became the state's duty to provide senior classes for children up to the age of fourteen, not just primary schooling. It was hoped to raise the school-leaving age to fifteen, though costs would make this impossible for some years. Labour once more attempted to tackle the housing shortage by committing the government to a fifteen-year scheme of expanding council housing available to rent. The bill passed easily through Parliament. The duty of the government to provide houses was becoming part of the post-war consensus, part of the ever greater expansion of the state's responsibilities for its citizenry. But although insurance for the unemployed was extended, Labour could find little more to do for them. Their number was still hovering about the one-million mark. It was an issue that Britain, the workshop of the world, had never had to tackle before.

Prime Minister Ramsay MacDonald, like many Labour people, was an idealistic socialist and committed internationalist. He had voted against Britain entering the war, believing that wars benefited only imperialists and arms merchants and destroyed the working classes, who were used as cannon fodder. He was a fervent proponent of international organizations to ensure that no war ever happened again and he attended League of Nations gatherings at Geneva which he hoped would remedy what was unsatisfactory about the peace treaties.

For Franco-German relations continued to be destructive and fraught with hatred. America and Britain were not part of the European continent, which had been menaced by Germany for half a century, so their statesmen possessed no intuitive understanding of France's feelings about her neighbour. She had agreed to a peace treaty which did not bring her frontier up to the Rhine because she believed that she had America's wing to shelter under. Once America refused to join the League of Nations, France, terrified once again for her security, became trigger-happy. Thus when Germany in 1923 defaulted on her reparations payments to France, French troops were rushed into the Ruhr Valley, Germany's industrial heartland, to make her pay. For a year the French occupied the Ruhr while German industry came to a halt in a show of defiance against the invader.

The French left in 1924, but they had already inflicted the damage on the German economy which made the German mark collapse. By the end of 1923, inflation was so out of control that one American dollar was worth hundreds of millions of marks. With the mark worth so little, people had to bring wheelbarrows full of paper money to pay even small bills. Germany was meanwhile bedevilled by assassination attempts and coups.

Nevertheless the internationalists in Europe like MacDonald were determined to help. Germany was not left to sink. In 1924 an American scheme, the Dawes Plan, adjusted the reparations burden to make it less harsh. By 1929 the Allied Reparations Commission had found the reparations to be disproportionately heavy on Germany, and they were reduced to less than a third of the total established in 1921. By the mid-1920s not all seemed bad. The German mark recovered.

A better era seemed to be ushered in for Germany under the gifted republican statesman Gustav Stresemann. Though Germany had never ceased to campaign to revise Versailles, in 1925 she at last appeared to have officially accepted her western frontier with France when she signed the Locarno Treaty. Germany was admitted to the League of Nations and the Rhineland was demilitarized. By 1926 she was no longer seen as a pariah nation. In 1928 the Kellogg–Briand Pact, produced by an American and a Frenchman, attempted to eliminate war as an instrument of national policy. Its multilateral treaty almost made up for America not joining the League.

The first Labour government had shown itself to be moderate and unexceptionable and contained reassuring personnel from Asquith's last Cabinet, such as Lord Haldane who became lord chancellor. Nevertheless a trade treaty and a loan which Labour tried to negotiate with Soviet Russia and what purported to be revolutionary instructions from the Soviet government did for the government. Four days before the general election in October 1924 the *Daily Mail*'s publication of a letter from one of the Russian Bolshevik leaders named Zinoviev which appeared to be addressed to Labour gave the country a fright.

The Conservatives returned to power under their new leader Stanley Baldwin. Although Labour was out, only forty Liberals were returned as opposed to 151 Labour and 413 Conservatives. The 1924 election is therefore interesting because it marks the real eclipse of the Liberal party. Labour had received one million more votes and had effectively become the second party in the British two-party system.

Baldwin now had a decent overall majority. Always seen chewing on his pipe he was a reassuring figure in troubled times, although his comfortable image disguised a mind like a trap. He was a formidable Parliamentary operator. The economic depression which began in 1921 had not ended, and indeed was about to get worse. Among Baldwin's Cabinet was Winston Churchill as chancellor of the Exchequer. He had last been a Conservative in 1903 when he had resigned over tariff reform. Many in the Conservative party believed that the only way to defeat the depression was to return to the pre-1914 monetary system, by which the pound sterling was fixed at a price reflecting its gold reserves. In 1925 therefore with Churchill as chancellor the country returned to the gold standard. It was a disaster that resulted in massive deflation and the overvaluing of the pound. Manufacturers exporting abroad found their order books diminishing because the strong pound made their products too expensive.

The economic depression created a crisis in the British coal industry. Until 1914 Britain had been the world's greatest exporter, but many industrialized countries had begun to mine their own coal. The coal industry would have declined more rapidly had it not benefited from France's invasion of Germany's Ruhr coalfields. By 1926 the writing was on the wall. As part of the war economy the huge industry had been taken out of private hands and run by the government. After the war the miners did not want the coalfields to return to private ownership because the wages offered were lower than those paid by the government. For several months they refused to return to work, though as a lure they were offered a seven-hour day. The simple truth was that British coal was too expensive. The mine owners asked for wage reductions and slightly increased hours. A Royal Commission of Inquiry achieved little, and the government eventually appeared to come down on the side of the owners when it recommended that the working day go back to eight hours. The miners took their case to the General Council of the Trades Union Congress. On 3 May 1926 a general strike was declared.

But this was not the start of the revolution in Britain that had been feared – and hoped for by Russia. Though the railwaymen, printers, and iron and steel trades came out in sympathy with their fellow workers, it was a social event rather than a political one. There was little professed desire to overthrow the government. The general strike – that formidable weapon by which workers could bring a country to its knees – was not applied very ruthlessly. The responsible, upright TUC had no wish to endanger the country's health; hospital and agricultural workers were excluded from the strike.

There was some violence by police and union members but after nine days, by 12 May, Britain could breathe again. The general strike had been called off, no revolution had taken place and Britain had kept going thanks to all kinds of enthusiastic volunteers from students to businessmen driving the buses. The working man had the Labour party to represent him in Parliament. Another Labour government would be a better way of making sure his voice was heard than the destruction of the general strike. Britain had no stomach for the way strikes were used abroad, with such lethal effects.

Only the miners remained on strike, staying out for another seven months until December 1926. Once their union funds were exhausted, they had to return to work. The strike had lasting effects on the coal industry. Many coalminers remained out of work because pits could not be reopened. The high rate of unemployment which followed in the industry forced lower wages and longer hours on the miners. To prevent another countrywide stoppage, in 1927 the Conservatives brought in a new Trade Disputes Act. General strikes were outlawed, and henceforth trade union contributions for political ends like supporting the Labour party had to be individually earmarked by the member concerned.

Although the Conservatives had weakened the trade unions, progressive social reform continued. One of the most notable effects of the war was that all parties now accepted that the state should play a far greater role in British life as a beneficent provider. The Ministry of Health, created to deal with insurance and health issues, was not disbanded after the war, as state provision for pensions and insurance continued to expand. The minister of health Neville Chamberlain, Joe's son, finally did away with the last remnants of the punitive approach to the destitute by abolishing the Elizabethan guardians of the poor. Instead the destitute became the responsibility of county councils, whose Public Assistance Committees provided new buildings and assistance for the old and sick who had nowhere else to go. The Conservative government, which in 1928 carried the Fifth Reform Act allowing women the vote at twenty-one in line with men, brought in a more generous state pension scheme. The Widows, Orphans and Old Age Contributory Pensions Act of 1925 allowed insured people to draw an old age pension at sixty-five and gave pensions to widows and allowances for bereaved children under fourteen.

The Conservatives also established the National Grid which provided cheap state-owned electricity across the country via a wire and pylon system run by the government-owned Central Electricity Board. By 1939 two-thirds of Britain had electricity, though in wilder parts of the country its supply could be less certain. Swans or snow on the line in the Highlands of Scotland often left local people without electricity for a day or two.

The British Broadcasting Corporation, created in 1927 by a group of radio companies, was also set up as a state monopoly owned by the government. Established by royal charter, the BBC was intended to have high ethical standards, which it has largely maintained. Its refusal to take advertising has always given it an editorial freedom and integrity. Soon most homes possessed a wireless. The BBC tradition of high-mindedness and public service broadcasting was encouraged by its first chairman, the Scot Lord Reith, who believed in a mission to improve Britain through his corporation. For many Britons, until the 1944 Education Act established free secondary schooling, BBC Radio served as a form of further education. The impartiality of the BBC, jealously guarded, made it one of the great British institutions of the twentieth century. Envied by other countries it remains a testament to the British love of fair play. The BBC Radio World Service has traditionally been a forum giving political exiles the chance to speak and broadcast to their homelands.

British women's lives changed dramatically during the war. With three and a half million men called up to fight in France, women had to take over many of their jobs on farms or in munitions factories. Those serving as nurses on the western front earned the heartfelt respect of the men. As a reflection of the new seriousness with which they were viewed, women were admitted to membership of Oxford University in 1920 – though it was not until 1948 that they could receive full degrees at Cambridge. Other acts of 1918 and 1919, recognizing their war work, revolutionized the civic position of women by removing sex qualifications for admission to the professions and to seats in the House of Commons. One of the best-known beneficiaries of this was the American-born Nancy Astor. She was the first woman to sit in the House of Commons when in 1919 she took over her husband Waldorf Astor's seat for Plymouth Sutton after he inherited his father's viscountcy. She remained an MP for twenty-five years.

When all British women over twenty-one became entitled to vote in 1928, they had stolen a march on their more protected French contemporaries – in France the vote for women only came in 1944. In Switzerland it was 1971. As a sign of their independence, skirts rose and women took up the fashion of bobbing or cutting their hair short, a fashion prompted by the need to keep it out of machinery during the war. The long lustrous locks piled up in elaborate folds so characteristic of the pre-war era vanished.

Jazz music, which began in the black part of New Orleans and spread throughout America, crossed the Atlantic to Europe in the 1920s and became all the rage. Millions of young people bought phonographs to hear recordings and dance the wild Charleston. Such enthusiasms showed that they belonged to the new world which rejected the boring and destructive ideas of the old. Inspired by sheer relief at the ending of the war and by the world's subsequent recovery, well-to-do people became hedonistic. Instead of being associated with the war, France exploited her holiday resorts such as Juan les Pins and Biarritz, to become the playground of the young, rich and gifted, particularly Americans like the writer Scott Fitzgerald.

Fitzgerald gave this short-lived breathing space between the wars its nickname, the Jazz Age. 'Seize the day' was its motto – with so many young people dead, who could say who would be alive tomorrow? A rather desperate frivolity reigned. From the mid-1920s onwards, London theatres were full of Noël Coward's bitter-sweet sophisticated comedies about world-weary, liberated young people. Divorce – a stigma before 1914 – started to become accepted as something that happened. Being realistic, being true to yourself, was what mattered now that so many of the old certainties of European civilization from religion to the army had disintegrated or been found wanting. The young Evelyn Waugh's cynical and often cruel novels, including *Decline and Fall* (1928) and *Vile Bodies* (1930) were hugely popular.

Despite the weakening of the trade union movement in the aftermath of the general strike, the Labour party returned to power for another two years in 1929. Though Labour had 287 MPs against Conservatives' 261, and the Liberals had a sorry 59, Labour was still in a minority. Once again an attempt was made to co-operate with the Liberals but it was not very successful. Nineteen-twenty-nine was the year the worldwide great depression began. It started with the Wall Street Crash in America, which wiped millions off the value of shares in October. The newspapers were full of ruined financiers committing suicide by jumping out of skyscrapers.

The Crash put an end to America's capacity to prop up the European monetary system, as she had done ever since the Great War ended. US financiers were forced to call in their loans. German banks failed. Between 1929 and 1932 the American economy shrank by almost 40 per cent. But the desperation of the unemployed in the dustbowl of America was as nothing to the political effects of the depression in Europe. The economic collapse wiped out responsible democratic governments which world statesmen were relying on to keep the peace.

The truth was that the European economic system had not properly recovered eleven years after the war had ended. In many ways it was not to recover for another seventy years. Europe's problems had been masked by America's readiness to bail out the post-war European economies, Germany's in particular. After the war German goods were not bought by other countries in the quantities needed to rebuild the German economy. They needed to restart their own economies and began to manufacture goods themselves which they had previously bought from Germany. The Russian market, a major source of revenue before the war, after the Revolution was effectively nonexistent. The war-guilt reparations imposed on Germany could not be paid without massive loans from the US, so when the American loans were withdrawn Germany's economy collapsed in 1929.

German foreign trade fell by two-thirds between 1929 and 1932, wiping out completely the savings of the middle classes. The situation was worse than that of 1923. Professional and well-to-do people went from leading an affluent life to penury, forced to sublet every room of their apartments. The effect hyperinflation had on Berlin, for example, may be vividly glimpsed in the writings of Christopher Isherwood. Conspiracy theories began to circulate, of which the most pernicious were 'The Protocols of the Elders of Zion', forged documents purporting to show that there was a Jewish conspiracy to take over the world and ruin everyone who was not Jewish. In their distress the German people not only lost their faith in democracy, they lost their faith in reason. They were looking for scapegoats, and the scapegoats put forward by Adolf Hitler and the National Socialist Party, or Nazis, who were attracting growing support, were Jews, big business controlled by Jews, foreigners, communists and the Versailles Peace Treaty.

In Britain the Conservatives had been voted out in 1929 for failing to solve the unemployment problem. But under Labour in the next two years unemployment soared to levels the country had never experienced before. Factories closed and men started being laid off in massive numbers in the north, in all the industries which had made Britain's fortune in the past: in coal, the iron and steel industries, shipbuilding, clothing. In some towns like Jarrow in Tyneside, once the home of the Venerable Bede, the unemployment level reached 75 per cent. Investors started to withdraw money from London. By July 1930 unemployment had jumped by almost a million. It was rising so fast that it was expected that one-third of the workforce would soon have no jobs. But the deepening industrial depression was beyond the control of any government because it was due to worldwide pressures and the way the war had thrown international trade into confusion.

This catastrophe left Labour reeling. A rich young Labour minister named Sir Oswald Mosley, influenced by the writings of John Maynard Keynes, in 1930 suggested greater state control of industry and more state-financed public works along the lines of the New Deal that President Roosevelt would use to get America on her feet again. But the Cabinet rejected these remedies and Mosley, who was hot-blooded and impetuous, resigned from the government and from his party. When the New party he attempted to found with six other former Labour MPs had no success, Mosley decided that Parliament was going to be no use to him. In 1932 he dumped the New party and created the British Union of Fascists. He had been deeply affected by a visit to fascist Italy where the system of public works, state monopolies of heavy industry and attempts at economic self-sufficiency gave the impression that the employment crisis had been solved.

Labour under its austere chancellor Philip Snowden believed that retrenchment and ultimately more loans from America were the only way out of the depression. But America had more stringent ideas for balancing the budget than Britain did. Her financiers would not lend the funds required unless the Labour government agreed to reduce the money spent by the state. When MacDonald proposed to the Labour Cabinet in August 1931 that unemployment benefit for the very poorest should be reduced by 10 per cent, as well as the incomes of teachers and members of the armed forces, ministers were so disgusted that most of them resigned. MacDonald therefore formed a National Government with the help of members of both the Conservative and Liberal parties to restore British credit abroad and maintain the value of the pound sterling. Three other Labour members of the Cabinet, including Chancellor Snowden, remained with him. Many members of the Labour party never forgave him for what they regarded as his class treachery.

To counteract severe unemployment in the north the national government in 1934 gave special statutory relief for depressed areas, but ministers seemed unmoved by deputations from the old heavy industries of the north-east, such as the Jarrow Marchers accompanied by their MP Ellen Wilkinson, begging for help. The means test introduced by the government for people unemployed for over six months – which involved public officials entering homes to assess whether household effects could be used to raise an income – intensified the anger of the Labour party against MacDonald. To many, the insensitive way the means test was carried out was a return to the era of the Dickensian workhouse. To this day the term 'means test' remains politically unacceptable.

The National Government never actually put through many of the economies which had caused so many Labour ministers to resign. Alarmed by a peaceful 'mutiny' by 12,000 sailors at Invergordon, the government modified the pay cuts. But because no more money could be borrowed, while £200 million in gold had been withdrawn from London since July, the government went off the gold standard in September 1931. It was feared that this might be disastrous, but in fact it was a great success as it made the pound cheap and British goods cheaper. The export trade began to revive.

Later that year MacDonald went to the polls to seek legitimacy, and the election produced an overwhelming mandate for the National Government, which won 558 seats (471 of these were Conservatives). The Labour party, which had only fifty-two seats, was led in opposition by George Lansbury. Though MacDonald remained prime minister, the National Government became increasingly Conservative in tone. With Neville Chamberlain back as chancellor – Snowden became lord privy seal – protection was adopted as a remedy for the economic crisis, a 10 per cent levy being slapped on most imports, especially manufactured goods. This resulted in the resignation of the Liberal free traders from its ranks.

In 1932 at the Imperial Conference in Ottawa Britain hoped to establish the policy of imperial preference in trade, giving advantageous tariffs within the empire. The Dominions, however, agreed only where it would not hurt their own produce. Ottawa thus achieved very little. But the national government managed to balance the budget and revive the national credit, so in 1934 the unemployment pay cuts were restored, and by 1936 Britain had come out of recession. At its height, just under three million people had been unemployed. Meanwhile the lack of American investment in Europe had been making it harder to pay reparations and war debts, so in 1931 the American president Herbert Hoover accepted a one-year moratorium. The following year Germany's reparations payments were permanently suspended after the Lausanne war-debts conference. Unable to repay the United States without being repaid herself, by 1933 Britain waived her allies' old debts and abandoned repayment of the £900 million she owed to the United States. This only increased America's view that meddling in the old world did her no good, and she continued to be strongly isolationist.

An extremely powerful disarmament movement took hold of the British people in the first half of the 1930s. In 1935 the Peace Ballot organized by the League of Nations Union and distributed by enthusiasts found that 90 per cent of the British people still favoured multilateral disarmament. There was more belief than ever before in 'collective security' and of submitting all disputes to the League of Nations to prevent the suffering of another war. In 1933 when the Oxford Union, the university debating society, passed the motion 'This House will not fight for King and Country', it was the high point of a distinctly anti-war feeling. People passionately believed that peace was the only option. But the early 1930s were also the time when it became clear that the Paris peace settlement based on collective security and orchestrated by the League would not last in its present form. For the system to work everybody had to obey the rules. In 1930 MacDonald presided over a London Conference on Naval Disarmament attended by Britain, the USA, France, Italy and Japan. Yet a year later Japan had seized Manchuria in China and pulled out of the League of Nations when it condemned her.

Despite the promises embodied in the Covenant of the League, no further action was taken against Japan. With most economies at a standstill League members could do nothing except express moral disapproval. The League's creators had not imagined that by the 1930s there would be governments which did not subscribe to the honourable conventions of the past and did not care if they lost the good opinion of the world. Once Japan had led the way the whole rationale of the League of Nations dissolved. Even so, people still believed in it, and the Word Disarmament Conference which met in 1932 at MacDonald's urging was the high point of the British government's acceptance of that belief.

But the conference was a dismal failure. The French would not agree to their arms being reduced to equality with Germany's official quota, unless British troops patrolled her eastern frontier. They were tormented by the prospect of German militarism reviving, for it was an open secret that Germany was rearming. Britain was in no financial position to send troops to guard the Franco-German borders and rejected the proposal. Meanwhile the Germans and their new leader Hitler, who had come to power in January 1933, chose to represent themselves as insulted by the French. By October that year Germany had withdrawn from the Disarmament Conference and left the League of Nations.

Adolf Hitler had been elected on a very clear programme: to destroy the humiliation of Versailles and to reclaim the land removed from Germany. In his book *Mein Kampf* ('My Struggle'), he had openly described his plans to exterminate races he believed were either evil like the Jews or stupid like the Slavs. He outlined a policy of occupying territory in the east to give the superior German race living space, or *Lebensraum*. But at the time the book was written in the 1920s no one could take *Mein Kampf* seriously. Hitler was then a would-be painter and political activist who had been imprisoned for a failed coup in Munich. Yet only a few days after he took over as chancellor he had removed civil liberties for Jewish people, and two years later racist laws were in place forbidding Jewish people to marry non-Jews; by 1938 half the Jewish population of Germany had left in despair.

Hitler's actions effectively destroyed the principle of collective security based on disarming to the lowest point, but its enthusiasts refused to accept that. For the rest of the decade Winston Churchill was one of the strongest voices urging action against Nazi Germany. As early as April 1933, he warned Parliament, 'One of the things which we were told after the Great War would be a security for us was that Germany would be a democracy with Parliamentary institutions. All that has been swept away. You have dictatorship, most grim dictatorship.' If Germany was allowed to rearm, he said, she would soon snatch back her lost territories – territories which bands of unemployed German youths were aggressively campaigning for, 'singing their ancient songs, demanding to be conscripted into an army, eagerly seeking the most terrible weapons of war; burning to suffer and die for their fatherland'. Churchill believed that MacDonald's ideas, for all their nobility, were a load of hot air, that while he talked of Britain dropping four air-force divisions, European factories were filling with arms. 'I cannot recall any time when the gap between the kind of words statesmen used and what was actually happening in many countries was so great as it is now,' he told the Commons.

After Germany's withdrawal from the Disarmament Conference the government acknowledged to some extent that the ideas of disarmament and reduction of armaments to the lowest point were no longer viable. In 1934 a new air-defence programme was announced, increasing the RAF by forty-one squadrons, and the following year the government published a White Paper which recognized the need for greater military provision. Nevertheless, at a popular level disarmament went on being the remedy for the world's ills. There was a general reluctance to contemplate the possibility of war. Moreover the British government, like many Britons, felt that Germany had been treated too harshly and was sympathetic to Hitler's revision of Versailles. For that reason, nothing happened in 1935 when Hitler told the world that he had created an air force, or when he started military conscription again to add another thirty-six divisions to his army. The British had thought they had protected themselves by signing a treaty with Hitler that limited the German navy to 35 per cent the size of the British, and submarine strength to 45 per cent.

At the same time, neither the British nor the French wanted to alienate Mussolini, the Italian leader. In April 1935, at the Stresa Conference called specifically to discuss Hitler's announcement that Germany would no longer be bound by the arms limitations of Versailles, Britain, France and Italy sought agreement on forming a common front against German rearmament. Nevertheless Mussolini had more in common with Hitler as a fellow dictator whose regime was based on violence than with the western democracies of France and Britain.

Despite joining the Stresa Front in October that year Italy, which had been very disappointed by the territories she had gained in the peace treaties, flouted the precepts of the League of Nations and invaded Ethiopia in pursuit of her dream of a north African empire. Reluctantly, because she still wanted Mussolini as an ally, Britain along with the rest of the League imposed sanctions on Italy. But the Italian forces did not withdraw.

The French and British governments now behaved very curiously: they decided to ignore the League of Nations and make a deal with Mussolini. By the secret Hoare–Laval Pact, signed by the British foreign secretary Samuel Hoare and the French prime minister Pierre Laval, they offered Italy a partition plan that gave her two-thirds of Ethiopia. In December the agreement leaked out and aroused such anger in Britain that Hoare had to resign. Italy nevertheless remained in possession of most of Ethiopia. The Anglo-French policy of appeasement, of allowing dictators to take chunks of territory at will in preference to fighting a war, had begun to take shape.

MacDonald the idealist grew too ill to remain in office and at the general election in November 1935 Baldwin became prime minister, his National Government winning a majority of 245. The public-school-educated barrister Clement Attlee had been elected to lead the Labour party, which, though it remained out of office, now had 154 seats in Parliament, a gain of one hundred.

Having seen that nothing had happened to Mussolini over Ethiopia, on 7 March 1936 Hitler moved his troops into the demilitarized Rhineland, proclaiming that Germany would no longer abide by the peace treaties. Versailles was at last visibly dead in the water. France was devastated by this move. The buffer between her and Germany had been removed, and she was left staring at a militarized frontier with Germany that now bristled with soldiers.

But Britain, France's ally, did not share her fears. British ministers were distracted by the many other issues demanding their attention which seemed just as important as containing the European dictators. In Mandated Palestine, British troops were required in greater numbers because of clashes between the indigenous Arabs and Jewish settlers. As the decade went on, growing numbers of Jewish refugees fled there from Germany, though a 1930 government White Paper on Palestine emphasized the resulting plight of the Arabs. It warned of the possibility that they might be swamped by a Jewish majority if there was not a temporary end to Jewish immigration.

But the real issue preoccupying British statesmen and British newspapers was India. In 1931 the architect Edwin Lutyens completed his masterpiece, the Viceroy's House in New Delhi, little knowing that it was only to be used for another sixteen years. All kinds of excuses continued to be found for preventing India from obtaining independence or even reaching Dominion status. There was now an articulate party called the Muslim League under Mohammed Jinnah, who like Gandhi was a lawyer. Jinnah was beginning to call for the partition of India to surmount the racial hatred between Muslims and Hindus.

With the great business of India linking so many members of the British middle classes, the subject of Indian independence obsessed Britain in the 1930s. Generations of Britons had been Indian civil servants, tea-brokers, planters and district commissioners; they were incensed at the way their businesses were being ruined by Gandhi's boycott of British goods.

By 1927, with Congress refusing to recognize the provincial legislatures because they would be satisfied with nothing less than full responsible government, Indian discontent produced a new Parliamentary Commission. Members of all three British political parties were sent to India to investigate her grievances. Though it was headed by the distinguished Liberal Sir John Simon, former attorney-general and home secretary, it did not contain a single Indian member. The viceroy Lord Irwin, the future Lord Halifax, who had become friendly with Gandhi, had already stated

in 1929 that Dominion status was the ultimate goal of the British government for India. But this was not good enough for the militant Indian
politicians, nor did the Simon Commission promise it when the report was
published in 1930.

Neither did the Government of India Act of 1935. This act was brought
in when it was at last acknowledged that talks with Gandhi were the only
solution, after 100,000 people had been imprisoned for taking part in his
civil disobedience campaigns. It created a federal structure so that the
national administration could reflect the diversity of the provinces within
the country, an arrangement which the Indian princely state rulers led by
the Maharajah of Bikaner agreed to participate in. But, although this gave
responsible self-government to the provinces, it still was not the self-
government of a Dominion. At national level despite a federal legislature
to which Cabinet ministers were responsible, the ultimate say on foreign
affairs, defence and religion continued to lie with the viceroy. The new
constitution was considered not to have taken into consideration properly
the rights of the Muslims and to have given too much power to the Indian
princes. It had nonetheless just begun to be implemented when the Second
World War broke out.

The Cambridge don E. M. Forster's *A Passage to India*, which highlighted the uneasy relationship between the British and their colonial
subjects, was published in 1924, and soon reached classic status in Britain.
Nevertheless complacency was an overwhelming characteristic of the
empire in the 1930s. This was partly because the empire and British
influence seemed as prevalent as ever. A treaty of 1936 put an end to the
occupation of Egypt, but British troops still guarded the Suez Canal, and
there was a clause allowing Britain to reoccupy the country in the event of
any threat to her interests.

British businessmen, officials, civil servants and advisers continued
knocking around in Shepheard's Hotel in Cairo and other famous British
expat haunts. Shrewd deals made in the nineteenth century ensured that
the empire still controlled parts of the Gulf States, such as Kuwait whose
foreign policy was run by Britain until 1961. To the growing number of
Arab nationalists in the Middle East, nothing much seemed to have
changed. When in 1924 the warlike Wahhabi tribe under their leader Ibn
Saud pushed the sharif Hussein out of Mecca, uniting the whole of Arabia
under what would become the Saudi royal family, they negotiated their
borders with the British.

Though Iraq was no longer a Mandate after 1932, rebelling Iraqi
tribesmen were still strafed by British aeroplanes. The Brooke dynasty of
white rajahs continued to rule Sarawak, a state in Malaysia on the island
of Borneo, as they had done for nearly a century. The Malaysian rubber

planters, as was candidly observed by the novelist Somerset Maugham, whiled away their time with chota pegs brought to them by natives they called 'boys', as if nothing would ever disturb the empire. Few of them took much notice that Britain was no longer absolutely assured of being able to defend the far eastern parts of the empire like Singapore and Malaya, whose rubber in the age of the motor car had become very alluring to the Japanese.

In Britain life went on much as usual. The publisher Victor Gollancz had started the Left Book Club in 1935, a vehicle for attacking fascism and promoting left-wing ideas which two years later had half a million subscribers. Gollancz and his supporters wanted to wake Britain up to the fact that in Italy fascism had destroyed free speech and imprisoned its opponents, while in Germany it had become a daily occurrence for Jews to be beaten up, robbed and sometimes killed. Yet the British and their government attempted to ignore what was going on in Europe. Britain continued to be a predictable, mainly tranquil land where all classes were passionate about games. Too many of her people were shutting their eyes to the impending cataclysm of world war.

Edward VIII (1936)
George VI (1936–1952)

The Failure of Appeasement (1936-1939)

Stanley Baldwin was a reassuring leader of a country whose people were longing for stability and the nostalgic sort of England which they remembered from before 1914. The dreamlike calm in which Britain existed between the wars was only briefly disrupted by the Abdication Crisis. In 1936, the year after Baldwin became prime minister, the popular king George V died. He and his wife, the redoubtable Queen Mary, had stored up a great deal of affection for the monarchy (George V had even nobly forsworn alcohol as part of the war effort), as was seen during the celebrations of their Silver Jubilee in May 1935.

But their son, the new king, Edward VIII, a handsome, weak-willed man-about-town, was quite unlike them. Showing none of the attentiveness to duty characteristic of the British royal family, frivolous and pleasure-loving, he was famed for his mistresses and his hedonistic way of life at Fort Belvedere, his country house. He had a soft-hearted and emotional side, however, and had earned some popularity by speaking out about the unemployed and about miners' conditions in Wales during the depression. But the bulk of his time was spent playing among the fashionable London fast set. He became enamoured of a hard-bitten, twice-married American named Mrs Simpson, who could not have adorned the throne and might in fact have endangered it. As the head of the Church of England, despite the anomaly that its founder Henry VIII had been married many times, the king, it was felt, could not be married to a divorcee. It was also believed that such an unsuitable marriage might be the last straw for the already fragile empire and Dominions, which were united by the crown.

Somehow, guided by Stanley Baldwin, Edward VIII had enough sense of his royal duty to abdicate, 'for the sake of the woman I love', as he put it dramatically in a speech broadcast to the world by the BBC. Edward took the title Duke of Windsor and retired to France. His younger brother the Duke of York, whose daughters were the ten-year-old Princess Elizabeth and the six-year-old Princess Margaret Rose, became King George VI. The

Duchess of York, the former Lady Elizabeth Bowes Lyon, became Queen Elizabeth. Thanks to Baldwin, the country and the throne survived tremors which could not have been less welcome. For the international situation had suddenly taken a turn for the worst.

Nazism seemed to win international respectability when the 1936 Olympic Games were held in Berlin, a venue arranged two years before the Nazis came to power. The Olympic stadium was tarnished by being draped with swastikas, and the Olympic experience by being associated with the Nazis, who used the Games to hand out leaflets about the superiority of the Aryan (non-Jewish German) race. But though the Germans won the largest number of medals, their racist propaganda was exposed for nonsense when the black American Jesse Owens won four gold medals. The impression that Nazism was socially acceptable was enhanced the following year when the Duke and Duchess of Windsor visited Germany to meet Hitler.

Despite Baldwin's kindness as a man, his readiness to respect views other than his own and his gifts as a Parliamentarian, his weakness as a prime minister was that he was not really interested in foreign affairs. Britain in the late 1930s with her slightly parochial air, reminds one of a jolly ocean-liner heading comfortably towards catastrophe. With its red telephone boxes (first seen in 1929), its red buses, its men in bowler hats, London was as orderly and safe as it had always been. And no real extremists flourished to either the right or the left despite the turmoil on the continent.

Few Britons joined Sir Oswald Mosley's British Union of Fascists, created in 1932 in response to what Mosley called the communist threat. He used his claim that Jews were behind the Russian Revolution as an excuse to unleash his own brutal quasi-military gang, the Blackshirts, on innocent Jewish people. The Blackshirts used to march through the East End of London where many Jewish people then lived and beat them up. That same year Parliament passed the Public Order Act which gave the home secretary the power to stop marches and banned the wearing of political uniforms. But like everything to do with Britain, for good or bad, it was felt that the home secretary could have moved a lot more quickly to stop Mosley than he had done. The tolerance traditional in Britain, where communism could attract intellectual sympathy but not inspire a large political party, allowed most people to think of Mosley as little more than a foolish man. He was permitted to carry on with his BUF rallies – he was knocked unconscious at one in Liverpool in 1937 – and was not interned until May 1940, nine months after war had broken out (he was released in November 1943).

However, to the young and intellectual, Britain's pragmatic indifference to extremism in foreign countries where it did not threaten her interests smacked of moral cowardice, of passing by on the other side. The Spanish Civil War, which broke out in 1936, was a case in point. Many believed that Britain should have done more to prevent the republican Spanish government being destroyed by right-wing forces under General Franco. The lack of support the republicans received from the liberal powers of Europe such as Britain and France drove brave young men from those countries and America, alarmed by the apparently unstoppable spread of fascism, to go out to Spain to help the republicans. But Baldwin and Chamberlain stuck to the view that it would be wrong to intervene in a civil war.

They also did not want to antagonize Italy, which they still wished to wean away from Germany, even though the two countries had combined to form an alliance called the Axis – and the Axis powers supported the right-wing side in the Spanish Civil War, while Soviet Russia armed the legitimate government.

Baldwin retired in 1937, having seen George VI safely on to the throne and the Duke and Duchess of Windsor off to permanent exile abroad. Neville Chamberlain took over as prime minister. He was a good, decent man, the author of much progressive social legislation. But he faced a very difficult international situation, which had given rise to the widespread belief that to oppose the dictator Hitler would plunge Britain into war. Chamberlain shared that belief, and as a result became associated with what after the Second World War would be regarded as the craven policy of appeasement. There was in fact little else Britain could do at a time when she was so weak militarily.

In the late 1930s the international situation began to spiral out of control. Even southern Ireland turned up the heat. By 1933 De Valera's Fianna Fáil had become the majority party, and immediately set about unilaterally dismantling Ireland's relationship with the British Empire and jettisoning the old constitution of the Irish Free State. Relations between Britain and Eire (Fianna Fáil's new name for southern Ireland) became even more bitter: De Valera repudiated the £100 million lent by the British government after the 1903 Irish Land Act which had enabled tenant farmers to buy more than nine million acres from their landlords, and a trade war began between the two countries. By 1937 Eire, in every way but name, was an independent republic. In 1949 that final detail was remedied and the Republic of Ireland was formally declared. She announced her neutrality at the outbreak of the Second World War but would not let Britain use her southern ports, thus endangering Britain's security.

Ever since Germany had broken the terms of the Versailles treaty, the danger she posed to international peace was all too evident to far-sighted people like Winston Churchill and an increasing number of Labour and

Conservative MPs. They believed that Britain should spend more on rearming and should stand up to the dictators who were destroying democracy in Europe by threatening to fight them if necessary. But the national government was still in power in London and its leaders still held to appeasement. They shrank from plunging Britain into another world war when she had scarcely got over the dislocation caused by the first.

In 1937 Lord Halifax was sent to discuss treaty revision in central Europe with Hitler. To the dismay of his critics, Chamberlain a year later made a more dramatic move to separate Mussolini from Hitler: the British government accepted Mussolini's conquest of Ethiopia by recognizing the King of Italy as its Emperor. But the foreign secretary Anthony Eden who had become convinced that this level of appeasement was a mistake, believed the price was too high and resigned in February 1938.

In March Hitler drastically began to reinvent the German Empire. A German army went into Austria in March 1938 and joined her to the Third Reich, or Third Empire. Welcomed by most Austrians, the 'Anschluss' had been expressly forbidden by Versailles, yet not a soul stirred to prevent it. The Nazi government had been confident that nothing would happen, because reports from its ambassador to London Joachim von Ribbentrop had assessed the British upper classes as being pro-German, mainly on the evidence of the appeasers he met at Nancy Astor's home, the so-called Cliveden Set. One of them, the editor of *The Times* Geoffrey Dawson, wrote his paper's pro-German editorials. Sir Oswald Mosley, whose admiration for the Nazis was so great that he would be married to his second wife Diana Mitford at Goebbels' house in Berlin, continued to be received by much of upper-class London society.

Hitler had only just begun. The German government, whose presses were pouring forth directives describing what the new German Empire demanded from its citizens, started churning out propaganda about the plight of the three million Sudeten Deutsch (or Germans) who lived in former Habsburg territory which the 1919 Treaty of St Germain had given to the new state of Czechoslovakia. It was quite obvious that Czechoslovakia was Hitler's next target, and in September he duly gave her an ultimatum. America's failure to guarantee the peace had driven France to make alliances on Germany's borders to protect herself more thoroughly. By the terms of one of these treaties she was bound to come to Czechoslovakia's aid. This meant war.

It was a war for which Britain was simply not ready. Moreover, since Europe was devoted to the right of self-determination there did seem to be good reason for the Sudetenland to be joined to Germany. Neville Chamberlain, who had had two earlier meetings with Hitler at Berchtesgaden and Godesberg, and had been persuaded that the Sudeten

Neville Chamberlain returns from Munich, 30 September 1938, waving the bit of paper which, he claimed, granted Britain 'peace in our time' by allowing Hitler to take Czechoslovakia's Sudetenland.

Germans had a point, flew to Munich to negotiate with the Führer. At the Munich conference attended by the French prime minister Edouard Daladier, Hitler, Mussolini and Chamberlain, it was agreed that Germany would take over the Sudetenland part of Czechoslovakia. Chamberlain returned clutching a piece of paper and saying in what would become a notorious phrase that he had achieved 'peace in our time'. Duff Cooper, the first lord of the Admiralty, resigned in protest at the betrayal of Czechoslovakia.

Nothing could have been less true than Chamberlain's belief that he had achieved peace for his time. He had bought a breathing space by throwing Czechoslovakia into the mouth of the wolf. And, as the clearest sign that appeasement did not work, Germany's military position became still more formidable once her tanks had rolled into the Sudetenland and appropriated forty divisions of the Czech army and most of the country's natural defences.

Whatever Chamberlain's feeling that it was 'horrible, fantastic and incredible . . . that we should be digging trenches and trying on gas-masks here because of a quarrel in a far-away country between people of whom we know nothing', it was becoming clear that even Britain could not insulate herself from Hitler's activities. By March 1939 the Führer had broken his word to Chamberlain and seized the rest of Czechoslovakia, the non-German Czech part – her steel mills, her industries and her population. All Chamberlain had bought was time, a year, for Britain to rearm and create an air force able to take on the Luftwaffe. Even he now saw that his policy of appeasing dictators had failed. Reluctantly Britain began to prepare herself for war. Appeasement formally came to an end on 31 March 1939 when guarantees of her territorial integrity were offered to Poland by France and Britain. Soon afterwards similar guarantees were granted to Romania and Greece.

Conscription, which even at the height of the First World War had appeared such an ethical problem and a threat to Britain's civil liberties, was introduced without prior discussion or much protest on 29 April, its first appearance in peacetime. The menace of Hitler, who had grabbed one country after another, made most Britons accept the need to begin military training. Once again Britain, which had been on distant terms with her First World War ally for too long, co-ordinated military secrets with the French.

Hitler had no fear of their preparations. Since 1936, if not before, many ordinary German factories had been turned over to manufacturing a huge arsenal for the drive to the east to recapture all the cities wrongfully given to Poland in 1919. That summer, more strenuously than ever, the German press pounded out demands to get Danzig and the Polish Corridor back where they 'rightfully' belonged. The only country which might prevent this was Soviet Russia. France and Britain now found themselves in a race with Germany to obtain an alliance with her new ruler Stalin.

But the dictator Stalin had not been impressed by the western powers' sacrifice of Czechoslovakia to save their skins, and Poland – with painful memories of her old ruler's savagery – refused to allow any of Russia's troops on to her soil.

On 23 August 1939, to the despair of the liberal western powers the German–Soviet Non-Aggression Pact was announced. It contained a secret agreement that Germany and Russia would divide Poland between them. Chamberlain warned Hitler that Britain would support Poland if she were attacked, and that pledge finally became an official Anglo-Polish Treaty on 25 August. But Hitler had obtained the go-ahead he needed. On the first day of September Nazi tanks supported by dive-bombers invaded Poland, spreading terror wherever they went. Two days later Britain and France declared war on Nazi Germany. The Second World War had begun.

The Second World War (1939-1945)

For the inhabitants of Britain, the Second World War began in a strangely hesitant way. A couple of thousand miles away, in the middle of the continental landmass, palls of smoke hung over the bombed-out cities of Poland. By the end of September 1939, more than 80,000 Polish soldiers had abandoned their homeland to avoid joining the 700,000 prisoners taken by the Germans and their allies, the Russians, who invaded Poland from the east that same month. But in Britain, Poland's ally, all was as quiet and peaceful as if she were not at war.

An army was created for Britain's defence, a Home Guard called the Local Defence Volunteers, and 146,000 men enlisted that summer. They were mainly Great War veterans, allowing young men to fight abroad. But, for all the noise of air-raid warnings, and the inconvenience of the blackout which put an end to street lighting and doubled road accidents, no enemy planes flew over Britain. The East End had been evacuated of half its children, many of whom were billeted in distant Cornwall to keep them out of harm's way when the Luftwaffe bombed the London Docks. But it never happened. After a few months the evacuee children went home again. No British or French soldiers fired a shot against the Nazis. In disgust, American newspaper correspondents called this period the 'Phoney War' and wondered what the two governments were up to. Would Britain and France in the end betray Poland as they had betrayed Czechoslovakia, and accept a peace offer?

In late 1939 the whiff of Munich continued to hang over the British government as a result of Chamberlain's delay in declaring war on Germany. While the civilized world watched with fascinated horror the newsreels which recorded the onrush of the German tanks through Poland, for two days the British government did nothing. It seemed an extraordinary hesitation; in fact it was a sensible hesitation reflecting the fact that Britain was in no position to wage war against anyone, let alone miles away in Poland. Nevertheless Britain was bound by her August Treaty to declare war immediately on Hitler, and it looked like cowardice that she had not done so.

Forty-eight hours after the attack on Poland, Prime Minister Chamberlain had announced to the House of Commons that if the German government withdrew its forces as far as the British government was concerned the situation could revert to peace as before! He was hoping that the Poles would offer Hitler Danzig to save England from war. Chamberlain still thought, even then, that he could bargain with Hitler. It took the threatened resignation of half the Cabinet to force Chamberlain to his senses as midnight approached. Earlier that evening, amid angry scenes in the House of Commons, the deputy Labour leader Arthur Greenwood

had remonstrated with Chamberlain about 'imperilling the very foundations of our national honour'. 'Speak for England, Arthur!' came the shout
from the angry Conservative backbenches when he stood up.

The next morning, 3 September, the ultimatum Chamberlain had been
made to give Germany expired. But though Britain and France were bound
to come to Poland's aid, their war on her behalf would take place in a
different arena. This was not immediately understood by those who were
anxious to make up for the betrayal of Czechoslovakia. But the speed of
Germany's campaign, as her forces unveiled her new method of warfare,
the *Blitzkrieg* or lightning strike – with tanks advancing a hundred miles a
day, in tandem with screaming dive-bombers – saw her overrun Poland in
two weeks. Though the Poles were brave fighters and superb airmen, their
equipment – they still deployed a prized cavalry division – was old
fashioned and swiftly annihilated.

Many people publicly urged that British bombers should cover a French
attack on Germany, but the service chiefs would not risk it. Britain did not
have the aircraft to defend herself if she were to attack German troops. The
government's policy of appeasement had left Britain with too few planes,
and parity with Germany would not be achieved until the spring of 1940.
With only a small professional army in readiness, Britain's initial response
to the war could only take place at sea, and not in Poland. Her powerful
navy was far larger than Germany's and would prevent food and fuel from
reaching her. But that was going to be a slow process.

The French army on the other hand was enormous and conspicuously
superb. Consisting of ninety infantry divisions, as opposed to Britain's ten,
if it had combined with the Polish army at the beginning of September they
would have fielded forty more divisions than the German army. Germany
had only left twenty-three divisions to guard her frontier with France and
they could have been speedily overcome.

But the French army never had a chance to invade Germany from the
rear to take the pressure off the Poles. The French reliance on conscript
armies – that is, on soldiers who held ordinary jobs in peacetime – meant
that the French mobilization in September 1939 took two weeks. During
that time, while Frenchmen left their jobs as lawyers, clerks, hoteliers, and
donned their uniforms, Poland was forced to surrender. Russia entered
Poland on the 17th of that month to complete her swift dismemberment
from the east. Accordingly, the order was given to withdraw the small
number of French troops who had already made a few skirmishes over
Germany's western frontier. Instead France settled down to defend the
Maginot Line, the defences of trenches, pillboxes and big guns that ran
along her frontier with Germany. The rest of Europe remained neutral, and
peace – other than in Finland, which Russia invaded on the last day of

November to re-establish herself on the Baltic – seemed to reign that winter.

The question now was where the allies should launch their attack on the Axis powers. From September onwards Britain and France sent their aircraft factories into frenzied production. Britain in particular was remarkably badly prepared for war. Even though the Royal Navy was hunting German submarines deep beneath the icy northern seas, the improved facilities required by the naval base at Scapa Flow, including a better anti-submarine boom, would not be ready until the following year. In October a German U-boat managed to penetrate the base and sink the battleship *Royal Oak*, killing 800 seamen. It would not be until March 1940 that twenty divisions of conscript soldiers would be trained and ready to cross the Channel to join the British Expeditionary Force, Britain's small professional army, in France.

That was one of the penalties of being a peace-loving, unmilitaristic nation. Britain started the war with one hand tied behind her back. Against the enormous professional armies of fascist Germany, whose torchlit parades throughout the 1930s had been a source of amusement to the irreverent British, was mustered an army of eccentric amateurs. The Germans also had the munitions and armies of Austria and Czechoslovakia to call on. On the other hand Britain had France and the vast resources of the British Empire at her back.

The British armies that fought the Second World War would be even larger than Kitchener's armies. By the end of the war, six years later, from Britain alone five million men would have been called up. But the shadow of the Great War, which had ended only twenty years before, made Britain and France in 1939 very reluctant to throw their armies into battle against the Germans and Russians. The all too recent memory of the trenches, and of the Somme in particular, had convinced the British forces chiefs that the war would have to be won in the air. But where was the war to be fought?

In the spring of 1940 the allies decided to put an end to the German export, via the Norwegian port of Narvik, of Swedish iron ore that was crucial for the German war effort, especially in the manufacture of shells, submarines and tanks. The plan involved laying mines in Norwegian waters. Meanwhile in vivid broadcasts on the BBC Winston Churchill, first lord of the Admiralty since 3 September, was advising the neutral states of Norway, Holland, Denmark, Belgium and Switzerland to join Britain and France against Nazism or they would be swallowed up too. 'Each one hopes that if he feeds the crocodile enough, the crocodile will eat him last,' he said. There was of course a second crocodile at work: the Finns' tiny but gallant army on skis – 'white death' it was called – consisting of only twenty-five divisions held down one hundred Russian divisions until 20 March 1940, when it was forced to surrender.

By this time the allied plan to mine Norwegian waters had become known in Berlin. Thus, in a surprise invasion, German forces landed in Norway on 9 April, shortly before the British were due to arrive. Backed by the Luftwaffe, they captured the capital Oslo and all Norway's main ports and airfields in only a few hours. On the very same day German tank regiments moved north across the German border to capture Copenhagen and overrun Denmark. British forces were soon landed in Norway, but her main ports remained securely in German hands. After moving out of Oslo to rally the country with radio messages broadcast from a secret mountain village, the King of Norway reluctantly agreed to evacuate. He left his country at the beginning of June 1940, on a ship bound for Britain with the last of the British soldiers.

His departure had been precipitated by news from the south which ruined all hope of saving Norway as allied territory. On 10 May, as guerrilla fighting continued in the icy fjords, German armies invaded neutral Holland and Belgium. At dawn, as in Norway, parachutists attacked Holland's two principal cities, Rotterdam and the Hague, capturing all their bridges before the Dutch could blow them up. By the 15th the Dutch had surrendered. A few hundred miles south-west Belgium was also fighting for her life, assisted by the British Expeditionary Force which had rushed to her aid from France. In another deadly surprise, only seventy-eight German parachute engineers were needed to capture the fort guarding the Albert Canal. Further airborne invaders prevented other crucial bridges being destroyed. Belgium too was soon overwhelmed. But this was just the prelude to Hitler's main objective, the capture of Belgium's vast neighbour France. For his ultimate game plane was to control France's Atlantic ports, and, after he had captured European Russia, to be prepared for the war between America and the future German empire, which he was convinced would one day take place.

While the French army and the whole of the British Expeditionary Force were rushing north-east to defend Belgium, to the south, unbeknown to them, German armies were invading France. German tanks were plunging through the thick woods of the Ardennes into France just above Luxembourg where the defensive Maginot Line came to an end. This weakness in the French border defences had been noted before the war by British strategists with some dismay. But the French military always reassured them that they considered the hilly, forested terrain of the Ardennes quite impassable by tanks. The Ardennes were therefore in no need of any great defence forces since they were a natural barrier in themselves.

The leader of the Panzer division which ploughed through the Ardennes was a man named Heinz Guderian who before the war had become fascinated by tank warfare. The British army had been leaders in the field and their experiments had been closely followed by Guderian. Not only was he convinced that tanks could be used like battering rams in wooded terrain, he had also become a master of strategy. His theory was that victory could be achieved by what the military historian Sir Basil Liddell Hart called 'deep strategic penetration by independent armoured forces' involving 'a long-range tank drive to cut the main arteries of the opposing army far behind its front'. Guderian would do just that to the allied armies.

The crucial point of the operation was to get the tanks across the River Meuse before the French realized what was happening. On 13 May at a point just west of the scene of another major French defeat, Sedan, German infantry crossed the river in rubber boats, attended once more by screaming bombers. As the French troops on the other side of the river were rounded up, pontoon bridges were constructed, over which soon trundled a stream of German tanks. While French attention was still focused on sending help to Belgium, the Panzer division began sweeping west to cut off the British and French armies in Belgium. They took Abbeville on the Somme, and then, having reached the coast, occupied Boulogne and Calais. They were now within fifteen miles of Dunkirk, just by the French border with Belgium – the only port from which the trapped British army could escape. But amazingly the German tanks went no further, because Hitler gave the order to halt. Although this is sometimes called Hitler's first mistake (his second was to invade Russia), he was following the advice of one of his senior commanders in France, General Gerd von Rundstedt, who wanted to preserve his tanks for the south, and that of Göring, who believed that the Luftwaffe would be sufficient to wipe out the British. Had the German army not stopped, the entire British Expeditionary Force would have been killed or captured. As it was it had to leave all its heavy artillery and tanks behind in France to be seized by the Germans.

The order to evacuate the British army from Dunkirk was given against the protests of the French. But it was evident that the British had to get out or be captured. On 26 May the mass evacuation began. In what became known as 'the miracle of Dunkirk', between 850 and 950 ordinary boats responded to the government's SOS and, organized by the Admiralty, rushed to France to help evacuate the army. They included cross-Channel boats, holiday steamers, hopper barges from the London County Councils, and nine tugs which towed barges behind them, as well as yachts, lifeboats and other private small craft. As the Luftwaffe bombed and strafed them, the exhausted soldiers waded through water up to their waists to get out to the hundreds of boats bobbing in the Channel. Some 224,000 British troops were retrieved from France and 95,000 French. Despite the murderous attacks by the Luftwaffe, thanks to the Royal Air Force and the weather, only 2,000 men died during the brilliantly executed evacuation.

On 9 June, as the Germans swept through France, her army crumbled and her government fled Paris for Tours. Meanwhile Mussolini, scenting spoils and a way to expand the Italian Empire, announced on the 10th that Italy (which had remained neutral until then) had entered the war on Hitler's side. On the 14th German troops goosestepped through the French capital, and two days later the French government asked for an armistice. It was granted on the 20th in the same place, Compiègne, and in the same railway carriage where the armistice of just over twenty years before had ended the First World War. The German revenge for Versailles seemed complete. When Churchill, who had just become prime minister in a turnabout for both his and Britain's fortunes, heard the news of France's defeat by the Nazis, he wept.

With the tragedy of the fall of France, the offshore islands of Great Britain were facing a hostile coastline of 2,000 miles. The most likely prospect was that she would be the next to be overrun by a regime which tortured and murdered anyone who got in its way or displeased it. Hitler assumed that Britain would make a separate peace, as the US ambassador to London, Joseph P. Kennedy, had predicted.

But Hitler had mistaken her nature. Ever since the invasion of Holland and Belgium, Britain had been led by a man who for a decade had been warning the world about the need to resist the evils of Nazism. During the Second World War Winston Churchill's superhuman energies could be used to the full. At last a real fighting spirit had become prime minister, ready to remind the British that this war was not 'a question of fighting for Danzig or fighting for Poland. We are fighting to save the world from the pestilence of Nazi tyranny and in defence of all that is most sacred to man.'

Had Chamberlain remained prime minister, it is possible that Britain would have given in; certainly some of the Cabinet had thoughts of a negotiated peace. With German planes and boats on the north coast of France and the whole of northern and western Europe overrun by German armies, logic would suggest that a country which was so highly dependent on imports for food should simply do a deal. Italy's entry into the war guaranteed that at any moment the tiny British armies in Egypt (36,000 men) and the Sudan (9,000) would be confronted by 200,000 invading Italians from their north African empire.

Nevertheless there were still the Dominions and colonies and their manpower ranged round the world, all of which had declared that they would support the empire. Many exiled governments, including those of

Norway, Holland and Belgium, found refuge in Britain; their fellow countrymen would start resistance movements from within their occupied countries. Moreover Churchill, who began negotiating with the US president Franklin D. Roosevelt almost immediately for matériel and above all credit, was hopeful that one day America would join the war.

Ever since Churchill had taken over the government on 10 May, the same day that the German invaders parachuted into Holland and Belgium, a new spirit had been infused into England. The acute national danger and the collapse of the Norwegian campaign made the House of Commons realize that it could no longer put up with Chamberlain's well-intentioned muddling. Now Britain had Churchill, an extraordinary public speaker and her most inspirational wartime prime minister. As he would so stirringly broadcast to the nation on 4 June 1940 after Dunkirk, Britain would never give in: 'We shall defend our island, whatever the cost may be, we shall fight on the beaches, we shall fight on the landing grounds, we shall fight in the fields and in the streets, we shall fight in the hills; we shall never surrender.' What has been called the bulldog spirit, a grip that refuses to let go even in its death throes, was epitomized in this magnificent, short, fat, bald Englishman. Although his generals often found him maddening, owing to his love of amateur strategy, Churchill's inventiveness, his refusal to accept defeat, above all his extraordinary eloquence roused the British people in their country's darkest hour. He said on his appointment, 'I have nothing to offer but blood, toil, tears and sweat', but it was enough. In his siren suit, cigar clamped in his teeth, fingers in a V-sign for victory, he represented hope.

In the mid-1930s Churchill's reputation had suffered as a result of his opposition to Indian self-rule and his support for Edward VIII. He was not popular among the Conservative grass roots thanks to his habit of changing parties. But in the Second World War his being above party was a huge asset. He immediately created a coalition ministry, bringing in four Labour ministers (Attlee was Lord Privy Seal) and one Liberal, as it was important to draw the nation together during such a crisis. While Churchill was orchestrating all parts of the war effort with the sort of bravura Lloyd George had shown in the First World War, Labour was left in charge of home affairs and began drawing up plans for social reform. Churchill was more of an official war leader than Lloyd George had been, he was less of an intriguer and he had better relations with the armed services. Moreover, by assuming the title minister of defence in May 1940, he had operational command of the Defence Committee of the War Cabinet.

One of Churchill's most important appointments was the flamboyant Canadian newspaper proprietor Lord Beaverbrook as minister of aircraft production. Under the tycoon's influence, production of aircraft increased threefold, though a shortage of trained pilots would prove a serious problem. The manufacture of arms also had to be dramatically increased after Dunkirk. If the Germans had landed in Great Britain at any time in the month after the fall of France the British would not have had the munitions to defeat them.

Seeking refuge in London was General Charles de Gaulle, a distinguished soldier who had escaped from France to carry on the struggle abroad. He made himself what he called the leader of the Free French forces and was thus a potential leader for all the French colonies. What was left of the Third Republic was a rump French state centred at Vichy in the south ruled by Marshal Pétain, the hero of Verdun in the First World War. The rest of France was occupied by the Germans. Many of the French felt betrayed by Britain. They believed that she could have lent them more fighter planes before the fall of France. And they were furious when, to prevent it being used by the Germans, the British navy sank the French Mediterranean Fleet at Mers El Kebir in July 1940 and killed 1,300 French seamen.

Sir Hugh Dowding, the head of Fighter Command, had refused to yield to the French pleas for aircraft because he had carefully calculated the number of planes needed to defend Britain. The Battle of Britain, which began about ten days after Churchill rejected a separate peace with Germany in August, was, to borrow from the Duke of Wellington, 'the nearest run thing'. Like Waterloo it resulted in a decisive victory for Britain.

When it was made very clear by the eloquent roar of Winston Churchill in August 1940 that Britain was continuing the war on her own against Nazism, Hitler decided to invade. This was Operation Sealion. All French Channel and southern North Sea ports from the River Scheldt to Boulogne became choked with invasion barges containing grey-uniformed soldiers waiting for the Luftwaffe to soften Britain up first. People began to fear that, as in the rest of western Europe, stormtroopers would soon be overrunning Britain. The Germans had occupied the Channel Islands on 30 June and established a concentration camp on Alderney. The Churchill government announced that Britain was about to be invaded. But first the Germans would have to dispose of the Royal Navy guarding the Channel – and those warships were protected by the Royal Air Force.

The Battle of Britain opened on 13 August 1940. That day the Luftwaffe made 1,485 sorties over Britain's south-eastern airfields. Day after day they flew in over Kent and Sussex dropping their deadly loads. Fortunately their effectiveness was greatly impaired by the secret use of radar, invented by Sir Robert Watson-Watt and developed by British research scientists between the wars. Radar stations set up at intervals all over the south and east coast of England from 1936 onward gave early warning of approaching planes, enabling RAF fighter pilots to rush to their machines and meet the foe in the air. On 15 August the RAF conclusively defeated a massive force of almost 1,800 German aircraft which could have wiped out the fighter aircraft which had been allowed for to defend southern England. The battle over the skies of England that hot August day was crucial in averting the invasion.

Nevertheless, if the German planes had continued to bomb the fighter airfields and aircraft factories, they probably would have done for the British in the end. But Hitler and the Luftwaffe leader Hermann Göring were infuriated when the RAF dropped bombs on Berlin in retaliation for the Germans mistakenly bombing London. Instead of continuing the assault on the airfields they ordered the attacks on London known as the Blitz. On 7 September, to the surprise of Londoners 900 German aircraft (300 bombers escorted by 600 fighters) roared overhead in broad daylight at about 4.30 in the afternoon, flying from the east in tight formation up the line of the Thames. Having bombed the Docks, they turned over central London and, like a monstrous flock of geese, flew back over the East End and down over southern England to France again. Then, at about 8.30 that evening, the night bombing began. Wave after wave of bombers came over until 4.30 in the morning. By then the whole London skyline seemed to be on fire, and about 2,000 people had been killed or badly injured. The East End and the Docks were ablaze. Meanwhile from the ground the searchlights of the anti-aircraft batteries – London's defences – raked the sky looking for German planes.

The number of German troop carriers in the Channel was growing daily, but the risk to Britain was over. Though in September a few church bells in southern villages were rung as an invasion warning, Germany was being defeated in the air. The boats in the Channel never disgorged their ferocious occupants to bring blood and death to England's quiet beaches. Although London continued to be bombed for fifty-seven consecutive nights, by 17 September the Battle of Britain had been won. Hitler was forced to postpone the invasion of Britain indefinitely, or at least until the following spring. By then his attention had turned to the conquest of Russia, and once again, as during the Napoleonic Wars, Britain remained free against a continental tyrant, a toehold from which the long struggle to overthrow him could begin.

At a cost of 900 aircraft, young British pilots – aided by gallant Poles determined to avenge the loss of their homeland – had fought off the Luftwaffe, downing about 2,000 enemy planes. The Battle of Britain was the first setback Nazi Germany had encountered anywhere since the war had begun a year before. Churchill would sum up the national mood in his tribute to the airmen: 'Never in the field of human conflict was so much owed by so many to so few.'

Even so, with brief respites the night attacks went on until May 1941. Many Londoners made use of the Tube network to take shelter until the all-clear was sounded; an official count on 27 September 1940 showed that 177,000 men, women and children spent that night sleeping in the Underground stations. Between September 1940 and May 1941 some 18,800 tons of bombs fell on London. But London was not alone. There were Blitzes on other cities. A thousand people were killed in Coventry on 14–15 November. There was heavy bombing of Birmingham on 29 November, and of Liverpool that same night and in early May 1941. Southampton and Plymouth were bombed on 30 November 1940; Bristol on 2 December, Manchester on 22 December; Glasgow on 18-19 March 1941, Belfast on four nights in April and two in May. Between 23 April and 6 June 1942 there were the so-called Baedeker raids on cities of historic interest in revenge for attacks on Lübeck; in these raids Exeter, Bath, York, Norwich and Canterbury suffered.

But Great Britain did not have just herself to defend. She had her Middle Eastern interests to consider, particularly Egypt and the route to India. The British stopped a pro-Axis group against the Iraqi regent in May 1941, and in an operation from Palestine with the help of Australian, Indian, British and Free French troops overran Syria and the Lebanon, where the Vichy-controlled administration was replaced by the Free French. The Italian troops in north Africa made a campaign there necessary. Britain also wanted to encourage any neutral states in continental Europe to turn away from the Axis. From the end of October 1940 there was a window of opportunity for the allied cause in the Balkans.

Mussolini, who had already seized Albania in May 1939, attempted to invade Greece in October 1940. Despite that year's Pact of Steel alliance between Italy and Germany, Hitler (who had already partially dismembered Romania to control her oilfields) was challenging Italy's natural hegemony in the Balkans, where Mussolini planned to extend his empire. The Greeks ejected Mussolini's forces, and by December 1940 they held part of Albania. A build-up of British troops began in Greece. But German forces were rushed across the Balkans to rescue the situation, and the window of opportunity began to close. The following March 50,000 British soldiers who had been enjoying a series of triumphs in the Western Desert of north Africa under General O'Connor and had almost succeeded in throwing the Italians out of north Africa – were suddenly diverted to Greece. In April Hitler attacked both Greece and Yugoslavia, which had declared against the Axis after a coup by General Simović. By mid-May it was all over – both countries were occupied by the Germans.

The British forces had to be evacuated to Crete, the island at the foot of the Greek mainland. On 20 May almost 30,000 British, Australian and New Zealand troops were defeated by another airborne invasion, of German soldiers. The allied troops had almost no air cover and, though they fought with great courage, they were evacuated as soon as possible. Not just north-western but southern Europe were now in German hands.

North Africa, which could have been clear of Italians by early 1941, was once more a desperate battleground. Because O'Connor had not been able to finish the job, there had been time for Hitler to ship his most brilliant general Erwin Rommel and his Afrika Korps tanks across the Mediterranean to help out the Italians, just as he had helped them out in the Balkans. Rommel drove the British out of Cyrenaica east along the coast and began menacing them in Egypt. Only Ethiopia remained secure. There British soldiers, Kenyans and other African peoples fought together to capture 200,000 Italians and restored the emperor Haile Selassie to his throne.

The Balkans campaign had been a failure for Britain. Yet it had an unlooked-for but crucial consequence. It delayed Hitler's invasion of Russia by six weeks while Germany overran Greece and Yugoslavia. Those six weeks were the invasion's undoing, because they ensured that it was not completed before winter set in. The German army was thus at the mercy of that powerful Russian ally, General Winter. For by March 1941 Hitler had begun planning for Operation Barbarossa, the invasion that summer of his ally Russia. As it had been for that other would-be world conqueror, Napoleon, Russia was where Hitler's campaign foundered irretrievably. Curiously enough, the Führer's invasion began on 22 June, the day before that of Napoleon had started in 1812. Operation Barbarossa put an end to the threat of invasion for Britain and pegged down German armies for years.

How did Hitler come to commit such a monumental error, one which would ultimately lead to his downfall? In fact he had always planned to invade European Russia and make her part of his empire, but he had intended to do it around 1943. His real hatred of Bolshevism meant that the Russo-German alliance was only ever going to be temporary. What brought the campaign forward was that in 1940 Russia's occupation of half of Romania threatened one of Hitler's most important sources of fuel, the Romanian oilfields. He could not use those of Iraq and Persia because they were occupied by the allies. Hitler also had designs on Russia's own oilfields in the Caucasus. His distrust of Stalin's intentions had been increased by his occupation of the Baltic states Lithuania, Estonia and Latvia in 1940, arousing the fear that Russia would invade Germany one day. By Christmas 1940 Hitler had secretly decided on a quick campaign against Russia to stop Germany being stabbed in the back by her rival, to be followed by a fight to the finish against England.

But unfortunately for Hitler the British knew his plans. The rescue of the German code machine, Enigma, early in 1941 from the U-Boat U-110, which was on the surface after her crew abandoned ship, enabled British cryptanalysts to decipher the codes in which messages were sent from the high command in Berlin to all the German armies. At Bletchley Park in Oxfordshire, a team of academics, mathematicians and crossword-puzzle fanatics sat up night and day working out variations on the codes and listening to German messages being tapped out across Europe. Thanks to Enigma Britain was able to recover after almost losing what Churchill in March 1941 called the Battle of the Atlantic. This was the war against German U-boats which since the occupation of France had threatened Britain's supply of food and oil from America. From ports on the French Atlantic coast, German submarines hunted in what were called wolf-packs and destroyed hundreds of thousands of tons of shipping.

The British codebreakers had already intercepted information about Operation Barbarossa passing from Berlin to the German armies in the east. But when the British government informed the Russians they refused to believe it. They thought it was a capitalist trick to divide Germany and Russia. But they were soon to realize it was nothing of the kind. Leaving only forty-four divisions behind to guard the west, on 22 June German army divisions advanced over a thousand-mile front between the Carpathian mountains in the south and the Baltic Sea in the north. Stalin's bloody purge of his generals in the late 1930s caused the British government to underestimate the Russian army's potential. But Russia had three times as many tanks as the Germans, a gigantic, deeply patriotic population and a high command with a careless attitude to soldiers' lives. Her roads were another secret weapon: they were so hopelessly bad that they prevented any invader getting very far. Unlike the level, tarmacked motorways of Holland, Belgium and France which had been a boon to German tanks, at a touch of rain the sandy Russian roads turned to mud. They were almost as effective at holding down German armies as the Russians themselves. It was the one feature of the Russian campaign that the Germans had not considered.

As they penetrated further into Russia, the Germans' methods of high-speed warfare could no longer work. A military campaign in Russia had to be different. There could be none of the swift moves forward as in the west. As for cutting the Russians off from their baggage trains – the Russians did not have baggage trains. Half starving, they lived off the land and any animal that moved. By December 1941 Hitler's armies, dug deep into Russia, had been brought to a standstill, struggling fruitlessly against the giant snows which blotted out all landmarks and froze their tanks. Nevertheless to the rest of occupied Europe it was not at all clear that Hitler was coming to grief.

However, that winter an event occurred that proved to be as important as Hitler's decision to invade Russia. America was attacked by Japan at Pearl Harbor on 7 December. Three hundred Japanese planes flew all the way to Hawaii in the middle of the Pacific Ocean. Without any warning, and without declaring war on America, they bombed the US fleet where it lay at anchor in the harbour. Three thousand American servicemen were killed, four out of eight American battleships were sunk and the ensuing uproar in the United States was momentous. America at last entered the war.

What had been a European war had thus become a truly global conflict with a new arena in the Pacific, and with Nationalist China brought in as America's ally against Japan. Fortunately Hitler declared war on America a few days later, on 11 December. Had he not done so, the American Congress might have insisted that their war should be confined to south-east Asia and the Pacific, which would have left Europe still struggling under Nazism. Until Japan's unprovoked attack on the US navy in Pearl Harbor much of America looked upon the conquest of Europe by Hitler as a European problem.

The far-seeing Roosevelt had been backing Britain unofficially since a plea for help by a beleaguered Churchill after the fall of France in the summer of 1940. The US president had lent Britain fifty destroyers in return for America being allowed to lease British bases in the West Indies. By the generous arrangement of Lend-Lease from March 1941, American food and matériel were supplied to Britain on credit. This had solved Britain's cash-flow shortage caused by the war's interruption to her usual business. But it was not at all the same thing as having American troops fighting alongside British soldiers as they were from 1942, or having the full weight of America's manufacturing engine on the allied side. But now that the United States, the greatest industrial nation in the world, had joined the fight, Nazism could be defeated. And Roosevelt agreed that Germany should be defeated before Japan.

One of the Axis powers since 1937 and long hostile to the western democracies, Japan had decided to take advantage of France's and Britain's predicament in the west to become the dominant power of the Pacific and south-east Asia. The French and British colonies of the Dutch East Indies, Indo-China and Malaya held 80 per cent of the world's rubber, a very important commodity in a twentieth-century world of tanks and cars, and would provide Japan with the oil and rubber she needed to become self-sufficient. Following a downturn in her economic fortunes, she was ruled by the army from 1940; a year later the aggressive General Tojo was head of the government. To him Japan's rightful dominance of the Pacific was being thwarted by the British base at Singapore and the American fleet stationed in Hawaii. Tojo regarded the American warships as 'a dagger pointed at the throat of Japan'. If Pearl Harbor were destroyed, Japan would be able to control the Pacific with impunity. The plan very nearly succeeded. Only a prolonged American campaign in the Pacific over the next four years prevented Australia from being occupied. But Japan was triumphant among outposts of the British Empire in the Far East. Both Hong Kong and the supposedly impregnable Singapore were in Japanese hands by mid-February 1942.

The Japanese also took over Burma, and their arrival at the border with India was used by the Congress Party in India to extract an assurance of post-war independence from the British, failing which they would welcome in Japanese troops to liberate them. The British slowly drove the Japanese out of Burma and down the Malay Peninsula to retake Singapore after three and a half years. Among many brave allied soldiers, the Chindits in Burma under General Orde Wingate became legendary for their daring.

Nevertheless, in late 1942 apart from Britain most of Europe, from the French border with neutral Spain to half-way across Russia was in Axis hands. It was not at all clear for how much longer the rest of Russia could hold out. The epic battle for Stalingrad, the city which controlled entry to the Caucasus and its oilfields had been raging since September. And despite Enigma the threat from the U-boats in the Battle of the Atlantic was still so severe that allied ships were being sunk at the rate of three a day.

The only positive feature of the way the Germans abused the countries they occupied was that it produced resistance movements in almost all of them, made up of heroic peoples of all kinds who kept the spirit of the country alive. Yugoslavia's partisans remained pro-British thanks to the daring activities of the commando Brigadier Fitzroy Maclean. He urged Churchill to back their leader Tito in 1943 and parachuted into Yugoslavia to arrange a supply of arms for them. For the rest of the war twenty-five German divisions were tied down by Tito's little band of partisans hidden in caves all over the mountains of Yugoslavia.

Both women and men like the mysterious French resistance hero Jean Moulin carried on deadly games of espionage on behalf of the allies to inform them of German troop movements, to sabotage the German defences and to help the allies' special forces which began secretly to be parachuted into occupied Europe. Their role was often to spirit Jews out of harm's way, for since 1941 with a monstrous project euphemistically called the Final Solution the Nazis had embarked on a programme of mass extermination of the Jewish race, gypsies and Slavs in death camps in

Poland. Once a country was occupied all Jews were rounded up, their property was stolen and they were sent by railway to the death camps of Auschwitz and Dachau.

The entry of America into the war raised the problem of strategical aims. As the larger country America was now the senior partner in the alliance with Britain, but her vision of the world she wished to see after the war did not coincide with Britain's. America did not want to spend money on troops to protect the British Empire. Equally, as Churchill put it, 'I have not become the King's First Minister in order to preside over the liquidation of the British Empire.' This underlying theme lent some tension to what were otherwise mainly good relations between the allies.

And there had been bad news for Britain's imperial interests in the Western Desert in the first half of 1942 when Tobruk fell to Rommel. It was as depressing for British morale as the fall of Singapore had been three months before. The British had to abandon the Egyptian frontier to the Germans as well as half of their Egyptian territory and make an urgent retreat right back inside Egypt to entrench themselves at El Alamein, only fifty-five miles from the key port of Alexandria. On 30 June Rommel moved his army right up to El Alamein to face them. The danger was so acute that the British fleet, which had been at anchor outside Alexandria, turned down the Suez Canal to take shelter in the Red Sea. The Egyptians believed that the British had lost the war for Egypt and were about to pull out. But they stood fast and, under General Auchinleck, managed to beat off Rommel in the first Battle of El Alamein that July. But it was not until late October, at the final battle of El Alamein, by which time the British had acquired a new commander, the dynamic General Montgomery, and massive reinforcements in the shape of American Sherman tanks, that the Desert Fox (as Rommel was known to the admiring British) was at last defeated. When this triumph was followed in January 1943 by the surrender of the German Sixth Army at Stalingrad, the turning point of the war had been reached.

Although Roosevelt did not like underwriting what he considered to be Britain's imperial aims, the American people needed to see something being done now that they had entered the war. Roosevelt therefore fell in with Churchill's plan to secure Egypt, by driving all German and Italian forces out of north Africa. By May 1943 this was successfully achieved, after British and American troops had landed in Morocco and Algeria the previous November.

At the beginning of 1943 Stalin urged the British and Americans to open a second front in Europe: if they landed in northern France it would take the pressure off the Russians. After some argument, it was agreed that such an invasion should not take place until sufficient troops had been gathered on the south coast of England to ensure as far as possible that it was a complete success.

But it was decided to put the Nazis on the retreat in mainland Europe by invading from the south via Italy. The Axis forces had made this easier to achieve because they had poured troops into north Africa and not left enough to defend mainland Europe. German plans were further thrown by a clever piece of deception on the part of the British with The Man Who Never Was. The body of a dead soldier was planted off the coast of Spain with plans in his wallet suggesting that the invasion of Europe was to take place on Sardinia. Sardinia was indeed a far more logical way of getting back into France, as it was almost directly south of the French port of Marseilles. In fact the allies landed in Sicily on 10 July. This would mean fighting their way up the Italian peninsula, but it offered a safer route back into Europe than the French coast, particularly as Mussolini had turned down Hitler's embarrassing offer of German troops to defend the Italian mainland. Capturing Sicily would help free up the Mediterranean which had more or less become an Axis lake. The island of Malta had held out so gallantly as the Axis air forces tried unsuccessfully to bomb it into submission that George VI awarded her people the George Cross.

A little cautious optimism was at last growing among allied leaders thanks to a *coup d'état* on 25 July 1943 which saw the overthrow of Mussolini. The new Italian government under Marshal Badoglio surrendered to the allies in September. Germany was then forced to fight her former Axis partners the Italians as well as the British and American forces. Nevertheless, the allied advance up the Italian mainland was extremely slow, and it took almost two years to reach the northern border.

So savage was the fighting that nine months later, on 4 June 1944, the allies had only just reached Rome, a four-hour train ride from Naples. But two days later in a tremendous amphibious operation allied troops under the overall command of the US general Dwight Eisenhower, landed on the coast of occupied France.

Thanks to the continued freedom of the islands of Britain, all the men and matériel needed for the invasion could be stockpiled on her southern coast, and camps set up for the training of 300,000 men steadily mushroomed. Despite their visibility, it was important to keep as much of the operation secret as possible. The camps revealed to the German high command that an attack was imminent, but they did not indicate where it would take place. Field Marshal von Rundstedt, the commander-in-chief of the Armies of the West, thought that the crossing would happen at the narrowest part of the Channel, with the invaders landing between Calais and Dieppe. Hitler and Rommel (now effectively in command of the Channel defences) both had an inkling it might be Normandy. Following his hunch, in the spring of 1944 Rommel ordered mines to be laid in the waters off the Normandy coast.

On D-Day, 6 June taking full advantage of allied air superiority, in an extraordinary logistical exercise the allies managed to land 156,000 troops, who were mainly British, Canadian and American, on the beaches of Normandy. Five days later, the rest of the soldiers had crossed from England along with 54,000 vehicles, and were creating an eighty-mile bridgehead, fanning out west and south. Although Field Marshal Montgomery, commanding the landing forces, would say that D-Day had gone like clockwork, its success was by no means a foregone conclusion. The weather was rough and stormy. Though this gave the expedition the advantage of surprise, as the Germans did not think the allies would risk a landing in such weather, there were very heavy casualties – some 10,000 among allied troops, with perhaps 2,500 killed outright on the beaches. But the losses might have been heavier had so many German divisions not been tied down in Italy. From small landing craft, thousands and thousands of gallant allied soldiers threw themselves on to the shore. Behind them the artificial 'Mulberry' harbours specially built for the landings were towed in, allowing the disembarkation of supplies. Meanwhile American airplanes rushed in and bombed the bridges all along the Seine and Loire, preventing Panzer divisions from racing up to Normandy to stop the allied soldiers.

The Normandy landings signalled the beginning of the end of the Nazi tyranny. By September 1944, from east and west, from Russia and France and Italy, the allies were sweeping the German armies before them. That month France was liberated. Britain was no longer plagued by the V1s, the flying bombs or 'Doodlebugs', now that their launch-sites had been captured, but for a few months the new V2 rockets caused limited destruction. Also in September Montgomery's advance into Germany suffered a setback at Arnhem in Holland when airborne troops dropped to seize bridges over the Rhine were killed or captured. But on the whole the allies were beginning to win.

In January 1945 Russian forces under General Zhukov captured Warsaw, the capital of Poland, which had previously been in German hands, and began moving through East Prussia. Soon less than 400 miles separated the Russians from their western allies' most forward positions. Hitler, more alarmed by the approaching Russians than by the Americans and British, decided to throw troops at the threat in the east on the River Oder. This freed up the Anglo-American forces in the west and enabled them to get across the Rhine. After that, the end came very quickly. By the end of April the Russians were in Berlin, Hitler then committed suicide and on 8 May Victory in Europe Day was proclaimed after Germany had at last surrendered. The war against Japan continued for another three months.

In Britain people danced in the streets. Light-hearted with relief, they flooded into Piccadilly and the Mall to cheer Churchill and the royal family, who had refused to leave London. Every London landmark bore the scars of war, including Buckingham Palace and the Houses of Parliament, and most major British cities had been hit by bombs too.

Some 60,000 British civilians had been killed by the Luftwaffe; nine million people had been working for one military organization or another; almost every family had lost a son, brother or a father in the war. They had dug potatoes for victory as exhorted to by Churchill so that they did not have to rely on imported food, and they had lived on tiny rations. They had also paid higher taxes. America, by helping to finance the war, had given Churchill the tools he had asked for 'to finish the job', and the British had at last finished it.

By the end of 1945 Britain was a very different place from what she had been in 1939. She was far more unified internally. The camaraderie of total war had dissolved many class differences. Churchill's government enjoyed unanimous support during the war and had outlined plans for social reforms that were welcomed by pretty well everyone. After such an epic struggle, most people in Britain believed that there should be a safety net to protect the poor and vulnerable, like the widows whose husbands had died for their country. There should be a good education for gallant soldiers' sons. There was a new idealism after the ordeal of war. People had a keen sense of the fairer country that Britain should become.

At the same time the world and Britain herself were full of a gloomy pessimism. The terrible, unimaginable figure of fifty-five million people had died worldwide, five times the number who had died in the Great War, and there were around twenty million refugees in Europe. Unspeakably cruel things had been done to human beings, by the Nazis to the Jews, by the Japanese to their allied prisoners. But the allies had also unleashed a weapon of destruction on the world which would overshadow it for more than forty years – the atom bomb. In order to end the war in Japan quickly and to prevent its occupation by Russian troops, two atom bombs were dropped on the Japanese cities of Hiroshima and Nagasaki. Each explosion killed approximately 80,000 people and caused birth defects to thousands more unborn Japanese children. Enormous mushroom clouds rising above white heat announced that man had discovered a power which could annihilate life on earth. Though nine-tenths of their shipping had been destroyed, the Japanese had been refusing to surrender, and they were still holding thousands of allied prisoners in conditions of extraordinary brutality. On 14 August 1945, one week after the bombing of Hiroshima, the Emperor of Japan announced that his country had surrendered unconditionally.

With the surrender of Japan the Second World War had finally come to an end. Though the British Empire still stretched far across the globe, it was a shadow of its former self. India was poised for independence, and the strength of anti-colonial feeling among British possessions in Africa and Asia suggested they wanted theirs too. Ties of affection between Britain and the Dominions of Canada, Australia and New Zealand had been strengthened by their shared struggle against Hitler. But after 1945 the Pacific Rim countries made treaties with America to protect them. It had after all been American forces which had saved Australia from the Japanese.

Reform at Home, Communism Abroad (1945–1952)

Peace came officially to a shattered Europe on 8 May 1945, when Germany surrendered unconditionally. Over that preceding week there had been a series of armistices on the different fronts in the west. Ever since the news that Hitler had committed suicide on 30 April the life had gone out of the German war effort, though it had been trickling away for some time. In early 1945, the sight of triumphant Russian armies swarming across Europe had brought a few high-up German officers like General Wolff of the Army in Italy into secret negotiations with the allies independently of Hitler. The Germans might hate the allied democracies, but they did not hate them quite as much as they feared the communism the Soviet Red Army represented. Many German officers believed that it would now be better to join the allies to defeat communism. But the allies' insistence on unconditional surrender, and terror of Hitler, prolonged the war. In Berlin, while Hitler cowered in his bunker a hundred feet below the Chancellery, civilians fought the Russians street by street, from the suburbs to the centre of the city. They had the crazed bravery of the desperate.

The German fear of the Red Army soon proved justified. It was spread right across eastern Europe and showed every sign of remaining there. Under the extraordinary General Zhukov, victor of Stalingrad, the heroic feats of the Russian army had acquired a legendary reputation. At the cost of twenty million dead, its soldiers had driven the Germans out of eastern Europe: first out of their native land, then out of Poland, Hungary and Austria; it had fought across half of Germany to reach Berlin. But in the process the Red Army occupied those countries and would continue to occupy them after the war was over. It was the price the allies now paid for allowing the Red Army to liberate the continental landmass from the Nazi tyranny.

Roosevelt and Churchill had proclaimed that their countries sought 'no aggrandizement, territorial or other', and that they respected 'the right of all peoples to choose the form of government under which they will live'. Their ally Stalin's war aims were exactly the opposite. But to keep Russia on the allied side Roosevelt and Churchill had to accept her demands that eastern Europe should become her sphere of influence. Stalin intended to re-establish Russia as the great power she had been before the end of the First World War. To prevent a strong central European power like Germany arising to threaten her, Stalin's plan was to ensure that all the countries which touched Russia's borders became her loyal satellites or client states – that is to say, ruled by communist regimes run by leaders trained in Moscow.

Unfortunately the American State Department took an overly benign view of Stalin, whom one historian has called 'that charming temporary gentleman Uncle Joe'. Unlike Churchill and the more wary British Foreign Office, the US made the naive assumption that Russia's eastern European client states would be set up on British or American democratic lines. The US government believed that Stalin would mysteriously change his spots and permit free elections throughout the Soviet sphere of influence.

President Roosevelt had been crucially important to Britain's war effort when she stood alone against a Nazi-controlled Europe, not least by unofficially financing Britain's fight-back before most of America would have been sympathetic to participating in the war. But he was not as interested in the shape of post-war Europe as he should have been, partly because he was a dying man. Unlike Churchill, he did not square up to Stalin at the strategy conference held at Yalta in the Crimea in February 1945. In the confusion after Roosevelt's death, with the excellent but very inexperienced President Truman at the helm, America's attention had not been focused on what Stalin was up to in eastern Europe. But Churchill's was.

With his usual sense of strategy, Churchill had seen that as the war ended it was important for the western powers to prevent the Red Army pushing too far west. Once the Russians entered a country it would be very hard to get them out without fighting them, which Britain did not have the manpower to do. If allied soldiers got to Prague, Berlin, Vienna and Warsaw before the Russians and liberated them there would be no reason for the Russians to go near those capitals. But American commanders were not interested in politics and there was no keen American president above them to order them forward, so they refused to press on further east. Churchill's desire to keep the Soviets at bay was thwarted. With Soviet armies stretching as far as the eye could see, Stalin was more formidable than ever.

It soon became clear as peace resumed that Russia's export of world revolution, which had been on hold during the war, had resumed. The Red Army was a far more effective way of spreading communism than the Comintern had ever been. Free elections in Poland after the war had been one of Churchill's demands to which Stalin had agreed. But Stalin had lied. In 1945 the wishes of the Polish government-in-exile in London were ignored – its leadership was in any case divided and ineffectual after the mysterious death of the premier General Sikorsky in 1943. Poles trained in Moscow appeared in Warsaw to set up a communist government, and non-communist leaders of the other political parties were arrested, taken for trial in Moscow and executed. And that was only the beginning of what Churchill would in 1946 call an 'iron curtain' descending over Europe from 'Stettin in the Baltic to Trieste in the Adriatic'. In country after country which had divisions of the Red Army stationed in them at the end of the war, voters – under the eye of soldiers with red stars on their lapels – returned communist regimes.

Poland, Bulgaria, Albania, Romania, Hungary and Yugoslavia all went communist, and would remain so for the next forty years. Indeed until they were liberated from the late 1980s onwards, when the *glasnost* era broke up the Soviet Empire, there seemed no reason why things should ever change. The countries of the eastern bloc appeared doomed to a one-party system of government in which dissent was punished by death. Despite their long and colourful histories, by 1946 a dreary grey uniformity had been enforced across what became known in 1955 as the Warsaw Pact countries: their peoples had little to eat, few medicines and lived their lives in fear. In 1948 Czechoslovakia became part of the unhappy band. When the foreign minister Jan Masaryk fell out of a window in his office in Prague, almost certainly having been pushed, it was the beginning of the end. By September Czechoslovakia had joined the Soviet bloc.

It was in Potsdam in occupied Germany at the peace conference held in July 1945 that the post-war governments of the democratic west and the autocratic secretive communist east rubbed up against one another. There were some hopeful omens. The United Nations, an international organiz- ation intended to keep the peace the way the League of Nations had never succeeded in doing, had been created at a conference in San Francisco the previous month. Fifty nations signed the organization's Charter and began to meet at the General Assembly, a sort of world Parliament in New York. Reflecting the UN's origins at the end of the war the great powers of the time, the United States, the Soviet Union, China, Britain and France became the only permanent members of the organization's Security Council, each of which possessed the right of veto.

But at Potsdam the burning issues were what should happen to Germany, Austria and, to a lesser extent, to Italian possessions. Though Italy had fought on the allied side at the end, she had to yield some of Istria and the city port of Fiume to Yugoslavia and the Dodecanese islands to Greece; she also renounced her African empire. Austria was to remain divided into British, French, US and Soviet zones of occupation until 1955, when she became strictly neutral.

It had been agreed that Germany was likewise to be divided into four zones to be occupied by those same four powers. Though France had been defeated in 1940, Britain argued successfully that she should be included in the army of occupation. The German capital Berlin was also divided into four sections among the four powers. Unfortunately Berlin lay some distance by rail and road from the zones of the western powers: it was situated in Russian-occupied territory in old Prussia. This was soon to raise problems.

Britain began with two representatives at Potsdam, Churchill (now heading a caretaker government pending a general election) and the Labour leader Clement Attlee. To the Tories' and his own surprise Attlee took Labour to a landslide victory at the end of July 1945. It was the first Labour majority government. The population might love Churchill, the great saviour of his country, but returning soldiers voted to have the country rebuilt by Labour. To the British people the Tories still seemed 'guilty men', even at the end of the war – guilty of not caring enough in the 1930s and guilty of the appeasement which had led to war. In short the population did not believe that they would get the sort of social reforms from the Tories they were determined to have after six years of total war.

Attlee had been Churchill's deputy prime minister. Although he looked disconcertingly like Lenin, he was a kindly former barrister who had spent much of his life on philanthropic projects in London's East End, but he was a good judge of men. Many were surprised that the stately role of foreign secretary went to Ernest Bevin, who had no diplomatic background and a reputation for calling a spade a spade. He was then best known for being the robust head of the Transport and General Workers' Union and minister of labour in the wartime coalition. But Bevin was an honourable, fearless man who had always been passionately interested in international affairs and was known for holding his own in any debate. He had been one of Labour's earliest critics of appeasement. Moreover, for many years he had fought the communists in the unions. Thus he had few illusions about the real nature of communist dictatorships and was ideally suited to dealing with the Cold War, as the continuous state of tension between Russia and her former allies was beginning to be known.

The Labour government began rapidly transforming Britain. The trade unions were liberated by the repeal of the 1927 Trade Disputes Act and allowed to recommence their fundraising. Heavy industries were nationalized. Plans were drawn up for new housing and an innovative free medical service. But the big problem Attlee and Bevin were wrestling with was what should happen to Germany after her division into zones.

It is hard to imagine more than half a century later the anger that was felt towards Germany at the end of the Second World War. German militarism had once again devastated the European continent and created a world war only twenty years after the first. The French had suffered three invasions, three destructions of their countryside, with two occupations of their capital Paris in seventy years. They simply did not believe that the Germans could be trusted with a national central government. Their experiences made them believe that the German nation was too warlike and powerful to be allowed to govern herself. The nature of the German people, the size of their country and her mineral resources made it inevitable that they would always want to dominate the continent. France's view overshadowed post-war discussions.

But there was considerable delay as the allies argued about what form post-war Germany should take. Some believed that there should only be local state governments as before German unification, and that any government at federal level should be controlled by Britain and France. Controls were imposed on German industries, and anything which could be turned to military manufacture was forbidden. At the same time the French drew up plans for the international management of iron and steel manufacture in Germany's industrial heartland, the Ruhr.

Aside from long-term political and geographical solutions, the devastated country also presented immense and more immediate practical problems. Not only was the countryside of Germany itself ruined and burned out, but Europe was filled with homeless peoples and marauding Russian armies. Two million Germans were fleeing from what had become western Poland as a result of Yalta. The occupying Russian soldiers, filled with fury against the German people whose soldiers had ruined their homeland, continually avenged themselves on the German civil populations, particularly by raping women.

The occupying American and British armies were at first forbidden to speak to the German people. British soldiers were so appalled by the death camps they had liberated at Belsen, one of the several sites where six million people of Jewish origin had died, whether gassed, killed by disease or worked to death, that they had no wish to fraternize with them. Germans in towns nearest to these sites were forced to rebury the dead in individual plots, so many of them having been thrown into mass graves. But, as the year wore on, the physical plight of the German people became so frightful that compassion crept into the allied powers' attitude to them. In a country with hardly a building standing they began to see the wisdom of Churchill's advice not to insist on punitive reparations. Thus, though the Nazi leaders were tried in the German city of Nuremberg by a multi-national court of judges for war crimes, crimes against humanity and genocide, reparations (except to Russia) would come to an end quite soon.

From the start relations were bad between the occupying powers. The British and American occupying armies were outraged by the callous and brutal behaviour of the Red Army. Although it had been agreed that the Russians should be allowed to remove German industrial machinery as reparation for the destruction inflicted on Soviet plants, Britain and America had not anticipated the level of asset-stripping to which the Russians would descend, carrying off whatever German industrial equipment they could get their hands on. From typewriters to telephone lines, from rolling stock to whole factories of superb German machinery, everything movable was loaded on to Russian lorries and disappeared into the east.

As the dust settled and the world began to spin in its own peaceful orbit again it became clearer that democracy had not completely died in Germany. Some pre-1933 politicians who had survived imprisonment by the Nazis were the best hope of future democracy in the western allies' part of Germany, such as Konrad Adenauer, the former mayor of Cologne. The western powers concluded that the whole country should be united under one government. But it became clear that Russia had no intention of allowing that to happen unless it was to be under the communist parties which soon controlled all the state governments in the eastern zone. Meanwhile, after free elections the whole administration of the city of Berlin was in the hands of democratic socialists, the SPD, despite Russian intimidation of its members through arrests and assault.

Matters came to a head with the brutal winter of 1947–8. The weather seemed to conspire with a simple lack of money to put back post-war recovery in Europe for twelve months. Britain ground to a halt because the extreme cold prevented fuel from being moved. For much of the time coal could not be mined, massively upsetting an already teetering balance of payments. With most of Britain's factories having been turned over to the war effort there was next to nothing to export to earn money. There were constant power cuts because of the weather and equally constant strikes in the newly nationalized coal industry.

The Labour government, however, continued to feel 'exalted', as Hugh Dalton, the chancellor of the Exchequer put it, at the thought of the changes it was going to make to life in Britain. But those reforms needed a great deal of money. And despite higher taxation lack of money was one of the most striking features of the post-1945 Labour government. American credit, American generosity, had made it possible for Britain to continue in the war after 1940. But directly the war in Japan had ended in August 1945 the Americans had cut off the Lend-Lease loans. From September that year Britain was left floundering.

Continually suspicious of Britain's imperialist aims, the US had given no consideration to the sacrifices made by Britain to fight Hitler, which had consumed about a quarter of her national wealth and all her overseas assets. In order to defeat Germany, Britain's manufacturing industries had been turned over to munitions factories, her heavy industry to warships, tanks and aircraft. America gave Britain no time to adjust to post-war dislocation. Two-thirds of the nine million people employed in the armed forces were going to be unemployed, even if it was only temporarily as old industries started up again. Nevertheless, returning to everyday production would be far from easy since many of the old pre-war overseas markets had been lost as the countries concerned had opened their own factories to replace British goods.

Dalton was allowed to borrow £1,300 million from America and Canada but only on condition that after twelve months the pound would be convertible to any other currency. But after six months the loan had been used up, and Dalton had made way for Sir Stafford Cripps, a high-minded but rather desiccated man whose name became a byword for austerity. In what is known as the convertibility crisis – a run on the pound as it was used to buy dollars to pay for the American goods which dominated the post-war world – the sort of measures employed in wartime Britain were implemented once again. Very limited amounts of cash were allowed out of the country. Rationing continued into the early 1950s as Britain did not have the money to import food nor the ability to grow it herself. The pound was devalued. Newspapers were permitted to print only four pages. Petrol could be bought for private use only for specific reasons listed by the government. The black market reappeared.

Britain was thus sinking psychologically under the combined effects of expensive domestic reforms and the cost of trying to reconstruct Germany when, like the rest of western Europe, she was rescued by the American Marshall Plan loan. Despite the western armies' best efforts, the British and French governments were unable to afford the level of reconstruction needed in Germany after the war, whether it was laying new sewage pipes or rebuilding homes in the rubble of bombed cities. Fortunately for Britain and France in 1947 President Truman at last woke up to the dire straits the allies' economies were in. Though he had none of FDR's elongated glamour, the small tubby Truman was hard working and sincere. He had become alarmed by the shape eastern Europe was taking with the barring of anti-communist parties in the Soviet zone of Germany, as well as in the other Russian-controlled countries. He proposed the Marshall Plan to put Europe back on its feet and proclaimed what is called the Truman Doctrine: 'to support free peoples who are resisting attempted subjugation by armed minorities or outside pressure'.

For 200 years America's attitude to Europe had been that the republic should hold itself aloof from the decadent Old World which the New World had been created to escape. The Versailles settlement had foundered on America's isolationist refusal to underwrite what President Wilson had devised. But from 1947 onwards the United States undertook to involve herself in renewing the prosperity of the Old World by underwriting the economic reconstruction needed so desperately after the war. Named for the US secretary of state General George C. Marshall, who announced it, the Marshall Plan poured £1,325 million into all the countries in Europe which requested funds through the OEEC, the Organization for European

Economic Co-operation. American dollars transformed the post-war European situation in return for very little. It was an altruistic action. This generous gift is sometimes regarded as a hedge against communism, but in fact it was offered to all countries irrespective of their political structures, but was turned down by Russia on behalf of all eastern European governments under her sway.

The Marshall Plan accentuated the line drawn down Europe by the Iron Curtain. On the western side the economies became prosperous. On the eastern side, however, the countryside was dotted with ramshackle buildings and rusty machinery. (Only in space was individual genius allowed to shine: Russia was the first country to put a man into orbit with Sputnik in 1957.) Stalin would not accept western aid. He continued to hope and believe that the capitalist contradictions in western democracies would make them collapse, as they should according to Marxist theory. The many partisan or resistance movements during the war throughout western Europe had had strong communist elements. The Russians were convinced that it was only a question of time before the communist parties took over.

As a result of the Marshall Plan, the western powers were able to reform the currency in their zones in Germany. The combination of a less punitive attitude towards German industry and agriculture had almost magical results when controls were removed. Until 1948 many industries using iron and steel had been banned in Germany, while any surplus produced by factories or farms above a certain level had been exported to allied countries as a form of reparation. Now, the black market died at a stroke, food appeared in shops, and money took the place of the barter system to which the German economy had sunk.

But the success of the western efforts in rebuilding Germany made the Russians feel threatened – they had been hoping that the whole of Germany would slowly go communist. When the western powers suggested spreading the helpful currency reforms to Berlin, the Russians reacted savagely. Believing that such reforms might lose them control of their zone, they took the extraordinary decision to close the roads from Berlin to the west. From June 1948 the Russians blockaded the city, even though a democratic local government was flourishing there, and even though it also contained the allied occupying forces of America, Britain and France. The Russians would allow nobody already in Berlin to go out, nor food to go in. These opening moves in the Cold War could have led to a third world war had it not been for Britain and America's calm response. The skills of the US and British air forces made the Berlin Airlift possible: 240,000 tons of everything human beings needed to survive – foods, clothes, baby milk – were flown into the city in an unending succession of plane loads. The Berliners became heroes of the hour for their refusal to give in to the Russians, and the whole episode did much to draw western Germany back into the community of European nations. In May 1949 the Russians gave up the gamble and Berlin was reopened to the west.

Nevertheless, the writing was on the wall: there was to be no reuniting of the four German zones for the moment. The western allies therefore continued to organize their zones to operate on their own. The small town of Bonn became the temporary capital of a West German government. By August 1949 a constitution for the German Federal Republic had been approved by the western allies, and a free election made Konrad Adenauer the first West German federal chancellor. In October of the same year the Moscow-controlled eastern zone set up the German Democratic Republic. Berlin continued nevertheless to be too much of a magnet for young dissatisfied East Germans because it was a gateway to the west. In 1961 the Berlin Wall was put up between the two halves of the city by the Russians to end the stream of emigration. Crowned with barbed wire and guarded by sentries who shot to kill, then dragged the bodies of their victims back into their sector, it was the very symbol of the Cold War.

After the furore of the Berlin Blockade, western attitudes towards Russia hardened. A military alliance became a necessity. Anxiety about Russian intentions thus created the North Atlantic Treaty Organization in 1949. A visible sign of the Truman Doctrine, NATO bound America in an unprecedented military alliance to protect western Europe. Britain had already attached herself to the Benelux countries (Belgium, the Netherlands and Luxembourg) and France in a mutual defence treaty. Now America, Canada, Italy, Norway, Denmark, Iceland and Portugal joined up with their own troops to create what became a formidable military system.

The formation of NATO put Russia on notice to tread more carefully. The United States, which had spread her wing over Europe, had the bomb and the dollars. In August 1949 the Soviet Union exploded her first atomic bomb, its programme greatly accelerated by the betrayal of critical data by the British atomic scientist Klaus Fuchs. The western alliance and the strength of the Cold War truce was to be tested only the next year by the outbreak of the Korean War. Once again this could have led to a mighty conflagration in the Far East, but all powers concerned were anxious to prevent it getting out of hand.

Korea descends from mainland China into a peninsula opposite Japan, her former ruler. From 1945 she was occupied by American troops in the south and Russian troops in the north. But on 25 June 1950 the communist government of North Korea sent troops into South Korea, armed with Russian tanks and supported by Russian aircraft. The brand new United

Nations sprang into action and asked its fellow members to support South Korea by sending a defence force to help her. Britain naturally contributed troops, though she could scarcely afford to. She continued to have important imperial commitments in Malaya and was anxious about Chinese communist influence there – for Chiang Kai-shek, China's nationalist leader, had been defeated and expelled by Mao Tse-tung the previous year.

The United States had a large number of troops in the region already owing to her occupation of Japan. At first US and UN troops under General MacArthur chased the North Koreans almost to their border with Manchuria. But communist China now began to throw her weight behind North Korea. Although there was a moment when it seemed that the world trembled on the edge of its third global conflict as American soldiers were directly engaged with Chinese troops, the conflict was contained – it never explicitly became an out-and-out war between China and the United States. The Americans did not attack Chinese territory, and did not use the atomic bomb. Russia too restrained herself. Despite the initial aid to the North Koreans, she did not send troops to the battle zone.

Seventy-five thousand South Koreans and United States servicemen died during the Korean War, but the conflict ended inconclusively. All concerned were anxious to show that they did not really wish for war. In 1951, a ceasefire was agreed upon and the country reverted to the *status quo ante*. The old frontier between North and South Korea at the 38th parallel was retained in a treaty agreed in 1953. That was also the year of Stalin's death, which caused the world to heave a collective sigh of relief. Nikita Khrushchev, who took over as secretary-general of the Soviet Communist party, denounced Stalin's dictatorship and his cult of personality. There seemed to be a distinct thaw in the Cold War: the Communist party congress in 1956 recommended a deStalinization process, as long as it did not go too far. Controls over Russia's client states in eastern Europe were loosened.

The expense involved in sending British troops to the Korean War was the final straw that broke the back of the Labour government, despite its remarkable achievements. It had made huge strides in changing the fabric of Britain, but the austerity measures it required of the public were very harsh because the costs of those changes were so huge. Nationalizing the coalmines cost hundreds of millions of pounds to acquire them from the private owners, and similar costs were incurred in nationalizing the railways, the utilities (that is, gas, electricity and water) and the iron and steel industries. Although they lost the 1951 general election (there had been another election the year before in which their majority had been drastically reduced), Labour had an enormous amount of which to be proud. There had been relatively little disagreement about their reforms. Many Conservatives agreed wholeheartedly with nationalization if it benefited the country as a whole as opposed to a few wealthy private owners. They too felt that the National Health Service was a benchmark of what the most enlightened twentieth-century democratic civilization could achieve.

And what twentieth-century governments represented was of course at the forefront of British politics in the aftermath of the war. The shame of the Nazis' treatment of minorities and of the vulnerable gave an additional edge to considerations of what post-war society ought to be like. In fact in the 1950s national politics were marked by their consensual nature: Labour and Conservative tended to implement programmes that moderates in all parties could approve of. This consensus politics came to be called Butskellism, taken from the names of the progressive Conservative chancellor of the Exchequer, R. A. Butler (author of the 1944 Education Act, which created universal free secondary education for all to the age of fifteen) and Hugh Gaitskell, his predecessor as chancellor, who became leader of the Labour party in 1955 when Attlee retired to the House of Lords. Their policies were remarkably similar, and (to a much lesser extent) elements of consensus were maintained until the arrival of Mrs Thatcher.

The most important contribution to national life made by Labour was the creation in 1948 of the welfare state, set up by two statutes: the National Insurance Act and the National Health Service Act. Its architect Sir William Beveridge, the 'People's William', proudly explained that this all-encompassing plan for national insurance would look after everyone 'from the cradle to the grave'. Every adult in Britain would contribute to it by paying national insurance, to ensure that everyone in British society was provided for. Every British citizen would be entitled to free medical care in free hospitals provided by the National Health Service. Child benefit was to be paid for every child after the first. There was to be cover for industrial accidents. State pensions were to be given to all citizens – to women at sixty and men at sixty-five.

Labour also took important decisions to reduce Britain's responsibilities overseas. India had been promised independence, but the division between Muslims and Hindus was so deep that it became clear that only partition would work – that the country was on the point of civil war. The Labour government announced that India's new viceroy Lord Mountbatten, a distinguished naval officer and member of the royal family, would hand over rule in June 1948 to an Indian government which would be set up by local parties. But once Mountbatten had arrived in the country he decided that independence had to be brought forward to a much earlier date,

15 August 1947. He believed that, if the subcontinent were swiftly divided into Muslim and Hindu states, this would cut down on the mounting death toll.

Pakistan, the new Muslim state, was to comprise those regions with large Muslim communities, concentrated in the north-west corner of India and above the Bay of Bengal, east of Calcutta. Unfortunately the two halves of the new state (known as West and East Pakistan) were a thousand miles apart. Worse still, the nine weeks during which Mountbatten organized partition saw the number of deaths rise to perhaps 200,000. Meanwhile the short period of time given to the Muslims of India to cross into Pakistan and the Hindus of the new Pakistan to cross into India created separate difficulties. During that two-and-a-half-month period, ten million people of rural origins, their bedsteads and belongings loaded anyhow on to oxen and carts, were on the move across the huge Indian subcontinent. They had to be within the freshly established frontiers before the stroke of midnight on 15 August. This vast movement of peoples, for whom shelter had to be found, was an additional source of strain for the brand-new governments of Hindu India and Muslim Pakistan.

The second enormous headache for the Labour government was Israel, another ancient country struggling to be born anew in the late 1940s. The problem of Israel and Palestine was as complicated as that of India. In the 1930s Nazi persecution of the Jews greatly increased their immigration into Palestine. By 1936 the Jewish population was almost 400,000 or a third of the whole. Conflict in Palestine brought about the Peel Report's 1937 recommendation of partition, but this was rejected by both sides. The last British government investigation into what was best for the mandate of Palestine in 1939 had produced the recommendation in a White Paper that the final number of Jewish immigrants be limited to 75,000. The mandate would be given up, Palestine would become independent under Arab majority rule. Previously Jewish emigration between the wars had been of an individual and unofficial nature. The situation, however, was dramatically changed after the Second World War by the sufferings of the Jews under the Nazis. From 1945 onwards the immigration into Israel threatened to become a flood which would upset the balance between Arabs and Jews in Palestine, when the American government asked Britain to allow unrestricted Jewish immigration into Palestine.

The British foreign secretary Ernest Bevin felt that if the Jews were allowed to immigrate into Palestine in the numbers the United States was proposing they would swamp the original Arab inhabitants. The Palestinian Arabs in any case refused to accept further Jewish immigrants. Britain had been entrusted to rule in the Palestinians' best interests by the League of Nations mandate, and Bevin believed she could not simply abandon them.

There were also the wishes of the Arab leaders of the Middle East to consider. These were important allies for Britain of long standing whom Bevin was anxious not to offend, who were already opposed to the Jewish National Home. Their importance was made greater by the west's increased reliance by mid-century on the motor car, fuelled by petrol converted from oil beneath the desert kingdoms of Iraq, Bahrain, Kuwait and, since 1938, Saudi Arabia. So when boatloads of illegal Jewish immigrants began to arrive in Palestine often visibly sick from their treatment by the Nazis, Britain felt compelled to use force to stop them from disembarking, though this was greatly deplored by the rest of the world.

Meanwhile a guerrilla war was being fought between the Palestin Arabs and Jewish terrorist gangs. Jewish terrorist attacks were also carried out on the British army, which was trying to keep the peace between the two warring sides. The British resident minister Lord Moyne was assassinated in 1944, the King David Hotel (headquarters of the British army) was blown up without warning in July 1946, killing ninety-one people, and two young British sergeants were hanged in July 1947. British public opinion became increasingly disenchanted with remaining in Palestine. Britain's duty towards the Arabs was offset by the high cost to an impoverished Britain of enforcing the mandate, in the year of austerity 1947. Britain could no longer afford to play the world's policeman. Moreover, with India gone in August 1947, the importance of Palestine to British interests fell away. Earlier that year Britain had referred the problem of Palestine to the newly founded United Nations in America, as an international arbiter. The UN recommended partition. In September the Labour government decided that British forces would leave in mid-1948, for Bevin would not use British soldiers to enforce partition on the Arabs who did not want it.

The day that the British mandate in Palestine expired, 14 May 1948, as the last British troops pulled out of the country, the Jews declared the existence of the independent State of Israel. It was to be open to any Jew throughout the world. David Ben Gurion became the first Israeli prime minister, while Chaim Weizmann was president. The Israeli Parliament, the Knesset, was set up in 1949. The reappearance of the State of Israel with all its historic biblical resonances for Jews and Christians, almost 2,000 years after vanishing from the map of the world, caused great rejoicing among many sympathizers. But the Arab leaders whose lands surrounded Israel on all sides were furious. Three days after the new state had been declared, Egypt, Syria, Jordan and others declared war. Astonishingly, in the tradition of David and Goliath the infant state defeated her mighty Arab neighbours and enlarged her territory by a quarter. The war ended in January the following year with the sacred city of Jerusalem divided in two between Israel and Jordan, which also occupied most of the UN-designated Palestinian state, and many of the 650,000 Palestinian Arabs homeless.

By 1951 Labour had run out of money for further domestic reforms – the first year of free dental and eye treatment alone had cost £400 million. Shortage of funds was so severe that all the medical centres the government wanted to build for free health care had to be postponed, while many people had started to live permanently in their 'pre-fabs' because there still was not enough money to build the promised new houses. When Labour realized that the only way out of these costs after the Korean War was to charge for medical prescriptions, Aneurin Bevan, the fiery health minister, and Harold Wilson resigned from the government in protest.

Some of Labour's spirit evaporated with the death in 1951 of Ernest Bevin, and by that time the British would have been superhuman not to have wanted an end to the rationing, hard times and retrenchment which they associated with Labour. They had had enough of sacrifice during the Second World War. At the 1951 election the Conservatives got in again with a majority of seventeen seats. That meant the return of the seventy-seven-year-old Winston Churchill. He was not quite Britain's oldest prime minister – Gladstone held that distinction, having been premier at the age of eighty-three – but he was made to seem distinctly elderly when King George VI died the following year, and his twenty-five-year-old daughter succeeded as Queen Elizabeth II.

Elizabeth II
(1952–)

Wind of Change (1952–1964)

To have Winston Churchill as prime minister gave the new queen Elizabeth's reign a wonderful beginning and sense of continuity. Elizabeth had been popular with her subjects ever since the war. In the service tradition of the British royal family she had gone into uniform and served in the Auxiliary Territorial Service, enabling her to change vehicle wheels with the best of them. In 1947 she had married her Greek cousin Prince Philip Mountbatten, and they soon had two children, Prince Charles (born in 1948) and Princess Anne (born in 1950).

A few days before Queen Elizabeth II's coronation in Westminster Abbey in June 1953, the New Zealander Edmund Hillary climbed Mount Everest. A year later the Briton Roger Bannister became the fastest man in the world when he ran the mile in less than four minutes. It seemed that an age of New Elizabethans had begun, ruled over by a new Gloriana who was photographed looking radiant and regal by Cecil Beaton. On the South Bank of the Thames a huge arts complex was rising like a strange modern city to house the nation's astonishing creative output. It would eventually contain the Royal National Theatre and the Hayward Gallery. The opening of its first building, the Royal Festival Hall, in 1951 had been the highlight of the Festival of Britain, organized by the Labour home secretary Herbert Morrison to demonstrate British cultural achievements a hundred years after Prince Albert had arranged the Great Exhibition to celebrate Victorian invention.

The 1950s would be a prosperous decade for Britain, as Japan's and Germany's industrial muscle would take another decade to rebuild and the British could export to their former markets. Britain continued to be an important world power, despite the increased acceptance that the days of the largest empire in the history of the world were coming to an end. There were bases and British administrations from Gibraltar to Malta, from Egypt and west Africa to Aden and Malaya. Educational and trade links reinforced a sense of common belonging between the far-flung countries of what was now called the Commonwealth. Britain was one of the three countries in the world to be sufficiently advanced to have built an atom bomb. As one of the Big Five on the Security Council she was able to veto the proposed actions of the United Nations.

Nevertheless the lands over which the young Queen Elizabeth II ruled were greatly diminished from Queen Victoria's day and about to diminish further. Under Labour, India had become two independent republics, the British mandate for Palestine had become the State of Israel, and the 1950s and early 1960s would see a speeded-up process of decolonization in the face of independence movements throughout the old British Empire in Africa. Britain simply could not afford to maintain what had become a very reluctant empire.

Even so, from the late 1940s she had to fight a jungle war in her colony of Malaya, which held two-thirds of the world's rubber plantations, and which had been badly battered by the Japanese invasion during the war. Now communist guerrillas from the native Chinese population threatened Britain's hold on the country. By 1956 the communist threat had been defeated but local antagonism to Britain made it pointless to delay independence. In 1957 Malaya became an independent state but remained within the Commonwealth.

But it was in 1956 that it was brought home to Britain how altered her position was in the post-war world. British power had been so substantial and so long-lived that the prime minister Anthony Eden – who had succeeded Churchill the year before – had assumed that Britain could continue to use military force if her interests were threatened. Eden was a conscientious, gentlemanly, Conservative politician of great integrity who had resigned over Chamberlain's policy of appeasing the dictators of the 1930s. Unfortunately the need to stand up to later dictators in case they should prove to be another Hitler obsessed him. When the new leader of Egypt, Colonel Nasser, nationalized the Suez Canal – which was still owned by France and Britain – Eden decided that the move had to be resisted by armed force, at the risk of war with Egypt.

The Arab nationalist Nasser had seized the Suez Canal zone when America and Britain had withdrawn an offer to fund the construction of a dam at Aswan on the Nile. In the midst of the Cold War America had become alarmed by the Nasser government's carelessness about its finances and about an arms deal it had agreed with the Soviet Union. Nasser seized the Canal zone declaring that its income would pay for the Aswan Dam. But Eden and much of the British public could not accept this. Although it had been agreed between the two countries twenty years before that British troops would leave the Canal zone in 1956 and that British influence over Egypt was at an end, Eden made plans to retake it with the connivance of the French government. The latter was closely involved with Israel, which had been buying French arms in quantity and saw this as a good opportunity to expand her territory at Egypt's expense. France was especially keen to see Nasser deposed because he was the chief source of arms for nationalist rebels in the French colony of Algeria.

Nasser was a dictator, yet he did not, as Eden believed, threaten the whole of the Middle East. However outrageous it was to seize the Canal, which had been built with British and French funds, it would have been wiser to accept it as a hazard of the post-colonial world. Though America warned Britain to hold herself back when dealing with Egypt, Eden was soon deep in a complicated plot with the French and Israelis to attack Egypt.

On 29 October Israeli troops marched into the Sinai Desert in Egypt, and a day later the French and British issued a pre-agreed call for both sides to withdraw ten miles from the Canal zone. When this was not done within twenty-four hours, French and British forces bombed Egyptian airfields. Four days later, to the world's amazement, French and British soldiers parachuted successfully into Egypt and captured Port Said. But within a further twenty-four hours, to France's fury, the Anglo-French action had been halted: the Canal zone had not been seized by the French and British paratroopers as planned because Britain had decided to withdraw from the operation.

Eden had been taken aback by the strength of world condemnation. Russia had threatened to launch rockets at the Anglo-French force, Australia had refused to back Britain's action, and Britain and France had been condemned in the United Nations by sixty-four votes to five. American pressure on Britain to withdraw from Suez, which she could not ignore because she needed another large loan from the US-controlled International Monetary Fund, brought the episode to an ignominious end. Eden ordered a ceasefire and a UN force took the place in the Canal zone of the British and French troops.

'Britain has lost an empire and not yet found a role', was the former US secretary of state Dean Acherson's much quoted epithet six years later. Britain and France were both humiliated by Suez, which had underlined the fact that they were not the great imperial powers they had been for two centuries and could no longer interfere in other countries' affairs when it suited them. Meanwhile the Soviet Union had taken advantage of the world's attention being focused on Egypt to move her tanks into Hungary to crush an uprising against communism prompted by Moscow's relaxation of controls over Iron Curtain countries after the death of Stalin. Britain's international reputation had been damaged because she had lost her moral edge. Arab countries were bitterly angry, and Nasser's stock had risen. Anglo-French diplomatic relations took two decades to heal, with the French feeling that they had been betrayed by Britain, which they saw as having become a poodle of the United States. This breach contributed to France's decision to veto Britain's application to join the Common Market in 1963.

The European Economic Community, or Common Market, had developed out of schemes in the late 1940s in the three Benelux countries and France to find a way of integrating German industry into Europe. Its forerunner was the Schuman Plan devised by the French foreign minister Robert Schuman, which in 1951 became the European Coal and Steel Community. By this treaty France and Germany were to produce their iron and steel under a joint higher authority. Despite the parlous state of Germany at the beginning of the 1950s, Schuman and the French statesman Jean Monnet believed that a country as large and resourceful as Germany would always revive. It was therefore important to absorb her within a federalist Europe.

Belgium, France, Italy, the Netherlands and Luxembourg were all attracted by the scheme, and so was Germany. Its very successful implementation for iron and steel was followed in 1957 by the Six (as they had become known) creating the European Economic Community (EEC) in order to include an agricultural policy. Although Britain was approached about joining, she regarded the insistence of the Six on the imposition of a single tariff towards the rest of the non-European world as incompatible with her preferential tariffs with the Commonwealth. Although Britain had been satisfied with the OEEC (the organization set up to implement the Marshall Aid plan) as a forum for communication between European countries, in 1960 she became a founder member of the European Free Trade Association (EFTA) with Sweden, Norway, Denmark, Portugal, Austria and Switzerland. This was a loose customs union between those countries which left all of them free to regulate their external trade.

At the beginning of the 1960s, however, the British government's attitude to the Common Market underwent a sharp about-turn. The ties linking the Commonwealth had been very much weakened by the independence that many colonies had gained from Britain in the previous decade, and statistics demonstrated that trade with the Common Market might offer a great deal more to Britain than trade with the Commonwealth. The catastrophe of Suez had been a salutary experience for Britain. Unlike France she had neither the political will nor the money to fight wars in order to keep her colonies.

Since the turn of the twentieth century much of the Colonial Office in London had tended to the view that Britain governed the colonies in trust for the indigenous populations until they were ready for democracy after a western-style education. But by the 1950s an elite in most of the countries had taken the same higher exams of English boards and the same courses at British universities as the colonial administrators. They had just as much knowledge of western political ideas. They also had experience of Parliamentary democracy, since every British colony (with the exception of the recently acquired Somaliland) featured an elected legislative assembly.

After India led the way there was considerable agitation in Africa for independence. The leader of the independence movement in the Gold Coast, Kwame Nkrumah, was at first imprisoned for his activities. But in 1957 Britain had bowed to the inevitable and he became prime minister of Ghana, the ancient African name of the country. In 1960 Nigeria also became an independent republic. Both elected to remain members of the British Commonwealth of Nations, as they are today.

This was the beginning of a widening process of decolonization that began under Harold Macmillan. Macmillan succeeded as prime minister when Eden resigned after Suez in January 1957. In 1960 in a speech made in South Africa Macmillan spoke of the 'wind of change . . . blowing through the continent'. Britain should yield to the strength of African national consciousness, he said. Thereafter, a stream of African countries obtained independence – Sierra Leone in 1961, Tanganyika (now Tanzania) and Uganda in 1962, Kenya and Northern Rhodesia in 1963, Nyasaland (now Malawi) in 1964, the Gambia in 1965, Basutoland (now Lesotho) and Bechuanaland (now Botswana) in 1966, Aden (now South Yemen) in 1967 and Swaziland, the last, in 1968. In all these countries black majority rule took the place of the white colonial administration. This was not true, however, for two former British colonies in Africa: in Southern Rhodesia (see below) and the Union of South Africa.

In 1948 the Boer Nationalist party defeated General Smuts's United party and began governing South Africa. To the consternation of the rest of the world they instituted a policy of separating citizens of African and Indian extraction from those of European, the white minority, by a system known as apartheid. Segregated schools, public lavatories, even swimming pools, were brought in to create a completely separate existence within one country. In 1961, as the apartheid system became increasingly barbaric and inhuman, South Africa was forced to withdraw from the Common-wealth and became an international outlaw, her goods boycotted for thirty years. Not until after the election of Nelson Mandela as president in 1994 did South Africa rejoin the Commonwealth.

Other former British colonies outside Africa also achieved rapid independence as part of the dismantling of the empire: in 1962 Jamaica, Trinidad and Tobago; in 1965 it would be Singapore's turn, in 1966 Barbados and British Guiana, in 1968 Mauritius. Most of them paid

Britain the compliment of remaining members of the Commonwealth. In Cyprus, which had been a British colony since after the First World War, a long war against the British began in 1954. Despite the presence of a large Turkish minority on the island the majority Greek population led by Archbishop Makarios desired *enosis*, or union with Greece, but Britain was loath to grant their wish and thereby lose an important base in the eastern Mediterranean and also upset Turkey, a no less important ally in the Cold War. But in 1960, after the rights of Greek and Turkish Cypriots had been guaranteed by both Turkey and Greece, Cyprus was given her independence. Since 1974, however, after an attempted coup by the then military government in Greece, the island has been divided into two.

Harold Macmillan has been compared to Disraeli, on account of his robust romantic patriotism and his historical sense of Britain's destiny. His wit and élan helped restore Britain's self-confidence at a time when she was still feeling her way in the post-war world. Despite his aristocratic languor and mournful-bloodhound looks, he was a ruthless personality. When he sacked most of his Cabinet, including his chancellor of the Exchequer Selwyn Lloyd, in July 1962, his action was dubbed the 'night of the long knives' after Hitler's assassination of the Brownshirt leaders in 1934. When his first chancellor and two other Treasury ministers had damagingly resigned a few years before Macmillan had laconically called it 'little local difficulties', but this time he was considered to have panicked.

The 1950s saw real growth in the British economy. With much of the rest of Europe still in ruins, for the present Britain had few competitors, and the retreat from empire and overseas responsibilities greatly reduced her costs. Like Disraeli, Macmillan never underestimated the importance of the nation's comfort; his government built hundreds of new houses with the end-of-empire dividends. By 1959 Harold Macmillan's boast that the British people 'have never had it so good' was evidently felt to be accurate. The Conservatives increased their majority by a hundred seats in the general election of that year.

Macmillan also addressed himself to defence options for Britain herself in a post-imperial age. Now that the atomic bomb had been invented, nuclear missiles offered a far cheaper way of defending Britain than conventional forces. Not having to support men and their families on military bases would save a great deal of money. It would end the unpopular and unBritish conscript 'national service' which had been in operation since the Second World War. But, although there was some experimentation in Britain with nuclear warheads, it became clear that America had perfected nuclear weapons to a higher degree than Britain could afford.

Britain's abandonment of her own nuclear-weapon research and the

Nassau Agreement of 1962, which signalled her dependence on America for such weapons, alarmed France. When Britain decided to apply for membership of the EEC in 1963, President Charles de Gaulle felt that Britain – and through Britain, America – would try to dominate the organization. The proudly nationalist de Gaulle did not accept France's reduced role in the world and feared British power at the centre of Europe. He had no wish to encourage America as a superpower. Britain's application was accordingly vetoed by France.

The humiliation inflicted by the EEC's rejection as well as the mockery made by Labour of the much vaunted 'independent British deterrent', which was 'neither independent, British nor a deterrent', was the beginning of the end of thirteen years of Conservative rule. At the height of the Cold War there was one spying scandal after another. Britain's security seemed deeply compromised in the early 1960s: there was the Portland spy ring, the Admiralty clerk William Vassal, as well as the intelligence officer George Blake who got forty-two years in prison for spying for the Russians. Questions were still being asked about the identity of the third man involved in the defection to Moscow of the high-ranking British diplomats Guy Burgess and Donald Maclean in 1951. Then the Profumo affair in 1963, when the secretary of state for war John Profumo was accused of sharing a call-girl mistress Christine Keeler with a Russian naval attaché, confirmed a growing suspicion that there was a careless decadence at the heart of the upper-crust government.

Although Profumo initially denied the relationship in a statement to the House of Commons, he eventually was forced to admit it and resigned. The senior judge Lord Denning's official report into the affair exonerated Profumo of espionage, but confirmed the sensational press stories surrounding Lord Astor's country home Cliveden. The affair sounded the death knell for an increasingly unpopular government. The trial for living off immoral earnings of Stephen Ward, a society osteopath who had introduced Profumo to Keeler and seemed to have provided mistresses for many Tory politicians, provided an unfavourable contrast with the situation in the country, where sterling crises prevented pay increases in the public sector. Since 1959 the Conservatives had put through little domestic legislation. Four new universities had been founded in 1961 and six more were planned in the wake of the 1963 Robbins Report, as were a number of new hospitals. Nevertheless the government gave the impression of being unwilling to put money into the maintenance of Britain's public buildings, not least her schools. The Commonwealth Immigrants Act, which restricted immigration from Commonwealth countries, looked racist. Hugh Gaitskell denounced it in the House of Commons as 'a plain anti-colour measure'. The Rent Act, which allowed far more competitive pricing, produced ruthless landlords like London's Peter Rachman, who terrorized innocent bedsit-dwellers in the then run-down area of Notting Hill.

Thanks to Macmillan's good relationship with President Kennedy, Britain became closely allied with America. Yet during the Cuban Missile Crisis of 1962 it was quite obvious that, however special the 'special relationship', so often said to exist between the two countries, Britain was not accorded the status of a partner by the United States. When an American spy satellite orbiting over Cuba spotted Russian missiles apparently pointing at the United States, a world crisis of terrifying proportions threatened. Though America belonged to NATO, John F. Kennedy, the youthful and charismatic American president, opted to play a lone hand against the Russian threat.

He put a blockade round Cuba and brought the world to the brink of a third world war without telling his allies, not even Britain. British civil servants and politicians began to see that an alliance with America did not really offer a solution for post-imperial Britain, for evidently there was to be no discussion among equals. Therefore, in spite of de Gaulle's rebuff, Britain began to revive her interest in the organization of European states. In terms of combined populations and of industrial and economic power, they made up as large a unit as America.

As a result of his theatrical abilities and his gift for presentation, Macmillan had become known to cartoonists as Supermac. But by the end of 1963 even his ability to convince the public was wearing thin. Although employment was high during the 1950s, the government's economic policy had never been very smooth. In order to prevent inflation, the Conservatives had resorted to 'stop-go' policies: if prices rose too sharply, tax was suddenly increased; if they fell, interest rates were reduced. All in all, Macmillan's administration was looking increasingly tawdry. At last, in 1963 illness forced him to resign dramatically in the middle of the Conservative party conference.

From his hospital bed Supermac made sure that it was a compromise candidate, the effete-looking fourteenth Earl of Home, who succeeded him as party leader and prime minister. Home gave up his peerage and became an MP as Sir Alec Douglas-Home. Had his principal rival, the multi-talented progressive R. A. Butler become prime minister in his stead, as many in the party wished, the 1964 election might have had a different outcome.

Unfortunately Sir Alex was a completely unreconstructed aristocrat, more interested in shooting on his grouse moor than in managing the House of Commons, which as a member of the Lords he scarcely knew anyway. Macmillan in a lordly way might pretend that the grouse moors were his natural habitat, but in reality he was a furiously energetic party politician beneath the apparently effortless superiority.

As the 1964 election approached the world was dominated increasingly by new scientific discoveries, symbolized by America's plans to put a man on the moon. The old certainties about Britain's role were vanishing. Who was more fitted to lead Britain into an ever more competitive future where new industries must take the place of the old and obsolete? A cadaverous and faint-voiced lord who said that he used matchsticks to count with, or an energetic young economics don who promised to introduce Britain to 'the white heat of technology'? Although it was a close-run thing there was not too much trouble deciding. Harold Wilson led Labour to victory by five votes in October 1964.

The Sick Man of Europe (1964-1979)

With the arrival of Labour in power in October 1964, the Swinging Sixties, as this progressive period is popularly known, really began. Prime Minister Harold Wilson was determined to modernize Britain. Her historic stability meant that the weight of tradition had a tendency to stifle change. The Ministry of Technology was created to thrust Britain forward into the modern age. By the late 1960s British and French engineers in happy collaboration trounced their American rivals by producing the Concorde aeroplane, which flew faster than the speed of sound. Consideration was even given to the amazing feat of submarine engineering to link the two countries which was finally achieved thirty years later, the Channel Tunnel.

Wilson's government coincided with a seismic shifting of the historical templates, with revolutions in thought in both Britain and abroad. In July 1964 Winston Churchill retired from Parliament after almost sixty years as an MP; the previous year the last young men had emerged from doing national service, marking a full stop to the era of wartime austerity and to the habit of clean-cut conformity among the nation's youth that the army required.

Youth's rejection of the older generation had been announced by John Osborne's play *Look Back in Anger* in 1956. By the mid-1960s 'angry young men' with long hair and outrageous clothing fresh out of university were not only the gadflies of the state, they set the tone for Britain. They became known for being 'anti-establishment', but in fact they were a new establishment whose allies were pop stars like the Liverpool group the Beatles, actors, photographers and models. With satirical TV shows such as *That Was the Week that Was*, and the satirical magazine *Private Eye*, which all made jokes not only about politicians but about the royal family, people in public life could no longer expect to escape criticism. The proliferating new universities – Sussex opened in 1961, Kent and Warwick in 1965, then eight more in 1966 – gave Britain a far larger undergraduate population. Since many students were the first in their family to experience tertiary education, the universities became hotbeds of radical thought.

The impresario and anarchic director Joan Littlewood had already challenged the notion that all plays should take place in drawing rooms with her championing of working-class dramas and actors in her Theatre Royal in the East End. One kitchen-sink drama, *A Taste of Honey* in 1963, unblinkingly showed the trials of an unmarried mother. Littlewood's 1963 musical *Oh What a Lovely War!* encapsulated the mood of the time in the scorn it poured on the officer class, an image from which they subsequently found it hard to escape.

The 1960s were the heyday of ideas and idealism and, paradoxically, of affluence. The young bought tellies, modern-looking furniture and bizarre fashionable clothes whose skirts were so short that only their generation could wear them. In 1966 young Britons began a consumer spree which has still not ended, and which their parents could never have enjoyed. Britain's first credit card, the Barclaycard, transformed the notion of credit, which hitherto had hardly been taken further than paying in instalments for a three-piece suite bought on hire purchase. It paved the way to what has today become a leisure explosion of clothes, household appliances and the package holiday, all of which could be put on the credit card. By August 2002, some 49 per cent of all Britons had credit cards and were using them to spend £540,000 a minute – a total of £285 billion in 2001 alone.

The 1960s opened with the trial of Penguin Books for publishing an obscene book, D. H. Lawrence's *Lady Chatterley's Lover*. They were acquitted, a verdict which brought the notion of literary censorship to an end. The jury's decision heralded an era of experimentation in all areas of life, with sexual permissiveness now made easier by the invention of the contraception pill. Under a great reforming home secretary, Roy Jenkins, the brilliant son of a miner MP, Labour moved Britain forward into a gentler, more humane society. Abortion was made legal in 1967 and thus safe for the poor (it had always been safe, though illegal, for the rich). This was part of an increasing sense that women were taking control of their destinies, the movement known as women's liberation, which flourished from the late 1960s onwards and reflected the growing number of young women being educated. In 1951 only one-quarter of the student population were women; by the end of the century it would be over half.

Prodded by the popular new disciplines of psychiatry and psychology at the more modern universities, the old British private educational system of repressive boarding schools began to seem barbaric. Public schools were now laughed at for producing an unimaginative kind of imperial administrator who was made to seem redundant with the end of the empire. Indeed, education was undergoing huge changes at all levels. Labour, with their commitment to social reform, were determined to break a vicious circle of a tiny number of the population being creamed off at eleven by the eleven-plus exams, which separated the gifted few and packed them off to grammar schools. The rest mainly sank in the secondary moderns laid down by the Butler Education Act of 1944. Labour embarked on a programme of building comprehensive schools so that children of all abilities would be educated together, in the belief that this would take care of the problem of late developers or children from disadvantaged backgrounds who were eternally condemned by the eleven-plus to the outer darkness of the despised secondary moderns.

After the 1967 Plowden Report, teaching at primary level entered an experimental and imaginative phase in which understanding the child took precedence over the rigorous discipline with which British schooling had previously been associated. A whole generation of schoolchildren grew up of whom it was said that they were very happy and superb at creating things out of yogurt pots but could scarcely read. Nevertheless, initially it seemed that a new heaven on earth was being created by enlightened people which had done away with the problems, mainly class-ridden, of the past. The bowler hat vanished, and young Etonians spoke mockney (mock cockney) to imitate the argot of young working-class photographers. It was a romantic age: hairdressers were working-class heroes and ran off with heiresses, pop stars ran off with countesses. Stiff British society swung; the idea of class was turned on its head. Money was uncool; upper-middle-class people gave up sending their sons to their old prep schools and sent them to the local primary school. The Labour MP Tony Benn, who had been educated at Westminster public school and had renounced a viscountcy, made Holland Park Comprehensive famous when he sent all of his children there.

In 1967 homosexuality between consenting adults was made legal, ending years of misery for men (homosexuality among women had never been a criminal offence) who had previously been liable to imprisonment. The painful procedure of divorce was made less cruel by removing the question of guilt and providing that after two years of separation a marriage could be ended on grounds of irretrievable breakdown. Perhaps most important of all, in 1965 Britain abolished the death penalty, though it was too late for many innocent victims of prejudiced trials such as Derek Bentley.

That same year Labour, by the Race Relations Act, set up the Race Relations Board to tackle racism. A growing number of Indian, Pakistani and Caribbean immigrants from the old empire had been encouraged since 1945 by successive governments to fill employment gaps in factories, hospitals and on the railways. In the mill towns of the north they were forming sizeable communities and cultural differences were being exploited by those who feared that immigrants would not adapt to the British lifestyle. The act made the incitement to racial hatred a criminal offence. In 1968 a second Race Relations Act rendered racial discrimination in employment, advertising and housing illegal, created new immigration-appeal procedures and gave the Race Relations Board power to act directly in the courts.

By now America was not only conquering space ahead of Russia by sending men to the moon and back, she was heavily involved in the former French Indo-China fighting communism in the shape of the North

746

Vietnamese, who, backed by communist China, had invaded South Vietnam.

The Labour government supported the American presence in Vietnam, though it declined a US request to send British troops. But as the war dragged on it became extremely brutal in its methods. Not only the left of the Labour party – which hitherto Wilson had been regarded as part of – violently disapproved of what they regarded as neo-colonialism, but millions of young Americans were outraged by it. One of the most important effects of the American anti-Vietnam War demonstrations was that protest movements became mainstream. By 1968 all over the world the young had gathered for revolution.

In Paris a student protest against poor teaching under the conservative Gaullist government turned into a massive strike, while in Prague behind the Iron Curtain there were the first attempts to break up the monolithic communist system. In what is known as the Prague Spring the Czech Communist party leader Alexander Dubček attempted to introduce 'socialism with a human face' by abolishing censorship and introducing multi-party elections. But it ended in August 1968 with Warsaw Pact tanks rolling into Prague to restore what was effectively Soviet domination. There were photos in all the world's newspapers of a despairing young Czech student named Jan Palach who burned himself alive in 1969, five months after the Prague Spring had failed to make it into summer.

Though British society was undergoing revolutionary change at all levels, Britain escaped revolutionary violence. Her problems were financial. Harold Wilson's TV persona – he liked to be seen pipe in hand wearing a raincoat – was intended to reassure the viewer of his down-to-earth British credentials, but he seemed always to be fighting a losing battle against economic instability, having found himself in the middle of a balance of payments crisis when he took office, set off by Tory fiscal irresponsibility. He and his chancellor of the Exchequer James Callaghan staved off a devaluation crisis for long enough to win another election in 1966, massively increasing Labour's majority to ninety-seven. But the British economy was failing. Industry was threatened externally by the rapidly reviving post-war economies of Germany, France and Japan and internally by the damage done by industrial action and strikes and soaring wage claims. The 1965 Trade Disputes Act made the strike weapon easier as it gave union leaders full legal protection to use it where there had been a threat of redundancy.

Wilson established the Prices and Incomes Board to investigate prices and wage demands with representatives from business and the trade unions, but when rising inflation necessitated giving the board legal powers to suppress soaring wage claims this angered the left in the Labour party as well as the trade unions themselves. Many felt that a Labour government with its roots in the trade union movement should not be in the business of preventing claims for higher wages. But Wilson had seen the figures: Britain could not afford the sort of claims which the unions were putting in. When he announced a statutory wage freeze to be put through Parliament to avoid devaluing the pound, there was uproar on the Labour backbenches. It would only get louder as the decade progressed.

Wilson's novel weapons of wage freeze and wage restraint did not stop Britain arriving at another sterling crisis by the autumn of 1967, precipitated by her renewed desire to enter the Common Market. Strikes threatened, and confidence in the pound fell to a new low, with gold reserves rapidly diminishing. In November the government was forced to devalue the pound, having been unable to raise any further foreign loans to prop up its value. This was a traumatic moment for Labour, who had been desperate to avoid further association with this drastic remedy after its deployment by the Attlee government in 1949. Although Wilson, the cunning communicator, insisted the next day that this did not mean 'the pound in your pocket' was worth less, no one believed him.

The new $1 billion loan arranged for Britain by the International Monetary Fund had the usual conditions of curbing government spending for what was becoming a cap-in-hand nation. Harold Wilson in the late 1940s had himself resigned from government when charges for spectacles were introduced by the Attlee administration. Twenty years later he was presiding over prescription charges on the NHS, building fewer council houses and putting off (until 1973) that key improver of children's lives, raising the school leaving age to sixteen.

Labour did not want to abandon all reforms, but they had to rely on emergency budgets to raise money. Worldwide, markets were in turmoil. Under Roy Jenkins, who replaced Callaghan as chancellor after the devaluation, there were price hikes on petrol, alcohol and cigarettes intended to control inflation. Austerity ruled at the gloomy Treasury. Once again, as in the late 1940s, Britons were allowed to take only £50 out of the country on holiday. It was not until the autumn of 1969 that economic recovery and a trade surplus put an end to a financial regime which Britons today would find unacceptable.

Meanwhile industrial action and the millions of days lost to industry were destroying the economy. Laws were needed to prevent wildcat unofficial strikes by left-wing shop stewards. Wilson and Barbara Castle, the secretary of state for employment and productivity, tried to use legislation to bring the trade union movement to heel, and in a famous White Paper entitled *In Place of Strife* they proposed that all strikes should first be approved by a ballot of the members. But MPs such as Jim

Callaghan, who in a job-swap with Jenkins was now home secretary, were extremely unhappy at the idea of introducing laws of which the Conservative party might have been the author. A backbench revolt combined with the TUC's refusal to accept fines or legislation against strikes ensured that by 1969 Wilson and Castle had to accept that the government had no chance of putting anti-strike legislation through Parliament, despite its enormous majority. They were forced to rely solely on the TUC's word that it would use its influence to prevent unofficial strikes.

Britain's revived attempt to join the Common Market was vetoed, for the second time, by de Gaulle shortly after the devaluation in 1967. Some comfort was derived from the resignation of de Gaulle in 1969, which suggested that next time it would be easier to be accepted into the Common Market. Britain therefore persisted with her negotiations for membership. Although Labour had set up a Ministry for Overseas Development to help the newly independent Commonwealth countries find their feet, the dynamics of nationalism had loosened ties between the old colonies and Britain. The increasing volume of trade with Europe made joining the Common Market seem inevitable.

Labour pressed on with relinquishing commitments, withdrawing what troops remained east of Suez. Under pressure from the African Commonwealth countries in 1965, the government imposed sanctions against the white Rhodesian politician Ian Smith when he made a Unilateral Declaration of Independence to evade the transition to black majority rule. Commonwealth pressure chimed in with Labour's natural idealism to stop Britain selling arms to South Africa in 1967, though many argued that this would lose thousands of jobs in the UK and that South Africa would obtain arms anyway from the French and the Israelis. Nevertheless Labour believed that they should not be seen to approve of a pariah nation. However, the support of the Wilson government for the Nigerian authorities when they refused to allow Biafra to break away and fought a bloody war (1967–70) angered many on both sides of the House.

During the campaign for the 1970 general election Labour seemed bound to win again. The government had been responsible for a remarkable quantity of improvements to the fabric of modern Britain. Establishing a Parliamentary Ombudsman to look into failures in Whitehall departments made the process of government more accountable to the people. But in 1970 it seemed Britons were dissatisfied by the rising tax demands and attracted by the Conservatives' patriotic reminders of Britain's great-power past. Despite all Labour's reforms their choppy financial record made the electorate turn to the more grandiose Conservatives, who denounced Labour's economic 'plans', higher taxation and incomes policies as interference in people's personal affairs.

The Conservatives presented a united front under their new leader Edward Heath, with his bright-blue eyes and booming voice. Heath came to power determined to succeed where Wilson had failed: he wanted to cut government spending and see off the unions. The millions of days lost in unofficial strikes continued to run down British industry and lose international markets, despite the TUC's vow of self-regulation. But the Conservatives came to grief in the epidemic of inflation which gripped the world at the beginning of the 1970s. There were enormous rises in world food prices and commodities which badly hit British shops.

The Conservatives were forced to devote large sums of taxpayers' money to saving some of Britain's most famous industries such as Rolls-Royce aero-engines and Clydeside shipbuilders. But the Heath government's decision to enforce a nationwide wage freeze when the TUC and the Confederation of British Industry together failed to reach a self-restricting wage limit outraged the unions. Their members were watching the price of milk and butter rise by 25 per cent a year. Heath set up two national organizations which were even more far-reaching than Wilson's: the Price Commission and the Pay Board which had to approve all pay rises affecting more than a thousand people.

The subject nearest Heath's heart was joining the European Common Market. This had always been one of his great enthusiasms (the others were yachting and music – he had been the organ scholar at Balliol College, Oxford). And fittingly it was under his government that Great Britain became part of the European Economic Community on 1 January 1973. To prepare for joining Europe, in 1971, the Conservatives brought in decimalization, the conversion of the British pound into a system based on tens to chime in with the continent. To a fanfare of national protest, the pound now comprised 100 new pence instead of 240 old pence; the sixpence was replaced by two and a half pence, and the shilling by five pence. Although Britain was also supposed to have converted to European kilometres, the majority of the population regardless of their age continue to talk about that ancient unit brought to Britain by the Romans, the mile. Nevertheless, kilograms and millimetres are now Britain's official units for weights and measures.

The Market's common external tariff ended Britain's very close relationship with Commonwealth countries such as New Zealand, which sent almost 90 per cent of her dairy products to Britain and in return received over half of her imports from Britain. Nowadays most of New Zealand's dairy trade is with Asian countries. The rupture of the former empire's trading links angered many politicians. They feared the end of cheap food from the empire and the effect on Britain's fishermen of not being allowed to fish at will in the seas surrounding Britain, given that each EEC country has its quota. The left wing of the Labour party began to turn anti-marketeer. So did some Conservatives who felt that the Commonwealth was being too swiftly abandoned for Europe.

Relations with the Commonwealth were made dramatically worse in 1971 when the government attempted to implement a harsh new Immigration Act. This would have prevented any further automatic immigration into Britain from former Commonwealth countries, while making it easier for EEC nationals. The bill aroused outrage on all sides of the House. MPs were still sensitive about the Conservative MP Enoch Powell's infamous 'rivers of blood' speech in 1968 in which he had proposed voluntary repatriation for Asians and West Indians. The legislation was altered: members of Commonwealth countries who wished to immigrate into this country who had a 'grandpatrial' connection, that is whose grandparents were from Britain, had preference over citizens of European Community countries. By accepting all 40,000 Ugandan Asians fleeing Idi Amin, the dictator of Uganda, in 1972 without a quibble, the Conservative government did something to restore good relations with the Commonwealth. So did the continuance of sanctions against Rhodesia.

As traditional supporters of the British arms industry, it was to be expected that under the Conservatives arms sales to South Africa would be resumed. That did not stop the increasingly assertive Commonwealth from condemning the move. In 1971 the Conservatives showed a return to a sort of mini-imperialism east of Suez by setting up a mutual defence pact with Australia, New Zealand, Malaysia and Singapore. Diplomatic relations were opened with Maoist China, which had been severed since 1949, an event memorialized by Beijing's gift to London Zoo of two giant pandas named Chi-Chi and An-An.

Not content with changing the currency and the country's trading orientation, the Heath government massively remodelled local government to reflect population trends. In six conurbations outside London new metropolitan counties came into being – Merseyside, South Yorkshire, Tyne and Wear, the West Midlands, West Yorkshire and Greater Manchester.

The Heath government also saw the intensification of a civil war in Northern Ireland which had erupted in the last year of the Wilson administration. Stormont, the local Parliament for home affairs established in 1920 on the edge of Belfast, had ruled Northern Ireland in the interests of the two-thirds Protestant majority. Protestants controlled everything, including housing and employment, leaving Catholics with very few civil rights. The Royal Ulster Constabulary, the province's police force, was Protestant to a man and discriminated against Catholics.

For forty years the Catholics of Northern Ireland had endured being treated as a lesser race. However, at the end of the 1960s the example of black people successfully asserting their civil rights in America inspired them to revolt. Civil rights organizations began to flourish in Northern Ireland, helped by a liberal reforming prime minister, Captain Terence O'Neill. The Royal Ulster Constabulary outraged world opinion by using violence against demonstrators, but no policeman was punished for this brutality and no attempts were made at government level to get Stormont to be more responsive to the needs of the Catholic community. So serious did the situation become, with clashes between Protestant and Catholic rioters and the burning of hundreds of mainly Catholic homes in Belfast, that in 1969 Wilson sent British troops to the province.

At the same time a deadly new splinter group called the Provisional IRA, or the Provos, started murdering Protestants in Northern Ireland. They believed that the only way things would ever improve for the Catholics was to obtain the unification of Ireland. The bombing campaign waged pitilessly by the Provos was answered just as bloodily by Protestant terrorist groups. When the British government insisted on introducing internment without trial, the prejudice against Catholics seemed to be confirmed even in the treatment of suspected terrorists, as no Protestant terrorists were being interned.

The watershed came one day in January 1972 that became infamous as Bloody Sunday, when thirteen members of a peaceful group of Catholic demonstrators were shot dead in Derry. With the province in uproar the Conservative government concluded that the fifty-year-old Stormont Parliament should be closed down. Direct rule would be imposed for twelve months while plans were drawn up for a fairer assembly and a power-sharing executive created from that assembly with equal rights for Catholics and Protestants.

The Heath government understood that one of the most important factors in obtaining peace in Northern Ireland was to involve Southern Ireland or Eire. At Sunningdale in 1973 the Council of Ireland was created, a body with members from both north and south. In return for gaining some say in the north's affairs, Dublin agreed to give up its fifty-year-old claim to Northern Ireland. Dublin also accepted that the province would never change its status and be reabsorbed into the south unless the majority of its citizens wished it.

Despite the importance of these exchanges, the sectarian hatreds of Northern Ireland prevented the assembly's rule of the province from getting under way as planned in January 1974. All the successful candidates in the elections to the new assembly, except one, were opposed to sharing power with the Catholics. Strikes took place all over Ulster in bitter protest against the Sunningdale agreement. The British government was forced to suspend Stormont and retreat to direct rule once more, with 20,000 soldiers now stationed in Ulster.

As Heath's initiatives in Northern Ireland ground to a halt, by the beginning of 1973 his industrial strategy was also being violently rejected. A series of massive strikes had been directed against his pay and price initiatives. Even normally restrained civil servants went on strike as the price of food soared and unemployment rocketed. The American dollar was devalued with knock-on effects on the pound. So ruinous and uncontrollable was the rate of inflation that Heath's chancellor Anthony Barber was forced to make emergency payments to those on social security and to subsidize the price of butter. He also handed over no less than £15 million to the mortgage companies to make sure they kept their interest rates down because the cost of living was rising too fast.

Unlike Labour, the Conservatives had not been divided among themselves over legislation to restrict the powers of the trade unions. They pushed through industrial relations laws and set up the National Industrial Relations Court. But this policy of confrontation did not stop the strikes. In 1972 the Conservatives had been humiliated when an inquiry awarded striking miners a pay rise three times the amount the government was offering.

In October 1973 the already spiralling inflation spun out of control, as it did all over western Europe, as a result of the Arab–Israeli Yom Kippur War. Enraged by western support for a victorious Israel, which had once again defeated the Arab nations, Arab revenge had been hardhitting. Countries which had supplied arms to Israel were boycotted, and oil prices were quadrupled. This pitched the economies of western Europe into recession. At this time of crisis it was more necessary than ever to keep a ceiling on wages and prices. But the miners rebelling against Heath's price controls realized that the moment gave them unique leverage. With fuel at a premium, they refused to work overtime unless they were given a pay increase above the government's norm. They were joined in fraternal solidarity by the electricity power engineers and by ASLEF, the Amalgamated Society of Locomotive Engineers and Firemen; this disrupted not only the running of power stations but the movement of coal.

As the icy winter of 1973 drew on the country began grinding to a halt. Heath felt he had to stand by his inflation strategy, but the result was deadlock. Once again the government was forced to employ emergency measures. British industry was rationed to working a three-day week to save electricity. A sense of despair pervaded the country. A government-imposed speed limit took the place of petrol rationing, but the effect on morale was the same. Television stations were forced to close down by government order at 10.30 each night. When the TUC stepped in to offer to negotiate a one-off settlement with the miners outside Heath's pay norm, the newspapers asked 'Who governs Britain?' But the miners refused to enter into further negotiations. They wanted a dramatic increase in wages, even though Britain could not afford it. When that was refused the miners declared that on 9 February 1974 they would strike. In response Heath called a general election for 28 February.

Heath had only been pursuing policies which Labour had pursued more cautiously. But, just as he had been defeated by the miners, he was defeated at the election – though so narrowly that he could approach the Liberals and ask them to form a pact with him. There was not enough common ground between the two parties, and so Harold Wilson formed a minority government, returning to power for the third time. In October that year he went to the country again, in search of an overall majority; he succeeded, but his majority was only three. Heath was challenged for the leadership of the Conservative party in February 1975 by Margaret Thatcher, his former education minister. With right-wing support she succeeded in replacing him.

In theory, an agreement known as the social contract between Labour and the TUC that had been reached before the February election should have made industrial relations less fraught. In return for the Labour government repealing Heath's anti-union legislation, the TUC promised once more to lean on the unions and dissuade them from demanding from the country more than it could afford. The miners' strike was indeed soon settled. Nevertheless, the rate of inflation ensured that the unions were not inclined to restrain themselves. By 1975 annual wage increases were averaging a grotesque 25 per cent a year, in line with inflation. Over the previous five years, the PSBR (the Public Sector Borrowing Requirement – the total borrowing of the government and of nationalized industries) had gone up by £8 billion. Once again in July 1975 the Labour government fell back on a statutory price freeze and a statutory prices and incomes policy, so that those earning over £8,500 a year were not allowed more money.

Labour fought a losing battle to keep down the cost of government. Mammoth amounts of money were still borrowed by the government and poured into British industries such as British Leyland Cars, Rolls-Royce and Ferranti. By 1976, once again, to the outside world Britain under Labour seemed to be sinking. In March Wilson retired without warning as prime minister. He was succeeded by James Callaghan, who had held the offices of home secretary and chancellor of the Exchequer in previous Wilson administrations and had been foreign secretary since 1974. He and his chancellor of the Exchequer Denis Healey's immediate task was to negotiate another vast loan of £3,900 million from the International Monetary Fund in Washington to prop up sterling. Once again, the conditions dictated to the British government by the IMF were to reduce public spending.

Denis Healey would implement deep cuts in health and education. But the Labour government was already committed to higher taxation as part of their policy of wealth redistribution. Healey's frappant remarks about soaking the rich could not be forgotten when supertaxes came in, with the highest rate pitched at a colossal 83 per cent. Many high earners chose to leave Britain now that they were only receiving seventeen pennies for every pound they earned. The new administration could not counter the widespread feeling that the unions ruled Britain. The weakness of the government was shown at every level.

A series of dismal by-elections had cut Labour's overall majority down to one. Only an agreement with the Liberals, the Lib–Lab pact, allowed them to continue in office, as Callaghan did not want to call an election. The Liberals under the youthful David Steel, 'the Boy David', made it a condition of their support that they should be able to veto every new Labour law. As ever the Liberals were hoping for electoral reform and proportional representation: in February 1974 they had polled six million votes out of a total of twenty-seven million, almost a quarter of the voting population, and yet had won only fourteen seats out of 635 in the House of Commons. But owing to an upsurge of Celtic nationalism, the Liberal vote started falling. When the Liberals decided to withdraw their support Callaghan was forced to turn to the newly powerful Scottish Nationalists, who had eleven seats by October 1974. The Scottish Nationalists demanded devolution and a Scottish Assembly in exchange for their support. The discovery of oil in the North Sea off the coast of Scotland in the late 1960s had given the Scots confidence that 'their' oil could finance an independent government. Their demands for Scottish independence obliged Labour to speed up an inquiry into the possibilities of devolution and regional assemblies for Scotland and Wales.

Sunny Jim, as the burly, commonsensical Callaghan was known, had begun his reign full of optimism and with the support of the unions. He was determined to unite left and right within the Labour party. But by the beginning of 1979 the unions were no more inclined to obey him or the TUC than they ever had been. They simply refused to be tied to the wage increases the government had asked for to keep down inflation. Almost all asked for double – and got it.

And the way they got it was by strikes. There was endless industrial action by transport workers and a reckless strike mentality spread into every industry in Britain. When in late January 1979 over a million workers in the public services, dustmen, ambulance drivers and water engineers, went on strike for a day it seemed that Britain was collapsing into its own filth. The dead could not even be buried. It was Britain's 'Winter of Discontent'.

In marked contrast to Callaghan's constant and ultimately feeble remonstrations with the unions was the voice of Margaret Hilda Thatcher, the new leader of the Conservative party. She did not mince her words as she watched the government's guidelines on incomes and industrial policies being destroyed by the unions. Increasingly most of the country agreed with her as the rubbish mounted outside their windows during a three-and-a-half-month dustmen's strike. At the end of March 1979 the Labour government had run out of deals. On a no-confidence motion in the House of Commons, it was brought down by one vote and an election was called for 3 May.

The Thatcher Legacy (1979–2002)

In a dramatic reversal of fortune the 1979 election gave the Conservatives 339 seats, against Labour's 268. With an overall majority of forty-three the Conservative leader Margaret Thatcher took office. With her elegant blonde coiffeur, her high court shoes, flowing skirts and handbag she looked no more threatening than the wife of the company director she was. But Mrs Thatcher's sedate appearance disguised the fact that she was a revolutionary, a revolutionary of the right.

By 1979 British industrial productivity had reached dramatic new lows. Britain was known as the Sick Man of Europe and was being held to ransom by the unions, whose legendary union-sponsored tea breaks made the country a laughing stock all over the world. The Labour government's stormy attempts to curb the unruly unions weakened Britain's international standing and undermined sterling. Restrictive union practices – for example, that such and such a worker could only do the job his union permitted – were holding back Britain from the sort of technological innovation without which industries die. The print unions were preventing the British newspaper business from using the computer technology that would have made their papers far cheaper to produce, because it would put the compositors out of a job – the people who each day pasted up the type for the hot-metal printing process invented in the fifteenth century. Japan and Germany were forging ahead because they had rebuilt their industries from scratch after the destruction of the Second World War, unimpeded by obstructive unions.

In 1979 the state not only owned practically every large industry from Vickers shipbuilding to British Steel, from Jaguar to British Gas, from British Airways to Rolls-Royce. It owned and maintained all the nation's council houses; it paid the salaries of the whole of the civil service and its myriad subdivisions which took care of tax collection and parking fines; its employees also included all the nurses and doctors employed in NHS hospitals and the cleaning staff too. It had to meet gigantic welfare bills. Since the beginning of the twentieth century the British state had been expanding its remit until it was the biggest employer and provider in the country. And yet Great Britain plc was going broke. She could not afford to run all the businesses she owned; she was constantly having to bail out many of the older industries like shipbuilding and coalmining with subsidies, because other countries could produce those products more cheaply. The spectre of mass unemployment in the communities that had grown up round shipyards and mines kept them open.

Mrs Thatcher was adamant that Britain could not go on borrowing immense sums from the International Monetary Fund to save failing state industries for what she considered to be sentimental reasons. She believed that Britain had drastically to reduce the overwhelming Public Sector Borrowing Requirement, and also to bring down the terrifying inflation rate, not by agreements with the trade unions but by controlling the money supply. Mrs Thatcher became famous for making Britain balance her books, for only paying what she could afford, and for a campaign to replace the culture of benefit scrounging with a nation of responsible home owners.

Though the Conservative party was traditionally a party of pragmatists who distrusted ideology, the Thatcherites were known for their slogans. They believed that they had a hard road to travel to rid Britain of the creep of socialist ideas, those post-war consensual assumptions Mrs Thatcher's mentor Sir Keith Joseph called 'well-intentioned statism'. Their most celebrated slogan summed up everything about the Thatcher Revolution. It was 'rolling back the frontiers of the state'. Privatization of numerous state activities was the Thatcher government's most significant contribution to British politics; in the process they invented what they called 'popular capitalism' through a 'stakeholder democracy'. British politics were turned on their head.

Almost all of the nationalized industries, most of which had become unprofitable monoliths, were sold off to private companies, or privatized, starting in 1980 with British Aerospace and British Airways. Private sector involvement was heavily encouraged in the public services. In the process Mrs Thatcher for most of the decade succeeded where her predecessors for the previous thirty years had failed: she broke the power of the trade unions once and for all and slew the dragon of inflation. By ridding the government of responsibility for inefficient and expensive state-owned industries, by the late 1980s she had raised £20 billion for the Treasury, and still more was raised when her creation of a deregulated, free-market economy helped spark a consumer boom.

By giving ordinary people who had never bought a share in their life a stake in the privatized industries and utilities of Britain, Mrs Thatcher intended to strengthen the bulwarks of the democratic process against socialism, by restoring people's pride in their independence. She believed that a dependency culture was eating away at Britain – too many people expected everything to be provided by the welfare state instead of by their own efforts. She was determined to create an enterprise culture instead where the sort of people who supported her were rewarded, not those who depended for everything on what she called the nanny state. In some ways Mrs Thatcher's convictions were simplistic. One of her favourite slogans was that Britain must return to 'Victorian values', when the state had been kept at arm's length by the self-reliant ethos which had made Britain great. She believed that if people owned their houses they would become more

758

upright citizens and take greater care of their environment. Her Council House Acts of 1980 and 1984 which enabled council-house tenants to buy their own homes with large discounts helped swing the working-class vote her way.

Mrs Thatcher had read chemistry at Oxford in the late 1940s, at that time a considerable achievement for a woman. As prime minister she stood out against her all-male Cabinet, as she did against the 635-strong House of Commons, for in 1979 there were only nineteen women MPs. She had shown similar robustness as education minister under Heath and had given some hint of the shape of things to come when she ended free milk in schools, gaining the nickname 'Mrs Thatcher, milk snatcher'. Some of her keenest supporters were self-made British Asian businessmen whose values of frugality, hard work and self-sufficiency were so similar to hers. But her followers came from a wide spectrum: they were not only bankers and financiers, they were small businessmen, shopkeepers and ordinary people fed up with the culture of Labour which seemed to be epitomized by inefficiency and the closed shop. The advertising slogan accompanying a posed photograph of a snaking dole queue which had helped win the Conservatives the 1979 election, 'Labour isn't working', said it all.

The arrival of the new government was overshadowed by two IRA assassinations, spectacular even after a five-year Provisional IRA campaign to get the British troops out by bombing the mainland. There had been bombs on the M62, and at pubs in Guildford and Birmingham, but when the IRA succeeded in penetrating the House of Commons car park and blew up Mrs Thatcher's mentor, the MP and Colditz escaper Airey Neave days before his protégé was elected prime minister, there was consternation over the threat to state security. It was followed at the end of August 1979 by the no less shocking murder of Earl Mountbatten and members of his family in a fishing boat in Ireland.

In its first months in office the Conservative government scored a remarkable diplomatic success. The seemingly intractable problem of the fifteen-year-old war in Southern Rhodesia yielded to the formidable foreign secretary Lord Carrington when he decided to deal directly with the guerrillas. Under the Lancaster House Agreement of 1979 Smith and the guerrilla leaders agreed to a ceasefire and democratic elections. The guerrillas handed in their guns in an orderly fashion at collection points, and free elections were arranged on the basis of one man one vote. Black majority rule brought the former guerrilla leader Robert Mugabe to power in February 1980. He became prime minister of the independent nation of Southern Rhodesia, which took the African name Zimbabwe.

The same year the amount of oil flowing from Britain's North Sea oilfields took a quantum leap five years after coming onstream and solved

Britain's fuel crisis. Cushioned by oil income – Britain in the early 1980s was extracting close to one-tenth of the world's production – Mrs Thatcher reinvented the British economy. Under her chancellor of the Exchequer Geoffrey Howe, Labour's swingeing taxation of the wealthiest was ended, the supertax of 83 per cent was cut to 60 and income tax reduced. A few years later the highest tax band would be 40 per cent. Mrs Thatcher believed that the pounds saved from the taxman would create a consumer boom. At the same time indirect taxation such as VAT was almost doubled, which (as some commentators noted) put the tax burden back on to those least able to bear it.

As the work of freeing the state of its vast burden and dismantling the enormously top-heavy public sector got under way, inflation fell towards single figures. Life slowly began to improve for many Britons as Mrs Thatcher and her team embarked on breaking up the state monopolies. Control over telephone equipment, for example, was removed from the Post Office in 1980. Once the telecommunications industry had been opened up to competition, the bad old days of a quarter of a million people waiting for phones, as they had done in the 1970s, were over. British Telecom, the new name of the privatized industry, was obliged to compete in the market. Overall Britain became far more efficient.

But the Thatcher success story and the Thatcherite mantra that the market must rule and the government not interfere had social drawbacks: massive unemployment and the contraction of the United Kingdom's manufacturing base. As a result of the new government's determination not to pour good money after bad, many state-owned and private businesses started to go bankrupt. In September 1980 the steel works at Consett, County Durham, which was the main source of work in the area, closed down. In historic manufacturing centres like Leeds, where engineering, textiles and printing had provided employment for more than a hundred years, the unprofitable, in the Thatcherite jargon of the day, had 'to go to the wall'. Manufacturing slumped from 52 per cent of the British economy to 32. All over the north, the centre of heavy industry, unemployment rose by leaps and bounds.

By the spring of 1982 more than three million people were out of work, figures which were worse than those seen in the great depression. Helped by the harsh economic climate, Mrs Thatcher's war against the unions was dramatically successful. She outlawed secondary picketing, reduced the scope of the closed shop and made it easier for employers to sack inadequate employees, which previously would have brought the unions out on strike. Unions could also be fined for unlawful industrial action. As unemployment climbed in the recession of the early 1980s the unions lost much of their power as a result of huge redundancies. They were not able to come out on strike because their membership had decreased so rapidly, and the TUC no longer encouraged strikes as they had in the past. In 1983 a newspaper publisher from Manchester named Eddy Shah paved the way for the computerized newspapers of our era when he launched a paper called *Today* without unionized labour.

In a failure of imagination born of her own comfortable circumstances and her own strong character, Mrs Thatcher could not visualize the plight of the poor or unemployed who through no fault of their own were living on benefit. To discourage reliance on the welfare state and force the unemployed into looking for jobs, her government deliberately set benefits to be increased at a rate 5 per cent below inflation. This was a saving at the expense of those least able to afford it, but Mrs Thatcher believed that harsh measures were the only way to break what she thought of as a vicious circle.

Mrs Thatcher's pronouncements to the effect that she did not believe in 'society' infuriated many of Britain's institutions – the universities and Churches, local councillors and the caring professions. The government's reputation could not but be dented by the unprecedented unemployment figures. The complaints that Thatcherism was cold and unfeeling began to be heard even among Tories, many of whom were of the One Nation Disraelian variety. They believed with Peel and Disraeli that Conservatism must not be the rule of the haves without reaching out to the have-nots. Mrs Thatcher herself divided her party into wets (One Nation Tories) and dries (her sensible followers). Britain's greatest asset in many people's eyes was that she was a uniquely caring society, the jewel in whose crown was the safety net of the National Health Service. But Mrs Thatcher and her brilliant Cabinet, whose grasp of the mysteries of economics could reduce opponents to silence, believed that this was the sort of talk that had driven the country massively into debt. Yet no matter how much hard men surrounding Mrs Thatcher suggested that the unemployed 'got on their bikes' and out of the social security offices to find work, too many areas had unemployment levels approaching 50 per cent.

In the spring of 1981 the tension in Britain suddenly exploded into inner-city riots. Brixton in south London was out of police control for several days. Although they were called race riots, the motive seems not to have been racial so much as the reaction of disadvantaged inner-city people who saw no future for themselves. Lord Scarman, a distinguished law lord who was chosen to chair an inquiry into the riots, was of that opinion. In Scarman's view the underlying problem was not criminal elements but unemployment and social despair in the decaying inner cities. Mrs Thatcher, however, refused to believe his evidence. Scarman also recommended that larger numbers of the police be recruited from the ethnic minorities and greater efforts be put into community policing.

Though Mrs Thatcher personally continued to believe in 'criminal elements', other members of the government nevertheless accepted that there was an urgent need for some state involvement to accelerate urban renewal. Grant-aided schemes for the unemployed were produced to help them start up their own businesses. The environment secretary Michael Heseltine launched a big northern initiative to help Liverpool's Toxteth district where there had been rioting for three days.

A few months after the Brixton riots the social fabric of Britain was strong enough to revive for the marriage of Prince Charles, the heir to the throne, to the enchanting blonde nursery-school teacher Lady Diana Spencer, in July 1981. She was a nineteen-year-old member of an old aristocratic landowning family with strong links to the court. Princess Diana's youth and spontaneous charm took the popularity of the royal family to new heights, as did her warm-hearted espousal of many difficult causes. She was admired for insisting on shaking hands with AIDS sufferers at a time when many thought that it was like leprosy and spread by touch. She would go on to do much to discredit the use of landmines throughout the world. The wedding at St Paul's Cathedral was watched by millions of people round the world and there were celebratory street parties all over the country.

Meanwhile Mrs Thatcher's success curve continued onwards and upwards: she moved from setting Britain's financial house in order to clawing back the nation's surplus contribution to the European Community budget, and by 1983 she had achieved a £450 million EC budget rebate to the UK. Nevertheless her revolution continued to antagonize many sections of British society, as did her close relationship with the ultra-conservative Republican administration in Washington. The election in 1980 of President Ronald Reagan, and the Soviet invasion of Afghanistan in 1979, restarted the Cold War after a promising period of détente which had seen work begin on a gas pipeline between Siberia and western Europe.

Most western European governments took a more pragmatic view of the Soviet Union's actions than the United States, believing the invasion of Afghanistan was a defensive measure against Muslim fundamentalism, which was threatening Russia's southern borders. But Reagan and his far-right supporters insisted that there should be a new arms race. Thanks to his imposition of sanctions against Russia, the growing exchange of information and technology between Iron Curtain countries and western Europe came to an abrupt halt.

When the Reagan administration announced out of the blue that it was extending the arms race into space by embarking on a 'Star Wars' programme to create a defensive nuclear shield over the American continent, European peace movements mushroomed. The Russians pulled out of arms-control talks, talks which American conservatives were threatening to stall anyway. Europe seemed to be on the edge of nuclear war. By 1981 more than 200,000 people in Britain had registered as members of CND, the Campaign for Nuclear Disarmament, an organization which had sunk from view after the Aldermaston marches in the 1960s.

The United States stationed the latest generation of nuclear missiles in western Europe to protect the west from 300 Russian SS-20s. But large numbers of European protesters became convinced that, with American conservatives in the driving seat bent on confrontation with Russia, their countries would form the theatre of nuclear war, while Americans remained safe 3,000 miles away. Women from all over Britain, young and old, built camps round the US airfield at Greenham Common in Berkshire when it was decided to locate cruise missiles there.

By the spring of 1982 Mrs Thatcher and Thatcherism were thus faced with a rising tide of unpopularity which threatened the whole experiment with early extinction. Abruptly and unexpectedly, in April that year she was rescued by Argentina's invasion of the tiny Falkland Islands. Although the islands are 300 miles off the coast of Argentina, the 1,800-strong population is entirely British and has continued to be British since it became part of the empire in 1833. On the orders of the military dictator General Galtieri a small force of Argentine soldiers overpowered the seventy-nine Royal Marines on the main island. With the governor of the Falkland Islands, Sir Rex Hunt, they were flown to Montevideo. Twelve thousand Argentinean troops were then landed on the islands, which were claimed for Argentina as Los Malvinas.

Britain had a choice of either giving in to Argentina or defending British nationals, even though they were 8,000 miles away. Under the warlike Mrs Thatcher, who was now compared by admirers to Boudicca, Britain chose to defend them. In a last gasp of imperial power a hundred ships of the Royal Navy steamed to Argentina accompanied by two aircraft carriers, one of which contained the queen's second son, Prince Andrew, a daring helicopter pilot.

By the end of June the Argentineans had been defeated (their military dictatorship was later overthrown as a result) at a cost to Britain of hundreds of millions of pounds. Mrs Thatcher said that what had been at stake was the safety of British nationals abroad. Nevertheless Britain no longer had the power, money or effectiveness to wage colonial wars in this fashion. It would have been impossible to go to war on such principles over Gibraltar or Hong Kong. Nor could Britain have won a war in the distant southern hemisphere without the support of the American administration in tackling the many logistical problems that arose.

The Falklands War made Mrs Thatcher a popular heroine at home. A fever of patriotism and traditional British xenophobia killed the beginnings of a revolt against her methods. At the June 1983 election, the ineffectiveness of Callaghan's successor as Labour leader Michael Foot, and by a left-leaning Labour manifesto later described as the 'longest suicide note in history', the Conservative party's majority rose from 43 to 144. As if to celebrate, a month later, £500 million of public spending cuts were announced.

Labour's share of the vote shrank to just over 25 per cent, a record low for a main opposition party. It had been split by the formation of the Social Democrat party in 1981 by four prominent members of the Labour shadow Cabinet, in protest against the influence of the hard left and the destruction of independent opinion within the Labour party. They included the former Labour foreign secretary Dr David Owen and Roy Jenkins, the former home secretary and chancellor. They believed that Labour was no longer a party dedicated to achieving its programmes through Parliamentary means. New rules allowed the deselection of sitting MPs if they offended grass-roots members, and gave trade union and other organizational blocs 40 per cent of the vote in the electoral college to choose the party leader. Labour had become backward looking and primitive in its anti-Common Market views and irresponsibly unrealistic in its adoption of nuclear unilateralism, the decision to rid Britain of nuclear weapons without asking others to do the same. A dramatic series of by-election wins parachuted the SDP leaders, known as the Gang of Four, into Parliament and made it clear that the Social Democrats were a force to reckon with.

But history was still with Mrs Thatcher. With such huge electoral approval, by 1984 Mrs Thatcher had begun limbering up to take on the miners. Having failed to close twenty-three unproductive pits in 1981, this time she was determined to win the war to reform the coalmining industry, whose subsidy cost the government £800 million a year. In some pits coal cost £20 a ton more to extract from the ground than it could be sold for. Since its heyday in the 1920s, when the industry employed a million and a quarter miners, British coal had been rapidly declining as a source of power and was being replaced by alternative methods that were cheaper and cleaner – nuclear-powered electricity stations, Middle Eastern oil, and now oil and gas from the North Sea. By the 1980s only 300,000 miners remained, 400,000 having taken advantage of excellent early-retirement deals to leave voluntarily in the 1960s and retrain.

In March the government announced that twenty pits had to be closed and 20,000 jobs lost. The leader of the National Union of Mineworkers Arthur Scargill, an old-fashioned Marxist, was determined to prevent it. For a year he kept the miners out on strike, but he did so without a national ballot, so he never had the entire industry's support. Moreover, under a new Trade Union Act in July, unions lost their legal immunity if they struck without a ballot. By October 1984 the High Court had ordered the sequestration of the NUM's funds. The NUM was penniless, and it was not going to be able to keep the strike going for long without money.

Despite the anti-union feeling among many Britons after years of being at their mercy, there was a great deal of sympathy for the plight of the miners and their families facing unemployment in areas where whole communities centred round the coal pit. At the same time the level of violence and intimidation on the picket lines against miners who wanted to work – in one incident a taxi-driver was killed by a concrete block being dropped on his cab – disgusted many. So did Scargill's financial links with the pariah terrorist state of Libya. That very year Gaddafi's diplomats had horrified their British hosts by firing at and killing WPC Yvonne Fletcher when she was escorting a demonstration against the People's Bureau of Libya in London's St James's Square.

Determined not to repeat Heath's mistakes and resort to a three-day week the Thatcher government stockpiled coal at power stations and made plans for non-union drivers to deliver it. It had also arranged for the mechanisms of many power stations to be adapted so that they could fire on oil as well as coal, and it organized the police so that they could be sent at a moment's notice to any trouble spot. Support for the strike within the mining industry itself was never unanimous: less than two-thirds of the pit supervisors voted in favour. Productive pits in the Nottingham area created a breakaway union, the UDM, whose members wished to continue to work.

By March 1985 the year-long strike was over. Under Ian McGregor, a Scot who had emigrated to Canada and who promised to re-examine decisions on pit closures, the National Coal Board succeeded in bringing the strike to an end. Neil Kinnock, the Labour leader who, after Labour's poor showing at the polls in 1983, had replaced Michael Foot, weakened his public standing by not condemning the picket-line violence. In fact he personally believed that Scargill was doing more to destroy the coal industry than the Tories were. Many pits, once closed, would cost too much to reopen. The strike cost the British government £3 billion, but the Labour party conference and the TUC had both backed it.

The miners' strike epitomized the conflict between old industries and the Thatcher government's determination to modernize British industry, between old-fashioned, obstructive unionism and progress. It had ended in a definitive victory for Thatcherism. It was followed the next year by the global tycoon Rupert Murdoch's successful defiance of the print unions in moving *The Times* and his other newspapers from Fleet Street to Wapping.

There he established union-free presses using the new technology and indirectly paved the way for the *Independent* newspaper, which was set up by journalists reluctant to cross the picket line. Thatcherism had begun to seem like the norm.

The defeat of the miners caught Labour at a low point in their electoral fortunes. The resounding Thatcher victory of 1983 was a sign that many in Britain were turning their backs on the trade union movement, partly because the working class (in the sense of manual workers) had shrunk to a third of the employed population. Though Mrs Thatcher's methods seemed insensitive at first, it was hard to deny and would become harder to deny that they were also very successful. She had broken the stranglehold of the unions and had made slimmed-down British industry an example to the rest of the world. Her success made it increasingly difficult for Labour as the client of the trade unions to be taken seriously as an electable party. Few people believed any longer that the trade unions could be relied on to create a viable wages policy. State capitalism had proved too expensive to work. Mrs Thatcher, who had drastically reduced government borrowing and inflation seemed to be proof that the free market first enunciated 200 years before by Adam Smith was the cure for Britain's ills.

The left-leaning progressive thought that had dominated the values of educated Britons was beginning to look obsolete. Yet left-wing extremists' control over Labour in the mid-1980s ensured that the party continued to insist that the way forward was through higher and higher spending. Each Labour party conference demanded more rather than less nationalization – though where the money was to come from was not discussed. As the British economic miracle took hold, it became as fashionable to hold right-wing views as it had been odious since the 1960s. Public schools and conspicuous consumption came back into fashion. The generation known as Thatcher's Children did not seem to have one atom in their bones of the old British yen for social reform that had been such a powerful legacy of the nineteenth century.

The final blow for all varieties of left-of-centre opinion seemed to have been dealt when Thatcherism contributed to the demise of Russian communism. Mrs Thatcher's success in privatizing state industries, in replacing stagnant state monopolies by economic competition, made the state planning of Warsaw Pact countries look old fashioned and ridiculous. Known in the Soviet Union as the Iron Lady, Mrs Thatcher was to achieve fame abroad comparable to that of Winston Churchill. For she continued on a roll. Her courageous conduct of the Falklands War cemented her warm personal relations with President Reagan. The special relationship with America sought by so many British post-war premiers genuinely

A new era in East–West relations 71 years after the Bolshevik Revolution: Margaret Thatcher and Mikhail Gorbachev, 1988.

existed in the 1980s thanks to the personal chemistry between Mrs Thatcher and President Reagan. She was a key player from 1985 onwards during the extraordinary period in east–west relations when under Mikhail Gorbachev the Cold War was ended and the Iron Curtain dividing Europe was put aside.

Gorbachev came to power as general secretary of the Soviet Communist party at a time when the economic and political contradictions of Marxism–Leninism were reaching crisis point. Given overwhelming moral force by the backing of the Polish pope John Paul II, the Solidarity movement in Poland was demanding greater autonomy, as were other Soviet bloc countries. Russia herself desperately needed European and American capital if she was not to sink into the dark ages just when the advances in telecommunications were remaking the modern world. Gorbachev understood that the almost bankrupt Russian state needed to be opened up to the same market forces that had benefited Britain under Mrs Thatcher. Russia no longer had the resources to compete in an arms race in space with America and maintain her increasingly ramshackle Iron Curtain empire. Twenty-five per cent of her national income was going on her armed forces. What had become known as the Brezhnev Doctrine of armed intervention in Warsaw Pact countries was no longer practicable.

Both superpowers agreed to arms reductions. Gorbachev allowed Mrs Thatcher to talk about democracy and human rights on Soviet television, which had never been done before. Mrs Thatcher's force and conviction were greatly to the taste of the Russian people (rather more by now than to that of her fellow countrymen) and she attained iconic status in many former Iron Curtain countries. In 1988 President Reagan's visit to Moscow was followed by a profound shakeup in Russia's institutions. A Parliament was elected and Gorbachev became president instead of general secretary; in 1990 the seventy-year-old communist dictatorship came to an end when the Soviet Parliament removed the party from the constitution and multi-party democratic politics were allowed. Gorbachev had also allowed free elections in the Soviet bloc countries. In November 1989 the Berlin Wall was torn down by the East Germans with disbelieving joy – not a tank moved to stop them and German reunification began.

But there were still more astonishing things to come. At the end of 1991 the Soviet Union was abolished after an attempted coup against Gorbachev by Russian conservatives. The new president of Russia, Boris Yeltsin forbade the Soviet Communist party from continuing in Russia, and the fifteen Soviet republics led by Russia, Ukraine and Belarus announced that they were forming the Commonwealth of Independent States. Gorbachev was no longer Soviet president because there was no Soviet Union.

These momentous events sounded the death-knell of the Marxist system and heralded a new post-ideological age. They have had endless inter-national repercussions, not least of which is that they have left the United States the only superpower in the world. America immediately agreed a series of arms-limitation treaties, as there were around 27,000 warheads in the new republics. Many eastern European countries applied to join the European Union, and ten who were accepted as members after signing the Treaty of Accession in 2003 are set to join the fifteen existing members on 1 May 2004. Former Soviet-bloc countries also joined NATO, the organization originally set up to counter the threat they presented as members of the Warsaw Pact.

In Britain the break-up of the Soviet system only underlined to the small group of Labour modernizers the desperate need for change if the party wanted to avoid becoming a dinosaur like the Soviet Communist party. Neil Kinnock saw that Labour must become more moderate if they wanted to return to office. Alarmed by the success of the SDP, whose electoral pact with the Liberals began eating away at the Labour vote in the mid-1980s, he spent the rest of the decade cleaning out the hard left from the Labour party. With the help of a communications director of genius, a young television producer named Peter Mandelson, grandson of the 1945 Labour home secretary Herbert Morrison, Kinnock began changing Labour's image. In 1986 at the party conference the outmoded revolutionary Red Flag was swapped for a softer red rose as the party's emblem. The next few years would see Labour abandon CND, nationalization and punitive taxation.

Kinnock's greatest challenge was the Trotskyist organization Militant, which had become entrenched within the Labour party. Militant believed in permanent revolution rather than Parliamentary democracy and were especially powerful in local government. They would prove extremely difficult to dislodge. Kinnock found an unexpected ally against Militant in Mrs Thatcher. In her second term of office, she embarked on her great experiment of controlling expenditure at local government level.

Militant had given town-hall funding a bad name by insisting on giving money to increasingly esoteric projects which suited their extremist beliefs, and this began to infuriate taxpayers. In 1984 with the introduction of rate-capping – enabling central government to 'cap' the rates if it considered them to be too high – Mrs Thatcher hoped to put an end to Militant's activities. Councils which overspent had their grants reduced, while those which kept within their limits would also have their grants reduced – it was a late-twentieth-century version of Morton's Fork and just about as popular. Although Britons were getting tired of strange projects belonging to what was now being called the loony left, they also disliked the way rate-capping limited local services. School buildings suffered, as did social services, housing and homeless shelters. In 1985 *Faith in the City*, a report by a Church of England commission, urged emergency action by the government to relieve the plight of inner cities.

In areas like Liverpool where many of the councillors were members of Militant, they refused to accept rate-capping and went on spending. This had been made illegal so that council leaders would be personally liable for costs, but Liverpool Council elected to go bankrupt when central government withheld its funds. The council had to borrow the unheard of sum of £30 million from a foreign bank to cover its debts. But the council still could not pay many of its workers. Militant's irresponsible behaviour enraged ordinary Labour supporters.

In June 1987 Mrs Thatcher won her third successive election with a reduced but still substantial majority of 101. Her final push to control local expenditure demonstrated that she had rather lost her political touch. She had already outraged liberal opinion with an attack on local freedoms in the form of Section 28 of the 1988 Local Government Act which forbade the promotion of homosexuality by local authorities. This provision was her response to media reports that local councils were promoting the idea of families with two gay parents.

Moreover in the late 1980s the gilt had begun wearing off the economic miracle of Thatcherism which had so mesmerized the world, with inflation reduced to 2.5 per cent in 1986. What had been boom was turning to bust.

In 1987 the pro-European chancellor Nigel Lawson slashed interest rates as the economy soared. He was shadowing the European Monetary System, the first step on the way to a single currency for the whole of Europe. At the same time a huge tax cut took the basic rate of income tax from 27 per cent to 25. Lawson believed the boom would last forever but low interest rates, low tax rates and double tax relief sparked a property-buying frenzy and house prices suddenly started rising by 34 per cent a year. Interest rates had to be sharply raised to cool the overheating economy as retail price inflation rose to 10 per cent in 1990 – and the Lawson boom was over.

In an excess of centralizing zeal Mrs Thatcher had abolished the Greater London Council in 1986 when it refused to reduce its expenditure. Now as Labour councils carried on raising the rates to counter the squeeze from central government, she decided that the only solution was to abolish the rates. In their stead she introduced the poll tax – poll being an ancient world for head. This tax had caused a revolt in the time of Richard II. It would have the same sort of effect in the reign of Elizabeth II.

Like many aspects of the Thatcher Revolution, the poll tax made logical sense to the Thatcherites but was hard for unbelievers to grasp. This time the Thatcherites' proud reputation for thinking the unthinkable was simply unthinkable, and a public-relations disaster. Mrs Thatcher and her researchers had hit on the fact that only a minority of the population were paying local taxes, less than half of the electorate of thirty-five million. Every man and woman able to vote would pay the one-off poll tax (its formal name was actually the community charge). That would soon keep council taxes down as voters hit in their pockets would vote for lower-spending (and so no doubt Conservative) councils.

Mrs Thatcher and her Cabinet believed the poll tax would unleash the angry citizenry on the town halls determined to curb their spending. But the government had badly miscalculated: instead the angry citizenry turned on the government in widespread poll-tax riots. The message which the British people picked up on was that the duke and the dustman were going to have to pay the same tax, and their sense of fair play was outraged.

Nevertheless Mrs Thatcher would not draw back. Her motto, she had once said, was 'This lady's not for turning.' But many in the Conservative party began to worry about her increasing inability to listen to the electorate or to the Cabinet. In 1989 Nigel Lawson resigned, chiefly because of Mrs Thatcher's reluctance to join the European Exchange Rate Mechanism, or ERM, although she had signed the Single European Act in 1986 which provided for greater European Community economic and social integration from 1992.

The poll-tax riots took place in March 1990. In August that year the dictator of Iraq, Saddam Hussein, invaded Kuwait, thus threatening Europe's oil supplies, and despite a UN Security Council resolution, failed to withdraw. Mrs Thatcher was at her courageous best encouraging the new United States president George Bush to lead a multinational coalition under UN auspices to war against Saddam when he refused to obey the UN. But disaffected Tories were worried by the way their party's lead was dropping in the opinion polls. The Thatcher revolution was running out of steam, even for her followers. Three months later Mrs Thatcher was to find herself stabbed in the back by a challenge to her leadership. That November John Major became British prime minister.

Mrs Thatcher had been in power for eleven years. There is no disputing her lion heart. Not only had she changed Britain almost overnight. Under her education minister Sir Keith Joseph, who was responsible for much of her regime's intellectual daring, she had paved the way for the greater testing and standardizing of education which began with the introduction of the national curriculum system in 1988. Tests for children at seven, eleven and fourteen, designed to show where schools were failing, signalled the end of thirty years of progressive teaching that had derailed into an undisciplined belief that it was more important for children to explore or 'find themselves' than to take in information.

Mrs Thatcher's Hillsborough Agreement in 1985 setting up an experimental inter-governmental Anglo-Irish Council was the beginning of the political solution that Catholic leaders had warned was the only way of ending the civil war in Northern Ireland. When half of the British Cabinet only just escaped death when their hotel was blown up in Brighton at the party conference in October 1984, Mrs Thatcher accepted that Britain could never win a war against the IRA. She was extremely shaken by the explosion. Even so she insisted that the local Marks and Spencer open early to provide outfits for ministers who had had to leave the hotel in their nightclothes. She was determined to chair a Cabinet meeting that morning. 'Business as usual,' she said, though two of her friends were dead and the trade and industry secretary Norman Tebbit's wife badly injured.

Despite protests from republicans and loyalists, the British government began to consult the Irish government on an official and regular basis about the administration of Northern Ireland and to hammer out a common policy for border security and justice. Eight years of Anglo-Irish co-operation would lead in 1993 to the Downing Street Declaration by the Irish and British premiers Bertie Ahern and John Major that welcomed Sinn Fein to all-party talks and ushered in an IRA ceasefire.

But, for all Mrs Thatcher's great gifts, by the early 1990s members of the Cabinet desired it to be more collegiate, for she had become increasingly dictatorial. There was also bitter disagreement over Britain's relations with

Europe. The Thatcher years coincided with a movement in France and Germany to accelerate the process of 'ever closer union' within the European Common Market, transforming it into a European superstate. The movement was led by Jacques Delors, the French president of the European Commission, and assisted by Chancellor Kohl of Germany and President Mitterrand of France. All three were on record as hoping that 80 per cent of legislation would soon be made by the European Parliament instead of at national level.

Mrs Thatcher fought Britain's corner on the principle of subsidiarity – a piece of EC jargon proclaiming the belief that all decisions should be taken at the lowest effective level, but used by the British as a euphemism for national decision-making. In October 1990, however, anxious not to lose her new chancellor of the Exchequer John Major and the equally pro-European foreign secretary Douglas Hurd, she took Britain into the ERM, a preliminary to joining the European Monetary System, itself the first step on the way to a single currency for the whole of Europe. The ERM was a system set up to create currency harmonization between EC members at the level of their national banks, and required national governments to intervene in foreign exchange markets to make sure that their currency kept its value within the system.

With Mrs Thatcher gone, a month later it was left to the new prime minister John Major and his chancellor Norman Lamont to weather the vicissitudes of the ERM. Unfortunately neither man had Mrs Thatcher's genius or political luck to ride out the two stormy years that followed. The high interest rates of the bust after the Lawson boom had already begun to strike at the heart of the enterprise economy that Mrs Thatcher had brought into being. But after Britain joined the ERM with the pound pegged to the German Deutschmark, the strongest currency in Europe, British interest rates started to go through the roof, with the British economy in deep recession. Germany's interest rates had to be kept high because of her economy's problems arising out of the reintegration of impoverished East Germany. By August 1992 her interest rates were forcing Britain's into double figures, way beyond what the economy could sustain. The economic miracle of the 1980s was on its way to becoming the economic disaster of the early 1990s. And on 16 September, Black Wednesday, Major and Lamont were forced into the ignominious decision to pull sterling out of the ERM immediately. At a stroke Britain's economy and European strategies were in tatters.

Despite the débâcle Lamont saw no reason to fall on his sword. But Black Wednesday had not only convinced Eurosceptics that Britain could never flourish in a single currency, it lost the Conservatives the reputation for being the safe managers of the economy which had been their greatest asset. From September 1992 Labour began to overtake the Conservatives in the opinion polls, while the Tories began a civil war over Europe which slowly tore them apart. In fact, after the initial shock, the effects of pulling out of the ERM were beneficial. Britain went on to enjoy ten years of low inflation, steady growth and falling unemployment, her economy grew faster than those of France and Germany, her inflation was lower and her jobless figures were lower.

Half the Conservative party had become violently anti-European and embarked on an internecine war in the media against pro-European Tories who composed much of the Cabinet. Nevertheless John Major did not pull back from his insistence on having the Treaty of Maastricht, which he had signed that February, approved by Parliament. The treaty revised the European Community's founding Treaty of Rome and turned the EC into the EU, the European Union – a further step towards 'ever closer political union'. But Major won the concession that Britain need not ultimately substitute the European single currency for sterling nor need she accept Delors' social charter (or Chapter, as it became known) guaranteeing minimum EU working standards, which it was believed would increase Britain's labour costs.

John Major was the son of an impoverished trapeze artist. He had reacted against his exciting origins and, as one wit said, ran away from the circus to join a bank. Perhaps memories of poverty in Brixton made him more compassionate than his old boss. Benefits were raised in line with inflation, and the poll tax was transformed into a council tax banded according to property values. The radical Thatcherite principles of privatization and reform of vested interests continued as before. But after Black Wednesday many felt that the Conservatives' day was drawing to an end.

The sentimental British public harked back to the old consensus politics; they did not like feeling that their country contained what some American sociologists were happy to call an underclass. The Conservative government actually increased the amount spent on the National Health Service each year, but ministers managed to give the impression that the NHS too would soon be a thing of the past, partly because they had introduced the internal market as a way to allow competition to make healthcare more efficient.

At the April 1992 general election, a Labour victory was widely expected. Middle England had had enough of tax cuts. It felt that the cherished infrastructure of the country was decaying under the Conservatives, and was dismayed by long hospital waiting lists (so many wards were being closed), potholes from underspending councils, poor social services and decaying schools. But ill-advised remarks by John Smith, then shadow chancellor of the Exchequer, made many people fear that the punitive taxation of the 1970s would be reimposed should Labour return to office. The upshot was the fourth Conservative victory in succession, with a modest majority of twenty-one seats. But a shadow still hung over Labour.

Neil Kinnock bowed out of the Labour leadership after his defeat, leaving the leadership to John Smith. Smith improved the voting system in the electoral college, while warning the unions they could expect no pay increases without productivity. But he died unexpectedly in 1994, and the leadership jumped a generation to the telegenic Anthony Blair, who was then under forty.

Blair, a former barrister and devout Christian with a formidable QC wife and three young children, (a fourth, Leo, would arrive in 2000, the first baby to be born to a serving British prime minister in 150 years), further modernized the party with the help of Peter Mandelson and Gordon Brown. They believed that people were still frightened of Labour and that it was their job to reassure them that the party had abandoned what had been known as the 'politics of envy', its commitment since 1918 to the redistribution of the nation's wealth by taxation. Blair excised Clause 4 from the Labour constitution, which promised 'common ownership of the means of production, distribution and exchange'. The unions were kept at arm's length and Labour embraced the European cause with fervour. Blair and Mandelson believed that New Labour, as they called the party, had to reach out to a wider audience.

On 6 May 1994, as a sign of closer relations between Britain and Europe, the Channel tunnel was opened. For the first time since the Ice Age Britain was linked to the continent. It had been dreamed of more than a hundred years before, but it was not until the late 1980s that Britain and France had the technology to build the tunnel, which runs 150 feet below the sea. The three tunnels, north, south and a service facility, required the removal of seventeen million tons of earth and cost £15 billion. It now takes just three hours to reach the centre of Paris from the centre of London.

But the triumph of the Eurotunnel and the excitement that it generated did nothing for the Tories' reputation. Labour was climbing higher and higher in the opinion polls, while the Tory government was slowly sinking into a self-inflicted mire of sleaze, lying ministers, illicit arms sales and money for votes.

The Tories even seemed unlucky on the question of Ireland, where by the beginning of the 1990s Mrs Thatcher's Hillsborough Agreement was having very positive effects. Although some Unionists saw the agreement as a form of betrayal, the Irish government reaffirmed that political union would come about only if the majority of citizens of Northern Ireland wished it. There was a change of attitude within the Sinn Fein leadership, who recognized that many of its supporters were exhausted by the war. By August 1994 the IRA had agreed a ceasefire, and this was followed by a loyalist paramilitary ceasefire in October. It was a great moment after twenty years of war. But decommissioning the IRA's weapons was the sticking point for the Unionist parties, which insisted that Sinn Fein could not participate in the political process until the Provisional IRA had destroyed their weapons.

In January 1996 the Major government turned down a proposal from the former American senator George Mitchell, President Clinton's adviser on Irish affairs, who headed the independent International Body to examine the process of decommissioning paramilitary arms, that the decommissioning should take place in tandem with all-party talks. Instead it began the election process without Sinn Fein. By way of response the following month the IRA bombed Canary Wharf in the Docklands. It was clear that the peace process had been derailed.

But it was the crisis over the spread of bovine spongiform encephalopathy (BSE, or mad cow disease) from cattle to humans that finally finished off the Conservatives. The public could just about accept ministerial prevarication over the Matrix-Churchill affair revealed by the Scott inquiry into the trial of three businessmen prosecuted by Customs and Excise for illegally exporting arms to Iraq, whose report was published in February 1996. This showed that several Tory ministers had been willing to let three innocent men go to prison rather than reveal that the defendants had been working for the British secret services. But when the Whitehall culture of secrecy endangered the nation's health, for Conservative ministers refused to come clean about how safe beef was to eat at a time when the television news was filming young people dying of CJD (Creutzfeldt-Jacob disease, thought to be a human variant of BSE), it was the end. As 4.7 million cows were slaughtered at a cost of £3 billion, after British beef had been banned round the world, eighteen years of Conservative rule collapsed. Unlike the Tories, the fluent and sensible Tony Blair, who had moved Labour far from their socialist roots towards the acceptable middle ground, looked like a man who could be trusted.

In May 1997 the people of England uttered a resounding no to the Conservatives. Labour won 419 seats, 101 of which were held by women, the so-called Blair Babes, and the Conservative vote was wiped out in Scotland. Blair swept to victory with a huge majority of 179 seats and proceeded to carry out extensive constitutional reform. John Major resigned as leader of the Tory party and was replaced by the thirty-six-year-old William Hague, a Parliamentarian of considerable gifts who had been secretary of state for Wales. But despite Hague's down-to-earth manner, as befitted his Yorkshire ancestry, the Tories failed to make any headway in the polls despite much soul-searching. After another landslide win for Labour at the election in June 2002 (a majority of 167), Hague too resigned, to be succeeded by an ex-soldier, Iain Duncan Smith.

The Labour government soon showed itself to be a modern administration. It incorporates a Women's Unit, though not yet a Women's Ministry, and provided the machinery since 2000 for an elected mayor of London, the capital's first, who took the place of the Greater London Council that Mrs Thatcher got rid of in 1986. The Bank of England was made independent in 1997 as soon as Labour took office and was given the sole power to decide interest rates, a power previously vested in the Treasury. Interest-rate decisions have thus been taken out of the political arena to avoid the boom and bust of the Lawson years and to create the economic stability required for economic growth.

After 120 years of delay, in 1999 the House of Lords began the first stage of being modernized when hereditary peers – other than ninety-two elected to oversee reforms – were excluded. This brings Britain well and truly into the third millennium. The reformed Lords will incorporate the best of its ancient traditions as a council of non-partisan professional experts and wise men who act as a delaying and revising chamber in the face of over-hasty legislation passed by the House of Commons. However, four years later, in July 2003, no decision had been reached on the construction of a reformed, representative second chamber which would not be a rival to the elected Commons.

Labour had promised regional assemblies to Scotland and Wales. After two referendums produced a vote in favour of devolution, the year 2000 saw both the opening of the Scottish Parliament and the Welsh Assembly. Reflecting Scotland's long history of independence and her separate legal system, the Scottish Parliament has powers to alter taxes raised at Westminster by 3 per cent and to legislate over internal affairs – the environment, social services, education and health. As befits a smaller country with a far longer history of being attached to England, the Welsh Assembly does not have the power to make laws though it may alter some designated Westminster legislation. The same number of Welsh and Scottish MPs will be retained at Westminster, leaving some commentators to wonder whether England should not, in fairness, have her own regional assembly too.

Labour came to power determined to end social division and chronic underinvestment in the public sector and manufacturing sector. Britain no longer has the absolute poverty with which Booth and Rowntree appalled middle-class consciences at the beginning of the last century. Nevertheless the respected charity the Child Poverty Action Group in 2002 estimated that nearly a quarter of the population, including almost four million children, are living in what is defined internationally as 'income poverty'. That is too high a figure for a civilized country to tolerate. Britain's infant mortality rates, once the lowest in the world, are on the rise, a sign that conditions among the poor are deteriorating and need to be improved.

Labour believe that the government has a social responsibility to foster growth in the economy by fighting unemployment, not just to let the market rule and the devil take the hindmost. But the lessons of the past have convinced them that government investment in industry cannot be afforded without the help of the private sector. Guided by the Scottish chancellor of the Exchequer Gordon Brown, the Labour government displayed a fiscal prudence that gained it a formidable reputation. Its auction in 2001 for licenses for the third generation of mobile phones raised the colossal sum of £22.5 billion. The City of London, traditionally a Tory stronghold, was reported, temporarily at least, to have become a Labour bastion. Labour also ended the internal market in hospital care, gave help to pensioners with heating bills and to the poor with tax credits, and introduced their New Deal intended to get people off benefit and into employment as soon as possible.

In July 1997 one of the last great outposts of empire was relinquished when Hong Kong was handed back to the Chinese. The lease on part of the Crown Colony had expired, but the whole of it was handed over following an agreement negotiated by the Thatcher government in 1982. Communist China undertook to allow Hong Kong considerable internal independence and leeway as a Special Administrative Region where capitalism would be permitted for the next fifty years at least, and it would continue to be a free port. In addition, the Basic Law for Hong Kong envisaged a freely elected legislature, and that has been honoured.

In August 1997 the former wife of the Prince of Wales, the beautiful Princess Diana, was killed in a car crash in Paris aged only thirty-six. For the previous sixteen years her sympathetic nature, youth and spontaneity had given her a considerable hold over the nation's affections. There was a great outpouring of sorrow at her death and for her bereaved sons, the fifteen-year-old Prince William and the thirteen-year-old Prince Harry.

Continental Europe of the 1990s was racked by the spectacle on the nightly television news of a vicious civil war between members of the federation of Yugoslavia in the wake of the changes in eastern Europe. The brutal massacres of around 250,000 Muslims and forcible expulsion of another two million from the Republic of Bosnia-Herzegovina by Serbs, who resisted their fellow Yugoslav republics' demand for independence and recognition by the European Union, generated a new expression that had echoes of the Holocaust – ethnic cleansing. In 1999 NATO warplanes bombed Belgrade to put an end to the Serb cleansing of the province of Kosovo of ethnic Albanians: 800,000 of them, many of them with babies and with their possessions in carts, were dying in the mountains. Although the Serb leader, Slobodan Milosević was deposed and handed over to a special tribunal set up by the UN at the Hague to be tried for war crimes, the refugee crisis caused by these dispossessed peoples continues to pose great problems for the EU.

But in Northern Ireland at Easter 1998 the twenty-six-year war finally came to an end. It was decided to allow the decommissioning of weapons to run in tandem with the devising of a new government. The only thing that Sinn Fein and the other political wings of paramilitary groups like the loyalist UDA had to do to participate was to get their paramilitaries to restore the ceasefire of 1994. The IRA had begun the process in July 1997.

On Good Friday 1998 an agreement was signed by all shades of opinion in Northern Ireland that set up a power-sharing Assembly whose creation had been deferred for over twenty-five years. Once more it was reiterated that it would be the will of the people of Northern Ireland, not those of Eire or Britain, that would decide their future. The withdrawal of troops from Northern Ireland put an end to the most dangerous tour of duty in every British soldier's career.

The peace process could have been derailed by a bomb set off at Omagh in August 1998 by a nationalist terrorist group beyond the control of the IRA. But Sinn Fein and the IRA condemned the tragedy in the strongest terms and the Assembly survived. Decommissioning remained an issue. However, the effect of the 11 September 2001 outrage in New York when the Twin Towers were destroyed by Islamic terrorists was to make Americans understand at first hand what terrorism does. So the IRA, despite its traditional American support, found that it had to alter its tactics, and in October that year a new effort at decommissioning began. Punishment beatings by both sides and mutual distrust continue to cause problems in Northern Ireland, however. Sadly, in October 2002 the Assembly was suspended (and remained so as at July 2003) and direct rule reimposed. After allegations of an IRA spy ring at Stormont, other parties refused to continue in government with Sinn Fein.

On 1 January 1999 eleven of the fifteen member states of the European Union abandoned their currencies for the euro, or single currency, which is managed by the European Central Bank. The eleven were Finland, Portugal, Austria, the Netherlands, Luxembourg, Italy, Ireland, France, Spain, Germany and Belgium, and they were joined in 2001 by Greece. To date Britain remains outside the euro zone; opinion polls show that around 60 per cent of Britain's businessmen are in favour of jettisoning the pound in its favour, but a similar portion of the public are opposed. Tony Blair promised Britain a referendum before sterling is abolished and Britain joins a single European currency. But in principle his government was in favour of joining the euro, and in February 1999 the prime minister published a national changeover plan outlining the steps being taken in preparation.

Britain's ancient democratic institutions mean she cannot view a European superstate without protest. The EU headquarters, where one man one vote seems irrelevant compared to the powers of appointed bureaucrats, appears to some to be a threat to British freedoms. From earliest times observers like Tacitus noted that the inhabitants of these isles have an obsession with their liberty. Today it may translate as a desire to preserve national sovereignty over matters like taxation, and to halt further attempts to harmonize national laws through the EU. On the other hand it might be argued that until the (European) Romans came there was much that was uncivilized about Britain, and that that remains true today. Britons interested in their freedoms will have noted that Europe is not short of liberties herself. The European social chapter, which Labour signed up to in 1998, has made Britain bring in legislation to ensure that the workplace is protected by far greater health and safety requirements and to set a minimum wage that she seemed incapable of introducing on her own. Successful appeals to the Court of Human Rights at Strasbourg, whether over the UK's harsh treatment of her children or over gender equality, show that there is much to learn from Europe. The Human Rights Act that Labour implemented in 1998, which incorporated into UK law the European Convention on Human Rights, is bringing Britain into line with a more humane way of life. Women, many of whom have not shared British liberties until recently – the Church of England only allowed women to be ordained vicars in 1993 – can especially look forward to the benign influence of Europe, which is committed to enforcing equal rights for women. Pay for women in Britain lags well behind other EU countries: as the Equal Opportunities Commission's witty poster of a young girl put it, 'Prepare your daughter for working life. Give her less pocket money than your son.'

Though women are hardly a minority, their lack of representation at the higher levels of the judiciary until very recently was mirrored by the ethnic minorities. In the twenty-five years since it was created to combat racism the Commission for Racial Equality has been extremely successful in harmonizing relations between ethnic and white Britons. Nevertheless in 1999 the failure of the parents of Stephen Lawrence to get their son's murder properly investigated seven years before led the High Court judge Sir William Macpherson to conclude that the British police were guilty of institutionalized racism, which he defined as a failure to provide a professional service to people because of their colour, culture or ethnic

Labour MP Paul Boateng, who became the first black Cabinet minister in British history when, in May 2002, he was made Chief Secretary to the Treasury. Seen here with Chancellor Gordon Brown.

origin. Most white Britons felt deeply shamed by the Macpherson Report, and it resulted in a massive shake-up in British institutions. There was an investigation by the Home Office into statistics on race and the criminal justice system, and a decision by the Labour government actively to combat hidden or institutionalized racism in other public bodies. The Race Relations Amendment Act of April 2001 imposes a legal duty on central and local government bodies to represent their ethnic minorities in proportion to their communities and this also applies to hospitals, schools, universities and public institutions like the BBC.

Prince Charles, who has taken a close interest in inner-city regeneration for three decades, has done much to bring together the many different elements in Britain's multicultural society. He says he intends to adapt the papal title bestowed on his ancestor Henry VIII and be, not the defender of the faith, but the defender of all faiths.

After more than half a century as queen, Elizabeth II lends grace, humanity and dutifulness to her position and continuity at a time of flux. In June 2002 the immense success of the Golden Jubilee to mark her fifty years on the throne was visible in the one million people who gathered in the Mall in front of Buckingham Palace to salute her. The deaths of the queen's sister Princess Margaret and of Queen Elizabeth the Queen Mother in the Jubilee Year only enhanced the sympathy felt for her.

The queen continues to live at Windsor Castle whose site above the River Thames was chosen more than nine centuries ago by William the Conqueror because it was a day's march from the Tower of London – it was intended to guard the western approaches to the capital. Though the M4 and a sprawl of housing and flyovers now lies between Windsor and the Tower, the queen's residence there reminds us of the extraordinary continuity the monarchy provides as a national institution and of Britain's great good fortune in not having been invaded since 1066. The monarchy's ancient roots provide an element of stability in an ever-changing world. Yet the queen herself has made a habit of moving with the times. Though her Rolls-Royce may look as old fashioned as her handbag, she insisted on her coronation being televised in 1953 in order to include as many of her fellow countrymen as possible. Today she even has her own web site.

Britain's days of pre-eminence as a great power are gone, as Antony Gormley's ironic statue *The Angel of the North*, a huge angel in rusty iron, reminds us, looking back to northern Britain's industrial and engineering past. All over the country, old industrial structures – whether the former Bankside power station in London or the Albert Dock at Liverpool – are being turned over to what is sometimes called the leisure industry. (Bankside and the Albert Dock became the art galleries Tate Modern and Tate Liverpool.) Britain's manufacturing base may continue to decline, but service or skills industries are more important than ever. In the twenty-first century Britain's expertise as a great imperial power enables the once informal arrangements between merchants waiting at wharves for their ships to arrive to be transformed into complex international insurance and maritime businesses. In the era of super-telecommunications, London's fortunate position equidistant between the time zones of Asia and America makes the City the world's leading financial centre, where 48 per cent of the global foreign equity market is traded. But 'leisure industry' seems a poor way of describing a mission to raise the British people's cultural expectations and range. In the age of the computer chip, the future for the European world seems increasingly to be in highly skilled work. Machines and computers have made much physical labour redundant where it is not already uncompetitive with the third world. Ford Cars closed its last British factory in 2001.

When an earlier Tyneside inhabitant, the eighth-century monk Bede of Jarrow, composed his history of the English people, ferreting out documentary evidence in the archives of English abbeys and in the papal registers at Rome, he was writing for a tiny audience, the few nobles who could read. In those days culture was then dispersed to the many, if at all, through priests' sermons or Bible readings at church. But one of Bede's most moving stories was that of Caedmon, the poor lay brother whose poetry earned him a place in the monastery. How pleased Bede would be to think that in the thirteen centuries since his birth a sense of inclusive cultural renaissance was gathering that has now exploded in a great new building on the River Tyne, the Baltic Exchange, which opened in August 2002. Tyneside, once a neglected and depressed industrial area, is reviving under the impact of cultural centres, cinema

London the day before Queen Elizabeth II's Golden Jubilee on 4 June 2002.
Crowds from all over Britain and the Commonwealth filled the Mall to show
their affection for Queen Elizabeth II after fifty years on the throne.

complexes, concert halls and cheap homes for young professionals.

Despite all the change, some things about Britain remain the same. For many people the most striking feature of the country is a sense of community-mindedness, a sense that – whatever Mrs Thatcher believed – society matters. The National Health Service was once described as the nearest thing the British have to a state religion. Thatcherism may have been a revolution, but now that the revolution is over, old beliefs in the state as a disinterested force for good cannot help resurfacing. The privatization Mrs Thatcher pioneered is looking a little less shiny. Railtrack in particular angered many, with the large dividends paid to shareholders instead of being devoted to the maintenance of the railways' infrastructure or to a proper inspectorate. When a broken rail caused an avoidable crash in Hertfordshire in 2002, the last of a line of terrible accidents, private finance initiatives began to look less good. The British expect political accountability in their public services, which many voters expected Labour to restore.

Britain has more or less gracefully withdrawn from the 400-year-old trading empire which made a great power out of some small north-westerly islands and their canny, energetic and not over-scrupulous natives. Though Britain has been reduced to her original area of a few offshore islands whose longest island is little more than 600 miles long, hers is the world's fourth largest economy and she is its fourth largest monetary power. Her influence persists in disproportionate relation to her small size.

Britain is now a fully signed-up member of the European Union. The question is what sort of Europe is Britain agreeing to be part of? Will it fall to England once more to take up her historic role of leading the resistance to a masterplan for continental tyranny expressed in European institutions which are not politically accountable enough?

I say England advisedly, because the country called Britain, which was invented in 1707 to describe the union of the Scottish and English crowns, may soon no longer exist. With the financial support of Brussels Scotland may find irresistible the national will to become an independent country again.

The British are a rather schizophrenic and mysterious lot where authority is concerned – the result perhaps of having had to adapt to so many waves of invaders, the Romans, the Anglo-Saxons, the Vikings and the Normans. The Welsh, Scottish and Irish spent many centuries fighting off the aggressive English state. There is both an official culture which the British subscribe to and a secret, rather Celtic, side of Britain which carries on regardless. It is helped to flourish by the nature of the country's geography. Her veiling fogs, dense forests, indented coastline and hidden valleys, particularly in the north and west, lend themselves to movements resisting all manifestations of central government, whether it be new dynasties or new religions. This inextinguishably individualistic side smoulders and periodically flares up, whether as Boudicca, Hereward the Wake, Catholic recusancy or Jacobite revolts. Who are Britain's' greatest heroes? Anti-heroes, that's who, from Robin Hood to Rob Roy.

Sir Howard Newby, the President of the British Association for the Advancement of Science, warned in 2002 that Britain must fight off what he calls 'increasing anti-intellectualism' and hostility to scientific progress which could leave Britain behind the rest of the world. The national passion for rural life as a sort of paradise on earth sometimes leads to a suspicion of all scientific inquiry whether over genetically modified food or the necessary use of animals for experimentation to cure disease. Yet from Isaac Newton onwards British life has always contained a very strong vein of scientific inquiry. Not content with inventing the steam engine, Britons have split the atom, produced the first test-tube baby and cloned the first animal, Dolly the sheep.

As Dr Tristram Hunt trenchantly reminded a Britain apparently overflowing with monarchists during the Queen's Jubilee, the island story is also 'a story of freethinking and restive inventiveness utterly at odds with the stifling conformity of court life. The Britain of Thomas Hobbes, Adam Smith and Jeremy Bentham is a tradition of pioneering political thought unrivalled in western Europe.' Although the Nonconformist conscience may have been identified as a national feature only in the seventeenth century, the rebellious British seemed genetically predisposed to make it their signature tune.

Pity the poor British then, despite their country's renowned stability. As with the seas that surround them they are continually washed by one current and then another. Their views seem as peculiar as their weather. Is it the changeable sea winds that make it impossible to predict how the British will react, one minute swayed by intense patriotism, the next supremely rational and suspicious of emotion? For the British contain within themselves two warring strains of thought that can never quite be reconciled. There is what amounts to a folk belief in the necessity of kings and queens. Yet that coexists alongside an equally powerful and living tradition of liberty and progress, expressed in some of the world's great reforming movements – Parliamentary democracy, the anti-slavery movement, penal reform, anti-militarism and municipal socialism.

From the middle ages onwards, Britain is generally held to have distinguished herself from other European countries by virtue of her highly mobile class system – considered to be one of the secrets of her prosperity. Yet foreigners complain that despite their apparently informal manners, there is no other people so hard to get to know as the British, and no country so class sensitive. As for Britain's position in Europe, there the Europeans believe she is a maddening law unto herself, neither wholeheartedly pro nor quite against. A curious and contradictory people indeed.

FURTHER READING

This book could not have been prepared without relying on the scholarship provided by the standard histories and reference books, in particular the Oxford History of Britain, *the* New Cambridge Modern History, *the* Dictionary of National Biography *and the* Pimlico Chronology of British History *by Alan and Veronica Palmer. The following is a list of suggestions for stimulating further reading – works by modern authors or translators which are in print or available from libraries.*

Ackroyd, Peter *Albion: The Origins of the English Imagination* (2002)
The Anglo-Saxon Chronicle, trans. G. N. Garmonsway (1953)
Aubrey, John *Brief Lives*, ed. Richard Barber (1975)
Ayling, Stanley *The Elder Pitt* (1976)
Bede, the Venerable *The Ecclesiastical History of the English People*, trans. L. Sherley-Price (1968)
Beevor, Anthony *Berlin: The Downfall* (2002)
Black, Jeremy *Culloden and the '45* (1990)
Blake, Robert *Disraeli* (1963)
Bragg, Melvyn *Speak for England* (1976)
Brewer, Derek *Arthur's Britain* (1985)
Briggs, Asa *A Social History of Britain* (1983)
Brooke, Christopher *The Twelfth-Century Renaissance* (1969)
Brooke, John *The Reign of George III* (1972)
Calder, Angus *The People's War: Britain 1939–1945* (1969)
Cannadine, David *Ornamentalism: How the British Saw their Empire* (2001)
Cannon, John and Griffiths, Ralph *The Oxford Illustrated History of the British Monarchy* (2000)
Churchill, Winston S. *A History of the English-Speaking Peoples*, 12 vols (1956)
Clark, Alan *The Donkeys* (1991)
Clark, Peter *Hope and Glory: Britain 1900-1990* (1996)
Cobban, Alfred *A History of Modern France* (1965)
Colley, Linda *Britons: Forging the Nation 1707–1837* (1997)
Coogan, Tim Pat *Michael Collins* (1991)
Cornwell, John *Hitler's Pope* (1999)
Curtis, Gila *The Life and Times of Queen Anne* (1980)
Davies, Norman *The Isles: A History* (2000)
Davies, W. *Wales in the Early Middle Ages* (1982)
Donaldson, G. and Morpeth, R. S. *Who's Who in Scottish History* (1973)
Duby, Georges *The Age of the Cathedrals: Art and Society 980–1420* (1981)
Edwards, Ruth Dudley *The Faithful Tribe* (1999)
Ehrman, John *The Younger Pitt*, 3 vols (1996)
Elton, G. R. *Reformation Europe 1517–1559* (1963)
Evans, Richard *In Defence of History* (2001)
Feiling, Sir Keith *The History of England* (1950)
Ferguson, Niall *The Cash Nexus: Money and Power in the Modern World* (2002)
Field, John *Kingdom, Power and Glory: A Historical Guide to Westminster Abbey* (1999)
Figes, Orlando *A People's Tragedy: The Russian Revolution 1891–1924* (1998)
Flenley, Ralph *Modern German History* (1968)
Foster, Roy *Modern Ireland 1600–1972* (1988)

Fraser, Antonia *Cromwell: Our Chief of Men* (1973)
Galbraith, J. K. *The Great Crash 1929* (1955)
Gardiner, Juliet and Wenborn, Neil, eds *The History Today Companion to British History* (1995)
Gash, Norman *Sir Robert Peel* (1972)
Gilbert, Martin *Churchill: A Life* (1991)
Gillingham, John *Richard the Lionheart* (1978)
Girouard, Mark *Life in the English Country House* (1978)
Glenny, Misha *The Fall of Yugoslavia* (1992)
Graham-Campbell, James *The Viking World* (2001)
Halevy, Elie *History of the English People in the Nineteenth Century*, vol. 5: *Imperialism and the Rise of Labour 1895–1905* (1951)
Hallam, Elizabeth and Prescott, Andrew, eds *The British Inheritance: A Treasury of Historic Documents* (1999)
Hampson, Norman *The Enlightenment: The Pelican History of European Thought* (1968)
Hibbert, Christopher *The Tower of London* (1971)
Hill, Christopher *Intellectual Origins of the English Revolution* (1972)
Hobsbawm, Eric *The Age of Revolution 1789–1848* (1988)
Horne, Alistair *How Far from Austerlitz?* (1997)
Hough, Richard and Richards, Denis *The Battle of Britain* (2001)
Howarth, David *Trafalgar: The Nelson Touch* (1997)
Huizinga, Johan *The Waning of the Middle Ages* (1955)
Hume Brown, P. A. *A Short History of Scotland* (1951)
Hunter Blair, Peter *An Introduction to Anglo-Saxon England* (1956)
Huntingdon, Samuel, P. *The Clash of Civilizations and the Remaking of the World Order* (1997)
Hutton, Will *The State We're In* (1996)
James, Lawrence *The Rise and Fall of the British Empire* (1995)
Jenkins, Roy *Gladstone* (1995)
Jenkins, Simon *England's Thousand Best Churches* (1999)
Johnson, Paul *The Offshore Islanders* (1972)
Kabbani, Rana *Europe's Myths of Orient* (1986)
Kee, Robert *The Green Flag* 3 vols (1976)
Keegan, John *The Face of Battle: A Study of Agincourt, Waterloo and the Somme* (1976)
Keen, Maurice *The Penguin History of Medieval Europe* (1991)
Kennedy, Paul *The Rise and Fall of Great Powers* (1988)
Kenyon, John *The History Men* (1983)
Kershaw, Ian *Hitler: 1889–1936 – Hubris* (2001)
La Guardia, Anton *War without End: Israelis, Palestinians and the Struggle for a Promised Land* (2002)
Lee, Christopher *This Sceptred Isle* (1997)
Lefebvre, Georges *The French Revolution* (1962)
Lewis, Bernard *The Middle East* (1997)
Lewis, Jane *Women in Britain since 1945* (1992)
Lloyd, Christopher *The British Seaman* (1968)
Longford, Elizabeth *Wellington* 2 vols (2001)
Mackay, Angus and Ditchburn, David, eds *Atlas of Medieval Europe* (1997)
MacKenzie, Alexander and Prebble, John *The History of the Highland Clearances* (1996)
Mattingley, Garrett *The Defeat of the Spanish Armada* (1959)
Medlicott, W. N. *British Foreign Policy since Versailles 1919–1963* (1968)
Monbiot, George *Captive State: The Corporate Takeover of Britain* (2000)
Monroe, Elizabeth *Britain's Moment in the Middle East 1914–1956* (1963)

Morgan, Kenneth O., ed. *The Oxford Illustrated History of Britain* (1984)
Morison, S. E. *Builders of the Bay Colony* (1931)
Namier, Lewis *The Structure of Politics at the Accession of George III* (1972)
Neale, J. E. *The Elizabethan House of Commons* (1976)
Nicolson, Harold *Peacemaking 1919* (1984)
Owen, Richard and Dynes, Michael *The Times Guide to the Single European Market* (1992)
Pakenham, Thomas *The Scramble for Africa* (1991)
Palmer, Alan *Victory 1918* (1998)
Palmer, Alan *The Kaiser – Warlord of the Second Reich* (1997)
Paxman, Jeremy *The English* (2001)
Pelling, Henry *A History of British Trade Unionism* (1971)
Pimlott, Ben *The Queen: A Biography of Elizabeth II* (1997)
Plumb, J. H. *Sir Robert Walpole: The King's Minister* (1973)
Pocock, Tom *Horatio Nelson* (1987)
Potter, T. W. and Johns, Catherine *Roman Britain* (1992)
Price, Munro *The Fall of the French Monarchy* (2003)
Ramm, Agatha, ed. *Grant and Temperley's Europe in the Nineteenth and Twentieth Centuries* (1984)
Ridley, Jasper *Lord Palmerston* (1970)
Roberts, Andrew *Salisbury: Victorian Titan* (1999)
Roberts, J. M. *The Penguin History of the World* (1995)
Robertson, Geoffrey *Crimes against Humanity* (1999)
Rose, Kenneth *George V* (2000)
Ross, Charles *Richard III* (1981)
Rowse, A. L. *The Story of Britain* (1979)
Runciman, Steven *A History of the Crusades,* 3 vols (1954)
Schama, Simon *A History of Britain,* 4 vols (2002)
Sebag Montefiore, Simon *Stalin. The Court of the Red Tsar* (2003)
Shannon, Richard *Gladstone: Heroic Minister 1865–1898* (1999)
Sked, Alan and Cook, Chris *Post-War Britain 1945–1992* (1997)
Somerset, Anne *Life and Times of William IV* (1981)
Starkey, David *Elizabeth* (2001)
Strong, Roy *The Spirit of Britain: A Narrative History of the Arts* (1999)
Tacitus *The Agricola and the Germania,* trans. Anthony R. Birley(1999)
Tacitus *The Annals of Imperial Rome,* trans. Michael Grant (1956)
Taylor, A. J. P. *The Struggle for Mastery in Europe* (1954)
Taylor, Barbara *Eve and the New Jerusalem: Socialism and Feminism in the Nineteenth Century* (1984)
Thomas, Charles *Celtic Britain* (1997)
Thomas, Hugh *The Slave Trade: The History of the Atlantic Slave Trade 1440–1870* (1997)
Thompson, E. P. *The Making of the English Working Class* (1963)
Thomson, David *Europe since Napoleon* (1962)
Thurley, Simon *The Royal Palaces of Tudor England* (1993)
Tillyard, Stella *Aristocrats* (1994)
Trevelyan, G. M. *History of England* (1926)
Tuchman, Barbara *The Guns of August* (1962)
Uglow, Jenny *Hogarth: A Life and a World* (1997)
Vincent, John *The Formation of the Liberal Party 1857–1868* (1966)
Williams, Neville *Henry VII* (1973)
Wilson, A. N. *The Victorians* (2002)
Worden, Blair, ed. *Stuart England* (1987)
Young, Hugo *One of Us: A Biography of Margaret Thatcher* (1989)
Ziegler, Philip *The Black Death* (1969)

KINGS OF ENGLAND 802–1135

including Kings of Wessex, Danish Kings, House of Godwin and Dukes of Normandy

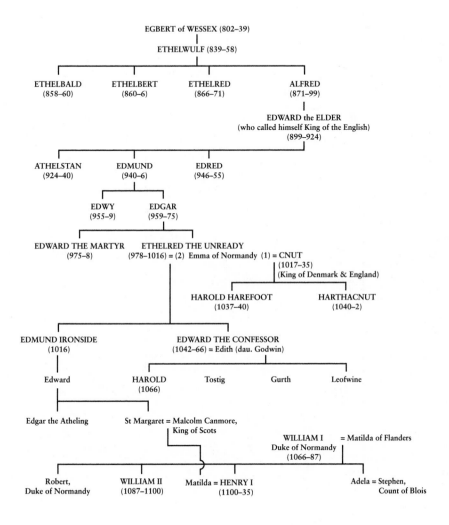

NORMAN AND ANGEVIN KINGS

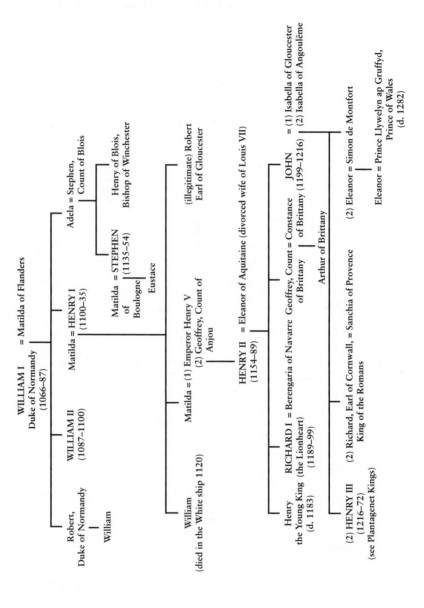

PLANTAGENET KINGS

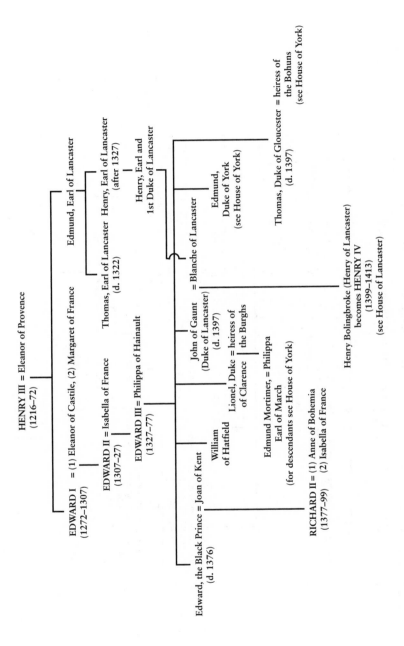

THE HOUSE OF LANCASTER

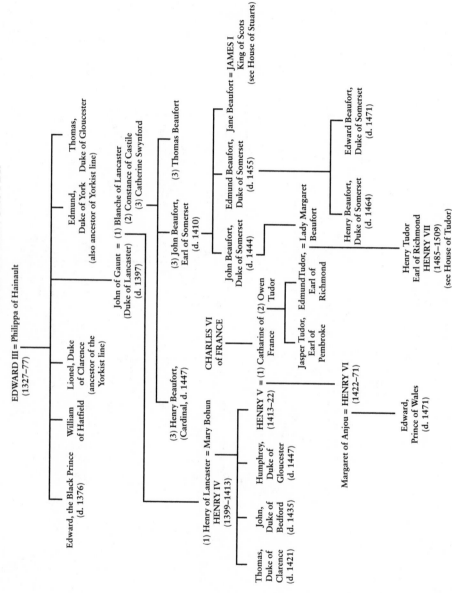

THE HOUSE OF YORK

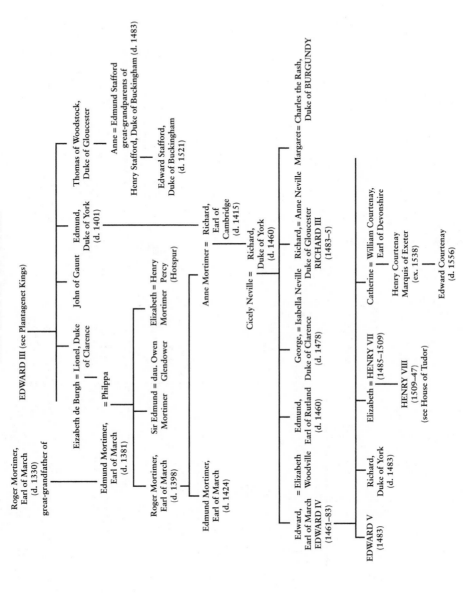

THE HOUSE OF TUDOR

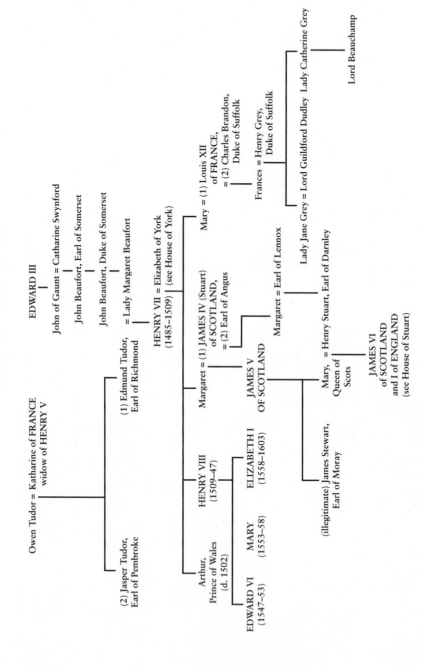

THE HOUSE OF STUART

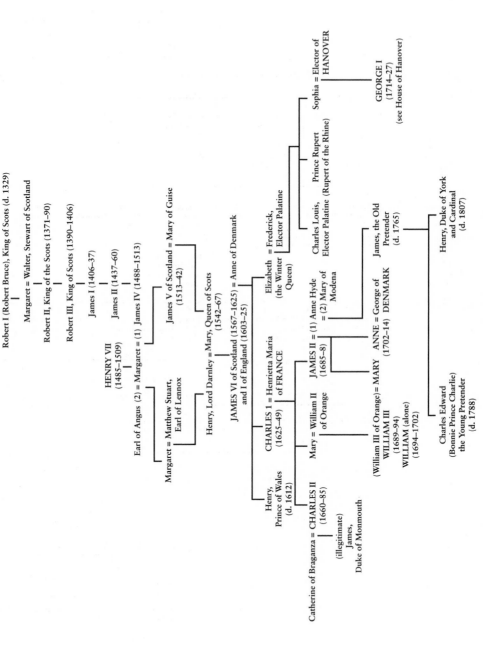

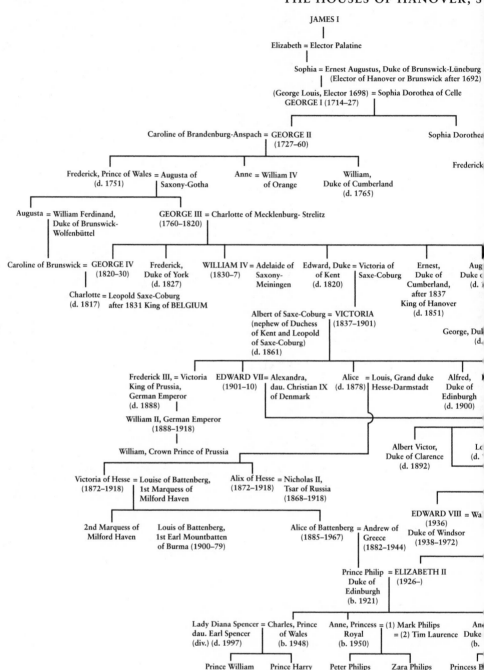

JAMES I

Elizabeth = Elector Palatine

Sophia = Ernest Augustus, Duke of Brunswick-Lüneburg
(Elector of Hanover or Brunswick after 1692)

(George Louis, Elector 1698) = Sophia Dorothea of Celle
GEORGE I (1714–27)

Caroline of Brandenburg-Anspach = GEORGE II
(1727–60)

Sophia Dorothea

Frederick

Frederick, Prince of Wales = Augusta of
(d. 1751) | Saxony-Gotha

Anne = William IV
of Orange

William,
Duke of Cumberland
(d. 1765)

Augusta = William Ferdinand,
Duke of Brunswick-
Wolfenbüttel

GEORGE III = Charlotte of Mecklenburg- Strelitz
(1760–1820)

Caroline of Brunswick = GEORGE IV
(1820–30)

Frederick,
Duke of York
(d. 1827)

WILLIAM IV = Adelaide of
(1830–7) Saxony-
Meiningen

Edward, Duke = Victoria of
of Kent Saxe-Coburg
(d. 1820)

Ernest,
Duke of
Cumberland,
after 1837
King of Hanover
(d. 1851)

Aug
Duke o
(d.

Charlotte = Leopold Saxe-Coburg
(d. 1817) after 1831 King of BELGIUM

Albert of Saxe-Coburg = VICTORIA
(nephew of Duchess (1837–1901)
of Kent and Leopold
of Saxe-Coburg)
(d. 1861)

George, Dul
(d.

Frederick III, = Victoria
King of Prussia,
German Emperor
(d. 1888)

EDWARD VII = Alexandra,
(1901–10) dau. Christian IX
of Denmark

Alice = Louis, Grand duke
(d. 1878) Hesse-Darmstadt

Alfred,
Duke of
Edinburgh
(d. 1900)

William II, German Emperor
(1888–1918)

Albert Victor,
Duke of Clarence
(d. 1892)

Lc
(d.

William, Crown Prince of Prussia

Victoria of Hesse = Louise of Battenberg,
(1872–1918) | 1st Marquess of
Milford Haven

Alix of Hesse = Nicholas II,
(1872–1918) Tsar of Russia
(1868–1918)

EDWARD VIII = Wa
(1936)
Duke of Windsor
(1938–1972)

2nd Marquess of
Milford Haven

Louis of Battenberg,
1st Earl Mountbatten
of Burma (1900–79)

Alice of Battenberg = Andrew of
(1885–1967) Greece
(1882–1944)

Prince Philip = ELIZABETH II
Duke of (1926–)
Edinburgh
(b. 1921)

Lady Diana Spencer = Charles, Prince
dau. Earl Spencer of Wales
(div.) (d. 1997) (b. 1948)

Anne, Princess = (1) Mark Philips
Royal
(b. 1950) = (2) Tim Laurence

An
Duke
(b.

Prince William
(b. 1982)

Prince Harry
(b. 1984)

Peter Philips
(b. 1977)

Zara Philips
(b. 1981)

Princess B
(b. 19

BURG–GOTHA AND WINDSOR

liam II

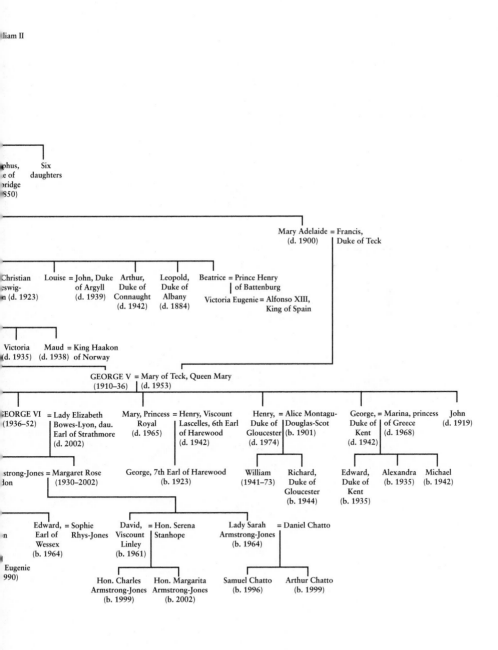

phus,
e of
oridge
850)

Six
daughters

Mary Adelaide = Francis,
(d. 1900) | Duke of Teck

Christian
eswig-
n (d. 1923)

Louise = John, Duke
of Argyll
(d. 1939)

Arthur,
Duke of
Connaught
(d. 1942)

Leopold,
Duke of
Albany
(d. 1884)

Beatrice = Prince Henry
| of Battenburg

Victoria Eugenie = Alfonso XIII,
King of Spain

Victoria
(d. 1935)

Maud = King Haakon
(d. 1938) of Norway

GEORGE V = Mary of Teck, Queen Mary
(1910–36) | (d. 1953)

GEORGE VI
(1936–52)

= Lady Elizabeth
Bowes-Lyon, dau.
Earl of Strathmore
(d. 2002)

Mary, Princess
Royal
(d. 1965)

= Henry, Viscount
Lascelles, 6th Earl
of Harewood
(d. 1947)

Henry,
Duke of
Gloucester
(d. 1974)

= Alice Montagu-
Douglas-Scot
(b. 1901)

George,
Duke of
Kent
(d. 1942)

= Marina, princess
of Greece
(d. 1968)

John
(d. 1919)

strong-Jones = Margaret Rose
Ion   (1930–2002)

George, 7th Earl of Harewood
(b. 1923)

William
(1941–73)

Richard,
Duke of
Gloucester
(b. 1944)

Edward,
Duke of
Kent
(b. 1935)

Alexandra
(b. 1935)

Michael
(b. 1942)

Edward, = Sophie
Earl of   Rhys-Jones
Wessex
(b. 1964)

David, = Hon. Serena
Viscount | Stanhope
Linley
(b. 1961)

Lady Sarah = Daniel Chatto
Armstrong-Jones
(b. 1964)

n

Eugenie
990)

Hon. Charles
Armstrong-Jones
(b. 1999)

Hon. Margarita
Armstrong-Jones
(b. 2002)

Samuel Chatto
(b. 1996)

Arthur Chatto
(b. 1999)

Prime Ministers

Party labels are only given where appropriate

1721	*April*	Sir Robert Walpole (Whig)
1742	*February*	Earl of Wilmington (Whig)
1743	*August*	Henry Pelham (Whig)
1754	*March*	Duke of Newcastle (Whig)
1756	*November*	Duke of Devonshire (Whig)
1757	*July*	Duke of Newcaslte (2nd) (Whig)
1762	*May*	Earl of Bute (Tory)
1763	*April*	George Grenville
1765	*July*	Marquis of Rockingham
1766	*July*	Earl of Chatham
1768	*October*	Duke of Grafton
1770	*January*	Lord North (Tory)
1782	*March*	Marquis of Rockingham (2nd) (Whig)
	July	Earl of Shelburne (Whig)
1783	*April*	Duke of Portland (coalition)
	December	William Pitt (Tory)
1801	*March*	Henry Addington (Tory)
1804	*May*	William Pitt (Tory)
1806	*February*	Lord Grenville (Whig)
1807	*March*	Duke of Portland (2nd) (coalition)
1809	*October*	Spencer Perceval (Tory)
1812	*June*	Earl of Liverpool (Tory)
1827	*April*	George Canning (Tory)
	August	Viscount Goderich (Tory)
1828	*January*	Duke of Wellington (Tory)
1830	*November*	Earl Grey (Whig)
1834	*July*	Viscount Melbourne (Whig)
	December	Sir Robert Peel (Con.)
1835	*April*	Viscount Melbourne (2nd) (Whig)
1841	*September*	Sir Robert Peel (2nd) (Con.)
1846	*June*	Lord John Russell (Whig–Lib.)
1852	*February*	Earl of Derby (Con.)
	December	Earl of Aberdeen (Peelite)

1855	*February*	Viscount Palmerston (Lib.)
1858	*February*	Earl of Derby (2nd) Con.)
1859	*June*	Viscount Palmerston (2nd) (Lib.)
1865	*October*	Earl Russell (2nd) (Lib.)
1866	*June*	Earl of Derby (3rd) (Con.)
1868	*February*	Benjamin Disraeli (Con.)
	December	W. E. Gladstone (Lib.)
1874	*February*	Benjamin Disraeli (2nd) (Con.); became Earl of Beaconsfield 1876
1880	*April*	W. E. Gladstone (2nd) (Lib.)
1885	*June*	Marquis of Salisbury (Con.)
1886	*February*	W. E. Gladstone (3rd) (Lib.)
	July	Marquis of Salisbury (2nd) (Con.)
1892	*August*	W. E. Gladstone (4th) (Lib.)
1894	*March*	Earl of Rosebery (Lib.)
1895	*June*	Marquis of Salisbury (3rd) (Con.–Unionist)
1902	*July*	A. J. Balfour (Con.–Unionist)
1905	*December*	Sir Henry Campbell-Bannerman (Lib.)
1908	*April*	H. H. Asquith (Lib.)
1915	*May*	H. H. Asquith (2nd) (coalition)
1916	*December*	David Lloyd George (coalition)
1919	*October*	David Lloyd (2nd) (coalition)
1922	*October*	Andrew Bonar Law (Con.)
1923	*May*	Stanley Baldwin (Con.)
1924	*January*	J. Ramsay MacDonald (Lab.)
	November	Stanley Baldwin (2nd) (Con.)
1929	*June*	J. Ramsay MacDonald (2nd) (Lab.)
1931	*August*	J. Ramsay MacDonald (3rd) (national)
1935	*June*	Stanley Baldwin (3rd) (national)
1937	*May*	Neville Chamberlain (national)
1940	*May*	Winston S. Churchill (coalition)
1945	*May*	Winston S. Churchill (2nd) (Con.)
	July	Clement Attlee (Lab.)
1950	*February*	Clement Attlee (2nd) (Lab.)
1951	*October*	Winston S. Churchill (3rd) (Con.)
1955	*April*	Sir Anthony Eden (Con.)
1957	*January*	Harold Macmillan (Con.)
1959	*October*	Harold Macmillan (2nd) (Con.)
1963	*October*	Sir Alec Douglas-Home (Con.)
1964	*October*	Harold Wilson (Lab.)
1966	*March*	Harold Wilson (2nd) (Lab.)
1970	*June*	Edward Heath (Con.)

1974	*March*	Harold Wilson (3rd) (Lab.)
1976	*May*	James Callaghan (Lab.)
1979	*May*	Margaret Thatcher (Con.)
1983	*June*	Margaret Thatcher (2nd) (Con.)
1987	*June*	Margaret Thatcher (3rd) (Con.)
1990	*November*	John Major (Con.)
1992	*April*	John Major (2nd) (Con.)
1997	*May*	Anthony Blair (Lab.)
2001	*June*	Anthony Blair (2nd) (Lab.)

Index